S0-BRB-781

The Complete Works of

WASHINGTON

IRVING

Richard Dilworth Rust

General Editor

JOURNALS AND NOTEBOOKS

Volume V

WASHINGTON IRVING

JOURNALS AND NOTEBOOKS

Volume V, 1832-1859

Edited by Sue Fields Ross

Twayne Publishers

Boston

1986

Published by Twayne Publishers
A Division of G. K. Hall & Co.

The Complete Works of Washington Irving
Volume V

Library of Congress Cataloging-in-Publication Data
(Revised for vol. 5)
Irving, Washington, 1783–1859.
Journals and notebooks.

(The Complete works of Washington Irving)
Vol. has imprint: Boston: Twayne Publishers.
Bibliographical footnotes.
Contents: v. 1. 1803–1806. 1819–1827, edited by W. A. Reichart. v. 5. 1832–1859, edited by Sue Fields Ross.
1. Irving, Washington, 1783–1859—Diaries.
2. Irving, Washington, 1783–1859—Notebooks, sketch-books, etc. 3. Authors, American—19th century—Diaries. I. Irving, Washington, 1783–1859. Works. 1976. II. Ross, Sue Fields. III. Wright, Nathalia, ed. IV. Title. V. Series.
PS2081.A2 1969 818′.2′08 69–16115
ISBN O–299–05320–2 (v. 1) varies
ISBN 0–8057–8504–3 (v. V)

Manufactured in the United States of America

for
C. Hugh Holman
(February 24, 1914–October 13, 1981)

Extraordinary teacher, scholar,
administrator, humanitarian

Beloved mentor and friend

ACKNOWLEDGMENTS

As is the case with anyone who undertakes a long and complicated project, I am indebted to far more people and institutions than I can mention in a limited space. I appreciate the opportunity to examine the Irving manuscripts in five libraries, and I wish to thank particularly the librarians at the Clifton Waller Barrett Collection of the University of Virginia Library; the Beinecke Rare Book and Manuscript Library at Yale University; the Folger Shakespeare Library in Washington, D.C.; the Edward Laurence Doheny Memorial Library at St. John's Seminary, Camarillo, California; and the Arents and Berg collections at the New York Public Library. My special gratitude for their good will and assistance goes to Mr. Paul Rugen, Ms. Jean McNiece, and Mr. John Stinson of the Manuscripts and Archives Division of the New York Public Library where most of these manuscripts are housed and where my visits were repeated and pleasant. Without reference librarians no editor could do his work, and I thank especially Ms. Pattie McIntyre and her staff at the Louis Round Wilson Library of the University of North Carolina at Chapel Hill; Mr. Don Berkebile of the Division of Transportation of the Smithsonian Institution in Washington, D.C.; and Dr. Mary Beaty of the E. H. Little Library of Davidson College. Mr. Archie Fields of the Circulation Department and Ms. Celia Poe of the Map Division of the Wilson Library at the University of North Carolina were also helpful.

For invaluable help with the preparation of the text—typing, proofreading, assisting in transcription—I thank Professor Boyd Davis, Ms. Christine Ross, Professor Connie Eble, Ms. Rita Snyder, Ms. Robin Mitchell, Ms. Roxanne Solomon, Ms. Joretta Archie, Professor George Poe, and the late Charmian Green.

I thank the National Endowment for the Humanities for a grant which helped fund the research; the Center for Editions of American Authors of the Modern Language Association, and Professor Matthew J. Bruccoli, its director during the preparation of the text; the English Department of the University of North Carolina for a Teaching Fellowship which gave me reduced teaching load in order that I might work on this research; and Davidson College for several weeks of study leave.

Deep is my appreciation to Professor Lewis Leary, in whose course I first became interested in Washington Irving and who has been an active Chairman of the Editorial Board of the Irving edition; to Professor Richard D. Rust, who has shared his skill as an editor and his encouragement as the third and present general editor of *The Complete Works of Washington Irving*; to Professor Joel Myerson, whose rigor and textual standards as vettor I admire; and most of all to the late C. Hugh Holman, with whom I studied and edited for twenty years. Professor Holman was in the original group which decided to undertake an edition of Irving's complete works; from the beginning he contributed to the policy-making sessions and was subsequently on the Editorial Board of the Edition.

Life-long gratitude is the only reimbursement for the debt I owe my parents, Reid and Christine Ross, for their moral and financial support during this and all of my academic pursuits.

S. F. R.

Davidson College

CONTENTS

ILLUSTRATIONS

INTERIOR ILLUSTRATIONS

Drawings and sketches made by Washington Irving
on pages of the journals

INTRODUCTION

When Washington Irving returned to America in 1832 after seventeen years in Europe, it was almost as if he were reliving the experiences of Rip Van Winkle, the character he had presented to the world thirteen years earlier. When he left America, his publications included the collaboration on *Letters of Jonathan Oldstyle* (1802–1803) and *Salmagundi* (1807–1808), the immediately popular *Knickerbocker's History of New York* (1809), and two biographical sketches, one of Thomas Campbell (1810) and one of James Lawrence (1813). His trepidation about his "re-appearance in literature" in 1819 with the first number of *The Sketch Book* seemed to be connected with his sense of separation from his literary roots. In an April 1, 1819, letter attached to the second number of that series, Irving asked his dear friend Henry Brevoort for suggestions about "themes &c [which] would be popular and striking in America; for I have been so long in England that things cease to strike me here as novelties & begin to wear a common place aspect."[1]

As early as 1820, when Irving had been away from this country for five years, he expressed to Brevoort his mixed feelings about returning:

> What would I not give for a few days among the highlands of the Hudson with the little knot that was once assembled there. But I shall return home and find all changed, and shall be made sensible how much I have changed myself. It is this idea which continually comes across my mind when I think of home, and I am continually picturing to myself the dreary state of a poor devil like myself who after wandering about the world among strangers returns to find himself a still greater stranger in his native place[.][2]

By 1827, Irving's sensitivity to the criticism of his countrymen prompted this affirmation of loyalty in an April 4 letter to Brevoort:

> I must confess that for a time I gave too much consequence to the attacks I had seen upon myself in the press and to anonymous

1. *Letters*, I, 546. For the convenience of the reader, I have removed textual symbols when citing these letters unless they are needed for clarity.

2. *Ibid.*, p. 593.

> letters which I received from some malevolent person seeking to persuade me that I was in a manner cast off by my countrymen. I am conscious that my long absence from home has subjected me to unfavorable representations and has been used to my disadvantage.... Do not let yourself be persuaded therefore that time or distance has estranged me in thought or feeling from my native country, my native places, or the friends of my youth.[3]

Even though Irving was by 1832 the best known American writer of the day, he was extremely apprehensive about his "re-entry" into his native land. By this time his works included *The Sketch Book* (1819–1820), which had appeared in numerous American, British, French, and German editions; *Bracebridge Hall* (1822); *Tales of a Traveller* (1824); *Life and Voyages of Christopher Columbus* (1828); *Conquest of Granada* (1829); *Voyages and Discoveries of the Companions of Columbus* (1831); and *The Alhambra* (1832).[4] As William Cullen Bryant said in a speech before the New York Historical Society in 1860, "All the trophies he had won in this field he brought home to lay at the feet of his country."[5] However, Irving dreaded his homecoming. According to Stanley T. Williams, Irving felt that his long absence from his homeland, the choice of European topics for his writing, and his favorable critical reception abroad had prompted the slander that he was "alienated in heart from [his] country."[6]

3. *Letters*, II, 225–26.

4. WI planned for the simultaneous publication of *The Alhambra* in England and America to precede immediately his arrival in New York. Serious problems arose between WI and his English publisher, John Murray, at the end of 1831. (See Ben Harris McClary, ed., *Washington Irving and the House of Murray: Geoffrey Crayon Charms the British, 1817–1856* [Knoxville: University of Tennessee Press, 1969], pp. 157–67; see also STW, II, 19–24.) In spite of this rift, apparently the "Spanish Sketch-Book" appeared in England (published by Colburn and Bentley) and in France (in translation) weeks before its publication in America on June 9, 1832. Pierre Irving found this delay puzzling, as the contract for 5,500 copies of *The Alhambra* with Carey & Lea was dated as early as March 17, 1832 (PMI, III, 17–18).

5. William Cullen Bryant, *A Discourse on the Life, Character and Genius of Washington Irving* (New York: G. P. Putnam, 1860), p. 31.

6. STW, II, 35. Philip Freneau, who died the year WI returned to America, lamented in an 1823 poem, "To a New England Poet," that American writers were not rewarded for their talents; he included these sarcastic lines about WI:

> Why stay in such a tasteless land,
> Where all must on a level stand,
> (Excepting people, at their ease,
> Who choose the level where they please:)

Irving's reception in 1832 allayed his fears: he found his public enthusiastic, his friends faithful, and his country different from the war-weary one he had left in 1815. The elegant dinner in Irving's honor at the City Hotel in New York City on May 30, 1832, helped to convince the wanderer that his Americanism was not suspect among friends. Bryant remembered that Chancellor Kent, who presided, "welcomed the historian of New Amsterdam back to his native city"; in his response, when asked how long he would remain, Irving exclaimed, "They know little of my heart who can ask me this question. I answer, as long as I live."[7] Perhaps the most moving account of the prodigal's feelings is in the introduction of the American edition of *A Tour on the Prairies* published in 1835. Irving confessed in print to his countrymen how afraid he had been to return in 1832, how mystified he was that his patriotism was ever doubted at home, and how grateful he was for his warm acceptance.[8] It is ironic that two years later Irving was defending himself against the vicious attacks of the *Plaindealer* which used as partial evidence of the author's patriotic duplicity the fact that *A Tour on the Prairies* had two introductions—one for his English readers and this "American" one.

According to Stanley Williams, it was early in the summer of 1832, after his return on May 21, that Irving decided to travel through his

---

See Irving gone to Britain's court
To people of another sort,
He will return, with wealth and fame,
While Yankees hardly know your name.

Lo! he has kissed a Monarch's—hand!
Before a prince I see him stand,
And with the glittering nobles mix,
Forgetting times of seventy-six,
While you with terror meet the frown
Of Bank Directors of the town,
The home-made nobles of our times,
Who hate the bard, and spurn his rhymes.

Why pause?—like Irving, haste away,
To England your addresses pay;
And England will reward you well,
When you some pompous story tell
Of British feats, and British arms,
The maids of honor, and their charms.

Attacks such as these in private and in print added to WI's trepidation.

7. Bryant, pp. 31–32.
8. *Tour*, pp. vii–xv.

native land, keep journals describing his exploration, and, finally, write a book about the American frontier.[9] It seems rather more likely that he had decided earlier, perhaps before he left the Continent, that, after seeing friends in New York and becoming reacquainted with his family, many of the younger generation whom he had never met, he would travel to New England to revisit the favorite haunts of his youth, then explore the frontier of his own state, much changed during his absence. The pressure to produce an "American" work would lead Irving to his time-tested formula for writing: careful notetaking in journals and notebooks, then creative culling from these accounts. The decision to travel in the Far West was largely an accidental one, as we learn from the August, 1832, journal 2, the first extant (and until now unpublished) journal written after Irving came home again.

Two members of what would later be called the "Irving party" were also chosen a bit by accident. Irving had met Charles Joseph Latrobe in Havre-de-Grâce before they sailed from France on April 11. Latrobe, an Englishman well born and educated, and his young charge, the Count Albert-Alexandre de Pourtalès, would naturally gravitate to the famous American; the friendship grew during the journey and was continued after they arrived in this country. Latrobe's reason for his trip to America is uncertain; perhaps it was to visit his uncle, Benjamin Henry Latrobe, who was a consulting architect for the original Capitol Building in Washington; perhaps it was, as he himself wrote, "to wander among the details of that sublime scenery which the fancy associates with the New World . . . and to be a guest in the lodges of that race, of whom men speak as doomed speedily to disappear from the face of the earth."[10] Latrobe was born in Leeds of a distinguished family; his father and grandfather were outstanding Moravian ministers, and, except for Latrobe's growing interest in botany and the out-of-doors, he would have followed in their footsteps, having himself been educated for the ministry. Latrobe lived in Switzerland from 1824 to 1827 and met the Pourtalès family, probably as a tutor of the children. Perhaps it was at the request of the parents to act as guardian-companion to their son, Albert, that Latrobe came to America.

The young Swiss count, Albert-Alexandre de Pourtalès, was educated in Geneva and Berlin, but as Latrobe noted, he was a person who "was bent like myself on forming opinions from observations."[11] Why a journey to America was appealing to the nineteen-year-old youth is not

9. STW, II, 36.
10. Latrobe, *Rambler*, I, 6.
11. *Ibid.*, p. 8.

known precisely. George F. Spaulding's discovery in 1965 of the manuscript of Pourtalès' journal helps us to guess. The count was born in Neuchatel, Switzerland, but because of the complexities of shifting rule he grew up as a Prussian. His great-grandfather became a member of the nobility under Frederick the Great, and his grandfather amassed great wealth. His father was a soldier of fortune—first commanding a Prussian regiment which was defeated by Napoleon in 1806, then becoming master-of-the-horse to the Empress Josephine in 1809. Pourtalès' mother was the Countess de Castellane-Norante, a member of the French nobility and the beautiful lady-in-waiting to Josephine. Perhaps Albert, their first son, wanted to follow the fashion of young men of quality by traveling in the New World; perhaps his outlook was international because of his background; perhaps his seeing the six Osage Indians who were brought to Geneva in 1827 piqued his curiosity; perhaps he came to America as a result of a family disagreement.[12] Whatever the reason, it appears that by the time the ship bringing Latrobe, Pourtalès, and Irving to New York had landed there on May 21, some plans for traveling together had been formulated. Irving found Latrobe and, initially, Pourtalès, to be "most agreeable travelling companions."[13] This favorable opinion of Latrobe continued.

During June, Irving traveled along the Eastern seaboard, primarily in Philadelphia, Baltimore, Washington, and New York. Latrobe wrote that the "series of common projects and common wanderings . . . kept us bound together as a trio for the greater part of the summer and autumn of this year."[14] He added that after their trip southward, apparently as far south as central Virginia, they made at the close of June "an excursion up the Hudson river, and to the Kaatskill mountains, lingering for a few days by the way, in a delightful retreat, in the bosom of the Highlands."[15] From two of Irving's letters to his brother Peter in Paris, it is possible to place outside limits as to the dates of this steamboat trip up the Hudson—June 28 and July 8, 1832.[16] Irving's companions were Latrobe, Pourtalès, and James Kirke Paulding, an old friend from Irving's younger days in New York. They visited West Point, spending three or four days with Gouverneur Kemble, another old friend, and then went twelve miles into the Catskill Mountains.

12. The information regarding Pourtalès is from George F. Spaulding's introduction and notes in Pourtalès, *Journal*, pp. 4–6, 4, n. 3.

13. PMI, III, 27.

14. Latrobe, *Rambler*, I, 25.

15. *Ibid.*, p. 37.

16. PMI, III, 25–27.

AMERICAN JOURNALS, 1832

Following the short trip was the excursion which actually began Irving's tour West and probably his first journal, a trip in July to Boston and the White Mountains of New Hampshire. Among Washington Irving's nine American journals, written from July until November, 1832, only numbers 3, 5, 6, 8, and 9 have been published.[17] The addition of journal 2 to the Irving cannon is significant for many reasons, primary among them that it reveals Irving's activities, acquaintances, and interests during August, 1832, only four months after he returned to America. Unfortunately, we can only piece together from Latrobe's account and Irving's letters[18] the events which were probably detailed carefully in the missing initial journal 1.

Apparently, Irving left New York alone; Latrobe wrote that during the second week of July, he and Pourtalès "prepared to follow Mr. Irving to Boston, where he purposed to give us rendezvous previous to our visit to the White Mountains, the highest group in the union."[19] Neither Irving nor Latrobe gave the date of their meeting in Boston. Irving had been in Boston five days in the company of Newton and his friends when he met the Englishman and the Swiss count at the Tremont Hotel, Boston's finest and by one travel account, the "most splendid hotel in the United States."[20] The first day's travel took the group from Boston over the Merrimac River to Concord, New Hampshire, a distance of approximately seventy miles. The second day they traveled to the shores of the Winnipisiogee Lake, along the way visiting a Shaker settlement. They paused for two days at an inn at the head of the lake and there, according to Irving, met a Mrs. L., whose party joined theirs for the remainder of the trip to the mountains.[21] Next they went to Conway and the base of the White Mountains and followed the valley of the River Saco to Notch. Latrobe climbed the third highest mountain in the range on one day (either Jefferson or Adams Mountain), and on the next day the party ascended the highest mountain, Mount Washington, which was enveloped in a heavy mist. The cold and wet travelers were disappointed by the lack of view. They descended via the Ammonoosuc River Valley, and on approximately July 26, after crossing the mountains, Irving left Latrobe and Pourtalès, who went to Lancaster, New

17. See the textual commentary, pp. lx–lxii below, for a discussion of the publication history of WI's Western journals.

18. Latrobe, *Rambler*, I, 52–64; PMI, III, 28–29; *Letters*, II, 709–13.

19. Latrobe, *Rambler*, I, 42.

20. *Northern Traveller*, p. 271.

21. PMI, III, 28–29.

Hampshire, then to Montpelier, Vermont. Latrobe wrote that they "'byde tryste' at Saratoga on the first days of August,"[22] actually setting the time at ten days from their parting. Irving began his trip southward, traveling by carriage down the valley of the Connecticut River to Springfield, Massachusetts, then to New York City. He wrote his brother Peter on August 3 from Tarrytown that he had just returned from Boston, the White Mountains, and New York City;[23] on the previous day he began journal 2 as he left New York for Tarrytown.

The possibilities for use of this journal, published here for the first time, are many. In addition to establishing a detailed chronology of Irving's whereabouts during the period between August 2 and September 1, 1832, we may also learn with whom he talked and visited.

Irving traveled during August in his home state, visiting places in which he had spent time in his youth, as well as exploring the state's "frontier." In August, 1803, he had gone from New York to Albany with the Hoffmans, the Ogdens, Ann Hoffman, and several other friends; they went to Ballston Springs, Saratoga Springs, Utica, Johnstown, Caughnawaga, among other places, with the young Irving keeping a detailed journal.[24] On August 2, exactly twenty-nine years and three days later, Irving left New York City in a steamboat and went up the Hudson to Tarrytown where he visited with members of his family. The next day found him traveling by wagon to Sing Sing, in a mail carrier to Peekskill, in a row boat to Caldwell's Landing, and in the steamboat *Constellation* to Albany. Because that city was besieged by the cholera epidemic of 1832, he left hurriedly by railroad the next day for Saratoga, where he met Latrobe and Pourtalès on August 5. Irving spent the next several days taking short trips out from Saratoga—fishing on two successive days at Saratoga Lake and visiting Schuylerville. From August 10 until his arrival in Cincinnati on September 1, Irving's itinerary can be determined from journal 2.

Leaving Saratoga by stage, Irving and his two friends traveled southwest through Galway to Johnstown, then west by wagon and stage along the Mohawk River to Little Falls. After spending the day of August 13 in Little Falls, the party went northwest, rejecting the more usual route through Utica to avoid the raging cholera epidemic and going through Middleville to Trenton Falls, where Irving remained from August 14 until the morning of August 18. Next, he bypassed Syracuse by again following a southwest route and someone's suggested itinerary

22. Latrobe, *Rambler*, I, 64.
23. PMI, III, 29.
24. *Journals and Notebooks*, I, 3–30.

which Irving had jotted on the inside front cover of this journal, "From Utica go by Onondaga Holl & not thru Syracuse"; they did indeed go through Trenton and Rome, visited Oneida Castle, passed through Onondaga Hollow, and spent two nights in Skaneateles. The party then traveled for two days in the scenic region now known as the Finger Lakes, going along the banks of Skaneateles and Owasco lakes and proceeding west to Auburn, Cayuga, Bridgeport, Seneca Falls, Waterloo, Geneva, and Canandaigua. After again turning northwest to Rochester and Sandy Creek, Irving led his party along the usual tourist route to Niagara Falls on the Ridge Road to Lockport, Lewiston, and Niagara where they stayed from August 23 to 26. Next they went south to Buffalo and embarked there on the steamboat *Niagara*, landing on August 27 at Ashtabula, Ohio. The following five days they traveled southwest to Cleveland, Medina, Wooster, Newark (near which Irving visited Indian mounds), Columbus, Springfield, Xenia, Lebanon; and they arrived in Cincinnati on September 1, 1832.

In addition to establishing details of Irving's whereabouts during those days in August, journal 2 reveals that Irving talked with men active in politics. Washington Irving's political beliefs, or lack of them, have been the subject of interest to the students of early American literature, as well as to his contemporaries. Irving left America in 1815, soon after his activity as an aide-de-camp and rank of colonel in the War of 1812. Although he regretted that conflict, he wrote with patriotic fervor in a biographical sketch of Perry published in the *Analectic Magazine*, of which Irving became editor in 1813:

> our feelings will ever accompany the flag of our country to battle, rejoicing in its glory, lamenting over its defeat. For there is no such thing as releasing ourselves from the consequences of the contest.... If the name of American is to be rendered honorable in the fight, we shall each participate in the honor; if otherwise, we must inevitably support our share of the ignominy.[25]

Irving's attempts during the intervening years at conciliation between England and America had often earned him the suspicion of both countries, but during his three years as secretary of the American legation in London, he had regained some of this earlier patriotic fervor. However, the country he left in 1815 and the one to which he returned in 1832 were very different.

James Madison was president on Irving's leaving; when he returned, Andrew Jackson had been elected and Jacksonian Democracy was the

25. PMI, I, 310–11.

political stance of the day. De Tocqueville had visited the country the year before Irving's return and had concluded that the old great race of American men—men of culture, talent, and character who had given this country the Declaration of Independence and a new democracy—was disappearing. We might infer from Henry Ellsworth, the commissioner to the Indians with whom Irving would travel west, that this comment would be of little concern to Irving; Ellsworth told his wife that Irving "dislikes political or polemic discussions" and that with "the great, he feels sufficiently acquainted—He desires most to ramble among the natural actions of men—He watches every spring and looks with microscopic eye into the hidden wheels that move men along, on the common walks of life."[26]

However, we learn from this journal that Irving met and had conversations with active New York state politicians, men such as Senator William L. Marcy, one of the "Albany Regency." Soon after this meeting with Irving, Marcy would be nominated as the Democratic party candidate for governor of New York.[27] We learn that Irving visited with Governor Enos Thomas Throop, another Democratic figure, and leader of New York, with Governor Duncan McArthur of Ohio, and with Mr. Kelley, probably Alfred Kelley, one of the first citizens of Ohio and of the country. By casually mentioning "Genl Harrison," who came to Cincinnati when there was only one log hut, Irving lets the reader of his journal know that he met and discussed the settlement of the West with William Henry Harrison.

This journal also supports the known fact that Irving was a man loyal to old friends and close to his family. He credited his friends with making him feel "indeed at home—and . . . it was a home of the heart";[28] journal 2 records his seeing old friends during his trip through the state, for example, Charles Graham, F. B. Cutting, Maxwell, and Aspinwall, his literary agent. When he was in Ohio Irving met members of the Ogden family. Even though he had at forty-six years old declared himself "an absolute old Bachelor,"[29] he was a devoted family man. Ellsworth noticed how dependent on Irving were many members of his family: "His affections are strong for his family connections. . . . He said his sister [Catharine Irving Paris] depended much upon him. . . . He could not read her letter without tears—she had lost her husband and [Irving?] was left the kind guardian of several nephews & ni[e]ces. . . ."[30]

26. Ellsworth, *Narrative*, p. 71.
27. See p. 7, n. 35 regarding Marcy.
28. *Tour*, p. xii.
29. *Letters*, II, 425.
30. Ellsworth, *Narrative*, p. 79.

One very human touch revealed by journal 2 is the fact that Irving, so long absent from his extended family, systematically listed all his relatives by families. He was like Rip Van Winkle, who, after a twenty-year absence, had to become reacquainted with his very changed family.

In the Sunday, August 26, 1832, entry of journal 2, Irving casually mentioned the meeting which would influence his travel plans and his career: "embark in Steam boat niagara for Erie—on board meet Mr Ellsworth . . . a commissioner to settle the Indians—agree to accompany him—." In retrospect, Irving elaborated on this important accidental meeting in a December letter to his brother Peter:

> On board of the steam-boat was Mr. E., one of the commissioners appointed by government to superintend the settlement of emigrant Indian tribes, to the west of the Mississippi. He was on his way to the place of rendezvous, and on his invitation, we agreed to accompany him in his expedition. The offer was too tempting to be resisted: I should have an opportunity of seeing the remnants of those great Indian tribes, which are now about to disappear as independent nations, or to be amalgamated under some new form of government. I should see those fine countries of the "far west," while still in a state of pristine wildness, and behold herds of buffaloes scouring their native prairies, before they are driven beyond the reach of a civilized tourist.[31]

It is, of course, probable that Irving would have traveled West whether or not he had met Ellsworth; his American public demanded that he write about America, and the West was intriguing to readers on both sides of the Atlantic. More important, Irving would have been led by his natural curiosity about the wilderness—its Indians, its settlers, its towns and posts, its manners, and particularly its philosophical milieu. The West was Jacksonian democracy realized. Therefore, what made the meeting and subsequent trip with Ellsworth significant was the possibility that Irving may not have gone as far into the Indian Territory, traveled and lived as primitively, nor seen as much firsthand had he not been a part of the government's commission to the Indians. The generally warm critical reception of Irving's *Tour* was due in part to the fact that a citizen of the world, a gentleman who was at home in the courts of Europe, was the American who took and described charmingly

31. *Letters*, II, 733–34. This letter was published in four Western newspapers in 1833 (*ibid.*, p. 737). Ellsworth's account of the meeting is retold in a letter written by his sister (*Narrative*, p. xvii, n. 3).

the dangerous trip West which other velvet-coated and felt-slippered men in Philadelphia, New York, or Boston did not undertake.

Removal of the Indians from their lands to the territory west of the Mississippi River had long been a government policy, but it was formalized into law on June 30, 1830, by the passage of the Indian Removal Act. The attendant charge by Congress that the president be responsible for implementation of the law, including land grants and payments for relinquished land and compensation for development of new land, prompted President Jackson's appointing in 1832 three commissioners to go into the Indian Territory to study the Indian Removal Bill of 1830 as well as the country it affected, to attempt to settle the disputes over land, mark boundaries, make peace with the Indians, and restore order. One of the primary problems of the removal, which added to the questionable morality of it, was the fact that most of the tribes in the old Southwest—the Choctaw, Chickasaw, Creek, Seminole, and especially the Cherokee—were agricultural and "civilized," and they were being sent into the territory of the Comanches, Apaches, Pawnees, and other hunting and more warlike nations. After several men refused this sensitive mission, the president appointed as the two other commissioners Governor Montfort Stokes of North Carolina and the Reverend John F. Schermerhorn of Utica, New York, as well as Colonel Samuel C. Stambaugh as secretary of the commission. When these three men did not arrive at the appointed time to meet Ellsworth, he asked Irving to replace Stambaugh as secretary, for which job Irving apparently received only remuneration for some losses, such as saddle, bridle, blankets, bearskin, and India mat.[32] The fact that this particular commission included a famous American writer made it one of the most completely reported government ventures of the period. The mission's political failure was matched by its literary success.

The discovery in 1965 and subsequent publication of the journal and letters of the Count de Pourtalès brought to four the number of "the Irving party" whose accounts of the journey West have been published. Irving's descriptions in print include *A Tour on the Prairies* (1835) and two editions of the journal versions, the first edited by William P. Trent and George S. Hellman in 1919 and the second edited by John Francis McDermott in 1944, with a second printing in 1966. In addition, Irving's *Astoria* (1836) and *Adventures of Captain Bonneville* (1837) were prompted by his first trip West. Throughout this volume of Irving's journals and notebooks, especially relating to the Western journals, I have referred to the other four accounts: the journals of Latrobe, Ells-

32. *Western Journals*, pp. 25–26, n. 41.

worth, Pourtalès, and Irving's *Tour.* From each of the four members of the party we learn something unique about the trip, the other members of the party, and particularly about that writer's own preconceptions, prejudices, personality, and style.

Published in 1835, the same year as Irving's *A Tour on the Prairies,* Charles Joseph Latrobe's book was dedicated to "Washington Irving, Esq. . . . In Token of Affectionate Esteem and Remembrance by The Author." Irving returned this compliment by writing that Latrobe

> had all the buoyancy and accommodating spirit of a native of the Continent. Having rambled over many countries, he had become, to a certain degree, a citizen of the world, easily adapting himself to any change. He was a man of a thousand occupations: a botanist, a geologist, a hunter of beetles and butterflies, a musical amateur, a sketcher of no mean pretensions, in short, a complete Virtuoso. . . . Never had a man more irons in the fire, and, consequently, never was man more busy or more cheerful.[33]

Latrobe's account is the most inclusive account of the four. In addition to the trip west, *The Rambler in North America: 1832–1833* includes the period before he and his young charge sailed for America, as well as the spring and summer in the city and state of New York, in cities along the east coast, in New England, and on the frontier. Volume 1 of Latrobe's *Rambler in North America* is divided into nineteen letters; the initial letter is an introduction and the remaining undated letters include descriptions and reflections of this careful observer, concluding when Latrobe and Pourtalès were back in Maryland on Christmas day, 1832.

Latrobe was a botanist by avocation, and although he wrote of the "character of the verdure,"[34] he did not concentrate on the flora of America. His accounts of the bee camp and the bison chase have been cited in studies of the West, but his descriptions of manners, rivers, Indians, traders, government, and his fellow travelers are equally revealing. About Pourtalès, he was the only one of the three older men who had generally positive things to say. Latrobe "laid some claim to the character of an old traveller";[35] he wrote with insight about the character of the New Englander, the absence of a national character, and about American and English travelers in the others' countries. He was often more succinct than the other keepers of journals on this trip; he described four major cities in America as follows: "New York is the

33. *Tour,* p. 20.
34. Latrobe, *Rambler,* I, 30.
35. *Ibid.,* p. 7.

most bustling; Philadelphia the most symmetrical; Baltimore the most picturesque; and Washington the most bewildering."[36]

Latrobe's style is clearly that of an educated nineteenth-century Englishman, but it is not euphuistic. He was writing to a person who was two years his junior and whose interests were presumably similar to his. He was often enthusiastic; when Irving and his friends accepted Ellsworth's invitation to join the party, Latrobe wrote, "So the tour in the Canadas was relinquished for the present, and it was now—hurra! for the Far West!"[37] His British sense of humor is often reflected in the journal, as when he described the "melancholy spectacle" of the missing boot of Pourtalès,[38] an event which Ellsworth used as evidence of the irresponsibility of the young Swiss count. Latrobe was also often romantic:

> The setting sun! You may have remarked how steadily for nearly the whole of this year we turned our faces towards that glorious spectacle;—how Spring found us day after day with our hopes and wishes directed there at the hour of eve, while we listened to the songs of the emigrant on the bosom of the sea: how evening after evening, we saw the purple and gold of the Summer sky reflected upon the vast liquid surface of the rivers of the New World; and now, when Autumn was spreading its gorgeous hues over the forest and prairie, we still pressed forward towards the glowing sky, and camped with our faces to the west.[39]

Discoveries of two manuscripts made Ellsworth's and Pourtalès' accounts available to the student of Irving and the West. Stanley T. Williams and Barbara D. Simison discovered the Ellsworth narrative while they were working on Irving's Western experiences, and it was published in 1937. Williams and Simison call the narrative a journal although it was written from Fort Gibson to Ellsworth's wife Nancy Allen Goodrich Ellsworth as a long letter dated November 17, 1832. Apparently, it was a transcript of the journals which the commissioner had kept on the trip. It reveals a man who is interested as much in the "receipt" for prairie tea as in the problems of the relocation of the Indians. Especially telling are long passages describing Irving, Latrobe, Pourtalès, and other members of the party. Ellsworth, like Latrobe, did not divide his narrative by date, and he was rather erratic about dating events.

36. *Ibid.*, p. 26.
37. *Ibid.*, p. 82.
38. *Ibid.*, p. 177.
39. *Ibid.*, p. 176.

Henry Leavitt Ellsworth, a native of Windsor, Connecticut, was the son of Abigail Wolcott and Chief Justice Oliver Ellsworth; his twin brother, William Wolcott Ellsworth, was also outstanding in law and government. Washington Irving seemed completely to forgive Ellsworth his Yankee background, this graduate of Yale (1810), student of law at Litchfield Law School, secretary of the Hartford County Agricultural Society, and president of the Ætna Insurance Company. Irving wrote of their "worthy leader" that he was "a man in whom a course of legal practice and political life had not been able to vitiate an innate simplicity and benevolence of heart. The greater part of his days had been passed in the bosom of his family and the society of deacons, elders, and select men, on the peaceful banks of the Connecticut...."[40] Ellsworth's background was perhaps responsible for his dim view of Irving's laughing at some of the Old Testament passages which he read from Pourtalès' French Bible; his judgmental, and actually incorrect, conclusion was that Irving did not read from the Bible often.[41]

Pourtalès, almost certainly sensing Ellsworth's disapproval of him, was scathing in his assessment of the commissioner's level of insight regarding Indians. The younger man thought it ridiculous that Ellsworth asked a missionary-cobbler about the Indians' methods of waging war, when traveling with the party was Colonel Auguste Pierre Chouteau, one of the most knowledgeable men in the West. In addition, "He questioned a half-blood hunter, who had probably never suspected that he had a soul, about their religious opinions."[42] The count wrote that Ellsworth's speeches to the Indians were simplistic to the point of irrelevance, actually producing hilarity among the natives, and that "the Lord Commissioner is one of those good old philanthropists" who after one of his speeches "imagined that peace would follow immediately and that the Indians would shake hands, would establish Plato's Atlantis, the living Utopia, and would retrace the era of the Golden Age for corrupt man."[43]

Although Irving's judgment was more benign, he did point out the humor in the situation of their arrival in this same "straggling Osage

40. *Tour*, p. 19.

41. Ellsworth, *Narrative*, p. 72.

42. Pourtalès, *Journal*, pp. 46–47.

43. *Ibid.*, p. 47. McDermott adds that there were others who felt that Ellsworth was inadequate for the job as commissioner to the Indians—S. C. Stambaugh, Governor Stokes, Colonel Chouteau, Colonel Arbuckle, and the other Fort Gibson officers (*Western Journals*, p. 11, n. 11). Historians have concurred in that this mission was a failure.

village" and Ellsworth's speech. The old Osage men shook hands and the women and children stared, chattered, and laughed. Irving continued:

> Here the Commissioner made a speech from on horseback; informing his hearers of the purport of his mission, to promote a general peace among the tribes of the west, and urging them to lay aside all warlike and bloodthirsty notions, and not to make any wanton attacks upon the Pawnees. This speech being interpreted by Beatte, seemed to have a most pacifying effect upon the multitude, who promised faithfully that as far as in them lay, the peace should not be disturbed; and indeed their age and sex gave some reason to hope that they would keep their word.[44]

As is true of most journal writers, Ellsworth revealed as much about himself as his subject. By his own admission to his wife, his purpose in the narrative was not "to give any opinion upon the Indian Country";[45] however, he showed that he was more astute than Pourtalès thought when he touched on the potential for the region's development in light of its minerals and timber as well as the potential for problems in light of the complexity of the Indian question. Ellsworth wrote,

> Politics are mixed up with the Indian question, and representation[s] are made, often, on both sides for party effect—As for myself, I am far, very far, removed from all the scenes of political strife, and as my feelings become every day more & more interest[e]d in behalf of the Indians, my mind withdraws *most willingly*, from the heart burnings & reckless detractions of political conflict. . . .[46]

Personally, Ellsworth was a frugal man; he often criticized the soldiers for their lack of that trait, and once he took Irving to task for his Epicureanism: "I was surprised to find Mr Irving opposed to any restrictions and ridi[c]ule the idea of taking thought for tomorrow."[47] However, Ellsworth appreciated in Irving his own ability to adjust to hardships when he wrote, "Mr Irving is curteous & even kind—cheerful in submitting to those circumstances which are incident to time & place, while he generally censures defects of every kind, which can with proper exertion be remedied."[48] Although the commissioner was rather stiff and judgmental, his ability to describe effectively the domestic

44. *Tour*, pp. 53–54.
45. Ellsworth, *Narrative*, p. 60.
46. *Ibid.*, p. 61.
47. *Ibid.*, p. 46.
48. *Ibid.*, p. 72.

details of life on the trail during plenty and want makes his *Narrative* often charming. Ellsworth's interests ranged from jerking venison, tasting pawpaws, washing woolens, brewing prairie tea, "casing" a doe, or baking bread without yeast, to buying provisions, hobbling the ponies, fording a stream, trapping a beaver, or creasing a wild horse. He was also a very sociable man, an aspect of his personality which Irving particularly appreciated, writing to his sister that Ellsworth was "a very gentlemanly and amiable person, and an excellent travelling companion."[49] Latrobe found Ellsworth "worthy of the respect which all entertained for him. His kindliness of spirit won our regard. . . ." Latrobe also praised him for leaving his comfortable Eastern home to "become a peace-maker among the rude tribes and inhabitants of the West."[50]

Three years after George S. Spaulding discovered the Pourtalès manuscript in 1965 while he and his wife were vacationing in Munich, the travel account of the fourth member of the "Irving party" saw light in print. Spaulding, who edited the volume, wrote in the preface that he and his wife found the manuscript in the Pension Biederstein, owned and operated by the count's great-granddaughter. The countess simply handed to Spaulding Pourtalès' 133-year-old diary and six letters to his mother, which the editor has inserted in their proper chronological sequence. In addition to having available another version of the trip and the travelers, we are especially fortunate to have access to this journal, because Irving's journal 4 (September 14–26) is missing, and Pourtalès wrote in detail about eight of those days, September 14–17 and 19–22. Irving's journal 7 (October 18–30) is also missing, and the young count included a rather full rendering of October 10 and 12–24.

Actually the most candid of the four, Pourtalès' account is full of undisguised nineteen-year-old criticism of his elders and enthusiasm about the trip, his Western clothes, his mounts, and especially the Indians. Irving wrote in the *Tour* that Pourtalès traveled with Latrobe "as his Telemachus; being apt, like his prototype, to give occasional perplexity and disquiet to his Mentor." He added that the young Swiss count was "full of talent and spirit, but galliard in the extreme, and prone to every kind of wild adventure."[51] At one point Pourtalès was separated from the group by the excitement of a hunt and was found only after he had spent most of two days and a night alone on the prairie without food; he wrote to his mother about this frightening experience and his warm reception by Irving, who "with tears in his eyes, shook my hand."[52]

49. PMI, III, 34.
50. Latrobe, *Rambler*, I, 146.
51. *Tour*, p. 20.
52. Pourtalès, *Journal*, p. 73.

Irving described this event in two chapters in his *Tour* (30–31), attributing to the count's "usual eagerness and impetuosity" his pell-mell pursuit of the herd.[53] According to Latrobe, Pourtalès conducted himself admirably during the crisis.

Throughout the diary and letters, Pourtalès was particularly enchanted by the Indians; he wrote that he had "become friendly with a chief named Beautiful Bird, a big sixty-year-old daddy," who presented to the young count his calumet and tobacco pouch,[54] relics subsequently found by Spaulding among the possessions of the countess. Pourtalès could contain neither his excitement over the "new acquisition, Mr. Manhattan . . . the handsomest male Indian that [he had] ever seen," nor his disappointment over that Indian's leaving the next day without a word.[55] He romantically imagined "the tears a sensitive girl cousin may have shed in order to keep this gentle Telemachus from leaving," and he lamented, "Good-by, then, oh mighty marksman."[56]

Pourtalès had seen six Osage Indians when they were on exhibit in Geneva, and it was the Osages about whom he now wrote, "They are hospitable, generous and love the whites with all their hearts."[57] While Irving compared the Osages to "noble bronze figures" with "Roman countenances"[58] and Ellsworth called them a "*dirty disgusting* set of beings" and shuddered at their nudity,[59] Pourtalès wrote that the "children exposed their natural parts with the ingenuousness of Grandma Eve before she stole the good Lord's apples."[60] Even prettier than the Osage squaws, thought the younger observer, were the Creek women; because of their dress, black hair, dark complexions, and dignity, he thought they resembled Roman women. He wrote coyly that the strict laws against adultery had "fallen into disuse" and "experts assure me that there are few Lucretias among them who resist advances accompanied by little gifts. . . ."[61] The disapproving commissioner hinted that the young count's parents had sent him abroad "to sow his wild oats in a foreign country . . . [which] I am sure will be done, unless his wild store is beyond measurement."[62] Ellsworth added that he was certain Pourtalès "will later in life, look back upon his western follies

53. *Tour*, p. 229.
54. Pourtalès, *Journal*, p. 38.
55. *Ibid.*, p. 44.
56. *Ibid.*, p. 48.
57. *Ibid.*, p. 37.
58. *Tour*, p. 29.
59. Ellsworth, *Narrative*, p. 18.
60. Pourtalès, *Journal*, p. 45.
61. *Ibid.*, p. 43.
62. Ellsworth, *Narrative*, p. 68.

(to say the least) with shame," especially when his "future domestic felicity" is disrupted "by the appearance of red progeny, who will rise up to call him father!"[63] When Ellsworth was deciding whether to take a young female Pawnee prisoner with them, he commented that "Mr Pourteles thought it would be an excellent plan—but his opinion, had little weight."[64]

However, among the four writers of journals on this trip West, it was Pourtalès who was most forthright about the Indians; even Irving, who carefully collected myths and recorded customs, tended to concentrate on the romantic. In spite of his boyish admiration of the Indians—their freedom, their ingenuity, their beauty—Pourtalès wrote rather perceptively:

> If ever I settle in America, it will be in this area, the only place in the United States which offers a romantic way of life plus absolute independence. I would surround myself with a double rampart of Osages to protect me against the Americans, those commercial Thebans of the New World. I would become the advocate of the Osages before the government, which each year pushes them back a little more into the wilderness and the grave. I would try to win them over by civilizing them, not by preaching the obscure and unintelligible dogmas of Methodism, but by helping them through my example and advice to cultivate indispensable arts and to develop agriculture. I would not have them leap into the maze of civilization and modern religion. I would instead have them pass through a kind of Middle Ages, convinced as I am that Catholicism is a necessary bridge between barbarism and the civilized state in which we find Europe today. It would be a beautiful life![65]

As fascinating as these three men and their journals are, it is how they relate to Irving and his journals that makes them particularly interesting to us. To Ellsworth's slight irritation, the commission to which he held a presidential appointment was known during the trip as the "Irving party." It was the writer who caused a flurry of excitement when the party arrived in a town or at a fort; his reputation as a literary figure and a note-taker preceded him. While he was in Cincinnati during the first days of September, Irving was visited by Timothy Flint, from whose major work, *The History and Geography of the Mississippi Valley* (1828), Irving frequently copied descriptions and opinions. Ellsworth

63. *Ibid.*, p. 67.

64. *Ibid.*, p. 19.

65. Pourtalès, *Journal*, pp. 62–63.

wrote that Flint was disappointed to find that Irving was "rosy faced and as plump as a partridge," not as he had expected—"a pale faced, lean man, who had worn himself down, over the midnight lamp."[66] When Irving and his companions spent the night of Wednesday, September 19 in Columbia, Missouri, he was mentioned in the local paper, *Missouri Intelligencer and Boon's Lick Advertiser.* The reporter wrote that Irving was surprised and pleased with Missouri and that in "his manners, Mr. Irving is unostentatious, affable and gentlemanly. He will no doubt acquire a valuable fund of materials in his progress, for interesting works or Sketches, which, ere long, we may have the gratification of perusing."[67]

The members of his party were aware that Irving, the American author, was taking notes for a purpose. In two letters to his mother, Pourtalès wrote that "Irving will certainly give the world some of the details" of the trip[68] and, more specifically, that "Our nomadic period will end brilliantly. Mr. Irving will probably publish two works on this summer's trip. He has spoken to us of the plan and the form of the work and has told us, in confidence, some of the anecdotes which he will include. That is the very great advantage of traveling in such company!"[69] Ellsworth recorded a dangerous crossing of the Arkansas River on October 15; after being the first to ford on the "tottering craft" fashioned from a buffalo skin, Irving had a short time alone in Pawnee country. Ellsworth remembered that after his own crossing, he was welcomed by Irving, "who was busily filling his little sketch book, with the interesting events of the day."[70] We also learn from the commissioner that before Irving "sits down to write his sketches or other works, he always washes himself up nice" and that Irving's "mode of recording events, is not to confide much to the memory, but to sketch in a little book every occurence worthy of remembrance and especially *dates* & *facts*—These he says are his foundations—he makes additional rooms when he builds his fabric and adds the rest[?] which he terms '*filligree work.*' "[71]

66. Ellsworth, *Narrative*, p. 73.

67. *Western Journals*, p. 19.

68. Pourtalès, *Journal*, p. 22.

69. *Ibid.*, pp. 35–36. At the conclusion of the trip, Pourtalès lamented that he had lost one of the notebooks of his own journal in the river; he told his mother that perhaps he would transform his "badly scribbled" notes into "an American sketchbook" just for her (p. 80).

70. Ellsworth, *Narrative*, pp. 41–42.

71. *Ibid.*, pp. 70–71.

Actually, there is much to recommend the "pre-filligree" account; these journals are more spontaneous than the literary version, *A Tour on the Prairies*, and, as a result, often more interesting to read. Also, *A Tour* includes material in the major portions of only two extant journals, beginning with p. [12] of journal 6 in early October, 1832, at Fort Gibson and ending with material in the concluding pages of journal 8.[72] Therefore, there are four extant journals which provide additional accounts of, and insight into, region and writer. Irving rather abruptly completed his *Tour* with this paragraph: "The next morning after breakfast, I again set forward in company with the worthy Commissioner, for Fort Gibson, where we arrived much tattered, travel-stained and weather-beaten, but in high health and spirits;—and thus ended my foray into the Pawnee Hunting Grounds."[73] A careful reading of Irving's entries for November 8 and 9 in journal 8 provides a much more charming account of the high spirits of the troop, the adventure of fording the Arkansas River, the excitement of first reading a newspaper, the beauty of the moonlight on the Verdigris, and the merrymaking at the garrison. In the final entry of journal 8 and the pages of journal 9, Irving recounted his hasty departure from the garrison and his trip down the plantation-dotted Verdigris River to the Mississippi River and Stack Island—events not included in the *Tour*.

In these journals we actually see America's most popular writer in 1832 without his mask. We learn immediately from the journals that one reason Irving was an excellent traveler is the fact that his Knickerbocker sense of humor was not merely a pose, but a way of looking at life. Although Irving was writing in these little leather books under trying circumstances and although his notebooks were only the jottings of facts and impressions to be used later by him alone, his genial, understated sense of humor is evident throughout. Once he described a "little dog looking on at shoeing horse as if studying the art or waiting for his turn" (October 10); earlier he had seen an "Old negro steward scolding young negros for lying—He aimes at a monopoly" (September 6).[74] He ap-

72. Journal 7 is missing. McDermott's edition of the *Western Journals* includes a well-documented introduction in which he outlines the daily experiences of the Irving party, suggesting from the other extant accounts (those of Ellsworth, Latrobe, and Pierre M. Irving) the events and geographical information which probably would have been described in WI's missing journal 4 (St. Louis to Independence) and journal 7 (Red Fork River to Little River).

73. *Tour*, p. 274.

74. For the convenience of the reader, I have referred to the dates of the entries and have removed from the passages textual symbols, unless they are needed for clarity.

preciated the Indian's sense of humor as he recorded the myth of the creation of the mosquito (October 4), and he enjoyed the story of Fort Gibson's desirable Widow Nix whose "Serenade was a horrible chorse voice that broke the sleep of man[,] woman & dog throughout the fortress" (November 9).

Often as much about a writer can be determined by what he omits from a description as by what he includes. In the early journals, Irving gave little information about the cities; even though he was in Cincinnati immediately following the publication of Mrs. Frances Trollope's devastating account of the *Domestic Manners of the Americans*, Irving had little to say except that he met several people. In contrast, Latrobe noted, "Whether the compote was justly and wisely compounded, I was in no way enabled to judge at the time, but it was very evident from the wry faces on all sides, and the aroused spirit of indignation, that the bitter herbs predominated over the sweet."[75] Other cities received from Irving equal lack of attention: for instance, Madison, Indiana, was a "Neat little place built of brick" (September 4); about Louisville, the "Quay of city presents a motley scene—fleets—steam boats—carriages—heaps of Iron[,] or Lead" (September 4). In the September 13 entry he noted that St. Louis was a "mixture of French & american character." Several inns visited and described by members of the group may well have occupied Irving's pen, but his journal depicting the trip from St. Louis to Independence (September 15–26) is missing.[76] City

75. *Rambler,* I, 99. Mrs. Trollope's book was based on her residence in Cincinnati from 1828 until 1830, and Ralph Leslie Rusk, in his excellent study of Western literature, says that it was one of the most popular travel accounts in this period even though it was "an ill-humored and ungracious rebuke to the people among whom she had lived"; Rusk adds that her judgments of their shortcomings were largely just. Defenders of the West responded with book-length rebuttal, satire, journal articles, and dramas (*The Literature of the Middle Western Frontier* [New York: Columbia University Press, 1926], I, 108–11; hereafter cited as Rusk, *Literature of the Middle West*).

76. Pourtalès said the inns of this area "are wooden chalets. They are generally very clean, but they often have only one bedroom in which up to seven or eight people sleep" (*Journal*, p. 35). On September 16 the group visited an "establishment" described by Latrobe as a typical dwelling on the prairie (*Rambler*, I, 121–24); in a particularly detailed three-page entry in his journal, Pourtalès presented this same thatch-roofed cottage not far from St. Charles in what his editor called a "grandiloquent description of a farmyard scene" (*Journal*, pp. 26–29, 26, n. 10). WI's journal 4 is not extant, but a two-page sketch of the "Lewis[?] Hotel" in the Olin Library, Washington University, reveals that he, too, was fascinated by this particular farm. In "The Log house Hotel," as WI called his sketch, he described the poultry yard confusion, arguments over whiskey, the Negro inhabitants, and conversations in dialect (John Francis McDermott, "An Unpublished Washington Irving Manuscript," *PELL*, 1 [Winter, 1965], pp. 369–73).

life was not Irving's primary interest in these journals; he concentrated on the wildness of the prairie, the lore of the Indians, or the beauty of a campfire scene, one which looked like "A robbers retreat" (October 15).

Irving's optimistic nature prohibited his mentioning in his journal, much less complaining, that he suffered a serious reaction to something he ate, a condition which Ellsworth described as a "swelling of the eye-lids and an erruption about the wrists. . . ."[77] Ellsworth also worried in print that the servants, particularly Tonish, did not show the proper respect to Irving and, in fact, were often rude to him. Irving was sometimes mildly critical about something specific that the men did, but the reader of his journals would in no way infer that Irving was aware of any lack of respect. The journals' narrator often understated difficulties; for instance, after leaving camp on October 14, Irving wrote that "In climbing a rocky hill the girths of my horse gave way and I have a fall, but am not hurt." Irving did not include this incident in the *Tour*, but Ellsworth found it frightening enough to comment at some length about the danger of Irving's falling on his hip "upon the sharp flinty ground" and the spooked horse's reaction.[78] When the party was exposed to a dangerous disease, Irving wrote simply that because Mr. Berryhill's family suffered "with bloody flux," the party pitched tents in the farmyard (October 10). Upon entering Pawnee country, the captain imposed restrictions on the men; Irving's rather casual remark that "it will be difficult to teach our young fellows caution—they are in the land of a silent, watchful crafty people" does not reveal the real danger in which the party was at that moment (October 15).

Something of the immediate spirit of the often exciting, dangerous, uncomfortable, and unpredictable journey is lost in the polished version of Irving's *Tour*. Also, Irving's attitude varied from entry to entry, from notebook to notebook, which moods have been "edited out" of his *Tour*. A close reading reveals a change in tone between journals 6 and 8. Irving's journal 7 is missing, but from the descriptions in the other accounts, the days between October 17 and 31 were extremely unpleasant.[79] Two typical days seemed to be October 18 and 19; on the first

77. Ellsworth, *Narrative*, p. 43.
78. *Ibid.*, p. 35.
79. See Ellsworth, *Narrative*, pp. 46–134; Latrobe, *Rambler*, I, 189–238; and Pourtalès, *Journal*, pp. 54–66, 68–74. In an October 18 letter to his sister, WI wrote that the party was "in high spirits. I was never in finer health, or enjoyed myself more, and the idea of exploring a wild country of this magnificent character is very exciting" (*Letters*, II, 729). No letters followed until November 16 from Montgomery's Point on the Mississippi River.

day, two of the men too sick with measles to go on had to turn back to Fort Gibson; Irving's $125 horse was too lame to proceed, and he hired two rangers to lead the horse back to the fort; Rian's son shot a bear and then lost the much needed plunder. On the following day, the party was lost for hours in the rain; Irving's horse was injured when jumping a ditch; the blankets and men were wet through as were the quinine and opium pills. As might be expected, there was dissension among some members of the party, and from Ellsworth's comments, Irving was in a rather bad temper. By the end of the time period included in the missing journal 7, the party had struggled against the forty-mile wide Cross Timbers, by everyone's account the most difficult of the journey; had changed directions from west to south, then to northeast; had overcome quicksand and horrible weather; and had lost and found Pourtalès. Irving also suffered a rash of some kind. Irving had concluded journal 6 with this enthusiastic picture of life on the Western trail:

> Delightful mode of life. Exercise on horseback all the fore part of the day diversified by hunting incidents–then about 3 oclock encamping in some beautiful place & with full appetite for repose, lying on the grass under green trees. in genial weather with a blue cloudless sky–Then so sweet sleeping at night in the open air & when awake seeing the moon & stars through the tree tops– –Such zest for the hardy, simple but savory meals the product of the chase. Venison roasted on spits or broiled on the coals–Turkeys fresh from the thicket–Honey from the tree–coffee–or delightful Prarie tea (October 16).

Journal 8 begins with the following entry:

> Encampt. on the little river–Canadian–In a day or two past discontent in the camp as among the children of Israel in the wilderness–want of bread–for a week past the troops have been out of flour. a corporal last night was put under arrest for mutinous talk on the subject–determined that we start from here direct for the garrison (October 31).

The tone of this journal continues to vary with the fortunes of the little band. The morning following the decision to return to the garrison, there is more optimism; however, as the weather and terrain become more treacherous, Irving used the word "fatiguing" often and complained of the "wretched travelling among rocks, quicksands &c" (November 5). He often included in these entries adjectives such as "miserable," "sterile," "cloudy," "dismal," "raw," "gloomy," "windy," as well as constant laments for falling, dying, or abandoned horses (one after having a colt). However, as the weather periodically cleared or the hunters were occasionally successful, Irving's mood lightened. For instance, he wrote in the evening after a difficult march, "Western horizon a clear apple colour then above a delicate lake then a deep purple blue—not a cloud—Steady chorus of Insects blended into one note—tinkling of horse bells—low murmuring talk of tired rangers round their fires" (November 1). He seemed relieved to write at one point that the "Land improves—fine praries like park scenery, now mellowed by the sober tints of autumn" (November 4). After describing the previous night as a "Clear moonlight frosty night," Irving casually added that "A cup of water standing by the head of my bed froze ½ inch" (November 7), a genial acceptance more like that of the earlier journals before the extremely difficult two weeks in October.

Entertaining to the reader of his journals are Irving's accounts of participating in the wolf chase (October 2) or the bee hunt (October 13), saving a mad dog (October 11), or losing and recovering horses (October 15–16). Perhaps more interesting than these narrative passages, which Irving mined thoroughly for his *Tour*, are the often sketchy but striking descriptions of a natural scene, a fellow traveler, an unusual custom, an early settler, or a solitary Indian. Like the Romantic poets and the Transcendentalists who would follow, Irving was much taken with the picturesque and the "transparent" aspects of nature; he was particularly fond of the picturesque scene as he took the long view of the march or reached the summit of a hill or approached the confluence of two rivers.

Although the imagery in the journals is usually directly descriptive, Irving occasionally used similes or metaphors to compare a natural scene to more civilized life. For instance, the prairie is "like park scenery" (November 4); "woody hills" look like "cultivated country" or the Saline looks "like Park Land" (October 6); one hill is rather strangely "like Pate de Strasborg" and another is described as "limestone rock & stones full of shells & miniature basalt like giant causeway" (September 30). In the more polished *Tour on the Prairies*, Irving compared the prairie rather elaborately to a European scene: "on the summit of a hill, was a singular crest of broken rocks, resembling a ruined fortress. It reminded me of the ruin of some Moorish castle, crowning a height in the midst of a lonely Spanish landscape."[80] Again he wrote that the prairies, rivers, and woodlands were "so beautifully interspersed as to appear to have been laid out by the hand of taste; and they only want

80. *Tour*, p. 133.

here and there a village spire, the battlements of a castle, or the turrets of an old family mansion rising from among the trees, to rival the most ornamented scenery of Europe."[81] In contrast, and more typical of the imagery in the journals, is this passage from the October 16 entry:

> The weather is in its perfection Golden sunshine, not oppressive but animating–Skies without a cloud–&[?] if there be clouds, of feathery texture and lovely tints–air pure, bland, exhilerating–an atmosphere of perfect transparency–and the whole country having the mellow tint of autumn. How exciting to think that we are breaking thro a country hitherto untrodden by whitemen, except perchance the solitary trapper. A Glorious world spread around us without an inhabitant.

Like most early Americans and especially early nineteenth-century travelers, Irving was fascinated by the rivers beside and on which they traveled and over which they made sometimes dangerous crossings–some of them the Ohio, the Mississippi (below Caledonia), Missouri, Osage, Neosho (including LaBette Creek and Cabin Creek), Verdigris, Arkansas, Red Fork, and the Great Canadian River. Irving's favorite scenes ranged from the tranquillity of a moonlit river viewed from camp site or boat deck, to the challenge of treacherous currents, runaway steamboats, and destructive snags, to the activity of a busy river port town. He was often effectively cryptic: the Arkansas River had "picturesque bluffs of tinted woodlands," banks which were "crumbling and abrupt" and which were "beautifully diversified by high bluffs of wood & rock–long willowed reaches–rich bottoms–and embowered promontories" (October 15). A lonely and still dawn on the Arkansas River near the mouth of the Illinois was "the Sabbath of the woods" (November 11). At one point on the Ohio River, Irving mentioned a show boat on the Illinois shore, then continued:

> Groups assembled there–rifle shooting–Horse race–along shore–negro laugh––Sunset–party breaks up–some in boat across glassy river singing ballad–others on horseback through the wood–some on foot–Some loiter on the shore–beautiful clear evg sky–moon nearly full rising over the Virginia shore above tufted forests–night hawks (September 8).

Irving's imagery included more suggestion of texture than color, more sounds than smells, and more details of dress than of diet. Per-

81. *Ibid.*, p. 136. In the notes at the end of journal 3, WI mentioned Mrs. Trollope's objection that there were "Few evergreens in the west," a rather strange selection of detail.

haps it was Irving's skill in sketching, his ability to pick a few extremely effective details that led to a fashion show of western dress in these journals. Black Hawk (not the famous Indian) was "a young river dandy. green marines short coat. domestic cloth trousers—low crowned broad brimmed white hat" (September 7). An old man had a "lantherned" jaw (October 11); the Negro Stewart was "very black with bright madrass handkerchief on head—large feet gold ear rings—Shirt collar up to his ears—white jacket & trousers checquered apron to his armpits" (September 4). When he first encountered young Captain Bean, Irving noticed that he was about forty years old "in leather Hunting dress & leather Stockgs" and that Dr. Holt was wearing "grey jacket. Linsey woolsey jacket & trousers—cloth hunting cap" (October 13). One young man wore a "straw hat not unlike a bee hive" (October 13). Irving noted Col. Chouteau's "calico surcoat after the Indian cut" (October 7) as well as describing the sophisticated Yankee Ellsworth as a Robin Hood "in half citizen half chasseur dress—embroidered leathern indian Pouch. Powder horn with red delicate worsted band" (October 10).

Irving's talent for describing dress in a few hastily jotted words and phrases was perhaps best spent on his Indians. In a camp scene, an Osage Indian "attempts to put blanket of ours on [his horse]—fine scene, figure of Indian—naked breast—blanket wild piebald Horse wild eyes—collar with red tuft of horsehair" (October 12). A cook in an Osage hunting party was "a tall man painted—head decorated with feather—Had an old great Coat, with a wolfs tail dangling below" (undated notes at end of journal 6). The more spectacularly dressed Creek Indians fascinated Irving, one "with turban, one end hanging over blue hunting shirt—horn rifle looked like Arab" and another with calico hunting shirt and "scarlet & blue &c handerchief round head—leather & scarlet leggings" (October 10). The following day, Irving wrote that they passed "several creeks, one with scarlet turban and plume of black feathers like a cocks tail. one with white turban & red feathers—Oriental look—like Sultans on the Stage" (October 11).

Related to Irving's attention to details of dress was his intense interest in the people who inhabited the West. He was alert to the reactions of early settlers, Negroes, and Indians to frontier life, and he included in the journals the negative as well as the positive aspects. He recorded that one man from Philadelphia who had been in the West for fifteen years said that if he had it to do over, he would not come primarily because there was "No means of educating his children" (September 9). One couple from Louisiana were "discouraged at the coldness of climate here" (September 12), and a woman from Nashville said that she and her husband would go back home when their four-year lease expired. Her primary complaint was that there was "no church in the neighborhood" and when a preacher did come, "the rude fellows pelt him & cut his horse loose & play[?] all kinds of tricks" (September 9). One French couple, he a blacksmith and she the proprietress of a café, told Irving of their being victims of an early American "flim-flam": a Frenchman named Lucas described land for sale in Kentucky "as a paradise[–]four roads turnpike met–diligence every day. The very place to set up." They came to America, turned down an opportunity to locate in New Orleans, and then "arrived at the promised land & found it a wilderness covered with trees–the four roads were 4 tracks thro forest–The Diligence a Stage waggon that plied 2 months in year when there was no steam boat" (September 10).

Irving was particularly interested in the Negro and the Indian, and he recorded in the dated as well as the undated portions of the journals stories told him around the campfire, on the boats, in the inns, etc. He was sensitive to the plight of the Negro living under the yoke of slavery, yet he did not seem angry about the institution. Irving wrote that after talking to a cheerful Negro woman on the Virginia side of the Wabash, "Mr Ellsworth asked about her children As the tears started into her eyes she got up crossed the hutt–I am not allowed to live with them–they are up at the plantation" (September 8). In the September 11 entry Irving wrote that one slave owner told him that "he never struck a negro since he was a boy. would not Sell one unless the negro wished to go away." Irving was also interested in the story of a thirty-six-year old Negro merchant who traded fowls down the river, for twelve years saving money by buying at one dollar and selling at three and who "lays up money to buy himself free. buries it. Cannot buy himself till next year Has wife & children but cannot buy them–Means to go when free where he can make most money but means to see[?] his wife & children occasionally & take care of them" (September 11). Irving also told the story of Governor Clark's slave York, one of three the governor set free, who fared poorly in his new state: "Damn this freedom said York I have never had a happy day since I got it" (September 13). Irving's ambivalence can be detected in this longer passage at the end of Journal 3:

> Negros–some prefer hoeing–others ploughing–others driving wagon. Some dislike wagoning because they have to take care of the cattle at night & on Sunday.
>
> Merriest people in these parts–If you hear a broad merry laugh be sure it is a negro–politest people. Fine Gentlemen–

> Evil of negroes they may be parted from their children—But are not white people so—by schooling—marriage—business &c.

As might be expected, it was the Indian to whom Irving was most attentive.[82] He attempted to imitate in writing Indian dialects; he enjoyed noting the superstitions of the Indians, such as the fear of killing an owl (October 13) and the joke/myth about the creation of the mosquito (October 4). Many of these myths found their way into the literary account of the journey West, and after presenting several of them, Irving wrote, "These are simple and artless tales, but they had a wild and romantic interest heard from the lips of half-savage narrators, round a hunter's fire, in a stormy night, with a forest on one side, and a howling waste on the other; and where, peradventure, savage foes might be lurking in the outer darkness."[83]

Irving's point of view changed rather significantly and naturally, depending on the persons with whom he was traveling or talking at the time of his jottings. These shifts are largely "edited" from *A Tour on the Prairies*. At the missions of the Reverend Mr. Dodge, the Reverend Mr. Requa, Mr. Vaill, and Mr. Jones, the emphasis in the journals was on the "civilizing" of the Indians, their education, and their beauty. At the agency of Colonel Chouteau or traveling with General Clark, both of whom were far from fond of missionaries, Irving paid more attention to the Indians' cunning, wily traits, tribal and religious customs, such as mourning and burial rites. This picture was a more varied one; for instance, Irving noted that a Pawnee boy at the Chouteau Agency was being prohibited from returning to his tribe because he would reveal the secrets of the agency including where the horses were kept (October 4). On the other hand, many of these stories are sentimental, such as the touching story of the little Indian girl who died and was buried with her favorite toys and her pony (October 4). Irving also tried to make character distinctions among the tribes: southern Indians were more intelligent than northern Indians (September 26); Osage warriors were of noble attitude (October 3); Choctaws were honest; Cherokees were sly, bargaining, avaricious, factious, electioneering; Osages were "Hunters—full of ceremonies & superstitions—We are poor people say they—we cannot farm & our hunting is failing us—The pride of the Osages is broken"

82. Journal 5, written when WI was traveling with Colonel Chouteau—who had lived among the Indians, traded with them, intermarried and had concubines among them—is especially full of the myths, customs, and descriptions of the Indians. See particularly the October 4 entry of that journal as well as the undated portions at the end of the journal.

83. *Tour*, p. 130.

(end of journal 6). Irving added that they steal horses, perhaps after having given "you a grand ceremony," but General Clark had earlier told Irving that "we ought not to set our faces agst Indians Stealing Horses, must not Shut up the only road left them to honour & promotion" (September 27). Irving also had an eye for the ladies: in two entries on successive days, he noticed and described in his journal the loveliness of naked Indian "nymphs" bathing on the banks of the Neosho River (October 6–7).

As curious as he was, Irving was not altogether comfortable with the merging of customs among white man, Negro, and Indian on the frontier in 1832. He described at length Colonel Chouteau's house and servants—an old Negro who was "mouth from ear to ear," Indians roasting venison and sitting on the floor with knees to chin, half-breeds, among them a sister of Chouteau's concubine—as well as assorted dogs, cats, hens, turkeys, and geese who wandered about the piazza or hall. Then this man of the East and citizen of the world concluded: "In These establishments the world is turned upside down[:] the Slave the master—the master the slave. The other has the idea of property[—]the latter the reality. The former owns[—]the latter enjoys it. The former has to plan & scheme and guard & economize—the latter thinks only of living enjoying[—] cares nothing how it comes or how it goes" (October 6).

THE DUTCH TOUR, 1833

The final dated entry of journal 9 of the Western journals was November 17, 1832, at Stack Island in the Mississippi River. Almost exactly one month later, on December 18, Irving wrote a long letter to his brother Peter from "Washington City," summarizing his tour West as well as the days following that final entry. He spent several days in New Orleans and then on a mail stage passed a "long and rather a dreary journey" from New Orleans "through Mobile . . . through Alabama, Georgia, South and North Carolina, and Virginia, to Washington."[84] He went on to say that although he had intended to proceed to New York after a few days in Washington, he had decided to "linger for some time" in the capital. He reaffirmed his delight in his native land, and his comments about politics are revealing in light of the degree to which he became immediately involved in the Jackson circle:

> You have no idea how agreeably one can live in this country, especially one, like myself, who can change place at will, and meet friends at every turn. Politics also, which makes such a figure in

84. *Letters*, II, 736.

> the newspapers, do not enter so much as you imagine into private life; . . . in fact, the mode of living, the sources of quiet enjoyment, and the sphere of friendly and domestic pleasures, are improved and multiplied to a degree that would delightfully surprise you.[85]

What happened in the subsequent months was that this "apolitical" literary man stayed in Washington and was everywhere "received with a cordiality, I may say an affection, that keeps my heart full and running over."[86] In this April 1, 1833, letter to Peter from New York, Irving explained that he had only recently returned home, having become fascinated with the political drama; that he had remained in Washington for the entire session of Congress, attending the sessions in the Senate so closely that he became acquainted "with the nature and operation of our institutions, and the character and concerns of the various parts of the Union, that I could not have learned from books for years."[87]

During this decade,[88] Irving's relationship with Martin Van Buren was important and stormy. In Andrew Jackson's first term as president (1829–1833), Van Buren was secretary of state; in August, 1831, he was appointed by the president as minister to the Court of St. James in London, where Irving was the secretary of the legation. Irving and Van Buren worked together for the next seven months until, after complicated political maneuvering on both sides of the Atlantic, Van Buren was not confined by Congress. Then Van Buren's political fortunes, like the phoenix, rose as he was chosen by Jackson as his running mate in the 1832 election. Van Buren's New York "Regency" background and his friendship with Irving during their London days prompted a personal and political association which belied Irving's disavowal of party politics. Irving told his nephew and biographer Pierre Irving in the summer of 1858 that in writing about George Washington, "I must deal cautiously with the party questions. I wish to stand in my history where Washington stood, who was of no party";[89] however, from 1833 until 1840, Irving was a political intimate of Van Buren—advising, interceding on behalf of family and friends, and traveling with Van Buren down the Hudson in the autumn of 1833, a trip he called his Dutch Tour.

85. *Ibid.*, p. 737.

86. *Ibid.*, p. 756.

87. *Ibid.*, pp. 756–57.

88. The most complete and helpful discussion of this period in WI's life is in chapters 27–30 of STW, II, especially "Citizen of the Republic, 1832–1837," STW, II, 48–71.

89. PMI, IV, 250.

On Tuesday, September 10, Irving wrote in his only extant journal during this decade in America, "Leave Albany with Mr Van Buren & John Van Buren for Kinder Hook"; following that entry is a rather erratically kept account of the trip from September 10 until September 25, 1833. Kinderhook was a town in Columbia County in New York twenty miles below Albany on the west side of the Hudson River. In 1830 its population was 2,706, and its most famous son was Martin Van Buren, who was born there in 1782. Irving seemed less interested in describing the scenery than he had in the August, 1832, journal 2 when he first returned from Europe and made the same trip in the opposite direction. In one undated section (probably September 21), he did note: "Surveying the varied valley of the Catskill[?]—and a rich broken country of vast extent watered by various Streams winding their way to bear their tributes to the Hudson." He listed people to whom Van Buren introduced him, and when they met the county clerk, Mr. Snyder, Irving wrote, "inspect old treaties in Dutch & English with Indians" (September 20). When he attended church in Goshen, he noted that it was a "good sermon from the Episcopal preacher Mr Clark of Brooklyn" (September 22). For obvious reasons, Irving seemed more interested in stories of André, in descriptions of Dutch clothes, and the names of mountain ranges. The two-week trip ended in Hackensack and Cummunipaw, notes about which Irving scribbled on page [1] of the journal.

The association with Van Buren became cooler toward the latter part of the decade. Irving was a "Jackson Democrat" in most senses of the word as was Van Buren, Jackson's choice as "heir" to the presidency in 1836. For instance, Irving was aligned with the Democrats on the controversial issue of nullification; but as he had done between England and America in his years abroad, Irving tried to walk a thin line between factions. He attempted to be the referee between Democrats Louis McLane and Van Buren; he frequently interceded with President Van Buren on behalf of one member of the New York group, James Kirke Paulding. Van Buren was surprised and probably hurt that Irving refused his offer in 1838 to be secretary of the navy and therefore in Van Buren's cabinet. Irving's letter of reply to the president includes the following revealing statement:

> I shrink from the harsh cares and turmoils of public and political life at Washington, and feel that I am too sensitive to endure the bitter personal hostility, and the slanders and misrepresentations of the press, which beset high station in this country. This argues, I confess, a weakness of spirit and a want of true philosophy, but

> I speak of myself as I am, not as I ought to be. Perhaps, had my ambition led me to a higher carreer, and aimed at official distinction I might have become enured to the struggle; but it has laid in a different and more secluded path, and has nurtured in me habits of quiet, and a love of peace of mind, that daily unfit me, more and more, for the collisions of the world.[90]

Irving's refusal to go "public" in politics, to take definite stands on one issue or another, angered both sides. Many were vicious in their attacks, especially James Fenimore Cooper, who was at once harshly critical of his country and passionately patriotic. That someone like Irving could view politics as a drama,[91] remaining largely aloof from its bloody battles, prompted Cooper and others to attack Irving personally and in print, the very outcome Irving had sought to avoid by not accepting Van Buren's offer of political office. Van Buren subsequently thought his friend a traitor to him and the party; in fact, Irving, Paulding, and Kemble "defected" in the 1840 election and actively supported William Henry Harrison and John Tyler who were running on the Whig ticket.

NEW YORK TO BAYONNE, 1842

By the early spring of 1841 when President Harrison had taken office and subsequently pneumonia (he died after one month in office), Irving's financial and literary fortunes were at a relatively low ebb. Investments made when he was enjoying the financial success of the early 1830's had been diminished by the Panic of 1837. The old method of culling travel journals and commonplace books did not seem to be yielding the literary fruit which had for so long kept his reputation high among his American and English readers. Emerson's "Nature" was published in 1836, and in spite of the rising transcendental star, Irving continued to be mentioned as one of America's leading writers, although often critics used the past tense when referring to him. He was still compared to that Englishman of an earlier era, Goldsmith, and Irving's two-volume *Life of Oliver Goldsmith* (1840) only served to reinforce this comparison. In contrast with Emerson's literary view of the world through a "transparent eyeball" was Irving's through a sentimental tear as he wrote a biography and described the *Poetical Remains of the Late Margaret Miller Davidson* in 1841. Irving relinquished his literary interests in Mexico to Prescott and was financially pressed to spend two and

90. STW, II, 68.
91. *Ibid.*, p. 64.

a half years in a field he said that he would never again pursue—journalism.[92] However, he was much read, and Philip Hone's pleased reaction to Irving's appointment as American minister to Spain in February, 1842, included the judgment that "He is a charming good fellow, a feather in the literary cap of his country."[93]

Still, it had been only a decade since Irving made his public pledge at the New York banquet that he would remain in this country "as long as I live."[94] The reader of his December 18, 1832, letter to Peter would have been prepared for this apparent change of heart, this willingness to return to Europe as minister to Spain a decade later:

> As to the kind of pledge I gave, you are correct in your opinion. It was given in the warmth and excitement of the moment—was from my lips before I was aware of its unqualified extent, and is to be taken *cum grano salis*. It is absolutely my intention to make our country my home for the residue of my days; and the more I see of it, the more I am convinced, that I can live here with more enjoyment than in Europe; but I shall certainly pay my friends in France, and relations in England, a visit, in the course of a year or two, to pass joyously a season in holiday style.[95]

The decade had taken its personal toll; in 1838, Irving's beloved Peter—brother and confidant—died. The same year his brother John Treat Irving died; subsequently, Irving's favorite niece and the family member who had partially taken Peter's place as trusted confidante, Sarah Paris, had married Mr. Storrow and moved to Paris. In a letter to her in July, 1841, Irving wrote that he "envied you your half wicked Parisian Sunday; at church in the morning and at S'Cloud in the afternoon" in contrast to his own Sunday surrounded by the "commonplace."[96] It is not surprising that for all of these reasons Irving accepted President Tyler's appointment to Spain in 1842.

After intense periods of study of the trade with Spain and Cuba, many discussions with Tyler and Daniel Webster, and some political unpleasantness over the appointment of the secretary of the legation (Irving's choice, Alexander Hamilton, was finally appointed), Irving set off from New York. At this point he began keeping his final extant journal, dated by him "April 10th. to July 20th. 1842" (Front cover); the April 10 entry includes his being taken by family members and friends to the

92. See the chapter, "At Sunnyside: 1837–1842," in STW, II, 92–118.
93. STW, II, 114.
94. See p. xix in this introduction.
95. *Letters*, II, 736–37.
96. STW, II, 97.

dock and a very brief summary of the voyage to England on the packet ship *Independence*, a crossing "without any incident of moment excepting the losing of a boy overboard...." They landed on April 29 in Bristol, and then on May 1, 1842, arrived in London. In the afternoon, Irving walked through the parks in the West End of the city, and his reaction to being once again in London is interesting: "Felt singularly low Spirited. Dreaded to throw myself once more into this turbulent Stream of life and to encounter the harrassing parade and dissipation of the great world" (May 1). The following day after calling on people and shopping, Irving "Returned home fatigued & dispirited" (May 2); however, on May 3, Irving called on his old publisher Murray and in light of the ten-year estrangement, the entry is revealing: "Called this day at Murrays. My heart was in my throat on finding myself in the drawing room the Scene of many an interesting literary meeting at the early period of my London Career. Kindly received by Murray and his family, promised to dine with them on my return to town." They did in fact dine together on May 10, and Irving's mood seemed infinitely lighter after this initial meeting with Murray. From May 1 until May 20, Irving's days were filled, as was his journal, with a whirlwind of social engagements—attending opera and theater, calling on and dining with the leading social, literary, and political figures of the day, including the queen, who was "pleasing in her appearance, acquits herself with grace and ease. Prince Albert tall, well formed a bland prepossessing countenance & demeanour" (May 5). During these three weeks, Irving went twice to Birmingham and was an honored guest at the Anniversary of the Literary Fund dinner. He wrote that "Prince Albert presided," and Irving, sitting "between Moore & Hallam," was "very nervous throughout the dinner knowing my health was to be drunk" (May 11). On May 21, Irving left London for Southhampton and the ship to LeHavre; he arrived in Paris on May 24, where he stayed with the Storrows. He was in Paris until July 11, during which time he kept a very erratic journal, omitting thirty-four days on the one hand and then writing an extremely full entry on June 7. On occasion, he seemed a typical tourist at the Invalids, fascinated by Napoleon's resting place (June 3), then he seemed rather casual about being presented to the king and his court (June 4). From July 11 until July 20, Irving traveled from Paris to Bayonne, spending four days at Bordeaux (July 15–19) along the way. The journal concludes with Irving's rather relieved comment that after the all-night diligence trip from Bordeaux to Bayonne, "Take bath. Stroll about the town" (July 20). This journal was his last.

Although it seems a bit strange, Irving apparently did not keep journals during his four years as Minister to Spain, but he did write long dispatches to the government in Washington as well as many letters to family and friends. According to Stanley Williams, Irving was a capable Minister. His tendency to view the affairs of state as a drama suited him for the role as diplomat more comfortably than as a party politician. The foreign service was during this century more often manned by amateurs than it is in our time, and Irving's popularity in Spain as a writer and as a person who appreciated Spanish castles and tales was a tremendous advantage to him and to his country's relationship with Spain in this crucial period. Irving worked diligently to understand the undercurrents of Spanish politics and by August, 1842, he sent home

> a summary of national conditions. At last, on November 5 he composed a long, characteristic message to Webster, who is said to have dropped sometimes all other business for the pleasure of reading the prose of his literary diplomat. This dispatch, like the rest throughout the four years, hardly adheres to the traditional barren form. Employing quotation and anecdote, it is touched with sympathy and satire.[97]

Williams concludes that "few Americans would have accomplished more for their country in Spain between 1842 and 1846 than did Irving."[98] In fact, the letter from Andrew Jackson to President Polk asking that one of Jackson's old political friends, Amos Kendall, replace Irving as minister to Spain, reveals more about Jackson than it does about the literary or diplomatic quality of Irving's endeavors: Jackson wrote, "There can be no delicacy in recalling Erwin . . . he is only fit to write a book and scarcely that."[99]

Irving returned to this country on September 18, 1846, and spent the remainder of his life being entertained by an admiring society, entertaining friends and family at Sunnyside, and receiving the attention of the next generation of American literary figures. He did not resume the habit of his earlier years in keeping journals; perhaps he realized that it would not be his personal recollections which would provide grist for his literary mill, but rather his life-long passion—his life of George Washington—and to that end he took voluminous notes. On Friday, May 20, on the way from Birmingham to London, Irving mentioned in his last journal that he stopped at Sulgrave, the "natal

97. *Ibid.*, p. 149. For a full discussion of WI's career as a diplomat in Spain, see chapters 21–24 in STW, II, 119–200.

98. *Ibid.*, p. 200.

99. Samuel Eliot Morison, *The Oxford History of the American People* (New York: Oxford University Press, 1965), pp. 423–24.

place of the Washington Family" and he included in the entry some family history and long descriptions of the landscape, Gothic churches, etc.

Irving had long been interested in writing about the man for whom he was named. In eighteen of his May, 1825, journal entries, he mentioned reading John Marshall's biography of Washington (Philadelphia, 1804–1807), from the May 2 entry when he "read 50 pages of Marshalls life of Washington" to the May 30 entry when he "finished Marshalls life of Washington before getting up."[100] In July, 1825, Irving "received overtures from Constable for a Life of Washington";[101] and in a July 31, 1828, letter from Seville to Mr. Everett, Irving said that Jared Sparks was then in London "prosecuting his researches and endeavoring to bargain with Murray for his correspondence, &c., of Washington. . . ."[102] Pierre Irving says that at the close of 1829, Irving was "bending his thoughts to a Life of Washington, and vainly flattering himself that he would begin upon it at once" and adds that years "were to elapse before this final labor of his pen was even commenced."[103] In a *New-York Mirror* article dated January 23, 1836, Irving was encouraged to write of Washington,[104] and an April 15, 1843, article in the same periodical proved that in "America it was known that Irving was at work upon a life of Washington."[105]

After Irving returned from Spain, he apparently began extensive research; in a letter to Pierre in October, 1847, Irving said that he was "much occupied, mind and pen, just now, on the History of Washington . . . ," a task Pierre says occupied Irving daily for several months.[106] Irving wrote Catharine Irving in December that he had "been very busy and very dissipated . . . at work all the mornings in the libraries."[107] Because of other publishing schedule demands, Irving once again laid aside this work, and in 1849 he expressed to Pierre "the most earnest

100. *Journals and Notebooks*, III, 480–89.

101. PMI, II, 238.

102. *Ibid.*, p. 335. Sparks would research his biography from 1828 until 1838, fearing all the while that WI's biography would be published before his and, because of WI's popularity, would undercut it (STW, II, 17, 332, n. 128). As it happened, Sparks' work was WI's chief source, and in 1841, when WI wrote to his bookseller, he asked that he be sent any works about Washington except those of Marshall and Sparks, which he already had. Sparks was very critical of WI's overuse and undercredit of his work, but Williams says that the latter's dependence on these limited sources has been exaggerated (STW, II, 227–28).

103. PMI, II, 424–25.

104. STW, II, 229, 397, n. 61.

105. *Ibid.*, p. 379, n. 75.

106. PMI, IV, 31.

107. *Ibid.*, p. 32.

desire to begin anew upon his Life of Washington," fearing that his health would fail before he finished this task.[108] Irving's two-volume *Mahomet and His Successors* was published in 1850, and beginning in 1851, the main thrust of Irving's writing was the Washington biography.[109] In an October 20, 1851, letter to Mrs. Storrow, Irving said that he was "fully engaged on the life of Washington. A task which was commenced nine years ago but which has been repeatedly interrupted and laid aside."[110] According to Williams, Irving was turning to "notes collected during some twenty-five years," and by 1853, the correspondence, library visits, pilgrimages to places relating to Washington, and gleanings from newspapers, government documents, and personal papers, and the conversations with innumerable people about Washington completely consumed him.[111] *Wolfert's Roost*, a collection of Irving's pieces from periodicals in the late 1830's and early 1840's, was published in 1855 with relatively little effort. The first volume of Irving's *Life of Washington* appeared in 1855, and he saw the final volume of the five through publication in 1859. Washington Irving died on November 28, 1859, at Sunnyside.

AMERICAN NOTEBOOKS, COMMONPLACE BOOKS

Reproducing notebooks and commonplace books as Irving wrote them helps the student of Irving to understand how he filled his leisure hours as well as how he worked. Irving was an inveterate keeper of notebooks, perhaps the result of his being in large measure a self-educated man. His creative process often included gleaning from a notebook, journal, or commonplace book the germ for a work. In discussing his research methods for his final work, *Life of Washington*, Irving admitted that he had no system. In fact, he said, "I never had any: you must go to Bancroft for that: I have, it is true, my little budgets of notes—some tied one way—some another—and which when I need, I think I come upon in my pigeon-holes—by a sort of instinct. That is all there is of it."[112]

Following his trip West in 1832, Irving collected from several sources "Notes Concerning the Far West," here published as "American Notebooks (1833)," numbers 1, 2, and 3. In the first of these three cardboard-bound notebooks, Irving gathered most of his information from Timothy Flint's *The History and Geography of the Mississippi Valley*, by 1833

108. *Ibid.*, p. 64.
109. STW, II, 216.
110. *Ibid.*, pp. 227, 397, n. 42.
111. *Ibid.*, pp. 216–17.
112. *Ibid.*, p. 229.

in its third edition. Irving had copied from Flint in the Western journals; for instance, at the end of journal 3 are several anecdotes about Indians from Flint. The topics which he found interesting enough to copy ranged from the difference between prairie grass and blue grass to the difference between the prairie wolf and the prairie dog. He made several notes about different types of birds of the West, particularly the owl.

In the second and third notebooks "Concerning the Far West," Irving quoted from two additional sources. In the second, he referred primarily to the Lewis and Clark journals. One especially long passage concerns the Osage Indians, the tribe with which Irving was more often in contact during the Western tour than any other of the tribes. Other subjects include Indian customs such as the Indian female's ritual of submission when she senses that death from an enemy is imminent, as well as ringing the antelope, making a Shoshone shield, and several religious "superstitions." In the third notebook, Irving quoted, usually closely, from Edwin James' *Account of an Expedition . . . under the Command of Maj. S. H. Long* (originally published in 1823). Subjects from "Long," as he called this work, which interested him were Indian mounds, various Indian beliefs, and prairie animals such as owls, bees, wild horses, and prairie dogs. About most of these topics Irving had made notes in the journals when he was "on the scene," and he seemed to be adding to the firsthand knowledge by reading these secondary sources. It is profitable to note how he used his sources at this point in his career by reading chapter 32 in *A Tour on the Prairies*, "A Republic of Prairie Dogs," and comparing it to the passages from Flint, Lewis and Clark, and Long as well as his own observations while on the prairie.

Although the three commonplace books here reproduced are undated, it becomes clear upon research that they are all earlier than the 1832 beginning date for the journals of this volume of the *Journals and Notebooks*. The initial and shortest of the three is a commonplace book, "Concerning Will Wizard, the Courts, Government, etc." The notebook contains long passages on Will Wizard's taste and personality (spoken in an "elbow-chair" tone) as well as opinions of government, courts of law, logocracy, customs, etc. In the introduction to *Salmagundi*, Martha Hartzog says that this undated notebook contains early descriptions of Will Wizard, particular ones of which would appear in numbers 7 and 14 of *Salmagundi*.[113] If this notebook antedates even these numbers, it

113. Bruce I. Granger and Martha Hartzog, eds., *Washington Irving: Letters of Jonathan Oldstyle, Gent.* and *Salmagundi: or The Whim-whams and Opinions of Launcelot Langstaff, Esq. & Others* (Boston: Twayne Publishers, 1977), p. 319, n. 2; hereafter cited as *Oldstyle* and *Salmagundi*.

would have been written before April, 1807. Stanley Williams says that the "idea of such a periodical had been simmering in Irving's mind since his first cigar with his friends in Hoffman's law office in 1806."[114] It is possible that this notebook, along with letters to Kemble and others of the "nine worthies," was written during this period in 1806. Hartzog goes on to say that in later years, James Kirke Paulding wrote that he and Irving were both under twenty years old when they thought of writing a little periodical for their own pleasure, and that each separately prepared an introductory paper;[115] if Irving wrote this notebook before he was twenty, its composition date would be during or before 1803.

In the December 21, 1823, entry in his French journal, Irving mentioned the desire of "Young Galignani" to republish *Salmagundi,* but at that point he had refused permission. Reichart points out that Irving did allow the papers to be reprinted by Galignani in 1824.[116] In a later entry in his journal, on January 7, 1824, Irving said, "Call this morng at Galignanis   agree to correct Salmagundi for him–."[117] One month later, on February 4, 1824, Irving wrote in the journal, "Correct Salmagundi . . . . Call at Galignanis & leave copy of Salmagundi."[118] Perhaps this notebook is a part of that revision.

Although many casual readers of Irving think of his life as one of genteel indulgence, there were extended periods during which he suffered major setbacks and, as a result, deep depression. One of the ways that he fought depression was to write—letters, sketches, or passages in commonplace books. At one point, he simply copied long passages from plays, here reproduced as "Passages from Elizabethan and Jacobean Plays," a manuscript housed in and dated by the Folger Shakespeare Library in Washington as ca. 1810, but which seems more likely to have been copied in 1817 or 1818.

Beginning in September, 1815, Irving spent approximately two years in a deep depression; during this time, failure of the business in which he was involved with his brothers, the death of his mother, and the illness of Peter, among other disappointments, led to his misery. In a November 6, 1816, letter to Brevoort, Irving apologized for not having written, but explained that "when I do take hold of my pen, I feel so poverty struck, such mental sterility, that I throw it down again in

114. STW, I, 79.

115. *Oldstyle* and *Salmagundi*, p. 319, n. 2.

116. *Journals and Notebooks*, III, 260, n. 383.

117. *Ibid.*, p. 266.

118. *Ibid.*, p. 283.

despair of writing any thing that should give you gratification."[119] At the end of July, 1817, Irving left Liverpool—the location of the failing business—and went to London, where he spent three weeks before he traveled to Scotland. He wrote to Brevoort about this London sojourn and reported that although the place was rather deserted, he explored interesting parts of the city, descriptions of which would later be included in *The Sketch Book.*[120]

Soon after Irving arrived in Scotland, he met Sir Walter Scott, and an association followed which seems to have lifted Irving's spirits. He wrote to his brother Peter on September 6, 1817, that he "never left any place with more regret" than he left Abbotsford and his daily ramblings with Scott.[121] Other letters from Scotland as well as his journal reveal a new optimistic spirit. He wrote to his brother William on December 23, 1817, that for "a long while past, I have lived almost entirely at home; sometimes not leaving the house for two or three days," and he added that his "future career must depend very much upon myself, and therefore every step I take at present, is done with proper consideration."[122] He wrote in a January, 1818, journal entry that it "has pleased heaven that I should be driven on upon my inner strength—and resort to the citadel[?] within me."[123] Irving also wrote that the "idea . . . suddenly came to return to my pen, not so much for support, for bread & water had no terrors for me, but to reinstate myself in the worlds thoughts—to raise myself from the degradation into which I considered myself fallen. I took my resolution—threw myself a stranger into London, shut myself up and went to work."[124] It was during this period that Irving took notes from *The Works of Sir William Temple* published in London in 1814,[125] the time which Williams calls "*The Sketch Book*'s prenatal period," when Irving became "a prospector on the trail of literary gold, and a rather anxious one."[126] According to Williams, Irving's "saturation in Elizabethan prose and poetry . . . reached its height between the years 1818 and 1822, during the composition of *The Sketch Book* and *Bracebridge Hall.*" Williams adds that "*Bracebridge Hall* alludes to some twenty writers of the sixteenth and seven-

119. *Letters*, I, 457.
120. *Ibid.*, pp. 494 ff.
121. PMI, I, 383.
122. *Ibid.*, p. 393.
123. Stanley T. Williams, ed., *Tour in Scotland, 1817* (New Haven: Yale University Press, 1927), p. 104.
124. STW, I, 155.
125. Williams, ed., *Tour in Scotland*, pp. 106–07.
126. STW, I, 155–56.

teenth centuries, and the notebook of 1818 is swollen with extracts from Spenser, Carew, and Robert Southwell."[127] It seems logical to assume that it was during this period that Irving systematically went through the collections of Dilke and Dodsley, among others, and copied extensively from dozens of Elizabethan and Jacobean dramatists. Of the twelve plays which Irving copied from the Dilke and Dodsley editions of *Old Plays*, only three were not used in some way in *The Sketch Book* or *Bracebridge Hall.* From Robert Davenport's "The City Nightcap," Irving derived almost the entire five-page sketch, "Wives," in *Bracebridge Hall.* He quoted in that sketch a total of fifty-seven lines of the play directly from his commonplace book, omitting from the sketch only twelve lines of the sixty-nine which he had copied from this play. The sketch is framed as the narrator's finding Lady Lillycraft's album "for which she claims the contributions of all her friends," and in which is a "series of poetical extracts, in the squire's handwriting. . . ." The narrator "took the liberty of copying them out. They are from the old play of Thomas Davenport, published in 1661, intitled 'The City Night-cap.' . . ."[128] Irving had misquoted Robert Davenport's name in the commonplace book as "Thos Davenport." It is for details such as these that it is important to have the commonplace books reproduced in full as Irving wrote them.

The third commonplace book, "Notes on Reading and Observations re: Manners, American Character, Economics, Navy, etc.," is also undated by Irving, but there are many external facts which provide evidence for its being dated 1825 or 1826. On February 2, 1825, Irving wrote to Murray that he was "in want of occupation for my leisure hours. I have been amusing myself for some time in reading Spanish authors and have an idea of making a translation of the novels of Cervantes."[129] On February 5, 1825, Irving wrote in his journal that he had a "Good night. Mind excited. Thinking over project of an Am: work."[130] At this time, Irving was suffering from indecision about what publication next to pursue; from criticism about his patriotic spirit; and from the critical judgment in *Blackwood's* that the American pieces in

127. STW, II, 283.

128. Herbert F. Smith, ed., *Bracebridge Hall or The Humourists: A Medley by Geoffrey Crayon, Gent.* (Boston: Twayne Publishers, 1977), p. 43. Smith notes WI's erroneous reading of "dead sea" for "dread sea," which he says went undetected in all editions of *Bracebridge Hall* (p. 377). There would be no reason for WI to correct the reading, because in the commonplace book to which he was referring, he had copied "dead sea."

129. *Journals and Notebooks,* III, 453, n. 14.

130. *Ibid.*, p. 453.

The Sketch Book were infinitely better than the English pieces and that because *Bracebridge Hall* was so very "English," it was far inferior to the *The Sketch Book.*[131]

There are many similarities between this commonplace book and Irving's dated journals of 1825; therein lies the most convincing evidence of dating this notebook 1825 or 1826. A close comparison reveals references to similar reading, for instance, Moore's *Life of Sheridan*[132] and Feijóo's *Theatro*. There are similar passages in the dated journals of 1825 and the commonplace book; in almost the same words as those in the notebook, Irving wrote in the journal from Bordeaux, November 26, 1825: "Sorrow & trouble soften the heart & render it tender & susceptible. It is quickly sensible to little gleams of pleasure."[133] There are other parallels which support the 1825 dating of the commonplace book, primarily the similarity in topics in the 1825 journals, the dated commonplace book, and this undated one. On the same day in many entries, Irving mentioned having studied Spanish and Latin, written Spanish, and rewritten an essay on manners, travel, etc. In the May 7, 1825, journal entry he had a "Spanish lesson[134] Read in Marshall[135] & Calderon"[136] and "rewrote English composit." Finally, there are similar passages in this undated commonplace book and the one Irving entitled

131. STW, I, 293.

132. In the entry on November 19, 1825, as well as those on November 20 and 23, WI said that he "read Moores life of Sheridan," that he "Read from 5 Oclock in Moores life of Sheridan[–]after breakfast wrote a little in Essay on Manners," and that he "Read in Moores Sheridan" (*Journals and Notebooks*, III, 545–46). In this undated commonplace book, he copied passages from this particular biography published in 1825.

133. *Journals and Notebooks*, III, 696.

134. With the exception of February 24, WI mentioned in every journal entry that month that he studied or had a Spanish lesson or read or wrote Spanish. On March 1, 1825, he said he "Bot Spanish Dictionary," which Reichart says was his second; he also owned a Spanish grammar for his study (*ibid.*, p. 460, n. 47). WI also mentioned in the random jottings at the beginning of that notebook, "Ovras de Feijoo teatro critico &c" (*ibid.*, p. 692). He apparently had a multivolume edition of that work (Benito Geronymo Feijóo, *Theatro Critico Universal, o Discursos Varios en Todo Genero de Materias*) in Paris during his Spanish lessons of February–May, 1825, because he copied three passages from one discourse in volume 7 (Madrid: Don Eugenio Bieco, 1753).

135. WI wrote in eighteen journal entries during May, 1825, that he was reading Marshall's *Life of Washington*, and in this commonplace book, he mentioned "The character of Washtgn as impressed on our constitution & nation" (p. [61]).

136. In a December, 1825, letter, WI asked Storrow to forward eight or nine volumes of Calderon to him from Paris; he quoted extensively from Calderon in the notebook titled "Notes, Extracts, &c" which Reichert dated 1824–1827 (*Journals and Notebooks*, III, 692 ff.).

and dated "Notes Extracts &c / 1825," for example, Chesterfield's *Letters to His Son* on the topic of good manners and good breeding and Cicero's work.

Apparently, Irving had begun a series of American Essays in 1823 in Dresden, continued working on the project in Bordeaux, but never completed it;[137] it seems likely that this undated commonplace book in the Berg Collection at the New York Public Library was a part of the process of gathering material for the series. The notebook is important for several reasons: first, because the essays were never completed or published in the form that Irving intended, this notebook is crucial in reconstructing the tone and matter of the essays. Moreover, the type of material which Irving was reading and from which he copied, including the Spanish writer Feijóo's *Theatro Critico Universal*, Moore's *Life of Sheridan*, Locke's *Conduct of the Understanding*, Chesterfield's *Letters to His Son*, Marshall's *Life of Washington*, among others, helps the student of Irving to determine some of his sources and methods of composition. By August, 1825, Irving had received no encouragement from Murray, and he wrote a rather discouraging note that he had "nothing ready for press, nor do I know at present when I shall have, my mind having been rather diverted from composition of late, and occupied by a course of study."[138]

ACCOUNT BOOKS, CONSULAR INFORMATION, AND MISCELLANEOUS MATERIALS

Completing this volume of the *Journals and Notebooks* of Washington Irving are four account books from this period, two notebooks filled with consular information which Irving made as part of his preparation for the position as Minister to Spain, and sixteen fragments included as miscellaneous materials.

The earliest of the four account books is dated January 6, 1830–July 2, 1831, and includes disbursements for contingencies of the American legation at London while Irving was secretary. When this ledger is reversed (Irving followed his journal pattern of writing back-to-front in a notebook if there were blank pages remaining), it includes personal expenses in 1841 after Irving had returned to this country. The three remaining account books include personal expenses—entertainment, travel, house and farm expenses. They are dated 1840–1841; April 10–

137. For an excellent discussion of these essays, see Richard Dilworth Rust, "Washington Irving's 'American Essays,'" *Resources for American Literary Study*, 10 (Spring, 1980), pp. 3–27.

138. *Journals and Notebooks*, III, 509, n. 64.

July 19, 1842, which coincides with Irving's trip to Spain to assume his duties as Minister; and one account book with entries in 1844, 1845, and 1846. It is helpful to the student of this period in our history to note what the head of a large household found necessary to buy and what the various items cost during that time.

Regarding the two "Consular Information" notebooks, Irving followed his usual pattern of filling notebooks with information which would be helpful to him later. In preparing to go to Spain in 1842, it was natural for him to do research regarding trade between the United States and Spain. In this first consular notebook, Irving copied from the letters of members of the Spanish legation, some dated January 14, 1842, and one as late as March 9, 1842. In a second notebook, Irving copied from a digest some notes on American trade with Spain and Cuba, including lists of principal exports and laws by which Cuba and her exports were governed. It is interesting to the student of Spanish-American relationships and to the student of Irving to read these two notebooks and to observe what the new minister to Spain in 1842 thought was important to note and to remember.

Because this is the final volume in the series of *Journals and Notebooks* of Irving, it is that one to which has fallen much undated and fragmentary material. These fragments, like the commonplace books, belong in most cases to an earlier period than the beginning date of the journals (1832). One of the undated fragments relates to the expenses of building a crib; some of the materials are commonplace book fragments, such as the "Notes for Life of Washington," a fragment until now unidentified and incorrectly cataloged as a portion of Irving's own "Trip Through the West." This fragment is actually an excerpt from Christopher Gist's *Journals* and was a portion of the research which Irving was doing for his *Life of Washington*. Some of the fragments are from early travel journals, such as Irving's accounts in 1805 of Naples and Palermo or the 1821 fragment relating to Paris. There is an interesting undated notebook fragment, "Variations on Goldsmith," and there are several fragments from *Bracebridge Hall*. Two fragments which have more literary importance are "Terms of Settlement with Publisher" (1828) and "Regarding Writing and Publishing Schedules" (1850).

TEXTUAL COMMENTARY

A textual discussion of the materials in this volume must include a consideration of the two previous editions of Irving's Western journals. It may seem, even to the serious student of early American literature, that these jottings in the small numbered notebooks have been sufficiently edited and published. Of the nine journals describing the Western trip, numbers 3, 5, 6, 8, and 9 were first published in volume 3 of *The Journals of Washington Irving*, edited by Willim P. Trent and George S. Hellman. To these men, subsequent editors owe much; as all of us who have transcribed initially from an original Irving manuscript will attest, the first contact is overwhelming. Only after many readings over a long period of time are we able to fill in the dozens of words that seemed hopelessly unrecoverable. However, the text which Trent and Hellman published is often misleading. There are many instances when a word, phrase, or sentence which is difficult to decipher is simply omitted without indication; words which have been guessed at are not questioned; many words are misread; and there is often silent editing. The journals are neither numbered nor separated except by a short line between the last and first entries, and there is very little annotation.

The second version of Irving's Western journals was edited in 1944 by John Francis McDermott as *The Western Journals of Washington Irving*; in the preface of what he called the second edition (actually a second printing in 1966), McDermott wrote that he was letting the earlier text stand except for some corrections of typographical errors. He indicated in the reprinted preface that he had prepared the text from "a microfilm of the originals and the Trent-Hellman edition. . . ."[139] McDermott significantly improved the text of Trent and Hellman, deciphering many words that had earlier been misread or omitted. He also added valuable notes based on careful research.

McDermott's improvements in the textual quality are evident throughout. For instance, in the undated portion of journal 9 (which McDermott numbered journal 5), Irving wrote "boots with ↑brass[?]↓ eagle[?] spurs"; Trent and Hellman transcribed as "boots with eagle spurs,"[140] omitting the word above the line, and McDermott transcribed "boots with [word illegible] eagle spurs."[141] The initial three lines of page [23] of the manuscript of journal 9 are in pencil and are difficult to read: "*Post of the Arkansas*—about here the speculator Law founded his colony." Trent and Hellman omitted the sentence without ellipsis;[142] McDermott transcribed the passage correctly.[143]

On the other hand, because McDermott did not use the original manuscripts, his text is not as exact as it should be. Microfilm often ob-

139. *Western Journals*, p. xi.
140. *Journals of WI*, III, 178.
141. *Western Journals*, pp. 162–63.
142. *Journals of WI*, III, 182.
143. *Western Journals*, p. 166.

scures strikeovers, does not clearly reproduce words written in smudged pencil, and does not separate marks on the film from punctuation marks or even letters. No machine can reproduce an indentation in the paper after the pencil lead with which Irving wrote either broke or ran out. These oddities the eye can often detect, although the number of questioned, illegible, and unrecovered words in this text suggests that even two or three fresh eye readings often leave the editor of Irving frustrated.

Also, it appears that sometimes McDermott followed the transcription of Trent and Hellman rather than referring to the microfilm. For instance, in journal 8 (McDermott's journal 4), there are two pages of manuscript text (pages [9–10]) omitted from the transcriptions of Trent and Hellman and McDermott. McDermott noted that there was not an entry for November 2;[144] on examination of the manuscript, we find the dated entry beginning approximately four lines from the top of page [9]. The subject of one sentence which concludes page [7] and the predicate of another sentence which begins page [10] combine logically; therefore, McDermott did not notice the error. It is possible that these two pages were not photographed for some reason. One curious thing about the error is McDermott's reading of the line which begins the following page of the manuscript: "resume our march [two words illegible] keeping easterly. . . ."[145] Trent and Hellman omitted the two words, which are "about one," without ellipsis;[146] it is therefore evident that McDermott looked at the microfilm of this page.

The two remaining journals in this edition were published in volume 3 of the journals of Irving edited by Trent and Hellman. The first is "American Journal, 1833," titled by Irving "Dutch Tour" with a subtitle "From Albany to Communipaw"; the second is "Journal, 1842," Irving's last extant journal, which he titled "New York to Bayonne." That portion of miscellaneous notes "Regarding Writing and Publishing Schedules [1850]" was published as Appendix IV in Ben Harris McClary's *Washington Irving and the House of Murray*.[147] The remaining notebooks, consular information, account books, commonplace books, and miscellaneous materials are published in this volume for the first time.

James Thorpe's admonition to the editor that his job is simply "to present the text which the author intended"[148] is at once a comfort and

144. *Ibid.*, p. 143, n. 9.

145. *Ibid.*, p. 143.

146. *Journals of WI*, p. 161. See p. 141, n. 33 for a more detailed discussion of this error.

147. *WI and the House of Murray*, pp. 217–20.

148. James Thorpe, *Principles of Textual Criticism* (San Marino, Calif.: Huntington Library, 1972), p. 50.

a curse to the editor of Irving. Nathalia Wright, whose initial volume in this series of journals has been a model of excellence to all of us who have come after, said that her aim was "to provide a reliable text, short of an absolutely literal transcription, which is manifestly impossible. . . ."[149] Irving's handwriting is difficult to read even when he sat at a desk copying from Flint's *Mississippi Valley* or Marlowe's *Lust's Dominion* or writing a letter to a friend. But when keeping a travel account or an account book which he never intended to have anyone read, Irving often wrote in haste, carelessly, and sometimes under difficult circumstances—at night, by firelight, in uncomfortable inns, and even while fording a river, an incident which Henry Ellsworth described in his own *Narrative*. The fact that Irving often used a pencil, particularly when jotting in his Western notebooks, adds to the difficulty of transcribing, because pencil is far more prone to smudge with carrying throughout the West and with handling through the years.

Several general editorial decisions were made at the outset of this project; for instance, the transcription does not indicate manuscript page numbers,[150] and pages in the manuscript are referred to by number only when there is some significant detail which makes the page noteworthy. Datelines have been regularized with the day of the week, the month, and the day's date underlined and flush left at the beginning of each day's entry (the year is given at the beginning of the journal, notebook, or miscellaneous item). Irving's actual indication of dateline is given for each entry in a footnote as he wrote it and in quotation marks. After the regularized dateline, the entry begins as a new paragraph on the following line, with no editorial comment as to Irving's paragraphing. Sometimes he began a new paragraph on the line following the date; often he continued writing with only a space, a dash, a comma, or a period separating the date from the entry.

When Irving wrote a word and then crossed it out only to rewrite it immediately, I have omitted the crossed-out word with no comment. Similarly, when Irving began a word with several letters at the end of the line, and then, perhaps realizing that he could not get the entire word on that line, went to the following line to write the complete word, I have silently omitted the false start.

These decisions are the simple ones; the difficulty begins when the editor, keeping in mind her dual goal of fidelity to manuscript and utility to the reader, finds that with almost every line there is some

149. *Journals and Notebooks*, I, xix.

150. Stanley Williams and Barbara Simison indicated manuscript page numbers in brackets in the text of Ellsworth's *Narrative*.

editorial decision to be made. For instance, Irving's patternless use of periods, dashes, commas, question marks, quotation marks, and parentheses, as well as his erratic use of spaces between syllables, words, lines, or paragraphs demand that the editor have some guidelines in making these decisions. Often common sense and a desire to be fair to Irving are the deciding factors.

Daily, the editor of Irving confronts his spelling inconsistencies ("Kelly" and "Kelley," "wagon," "waggon," "prarie," "prairie," etc.) and his tendency to spell phonetically or incorrectly. Variations in spelling of the same word are rendered as Irving wrote them, as are his misspellings. Place names and proper names are spelled correctly in the note, when the correct spelling could be determined from external evidence; often information about Irving's particular spelling is given, if it seems helpful. For no reason is "[*sic*]" used in the text; if a misspelling causes confusion, an explanatory note is given, or when Irving's elision obscures meaning, the omitted letters are added in brackets. Readers of this text must assume that any spelling error is Irving's, not the editor's—an act of faith which I hope is justified.

Irving's use of punctuation, or lack of it, deserves some comment. He seldom used periods to end sentences or to indicate abbreviations, often simply skipping a space or using a dash when he shifted from one thought to the next. I have not added periods, but if the first word of the followig sentence begins with a lowercase letter or if the uppercase beginning is a proper name and the absence of a period might cause misreading, I have added a period or a dash in brackets, depending on the context. Irving irregularly employed punctuation in abbreviations; I have transcribed "M^{r}" and "Mr" as "Mr" in the text; Irving's "M^{r}", "M^{r-}", "M^{R}", "M$^{r.}$", "Mr-" are rendered as "Mr." in the text. Irving often used the ampersand and the combination "&c" to mean "and so forth," which habit has been faithfully rendered. The abbreviations with and without periods for elisions of verb endings also have been followed in the text, so that "serv^{d}" and "servd" are "servd" in the text; "serv^{d}", "servd-" "serv^{d-}", and "servd." are rendered similarly as "servd." in the transcription. Irving's "ing" often resembles a or ; in these cases, he is given the benefit of the doubt, and the symbol becomes "ing" in the text.

Irving used dashes frequently to separate sentences, words, and thoughts; they vary greatly in length and position in the manuscript, from a long extension of a crossed *t* to a line not much longer than a period. I have attempted to be as faithful to Irving's intention as it can be determined; dashes have been added in brackets only if they are necessary to prevent misreading. In the account books, Irving intermittently and irregularly used a combination of dashes and periods to connect the item in the left column with the figure in the right. Except when the dash seems to relate directly to the word, I have omitted all of these marks, realizing that in the printed text the correlation between columns would be clear. If other punctuation marks have been added to the text to aid the reader—question marks, the second half of quotation marks or parentheses, or commas—they are in brackets.

Perhaps the most difficult of Irving's idiosyncrasies to deal with in the text is his spacing. There are often spaces at the ends of lines; sometimes one-half or two-thirds of a line will be left blank for no reason. There is often space between words, between syllables, between lines, at the end of pages, and at the beginning of lines or pages. Spaces between syllables and compounds have been rendered as Irving skipped them, for instance in "O clock," "to day," or "steam boat." If Irving simply lifted his pencil from one syllable to the next, as he often did to begin the following letter at the top of the line, I have given him the benefit of the doubt and transcribed as one word. Similarly, if Irving did not lift his pencil between compounds, as "steamboat," I have not added a space to make him seem consistent. On the other hand, if he did not lift his pencil between words clearly meant to be individual words, as "wearehappyas," "ofthe," "tothe," "tofind," "ExtraStage," and my favorite, "fromit," I have rendered as separate words with no note. If the space is an apparent accident, the result of haste or fatigue (there are successive pages in which many of these run-together words exist, and other pages in which this habit rarely appears), it is not noted. If it seems that Irving intended to add information in a blank space later, such as a place name or a proper name, I have indicated "[*blank*]" in the text. Sometimes he provided his own blank as "Judge ———." If the space was used by Irving to separate sentences and the following sentence begins with an uppercase letter, I have skipped two spaces between sentences in the text, following his pattern.

Spacing is also related to the difficult task of paragraphing. If the paragraph is not indented by Irving (his left margins are challengingly irregular), but it is clearly intended as a new paragraph, I have indented in the text. Some of the frequent reasons for indenting are as follows: paragraphs separated by several skipped lines; the last portion of the preceding line left blank; all lines in the paragraph indented, so that the left margin is more or less uniformly moved to the right; a long dash covering the space of several words; and a change in topic. Occasionally Irving's paragraph beginning flush left has been rendered as such in the text, if the context provides evidence that the paragraph is a new one (for example, if Irving has drawn a line between paragraphs).

One of the most exasperating problems to the editor of Irving is that of upper- and lowercase letters. Nothing short of a vernier caliper provides a sure rule to be followed when transcribing in this area, and even measuring the height of letters, as foolishly pedantic as it may seem to the outsider, is actually ineffective. Often the word preceding and the one following the word whose initial letter is in question will vary in height of letters to so great a degree that there is nothing against which to compare for size. Often Irving used the old practice of uppercase letters for nouns, but not consistently; often he used lowercase letters at the beginning of sentences or for proper names, but certainly with no regularity. The fact that many letters of both cases were formed similarly by Irving—*a*, *c*, sometimes the *g*, *m*, *n*, *o*, *u*, *v*, *w*, *x*, and the *y*—means that the size relative to the other letters in the word and words in the sentence must be a determining factor. Here the term "relative" is a key, for often the sizes of the letters of an entire word or phrase vary within a sentence for no apparent reason. The letters *b*, *d*, *e*, *f*, *h*, *i*, *j*, sometimes *k*, and *l* have distinctive enough versions for upper- and lowercase letters that they present little problem; however, the letters *r*, *s*, and *t* are frustrating. Irving's uppercase S may be formed as , , , and the lowercase *s* may be or , of varying height. Irving's uppercase *R* may be the standard R or . The uppercase *T* is usually but it may be or . If the letter is obviously lower- or uppercase, no matter what the context, I have been faithful to the manuscript; if, however, there is no clear distinction, I have been kind to Irving. The reader may be certain that at all times silent editing has been kept to a minimum, being used only to cover matters of common sense.

NOTE ON SOURCES

Indispensable to the textual critic are the atlas, gazetteer, guide and travel book, encyclopedia, and biographical dictionary; in order that this text be as uncluttered as possible, general information derived from these standard sources ordinarily is not noted individually. Because the geographical material in the notes relating to the American journals and notebooks is essentially a compilation of information from four sources, they should be noted, here in chronological order: Bishop Davenport, *A New Gazetteer, or Geographical Dictionary of North America and the West Indies* (Baltimore: George M'Dowell & Son, 1832), hereafter cited as Davenport, *Gazetteer*; William Chapin, *A Complete Reference Gazetteer of the United States of North America* (New York: T. & E. H. Ensign, 1844), hereafter cited as Chapin's *Gazetteer*; Thomas Baldwin and J. Thomas, *A New and Complete Gazetteer of the United States* (Philadelphia: Lippincott, Grambo & Co., 1854), hereafter cited as Baldwin and Thomas, *Gazetteer*; and Leon E. Seltzer, ed., *The Columbia Lippincott Gazetteer of the World*, 2nd ed. (Morningside Heights, N. Y.: Columbia University Press, 1962), hereafter cited as *Columbia Lippincott*. Particularly helpful in working with the New York portion of Journal 2 was a detailed folio-sized map of each county in 1829, only three years before Irving's trip: [David H. Burr], *An Atlas of the State of New York* (New York: David H. Burr, Rawson Wright & Co., 1829), hereafter cited as Burr's *1829 Atlas*.

Also extremely useful were contemporary guide books; I used extensively four of these which were published in the 1830's, one of which Irving himself used and two others which he might have found helpful: Irving often copied passages into later journals from Timothy Flint's *The History and Geography of the Mississippi Valley*, published in 1828, with a second edition in 1832, and a third, which I have used, in 1833 (Cincinnati: E. H. Flint), hereafter cited as Flint, *Mississippi Valley*; other guidebooks which I found particularly helpful were [Robert Baird], *View of the Valley of the Mississippi: or the Emigrant's and Traveller's Guide to the West* (Philadelphia: Published by H. S. Tanner, 1832), hereafter cited as Baird, *View; The Northern Traveller and Northern Tour* (New York: Goodrich & Wiley, 1834), hereafter cited as *Northern Traveller*; H. S. Tanner, *The American Traveller; or Guide*

Through the United States, 2nd ed. (Philadelphia: Published by the Author, 1836), hereafter cited as Tanner's *Guide*; and *The American Guide Book; Being a Hand-Book for Tourists and Travellers Through Every Part of the United States* (Philadelphia: George S. Appleton, 1846), hereafter cited as *Appleton's Hand-Book*.

Biographical information concerning the many people Irving claimed as friends, enjoyed as family, knew in government, or simply met and mentioned has been derived from hundreds of sources, primary among them the standard biographies by Irving's nephew, Pierre M. Irving, and by Stanley T. Williams (see list below for full reference). When the information could be classified as general knowledge regarding the people whom Irving mentioned and who were outstanding enough to be included in the standard biographical dictionaries and encyclopedias, I have used these sources without individual bibliographical notation; if I quoted from the source or used material which seemed controversial or unusual, I cited the short-titled reference as indicated in the following list of frequently used works: J. Balteau, M. Barroux, and M. Prevost, eds., *Dictionnaire de Biographie Française*, vols. 1-15 (Paris: Librairie Letouzey et Ané, 1933-1979); J. L. Blake, *A General Biographical Dictionary*, 5th ed. (Philadelphia: James Kay, Jun. and Brother, 1842); John Howard Brown, ed., *The Cyclopædia of American Biographies*, 7 vols. (Boston: The Cyclopædia Publishing Company, 1897-1903); George Derby, ed., *A Conspectus of American Biography* (New York: James T. White & Co., 1906); Francis S. Drake, *Dictionary of American Biography* (Boston: James R. Osgood and Co., 1872); Evert A. Duyckinck and George L. Duyckinck, *Cyclopædia of American Literature*, 2 vols. (New York: Charles Scribner, 1856); *The Encyclopædia Britannica*, 11th ed., 29 vols. (Cambridge, England: University Press, 1910-1911); James D. Hart, *The Oxford Companion to American Literature*, 3rd ed. (New York: Oxford University Press, 1956); Paul Harvey, *The Oxford Companion to English Literature*, 3rd ed. (Oxford: Clarendon Press, 1946); Francis L. Hawks, ed., *The Pictorial Cyclopædia of Biography* (New York: D. Appleton and Co., 1856); Allen Johnson, ed., *Dictionary of American Biography*, 20 vols. (New York: Charles Scribner's Sons, 1928-1937), hereafter cited as DAB; *The National Cyclopædia of American Biography*, 63 vols. (New York: James T. White & Co., 1891-1984); *The National Portrait Gallery of Distinguished Americans*, 4 vols. (Philadelphia: D. Rice & A. N. Hart, 1856); *Nouvelle Biographie Universelle*, 46 vols. (Paris: Firmin Didot Frères, 1852-1866). I found especially helpful the long biographical essays in the *Dictionary of National Biography*, vols. 1-21 ed. Leslie Stephen, vols. 22-26 ed. Leslie Stephen and Sidney Lee, vols. 27-63 ed. Sidney Lee (vols. 1-49 London: Smith, Elder & Co.,

1885-1897; vols. 50-63 New York: The Macmillan Co., 1897-1900); even though I relied heavily on the biographical information in this source, particularly in the notes relating to the 1842 Journal, I rarely cited the source individually as I considered the information general; if I quoted material or if the information contradicted other generally held positions, I cited the source as DNB. Also, in working on the 1842 Journal, I found the Burke volumes invaluable: *Burke's Genealogical and Heraldic History of the Landed Gentry*, ed. Peter Townend, 18th ed., 2 vols. (London: Burke's Peerage Limited, 1965); *Burke's Genealogical and Heraldic History of* the *Peerage, Baronetage and Knightage*, 99th ed. (London: Burke's Peerage Limited, 1949); *Burke's Guide to the Royal Family* (London: Burke's Peerage Limited, 1973); *Burke's Royal Families of the World*, vol. 1: *Europe & Latin America* (London: Burke's Peerage Ltd., 1977); hereafter cited as *Burke's Royal Families.* Also helpful were the thirteen volumes based on George Edward Cokayne's work, *The Complete Peerage of England, Scotland, Ireland, Great Britain, and the United Kingdom*, 2nd ed. (London: St. Catherine Press Ltd., 1910-1940).

CHRONOLOGICAL TABLE, 1832–1859

1832: January, remains at Newstead Abbey, after previous month's tour with Van Buren through Oxfordshire, Warwickshire, and Derbyshire; March 6, edition of *Poems by William Cullen Bryant, an American*, with introductory letter and dedication, published by John Andrews in London; March 23, sells manuscript of *The Alhambra* to Colburn and Bentley, the climax of estrangement from John Murray continuing until 1835; April 3, sails from Southampton for Le Havre to bid farewell to Peter Irving; April 11, embarks for America on *Havre*, on board meets Charles Latrobe and Count de Pourtalès; third or fourth week in April, *The Alhambra* published in London; May 21, lands in New York; May 30, attends dinner in his honor at City Hotel, New York, with 300 outstanding guests; June, travels with Latrobe and Pourtalès along Eastern seaboard, particularly to Washington on political business, then to Baltimore, Philadelphia, and Virginia; June 9, *The Alhambra* published in Philadelphia by Carey and Lea; June 28–July, makes steamboat trip up the Hudson to West Point and Catskill Mountains; August 2–26, travels up the Hudson, to western New York, and Lake Erie, meets Henry Ellsworth and accepts invitation to join his Commission to the Indians; August 27–September 1, Ashtabula to Cincinnati; September 3–14, Cincinnati to St. Louis; September 14–24, St. Louis to Independence; September 27 to October 8, Independence to Fort Gibson; October 9–November 9, Fort Gibson into Indian Territory west as far as the Cross Timbers and the Great Canadian River, then back to Fort Gibson; November 11–December 15, travels down the Mississippi, visits New Orleans, then by mail stage returns to Washington via Alabama, Georgia, South and North Carolina, and Virginia.

1833: Until March, remains in Washington with the McLanes; adviser to Van Buren and active in national politics; March, detained in Baltimore for three weeks, meets John Pendleton Kennedy; by March 28, returns to New York, lives at Ebenezer Irving's place at 3 Bridge Street, receives notice of the honorary Doctor of Laws Degree awarded by Harvard University on June 27, 1832; maintains active social and political life in New York, Baltimore, Washington, Charlottesville, Saratoga Springs, etc., begins work on an "American book" from the Western journals; September 10–15, takes the "Dutch Tour" from Albany to Communipaw with Van Buren and his son.

1834: Fall, refuses nomination by Jacksonians for Congress; September, approached by John Jacob Astor to write about his enterprise, arranges with Pierre M. Irving to move to Hell Gate, Astor's place, to organize materials; November, completes work on Western tour.

1835: February, purchases "neglected cottage" and ten acres two miles south of Tarrytown (deed recorded in June and architect begins work which continues through the fall, 1836); March, *Crayon Miscellany, No. 1: A Tour on the Prairies* published by Murray in London; mid-April, publication of *Tour* in Philadelphia by Carey, Lea, and Blanchard; May 1, *Abbotsford and Newstead Abbey* published in London; May 30, publication follows in Philadelphia; July, revises and sees through publication John Treat Irving's *Indian Sketches*; August, moves into Astor's home to work on *Astoria*, meets Captain Bonneville; October 2, completes first draft of *Astoria*; October, *Legends of the Conquest of Spain* published in Philadelphia; December, publication follows in London.

1836: February, completes *Astoria*; June, Peter Irving arrives in New York; October, moves into remodeled home, Sunnyside; October, *Astoria* published in Philadelphia, London, and Paris, financial investments fail; begins work on materials purchased from Bonneville.

1837: January 14, attacked in *Plaindealer* by William Leggett for being an Anglophile; January 28, answers charge in *Plaindealer*; February 18, apologizes to William C. Bryant in *Plaindealer*; March, *The Rocky Mountains . . . from the Journal of Captain B. L. E. Bonneville* printed but not sold in America until June; early summer, publication follows in London with altered title, *Adventures of Captain Bonneville.*

1838: March 15, death of brother John Treat Irving; March 21, offered and declines the Democratic nomination for mayor of New York; April 23, offered position as secretary of the navy; April 30, declines in a letter to President Van Buren on the grounds of a too-sensitive nature; June 27, death of brother Peter Irving; deep depression follows; fall and winter, works on the history of Mexico's conquest, approached by Joseph Cogswell about the conflicting enterprise of William Prescott, yields the subject to Prescott.

1839: February 7, signs contract with *The Knickerbocker, or New York Monthly Magazine*, contributes twenty-nine articles from March, 1839, until October, 1841; spring, negotiates for publication of *Mahomet*, offered to Murray eight years earlier.

1840: Fall, edits *Life and Works of Oliver Goldsmith* in two volumes for *Harper's Family Library* with a biographical essay of 186 pages, an extensive reworking of his three previous introductions to Goldsmith's works; summer and fall, works against Van Buren's reelection in favor of Whig slate, William H. Harrison and John Tyler.

1841: March 31, sees Sarah Paris married to Thomas W. Storrow; May 1, they leave for Paris to live; deep sadness follows; early summer, asks for materials regarding Washington and resumes work on that project begun in 1825; July–August, visits the Highlands, mining regions, and Gouverneur Kemble and Henry Brevoort in their homes on the Hudson; March, sends to Lea and Blanchard the manuscript of *Biography and Poetical Remains of the Late Margaret Miller Davidson* published in the late spring in London and Philadelphia; April 4, President Harrison dies after one month in office; Tyler succeeds him.

1842: February 10, nominated as Envoy Extraordinary and Minister Plenipotentiary to Spain; February 18, accepts by letter to Secretary of State Daniel Webster, who recommended him; February 18, presides (and "broke down") at the dinner for Charles Dickens at the City Hotel; February–March, entertained with Dickens at numerous dinners, prepares actively for establishing mission in Spain—selects staff (with some controversy), is briefed in Washington, reviews government documents; April 10, sails aboard the *Independence*; April 29, lands in Bristol; May 1–15, reenters the social scene of London, presented to Queen Victoria twice, meets staffs of British and American diplomatic corps; May 10, honored at dinner at Murrays; May 11, attends the dinner of the Anniversary of the Literary Fund, with Prince Albert presiding and English literary notables present; May 15–20, visits sister Sarah Van Wart in Birmingham; May 21–24, London to Paris; May 24–July 11, remains in Paris with Sarah Storrow, active in Paris social and diplomatic life, presented to the king; July 11–25, Paris to Madrid, with four days each in Bordeaux and Bayonne; organizes legation.

1843: February–May, suffers illness; mid-summer, Carlist revolution, joins with British legation to protect the young Queen Isabella II, who is declared of age and becomes queen without regency; September–December, goes to Paris to recover from illness.

1844: June 29, removes to Barcelona, the summer residence of the Spanish court, is a favorite of the court; July 29–31, Barcelona to Marseilles; July 31–August 21, Marseilles, Paris, Le Havre; August 21, embarks on steamer for England and Birmingham for a three-week stay with ill sister Sarah Van Wart; mid-September to mid-November, Paris; November 17, returns to Madrid.

1845: Winter (1844–1845), enjoys good health, an active social life, and the beginning of an effective year as diplomat; spring, begins to write, works on the Washington and Mahomet projects; September, Madrid to Paris; late September through December, Paris; December 29, sends resignation as Minister to Spain by steamer; December, urged by McLane to come to London to help negotiate the Oregon question.

1846: January, resides in London and in Birmingham; February, Paris; March 6, returns to Madrid; July 22, replaced as Minister but remains to effect transition; July 29, sees the "little Queen" for the last time; early August, goes to London; early September, embarks for America on the *Cambria*; September 18, arrives in Boston and proceeds to New York; fall, begins close relationships with John P. Kennedy as friend until death and with Pierre M. Irving as agent, secretary, and biographer; winter and spring, remodels Sunnyside; works diligently on life of Washington; begins a two-year, systematic revision of complete works for Putnam.

1848: February, puts aside work on Washington; March 29, death of John Jacob Astor, named one of six executors of the estate, contributes to settling of estate and organizing the Astor Library (through 1849), named the first president of the library; May 17, death of lifelong friend, Henry Brevoort; July 26, signs contract with G. P. Putnam for Hudson Edition; fifteen volumes published from September (*History of New York*) until August, 1850 (*Conquest of Granada*); fall, announces membership in the Protestant Episcopal Church, which he had joined in early youth; becomes active in Christ Church; November 19, death of sister Sarah Van Wart in Birmingham, England.

1849: April 15, announcement by Putnam of the publication of *Book of the Hudson*; December 25, death of sister Catharine Paris in New York; late December, volume 1 of *Mahomet and His Successors* published in New York by Putnam and in England by Murray with altered title, *Lives of Mahomet and His Successors.*

1850: April, volume 2 of *Mahomet* published in London and New York.

1851: Continues life as a famous American man of letters, receives guests at Sunnyside from abroad and from home, begins correspondence with an admiring Hawthorne, reads tributes published in magagines such as the April *Harper's*, works in earnest on Washington's life; becomes warden in Christ Church; controversy in England among publishers Richard Bentley, Henry G. Bohn, and John Murray regarding copyright erupts into lawsuits.

1852: February 24, attends Memorial Service for Cooper, having served as a member of the committee on the memorial for his old literary enemy; summer, travels to Saratoga Springs.

1853: January–June, works incessantly on Washington's life, including intensive work in libraries, correspondence, and trips to New York, Baltimore, Washington, Mt. Vernon, etc.; February 27, guest of honor at dinner in Washington to meet William Makepeace Thackeray; March 4, attends the inauguration of President Pierce; June, exhausted, lays aside his pen; June 30–July 11, travels through Virginia and Maryland, then to Saratoga Springs and western New York until August 17; September, removes remains of family members buried in the New York Brick Church Cemetery to the Sleepy Hollow Cemetery; Fall, and through the year 1854, continues in a state of restlessness, exhaustion, and ill health.

1855: January or February, *Wolfert's Roost and Other Papers* published in New York by Putnam, in London by Henry Bohn, and in Edinburgh by Thomas Constable; April or May, volume 1 of *Life of George Washington* published in New York by Putnam; December volume 2 of *Washington* published.

1856: July, volume 3 of *Washington* published; declines in health; works intensely on fourth volume of the biography.

1857: May, volume 4 of *Washington* published; declines rapidly in health; labors on final volume through the end of 1858; suffers intensely.

1859: January, submits the first three chapters; February, 200 pages in print; March, completes work; April, volume 5 of *Washington* pub-*lished*; November 2, dies.

EDITORIAL SYMBOLS AND ABBREVIATIONS

[roman]	Editorial additions
[*italic*]	Editorial explanations
⟨ ⟩	Restorations of canceled matter
? ? or [?]	Doubtful or alternate readings. The former are used within square or angle brackets. The latter is used for a single doubtful word and appears immediately after the word or character in question, with no intervening space.
unrecovered	Undeciphered word. When more than one word is involved, the fact is indicated ("*three unrecovered words*," or "*two unrecovered lines*").
illegible	Hopelessly unrecoverable word
↑ ↓	Interlinear insertions, above or below the line
/river/Red/	Irving's alternate readings. The first word was written on the line; the second, immediately above the first.

^	Irving's caret, in text where he inserted it
⟨8⟩9	Strike-over; an initial number written over by a second number
grass/hopper	Compound divided by end of line with no hyphen
grass-/hopper	End-line hyphenation
grass-/-hopper	End- and beginning-of-line hyphenation

Editorial situations not covered by these symbols are explained in the notes. For details of the editorial procedures followed, see the general introduction to volume 1 of the *Journals and Notebooks.*

Ellsworth, *Narrative*	Henry Leavitt Ellsworth. *Washington Irving on the Prairie: or a Narrative of a Tour of the Southwest in the Year 1832.* Edited by Stanley T. Williams and Barbara D. Simison. New York: American Book Company, 1937.
Latrobe, *Rambler*	Charles Joseph Latrobe. *The Rambler in North America: (1832–1833).* 2 vols. London: R. B. Seeley and W. Burnside, 1835.
Letters	Ralph M. Aderman, Herbert L. Kleinfield and Jenifer S. Banks, eds. *Washington Irving: Letters.* Vol. 1. *1802–1823.* Boston: Twayne Publishers, 1978; Vol. 2. *1823–1838.* Boston: Twayne Publishers, 1979; Vol. 3. *1839–1845.* Boston: Twayne Publishers, 1982; Vol. 4. *1846–1859.* Boston: Twayne Publishers, 1982.
Journals and Notebooks, I	Nathalia Wright, ed. *Washington Irving: Journals and Notebooks.* Vol. 1. *1803–1806.* Madison: University of Wisconsin Press, 1969.
Journals and Notebooks, III	Walter A. Reichart, ed. *Washington Irving: Journals and Notebooks.* Vol. 3. *1819–1827.* Madison: University of Wisconsin Press, 1970.
Journals of WI	William P. Trent and George S. Hellman, eds. *The Journals of Washington Irving (From July, 1815, to July, 1842).* 3 vols. Boston: Bibliophile Society, 1919.
PMI	Pierre M. Irving. *The Life and Letters of Washington Irving.* 4 vols. New York:

	G. P. Putnam; Hurd & Houghton, 1862–1864.
Pourtalès, *Journal*	George F. Spaulding, ed. *On the Western Tour with Washington Irving: The Journal and Letters of Count de Pourtalès*. Translated by Seymour Feiler. Norman: University of Oklahoma Press, 1968.
STW	Stanley T. Williams. *The Life of Washington Irving*. 2 vols. New York: Oxford University Press, 1935.
Tour	Washington Irving. *The Crayon Miscellany. No. 1. Containing A Tour on the Prairies*. Philadelphia: Carey, Lea & Blanchard, 1835.
Western Journals	John Francis McDermott, ed. *The Western Journals of Washington Irving*. Norman: University of Oklahoma Press, 1966.
WI	Washington Irving.

Other works cited often enough to warrant some form of shorter notation are given full bibliographical identification in the first note and are short-titled thereafter.

JOURNALS AND NOTEBOOKS

Volume V

AMERICAN JOURNALS, 1832

Number 2[1]

New York to Cincinnati

This manuscript journal is in the Estelle Doheny Collection of the Edward Laurence Doheny Memorial Library at St. John's Seminary, Camarillo, California, where it bears the accession number A–435. It consists of 45 leaves with leaves 1, 30, and 33 having been torn out. Its remaining 84 pages of unlined paper measure 2¹³⁄₁₆ x 3¹³⁄₁₆ inches and are held together with binding thread at the top of the notebook between leaves 7 and 8; 23 and 24; 39 and 40, and at the bottom of the notebook with a brass latch. Its cover of soft red-rust colored leather measures 3 x 3⅞ inches with a small cylindrical leather pencil holder attached to the left edge of the cover. The notebook is housed in a red leather slip case. The writing is in pencil, and pages [4], [62], [64], [68], [78], [80], [81], [84], [85], and the inside back cover are blank.

[*front cover*]

No 2 1832
1832, August 2d.[2]

[*inside front cover*]

36 Neph
27
―――
63

Hank–(Hendrick)[3]

1. The first of these journals, number 1, has not been found. It probably contained details of WI's trip from New York City to Boston and the White Mountains of New Hampshire, and back to New York during the last two weeks in July, 1832. See Introduction, pp. xxii–xxiii for information concerning this trip.

2. "No 2" is written in ink directly on the leather binding. Beneath it on a paper seal pasted on the leather are the words "1832, August 2d." The handwriting appears to be WI's.

3. In the upper left-hand corner of the inside front cover, pasted along its top

Mr Gill[4]–
Oak St.[5] first of 2 marble Houses
From Utica go by Onondaga Holl & not thru Syracuse[6]

[*p. [4] blank*]

Thursday, August 2[7]

Left NYork at 7 OClock in steamboat for Tarrytown[8]–arrived there

---

edge, so that it can be lifted, is a square bookplate that reads "Ex Libris William Harris Arnold"; the column of addition is written under this bookplate and can be read by lifing it. The figures seem to be WI's estimate of the number of his nephews and nieces, a detailed accounting of which he will determine later (see n. 231 below). William Harris Arnold (1854–1923) was a noted book collector and the author of *First Report of a Book Collector* (New York, 1898) and *Ventures in Book Collecting* (New York, 1923). This journal was sold at the auction of the Arnold Collection on November 10–11, 1924, at the Anderson Galleries in New York City, probably to W. M. Hill, Chicago. Presumably Hill sold it to Frank Harris. In the upper right-hand corner of the inside front cover is pasted an oval bookplate that reads "Ex Libris Estelle Doheny." Mrs. Carrie Estelle Betzold Doheny (1875–1958) was the wife of Edward L. Doheny (1856–1935), the noted oil tycoon. Mrs. Doheny was one of the first outstanding women book collectors. A white card kept in the note-book reads "To Estelle, in whose home one of us read Irving's Sketch Book in parts. With love. Mamie & Frank. Christmas, 1933." Frank and Mamie were Mr. and Mrs. Frank J. Hogan, he, an attorney and book collector. According to Mrs. James Gayle, librarian of the Estelle Doheny Collection, Mr. Hogan and Mrs. Doheny began their collecting by each attempting to acquire the entire list in Merle Johnson, *High Spots of American Literature* (New York, 1929). Mrs. Doheny won.

4. WI wrote together as "MrGill." Page [1] contains notes and directions for the trip which WI was about to take; in Albany he would "Dine at Gills" (see August 4, 1832, entry).

5. According to an 1876 map of the city of Albany, Oak Street was only three blocks long, perpendicular to and running from Lumber Street to Second Street; it did not appear on earlier (1856 and 1843) maps of Albany, apparently because it was on the city line or considered outside the city (*City Atlas of Albany, New York* . . . [Philadelphia: G. M. Hopkins, 1876], 6–7).

6. The recommended westward route across the state of New York from Albany to Niagara Falls included following the Mohawk River to Utica, then to Syracuse and Rochester. WI made this note to vary the route by going south from Utica through Onondaga Hollow (see the August 20 entry).

7. WI wrote "1832." in the middle of the first line of page [3] in larger than usual numbers, and then "Aug. 2d" at the beginning of the next line.

8. WI failed to connect the last syllable with the first two. Tarrytown, New York, was in the northwestern corner of Greenburg township (it is also spelled "Greens-burgh" and "Greenburgh"), Westchester County, 27 miles north of New York City on the eastern bank of the Hudson, or, as it was called at this point, the Tappan Sea or Tappan Bay. This village was famous as the setting of "Rip Van Winkle" and as the scene of Major André's capture upon his return from his interview with General Benedict Arnold (see pp. 192–93, nn. 69–71).

at ½ past 10. Found Mrs Paris[9] & all well. Ebens[10] family staying with her At Oscars[11] were Pierre M & his wife.[12] Irving V W & wife[13] Julia Irving[14] Helen Dodge[15] Ogden Irving[16]–

Thunder storm–⟨all⟩ 9 of us rode home in waggon

Friday, August 3[17]

Drove in wagon with Oscar[,] E Irving[18] & W V W.[19] to Saw mill

9. WI's sister, Catharine Rodgers Irving (1774–1849) married Daniel Paris, and they had nine children. At this time Mrs. Paris was living in a cottage at Tarrytown, about which WI wrote, "Here I am in a little cottage, in which is Mr. Paris's family, and a number of the Bramin's young fry, among which are his two oldest daughters, whom I have now seen for the first time." The "Bramin" was Ebenezer Irving (PMI, III, 29). Ebenezer's girls were Catharine Ann (1816–1911) and Sarah (1817–1900), the oldest daughter Eliza having died (1814–1819). (See tables 1–4 in STW, II, 253–54, and opposite p. 255; "Irving Family Genealogy," *Letters, IV*, pp. 879–95.)

10. Ebenezer Irving (1776–1868), WI's older brother and the father of thirteen children (see note above).

11. Oscar Irving (1800–1865) was WI's nephew, the son of his brother William. Oscar lived two miles below Tarrytown adjoining the property which WI was later to buy (Sunnyside) and about which he wrote to his sister Mrs. Paris in November of this same year, "I am more & more in the notion of having that little cottage below his house and wish you to tell him to endeavour to get it for me. I am willing to pay a little unreasonably for it; and should like to have it in time to make any alterations that may be advisable as early as possible in the Spring" (*Letters*, II, 731–32).

12. Pierre Munro Irving (1802–1876) was WI's nephew and the author of a four-volume biography of Irving. In the preface PMI quoted WI: " 'Somebody will be writing my life when I am gone,' said he to me some years before his death, and after having resisted repeated applications for an autobiography, 'and I wish you to do it. You must promise me that you will' " (PMI, I, 5).

13. Irving Van Wart (1808–1896) was WI's nephew, the son of his sister Sarah Irving (Mrs. Henry) Van Wart (1780–1848). Irving Van Wart had married Susan Anne Irving (daughter of William Irving and, therefore, his first cousin) in July, 1832.

14. Julia Irving (1803–1872) was WI's niece, the daughter of his brother William.

15. Helen Dodge (1802–1885) was WI's niece, the daughter of his sister Ann Sarah Irving (Mrs. Richard) Dodge (1770–1808). She later married her first cousin, Pierre Munro Irving.

16. Henry Ogden Irving (1807–1869) was WI's nephew, the son of William.

17. WI wrote "3d–."

18. Ebenezer Irving (see above, nn. 9–10).

19. William Van Wart (1814–1868) was WI's nephew, the son of Sarah.

River[20] ⟨to be[?]⟩ visited with John[21] & Stephen[?] V W wife[22]—Oscars ⟨D⟩ home—at 3 oclock. Lewis G Irving[23] drove in to Sing Sing[24]—from thence ⟨dr⟩ took seat in waggon of mail carrier to Peekskill[25]—beautiful drive along Croton River[26] & highlands beyond. from Peekskill crossed to Caldwells landg[27] in row boat to wait for Steam boat. bathed in river[28]—glorious clear sunset—apple grey sky—oily line of the wooded Hills

Got[29] on board of the Steam boat Constellation at ½ past 8. (Arrive

20. Sawmill Creek, or Saw Mill River, rises in Westchester County, northeast of Tarrytown, flows in a southwesterly direction to the east of Tarrytown and Dobbs Ferry, and into the Hudson at Yonkers.

21. John could be WI's brother, John Treat Irving (1778–1838), or his brother's son, John Treat Irving, Jr. (1812–1906).

22. Sarah and Henry Van Wart (WI used the initials *V W* to indicate the Van Wart part of the family) had six children—Henry, Irving, William, Matilda, Marianne, and George—none of them a "Stephen." Perhaps this person was a Van Wart in-law; WI did not mention him or his wife in the list at the conclusion of this notebook when he named and divided his brothers, sisters, nieces, nephews, etc., into families.

23. Lewis Graham Irving (1795–1879) was WI's nephew, the son of his brother William.

24. Sing Sing, or Singsing, incorporated in 1813, was a post-village of Mount Pleasant township, Westchester County, New York, on the east side of the Hudson River, 33 miles above New York City. Its elegant villas and view of the Hudson 200 feet below made it a "picturesque" spot, according to contemporaries. It was known for the Croton Aqueduct and the Mt. Pleasant State Prison.

25. Peekskill was a thriving post-village in Cortland township, Westchester County, New York (incorporated as a village in 1816, as a town in 1837), on the east bank of the Hudson River, approximately 42 miles north of New York City and 100 miles south of Albany.

26. Rising in south Dutchess County, New York, the three branches of the Croton River flow south through Putnam County and join near the Westchester County line; the stream enters the Hudson River above Sing Sing about 35 miles north of New York City.

27. Caldwell's Landing, or Gibraltar, was on the west side of the Hudson River in Rockland County, New York, 42 miles from New York, 101 miles from Albany. The landing was at the south entrance of the "Highlands" and was the first stop up the Hudson for large steamboats.

28. Hudson River.

29. This word could be the present tense, "Get."

at Albany [*illegible*]⟩[30] find Charles Graham[31] on board–arrive at Albany[32]

Saturday, August 4[33]

at ⟨8⟩9 oclock. Albany half deserted on a/c of the cholera.[34] ⟨Dinner⟩ meet Mr Marcey (Senator)[35] &c–Dine at Gills[36]–leave in rail road line[37] ⟨½ past⟩ 3 oclock. at 7 arrive at Saratoga[38] & put up at Congress

30. The word could be "we" or "ne."

31. Charles Graham is one of the group of New Yorkers who had given WI the public dinner on May 30, 1832, welcoming him back to the United States (see a copy of the invitation with its signers in STW, II, 336, n. 41).

32. Albany, New York, was the capital of New York State; on the west side of the Hudson River, in Albany County, it was 144 miles north of New York City. Settled by the Dutch in 1612 and called Aurania, it was the second colony "planted" in America. In 1830 its population was 26,000; it was a wealthy and prosperous city, active in trade because of the Hudson, the Erie and Champlain Canals, many stage coach lines, and the Schenectady Railroad.

33. WI wrote "Aug 4."

34. The plague prompted Latrobe to write that during the "second week in July, after being witnesses of the panic caused in New York by the outbreak of the cholera, we prepare to follow Mr. Irving to Boston" (*Rambler*, I, 42); this same plague was still raging in New York in early August and caused WI's early departure.

35. William Learned Marcy (1786–1857) was at this time a senator from New York in the 22nd Congress (December 5, 1831–July 16, 1832; December 3, 1832–March 2, 1833). In 1821, when the Clinton-Van Buren rivalry for leadership in New York State was at its height, Marcy replaced the Clinton man as adjutant general; with two other Van Buren men, Marcy helped to improve the political climate of New York. The power of this "Albany Regency" was derived from these men's ability and integrity. Soon after this meeting with WI, Marcy was nominated at the party convention in Herkimer in September, 1832, as the democratic candidate for governor. He was elected after a difficult campaign and served as governor for three terms. He was subsequently secretary of war (1845) and secretary of state (1853). For a discussion of Marcy and his relationship to New York politics, see DeAlva Stanwood Alexander, *A Political History of the State of New York* (New York: Henry Holt, 1906), I, 287–94, 385–91, 394–97; hereafter cited as *Political History*; see also Ben: Perley Poore, *The Political Register and Congressional Directory* (Boston: Houghton, Osgood, 1878), p. 80; hereafter cited as Poore's *Register*.

36. On page [1] of this journal, WI wrote "MrGill" and then noted directions to a house in Oak Street.

37. One suggested route to the Springs from Albany was the Mohawk and Hudson Railroad to Schenectady (sixteen miles), the Saratoga and Schenectady Railroad to Ballston Spa (fourteen miles), and then on to Saratoga Springs.

38. Saratoga Springs, incorporated in 1816, was in Saratoga township, in Saratoga County, New York, approximately 38 miles north of Albany; it was "the most fashionable watering-place on the American continent, as well as the most in repute for the medical virtues of its waters. Here assemble from every quarter of the

Hall[39] where I find Chas Graham–Maxwell–Mr Cutting & family–Mr Greenway & &c[40]–⟨meet⟩

Sunday, August 5[41]

Meet with Latrobe[42] & Pourtales[43]–In the afternoon drive to Saratoga lake[44] [–] fish–

Monday, August 6[45]

at ½ past 6. Set off with Latrobe & Pourtales for Saratoga lake Break-

---

Union the devotees of pleasure and the victims of disease . . ." (Baldwin and Thomas, *Gazetteer*, p. 1051). There were seven springs and approximately 75 hotels, many of them elegant.

39. Congress Hall was one of Saratoga Springs' finest hotels and was listed in contemporary guide books as either the first or second best. There were rooms for 150 persons, and the board was $10 per week in 1834. It was located near Congress Spring, the most popular of the mineral springs.

40. Pierre Irving said of his uncle on this occasion, "Among the visitors to the Springs he found many old friends, with whom he resumed acquaintance. 'It quite delights me,' he writes to Peter, 'to find how soon I fall into the current of old intimacies, and forget the lapse of years' " (PMI, III, 30). Stanley T. Williams wrote that the signers of the invitation to the May 30, 1832, dinner welcoming Irving back to his native city suggest his friends for the next ten years (STW, II, 336, n. 41). Charles Graham and F. B. Cutting were New Yorkers connected with that dinner. WI mentioned in his 1805 journals that he called on the American gentleman, Mr. Maxwell, in Rome and that he was visited by him in Paris; Nathalia Wright suggested that this person was Dr. Joseph William Maxwell, an American who was graduated in medicine from the University of Edinburgh in 1803 (*Journals and Notebooks*, I, 262, n. 289; see also pp. 268, 296, 419–21, 424 for references to Maxwell). Cutting is mentioned often by WI in his November 5, 1825–February 8, 1826, "Bordeaux journal"; on December 13, 1825, Cutting and Maxwell were with WI for long periods of time (*Journals and Notebooks*, III, 551).

41. WI wrote "Aug 5–Sunday–."

42. Charles Joseph Latrobe (1801–1875). See Introduction, p. xx.

43. Count Albert-Alexandre de Pourtalès (1812–1861). See Introduction, pp. xx–xxi.

44. Saratoga Lake, approximately eight miles long and two miles wide, was frequently visited by guests of Saratoga Springs (five miles southeast of the lake); "At a considerable distance from the shore, is erected a stage, 16 by 14 feet, a little raised above the water, and capable of containing thirty people. The lake is there about seven feet deep, and the spot is excellent for fishing. Parties of ladies and gentlemen are taken off in boats, and in hot weather an awning is spread to shade them from the sun" (*Northern Traveller*, p. 124).

45. WI wrote "Aug 6."

fast at Williams[46]—. ⟨Wo[?] Broi[?]⟩ Perch—Pickerell.[47] Broiled wood-duck &c embark on the lake with Latrobe—attended by "David" a boatman & Alonzo Stickney, a boy—catch perch & Bullhead[?] & pickerell——pleasant air—awning[?] to boat[?] ⟨it[?]⟩ delightful in summer to be thus between sky and water—Sound of wood cutter axe—King fisher—with his ⟨ha⟩[48] plunging & swaying[?] flight ↑wood duck—↓. Locust his sultry note like spinning—crow barking.

⟨Mid day⟩—noon—Horns sound/-ing from distant farm house for dinner Skiff shooting across the lake—↑light↓ blue ⟨tint⟩ airy tint of distant islands & promontories—Silver waves with dark ripples laving the sandy shore—pond lilies—⟨*illegible*⟩ Marsh long blades[?] of water winds[?] with diamond drops—⟨fa[?]⟩

Luke Moore who ⟨lives in⟩ fishes & shoots about the lake & makes 20 to 30 $ per month—Sells fish at Saratoga—at present em-/-ployed by Williams—about 40 years of age. Has small ⟨*illegible*⟩ house on little river that runs into lake—wife, cow & potato patch. Knows all the deep holes and fishing places—what places what streams—what creeks & bait to choose—

At dinner meet a Scotchman and an Englishman—The former claims cousinship with Campbell[49]

On the way homeward stop at old Barcuths[?]—a mill wright who fixed himself 2 miles from the springs 35 years since—His millpond abounds with trout & trees[?] ⟨to⟩ became a source of wealth bringing company to his farm[?].[50] He is of dutch or flemish extraction—His wife of German—her parents from Hamburgh. She[51] speaks a little German & reads more[?]. Has an old German bible & prayer book—Barcuth tall, thin white headed. ⟨*illegible*⟩ His farm 200 acres—60 cleared—but does not consider himself a farmer. Independent—sometimes cross—though

46. According to one contemporary guide book, there was "a good house on the shore" (*Northern Traveller*, p. 124); Williams could be the proprietor of that resort. Latrobe mentioned the "pretty inn on [the lake's] banks" (*Rambler*, II, 131).

47. Flint wrote that "esox" or pike was also called pickerel, jackfish, or by the Indians of the Wabash and the Illinois, "piccannau." They vary in size from a half-pound to twenty pounds and in species (*Mississippi Valley*, I, 87).

48. These letters could also be "Le," "he," "La."

49. Thomas Campbell (1777–1844), Scottish poet and critic, was best known in America for *Gertrude of Wyoming* (1809). WI edited Campbell's poetry in America in 1810, and they were friends from 1816. While in Dresden, WI mentioned the reading from Campbell's poem "Pleasures of Hope" during after-dinner music and conversation on Friday, April 25, 1823 (*Journals and Notebooks*, III, 357, n. 805, 143).

50. This word might be "place."

51. This word could be "He."

to[52] us very civil. His wife a decent matronly old woman seated with spectacles—mendg[53] stockings. Their house in the forest—tall primitive pines & oaks about it deep dark mill pools—view in one direction of distant mountains—Joseph Bonapart[54] wanted to buy the land of old Barcuth but the old man asked too high.

(Mr Pell wanted to buy farm at Communipaw[55] but the Dutch man refused—He wanted to buy 4 or 5 acres. Dutchman said if you were to cover it with dollars I would not part with it. His daughter ⟨re-/-buked him⟩ remonstrated but he rebuked them. What do we want of the money—we are happy as we are, so let us be content—)

Wednesday, August 8[56]

⟨ride to⟩ ⟨Drive[?]⟩[57] Excursion to Schuylerville[58] in Dearborn[59] of Mr Glover with Graham & Bremnor[?]. Mrs Schuyler and her bashful daughters. House situated on old battle ground[60]—Hudson river—Vermont Hills beyond.[61]

52. Written together as "thoughto."

53. WI's abbreviation for the word "mending."

54. Joseph Bonaparte (1768–1844) was born in Corsica, the brother of Napoleon. After Napoleon's defeat at Waterloo, Joseph helped with plans for the emperor's escape to America; in fact, it was Joseph who went to Bordentown, New Jersey, after Napoleon's surrender.

55. Communipaw was a small village in Bergen County, New Jersey, two miles south of Jersey City, on the west side of New York Bay. Communipaw, which is an Indian word for "good fishing," was made famous in Book II of Diedrich Knickerbocker's *A History of New York.*

56. WI wrote "Aug ⟨7⟩8—."

57. The word also could be "Dearborn," with the separate line crossing it out, thus suggesting that WI made two false starts on this sentence.

58. Schuylersville was a post-village in Saratoga township, Saratoga County, New York, on the Hudson River at the mouth of Fish Creek; it was 35 miles northeast of Albany, twelve miles east of Saratoga Springs, and seven miles north of the battleground.

59. The Dearborn wagon was a lightweight, one-horse, passenger vehicle, resembling a surrey, also used as a freight wagon, and named for General Henry Dearborn who used it in the field during the War of 1812. For drawings and specifications of the Dearborn, see *Carriage Monthly*, 14 (February, 1878), plate 89, p. 204; and "The Apprentice," *Carriage Monthly*, 24 (1889), 14–15, 50–51.

60. According to one guidebook, "*The house of Gen. Schuyler* stood on the spot now occupied by that of his grandson. It was burnt by Burgoyne on his retreat, together with his mills; notwithstanding which, the British officers were afterwards received at his house in Albany, and treated with great kindness" (*Northern Traveller*, p. 126).

61. WI left the second half of p. [14] blank, apparently so that he might recount the activities of August 9.

Friday, August 10[62]

Leave Saratoga at 9 oclock in stage for Johnstown[63]—⟨Dine⟩ 32 m—Dine at Fondas Bush[64]—Pleasant range of the Mayfield mountains[65]—arrive at Johnstown[66] ½ past 3—On the road pass Stimsons at Galway.[67]

Sunday, August 12[68]

Leave Johnstown[69] 2 oclock in waggon with Wm Dodge[70] & Sarah

62. WI wrote "Aug. 10—."

63. At this point, WI and his party changed direction, going west away from the Hudson River.

64. Fondasbush, a little village south of Fish House and north of Amsterdam, was the county town of Montgomery County, New York, on the north bank of the Mohawk River, and 42 miles northwest from Albany.

65. The northern part of Montgomery County is hilly; one range, called Klipse (or Mayfield) Mountains, extends south from the Sacandaga to the Mohawk River at the "Nose."

66. Johnstown, four miles north of the Mohawk and of Fonda, connected to it by stage, and 41 miles northwest of Albany, was an old town settled by Sir William Johnson, whose family played a significant part in the early Indian wars. It was the county town of Montgomery County, and in 1830 the population was 7,359. Pierre Irving wrote that because of Johnstown's historical significance and its geographical setting, the colonial town "still boasted . . . quite a gay and cultivated society" (PMI, I, 39).

67. Galway, between Saratoga and Fondasbush, was in Saratoga County, eight miles west of Ballston and 31 miles from Albany. The population in 1830 was 2,710. The place which WI called "Stimsons" at Galway was apparently well known enough to warrant a long description in a contemporary guidebook: "*Mr. Simpson's Farm in Galway*, is 11 miles west from Ballston Springs, on a high ridge of land; the farm contains 800 acres, 360 of which are cultivated, principally for grain and grass. . . . The place enjoys so fine and healthy a situation, and the inn is so well kept, being one of the best in this part of the country, that it is the resort of many visiters from different quarters, who frequently spend days or weeks there. The charges are more moderate than at the Springs. The view is commanding, and the air fine" (*Northern Traveller*, pp. 120–21).

68. WI wrote "Aug 12."

69. We have corrected WI's misspelling, "Johhstown."

70. WI wrote as "WmDodge"; William Irving Dodge (1790–1873) was WI's nephew, the son of Ann Sarah Irving Dodge (1770–1808). She had married Richard Dodge (1762–September 20, 1832) in 1788, had six children, and in the spring of 1808 died in Johnstown. Two of WI's sisters, Ann Dodge and Catharine Paris, lived in Johnstown, and he visited them at length in 1800 and again in 1802; it was from Johnstown on July 2, 1802, that WI wrote the earliest letter which Pierre Irving collected (PMI, I, 39, 45).

Ann[71] & the two boys for Caugh-/-nawaga.[72] cross the river[73] to Fultonville[?][74] call at Mr Voorhees[75]—return to Fonda's where the stage arrives[76] ¼ past 4 with Latrobe and Pourtales—take seat in the [*unrecovered*][77] and arrive ½ past 7[78] at Little Falls[79]

Woods along the Mohawk. ⟨Strong⟩ Walnut butternut, chest-/-nut—country of abundance—comfortable german farm house—Teniers groupes—[80]

Hum of spinning wheel

⟨Bee country a buzz headed thistle⟩

71. Sarah Ann could be an error for his niece Jane Ann (1799–1875), the sister of William Dodge (see chart in STW, II, opposite p. 255); however, when WI made his list of the families at the end of this notebook, he indicated that William Dodge was married and that his family contributed six great-nephews and great-nieces to WI's list, one of whom he named Sarah Ann. It is probable, therefore, that this Sarah Ann could be William Dodge's daughter (therefore, WI's great-niece) Ann Sarah (1816–1886). The boys are certainly William's two oldest sons, William James (1822–1879) and Richard, as Washington Irving Dodge was only one year old at this time (*Letters*, IV, 886).

72. Caughnawaga was a small village in Montgomery County on the Mohawk River, 39 miles from Albany. Johnstown was four miles north of the canal and Caughnawaga.

73. The river is the Mohawk.

74. Across the Mohawk River from Caughnawaga is Fulton; Irving's spelling could be "Fullminster" or "Fultonmster" or as a modern gazeteer indicates, "Fultonville," which is a village, population 840, in Montgomery County, New York, on the Mohawk River opposite Fonda and ten miles west of Amsterdam.

75. There was a village just southeast of Fulton called Voorheesville.

76. It is interesting that WI went back to Fonda and took the stage rather than going to Utica by water; the distance by the canal from Schenectady to Utica was 79½ miles and by road, 81 miles.

77. This word is apparently a part of the stage, but the editor has been unable to decipher it; it could be "Salipn," "Lalipn," etc.

78. This journey by stage of 2¾ hours was approximately 22 miles and took the Irving party past Spraker's and Anthony's Nose, a high hill on the southern bank of the Mohawk River at whose top was a great and unusual cavern. The last points of interest along this route before reaching Little Falls were the Mohawk Castle and the brick house which was home and site of the death of General Herkimer.

79. Little Falls was a busy post-village in Rockton township, Herkimer County, New York, 75 miles west-northwest of Albany. The Mohawk River flows through the village, which was connected by a handsome stone or marble aqueduct 214 feet long, sixteen feet wide, with three arches (the span of the middle arch was sixty feet). In 1830 the population was 2,539; there were factories driven by the power of the falls and "a large and comfortable inn, with canal boats and stage coaches passing very frequently" (*Northern Traveller*, p. 52). Before beginning his entry on the next page, WI drew a one inch line at the top.

80. David Teniers (1582–1649), a Flemish painter, or his son David (1610–1690), who like his father was a noted genre and landscape painter.

Monday, August 13[81]

morng—½ past 10. Seated in a grassy nook beside a rock at the foot of a /⟨c⟩Cedar/Pinetree/ and oak on the banks of the Mohawk. ¾ mile below little falls.[82] River makes a basin surrounded by perpendicular lime stones with shrubs & weeds growing out of their fissures—and covered by groves of bush[?]-oak beech—pine &c eagle sailing above the woody heights—grass-/hoppers ⟨of[?]⟩[83] skipping & fluttering—buzz of bee about buzz headed thistle—quick strong hum of fly jerking by—note of cat bird—spinning of locust. sultry note of insects—Swallows in the air—trees rotting in the water, with fish lurking about their mouldy trunks distant sound of axe or hammer—Sunny faces of rocks, looking out from among sun gilt trees—⟨blue Mount[?]⟩ airy tints of woody crests of mountain with crows wheeling & cawing about them—terrapin bathing in sun & sliding off of ⟨*illegible*⟩ drift wood—headlong plump of the ⟨fog⟩ ⟨f⟩Frog.

Insects gamb[o]ling on the water chasing each other

Dragonfly or Devils darning needle flying athwart the grove

fish leaping

—Summer note of insects an universal hum & buzz & chirp reduced to a monotonous lulling note

broad leaved sycamore

The crow flies to the woody breast of the mountain

Sparkling grass & weeds on the sunny point, reflected in the water leaf by leaf & blade by blade—

Pond lillies—

leaf losing freshness in the sun.

distant sound of water fall like a breeze springing up in the woods.

Note of chipi clear

Butterfly pursuing its irregular flight across the basin—Keeps forward agst wind—Meets another butterfly from opposite course. both ⟨to⟩ exchange saluta-/-tions. Coy together. flutter up a little & waltz in the air and then each resumes his original course

Evg—Several gentlemen call on me

81. WI wrote "Aug 13—Monday morng—."

82. The adjective seemingly universally applied to this scene by the guidebooks and gazetteers is "romantic," suggested by the combination of a chain of the Catsberg Mountains whose rugged cliffs rise above the town of Little Falls, the rushing waters of the Mohawk which have widened a gap in the mountains and revealed layers of sandstone and blue limestone, and the perpendicular masses of dark rocks and evergreens.

83. This crossed-out word could be WI's symbol, "&c."

Tuesday, August 14[84]

leave Little Falls at ½ past 8—in open carriage for Trenton falls, 26 miles, in compy with Latrobe & Pourtales rough road[85]—fine view from Hales Hill—pass through very pretty town of Middleville.[86] Stop to change horses at Newport Factory[87]—beautiful scenery along ⟨the⟩ West Canada Creek[88] arrive at Trenton Falls[89] about 2. very hot day—Evening thunder showers

Wednesday, August 15[90]

⟨on⟩ 8 oclock morng. on Piazza of Hotel.[91] Still pleasant morning—country moist from late rain—the mists have been steaming up

84. WI wrote "Aug 14."

85. One route from Little Falls to Trenton Falls was to follow the road along the river for six miles through the rich alluvial section called the Herkimer and German Flats to Lock No. 48 where the West Canada Creek joins the Mohawk River, then to take a carriage from Herkimer to Trenton Falls.

86. Middleville was a post-village of Herkimer County on the West Canada Creek, about fourteen miles east-northeast from Utica. It was a manufacturing town (cotton, principally). WI and his party were now traveling almost due north along the east bank of the West Canada Creek.

87. Newport Landing, or Newport Factory, was on the West Canada Creek, in Herkimer County, New York, 85 miles west-northwest from Albany and twelve miles northeast of Utica.

88. West Canada Creek formed a small part of the boundary between Herkimer and Oneida Counties and flowed through Herkimer County and into the Mohawk River just east of Herkimer.

89. Trenton Falls, a post-village in Oneida County, New York, was on the West Canada Creek, two miles east of the village of Trenton. Within two miles the river descended 312 feet over six cascades or falls (Upper Falls, Cascades, Mill-dam, High Falls, Sherman's Falls, and Conrad's Falls) and presented wild scenery, boiling pools, rocky beds, eddies, smooth falls (almost like a mill dam), wooded banks, and rocky cliffs. On August 15, 1832, WI wrote Peter that the "falls are uncommonly beautiful" (PMI, III, 31), almost the same words used by a contemporary writer of an atlas when he called the falls "wildly picturesque and uncommonly beautiful" (Burr's *1829 Atlas*). Other writers described the danger of the setting, one mentioning a "melancholy accident [which] occurred in 1827. A lady from New-York was drowned by slipping from a low bank; unseen, although her friends and parents were near her" (*Northern Traveller*, p. 56).

90. WI wrote "Aug 15."

91. WI commented in a letter to Peter that nowhere outside of England had he found "such excellent hotels, and such good fare, in places remote from cities." He commented particularly about this hotel in Trenton Falls, "a clean, airy, well-furnished hotel, on a hill with a broad, beautiful prospect in front, and forests on all the other sides. My travelling companions and myself have the house to ourselves. Our table is excellent. . . . In fact, I return to all the simple enjoyments of old times with the renovated feelings of a schoolboy, and have had more hearty,

from the brooks & glens—universal ⟨*illegible*⟩[92] spinning of cricket & ↑grasshopers↓ cicadas, for summer heat distant roar of waterfalls wide prospect of woodland and distant field with misty haze. Notes of various birds—goldfinch

Cocks crowing—flies ⟨seen hovering⟩ wafting lazily in the air distant crow of rival cock from some farm house among the woods[93]

Saturday, August 18[94]

Leave Trenton Falls—½ past 7—in post waggon Stop at Trenton[95]

Knot of gaping worthies at door of Store, with hands in pockets. village jaunties—straw hat, with band half up[96] it. Short ragged coat[,] flat, bagging trousers

Pass through [*blank*][97] Country hereabouts settled by Welsh—who came out to Trenton[?]—industrious—frugal but dirty & given to whiskey—↑—rich, level country↓

½ past 11. arrive at Rome[98]—At the Flints inn find Mr Clark in parlour adjustg a/cs. dry head—thin—Little man in loose[?] stuff black

---

homebred delights of the kind since my return to the United States, than I have ever had in the same space of time in the whole course of my life" (PMI, III, 31).

92. These letters could be "note," "hu," "bu," or "wa."

93. There are no entries for August 16 and 17.

94. WI wrote "Saturday Aug 19," thereby misdating the entry.

95. Trenton was usually listed as the post-township which includes the village of Trenton Falls, but here WI makes a distinction between the town of Trenton, about two miles west of the falls, and Trenton Falls. Trenton was in Oneida County, New York, twelve miles north of Utica; its population in 1830 was 3,221.

Whether the decision to change routes was made as a result of news he heard in Trenton or whether he had made the decision earlier is not clear; at any rate, WI decided that the cholera which was rapidly spreading through the northern part of the United States and had reached Utica, New York, imposed too great a threat and he wrote to Peter: "I shall leave that place out of my route . . . though hitherto I have never avoided the malady, nor shall I do so in the course of my tour; simply observing such general diet and habits of living as experience has taught me are best calculated to keep my system in healthful tone" (PMI, III, 32).

96. This word could be "of[f]."

97. WI left the name of the town blank; unfortunately, so did the folio-sized map of Oneida County in Burr's *1829 Atlas* (plate 29). There is only a dot to indicate a town between Trenton and Rome.

98. Rome was a post-township in Oneida County, New York, on the Erie Canal between the Mohawk River and Wood Creek at the southern point of the Black River Canal. It was fifteen miles west of Utica and, in 1830, had 4,360 residents. One gazetteer called Rome the "semi-capital" of Oneida County because some of the county buildings were at Whitesborough and some were here (Baldwin and Thomas, *Gazetteer*, p. 1005). Rome was built on the site of Fort Stanwix, important in the Revolutionary War. The *American Journal of Science* in 1829 reported that when

clothes & big hat comes in to Settle a/cs—large features ↑long nose↓

Judge ———[99]

Pink complexion—blue eyes—shy downcast look.

Jasper Lynch calls on me—Dinner 25 cents

Dearborn waggon to Oneida Castle[100] 2$—

pleasant drive to Oneida—The latter a small village on a pretty creek[101] —fine wooded hills inhabited by the Oneida Indians[102]—find the Count at Oneida ⟨villa⟩ Castle Stroll out with him to Indian village—Indian ill with fever. Gentlemanlike fellow—handsome squaw have picture of GWashtn.—worked mat—Squaw light—slender make [—] small feet & ⟨arm⟩ hands—Soft talk[.] walked up between cornfields to hill commanding a view over the rich plain[103]

———

/Landlord/Parkhurst/[104] of the Inn—a little knotty, patchwork fellow, with ⟨cross⟩ small cross eyes—red sharp triangular face—big hat & bushy irongray hair—tumbles over pigeonholes full of old undelivered newspapers to find me a late one—but in vain—His daughters, with fine names (Emmalina[105] & [*blank*]) and hair in long ringlets—pale & mawkish—Big room up stairs that might serve for justice room Ball

---

the canal was opened through the diluvial formation near Rome, live clams were discovered and eaten by the workmen (*Northern Traveller*, p. 58).

99. WI drew a half-inch line to indicate, perhaps, that he would later add the judge's name.

100. From Rome there was a stagecoach road southwest to a village called Oneida Castleton on the Oneida Creek. Oneida Castle was a post-village of Oneida County, New York, twenty miles west of Utica and "on the confines of a tract of reserved land belonging to the Indians of the Oneida nation. The principal residences of most of the Indians in this part of the country were formerly fortified in a manner corresponding with their ideas of warfare, and hence the name of castle attached to this village . . ." (*Northern Traveller*, p. 58).

101. Oneida Creek, flowing northwestward, formed the boundary between Madison and Oneida Counties until entering Oneida Lake.

102. The Oneidas were one of the original five Nations. According to one contemporary, "a few years ago the nation renounced their ancient superstitious rites, and declared in favor of Christianity" (*Northern Traveller*, pp. 58–59). Frederick W. Hodge wrote that the name means "a rock that something set up and is still standing" which refers to a boulder near one ancient Oneida village. The Oneidas were a tribe of the Iroquois confederation, and they were the second tribe to accept the proposition to form a league of all tribes for defense and offense. Between 1788 and 1842 they held no fewer than thirty treaties with the state of New York (*Handbook of American Indians North of Mexico* [Washington, D.C.: Bureau of American Ethnology, Bulletin 30], II, 123–27; hereafter cited as Hodge, *Handbook of Indians*).

103. WI drew a line three-fourths inch long to separate paragraphs.

104. This interlinear insertion actually represents an alternate reading; WI wrote "Landlord" on the line and "Parkhurst" immediataely above it.

105. The spelling could be "Emmilina."

room, Meeting house &c—now antechamber to our apart-/ments. crazy[106] frame with black skirt stretched in it to be worked—about the room religious newspapers—tracts &c prevalence throughout the country of religious tracts & singing books

Sunday, August 19[107]

all night rain in torrents—brooks swoln. house overflowed—

Leave Oneida about 11. ride outside—rain holds up[—]dine at Manlius[108]—pass thro Onondaga hollow[109]

Evg. ½ past 10. arrive at Skeneatales[110]

Monday, August 20[111]

neat hotel[112]—Sherwood mine[?] host—a falstaff[113] in form—⟨c⟩good humoured—called ⟨T⟩the Squire—

His neighbor who has a neat house opposite the way on the border of the lake.[114] passes his time in a corner of Sherwoods piazza setting

106. This word is rather difficult to transcribe, with one possible reading as "decayg"; however, the context and the rather clear "azy," suggests "crazy" as the better reading, perhaps as in a crazy quilt frame.

107. WI wrote "Sunday morng 20," thereby misdating the entry.

108. Manlius township had a population in 1830 of 7,375; in the eastern part of Onondaga County, New York, eight miles east of Syracuse, it contained both the post-villages of Manlius and Manlius Centre. Two miles east of Manlius Centre and approximately fifty yards from the Erie Canal, sulphuretted hydrogen, which is inflammable, rose from a spring.

109. Onondaga, the post-township and apparently formerly the county seat of Onondaga County, New York, was pleasantly located on a hill; it was an agricultural town as well as a town of many mills, and its population in 1830 was 5,668, growing very little within the next twenty years. The Indian word "Onondaga" means variously a "swamp at the foot of a hill" or "on, or on top of, the hill or mountain." The Onondagas were an important tribe of the Iroquois confederation; they lived formerly in the area of the mountain, lake, and creek named for the tribe (see Hodge, *Handbook of Indians*, II, 129–35).

110. "Skeneateles" was the less preferred spelling of "Skaneateles"; in the western section of Onondaga County, New York, seven miles east-northeast of Auburn and 146 miles west of Albany, it was located at the northwestern end of Skaneateles Lake. The population in 1840 was 3,981.

111. WI wrote "Monday 20," the correct day and date after the two previous errors.

112. Andrew's Tavern was the only inn listed in Skaneateles by Elise Lathrop, *Early American Inns and Taverns*, 4th ed. (New York: Tudor Publishing Company, 1946), p. 253.

113. The initial letter could be transcribed as either *f* or *F*.

114. Skaneateles Lake was about sixteen miles long and from three-fourths to two miles wide; the northern part of the lake was in Onondaga County, New York, and

his dog Turk on the pigs[.] John the omnibus of the stable yard—tall thin, pale laughing & careless—platterbd.[115] old hat, foxy & slouching—thin bagging pantaloons &c

The bar keeper, who acts as master of ceremony & intro/duces every one to us—makes us drink wine with him at parting—⟨fa⟩ Loungers who gape in at every window wonderfully ⟨att⟩ angular atti-/-tudes of loungers—

In the course of the night Latrobe arrives

[*p. [36] blank except for* ⟨*Tuesday 21*⟩]

Tuesday, August 21[116]

at 9.—Set off in carriage, accompanid by Mr Aspinwall.[117] ride up the west side of the lake—then across to [*blank*][118] Lake—visit Gov Throop.[119] find his mother[120] & his sister Mrs Martin there also Genl Brenker-

---

the southern part was between Onondaga and Cayuga Counties. The lake was picturesque and abounded with fish.

115. The mark after the word "platterbd" may be intended as an underlining (transcribed as period) to indicate an abbreviation, or it may be a dash.

116. WI wrote "Tuesday 21."

117. Colonel Thomas Aspinwall (1786–1876) had been since 1824 Irving's literary agent; he was the American consul-general in London from 1815 to 1853, and, during 1824–1825, Irving saw him frequently in Paris (*Jourals and Notebooks*, III, 319, n. 641).

118. The name which WI apparently intended to fill in later was Owasco Lake, which is west of Skaneateles Lake and almost parallel to it. Owasco Lake was in Cayuga County, New York; eleven miles long and 1½ miles wide, it runs into the Seneca River.

119. Enos Thomas Throop (1784–1874) was born in Johnstown, New York. He studied law, practiced at Auburn, New York, and was subsequently a state representative and circuit judge. He was elected lieutenant governor in 1828, and, when Van Buren left the governorship seventy days after election to become secretary of state, Throop became acting governor; he was elected governor of New York State in 1830 and served the full term. However, by the time of this meeting with Irving, Throop was, according to Alexander, being "practically ridiculed into retirement. He was nicknamed 'Small-light,' and the longer he served the smaller and the more unpopular he became" (*Political History*, I, 394). William L. Marcy replaced Throop as his party's nominee for governor at the party convention in September, 1832. Throop was later appointed naval officer at the port of New York (1833–1838) and minister to Naples (1838–1842).

120. Governor Throop's mother was Abiah Thompson, the daughter of Enos Thompson; she married George Bliss Throop, was widowed in 1794, and afterward remarried.

hoff[?][121] & lady– ⟨parting⟩ leave taking[122] of latter–difficulty in drawing on her gloves.–

Auburn[123]–Hotel kept by Noyes.[124] built of stone by Sherwood–cost 25000 $–neat Stone buildings in Auburn.–Penitentiary[125]–Theological Seminary[126]– –Met at Auburn Professor [*blank*] of Geneva–⟨drove from⟩ dined–after Dinner ⟨c⟩took extra Stage Drove to Cayuga[127]

121. Although it is difficult to determine which of the many Brinkerhoffs connected with New York WI met, one possibility is Henry R. Brinkerhoff (1788–1844). He was born in Pennsylvania, but his family moved soon afterward to Cayuga County, New York. Brinkerhoff commanded a company of militia in the War of 1812, was a member of the state legislature, and served as a major general in the New York State militia. Brinkerhoff moved to Huron County, Ohio, in 1827, and was elected to the 28th Congress as a Democrat from that state in 1843 (Poore's *Register*, p. 300). Two other possibilities are George R. Brinkerhoff and Jacob Brinkerhoff.

122. WI left space between these words, but, as was often his habit, he failed to lift his pen; therefore, we have transcribed as two words.

123. Auburn was the capital of Cayuga County, New York, on the Albany-Buffalo Railroad, approximately 173 miles west of Albany, and 2½ miles northwest of Owasco Lake on the north bank of the Owasco River. Its beauty was noted by writers of gazetteers and travel books; in 1830 the population was 4,486.

124. The principal hotels were the American Hotel, the Auburn House, and the Western Exchange.

125. The state prison at Auburn, located in the northern part of town and on the north side of the Owasco outlet, was considered a celebrated feature of both the town and the prison system. The Auburn prison was founded in 1816 with cost estimates from $300,000 to $500,000. In the shape of a hollow square, its five stories were constructed so that prisoners could neither converse nor make signs to each other. Travelers were intensely interested in the rival American prison systems in Philadelphia and Auburn, the former prescribing solitary confinement without labor so that prisoners could contemplate wrongdoings and repent. The Auburn system allowed the prisoners to work together during the day without communication and separated them at night in the 730 solitary cells. At the end of 1829 there were 639 convicts at Auburn, and in 1831 one visitor wrote of representatives of the French government observing this model system confining 700 men and thirty women. Jane Louise Mesick cites many other accounts of visitors to this prison, with Harriet Martineau's objecting to the surveillance of prisoners without their knowledge (*The English Traveller in America, 1785–1835* [New York: Columbia University Press, 1922], pp. 117–20).

126. The theological seminary was founded in 1821 by the Presbyterian Church; its four professors and library of 5,000 to 6,000 volumes were housed in a single stone building of four stories.

127. Cayuga, sometimes called Cayuga Bridge, was a small village in Aurelius township, in Cayuga County, New York, ten miles west of Auburn and on the eastern shore of Cayuga Lake. Two bridges crossed this lake (which is 38 miles long and from 1½ to four miles wide); one was the railroad bridge, and the other connected Cayuga to Bridgeport.

⟨to⟩ crossed bridge—⟨passed through⟩ white sails on lake[128] at a distance—passed through thriving town of Seneca falls.[129] drove along Seneca river[130]—a fine Stream Stripped of its trees—Waterloo[131] a very neat town—

arrived at Geneva[132] at Dusk. ⟨fine⟩ thriving place. large Shops—pavd streets. excellent Hotel—(Franklin)[133]—

Wednesday, August 22[134]

leave Geneva at ½ past 9. in Stage coach: to Canandaugua[135]—⟨There take⟩ pretty town—Court in Session—There take an extra and ⟨keep on till[136] until 10 at night when we stop⟩—Stop at Rochester[137]—dine

128. Apparently WI began this word with another letter, either *S* or *d*, then over it wrote both *l* and *L*.

129. The stage road connecting Bridgeport to Seneca Falls was, according to one travel manual, not as scenic as the less direct steamboat ride from Cayuga Bridge via Cayuga Lake and Seneca River. Seneca Falls was a post-township in Seneca County, New York, five miles west of Cayuga and fifteen miles west of Auburn. Located on both sides of the Seneca River, the town was erected after the 1820 census, incorporated in 1831, and by 1840 its population was 4,281.

130. The Seneca River, formed by the overflow of the Seneca Lake, at this point flows east-west from the foot of the Seneca Lake to the foot of the Cayuga Lake; five other lakes flow into this river, which is 65 miles long.

131. Waterloo, a post-township, was the semicapital of Seneca County, New York; the other county buildings were at Ovid. It is located on both sides of the Seneca River about four miles west of Seneca Falls and seven miles east of Geneva. Called a "handsome village," it was incorporated in 1824, and by 1840 its population had grown to 3,036.

132. Geneva, a post-village of Seneca township in Ontario County, New York, seven miles west of Waterloo, was beautifully situated at the northern end of Seneca Lake and called "one of the neatest villages in the state." Incorporated in 1812, its population in 1838 was about 3,400; noteworthy was Geneva College, an Episcopal institution founded in 1823 and by 1832 having a president, nine instructors, and a library of 1,500 volumes.

133. WI's dash cuts across the final parenthesis.

Several contemporary sources remarked on the fine hotel accommodations in Geneva, and the Franklin was one of those particularly mentioned.

134. WI wrote "Wednesday 22."

135. Canandaigua, approximately 23 miles west of Geneva, was the county town of Ontario County. Its Indian name, which means "a chosen place," supports one contemporary's conclusion: "Perhaps there is no place in the United States which exhibits more pleasing evidences of a finely cultivated taste, both in the architecture of the buildings and their rural embellishments, than Canandaigua" (Chapin, *Gazetteer*, p. 50).

136. Before WI crossed out lines 6 and 7 on page [38] ("keep . . . stop"), he seemed to write over the word "at" or "all," the word "till"[?].

137. Rochester, the capital of Monroe County and situated on both sides of the Genesee River seven miles from its mouth, was only four miles from Canandaigua

there & continue on to Sandy Creek[138] where we ⟨dine⟩ sleep—comfortable Inn—

Thursday, August 23[139]

Continue along the ridge road[140] to Lock/port[141] ⟨by the⟩ dine there & from thence to Lewis-/town[142]—take an extra there & continue on to

---

and seven miles south of Lake Ontario. It was founded in 1812 by Nathaniel Rochester, William Fitzhugh, and Charles Carroll of Maryland, incorporated as a village in 1817 and as a city in 1834. Its population grew rapidly from the first: 1,502 inhabitants in 1820; 9,269 in 1830; and 20,191 in 1840. It was a well-built city with a splendid aqueduct by which the Erie Canal crossed the Genesee River; the power derived from this great river (which dropped 268 feet over falls and rapids within the city), the fertility of the land, and accessibility to the other areas of the country gave Rochester its early growth and its promise for the future.

138. The road from Rochester to Niagara Falls was 87 miles; from Rochester (through Carthage Falls, Parma, Clarkson, Hartland) to Sandy Creek, 39 miles. Sandy Creek entered Lake Ontario in Monroe County about twenty miles northwest of Rochester. The village was in Orleans County, New York, and in 1840, had a population of about 200; it was on the stage route and in Burr's *1829 Atlas* was called Sandy Creek Ville (plate 45).

139. WI wrote "Thursday 23–."

140. One of the principal features along this route, according to a writer in 1834, was this Ridge, "a remarkable elevation, of little height, and for the most part very narrow, extending a great part of the distance from Rochester to Lewiston. It is often perfectly level for several miles, and affords an admirable foundation for the road, which has, in consequence, been laid along its top. Some have imagined that the ridge was, at some long past period, the shore of Lake Ontario, and was thrown up by its waves" (*Northern Traveller*, p. 68).

141. Lockport, the county seat and largest town of Niagara County, New York, with a population in 1830 of 3,823, was on the Erie Canal, thirty miles northeast of Buffalo and 65 miles west of Rochester. Two ranges of locks compensated for the canal descent of sixty feet from the level of Lake Erie to the level of the Genesee River and provided hydraulic power for manufacturing.

142. Lewiston, a village and township, was seven miles below, or north of, Niagara Falls, seven miles above, or south of, Lake Ontario; it was a port of entry of Niagara County, New York, and was on the eastern side of the Niagara River. Destroyed in the War of 1812 and rebuilt in 1815, its population in 1830 was 1,528. A mile east of Lewiston was the Tuscarora reservation on which lived Indians who emigrated from North Carolina by invitation of the Five Nations.

Niagara[143] where we arrive ⟨before⟩ in time to see the Falls[144] by sunset

Friday, August 24[145]

Beautiful view of Falls on Cloudy morng. at first the prospect in cloud[?] colouring then a break of Sunshine lighting up opposite side & gradually passing athwart the whole abyss— —descend to the foot of the falls—

Afternoon cross to the English side[146]—Great yawning Hotels overlooking the falls.[147]

Swallows playing about in the mist of the falls

143. After traveling almost due west from Lockport to Lewiston (approximately eighteen miles), WI's party was now traveling south, along the eastern bank of the Niagara River, to reach the village of Niagara Falls (approximately seven miles). At this time, Niagara Falls, only a post-village, was in the Niagara Falls township in Niagara County, New York. It was on the northeastern side of the Falls, 22 miles from Buffalo; its population in 1840 was 560. Latrobe wrote that there were several reasons for their choosing this village for their "halting place," among them that the hotel on the Canadian side was "garish," that the distant view of the Horse-shoe Fall was grand, that access to both falls was facilitated by the bridge to Goat Island, and most important to Latrobe, that Niagara village was more rural and secluded, and the village and inns exhibited more taste than its Canadian competition (Latrobe, *Rambler*, I, 77).

144. Latrobe confessed to being "a notorious cascade-hunter"; he was disappointed that the "Cataract of the wilderness," which at the turn of the century was rarely visited and sparsely settled, had become a tourist attraction, with the forest first having "yielded to the axe," then to hotels, "museums, mills, staircases, tolls, and grogshops." Yet he said of his first view of the falls, "I shall never forget the real anxiety with which we looked out, on our ascent from Lewiston, for the first appearance of the object of our visit. . . . We all agreed that we could even then grasp the idea of its magnitude, and that all we had seen elsewhere, and all we had expected, was far surpassed by what was then shown to us" (*Rambler*, I, 75–76). For a later, detailed description of the Falls and surrounding area, as well as many quotations about the Falls from visitors, some contemporaries of WI, see the section "Niagara As It Is: A Complete Guide," in *Pauls' Dictionary of Buffalo, Niagara Falls, Tonawanda and Vicinity* (Buffalo: Peter Paul Book Co., 1896), pp. 171–265; hereafter cited as *Pauls' Dictionary of Buffalo.*

145. WI wrote "Friday 2⟨2⟩4."

146. Latrobe began his description of this early morning view, "What a glorious scene!" and continued in great detail (*Rambler*, I, 77–78). On the American side of the falls, the traveler could descend to the river by the "Biddle stair case," built in 1829 at a cost of $300 by the late Nicholas Biddle; he then reached the British fall by ascending one of several paths.

147. Two large hotels overlooking the falls on the Canadian side of the river, whose splendid views were noted, were the Pavilion, standing on the upper bank and kept by Mr. Forsyth, and the Clifton House on the brow of the bank near the ferry with the best view of the falls; on the American side was the Cataract House,

Saturday, August 25[148]

½ ↑past↓ 9 oclock morng. on the stage over the falls. beautiful trans/parency of the water bright ⟨chrys[?]⟩ feathery look of water—mist ⟨bri[?]⟩ all illuminated—rainbow forming a halo. The whole wonderfully brilliant & light—drops like chrystal chandolier ↑and↓—foam below[?][149] like snow

12 oclock. By the cabin beside the American Fall. ⟨*illegible*⟩ Seated on a stone in fine grove of oaks & maples—Spray of ⟨f⟩ water falling on me—⟨Gran[?]⟩[150] view on the Am. fall to the Horseshoe[151] looks like one constant fall[?]—lulling sound of water—Cool breeze from the falls—place for Summer nap.

After dinner cross to Canada side. drive to Brocks Monument[152] & back. Evg. Judge Rochester of Buffalo & party arrive at Niagara
—walk by night round Goat Island,[153] with Pourtales[154]

Sunday, August 26[155]

Set off⟨in⟩ at 5 Oclock in morning for Buffalo[156]—embark in Steam

---

"a part of it almost overhanging the rapids between the shore and Goat island" (*Appleton's Hand-Book*, pp. 147–48).

148. WI wrote "Saturday 25."

149. This word could be "blows"; Latrobe talked of the "heavy white cloud of spray which rose from the depth of the boiling basin" and then of "the floating sheets of foam and spray which the wind of the mighty cataract drove backward and forward over it like innumerable clouds of thin floating gauze . . ." (*Rambler*, I, 78).

150. These crossed-out letters could be "Grea."

151. The Canadian part of the falls, between Iris Island and the Canadian mainland, was called the Horse-shoe Fall because of its shape. The distance around the Horse-shoe Fall was 144 rods, and directly across, it was 74 rods.

152. General Brock's Monument was in Queenston Heights on the Canadian side of the Niagara River, just south of Queenston and southwest (and across the river) from Lewiston. The monument, 126 feet high, was at the scene of Sir Isaac Brock's death during the Battle of Queenston, October 13, 1812, when American troops under the command of General Van Rensselaer at Lewiston crossed the river to capture the heights; the victory went to the British as the Americans lost 1,000 men (*Pauls' Dictionary of Buffalo*, p. 81).

153. The following description by Latrobe of these walks supports our reading of "Goat": "The scene at sun-set, day after day, was no way less majestic, when the sun glancing from the Canadian side of the river, lit up the precipices and woods of Goat Island, and the broad face of the American Fall, which then glowed like a wall of gold. . . . Morning, noon, and night, found us strolling about the shore, and on the island, which is an earthly paradise" (*Rambler*, I, 78).

154. For reference to Count de Pourtalès, see p. 8, n. 43.

155. WI wrote "26th."

156. Buffalo was a city, port of entry, and the county seat of Erie County, New York, and two or three miles south of the head of Niagara River; both the Erie Canal and the Central Railroad terminated at this city. Previously a trading out-

boat niagara[157] for Erie[158]–on board meet Mr Ellsworth[159] & Mr. [*blank*][160] The former a commissioner to settle the Indians–agree to accompany him[161]–

Lake[162]–pale green range of blue long hills–Span[?] of the Allegany[163][.] white sails at distance Water of the lake pure[,] clear–the breezes from it sweet & wholesome. no swamps or marshes around it–

---

post, Buffalo was laid out by the Holland Company in 1801; it became a military post in 1812 and in December, 1813, was burned by a party of British and Indians, a disaster partially compensated for by the U.S. Congress in the sum of $80,000 to the residents. In 1822 Buffalo was incorporated as a village and in April, 1832, it was incorporated as a city. Its population showed predictable growth: in 1820 there were 2,095; in 1830, 8,653; and in 1840, 18,213. With the completion of the Erie Canal, Buffalo became a major center of manufacturing and commerce.

157. Buffalo's harbor formed by Buffalo Creek was twelve to fourteen feet deep and large and protected enough to accommodate several hundred steamboats at once.

158. There were several towns and villages called "Erie" on Lake Erie; even though, from Latrobe's account (*Rambler*, I, 80–81), we might infer that WI's Erie was the township in Ottawa County, Ohio, the more obvious choice is Erie, Pennsylvania. The recommended steamboat route westward included Buffalo, Dunkirk, Portland, then to Erie, Salem, Ashtabula, Grand River, etc. (*Northern Traveller*, p. 383). Incorporated in 1805, Erie was the port of entry and capital of Erie County, Pennsylvania, 90 miles southwest of Buffalo, with a population in 1840 of 3,412. Its harbor across from Presque Isle was one of the best on the lake, and its shipbuilding industry made it a fast-growing town in the first part of the nineteenth century. (See Charles B. Galbreath, *History of Ohio* [Chicago: American Historical Society, 1925], I, 572–73; hereafter cited as Galbreath, *History*.)

159. Henry Leavitt Ellsworth (1791–1858), whom Latrobe called "Judge E. of Hartford"; see Introduction, pp. xxix–xxxii, for discussion. Following this time as commissioner to the Indians, Ellsworth was mayor of Hartford for a short time in 1835 and the first United States commissioner of patents, in which office he precipitated the first government appropriation for agriculture, making him the "Father of the Department of Agriculture."

160. We have not identified this person, perhaps a traveling companion of Ellsworth.

161. WI's rather casual reference to this change in plans belies its importance; at this point he intended to leave Pourtalès and Latrobe, who regretted the impending "separation from our friend Washington Irving," and return to New York by way of the Ohio. Latrobe and Pourtalès were going to Canada (*Rambler*, I, 80).

162. Lake Erie.

163. WI used the "New York spelling" of the Allegany Mountains. As late as 1853, Baldwin and Thomas were calling for a uniform spelling ("Alleghany"), because even on the same map, the river and mountain range were variously spelled "Allegheny," "Allegany," or "Alleghany." With a mean height of 2,500 feet, the Alleghany Mountains extend southwestward and parallel to the Atlantic coast for approximately 300 miles; more often the section of the Appalachian Mountains referred to as the Alleghanies is that part lying southwest of the Hudson River and

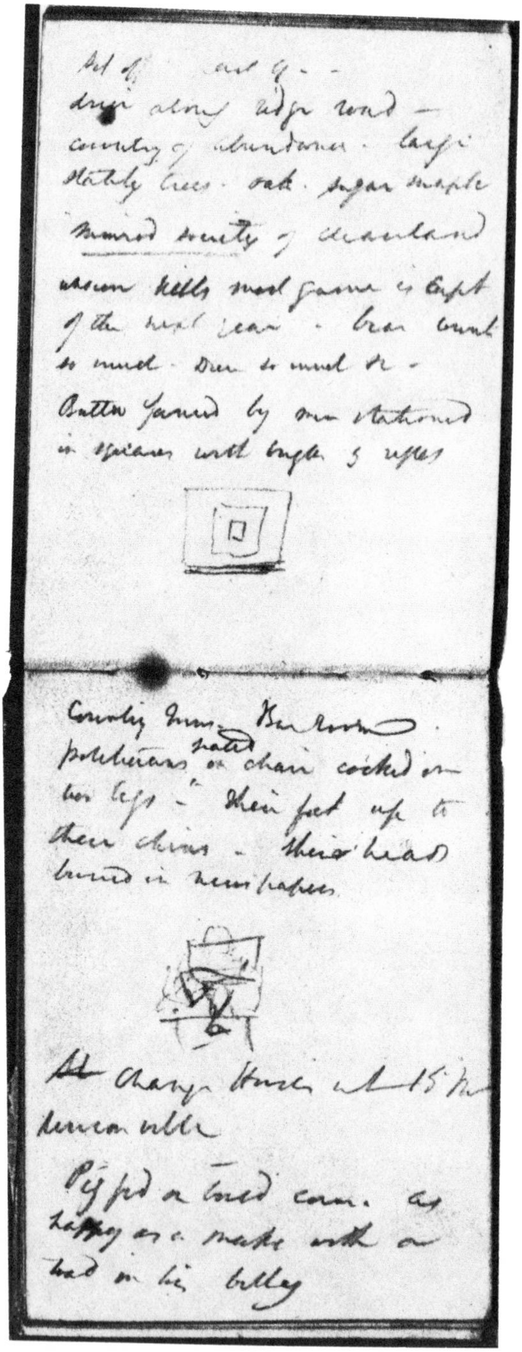

Fig. 1. Top, Drawing of three boxes within boxes on bottom third of notebook p. [48]; *bottom,* small crude sketch on p. [49] of man "seated on chair cocked on two legs–Their feet up to their chins–Their heads buried in news papers."

Mr. Kellys[164] eulogium on corn bread[165]—(virginia)—

Monday, August 27[166]

at 6 oclock. Land at Astabula[167] ↑(Ohio)↓—mouth of river[168] of same name 40 miles from Erie—Get a waggon to convey us to the village—about 2½ miles distant—where we ⟨eng⟩ breakfast and take an Extra Stage for Cleaveland.

Hubbards Hotel[169]—Sluts[?], flies & squalling children

Set off ½ past 9— —drive along ridge road—country of abundance—large stately trees—oak, sugar maple

Nimrod society[170] of Cleaveland[—] who ever kills most game is ⟨c⟩Capt of the next year—bear counts so much—Deer so much &c—[? Battle formed?] by men stationed in squares with bugles & rifles

[*Drawing of three boxes within boxes on bottom third of p. [48]*]

Country Inns—Bar Room politicians ‸↑seated↓ on chair cocked on two legs—Their feet up to their chins—Their heads buried in news papers

[*Small crude sketch of man so seated and reading, p. [49]*]

⟨St⟩ Change Horses at 15 Mi[.] Unionville[171]

———

dividing the waters flowing east to the Atlantic and those flowing west to the Mississippi (*Gazetteer*, p. 34).

164. Mr. Kelly (see n. 181 below).

165. There are many variations of Southern corn bread—hoecake, griddle cake, corn pones—but all are made simply with cornmeal, water, and salt, and then fried or baked. Corn bread is different from corn muffins which have eggs, milk, baking powder, etc.

166. WI wrote "27th."

167. Ashtabula, a post-township on Lake Erie, was about twelve miles north of Jefferson, three miles from Lake Erie, and on Ashtabula River, the harbor at the mouth of which steamboats visited on the trip from Buffalo to Detroit. The population in 1840 was 1,704.

168. Ashtabula River or Creek, approximately 40 miles long, rose in east Ashtabula County, flowed north and west, and entered Lake Erie at Ashtabula.

169. Apparently, after leaving the steamboat at Ashtabula and taking the stage for Cleveland, WI's party followed the stage road parallel to Lake Erie; Hubbard's Hotel could have been in the village of Ashtabula or in Saybrook, between Ashtabula and Unionville.

170. We have been unable to identify the Nimrod Society of Cleveland; it apparently was a hunt club.

171. Unionville, Ohio, one of the largest villages in Geauga County, was near the Cleveland and Erie Railroad.

Pig fed on wild corn. As happy as a snake with a toad in his belly

Sign.[172]

[Going out to work done[?] in this back room.]

Magnificent[173] woods—Golden repose of the country—As if heaven smiled down upon it & it smiled back again—

[? Trees[174] prof[f]ering ?] exhuberant fertility—offering their treasures—⟨ma⟩ Neat log huts—Stage breaks main chain—call at log hut—Young woman. 2 children—play with one & a big mastiff—young woman has been there 7 years—Spinning wheel

dine at Paynesville[175]—beside Grand river[176]—nice help at dinner named Grace—The daughters of landlords help at dinner & then have the servant woman to remove things—

Serene evening—quiet green lawns bordered by noble forests—deep lake tinge of sky—night hawks—

arrive about 8 oclock at Cleaveland.[177]

172. The words of the sign are divided into two lines, and the brackets are WI's. The questioned word could be "down."

173. Over two letters, perhaps "wo," and what seems to be a line crossing them out, WI wrote the initial letters of this word.

174. The initial word of this difficult sentence was written over other letters, one perhaps an *F*; the process could have been reversed with the word being "Four" rather than "Trees." The second word could possibly be "pledging."

175. Apparently WI first wrote "Payns" and then added between the *n* and the *s* what appears to be an *a*, and over it an *e*; the fact that there is a village in Onondaga County, New York, with this spelling might have influenced his "correction."

Painesville was a post-township, and after the formation of Lake County in 1840 from portions of Geauga and Cuyahoga Counties, it was the county town. The township, which had been named for General Edward Paine, a Revolutionary War officer from Connecticut, was three miles from Lake Erie and contained three villages—Fairport, Richmond, and Painesville, the one WI visited. The village was situated on the left, or west, bank of the Grand River at the lower rapids and had a population in 1840 of about 1,100.

176. Rising in northeast Ohio, the Grand River flowed into Lake Erie about three miles from Painesville.

177. WI may have spelled this city "Cleaveland," because in 1832 it was one of the acceptable spellings of Cleveland, New York; also, the city was named for General Moses Cleaveland (a kinsman of President Grover Cleveland) whose family used the *a* spelling; when the town took the general's name, printers dropped the *a*, leaving it with its present spelling.

Cleveland, port of entry of Ohio, and county seat of Cuyahoga County, was a trading post as early as 1786. It was incorporated as a village in 1815; in 1824, the first steamboat was launched in its harbor, and when the Ohio Canal was opened in 1827 and completed in 1832, it became more important as a trading town. Its population grew rapidly: in 1820, it had 600 people; in 1830, 1,076; and in 1840, 6,071.

Tuesday, August 28[178]

At Cleaveland, exit of Ohio Canal[179]—⟨visit[?]⟩[180] walk about the place with Mr Kelley.[181] introduced to his brothers[182]—to Mr Ogden[183]

178. WI wrote "↑Tuesday↓ 28, Aug."

179. The Ohio Canal, sometimes called the Ohio and Erie Canal, was begun on July 4, 1825, with speeches by Governor Clinton of New York and Governor Morrow of Ohio. Some people bitterly opposed its construction; 1,185 feet of lockage had to be constructed, as well as numerous aqueducts over rivers and creeks. However, on June 27, 1827, the canal, which was 40 feet wide and four feet deep, was opened from Lake Erie at Cleveland to Akron; it was completed to Portsmouth in the summer of 1832, a total of 307 miles. According to Galbreath, the canal "was the beginning of prosperity in Ohio" (*History*, I, 431).

180. Another possibility for the reading of this crossed-out word is "with."

181. Probably Alfred Kelley (1789–1859), who was known as the "Father of Ohio Canals"; his name and Cleveland's grew in importance together. Born in Connecticut, educated in New York, Kelley moved to Cleveland and was admitted to the Ohio bar in 1810, making him Cleveland's first lawyer. As the prosecuting attorney from 1810 to 1822, as the first "president" of the village of Cleveland, and from 1814 until 1857, as a member of the Ohio House or Senate through twelve sessions, his political record was outstanding.

Apparently WI met him the same day he met Ellsworth (see the August 26 entry), the day they all embarked on the steamboat *Niagara* for Buffalo, and had traveled with him for two days until they reached Cleveland. By this time, Mr. Kelley had moved with his large family from Cleveland to Columbus, Ohio, where he lived from 1830 until his death. In his later career, Kelley was president of many important railroad companies, but it was his part in establishing the canal system in Ohio that was his most outstanding contribution.

182. Alfred Kelley was the second son of Daniel and Jemima (Stow) Kelley; he had five brothers, who, with their father, joined him in Cleveland after he became established. The elder Kelley followed his son Alfred as "president" of Cleveland (1816–1819). One brother, Irad Kelley, was the local postmaster from 1816 until 1830; Alfred, his father, and two brothers—Irad and Datus Kelley—were among the incorporators of the Cleveland Pier Company.

183. Written together as "toMr" or perhaps "toWm." The Ogden family was in early nineteenth-century America outstanding and large. (See William Ogden Wheeler, *The Ogden Family in America* [Philadelphia, 1907].) Thomas Ludlow Ogden (1773–1844) was a vice-president of the dinner given in New York to honor WI on his 1832 homecoming, and the "Mr Ogden" to whom WI here refers is probably Ludlow Ogden's nephew, William Butler Ogden (1805–1877), who was the son of Abraham and Abigail (Weed) Ogden and was born in Walton, New York. When he was only fifteen years old, his father suffered a paralytic stroke, and William took over his father's business interests in an undeveloped country. With the same financial capability which had marked his early career as land developer, he became a rich man, the first mayor of Chicago when it was incorporated as a city in 1837, as well as a railroad executive.

son of Abraham O[184] to Mr Clinton[185] &c &c.

Leave Cleaveland at ½ past 1. drive through woody country to [*blank*][186]

Latrobe shoots young Eagle

Sleep at Medina,[187] 28 miles from Cleaveland

Wednesday, August 29[188]

Breakfast at Medina—with passengers in the Stage that comes in—imposition of Stage proprietor—Sending in a full stage—Gentm. wife & 4 children to ⟨ha⟩ occupy 3 places[189]

mount outside. drive to Wooster[190] great part of the way thro woods. monotonous—at Wooster (28 mi) dine & procure extra Stage. Story of clock pedlar who insisted on leaving his clocks on trial. at the end of 6 months called to know if they would take them—women always colleagued to make their husbands buy them as they could cook—boil their Eggs by them &c Clocks that cost 5 $ sold for 30 $. Had 100 clarks engaged in pedling clocks[.] had sold 30000 $ worth

Afternoon drive[?][191] through woods. rough road—a thunderstorm comes up—dark blue clouds—with pale streaks & ragged edges—

Arrive after dark at Browns[192]—a small but very clean house—civil

184. Mr. Abraham Ogden (1775–1846), the father of the previously mentioned Ogden. Nathalia Wright suggests that the "Mr. Abm. Ogden" whom WI gratefully acknowledged as being responsible for the kind attentions paid him in Marseilles in September, 1804, was the brother of T. L. Ogden (*Journals and Notebooks*, I, 475, n. 35).

185. We have been unable to identify Mr. Clinton.

186. Irving and his party had now changed directions; one town between Cleveland and Medina along his route which WI might have meant to add later was Berea, a village in Cuyahoga County, twelve miles southwest from Cleveland.

187. Medina, in the central part of Ohio, 28 miles south-southwest from Cleveland, was the county town of Medina County. The township, settled in 1813, was named Mecca (indicated as such on early maps) and later Medina, a change from the birthplace to the burial place of Mahomet. In 1840, its population was approximately 650.

188. WI wrote "29th. Wednesday."

189. WI began the word with an S or a "ch," then over that wrote "places."

190. Wooster, the county town of Wayne County, Ohio, was 52 miles southwest from Cleveland. Named for General David Wooster, a Revolutionary War officer, it was laid out in 1808 on a site 337 feet above Lake Erie on Killbuck Creek. Wooster became a center of trade and carriage making, and in 1840, its population was approximately 1,100.

191. WI completed his final *e* unusually—above the line, resembling a *d*. The word could also be "down."

192. WI could be referring to an inn south from Wooster; however, there were Brown townships in Ohio in seven counties. If WI referred to a township, it was

people[—]good supper—crowded bed room. crying child in next room. hot night—⟨s⟩ dress[,] go down & sleep in Stage Coach—

———

Thursday, August 30[193]

Set off at ½ past 4 in consequence of impertinence of driver—drive to Wooster[194]—fly/[195] blown hotel—get Stage to Newark—ride through more open country, rich loamy soil—noble trees—Stop at Utica,[196] small town or village—⟨p[?]⟩[197] Inn a Small & plain house, but extremely clean—contrast between large showy, flyblown house & small clean humble one Arrive at Newark[198] about 3 o'clock

⟨Whitewoods, elms straight tall carried into high air⟩[199]

Newark[200]—

---

probably the one in Knox County, about twelve miles northeast from Mount Vernon and between Wooster and Newark.

193. WI wrote "30. Thursday."

194. Apparently, WI doubled back over already traveled ground, now going north to Wooster to get another stage bound for Newark, Ohio, which was south of both Brown and Wooster.

195. WI first spelled the word "fly," then after the *y*, added another *y*, letting the loop of the first be an *l*; the word in the manuscript appears to be "fyy," but with Irving's correction his intention is clear: "fly."

196. Utica was a post-village in Licking County, Ohio, twelve miles north of Newark and on the railroad between Sandusky and Newark.

197. This letter could also be an S.

198. Newark, the county town of Licking County, was platted in 1801, after the plan of Newark, New Jersey; it was incorporated in 1826, and in 1832, had 250 houses. It was at the confluence of the three main branches of the Licking River as well as on the Ohio and Erie Canal, 176 miles from its outlet in Lake Erie. Quarries of sandstone and a mine of cannel coal were worked here.

199. This difficult passage is the first attempt to describe the forest; WI came back to this idea on the following two pages of the manuscript.

200. It is not surprising that Irving was interested in the earthworks near Newark; they were, and are today, "among the most interesting and diversified of the entire state, which is famous for its mound builder remains" (Galbreath, *History*, I, 377). Baird wrote in 1832, "In the vicinity of Newark, Ohio, is found a fort containing forty acres within its walls, which are about ten feet high. It has gate ways and walls in front of them for protection. Another fort contains 22 acres, and has an observatory, partly of earth, and partly of wood, in the middle of it. There is another circular fort, containing 26 acres. There are also parallel walls, with watchtowers. It is said that there are more than 1000 wells, many of them exceeding 20 feet in depth, in the vicinity of the same town" (*View*, pp. 85–86). Timothy Flint commented at length on the "monuments" of the Mississippi Valley, using them to answer the literary complaint that America had "nothing to connect the imagination and the heart with the past" (*Mississippi Valley*, I, 131–34). William Henry Harrison, whom WI was to meet several days later (see September 1, 1832, entry), wrote extensively on these earthworks in his "Discourse: On the Aborigines of the Valley of the Ohio," published in the *Transactions of the Historical and Philosophical*

Circular fort–

Oak three mens arms at mans height–

Inside 35 feet to 40 feet–ditch[?] within, formed[?] by churning up mud[?][201]

mound 30[202] feet wide[?] of open pastur[?]

Trees oak, butternut &c rich soil–robins Jays–cowbell[203] Immense trees crashed down[?] some cut by man

whitewood–elm–Oak[?][204] into mid air–

rushing blast far above–⟨wh⟩

They[205] who found them must have ⟨known⟩ cleared the forest– –

ditch mud–Mound lawn without

Area filled with Gigantic trees Silence below–rushing blast in the high tree tops

Mr Ellsworth never saw exhibition of larger & finer forest trees–oak &c than those within & in forest

Holes of wood chuck[,] noise of wood cutters axe[,] gun

[*p. [62] blank*]

Leave Newark at [*blank*] and drive 9 Miles to Lima[206][–] Country House of ⟨Van Dorn[?]⟩ ↑Humance[?]↓–an honest fellow from New Jersey–House small, dirty, people good humoured to a mensch. All assembled ⟨talki⟩ cutting apples in a huge trough & talking & laughing–Supped. passed a hot Sleepless night–

Friday, August 31[207]

rose at earliest dawn–talked with landlord–tall good looking round

---

Society of Ohio, vol. 1, pt. 2 (Cincinnati: Geo. W. Bradbury, 1839), pp. 217–59. Harrison maintained that the Newark and Circleville works were "never intended for military defences" (p. 225).

201. This word could be read "soil" or "dirt."

202. This number could be "70."

203. These last five words are difficult to decipher; Flint described the predominance of deciduous trees and deep forests and the fact that "in the richest soils the trees are rather distinguishable for their straightness than their size" (*Mississippi Valley*, I, 395).

204. This word could be "tall," with a shorter than usual final *l*.

205. WI first wrote the word "these," then over the final *e*, a *y*.

206. Lima was a township in the southwest part of Licking County, Ohio. Galbreath commented on the mixed quality of the population of this county, settled by people from Pennsylvania, New Jersey, Virginia, New England, Wales, and Germany (*History*, I, 375); we have been unable to identify the owner.

207. WI wrote "hot Sleepless night ↑Friday Aug 31↓–rose at earliest dawn"; the day and date seem to have been added later in heavier writing.

Fig. 2. Drawing of fort, perhaps at Newark on notebook p. [67].

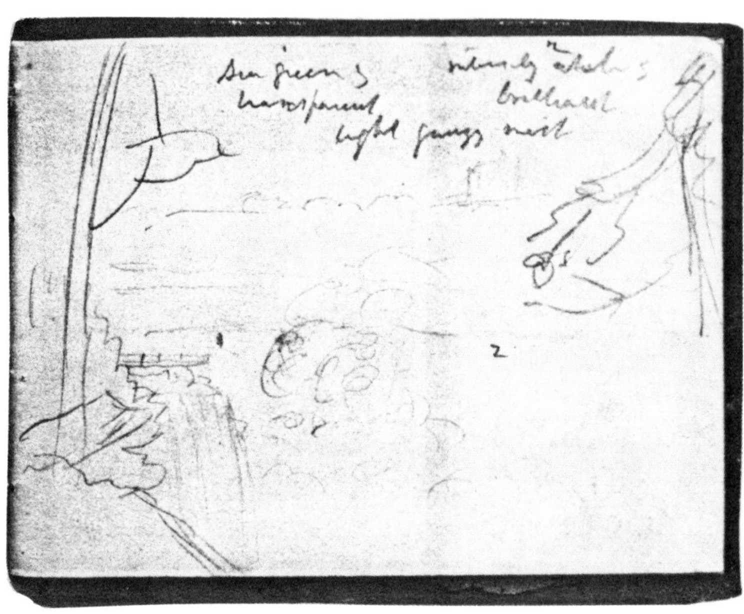

Fig. 3. Sketch on notebook p. [69], perhaps of Niagara Falls with sections numbered "1" and "2" and titles.

bellied fellow. pleasant dark eye. oily[,] good temper[,] talks without nasal accent contrast to Yankees

[*p. [64] blank; pp. [65–66] torn out*]

[*p. [67] is a drawing of fort, perhaps at Newark.*]

[*p. [68] blank*]

[*p. [69] is a sketch, perhaps of Niagara Falls with sections numbered "1" and "2." Above the section numbered "1" are the words, "1 Sea green & transparent"; above the second section are the words, "2 intensely white & brilliant"; in the center of the page are the words, "light gauzy mist." Irving turned the notebook counterclockwise before sketching so that the top of the sketch is along the right edge of the page.*]

ride from [*blank*][208] to Columbus–rugged–corduroy–pass Welshmans cottage with whom I have a parley–

Meet two huntsmen–one old ruddy grey headed–short hunting coat with broad short Skirts–belted

Arrive about 12 at Columbus[209]–neat flourishing tho Small place.

208. The stage road from Newark to Columbus passed through Hebron and Etna, respectively 27 miles and 17 miles east of Columbus, and both in Licking County, Ohio.

209. Columbus, the capital of Ohio and the county seat of Franklin County, was situated in the center of the state and the center of the county, on the east bank of the Scioto River, 90 miles from its mouth, just below the confluence of the Whetstone River with the Scioto; it was 112 miles northeast of Cincinnati. It began with a cabin on the Scioto River in 1797 and was designated as the state's capital when it was laid out in 1812 in the middle of a dense forest. In 1824, the county seat of Franklin County was moved from Franklinton across the Scioto to Columbus. As WI visited it, only twenty years after its being carved out of the wilderness, its population was approximately 3,000; by 1840 it would grow to 6,048. Contemporary writers commented on the beauty of the town. Important factors in the early development of Columbus, in addition to the fact that it was designated the capital of the state, were the building of the National Road, or the Cumberland Road, which was completed to Columbus in 1833, and the construction of state plank-roads and a lateral branch of the Ohio Canal, through which the first water and boat made their way in September, 1831. (See especially Galbreath, *History*, I, 335–46; Henry Howe, *Historical Collections of Ohio* [Norwalk, Ohio: Laning Printing Co., 1896], I, 614–25; hereafter cited as Howe, *Collections*.)

capitol of Ohio. Situated on Scioto[210]—walked out to see the canal[211]— ⟨*illegible*⟩

After[212] dinner ⟨&⟩ introduced to Genl McArthur,[213] Governor of Ohio—to the Secretary of State[,][214] the Auditor[215] &c &c &c

—Hired extra stage 4 places for 12 $. in some places would have been 10 $.

drove through fertile country, to Springfield,[216] ⟨on the Miami⟩[217] arrive there 10 oclock. Sleep there—

210. Flint distinguished this river from the Little Scioto, calling it the Big Scioto, or the Scioto. Rising in Hardin County, its direction was southeasterly until it received its principal branch at Columbus, then it flowed south until entering the Ohio at Portsmouth. It was navigable for 130 of its 200 miles, and on its banks near Columbus was a large quarry of marble (*Mississippi Valley*, I, 401, 404–05).

211. The feeder canal of ten miles from Columbus to the Ohio and Erie Canal at Lockbourne was probably the one to which WI referred.

212. The word "After" is written to the left of the margin. WI also wrote that word over another, perhaps "ate" or "at."

213. Duncan McArthur (1772–1840) was born in New York and as a boy moved with his father to the Pennsylvania frontier. Beginning as a laborer, his rise included time as a soldier, surveyor, spy against the Indians, businessman (real estate), member of the state legislature and Congress, brigadier general, commander of the Northwestern Army, commissioner to the Indians, and speaker of the Legislature. McArthur was governor of Ohio from 1830 until 1832, having defeated Robert Lucas by only 482 votes (of 98,854 cast). Because he had suffered an accident in 1830 which left him maimed physically and, subsequently mentally, the governor decided not to seek a second term. (See Galbreath, *History*, II, 499–503; Howe, *Collections*, II, 505–07.)

214. Moses H. Kirby was secretary of state of Ohio, having in 1830 defeated Jeremiah McLene, who had held that office for 23 years.

215. Ralph Osborn had been state auditor for eighteen years; he was defeated in 1832 by John A. Bryan.

216. Springfield, the county town of Clark County, Ohio, was on the National Road, 43 miles west from Columbus. Incorporated as a town in 1828, it was located at the confluence of Mad River and Lagonda Creek, both of which are capable of providing great water power, and the first grist mill was built in 1804; soon other plants were built, and it came to be known for its manufacture of machinery, especially turbine water-wheels and Champion reaper and mower works. Its population in 1830 was 1,080 and in 1840, 2,094.

217. The Mad River, rising in the west-central part of Ohio, flowed into the Miami River at Dayton and was its largest affluent from the east. The eastern fork of the Mad washed the town of Springfield on the north; Buck Creek, or Lagonda Creek, also rushed through the town; there were more than twenty old mill seats within a few miles of Springfield. Apparently WI realized his mistake.

Saturday, September 1[218]

Leave Springfield at 5 Oclock–drive 8 miles to Yellow Springs[219][–] pretty place–park scenery behind the house–from thence thro pleasant scenery to Xenia[220][,] a neat well built place. 18[221] miles from Spring-/ field–where we arrive at 8.

Hence to Lebanon. Through a beautifully wooded country–some part like park scenery. Open forests Great Cotton woods–

Flight of Turkey Buzzards sailing over the forest–Wide ⟨Scen⟩ prospect of rich cornfields meadows and forest trees with Cloudless sky & golden sunshine–smoke rising from a woody Hill side–

arrive at Lebanon[222] about ¼ before 1.

scene at breakfast at Xenia. little negro girl with big head & white eyes Standing like an automaton brushing away flies with bunch of ragged peacocke feathers[,] dirty boy to aid in attending

218. WI wrote "Sept 1. Saturday–."

219. Yellow Springs, only a post-village at this time, was in Greene County, nine miles south from Springfield, nine miles north from Xenia, and on the Little Miami River. It was settled about 1820 when it became a health spa; the chalybeate spring discharged more than 100 gallons an hour. Flint wrote of Yellow Springs that its "elevated position, the grand and romantic scenery, and the cool and salubrious air probably contribute as much to the restoration of invalids as the waters, which are, however, strongly charged with iron in solution"; he concluded that the resorts of Pennsylvania and Virginia cannot "surpass this place in grandeur, or equal it in amenity of prospect" (*Mississippi Valley*, I, 406–7).

220. Xenia, the county town of Greene County, was 55 miles southwest from Columbus and handsomely situated on Shawnee Creek. In 1832, its population was 919, and its court house was one of the state's finest, by some accounts, the most elegant. At one grist mill on the Little Miami, about three miles from Xenia, lived William Dean Howells, who came to this area with his family when he was fourteen.

221. The second digit of this number resembles neither WI's rather unusual "6" nor his "8." Because Yellow Springs was half way between Xenia and Springfield, and nine miles between Yellow Springs and Xenia was the usual figure mentioned, the logical reading of the distance is "18."

222. Lebanon, located in the beautiful Turtle Creek Valley between its branches, was four miles west of Little Miami River, 80 miles southwest from Columbus, and 30 miles northeast from Cincinnati. It was at this time a post-village of Turtle Creek township, and the county town of Warren County, Ohio. In 1820, Lebanon had a population of 1,079; in 1840 it was 1,327.

Beautiful approach along the bottom road[223] to Cincinnati[224] where we arrive about ½ past 6 & put up at the Cincinnati Hotel[225]

At Cincinnati become acquainted with Mr [*blank*] Mr & Mrs Huntz[?],[226] Genl Harrison[227] who came here as ensign when there was but one Log Hut—40 years Since &c

[*p. [76] is a drawing of a man sitting on tilted chair reading newspaper. The notebook has been reversed.*]

223. WI's description of the approach to the city was well founded; Cincinnati was situated beautifully on the northern shore of the Ohio River opposite the Licking River and surrounded by wooded hills, sometimes 300 feet high. Flint wrote that from "the summit of any of these hills, the town spreads a panoramic map of exquisite painting," and the combination of mansions, smoke, the river, the steamboats and flatboats, the villages opposite the city "taken together, offer such a picture of beauty, wealth, progress and fresh advance, as few landscapes in any country can surpass" (*Mississippi Valley*, I, 412–13).

224. Cincinnati was at this time second only to New Orleans in population and importance in the Western states and often called "The Queen of the West." It was built on the site of ancient works and called Losantiville (L[Licking] + *os*[mouth] + *anti*[opposite] + *ville*[city]), a name it retained until 1790 when Governor St. Clair renamed it in honor of the Revolutionary Army Society of Cincinnatus, of which he was a member. The first houses had been built in 1788 and Fort Washington in 1789; in 1790, Cincinnati was made the capital of Hamilton County, only the second county established in the Northwest Territory. Because of its location between Pittsburg and the mouth of the Ohio, it was fast-growing: incorporated in 1802 as a town and in 1819 as a city, its population grew from 750 in 1800 to 28,014 in 1831. According to Rusk, the leadership of the early West passed from Kentucky to Ohio, and by 1830, Cincinnati "had become the cultural as well as the commercial capital of the frontier" (*Literature of the Middle West*, I, 29). In 1832, among other industries, 130 steamboats were built here, the total value of manufactures exceeded $2,500,000, and exports were estimated at four million dollars. (For helpful accounts of Cincinnati's founding, see Howe, *Collections*, I, 747–51; see also Judge Jacob Burnet's letters written from Cincinnati in 1837–1838 and published as "Burnet's Letters" in *Transactions of the Historical and Philosophical Society of Ohio*, vol. 1, pt. 2, pp. 9–180; for descriptions of the city in 1832, see Baird, *View*, 137–40; Flint, *Mississippi Valley*, I, 412–18, as well as Flint's *Recollections of the Last Ten Years*, ed. C. Hartley Grattan [New York: Alfred A. Knopf, 1932], pp. 38–54; hereafter cited as Flint, *Recollections*.)

225. Latrobe wrote that "such was the crowded state of the only large hotel in the place, two having been burnt in the course of the spring, that we deemed ourselves fortunate to find a speedy opportunity of departure on one of the splendid steam-boats with which the landing place was crowded" (*Rambler*, I, 99).

226. We have been unable to identify Mr. and Mrs. Huntz or Heintz.

227. It appears that Irving began to form the letter *H* and went into the *G* of "Genl." William Henry Harrison (1773–1841) was born in Virginia, educated at home and at Hampden-Sidney College, and studied medicine from 1790 until his father's death in 1791. Through President Washington's influence, young Harrison

Fig. 4. Top, drawing of a man sitting on tilted chair reading newspaper; *bottom*, sketch of same man. Both are upside down. Notebook has been reversed here.

[*p. [77] is a sketch of same man also upside down.*]

[*p. [78] blank*]

[*to p. [79] is attached a printed poem:*

A WOMAN'S LOVE.[228]

A woman's Love is of man's Life
The dearest, brightest part;
It soothes him in the hour of strife,
And cheers his lonely heart;
And blest is he who back repays
Affections smiles and tears—
A woman's Love shall gild his days,
And smooth the lapse of years.

---

was commissioned in 1791 and assigned to Fort Washington, Ohio. The teenaged ensign distinguished himself early by leading a detachment safely through snow and hostile Indians to a distant destination, and he rose quickly in the army. In 1798, Harrison resigned his commission and the command of Fort Washington because he did not approve of the idleness and dissipation of garrison life. Other positions followed—secretary of the Northwest Territory and its delegate to Congress and the first governor of Indiana—but it was his role in the War of 1812, including defeating the Prophet at Tippecanoe as well as a large British force and Tecumseh in Canada, which brought him national recognition. After the war his positions in government included Indian commissioner, member of the Ohio state senate and the U.S. Congress and Senate, and minister to Columbia, a position from which he had been recalled under political fire in the summer of 1829, returning to his farm in Ohio in October of that year. When WI met him, Harrison was in the midst of financial and family misfortunes, but his political star rose again, and in 1840, he was the first half of the "Tippecanoe and Tyler too" Whig ticket; he died of pneumonia exactly one month after his inauguration.

228. This poem was apparently torn from a periodical. In the right margin of the poem, after the page is rotated counterclockwise a quarter turn, written in pencil, are the words "Remember / Mary land." The paper is very thin and measures approximately 2⅝ inches wide and 3¼ inches long. At the bottom of the page, after the poem and also in print is a line 1½ inches long and then the words "We have had [*torn page*]." On the reverse side of the scrap of paper is printed what seems to be a listing of property by date, name, and number of lots; for example,

"1827 to 1829	Ferris Pell	17 lots
1830	Solomon J. Degroff	
1830	A. Alvoid	House and lot"

Other names in the list are David Wagstaff, Francis Price, Patrick Quin, Abraham Stagg, Patrick Monaghen, Asa Holden, Aaron Drake, – Hart, Asa Longworthy, William Tvack, and Thomas Thomas. The earliest date is 1827 and the latest, 1830.

A woman's Love is like the shade
  Upon the snow's white breast;
Each fleecy cloud o'er sunshine laid
  Disturbs its fretful rest,
And blest is he whose anxious care
  Can chase those clouds away;
On him shall beam those graces rare,
  That melt the soul away.

A woman's Love is like a wave,
  By every tempest shaken;
Nourish'd—it blooms unto the grave,
  But withers—if forsaken;
And blest is he by whom 't is nurs'd,
  For him 't was made and given.
Of all perfections, blest and first,
  A woman's Love is Heaven!]

[pp. *[80–81] are blank; p. [82] is a drawing of elaborate building with woman and girl.*]

[*p. [83] is a drawing of boat on river approaching town.*]

[*pp. [84–85] blank. Beginning with p. [86], materials in this notebook are reversed; Irving apparently began writing at the back of the notebook, p. [90], and wrote to p. [86]. This material is given in the order in which Irving seemingly wrote it.*]

You[229] wish to know the cause of the lateness of the mails. It is owing to the time lost ⟨by chattering[?] post a⟩ in exam/ining the mail bags and in changing the horses between New Haven & NY. ⟨I would especially point o⟩ This is expecially the case after the change of carriages which took place ⟨late⟩ after leaving NHaven, where we had a saucy

---

In the margin after the paper is rotated clockwise a quarter turn are the words "for[?] Mr. Irving" written in almost imperceptible pencil; the hand seems to be one which wrote "Remember Maryland" on the other side.

229. This entry on p. [80] may be a first draft of a letter, perhaps to WI's brother Peter, who was then in Paris; it contains the only use of second person in the notebook. In a letter dated July 9, 1832, WI discussed problems regarding the mails (PMI, III, 27); however, it was probably three weeks later that he wrote this entry, after having visited Boston and the White Mountains, a trip which was perhaps described in the missing journal number 1 (see Introduction, pp. xxii–xxiii).

Fig. 5. Left, drawing on p. [83] of boat on river approaching town; *right*, drawing on p. [82] of elaborate building with woman and girl.

chattering coachman impertinent to the passengers [? and to get horses [*illegible*] at the Inn [*illegible*] ?][230]

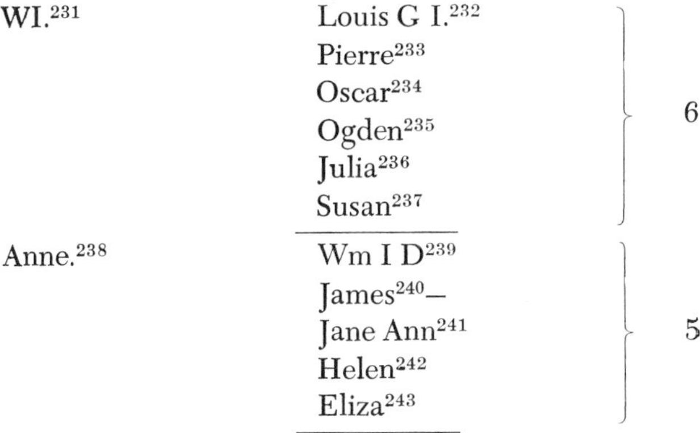

WI.[231] Louis G I.[232]
Pierre[233]
Oscar[234]
Ogden[235]
Julia[236]
Susan[237] } 6

Anne.[238] Wm I D[239]
James[240]—
Jane Ann[241]
Helen[242]
Eliza[243] } 5

230. The last three lines of p. [80] are difficult to decipher because of the smudged writing and the frayed bottom edge.

231. On August 3, 1832, WI wrote to Peter that he was now "in a little cottage, in which is Mr. Paris's family, and a number of the Bramin's [Ebenezer's] young fry, among which are his two oldest daughters, whom I have now seen for the first time" (PMI, III, 29). The realization that his sixteen- and fifteen-year-old nieces, Catharine Ann and Sarah, were strangers to him might have prompted WI to make a list of names and numbers by families; he also had available for assistance his sister Catharine Paris, his brother Ebenezer, and his nephew Oscar. For information regarding the dates and full names of these members of WI's family, see the genealogies in STW, II, opposite p. 225, and in *Letters*, IV, Appendix VI, pp. 879–95.

"WI" was William Irving (1766–1821), WI's oldest brother. He married Julia Paulding in 1793, and they had nine children, six of whom lived and WI listed here, not in chronological order.

232. Lewis Graham Irving (1795–1879) married Maria Carleton Hale.

233. Pierre Munro Irving (1802–1876) married in 1829 Margaret Ann Berdan (1808–1832), who died in October; he married Helen Dodge, his first cousin, in 1836.

234. Oscar Irving (1800–1865) married first Catherine E. C. Dayton (1800–1842) and later Eliza Dodge, his first cousin, in 1845.

235. Henry Ogden Irving (1807–1869).

236. Julia Irving (1803–1872) married Moses Hicks Grinnell in 1836.

237. Susan Anne Irving (1811–1836) married Irving Van Wart, her first cousin, in July. After Susan's name there is a line approximately 1¼ inches long, separating William's family from Anne's.

238. WI's sister, Ann Sarah Irving (1770–1808), married Richard Dodge in 1788; they had six children, one of whom, Samuel, died in infancy (1798).

239. William Irving Dodge (1790–1873).

240. James Richard Dodge (1795–1880).

241. Jane Ann Dodge (1799–1875). Written together as "JaneAnn."

242. Helen Dodge (1802–1885) married Pierre Munro Irving, her first cousin (see n. 233 above).

243. Eliza Dodge (1801–1887) married Oscar Irving, her first cousin (see n. 234 above). After Eliza's name is a short line (¼ inch) separating families.

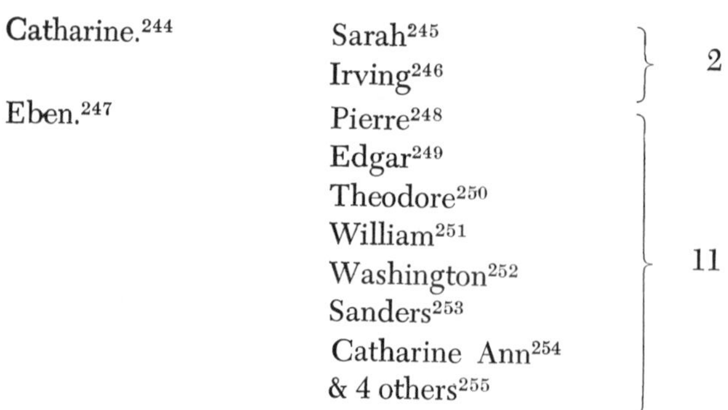

Catharine.[244]	Sarah[245] Irving[246]	2
Eben.[247]	Pierre[248] Edgar[249] Theodore[250] William[251] Washington[252] Sanders[253] Catharine Ann[254] & 4 others[255]	11

244. Washington Irving's sister, Catharine Rodgers Irving (1774–1849) married Daniel Paris; according to Alice R. Aderman, they had nine children, seven who had died by this time, the most recent one Catharine (1807–1828); there were two remaining Paris children (nn. 245–46) (*Letters*, IV, 881).

245. Sarah Sanders Paris (1813–1885) married Thomas Wentworth Storrow in 1841.

246. Irving Paris (1816–1879), WI's nephew whom Williams neither named nor identified. WI had visited the Paris household on August 3, 1832 (PMI, III, 29), not long before this list was compiled; the fact that five of the Paris children had died while WI was in Europe adds poignancy to WI's list.

247. WI's brother, Ebenezer Irving (1776–1868) married Elizabeth Kip in 1805; they had thirteen children, two of whom had died when WI completed this list: Eliza Irving (1814–1819) and Jane Irving (1818–1827). See Table IV, "The Children of Ebenezer Irving and Elizabeth Kip," in STW, II, opposite p. 255.

248. Pierre Paris Irving (1806–1878) married Anna Henrietta Duer in 1826.

249. Edgar Irving (1808–1873) married Amanda Tenant in 1834.

250. Theodore Irving (1809–1880) married first Jane W. Sutherland in 1838 and second, Louisa Ketching in 1857; a third wife was Maria.

251. William Irving (1811–1854) married Sarah Mann in 1844.

252. Washington Ebenezer Irving (1822–1894) married Guadaloupe Gomez in 1866.

253. Sanders Irving (1813–1884) married Julia A. Granger in 1840.

254. Catharine Ann Irving (1816–1911).

255. The "4" are all girls: Sarah Irving (1817–1900); Julia Irving (1818–1861), whose twin sister Jane died in 1827; Mary Elizabeth Irving (1820–1868); and Charlotte Van Wart Irving (1824–1911), who married William R. Grinnell in 1847.

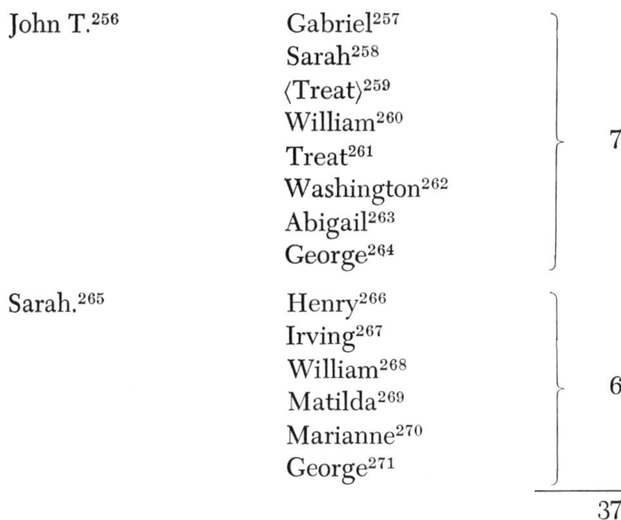

John T.[256]
Gabriel[257]
Sarah[258]
⟨Treat⟩[259]
William[260]
Treat[261]
Washington[262]
Abigail[263]
George[264]
7
Sarah.[265]
Henry[266]
Irving[267]
William[268]
Matilda[269]
Marianne[270]
George[271]
6
37

256. WI's brother, John Treat Irving (1778–1838) married Abigail Spicer Furman in 1806 and they had seven children, as two had died by this time.

257. Gabriel F. Irving (1807–1845).

258. Sarah Irving (1811–1836).

259. WI seems to be making an attempt to name the children in this family in chronological order, striking Treat's name here and adding it after William's name; however, according to Alice Aderman's genealogy, the order is as follows: Gabriel, William, Sarah, John Treat, Washington, Abbey, and George.

260. William Irving (1809–1832).

261. John Treat Irving, Jr. (1812–1906) married Helen Schermerhorn in 1838. This nephew of WI shared his interest in the West; the year following WI's journey, Treat went with Ellsworth to the same region, and he wrote an account of that trip, *Indian Sketches. Taken During an Expedition to the Pawnee Tribes* (Philadelphia: Carey, Lea, & Blanchard, 1835); this first American edition followed WI's *Tour* by two months. Two years later Treat Irving wrote *The Hawk Chief: a Tale of the Indian Country* (English edition entitled *The Hunters of the Prairie: or, The Hawk Chief*); other works include *A Chronicle of Nieuu Amsterdam* (1840); *The Attorney: or, the Correspondence of John Quod* [1842]; and *Harry Harson: or, The Benevolent Bachelor* [1844].

262. Washington Irving (1814–1894), apparently named for his uncle.

263. Abigail Irving, or Abbey (1822–1906).

264. George Irving (1824–1908).

265. Sarah Irving (1780–1848) married Henry Van Wart in 1806, and they had seven children whom WI names in order; Washington Irving Van Wart died in 1823.

266. Henry Van Wart (1806–1878).

267. Irving Van Wart (1808–1896) married his cousin Susan Anne Irving in 1832 and Sarah Craig Ames in 1839.

268. William Van Wart (1814–1868).

269. Matilda Van Wart.

270. Marianne Van Wart (d. 1887).

271. George Van Wart (1818–1903).

⟨Louis G. I.⟩[272]	37
⟨M⟩ Louis G I's wife[273]	1
Oscar– ”[274]	1
Pierre ”[275]	1
Wm I Dodges wife–[276]	1
James D– ”–[277]	1
Jane anns Husbd–[278]	1
Eliza– ”[279]	1
Pierre P. wife[280]	1
Gabriels– ”–[281]	1
Sarah: Husb–[282]	1
Henry V W. wife[283]	1
nephews & nieces[284]	48

272. WI began a new page at this point, and, after striking through the name of the oldest child of his oldest brother, he carried over from the previous page the total number of his list of nieces and nephews. WI wrote together as “LouisG.”

273. Maria Carleton Hale (1797–1869).

274. Oscar's first wife was Catherine E. C. Dayton (1800–1842); his second wife, whom he married in 1845 after this list was compiled, was Eliza Dodge (1801–1887).

275. Pierre Munro Irving's first wife, Margaret Ann Berdan (see n. 233 above).

276. William Irving Dodge's wife, Patience Akin (1793–1879).

277. James Richard Dodge's first wife, whom he married in 1826, is unidentified.

278. Jane Ann Dodge's husband, John Frost Frothingham (1789–1868).

279. Eliza Dodge first married in 1828 Theodore F. H. Romeyn, who died in 1833, and then she married her first cousin, Oscar Irving, in 1845. Interestingly, when compiling this list, WI did not indicate in any way that Susan Anne Irving had married Irving Van Wart (July, 1832) because both were included in the list of 37 nieces and nephews.

280. Pierre Paris Irving's wife was Anna Henrietta Duer (1807–1874), whom he married in 1826.

281. Gabriel F. Irving's wife, Eliza Eckford (1813–1866).

282. Sarah Irving's husband, Edwin Clark (1802–1878).

283. Henry Van Wart's first wife, Susan Clark Storrow (1807–1843); he married Abbey Irving in 1845.

284. Before writing the total number of his nephews and nieces, WI drew a line 1¼ inches flush right.

Gt. Nephews & nieces ———

Wm I Dodge[285]—Sarah Ann Julia I. ⟨Richd.⟩ James Richard Elizabeth W Irving[286]	}	6
James D—[287]		3
Jane Ann[288]		7
Louis G. I.[289]		3
Oscar[290]		2
Pierre P.[291]		3
Gabriel[292]		1
		25

48
25
73[293]

[*inside back cover blank*]

[*back cover blank*]

285. William Irving Dodge's children were Ann Sarah, Julia Irving, William James, Richard, Elizabeth Russell, and Washington Irving (see n. 71 above).

286. Written together as "WIrving."

287. James Richard Dodge's children were Richard Irving (1827–1895), Susan Taylor (b. 1829), and Ann Sarah (b. 1831); Mary Helen was born in 1835.

288. Jane Ann Dodge Frothingham's children were Thomas (1789–1868), Richard Dodge (1820–1880), Washington (1822–1914), Augustus (1825–1874), John (1827–1869), William (1830–1885), and Catharine Paris (1832–1914); there would be three more children.

289. Lewis Graham Irving's three children were Lewis (1825–1861), Charles (1826–1895), and Paulding (1832–1851); one had died and four were to be born.

290. Oscar Irving's sons by his first wife were Nathaniel Paulding (1826–1869) and William (1827–1859).

291. Pierre Paris Irving had at this time three children: Pierre Leslie (1828–1891), Ann Duer (1830–1884), and John Duer (1832–1836); he and his wife would have seven more children.

292. Gabriel F. Irving (1807–1845) had a daughter, Henrietta Eckford (1832–1921); he would have another.

293. After listing in the right margin the number of great-nieces and great-nephews in each family, WI drew a line 1¼ inches flush right and totaled the figures. Then after writing the two subtotals—48 and 25—he drew a ¾-inch line and added the numbers. He counted 73 relatives in the greater Irving family.

AMERICAN JOURNALS, 1832

Number 3
Cincinnati to St. Louis

The manuscript journal is in the Seligman Collection of Irvingiana in the Manuscript Division of the New York Public Library, where it is cataloged as #22–3300, Journal 25. It consists of 38 leaves of unlined paper whose edges have faded red and green designs; its 76 pages measure 2 13/16 x 3 13/16 inches. It is bound in soft reddish-brown or rust leather and held together at its top with a string tied between pages [38] and [39][1] and a brass latch at its bottom. The writing is in pencil except for the black ink on one-half of page [75], three-fourths of page [76], and the front cover. Blank are pages [2], [54–64], and the back cover. On page [1] is a drawing in pencil of a street scene in Cincinnati dated "Sept 3rd." Pages [1–30] and [47–76] are loose; pages [31–32], [45–46] are partially loose. After page [53], Irving reversed the journal and wrote backward from the inside back cover to page [65].

[*front cover*]

No 3.

1832
Sept 3d.

[*inside front cover*]

18[2]

1. Between 1973 and 1975, there were some changes in the condition of this journal: all of the pages have come loose from the binding, and there is no string between pp. [38] and [39], although there is a faded spot where the string once was tied. Whereas conjugate leaves 19 and 20 are almost wholly connected, leaves 18 and 21 are connected only at the edges, and leaves 17 and 22 are not connected at all. In addition, someone has added in pencil "Journal 25" at the top left of the inside front cover.

2. The number "18" does not seem to be in WI's handwriting; it has been added in pencil in the upper right corner (notebook has been rotated counterclockwise a quarter turn).

[*p. [1] consists of a page-size drawing of a street scene of Cincinnati, with a girl in the lower left corner. In the lower right corner Irving has labeled the drawing as follows:*]

Sept 3rd.
Cincinnati

[*p. [2] blank*]

Monday, September 3[3]

Le⟨ave⟩ft Cincinnati at 5 oclock on the Steam boat Messenger,[4] for Louisville. Thunder Showers—After which a remarkably clear tract in the west—Moonlight night—mist on river—passenger on board ⟨wound⟩ with slash on the face—

At Cincinnati saw Mr Wood[5] with whom I once travelled in Rhode Isld [*three words illegible*]

3. WI wrote "↑*Monday*↓ Sept ⟨4⟩3, 1832."

4. Latrobe reported that they felt "fortunate to find a speedy opportunity of departure on one of the splendid steam-boats with which the landing place was crowded" (*Rambler*, I, 99). In 1842 Charles Dickens traveled from Pittsburgh to Cincinnati on the 130-ton *Messenger* built in 1825: "The *Messenger* is a high-pressure boat, carrying forty passengers, exclusive of poorer persons on the lower deck. There was no mast, cordage, tackle, or rigging, only a long, ugly roof, two towering iron chimneys, and below on the sides, the doors and windows of the staterooms; the whole supported on beams and pillars, resting on a dirty barge, but a few inches above the water's edge, and in this narrow space between the upper structure and this barge's deck are the furnace fires and machinery, open at the sides" (Ralph K. Andrist and C. Bradford Mitchell, eds., *Steamboats on the Mississippi* [New York: American Heritage, 1962], p. 82). The steamboat trip from Cincinnati to Louisville was 132 miles on the Ohio River and cost $3.00, a trip by stage of 95 miles.

5. Although it has been impossible to make a certain identification of the "Mr Wood" with whom WI once traveled, there are two attractive possibilities. George Wood (1799–1870), the author who would later contribute to the *Knickerbocker Magazine* (1846–1847), was born in Newburyport, Massachusetts, was clerk in the War Department and in the Treasury Department, and was eventually the chief of its navigation division. Another possibility is Reuben Wood (1792–1864), born in Middletown, Vermont, and educated in Canada; in 1812, when he was drafted to fight against his country, he escaped and enlisted in the American army. In 1818, he went west to Cleveland, Ohio, practiced law, was elected to the state senate, appointed presiding judge of the court of common pleas of the district, promoted to the supreme court bench (in December, 1832), and made chief justice of the supreme court during the latter part of his term. Later he was the first governor of Ohio and the U.S. consul to Valparaiso.

Fig. 6. Drawing, on p. [1], of street scene of Cincinnati, with girl in lower left corner.

Tuesday, September 4[6]

Grey morning—In the night steam boat stops here & there when lights gleam on the wooded shore[7]—

Stop at Madison[8] in Indiana. Neat little place built of brick—

Old negro Stewart very black with bright madrass handkerchef on head—large feet[,] gold ear rings—Shirt collar up to his ears—white jacket & trousers ↑checquered↓ apron to his armpits

Clearings on the banks of river Solitary log hut with corn field among the forests—canoe by the shore

arrive at Louisville[9] ½ past 12. dine at Throgmorton[10] (Take pass [?]⟩ Quay of city presents a motley scene—fleets—steam/boats—carriages—

6. WI wrote "↑*Tuesday*↓ Sept 4."

7. Between Cincinnati and Madison, there were several small villages on the Ohio River: Lawrenceburg, Aurora, Rising Sun, Fredericksburg, Vevay, and Port William.

8. Madison, the county town of Jefferson County, Indiana, beautifully situated on the Ohio River, approximately 90 miles below Cincinnati and 44 miles above Louisville. The first settlers came in 1808; in 1829, between forty and fifty brick buildings, some three stories high, were added, so that when WI saw it, it contained more brick buildings than were usually found in Indiana. Its population in 1832 was between 2,000 and 2,500, making it the most populous in the state, and it was the landing place for imports from the Ohio to the fast growing Indiana towns and counties.

9. Louisville, the county town of Jefferson County, was approximately 132 miles by steamboat from Cincinnati and was for the Irving party the "next halting-place . . . another large and thriving city, situated on the Kentucky shore, just above the Falls of the Ohio. Its position on one of the great bends of the river, with the islands and rapids below, forms one of the most striking among all the beautiful scenes with which the Ohio bounds" (Latrobe, *Rambler*, I, 99–100). Contemporaries also commented on its "bustle" and rate of growth: calling it "a great thoroughfare for the Valley of the Ohio," Baird wrote of the flat boats by the thousands and steamboats by the hundreds which arrived yearly in Louisville (*View*, p. 182). It grew from 600 residents in 1800 to 10,336 in 1830, and by 1832 its population was more than 13,000. Louisville stood on a "vast alluvial bottom," and its rich sloping plain was very fertile. The main street, which was a mile long, was "as noble, as compact and has as much the air of a maritime town, as any street in the western country" (Flint, *Mississippi Valley*, I, 359). To answer the only printed criticism in the guides that during August and September "bilious fevers prevail to a considerable degree" (Baird, *View*, p. 182), Flint said that most of the ponds and marshes had been drained and now it was "nearly as healthy as any other town in the same latitude on the Ohio" (*Mississippi Valley*, I, 359).

10. According to McDermott, WI was probably referring to Aris Throckmorton, who was the landlord of the Lower Blue Lick Springs Hotel and, by the time Dickens made his stop there, was the landlord (from 1835–1865) of the Galt House in Louisville (*Western Journals*, p. 70, n. 5).

heaps[11] of Iron[,] of Lead–Leather &c take places on board the steamer Illinois[12] from Louisville[–]after going on board ⟨*illegible*⟩ run agst post–break some of the machinery & have to remain all night[13]

called in Evg on the mayor Mr. Burkland[14] who once boarded with me at Mrs Ryckmans[15]–Mr smith[16] &c. &c. &c.–

Took warm bath

Wednesday, September 5[17]

all day detained by arrangt of machinery–after dinner drove out in compy with fellow travellers & Capt Chambers[18] to Judge Ormsby.[19]

11. This word could be "barges."

12. The steamboat *Illinois* later was called by Latrobe "only third-rate" (*Rambler*, I, 111); he said also that it "was certainly not a fortunate boat, in spite of the horse-shoe nailed to the capstan" (I, 113–14).

13. The greatest fall on the Ohio River is this one just below Louisville; except for two months of the year when the rocks and shallows were covered by water, passage was a problem solved by the boats' lying by and the goods' being unloaded, transported by land, and reloaded. Latrobe reported that the shallowness of the water prohibited even the smallest steamboats from crossing over the falls, and they had to use the "newly-constructed canal, which, by the aid of three noble locks at the lower end," opened the Ohio River for navigation (*Rambler*, I, 101). On December 21, 1829, the first steamboat, *Uncas*, had passed through the Louisville and Portland Canal. Cut through solid limestone, it was 2½ miles long, 40 feet deep, and had 22 feet of lockage (five locks); its cost was $750,000. The canal only partially solved the problem: the toll charges were prohibitive (steamboats were charged sixty cents a ton until the early 1840's when the charge was fifty cents a ton), and the lock chambers were too small to allow the most efficient steamboats to pass. In addition, the direction and strength of the current at the locks often caused navigational problems and accidents, as WI and his party learned. (See for additional information, Louis C. Hunter, *Steamboats on the Western Rivers: An Economic and Technological History* [Cambridge, Mass.: Harvard University Press, 1949], pp. 233–34, 371.)

14. According to J. Stoddard Johnston's *Memorial History of Louisville* (I, 645, 86), John C. Bucklin was Louisville's mayor from 1828 until 1833 (McDermott, *Western Journals*, p. 70, n. 6).

15. WI left Washington in May, 1811, and took temporary lodgings with Henry Brevoort at Mrs. Ryckman's at 16 Broadway, New York, near Bowling Green; he lived there until they moved to the boarding house of Mrs. Bradish (at the corner of Greenwich and Rector Streets) soon after Brevoort's return from Europe, probably late 1813 (STW, I, 128, 143, 413, n. 125, 417, n. 87).

16. Could be "Dr smith."

17. WI wrote "Sept 5."

18. Captain Chambers, perhaps the captain of the *Illinois*.

19. Stephen Ormsby, who was admitted to the Louisville bar in 1786 after having come from Ireland, was elected to Congress (1810–1817), served in the judiciary, and died in 1846 in Louisville (McDermott, *Western Journals*, p. 70, n. 7).

20. The words might be "Chairs opp."

Popler 13 feet diameter ruin[?] of tree 45 feet round roots Entrance straggling road thro butternuts—grape vines—a wild stream running across the land—⟨Neg⟩ old negro & dogs[—]gate way built in stone—Swiss barn.

↑wooden↓ House among [*blank*] trees flanked by negro homes[.] negros of all ages—lighter[?] barefoot negro—On our approach a little negro head seen at [*illegible*] windows of hut opposite [*two words illegible*][20] few chairs—brass andirons broken hole in ceiling over fire place—old tables[?] of all kinds

bugle sounds to call Mr Ormsby. shy figure of negros & white children stealing about house

little‸ ↑well dressed↓ negro girl brings in Salver of peaches

↑fat↓ Negro wenches drying apples & peaches on board under trees[?]

wild goose, fowls &c &c about lawn[21]

In neighboring field negro boys exercising race horses—⟨Mr Orms⟩ flower garden—Iron gate on [?cotton wooden?] stanchions—flowers & fruits of various kinds—

Mr. Ormsby the younger comes home. Son of Judge by an Irish servant woman. The latter is crazy & lives in a log hut on the farm—young Ormsby married[22]—pretty wif⟨n⟩e—walk with him to see Elks[,] pack of tame[?] wild geese[23]

Thursday, September 6[24]

Start at 9 oclock Get to canal[25]—machinery damaged[?][26]—Get thro about 3

Evg Scene on Ohio—Steam/ boat aground with 2 flats each side of her[.] we take part of cargo on board—

—Moonlight—light of fires[—]chaunt[?][27] & chorus of Negro boat man—Men Strolling about docks with cigars Negros dancing before furnaces Glassy Surface of River. ⟨wide[?]⟩ undulations made by boat—wavering[?] light of moon & stars Silent, primeval forest sleep-

21. Trent and Hellman transcribed as "wild gorse, flowers, etc., about house" (*Journals of WI*, III, 102); McDermott interpreted as "wild gorse, flowers, &c, about house" (*Western Journals*, p. 71).

22. McDermott interpreted as "normal" (*Western Journals*, p. 71); Trent and Hellman omitted this paragraph (*Journals of WI*, III, 102).

23. WI separated paragraphs with a line one-sixteenth inch long.

24. WI wrote "Sept 6."

25. Louisville and Portland Canal (see above n. 13).

26. This word could be "deranged." Latrobe wrote of this incident that they were detained "by some disarrangement in the machinery" (*Rambler*, I, 100).

27. The initial letter was written "⟨n⟩c."

ing in sunshine on each side ⟨*illegible*⟩[28] Still forest–forest–forest–

Old negro steward scolding young negros for lying–He aimes at a monopoly.

Friday, September 7[29]

At 5 oclock Morng Stop to take on wood & wait till fog rises–neat log hut[,] woman & 6 children–the latter half civilized & ignorant–abundance round the house[–]cattle, hogs, poultry, corn forest &c. See patch of cotton plant in blossom

9 oclock–river glassy–Golden Sunshine on forests–rude ark rowed by one man. Roofed with chimney &c.[30]

ducks in couples in the river[–]cloudless Sky. Mellow weather[–] passengers on board–Black Hawk[31]–a young, ⟨Ke[?]⟩ river dandy. green marines[32] short coat. ⟨linsey corduroy⟩ ↑domestic cloth↓ trou/ -sers –low crowned broad brimmed white hat–plays cards with a kindred genius. ⟨*illegible*⟩

All[?] Serenity–a quakeress[–] The princess Hullabulloo

Saturday, September 8[33]

detained from 10[?] last night until ½[?] past 7[34] this morng by fog–an Intelligent man having [*illegible*][35] comes on board–gives us a/c of his farming &c.

9 Oclock. Serene sunny morng–Clear reflection of objects–small flock of wild ducks doubled in the Stream[–]bland atmosphere

28. This word could be "Ohio" or "Old."

29. WI wrote "Friday Sept 7."

30. Latrobe's was a more detailed description of "a broad flat boat with a deck of two or three feet elevation above the water. They have generally a small window fore and aft, and a door in the middle, a peep into which will show you a goodly store of pots, pans, or flour-barrels. A narrow ledge runs around them for the convenience of polling. A small chimney rises above; racoon and deer-skins, the produce of the hours spent ashore, are nailed on the sides to dry. The larger are generally propelled by four oars, and I have occasionally seen them surmounted by a crooked mast and top-mast" (*Rambler*, I, 112).

31. This Indian is not the famous Black Hawk whom WI would see several days later (see September 14, 1832, entry).

32. Trent and Hellman and McDermott deciphered the word "merino" (*Journals of WI*, III, 103; *Western Journals*, p. 72).

33. WI wrote "Saturday Sept 8."

34. Trent and Hellman rendered as "from ten last night till seven" and McDermott changed only the last word to "7" (*Journals of WI*, III, 103; *Western Journals*, p. 72).

35. There may be nothing written in this space; the first half of the page is badly smudged.

Pass Diamond Island[36]—well wooded.

Near Wabash[37] Horses ranging along sandy shore—long glassy reach of river smoke rising on sunny shore Stop for wood near Wabash on Virginia side[38]—negro woman in Log hut—who cooks for the men who cut[?] wood—a cheerful contented being—plenty to eat & drink—⟨fi[?]⟩ good clothing[?]—no one to [*illegible*] or trouble her—[*three lines illegible*][39] Since—does not think shell marry again. Mr Ellsworth[40] asked about her children As the tears started into her eyes she got up crossed the hut—I am not allowed to live with them—they are up at the plantation—

Pourtales[41] killed a raccoon in the woods adjacent—

½ past 1 pass mouth of the Wabash—farm on left bank opposite the mouth on[42] wooded island Wabash island

Wabash enters peacefully into the peaceful River[43]—water clear. ⟨green⟩ ↑greenish↓ blue[—] Ohio yellow

36. Diamond Island was in Henderson County, in northwest Kentucky, in the Ohio River approximately 30 miles above the mouth of the Wabash and ten miles west of Henderson. In WI's day it was known as a refuge for bandits. Diamond Island was the only place-name which WI cited between Louisville and the mouth of the Wabash River; the towns he passed were Philadelphia, Fredonia, Rome, Troy, Rockport, Owenboro, Evansville, and Henderson.

37. The "noble" Wabash, "great river," was one of the most important tributaries of the Ohio River; it rose in western Ohio in Mercer County, changed directions several times, and entered the Ohio approximately 140 miles above the mouth of that river and thirty miles above the Cumberland River. Approximately 550 miles long, the Wabash was navigable in 1832 for keelboats for 400 miles and steamboats for 370 miles above the Ohio to Lafayette; in February–April of 1832, 60 steamboats arrived in Lafayette, and some steamboats had ascended 25 additional miles. One estimate during this period was that 1,000 flatboats entered the Ohio from the Wabash.

38. Even though "the country now called Kentucky, once belonged by charter to Virginia" (Baird, *View*, p. 184) and was set apart from Virginia in 1790 and admitted as a state to the union in 1792, WI called the Kentucky side of the river the "Virginia side" twice in this journal. Perhaps WI's cultural lag was a result of his long absence from his native land.

39. Trent and Hellman read the difficult passage, "good whistling—no one to worry or trouble her—does not think she'll marry again"; McDermott used their reading (*Journals of WI*, III, 104; *Western Journals*, p. 72). In the three illegible lines at the bottom of p. [15], some words to the left of the page could be "buys plants & . . . broken arm left . . . but her husband. . . ."

40. See Introduction, pp. xxxi–xxxii.

41. See Introduction, pp. xxxii-xxxiv.

42. This word could be "is."

43. The Ohio River was in WI's day one of the most important in the country. On the boundary of Ohio alone, it flowed nearly 500 miles of its 950 miles; the contemporary estimates of the navigable waters of the Ohio and its tributaries reached

Men on sand bar with a seine sack[44]

Aground near natives House.[45] Show boat on the ⟨Indiana⟩ ↑Illinois↓[46] shore with flag. Groups assembled there–rifle shooting–Horse race–along shore–negro laugh– –Sunset–party breaks up–some in boat across glassy river singing ballad–others on horseback through the wood–some on foot–Some loiter on the shore–beautiful clear evg sky–moon nearly full rising over the Virginia shore above tufted forests–night hawks[47]

———

Gross plenty that prevails throughout the country–in Hotels[,] steam-bots &c–Meats, poultry[,] vegetables, excellent bread, pies[,] puddings–Food seems to be wasted–as if of no value.

———

Passengers in steam boat from every part of Union–mercht from N York, smug, dapper a[?] calculating Yankee. Reckless boastful Virginian. Black Hawk [48] from Kentucky–Swiss Count

---

5,000 miles. The French called it "La Belle Rivière," and the Indian "translation" of that name suggested the word "Ohio." Formed by the confluence of the Alleghany and Monongahela Rivers at Pittsburg, the Ohio entered the Mississippi 1,216 miles from its mouth. The river's mean width was 600 yards, varying from 400 to 1,400 yards, but below the Cumberland River, it averaged 1,000 yards in width. It contained more than 100 significant islands; its fertile valley varied two to ten miles in width; and the guides used adjectives such as "sublime," "picturesque," "romantic," and "beautiful" in their descriptions of river, bluffs, valleys, forests, islands, etc. Timothy Flint wrote enthusiastically about the Ohio in comparison with the Mississippi, the more often romanticized in early Western literature: "If the Mississippi has more grandeur, the Ohio has clearly more beauty. If the Mississippi rolls along its angry and sweeping waters with more majesty, the Ohio far exceeds it in its calm unbroken course, which seldom endangers the boats on its bosom, except there be mismanagement or storms. No river in the world rolls for the same distance such an uniform, smooth, and peaceful current. Its bluffs and bottoms have a singular configuration of amenity or grandeur. Sometimes lofty bluffs, three hundred feet in height, impend the river and cast their grand shadows into the transparent waters" (*Mississippi Valley*, I, 398).

44. Apparently the men were fishing, using a net with weights and floats on opposite edges.

45. Latrobe complained that "when we descended below the Wabash, our opportunities of going on shore became a little too frequent" (*Rambler*, I, 113).

46. Below Terre Haute, the Wabash River, flowing southward, formed the boundary between Indiana and Illinois; WI was on the Ohio River, looking north toward the mouth of the Wabash; in the right quadrant was Indiana, and to the left was Illinois.

47. WI drew a line approximately one-eighth inch long to separate thoughts.

48. See n. 31 above.

Sunday, September 9[49]

Still ashore[–]go to shore—log house with cornfield in wood—man & his wife from Philadelphia County[50][–]good looking man & woman, children decently clad—been here 15 years[.] If it were to be done over would not come here—No means of educating his children.[51] Wants neighbors—people in neighborhood rough & rude—some live by hunting[,] poaching &c—Says he finds a great difference in himself since he has been here—His[?] sons prefer hunting to learning—pays 1½ dolls an acre for land—Indian corn 15 feet high

Stop at log house on ↑the↓ shore pretty delicate woman from near Nashville Tennessee wishes herself back—no church in neighborhood—people rude— —If there comes a preacher the rude fellows pelt him & cut his horse loose & play[?] all kinds of tricks[.] Her husband a good looking young man. Has lease for 4 years after which will return to Tennessee—

The fete yesterday was shooting[?][52] for merchandize &c[?] pedlars bout— —a quarrel occurred & fighting

Enormous sycamores—cotton wood trees &c—vines—

white cranes

Get off at 3 oclock. ⟨?river to pa?⟩[53] Land at Rock cave [54]—a ⟨Cavern⟩ limestone cavern—

49. WI wrote "Sunday 9th. Sept."

50. Philadelphia County is in the extreme southeast part of Pennsylvania, containing from 120 to 150 square miles, depending on the account. In 1830, its population excluding the city of Philadelphia was 108,509; its primary products were Indian corn, wheat, oats and potatoes, as well as manufactured goods.

51. This mark could be a period or an accidental mark.

52. This word could be "looking."

53. The crossed-out words are very difficult to decipher; alternate readings could be "limesto pa," "cavern to pa," "limesto La," "arrive to La," and several combinations of these words and syllables. Line 5 begins with the last syllable. Trent and Hellman read as "o'clock—see land at Rock Cave" (*Journals of WI*, III, 105); McDermott read as "oclock—to see land at Rock Cave" (*Western Journals*, p. 74).

54. It seems strange that WI did not use the more common name, "Cave-in-Rock," as did Latrobe (see below, n. 56). This limestone cave on the bank of the Ohio approximately 25 miles below Shawneetown had long been "pointed out to passengers on the Ohio, as a great curiosity"; Flint went on, "The entrance to the cave is just above high water mark. It has an arched roof of 25 or 30 feet high, and extends back 120 feet" (*Mississippi Valley*, I, 335). Among the early dangers of river travel in the West were pirates, and the most notorious gang used "Cave-in-Rock" as the chief gathering place, "long a spot approached with apprehension and passed with relief," according to Seymour Dunbar. The river pirates' typical pattern was to attack a richly laden boat, attach its own crew, and take the boat to New Orleans or some other place, sell the goods, and return with the spoils. Early in the century, Kentucky organized militia which fought and defeated the largest band quartered here (*A History of*

9 oclock Evg. arrive at mouth of Cumberland river[55]—land passen/ -gers[—]get aground & remain aground all night[56]

Monday, September 10[57]

8 oclock Still aground—Shower of rain—procure Keel boat from Smithland[58] ⟨and⟩ to take part of cargo and at ½ past 12 get off—

fat old fellow in flat rowed by negros, with cargo of flour to sell[.] after dinner Stop at Paduca[59] a small village or town & quite new. Court holding in Piazza of post office. Judge in linsey corduroy coat & trousers. & deer skin sandals with hat on—⟨se⟩[60] Seated on chair ⟨&c[?]⟩ lolling back. farmers discussing their cause with hats on[.]

meet[?] with an Irishman who has been out 6 years—56 years of

---

Travel in America, 2d ed. [New York: Tudor Publishing Company, 1937], 298–300, 649–50; hereafter cited as Dunbar, *Travel*). "Cave-in-Rock was also the subject of writers of fact and fancy: one of Thomas Ashe's 1806 tales of adventure described "his thrilling experiences while exploring Cave-in-Rock, the headquarters of a notorious outlaw band . . . ," and three years after WI's trip, Charles A. Jones published a volume of poems, the title poem of which, "The Outlaw," was set in the "notorious Cave-in-Rock, on the lower Ohio" (Rusk, *Literature of the Middle West*, I, 102–3, 347).

55. Rising in southeastern Kentucky in the Cumberland Mountains, the Cumberland River ran westward and southwestward until its circuitous route took it in and out of Tennessee and Kentucky and finally into the Ohio River at Smithland, eleven miles above the mouth of the Tennessee River, and approximately 60 miles above the Ohio's junction with the Mississippi. At the Cumberland's entrance its mouth was 300 yards wide, and it was navigable for 400 or 500 miles of its total 600 miles, with steamboats traveling to Nashville during several months and keelboats able to travel 300 miles farther during normal times.

56. Latrobe described this 48-hour period in more detail: "it was our lot, somewhere above the remarkable cavern called the 'Cave in Rock,' to share the fortune of two other steamers, and get so irreparably shoaled about sunset, that, after many hours spent in attempting to extricate ourselves, by carrying out anchor after anchor, the use of the lever, and furious press of steam, it was decided, that whether the prospect were agreeable or not, the vessel must be partially unloaded, and for this purpose lighters were procured from the nearest settlement." He concluded his account with the welcomed fact that "on the night between the 10th and 11th of September, [we] entered the 'Father of Waters' " (*Rambler*, I, 113–14).

57. WI wrote "Monday, Sept 10th."

58. Smithland, a village on the left or eastern bank of the Ohio three miles below the entrance of the Cumberland, was in Livingston County, Kentucky; its population in 1830 was 388 but it was considered an important town because of its location.

59. The fact that Paducah, laid out in 1827, was "quite new" is supported by its absence from the contemporary guides. Baird (1832) simply mentioned it as one of the other towns on the Ohio "at the entrance of the Tennessee river" (*View*, p. 182). It is not mentioned among dozens of Kentucky towns in Flint, and Davenport did not include it in his *Gazetteer*.

60. These letters could be "far."

age. Lets me know immediatel[y][61] that he is a rich imigrant—talks of his neighbor Lord Castlereagh[62] who was the greatest statesman in Europe

Take on board here a little Frenchman & his wife who are rolling a big box through the country like a pair of tumblers[.] He is a blacksmith—she kept a caffé ↑in Touraine↓[63] natives of Tours. beguiled out here by frenchman ↑the same Lucas↓ [64] who had bought[65] land in Kentucky & represented it as a paradise[—]four roads[?] ↑turnpike↓ met—diligence[66] every day.[67] The very place to set up ⟨blacksmith shop⟩[68] & caffé. ↑tells her to bring all the linen she cd.↓ The little frenchn & his wife packed up all their worldly effects in three pine boxes—bundled up their bed & embarked. Landed at New Orleans Good opportunity presented to fix themselves, but recd[69] letter from their friend pressing[?] them to come on. Embarked in steam/boat, arrived at the promised land & found it a ⟨f[?]⟩ wilderness covered with trees—the four roads were 4 tracks thro forest—The Diligence a Stage waggon that

61. This word could be "incidental."

62. Trent and Hellman identify as Robert Stewart, Viscount Castlereagh (1769–1822), who was the second marquis of Londonderry; he committed suicide (*Journals of WI*, III, 106, n. 1).

63. Touraine is an old province in west central France; it is crossed by the Loire River on which is its principal city, Tours (approximately 140 miles southwest of Paris). The area is famous for its fertile Loire River valley and its beautiful châteaux.

64. Trent and Hellman identified as one of Napoleon's soldiers, Frederick Lucas, who, after the Battle of Waterloo, came to America and settled in the West (*Journals of WI*, III, 106, n. 2).

65. Immediately above this word between lines 11 and 12, there is a mark, apparently the beginning of the word "who" following the inserted words from the line above, "the same Lucas"; when WI realized he had written "who had" on the line above, he crossed out the "wh."

66. There is a line through the word "diligence" from the *l* to over the *n* which makes the word difficult to decipher. The diligence, from the French word meaning "speed" and originally a French wagon, was adopted by the English; in eighteenth-century America, advertisers for diligence wagons emphasized the fact that they were beginning to imitate coaches and that they were extremely fast. In a contemporary description of a sixteen-hour trip from New York to Philadelphia, the wagon—also called a "stage" and "carriage"—was named the *Flying Diligence* (Belknap's *History of New Hampshire* as quoted in Dunbar, *Travel*, p. 186).

67. Trent and Hellman and McDermott read this difficult passage as "from turnpike could meet diligence every day" (*Journals of WI*, III, 106; *Western Journals*, p. 75). Another possible reading is "four lanes ↑turnpike↓ met" with WI's caret over the *e* of "lanes" making it resemble a *d*.

68. It is possible that these words are not intended to be crossed out; the line through them could separate the interlinear line (between lines 1 and 2) from the last part of line 1 (line 2 begins with "& caffè").

69. WI's abbreviation for "received"; this word could also be "read."

plied 2 months in year when there was no ⟨stage⟩ steam boat. They re embark to return to New Orleans.

A little Canadian who had been passenger in our boat hither/-to, was making arrangt with captain for them—⟨I⟩ & wanted to know if no one on board spoke French. I offered my services—[70]

———

8 at night—arrive at Caledonia[71]—at the point of confluence of Mississippi & Ohio.[72] Land part of cargo—

Little Frenchman & wife go ashore. I speak to the landlord for them & put them under care of a passenger[—] Rolled their big Box up bank. Carried bedding up to ⟨hous⟩ Inn Little Frenchman remained on bank—put all his boxes together—lit fire—mounted guard by moonlight—Left him humming tune & watching—

at 1 oclock at night get under way—enter Mississippi[73] by moonlight—

70. WI drew a line one-sixteenth inch long to separate paragraphs.

71. On maps that WI was using, this village was called America. It was the county town of Alexander County, Illinois, and was situated on the right, or west, bank of the Ohio approximately fifteen miles above its mouth. Flint said that its position, "a point to which large steam boats can ascend from below, to wait for the smaller boats, that ascend the Ohio in low stages of the water," will make it a town of "consequence" (*Mississippi Valley*, I, 331). It was subsequently called Caledonia and became the county town of Pulaski County.

72. WI's surprising lack of enthusiasm upon reaching this geographical milestone might be explained by Flint's recollection of the same scene: "The junction of the Ohio and Mississippi does not impress that idea of physical grandeur, which fills up your anticipations" (Flint, *Recollections*, p. 84).

73. At this point, the "Great Water" had been joined by its principal affluent, the Missouri River, as well as by the Illinois, Maramec, Kaskaskai, and the Big Muddy. It had flowed approximately 1,800 miles from its source; Henry Roe Schoolcraft (1793–1864) discovered in 1832 that its extreme source was the Itasca Lake, but other writers debated that fact. It flowed generally north to south, and even though it was 1,600 miles from the mouth of the Missouri to the source, the Mississippi was navigable only to the Falls of St. Anthony. The river's speed averaged two miles an hour, and its height varied from fifteen to four feet at flood and low water; its width varied from 1½ miles at the mouth of the Missouri to an average of three-fourths mile over the winding distance of 200 miles from there to the mouth of the Ohio. Flint wrote that with the confluence of the Missouri, the Mississippi's character changed from "the gentle, placid stream, with smooth shores and clean sandbars; but has a furious and boiling current, a turbid and dangerous mass of sweeping waters, jagged and dilapidated shores, and, wherever its waters have receded, deposits of mud. . . . The bosom of the river is covered with prodigious boils, or swells, that rise with a whirling motion, and a convex surface, two or three rods in diameter, and no inconsiderable noise, whirling a boat perceptibly from its track" (*Mississippi Valley*, I, 97–98). Flint also described the "points and bends" and the navigational skill necessary to negotiate the resulting currents, eddies, crumbling alluvial soil, sandbars, etc. (pp. 104–5); he said that steamboats "which

(—Mem.[74] This evg a Splendid sunset in Ohio— ↑full↓ moon rose from behind forest, attended by a virgin star—)

Tuesday, September 11[75]

On the Mississippi broad turbid stream. Sand bars, low alluvial shores with forests—Chemin de forge of Snags[76]—Streaming files of ducks & geese— —½ past 8 land for wood on Missouri side—corn field—where crops of corn have been raised for 28 years successively, without manure —rich covering[—]sandy soil—level—Grow[77] seed corn 20 rows on a cob. —country still—lonely

Travellers—Some adventurers embark without money—are put ashore —at wood piles—remain there till next boat comes along—hoist a handkerchief on pole—taken on board—⟨Get on under⟩ boat under way—too late to Set them ashore[—]carry them to next pile—So they work their way from wood pile to wood pile

Woman with family of children applies[78] to capt occasionally Get passage for nothing—a subscription among passengers

⟨Ohio⟩ ↑Illinois↓ mercht on board—says he trusts for a year ⟨the⟩ Then 25 per cent—

If man cant pay he hangs about him like fever & ague whispering[79] to him until he pays—does not lose above 5 p cent

---

can be changed in a moment, to reverse the impulse and direction of the boat, are exactly calculated to obviate the dangers of this river" (p. 98). The first steamboat on the river was built in 1811; in 1829, there were 230 in use (see Flint, *Mississippi Valley*, I, 91–107; Baird, *View*, pp. 18–21, 234–40, and an excellent chapter on steamboating in 1832, pp. 313–29).

74. WI's parenthesis cuts through the dash here and at the end of the parenthetical sentence.

75. WI wrote "Tuesday Sept 11."

76. McDermott said that this French term means "raft"; however, it is not in French dictionaries and may have been a coined river term. "Chemin de fer" means "railroad" or "way of iron," and WI may have been referring to a snag boat, a boat which forges its way or makes its way by force. Captain Shreve's snag boat, the *Heliopolis*, was at work on the upper Mississippi during this particular fall; the snag boat "marches up the stream with a tremendous pressure of steam, and takes the visible part of the snag (which is the top of the tree) between the bows of the boat, and by the strong cross beam, lifts it up, and as the boat urges her way onward, the snag is raised up, until the whole tree almost stands on its end. Then the boat stops, holds it there, while the hands cut it in pieces of twenty or thirty feet, and let them float away" (Baird, *View*, pp. 238–39).

77. Trent and Hellman (*Journals of WI*, III, 107) and McDermott (*Western Journals*, p. 76) deciphered as "sound." It could also be "Grand" or "Gourd."

78. This word could be "appld" or "appeals."

79. This word is probably "whispering" although the *p* looks like a *k* or an *h*, with no loop below the line.

–Go to farm house. woman spinning–Young lad sitting idle– their beds in room–full of negro children–Fat little gourd shaped one cries–the lad tells another child to amuse it by rolling ball on floor–Have lived here 33 years. Man says he never struck a negro since he was a boy. would not Sell one unless the negro wished to go away–

House open to the weather ⟨Frenchman[?]⟩ pigs–fowls–corn–vegetables–fruit[–]pure[80] well of water–

neighboring cypress swamp [–]Deer[,] bears, panthers[,] wild cats–Turkeys in abundance no Snakes

Wind now–pure Soft air

Frenchman–the same Lucas who came to Touraine in grand air[?][81] in winter & has not 2 negroes[82]

–pass lime stone cliffs looking like old castle towers–light foliage below–wild ducks–Sand bars–after sun set stop at apple[83] orchard–Mr Kemmels new store & house–thriving place. children ill with fever[,] wife "first rate woman" educated in convent about 18 miles off where there is also a seminary.[84] She is from Kentucky

Saw at the landing ⟨A⟩a negro merchant 36 years old–Going to New Orleans with 40 doz fowls–had canoe[,] a boat[85] with corn to feed them[–]goes down in Steam boat–gets passage for nothing from some–buys 1 $ doz sells 3 $–has followed the business 12 years. brings back nothing but money–pays his master 50 $ a year[–]lays up money to buy himself free. buries it. Cannot buy himself until next year[.] Has wife & children but cannot buy them–Means to go when free where he can make most money but means to see[?] his wife & children occasionally & take care of them.

80. This word could be "fine."

81. Trent and Hellman transcribed as "way," as did McDermott (*Journals of WI*, III, 108; *Western Journals*, p. 77); this reading is a possible one.

82. For reference to Lucas, see September 10, 1832, entry and n. 64 above.

83. Following this last word on the line there is a mark which could be a hyphen, "apple-/orchard."

84. The geography and the strongly Catholic community suggest St. Geneviève, Missouri, as the town in which the young woman studied (see below, n. 91). In his overview of colleges and universities in the West in this period, Baird mentioned several Catholic schools, among them the "seminary in Perry county, at Perryville, about eighty-five miles south of St. Louis, which has three departments,—one for boys, in which are nearly 100 youth, many of them from the West Indies and Louisiana, receiving an education; another for girls, where there is a large number; and a third for young men, who are preparing for the priesthood" (*View*, pp. 302–03).

85. WI might have written "canoe or boat."

The Lady of the House says that there are different meetings here—Catholics—Presbyterians—Methodists &c

Beautiful moon rise—on Illinois—fire of wood/-man at point[?][86] of island[—]red-yellow moon—silver star—calm whale[?] green[87] sky reflected in river—here & there at far distances solitary ↑a↓ light twinkles from some log house among the trees

Moon regent of Lakes & woods

Wednesday, September 12[88]

Fog comes in about ½ past 4—Stop at wood yard ⟨a little⟩ a few miles above Kaskaskia river[89]—visit Log house—people from Louisiana—discouraged at the coldness of climate here—Soil abundant—Game plenty—Hunt Turkeys by moonlight. The settlers emotion[?] anxious[90] to return to Louisiana

S Geneviève[91]—fine level with range of hills behind it to the north: one of the oldest French settlements—people live in the[92] village where the houses are private property—20000 acres in front in common. Each one has a right to cultivate a portion for his own use—Strangers apt to marry the Genevieve girls to get the right—College on hill back of the

86. McDermott read this word as "front" (*Western Journals*, p. 78).

87. Trent and Hellman and McDermott read as "calm, cobalt-green" (*Journals of WI*, III, 109; *Western Journals*, p. 78).

88. WI wrote "Wednesday Sept 12."

89. The Kaskaskia, "a beautiful stream," rose in east central Illinois, "nearly interlocking with the waters of Lake Michigan," and flowed southwestward for approximately 250 miles; its branches were many, its region fertile, and its course largely navigable during high water. It entered the Mississippi approximately 100 miles above the mouth of the Ohio, and its lower course was called "Okau" by the considerable surrounding French community.

90. Trent and Hellman read as "the settlers—mother anxious" (*Journals of WI*, III, 109); McDermott read as "the settlers northern—anxious" (*Western Journals*, p. 78).

91. St. Geneviève, the county town of St. Geneviève, Missouri, stood a mile west of the river opposite Kaskaskia, 120 miles above the mouth of the Ohio and 64 miles below St. Louis. On a navigable creek, the Gabourie, the town was situated in a beautiful alluvial fertile prairie, 3,000 to 6,000 acres (estimates varied) of which were fenced and cultivated in common. Nearly a century after its settlement by French Canadians, it still retained its French characteristics, including language, wooden houses surrounded by porches, and a theological school. The population had diminished from an earlier 7,000 to approximately 1,600 in 1832. Flint remarked on the "handsome building erected for an academy" located west of town on a hill with a "magnificent view of the village, the bluffs above, the prairie below, and the Mississippi sweeping in the distance" (*Mississippi Valley*, I, 310–311).

92. This word could be "this" or "their"; it appears that WI wrote over the initial letter.

town—above the settlement pretty openings and views[?][93] as through side scenes of a theater—low banks of cotton trees—willows &c

StGenevieve—tall[?][94] man comes on board with saddlebags—⟨traps⟩ steel traps. bundle[—]conducted by man in blanket coat, & mockasins. Turns out to be Col Menard—who accompanied atwater on the Indian Expedition[95]

Herculaneum ⟨??⟩Gl[96] Store ⟨leadn[?]⟩ shot tower on brink of limestone[97] precipice Beautiful ⟨with[?]⟩ precipice of lime stone ⟨with⟩ like towers of ruined castles— —with many tinted virginia creepers. ⟨*illegible*⟩[98] hanging about the cold grey—Land on Island—immense cotton/wood trees—Uncle Sams land, with poachers cutting & selling wood.

Evg. 9 oclock—crash!—a steamboat, the yellow/stone, coming down the Stream at the rate of 15 Miles an hour runs on us & ⟨tears⟩ Staves in the upper works of our side— — the wheel box—privy &c ⟨Splash[?][99] of the b[?]⟩ General alarm—some think the boat sinking—Kentucky lady threw herself into her husbands arms—⟨d[?]⟩[100] Alarm subsides—make for land to repair damages & mend wheel.[101] Speech of black fire man. They have torn the [?d— b—?] all to sallad—

93. This word could be "scenes."

94. Apparently WI wrote over some unrecovered letter or letters what seems to be the word "tall."

95. According to McDermott, "Pierre Menard (1766–1844) was born in Canada and, after some years at Vincennes, settled at Kaskaskia in 1790. He served as an officer in the Illinois militia, as a member of the Territorial legislature (1812–18), and as lieutenant governor (1818–22); he was also an important figure in the fur trade. . . . In 1829 Caleb Atwater (1778–1867) was appointed a commissioner to serve with Pierre Manard and General John McNeil of the United States Army in making treaties with the Indians at Prairie du Chien" (*Western Journals*, p. 79, n. 26).

96. Herculaneum, on the west bank of the Mississippi 21 miles above St. Geneviève and 30 miles below St. Louis, was the county town of Jefferson County, Missouri, and a very small town. Lead from the mines in Washington County, approximately 40 miles west of this point, and the shot manufactured in Herculaneum were deposited and exported by steamboats from this town and St. Geneviève.

97. Over the last syllable of this word is an illegible mark.

98. These letters could be "Lan."

99. This word could be "Break."

100. This letter could be *L*.

101. The *Yellowstone* was based in St. Louis and the year before, on its first voyage, had traveled up the Missouri River almost to the Yellowstone River, an amazing distance of 1,400 miles from St. Louis. WI wrote almost identical accounts to his brother Peter in a letter of December 18, 1832, and to his sister Catharine Paris, in a letter one day after the incident: "The last evening of our voyage we were nearly run down & sent to the bottom by a huge Steam boat ⟨'⟩The 'Yellow Stone' which came sweeping down the river under the imp[e]tus of 'High pressure' and a rapid current. Fortunately our pilot managed the helm so as to receive the blow

arrive at St Louis[102] about 11. ⟨remain⟩ ↑sleep↓ on board—

Thursday, September 13[103]

St Louis—Mixture of French & american character. French billiard room—market place[104] where some are Speaking French[,] some English—put up at union Hotel[105]—See Mr Chouteau (pere et fils[106]—Dr

---

obliquely, which tore away part of a wheel and staved in all the upper works of one side of our boat: we made shift to limp through the remainder of our voyage, which was but about twelve miles" (*Letters*, II, 722–23). Pourtalès, as would be expected, wrote the most sensational version of the three, concluding that the "weaker sex, consoled by members of the stronger one, stoppd their cries" and that "the crew merely cursed the pilot of the other boat with the strong oaths which usually season the speech of western Americans" (*Journal*, p. 23). The *Yellowstone* was built the year before in Louisville for the American Fur Company and was owned in part by John Jacob Astor, who was later to be important to WI.

102. When WI visited St. Louis, the county town of St. Louis County, it was still a trading post town about to undergo explosive growth in the next ten to twenty years. Situated on the west bank of the Mississippi eighteen miles below the mouth of the Missouri and 200 miles above the mouth of the Ohio, the site was selected by Pierre Laclede because of its favorable location for trade; the town was founded in 1764 and chartered as a city in 1822. In 1820, there were approximately 600 "American houses" (that is, of brick) and 4,598 people, with a two to one ratio of American to French; by 1830, the population had grown to only 6,694, of those 1,668 were slaves, but in ten years the population doubled and in twenty years multiplied by fourteen. St. Louis College, founded in 1818 and taken over in 1827 by Jesuits, was chartered as St. Louis University only three months after WI was there. As the commercial capital of the state with promise of immediate and tremendous growth, extensive warehouses were being built, and in 1832 as many as twenty steamboats could be seen at one time at its wharves, and the revenue of the city was $4,766; in twenty years that revenue was almost 40 million dollars. The lead industry influenced growth, and the fur trade seemed limitless, particularly Astor's American Fur Company which employed 1,000 men in town, on the prairie, and at the outposts. Drawn to this mile-long town were diverse types of people, among them Indians, French, Americans, trappers, hunters, immigrants, many "desperate and abandoned characters," and adventurers who found it relatively easy to be absorbed into "society." St. Louis had an air of lawlessness typical of an early frontier trading town; however, in 1832, several writers noted that a moral revolution was beginning to gain momentum: respect for the Sabbath and interest in religion were gaining, tendency to duelling disappearing, number of police growing, and respect for laws increasing.

103. WI wrote "Thursday Sept 13—."

104. A mark between the words "market" and "place" could be a hyphen or the crossing of the *t*.

105. According to the *St. Louis Directory for 1836–37*, the Union Hotel was kept by Mr. Farrish and was located at Prune and First Streets (McDermott, *Western Journals*, p. 80, n. 30).

106. There were four Messrs. Chouteau important in the history of this section; the oldest of the four was René Auguste Chouteau (1749–1828), born in New

Orleans. His mother, Marie Thérèse Chouteau, left his father soon after Auguste was born and began a relationship with Pierre Laclede, whom she never married. In 1763, when he was only fourteen years old, Auguste went with his "stepfather" to select the site for a new town, and in several months Laclede put Auguste in charge of the expedition to begin the building of the village which would become St. Louis. He was the chief manager of Laclede's business ventures, and ultimately "Col. Auguste" was the wealthiest and one of the most respected men in the city.

Nine years younger than his half brother was Jean Pierre Chouteau (1758–1849), also born in New Orleans, the son of Marie Thérèse and Pierre Laclede, but using his mother's surname, Chouteau, because of the French custom; Pierre is probably the "pere" of whom WI wrote. He had come with his mother to St. Louis in 1764 and, from his earliest days, had a great facility for friendship and business with the Indians, particularly the Osages. He lived and traded among the Osages as commandant of Fort Carondelet and in 1804 was appointed U.S. agent for the Osages by President Jefferson. He was active in the militia, advancing to major. He joined with his half brother and several others including William Clark and Manuel Lisa to form the St. Louis Missouri Fur Company, the first company formed to organize trade in the western region and subsequently a rival of Astor's company. For almost thirty years, from 1820, Pierre lived in semi-retirement receiving guests at his "plantation" outside St. Louis.

The older of Pierre Chouteau's two famous sons was Auguste Pierre Chouteau (1786–1838), born in St. Louis. He went to West Point from 1804–1806, was graduated as an ensign in the infantry, was an aide to Gen. Wilkinson and was made a captain of the militia during the War of 1812; however, Auguste Pierre's appellation of "Col. A. P." was bestowed on him by his fellow citizens. At 23, he was one of the partners in the Missouri Fur Company. Like his father and his uncle, Col. A. P. Chouteau was a man at home in the West with white man and Indian alike—as a successful businessman or as an advocate for Indian rights; as the trader persuading the Osages to relocate when a government "treaty" interfered with his agency's business; as a close friend of Sam Houston, who from 1829–1832 also lived among the Indians; and as an appointee of the secretary of war to negotiate peace treaties with Indians at war. He was important in the taming of the frontier. In September, 1832, he happened to be in St. Louis and offered to lead the Irving party to his home and agency on the Verdigris, near the mouth of the Arkansas.

The other candidate for WI's "Chouteau fils" was Pierre Chouteau (1789–1865), born in St. Louis and known among his friends as "Cadet," the French word meaning *younger, junior of two.* From the beginning, he was more interested in business than in frontier association with the Indians, and in 1831, he became a member and then a partner of a large firm which in 1834 bought the American Fur Company's Western Department which became Pierre Chouteau, Jr. & Company. Living for long periods in New York, he became a leading American financier with companies in fur trading, iron works, rolling mills, and, finally, railroads. For additional information on the Chouteaus, see John Joseph Mathews, *The Osages: Children of the Middle Waters* (Norman: University of Oklahoma Press, 1961); hereafter cited as Mathews, *Osages*; see also Grant Foreman, *Indians and Pioneers: The Story of the American Southwest Before 1830*, rev. ed. (Norman: University of Oklahoma Press, 1936); hereafter cited as Foreman, *Indians and Pioneers*; and Grant Foreman, *Advancing the Frontier: 1830–1860* (Norman: University of Oklahoma Press, 1933); hereafter cited as Foreman, *Advancing the Frontier.*

O'Dwyer—Judge Peck[—]Mr Bates[107]—

Drive ⟨across⟩ out to Gov Clarkes.[108] cross prarie—Flowering & fragrant shrubs—The Govs.[109] Farm. small cottage—Orchard bending & breaking with loads of fruit—negros—with tables under trees preparing meal—fire ⟨Sitting room⟩ in open air—little negros, whooping[110] & laughing—Civil negro ⟨*illegible*⟩ major domo who asks to take horses out, invites us to walk in the orchard—& spreads table with additional cov-

107. McDermott identified the three men as follows: Dr. Thomas O'Dwyer was stationed at Fort Smith as an assistant surgeon; James Hawkins Peck (ca. 1790–1836) came from Tennessee to St. Louis in 1818 and in 1822 was appointed the U.S. District Court's first Judge in Missouri; Edward Bates (1793–1869) was admitted to the bar in 1816, two years after he came to St. Louis; subsequently, he was elected to Congress and to the state senate, serving from 1830 to 1834, and was President Lincoln's attorney general (*Western Journals*, pp. 80–81, n. 31).

108. Known by both titles, Governor William Clark (1770–1838) was one of the most famous and knowledgeable men in the West; having moved with his family from Virginia to Louisville in 1784, Clark was a member of many successful military expeditions into Indian territories from 1791 until 1796; in 1803 he was called out of "retirement" by Captain Meriwether Lewis, who requested that the young lieutenant join his expedition ordered by President Jefferson to find a route to the Pacific—and the Lewis and Clark expedition set off from St. Louis in May, 1804. The success of the mission was due in large part to Clark's insight regarding the ways and means of the Indians, his ability in map making and sketching, and his common sense. He resigned from the army in 1807 and was appointed brigadier general of the militia for Louisiana.

In 1808, General Clark was married, began a thirty-year residence in St. Louis, and was appointed to fill the governorship vacated by the untimely death of his friend, Governor Lewis; he declined the appointment but in 1813 accepted the appointment of President Madison as governor of Missouri Territory, which office he held until 1820. In 1818, on a lot on the corner of Main and Vine Streets, he built "his large brick mansion, and afterward his brick row south of it for his Indian council-house and museum of Indian curiosities" (Coues, I, lxxviii), in which he had a large collection. Although Clark was not elected in the first race for governor of Missouri in 1820, he was appointed superintendent of Indian affairs in 1822, a position he held until his death. Known to the Indians as the "Redhead" and trusted by them, one of the most important treaties he effected was the Prairie du Chien relating to the lands of the Creeks, Chickasaws, and Choctaws, among other tribes; the treaty was broken twice in 1827 and once in 1832 when Black Hawk led the Sauks in war. Governor Clark helped in settling that matter, including the capture and holding of Black Hawk in Jefferson Barracks just before WI arrived. Clark was surveyor general of Missouri, Illinois, and the Arkansas Territory from 1824, and he was also a successful "man of affairs, who could turn a trade as well as he did various other things" (Elliott Coues, ed., *History of the Expedition under the Command of Lewis and Clark* [1893; reprint ed., New York: Dover, 1965], I, lxxvii; hereafter cited as Coues, ed., *Lewis and Clark*. See "Memoir of William Clark," I, lxii-xcvii).

109. This word could be "Genls."

110. This word could be "whispering."

ers.[111] Sitting room. rifle & game bag &c in corners—Indian calument[112] over fire place—remains of fire on hearth—showing that morng has been cool—lovely day—golden sunshine—transparent at-/-mosphere—pure breeze—

Fine nut trees—peach trees[,] grape vines ↑Calalpas↓[113] &c &c above the house look out over rich level plain or prairie—green near at hand—blue line at the horizon ⟨*illegible*⟩ universal chirp & spinning of insects—fertility of country

grove of walnuts in the rear of the house.

Bee hives—Dove cote[—]Canoe.

Genl arrives on horseback with dogs—⟨Gen[?]⟩ Guns—His grandsons[114] on a calico poney—hallowing laughing—Genl on horseback—Gun on his shoulder ‸↑cur↓—House dog[115]—bullying setter—

⟨Genl⟩ Gov Clark fine healthy robust man. tall about 56—perhaps more. His hair, originally light, now grey falling on his shoulders[—] Frank—intelligent—

111. This word could be "courses."

112. Calumet is a long-stemmed and highly ornamental ceremonial pipe of the North American Indians. Pourtalès mentioned exchanging gifts with an Osage Indian: "In our first and only meeting he gave me his calumet and his tobacco pouch. I returned his courtesy by giving him my powder horn" (*Journal*, p. 38).

113. WI probably meant to cross the *t* and list catalpa as one of the trees; Flint said that the catalpa is common to Louisiana, Louisville, and Nachitoches (*Mississippi Valley*, II, 201, 203, 211); he added, "Some have undertaken to say that this is not a tree indigenous to the country. For our part, we have no question on the subject" (*Mississippi Valley*, I, 44). The catalpa is chiefly a North American tree, of the trumpet creeper family, having large cordate leaves and long pods. It is sometimes called "Indian bean."

114. The Christmas before WI visited him, Governor Clark's second wife had died, leaving two sons and a daughter by her first husband, Dr. Radford, and an eight-year-old son by Clark; this boy, whose name was Jefferson, was probobly the child whom WI called Clark's grandson. The Radford sons were William, who at that time was twenty-five and apparently unmarried, and John, who was sixteen. The oldest child of William Clark's first wife, Julia Hancock, was Meriwether Lewis Clark (see below, n. 116), who did not marry until 1834, and William Preston Clark, who was twenty-one at this time and unmarried; the third son, George Rogers Hancock Clark, was sixteen at the time, and the fourth son had died in St. Louis the previous fall when he was thirteen years old (Coues, ed., *Lewis and Clark*, I, lxiv–lxvii).

115. This word could be "Houndog"; WI did not lift his pen between syllables or words.

His son—a cadet of W P. now in the army aid deCamp to Genl Atkinson[116]—⟨Hands⟩[117]

———

Dinner plentiful[—]good, but rustic—fried chicken—Bison & Game—roast beef—Roasted[?][118] potatoes—tomatos, excellent Cakes—bread—butter &c

—⟨Genl⟩ Gov C. gives much excellent information ⟨as⟩ concerning Indians.[119]

———

His slaves—Set three free—⟨one, his famous man York⟩[120] one he placed at a ferry—another on a farm giving him land, horses &c—a third he gave a ⟨farm[?]⟩ large waggon & team of 6 horses to ply between Nash-/ville & Richmond

116. Governor Clark's son, Colonel Meriwether Lewis Clark (1809–1881), was born in St. Louis, named for his father's fellow explorer, graduated from West Point in 1830, and was stationed at Jefferson Barracks near St. Louis until 1833. As aide-de-camp to General Henry Atkinson (1782–1842), young Clark served a man whose reputation in settling this part of the West was second only to his own father, Governor Clark. Born in North Carolina, entering the Infantry in 1808, and rising to the rank of adjutant general in 1821, he was respected as one capable in Indian affairs; in 1825, he led an extremely successful expedition from St. Louis to the Yellowstone to make treaties with the Indians. While he was at the Yellowstone post, he met General Ashley (see n. 127) and subsequently provided him and his furs safe passage to St. Louis; all this he accomplished without losing a man or a boat. In 1826 General Atkinson selected the site, oversaw the building, and assumed command of the post of Jefferson Barracks, leaving only periodically to help with removal of Indians or to settle Indian uprisings, among them the Black Hawk War in 1832 during which he was in general command and in immediate command on the second day (August 2) when Black Hawk's men were defeated at Bad Axe.

117. Following this paragraph is a line one-sixteenth inch long.

118. WI could have written "Butterd" or two words, "Hot ro[a]st"; WI lifted his pen between syllables or words.

119. Following this paragraph is a line three-sixteenths inch long.

120. The "black servant belonging to Captain Clark" was indeed famous; astonished Indian squaws, for instance, paddled small canoes through rough water to get a look at York, "a remarkable stout, strong negro," according to an October 9, 1805, entry. "They had never seen a being of that color, and therefore flocked around him to examine the extraordinary monster. By way of amusement he told them that he had once been a wild animal, and caught and tamed by his master; and to convince them showed them feats of strength which, added to his looks, made him more terrible than we wished him to be" (Coues, ed., *Lewis and Clark*, I, 159). Once, the curious chief of the Minnetarees, who wished to verify the rumor about the presence of a black man, "examined [York] closely, and spit on his finger and rubbed the skin in order to wash off the paint; nor was it until the negro uncovered his head and showed his short hair, that La Borgne could be persuaded that he was not a painted white man" (*ibid.*, I, 243). According to Elliott Coues, a con-

They all repented & wanted to come back–

The waggoner was York the hero of the Missouri ⟨jour[?]⟩ expedition & adviser of the Indians– –He could not get up early enough in the morngs–his horses were ill kept[–]two died–the others grew poor. he sold them, was cheated–entered into service–fared ill–Damn this freedom said York I have never had a happy day since I got it. He determined to go back to his old master[–]set off for St Louis, but was taken with the choke[121] in Tennessee & died–

Some of the traders think they have[122] met traces of ⟨?⟩Yorks crowd[?][123] on the Missouri[124]

Returned by another route escorted by Young Clark–ride thro prarie –flowers–Hazle nuts[125]–&c pass by a little farm–every/thing in abundance. pass by a circle of Indian mounds,[126] on one of them Genl. Ash-

---

temporary, York was a "wag." After he returned to St. Louis and was a free man, York was given to drinking and entertaining his fellow revellers with amusing and tall tales, one of them about a "nation of bearded, blue-eyed, and red-haired Indians on the Upper Missouri" (*ibid.*, I, 159, n. 31).

121. McDermott transcribed as "cholera," a logical reading but one which is not supported by the formation of the second half of the word. It could be "choler," or a coined medical term describing the symptom. One day during the expedition, Lewis reported that York was not well and Clark "gave him a doze of tartar emettic which operated very well and he was much better in the evening. [T]his is a discription of medicine that I never have recourse to in my practice except in cases of intermittent fever" (Coues, ed., *Lewis and Clark*, II, 405, n. 22).

122. Apparently, WI wrote over a *g* or *y*, the *v* of "have."

123. This word could be "brood": WI might have been referring to one of the inebriated York's favorite tales about the blond, blue-eyed Indians up the Missouri (see above, n. 120), or he could have meant York's possible progeny.

124. After this word, WI drew a line three-sixteenths inch long to separate paragraphs.

125. Flint included the Hazel nut in his list of "Flora of Louisville" (*Mississippi Valley*, II, 203, table 3). The hazelnut is a small tree common to the British Isles, Europe, and Asia; the American species are *Corylus cornuts* and more often *Corylus americana*; the edible "woody nut" of the hazel is in a brown smooth hard shell.

126. See pp. 29–30, n. 200, for discussion of mounds.

ley[127] has built his[128] house so as to have the summit of it as a terrace in the rear[129]

St Louis—old rackety gamb-/-ling house. Noise of the queue[130] & the billiard ball from morning till night—

old french women accosting each other in the street

Friday, September 14[131]

Drive out with Judge Peck[,] Judge Andre[?][132] & our party to Fort Jefferson[133] to See Black Hawk. Ride thro open country—formerly forest. Drive to Genl Atkinsons quarters—

Black Hawk.[134] old man upwards of 70 with aquiline nose. finely formed head—organs of benevolence—His two sons, oldest a fine look-

127. General William Henry Ashley (ca. 1778–1838) was another outstanding citizen; his "magnificent residence in north St. Louis" (*DAB*, I, 392) built in 1826 was unusual in its position on an Indian mound, its landscaped eight acres, and its fountain in front of the house (McDermott, *Western Journals*, p. 82, n. 37). Ashley was born in Virginia, was settled in Missouri by 1805, and was early a success in the manufacture of saltpeter and gunpowder. In the territorial militia, he rose from captain to general from 1813 to 1822; in that year he founded his own fur company, establishing a post at Yellowstone in 1823 and becoming an adventurer and experimenter in the lucrative fur trade in South Dakota, Nebraska, Colorado, and Wyoming. (See Harrison Clifford Dale's edition of the *Ashley–Smith Exploration and the Discovery of a Central Route to the Pacific* [1819].) Ashley was elected lieutenant governor of Missouri in 1820 and defeated for governor in 1824 and for U. S. Senate in 1829; the year before WI observed his house in St. Louis, Ashley had been elected to fill a seat in Congress vacated because of a duel death.

128. Just below the *s* of this word, there is a mark, apparently a mistake, which might be confused with a *y* or *g*.

129. WI added a line one-fourth inch long to separate thoughts.

130. WI used the French spelling for "cue," the leather-tipped rod used to strike a billiard ball.

131. WI wrote "Friday Sept 14."

132. Trent and Hellman deciphered as "Judge's uncle" without identifying him (*Journals of WI*, III, 112); McDermott used this reading but suggested that WI might have written "Easton"; he then identified Judge Rufus Easton (1774–1834), who came to St. Louis in 1804 as one of the first judges of Louisiana Territory (*Western Journals*, p. 83 and n. 39). See inside back cover; the second name in the list appears to be the same as this one.

133. According to Baird's 1832 description, Jefferson Barracks was "ten miles below St. Louis. The Arsenal is still nearer to that city. This is the most important military post in the west. It is immediately on the bank of the river. The buildings are all of stone, and sufficient to accommodate from five hundred to seven hundred men. There are about five hundred here at present" (*View*, p. 227).

134. Black Hawk (1767–1838), whose Indian names varied throughout his life, was born in Illinois, was the adopted brother of the chief of the Foxes, and al-

ing young man. His brother in law the prophet[135]—The little Indian Stables[136]—

⟨*illegible*⟩[137] They were all chained arms & ankles, with cannon

---

though not a Sauk by birth was reared as one and became a Sauk chief by the age of twenty-one. From the beginning, his policies and practices grew out of his dislike and mistrust of the whites, including his supporting the British in the War of 1812. The Black Hawk War in 1832 grew out of the chief's disapproval of earlier treaties into which some of the Sauks had entered and his refusal to adhere to them, especially the order to leave his beloved Rock Island, Illinois, and move across the river to Iowa. The issue became acute in 1831 when whites moved into the area and, according to Black Hawk, farming rights were violated, the Sauk women were mistreated, and the promised guns were withheld. A strong government show of force averted war until the following year when Black Hawk's forces—500 people including entire families—crossed the river and refused to return. The Sauk chief had used the unrest of the southwestern Indians, especially the Osages as well as the Pawnees, Delawares, Comanches, and Wichitas, to incite them to attack and retaliate. General Atkinson's 3,000 men ultimately defeated the Indians; those remaining retreated to the mouth of the Bad Axe where they were massacred on August 2. Even then, Black Hawk escaped only to be chased by Sioux, captured by a few Winnebagoes, and handed over to the army for a reward; his incarceration at Jefferson Barracks on September 7, 1832, preceded WI's visit there by only one week. In a letter to his sister, Catharine Paris, WI wrote that the "redoubtable Black Hawk who makes such a figure in our Newspapers is an old man upwards of Seventy: emaciated & enfeebled by the sufferings he has experienced and by a touch of cholera. He has a small, well formed head, with an aquiline nose and a good expression of eye . . ." (*Letters*, II, 723). Even though the local phrenologist had pronounced Black Hawk benevolent, WI reluctantly admitted to Mrs. Paris that the Indian was accused of many cruelties. See Foreman, *Indians and Pioneers*, pp. 21–24; Foreman, *Advancing the Frontier*, pp. 107–14; Kenneth M. Stewart, "Black Hawk War," in *Dictionary of American History* (New York: Charles Scribner's Sons, 1976), I, 311–12; hereafter cited as *DAH*.

135. There is much conflicting information about the members of Black Hawk's contingent, including WI's own report that the Prophet was Black Hawk's brother-in-law. An early source indicated that Black Hawk's two sons were the Prophet and Naopope (*Cyclopædia of Am. Biography*, IX, 477). Largely based on *Black Hawk: An Autobiography*, edited by Donald Jackson, the conclusion is that the Prophet was White Cloud (Wabokieshiek), born in 1794 and no relation to Black Hawk; Neapope was White Cloud's adopted son and a Sauk chief. The name of the older of Black Hawk's two sons was Nasheaskusk (Loud Thunder) or Nah-se-us-kuk (Whirling Thunder), a man whom one observer described as the "embodiment of ideal manly beauty." One authority gave the younger son's name as Wa-saw-me-saw (Roaring Thunder) and another version was Nasomsee or Gamesett. See references cited in note above; also see McDermott, ed., *Western Journals*, 83–84, nn. 41, 43, 45; *Letters*, II, 724–25, n. 7.

136. An alternate reading might be "stature."

137. These letters could be "restr[ained]."

but[?][138] are allowed to walk about—escorted by soldier[139]

———

Old french town [*blank*] Nick named Vaide Poche[140]—Old french settlers retain their dress[,] manners &c—cared little for money or lands but avaricious[?] about their negros. met two or three times a week to dance. Very sober & temperate tho Gay—Kept aloof from americans, but began to intermarry with them

Black Hawk[141]—Had a Skin of a black Hawk in his hand & fanned himself with the tail

[*pp. [54–64] blank*]

[*Beginning with p. [65], the journal is reversed. Irving wrote from the inside back cover forward to p. [65]; for the convenience of the reader, the journal is transcribed in that order.*]

[*inside back cover appears to be a list with many items illegible*]

g[142]

Genl Ashley
Judge Wash[143]
[*two lines illegible*][144]
Musquito[?] [*illegible*][145]
[*two[?] words illegible*][146]

138. This word might be "ball."

139. After this word, WI skipped two lines and added a line one-sixteenth inch long to separate paragraphs.

140. On a contemporary map of the "Environs of St. Louis," this town is "Carondelet," the name WI probably intended to fill in later; however, it was called "Vide Poche," meaning "empty pocket." A small village on the west bank of the Mississippi just below Jefferson Barracks and across the river from Cahokia, it was "inhabited by French, or rather a mixture of French and Indian, called by boatmen of this region, *Gumbo* French" (Baird, *View*, p. 227). The people were avid gardeners, and many vegetables sold at market in St. Louis were raised here (Flint, *Mississippi Valley*, I, 312).

141. WI's underlining.

142. At the top of the inside back cover, there is a brass latch; in the upper right corner, there is what seems to be the letter *g*.

143. This word may be the same as the second judge mentioned in the September 14, 1832, entry.

144. The page is badly smudged and stained; there may be no writing on these two lines.

145. This word might be "Bar."

146. The first of these words seems to begin with a *B*.

Greenback[?][147]
Shoes
leather
Cafè[148]

Cumberland mounts Tenness[?] enchanted mounts[149]

On some Spurs of the Cumberland Mounts called the Enchanted Mounts—are marked in the solid lime stone[,] footsteps of men, horses & other animals, as fresh as though recently made, and as distinct as tho impressed upon clay mortar. The tracks often indicate that the feet which made them had slidden, as would be the case in descending declivities, /of$_\wedge$/in/ soft clay[.] They are precisely of the same class with the impress of two human feet found in a block of solid lime[150] stone, quarried on the margin of the Mississippi. The manner in which they were produced is utterly inexplicable

Flint Geog. [151] Vol II.
Tennessee.

———

Screaming of the Jay in the solitude of the woods & mountains—

Pine woods. Solemn sound of the wind thro them—no whispering— among leaves.

147. This word might be "Greenhawk."

148. There is a mark above the final letter of this word—possibly, a smudged grave.

149. The Cumberland Mountains are part of the Appalachian range, beginning in the southwestern part of Pennsylvania and named in Virginia the Laurel Mountains. As the range passes through Kentucky and Tennessee, it forms a portion of the boundary between Kentucky and Virginia and between Tennessee and North Carolina. Its notable features were its "stupendous piles of craggy rocks," thin covering of trees, and alum-filled springs.

150. The *l* is crossed.

151. Trent and Hellman and McDermott read this word as "Essay" (*Journals of WI*, III, 114; *Western Journals*, p. 85). The passage which follows is almost a word-for-word transcription of Flint's description. In the 1833 edition of the *History and Geography of the Mississippi Valley*, this passage is in I, 343; in the earlier edition, it is in II, 12–13. It is not surprising that WI, an avid reader and habitual note-taker, would have Flint's *Geography* with him as he traveled west and would copy from it into his journal. It is also not surprising that WI was drawn to Timothy Flint's specific descriptions of the landscape in this particular book, because it "contained enough of the glamour of the West to cause one contemporary to complain that it was too interesting for reference" (*DAB*, VI, 475).

Timothy Flint (1780–1840) was born near North Reading, Massachusetts, and attended public schools, Philips Academy at Andover, and Harvard University from which he was graduated in 1800. After two years of theological training and preaching, he accepted a call to a Congregational Church in Massachusetts, from which he was forced to resign when parishioners accused him of "counterfeiting coin" in his

Few evergreens in the west—objected by Mrs Trollope[152]—a ⟨sign of fertility⟩[153]

The cypress grows in deep & Sickly swamps[—]the haunts of fever, mosquitos[,] moccasin snakes[,] alligators & all loathesome & ferocious animals &c ⟨that congrega⟩

It loves the deepest, most gloomy & inaccessible and inundated swamps, and south of 33° is generally found covered with the sable festoons of long moss hanging as it seems, a shroud of mourning wreaths almost to the ground. It flourishes best where water covers its roots for half the year

Flint. V. I P 62[154]

Hunters a/c of himself—His fathers log hut solitary on margin of river surrounded by forest. mode of living—careless—plenty—shoot deer, wild turkey—children half wild—without education—two or three books which they could not read

Big rivers all peaceful & gentle—mouth[?][155] ohio
Little rivers noisy & unruly
invincible[?] strength of big giant rivers

---

laboratory. After working in missions in New Hampshire, he and his family went west to Cincinnati in the fall of 1815 under the sponsorship of the Missionary Society of Connecticut. Subsequently he moved farther west, did mission work for eight years, and was the first Protestant to administer communion in St. Louis; also, he researched the flora, fauna, Indians, traders, history, and geography. In addition to books already mentioned, other resulting works were *Recollections of the Last Ten Years Passed in . . . the Valley of the Mississippi* (1826); *The Geography and History of the Mississippi Valley* (1827); *A Condensed Geography and History of the Western States* (1828); *Indian Wars of the West* (1833).

152. In addition to her objections to the manners of Americans, Mrs. Trollope (see p. xxxvii, n. 75), who was traveling west in 1828, also was displeased by most American rivers, valleys, mountains, and forests. The passage to which WI was referring was as follows: "Near New Orleans the undergrowth of palmetto and pawpaw is highly beautiful, but in Tennessee, Indiana, and Ohio, I never found the slightest beauty in the forest scenery. Fallen trees in every possible stage of decay, and congeries of leaves that have been rotting since the flood, cover the ground and infect the air. The beautiful variety of foliage afforded by evergreens never occurs, and in Tennessee, and that part of Ohio that surrounds Cincinnati, even the sterile beauty of rocks is wanting. On crossing the water to Kentucky the scene is greatly improved . . ." (*Domestic Manners of the Americans* [London: Whittaker, Treacher, 1832], p. 32).

153. After this word, WI began another passage from Flint's book.

154. This passage is almost an exact transcription from Flint's *Mississippi Valley* (in the 1833 edition, I, 41–42; in the earlier edition, I, 62).

155. This word could be "south" or possibly, "smooth"; Trent and Hellman transcribed the phrase as "gentle—Ohio—little" (*Journals of WI*, III, 115); McDermott called the word illegible (*Western Journals*, p. 85).

Two Kentuckyians quarrelling—one says put down that rock & Ill fight you

The rock was a stone as big as an apple

double barreld[156] gun

⟨my [*illegible*]⟩

Mighty little giving[?] about the lock.

[?lock gunman[157] the rifle also a/c?]

moon

handmaid a virgin star

Missouri[158]—50 miles above confluence of ohio & Mississippi

Indian corn—38 years successive crop—gourd seed[159]—20 rows

Negro driving team of 6 oxen in Louisville—exclaims—

Get along you fat money making rascals—.

Negros—some prefer hoeing—others ploughing—others driving wagon. Some dislike wagoning because they have to take care of the cattle at night & on Sunday.

Merriest people in these parts—If you hear a broad merry laugh be sure[160] it is a negro—politest people. Fine Gentlemen—

⟨Agst[?]⟩

⟨Negr⟩

Evil of negros ⟨tho[?]⟩ they may be parted from their children—But are not white people so—by schooling—mar-/-riage—business &c[?]

Observation of French trader in West Indies on shutting up counting[?][161] House. If I could go home & not think till morng I should ⟨buy⟩ be a happy man—but this thinking will kill me

156. WI failed to lift his pen between words; therefore, we might also read as "doublebarreld" or "double-barreld."

157. This word might be the two words, "gives me."

158. WI's figure is confusing here, because he would have known by experience and authority that the Missouri River enters the Mississippi approximately 200 miles above the mouth of the Ohio. Apparently jotting unrelated notes as someone, perhaps Governor Clark, was talking about the geography and people of the West, WI may have been referring to the small village of Missouri, which is on the west bank of the Missouri River above St. Charles and somewhat less than fifty miles above the confluence of the Missouri (rather than the Ohio) and the Mississippi. Cape Girandeau is the town in Missouri on the west bank of the Mississippi which was approximately 50 miles above the confluence of the Ohio and the Mississippi.

159. Trent and Hellman read as "crops—ground rich" (*Journals of WI*, III, 115); McDermott used their reading (*Western Journals*, p. 86).

160. WI's initial *s* is unusually formed, beginning below the line and resembling the first of his double *s*'s; an alternate reading might be "laugh &c find it is a negro."

161. This word might be "country."

Ice Spring between Niagara & Hamilton—frozen in summer[—]thawed in winter

Illinois—famous for children & dogs—a house with 19 child/-ren & 37 dogs[162]

———

Cherokees & Kickapoos[163] used to say we'll fight[,] fight[,] fight until we are all dead & then our bones will fight together—but they are now neighbors & friends—thro necessity

—The various western tribes call the Delawares their grandfather—& mediator If one kills another ⟨rela[?]⟩ a friend—relative of the murderer hastens to the ⟨Cherokees⟩ Delaware—who interposes & prescribes a certain quantity of Wampum to cover the deceased

Indians never quarrel ↑& fight↓ when sober—only when in liquor & then lay it all to whiskey—When one Kills another he considers himself doomed—Sometimes mounts his horse & proclaims it—but says come and take me who can

162. After this word, WI drew a line three-eighths inch long between paragraphs.

163. Although not infamous enemies, the Cherokees and Kickapoos were tribes whose background and inclination would often put them on opposing sides of a dispute. The Cherokees, one of the "five civilized tribes" discussed by Grant Foreman in his book by that name ([Norman: University of Oklahoma Press, 1934], pp. 281–420), were of the Iroquoian family but detached from it. They were early called "cave people" because of their location in the southern Alleghenies, before they were tragically removed to Oklahoma in 1838–1839 along what came to be called the "Trail of Tears." They were historically influenced by white settlers, and they were generally loyal to the government in the War of 1812 and the French and Indian War. Their more natural enemies were the Osages. They were also an agricultural and sedentary people, unlike the Kickapoos, whose name means "he moves about."

The Kickapoos were of the Algonquian family and a part of the Sauk and Foxes, tribes they often joined in hostilities on the prairie. They were naturally hunters, horse thieves, daring, and rather savage, reportedly eating parts of the flesh of their enemies as warning. The Kickapoos helped Tecumseh against the United States during the War of 1812, and many helped Black Hawk, a Sauk chief, in his war in 1832 (see n. 134). Because they were hunting acquaintances of the more savage Indians of the plains, the Kickapoos and several other tribes provided a kind of buffer between those hostile Indians and the whites and civilized Indians such as the Creeks. Occasionally roving bands of the Cherokees and the Kickapoos joined to annoy others such as the Chickasaws by stealing livestock, particularly horses, and Negroes (Hodge, *Handbook of Indians*, I, 245–49, 684–86; *Dictionary of Indian Tribes of the Americas* [Newport Beach, Calif.: American Indian Publishers, 1980], I, 525–28; II, 364–67).

AMERICAN JOURNALS, 1832

Number 5

Independence, Missouri, to Cabin Creek, Oklahoma

The manuscript journal is in the Seligman Collection of Irvingiana in the Manuscripts and Archives Division of the New York Public Library, where it is cataloged as #22–3300, Journal 26. It consists of 17 leaves, the first 32 pages ruled with two vertical columns on the left (one of these lines is actually two very closely approximate lines) and one on the right; the last leaf is unlined and loose, and the original first leaf is missing. The pages measure $3^{11}/_{16}$ x $5^{11}/_{16}$ inches; the journal is bound in brown leather, held together with a brown string tied between pages [16] and [17]. The writing throughout is in pencil, except on the front and back covers which is in ink. Blank pages are the inside front cover, the inside back cover (except for number "13" added in pencil in the upper left corner), and page [33]. After the first one-third of page [26], the journal has been reversed, and Irving began writing back to front and upside down from page [34] to page [26].

[*front cover*]

No 5[1]
1832[2]

[*inside front cover blank*]

1. WI's journal number 4 relating events of the journey from St. Louis to Independence is missing; fortunately with the discovery and publication of Count de Pourtalès' journal and letters in 1968, we have a detailed account of those days. According to Spaulding, the editor, Pourtalès "began his journal the first day out of St. Louis and was faithful to it for seven days. He started in a heavy, grandiose style, as if hoping to compete with his associate, the famous Washington Irving. Fortunately, he soon tired of this effort and settled down to writing simple and effective narrative and description, sprinkled here and there with appropriate references to mythical and historical characters and incidents, an evidence of his classical education" (Pourtalès, *Journal*, pp. 12–13). Of course, Latrobe's account continues during this period (*Rambler*, I, 117–43).

2. "1832" was apparently added later.

Wednesday, September 26[3]

Independence[4]

Arrived at the Globe Hotel—Mr Dodge[5] a former missionary among the Osages[6]—comes in a covered waggon with his son &c Disagreed

3. WI wrote "Independence" on the first line of p. [1]; he then began the next line flush left with "Wednesday Sept. 26th." and the third line with a new paragraph describing his arrival at the hotel.

4. Independence, Missouri, a village five miles south of the Missouri River and on the western border of the state, had been settled only seven years when WI visited; the site was initially visited by Daniel Boone, and the town was platted in 1827 as the county town of Jackson County, which had been formed and named in 1826. The first blacksmith shop and wagon factory were built in 1830. In 1831, five Mormon missionaries sent by Joseph Smith arrived to claim this spot as the New Zion, and the following year in June a Mormon newspaper, the *Evening and the Morning Star* began publication. The sect grew too quickly, bought too much land, and was too clannish to suit local residents; conflict ensued and by 1838–1839, they were evicted from the state. Independence was from its beginning one of the major jumping-off places to the West; it was visited and described in May, 1831, by Josiah Gregg as "the general 'port of embarkation' for every part of the great western and northern 'prairie ocean.' Besides the Santa Fé caravans, most of the Rocky Mountain traders and trappers, as well as emigrants to Oregon, take this town in their route. During the season of departure, therefore, it is a place of much bustle and active business" (*Commerce of the Prairies: or the Journal of a Santa Fé Trader* [1844; reprint ed., Philadelphia: J. B. Lippincott, 1962], I, 12; hereafter cited as Gregg, *Commerce*). Latrobe's account of pursuing his duties as the Irving party's unofficial "Commissary-general, and minister of finance to our mess . . . to buy and sell—higgle and haggle—chaffer and cheat, and be cheated . . ." in the "rising city of Independence" is amusing (*Rambler*, I, 139–40).

5. According to McDermott, Nathaniel B. Dodge (1781—1884), born in Vermont, came to Harmony Mission in 1821 and served as its superintendent until 1829 when he moved to Independence. In 1830, he founded Boudinot Mission on the left bank of the Neosho River below Four Mile Creek near an Osage village. The Reverend Mr. Dodge and his family served this mission until 1835; his sons were Leonard, Nathaniel, Jonathan Edwards, Samuel, and Thomas. The trip WI mentioned was initiated by Dodge on September 17 to find schooling for "some of our young men" (*Western Journals*, pp. 89–90, n. 3; p. 99, n. 31).

6. One of the five tribes in the Dhegiha group of the Siouan linguistic family, the Osages were a hunting people, excellent judges and traders of horses. A 1673 map located them on the Osage River, but they ranged from the Red River to the Missouri and from the Mississippi to the Rockies; when the supply of buffalo waned, they went westward to hunt and steal horses. They were aggressive and warlike, generally feared and at war with other Indians, especially the Kiowa, Comanche, Pawnee, Cherokee, Choctaw, Creek, Caddo, Chickasaw, Shawnee, among others, who "spoke of the Osage with abhorrence and called them a barbarous and uncivilized race" (Foreman, *Indians and Pioneers*, p. 23). However, they were generally friendly to the whites and were the first Indians in the Missouri valley to trade regularly with them. The Osage ritual was highly symbolic; their huts were rectangular (very unusual); their dress and many individuals in the tribe

with the Indians. Is settled near the White Hairs,[7] among the Osages[–] keeps school–feathers his nest–

The Southern Indians more shrewd and intelligent than the northern[8]

Mr McCoy[9]–son of missionary–employed as surveyor–

---

were made famous by the artist George Catlin in 1834 (see below, n. 7). The tribe separated into three major groups, largely based on geographical location; dividing in the eighteenth century were the Great Osage, located primarily near the mouth of the Marmiton River, and the Little Osage, located six miles west on the west side of the Little Osage River. The third group, the Arkansas Band, broke off as the result of their relationship with the Chouteau brothers (see pp. 58–59, n. 106); when a treaty at the turn of the century favoring Manuel Lisa threatened to cut into the almost exclusive rights of the Chouteaus to trade with the Osage, the brothers persuaded a large group of Osages to move in 1802 to the Arkansas River near the mouth of the Verdigris. According to Pike, in 1806 there were 1,909 Great Osage, 926 Little Osage, and 1,700 Arkansas Osage (Foreman, *Indians and Pioneers*, p. 23, n. 56). In 1808, the first treaty was signed at Fort Clark in which the Osages ceded to the government one-half of the state of Missouri and northern Arkansas; between 1825 and 1836, the tribe was removed from the Osage River to a fifty-mile wide reservation in Kansas established by a treaty signed in St. Louis in 1825, at which time there were 5,200 Osage Indians. Before 1836, the government maintained an Osage subagency at the Chouteau trading post by the falls of the Verdigris; there were many other posts which connected the Chouteaus and the Osages. (See Mathews, *Osages*; Hodge, *Handbook of Indians*, II, 156–59; and Muriel H. Wright, *A Guide to the Indian Tribes of Oklahoma* [Norman: University of Oklahoma Press, 1951], pp. 189–98; hereafter cited as Wright, *Indians of Oklahoma*; for a detailed account of many Osage hostilities, see Foreman, *Indians and Pioneers*, 10–25, 63–79, 90–112.)

7. The White Hairs were the Arkansas band of Osages who followed White Hair, also called "Pahuska," "Cheveax Blancs," or "Paw-Hiu-Skah"; Foreman wrote that the Indian "derived his appellation of 'White Hair' from a gray wig, or scratch, which he had taken from the head of an American at the disastrous defeat of General St. Clair." Old Clermont, or Claremore, the chief of the Osages, died in 1828, and his son Clermont was the new hereditary chief; however, White Hair was able to usurp the position when Clermont was only an infant. White Hair was very active in the trade controversy (French versus Spanish) and was influenced by the Chouteaus; in fact, according to Foreman, he "was a chief of Chouteau's creating . . ." (*Indians and Pioneers*, pp. 19–20, p. 20, n. 41). White Hair died in 1808, and Young White Hair, who followed him, died in 1833. Portraits of White Hair the Younger and Clermont, painted by Catlin in 1834, are in the Smithsonian Institution and are a part of that museum's Bureau of American Ethnology (see George Catlin's *Letters and Notes on the Manners, Customs and Conditions of the North American Indians*, 2 vols. [London, 1841]).

8. WI added a line approximately three-sixteenths inch long between paragraphs.

9. The father, Isaac McCoy (1784–1846) was born in Uniontown, Pennsylvania, the son of a Baptist minister who moved to Kentucky when Isaac was five. Having married Christiana Polke in 1803, Isaac was "called" to the ministry in Vincennes, Indiana, in 1804; four years later he was licensed to preach and founded a

Thursday, September 27[10]

This morng Mr Ellsworth & Dr ODwyer[11] arrive in old flimsy carriage with two horses driven by a tall negro. Had left the steamboat aground & come by land[12]—

preparations—packing of waggons—Genl Clark.[13] ⟨Thinks[14] the⟩ clergymen the only class of people on earth that he hates—

---

church on Maria Creek. A wheelwright by trade, he was appointed by the Baptist Missionary Convention as the first missionary to Indians in counties in Indiana and Illinois, and he established missions in several states for preaching and teaching. He recognized the resulting problems involved in whiskey trade with the Indians (see Foreman, *Advancing the Frontier*, pp. 25–34) and, as a result, recommended to the government a colonization plan to keep offending whites away from Indians. In 1826, he was made head of the Shawnee Mission in Oklahoma and for ten years made surveys for Indian Reservations (with the help of his sons), established schools, preached, and ministered to the Indians. He received attention for his pamphlet, "Remarks on Indian Reform" (1827); traveled many times to Washington; led surveying parties to mark the Cherokee nation boundaries in 1830–1831; published *History of Baptist Indian Missions* in 1840; and moved to St. Louis in 1842 to become the secretary of the American Indian Missionary Association. Isaac McCoy and his wife lost ten children, five of whom died while he was away on missionary trips; the son mentioned by WI may have been John Calvin McCoy, whom Foreman mentioned as having conducted, under his father's direction, in November 1831 a survey of the Arkansas and Canadian rivers (*Advancing the Frontier*, p. 18, n. 9).

10. WI wrote "Thursday—Sept 27."

11. For references to Dr. Thomas O'Dwyer, see WI's journal entries for September 13, 1832, and October 3, 1832; see also p. 60, n. 107. Latrobe said of "the Doctor" that he was "quite an unnecessary appendage, and I believe he would have felt no disappointment, had his lot been cast otherwise, as this kind of adventurous life was not consonant with his tastes. He had not made up his mind to all those petty troubles which are unavoidable beyond the pale of civilization, and you will always find that such men are sure to meet with more mischances than their neighbours" (*Rambler*, I, 146). Ellsworth's opinion of "Doct O Dwyer" was a contrasting one (see *Narrative*, p. 61).

12. Latrobe described the gathering of the party, calling Ellsworth and O'Dwyer "the laggards of the party" because their steamboat had met with numerous groundings, the final one 100 miles below Independence, and they were forced to make their way through the woods (*Rambler*, I, 127).

13. McDermott included in his introduction a letter from Ellsworth to the secretary of war, Lewis Cass, in which he mentioned his "opportunity to see Gen. Clark, agent of the Kanzas" on the way to Independence (*Western Journals*, p. 24); he identified the agent as Marston G. Clark (*ibid.*, p. 90, n. 6). Clark, as well as other knowledgeable observers of the Indians, including Zebulon Pike, understood that all the Indians, especially the Osages, "secured their horses by stealing them from other tribes; horse-stealing raids formed a considerable part of the normal activities of these Indians; a man's skill as a horse thief advanced him in the esteem of his fellows" (Foreman, *Indians and Pioneers*, p. 21, n. 45).

14. There is a line above this word approximately three-fourths inch long which might be the crossing of the *t* or a line intended to separate paragraphs.

Thinks we ought not to set our faces agst Indians Stealing Horses, ⟨th[?]⟩ must not Shut up the only road left them to honour & promotion

waggons set off at ½ 2 oclock—Mr Ellsworth & Mr Latrobe set off about 3 with Genl Clark for Mr McCoys[15]—I set off at ⟨½⟩ 4 with Mr Choteau[,][16] Pourtales & the Dr.[17]

lose our way in the Praries—after a while get to where the waggons are stationed, by Mr Yates[18] ⟨*illegible*⟩[19] Scene at Mr Yates—⟨Lar[?]⟩ Log hut—large fire—tell stories to children

—Camp—Fire—meat roasted on sticks—Savory—our salon of trees lighted up by fire—sky & stars in the centre—but flitting across—faces of men & black boy roasting meat—greyhound with spectral face[20]—we sit on bear skins & the meat put on spits before us—cut it off with knife & eat—coffee—Mr Yates comes & sits with us. Tall strong pleasant faced fellow—Stretch a tent on cords. spread our mats and sleep—Mr Choteau sleeps at foot of tree. Dr ODwyer in waggon. men on ⟨mat⟩ blankets with feet to fire

15. Latrobe said that on September 27, he and Ellsworth went alone to the "Shawanese Agency on the frontiers and the following day we struck across the wide prairies to overtake our companions, who had meanwhile left Independence, cutting the Santa Fe traders' trail, and, finally bending more to the southward, hit upon that of our own party, which we followed till we found them encamped in the twilight . . ." (*Rambler*, I, 143). Ellsworth reported in the letter to Cass that they also saw Harmony and Union missions and McCoy at his house, where Ellsworth was disappointed that McCoy's surveys were not ready for this particular commission (letter cited in McDermott, *Western Journals*, pp. 24–25).

16. Latrobe described Colonel A. P. Chouteau as a "fine, good-humoured, shrewd man, of French descent . . ." with "courteous manners, and extensive information on every subject connected with the country and its red inhabitants . . ." (*Rambler*, I, 145); see p. 59, n. 106.

17. Dr. O'Dwyer. George Spaulding, in his usually reliable notes, indicated that the doctor was Dr. David Holt and that Dr. O'Dwyer had left the party at Independence (Pourtalès, *Journal*, p. 41, n. 32); however, WI mentioned Dr. O'Dwyer by name several times during this part of the journey, and Holt did not join the party until later (see p. 113, n. 88).

18. Trent and Hellman read as "Mr. Yates" (*Journals of WI*, III, 117); McDermott also reads as "Mr. Yates" but adds a note that the name may be "Gates" (*Western Journals*, p. 91, n. 8). There was a Captain George W. Yates mentioned as participating in a council meeting at Drum Creek in 1868 (Mathews, *Osages*, p. 667). The name could also be read as "Eaton."

19. The word or letters could be "MrY," "MrL," "not."

20. Latrobe mentioned the eight dogs belonging to Colonel Chouteau, whose sense of humor and political feelings prompted such names as "Henry Clay, a greyhound; Jackson, a bull-dog; and Mrs. Trollope, a hound with a number of whelps" (*Rambler*, I, 148). See Latrobe's description of the domestics, *Rambler*, I, 146–48.

Friday, September 28[21]

At peep of day fire made in the ⟨k[?]⟩Camp—preparations for cooking —water brot from neighborg brook. Dogs prying about for food—showers of rain—mats &c spread over waggons—day breaks—find ourselves in a light grove on the edge of a prarie.

horses led in strings to water[—]man riding one[,] leading others [—]whooping to hounds who follow.

Breakfast like supper. Spits placed before us as we sit on mats & cut off strips—

Leave at ¼ to 8. ride along ⟨rig⟩ ridge & over grassy praries—meet people going to Camp meeting—encamp at 12 beside a brook to wait for Ellsworth & Latrobe who are to come in by McCoys trail

A couple of Bee Hunters arrive at the brook, with waggon drawn by 4 ⟨⟨horses⟩oxen⟩ oxen—with Barrels &c to contain Honey—Going to Grand River[22] about 2 days journey from independence—all the country down here being hunted out—Bee hunter 23 years of age[—]plaid upper coat, tan cloth trousers with deerskin tied over them—His companion lying in waggon with rifle—Prarie Hen that they had shot—

Midday Camp—men dispersed cutting wood—one making fire, blowing of spark among dry leaves—Horses turned loose[—]some hobbled—others free rolling on grass—Saddles put round foot of tree Dogs scattered about, nosing & prying ⟨to⟩ Dr ODwy ⟨draw⟩ dragging dry branches [—]wind rustling thro tree tops but passing over the hollow in which we are placed—

Dogs lying down watching with hungry eye all the cooking operations ⟨After dinner⟩ At dinner. Stories Joke[s] &c

After dinner another gang of Bee Hunters—waggon 4 ⟨horses⟩ oxen—2 saddle Horses—long fellow with rifle[—]two Younger ones with rifles ⟨Ge⟩ says they get 37 cents gallon for Honey—collect 100 or 150 gals—Go for amusement as much as any thing else, being a time of year they have little to do—shoot deer[,] Elk &c for their food—

In the Evg Mr Ellsworth[,] Mr Latrobe & young Mr McCoy arrive with another dearborn waggon[23]

—encamp for the night

21. WI wrote "Friday 2⟨7⟩8."

22. The Grand River is another name for the Neosho River, one of the chief tributaries of the Arkansas River. Rising in what is now Morris County, Kansas, and flowing generally southeastward, it received the Cabin de Planche Creek at Hopefield Mission and joined the Arkansas on the right just above Fort Gibson and one-half mile below the mouth of the Verdigris River. The Neosho River is approximately 460 miles long.

23. See p. 10, n. 59, for description of a Dearborn.

Saturday, September 29[24]

Start after breakfast—Mr Younger[25] who was to have driven our new Dearborn deserts—Mr Ellsworth drives—road winds along a ridge, with prarie sloping down into[?] beautiful copses[26]

Stop at log house—pretty young married woman with pretty Sister & fine children[27]

Encamp at Midday after 18 miles—⟨under⟩ ↑in↓ pine[28] grove—repast under tree—preparations of guns—Latrobe arranging plants[29]—Dogs lying about—Plan for Antonio[30] to go deer hunting while we journey this

24. WI wrote "Saturday 20—."

25. Mr. Younger has not been identified.

26. Latrobe noted that there were few farms and clearings and that their journey was through "wide open prairies with long lines of timber trees skirting the course of the creeks and rivers, many of which rose in this elevated corner of the country. The road was merely a track over the natural sod of the prairie, and though practicable in the dry season for such light four-wheeled vehicles as those in our train, the swollen state of the streams often rendered it impassable for weeks" (*Rambler*, I, 148).

27. The lead in WI's pencil ran out after the "child" of "children," but the indentation in the paper of the manuscript makes the last syllable of the word clear.

28. This word could be "fine."

29. Ellsworth described Latrobe's interest in the science of botany: "He always has a little bag slung to his coat button, to receive a new variety—from every kind of stalk and limb (not excepting the grasses) he makes a gathering, and the collection of months is thrown promiscuously together, to be sown in Europe—What a collection!" (*Narrative*, p. 69). Pourtalès, saying that Missouri even during the early fall "is a limitless mine for a botanist," commented: "Latrobe has gathered more flowers here in a week than in the rest of America in five months" (*Journal*, p. 34). Latrobe's enthusiasm is obvious as he went on for two pages naming, describing, and summarizing "a thousand other flowers which I cannot undertake to describe" (*Rambler*, I, 125–26). At one point, he mentioned his "botanizing" (*ibid.*, I, 156).

30. Antoine Deshetres (1791–1854) was born in Florissant, the son of Hyacinthe Deshetres and Francoise Normandeau; he was married in 1812 to Camille Mercier of Florissant. He was connected with the Chouteaus as hunter, trader, and guide; when WI's party hired him, he had recently returned from guiding a party of Seneca Indians who were being removed to the Neosho River. WI's spelling of Antoine's name varies; in these earlier references, he tends toward the "Antonio" spelling. Because the journal from St. Louis to Independence is lost (journal number 4), we do not have WI's initial description of Tonish; Latrobe introduced him as follows: "We had secured the services of a French Creole, accustomed to the country and mode of travelling, who was to serve us in the several capacities of guide, groom, driver, valet, cook, interpreter, hunter, and jack-of-all-trades; and as he became consequently a prominent character, you shall not have to complain of his being kept in the back-ground" (*Rambler*, I, 117). Later, Latrobe continued his account of Antoine, whom they called Tonish, including the fact that he was "Light, active, in the prime of life. . . . Full of make-shifts, and unspeakably useful

afternoon—yelping of young hounds, wind rushing thro trees—Fire of[31] our Kitchen at root of gigantic old tree, threatening to undermine & bring it down. Autumnal tint of trees

Evg encampt. about 5 Oclock on a beautiful plat of land made by the winding of a sluggish brook[—]Fine oak & walnuts—herbage full of flowers—opposite bank of brook fine woods—Mr Latrobe saw two stags—Antonio returns without game

Barking of dogs at wolves prowling round the Camp—Hooting of owl—Pond nuts like fresh almonds—⟨rich[?]⟩ dined Buffalo meat—rich

---

Sunday, September 30[32]

Morning, rise before day/break—breakfast by light of fire—day breaks thro forest—

after breakfast set off with Portales on horseback ahead of the rest—to look for Prarie hens—Mr Latrobe precedes us on foot—

scale a hill—limestone rock & stones full of shells & minature basalt like giant causeway—boundless view of silent Praries[33]—distant hill like Paté de Strasborg[34]

---

in the woods. . . . He was garrulous to excess, in spite of an impediment in his speech. . . . He was a weaver of interminable stories, all about himself and his hunting exploits. We soon found out that he was a most determined and audacious braggart; but it was some time before we all came to the unanimous conclusion, that, for lying effrontery, none of us had ever seen his equal" (*ibid.*, I, 147–48). Ellsworth identified Tonish as "cook as well as hunter and driver of the pack horse" (*Narrative*, p. 11), and Pourtalès called him "our male Antigone, our pioneer, factotum, and guide, Antoine, a little, old, wrinkled Creole, who looked somewhat like an Osage, but dressed like a Creek" (*Journal*, p. 25). In the introduction to WI's *Western Journals* (pp. 49–62), McDermott went into great detail in discussing Tonish as an example of the relationship between fact and fiction in *Tour*, in which WI described this man as a "swarthy meagre, French Creole . . . a kind of Gil Blas of the frontiers . . ."(*Tour*, p. 21).

31. It seems that WI first wrote "at," then drew a loop below the *t* to form an *f* and the word which we read as "of."

32. WI wrote "*Sunday 30*" above the line and flush left.

33. Latrobe added that the view of "vast grass-covered Prairies . . . is monotonous to a certain degree; yet . . . we did not find our journey wearisome. . . . Here and there the country swelled up to a higher level than ordinary, into singular ranges of lime-stone hills, surmounted by what are called 'flint knobs,' which rise not unfrequently some hundred feet above the general level of the country. Over such a chain, called the Mounds, we passed on the last day of the month, and were greatly struck with the regular form and mould of the southernmost excrescence in particular, which rose up in the exact form of a truncated cone" (*Rambler*, I, 153–54).

34. Trent and Hellman said that WI was referring "to the shape of the famous goose liver pâtés made in Strassburg" (*Journals of WI*, III, 120, n. 1).

overtake Latrobe 12 miles off by a brook—waggons [? do n ?][35] not arrive—wait for them[.] Scene on knoll—lying among prarie grass with guns—dogs—game—Horses grazing by us—one & the other go alternately as scouts to edge of distant hill to look out for waggons—

give up hopes of being rejoined and resume our route—Mr Latrobe on foot & Pourtales & myself on horseback—fatiguing ride—wide bare praries—small strips of wood land. 12 Miles further come to a clearing in wood. Log house[.] Mr Fuller of East Hadham[?][36]—his wife daughter of Dr [*blank*] of Philadelph[.] Hospitable reception Good wife[—] busy baking cakes Gets dinner for us—countryman arrives who brings tidings from the Camp[—]Horses had strayed—while at dinner Mr Ellsworth arrives—then Col. Choteau & Dr. ⟨Mr⟩ Take leave of Mr Fuller who refuses compensation—ride with Mr Latrobe by Moonlight to Harmony Mission.[37] arrive at Mr Brights[38]—⟨Sup⟩[39] Kind reception—blazing fire—Half breed Indian girl who waits on us—Mr Requa[40] a missionary—

35. These letters could be "&c do[?]."

36. "Mr. Fuller of East Hadham" which is probably East Haddam, Middlesex County, Connecticut, has not been identified.

37. In 1821, the year following the founding of Union Mission, Harmony Mission was founded among the Osage Indians by the American Board of Commissioners for Foreign Mission; it was on the banks of the Osage River (on some maps, the Marais des Cygnes River), approximately six miles above the confluence of the Osage and Little Osage rivers and 76 miles above the settlement of the White Hairs on the Neosho. The stated purpose of the three missions—Dwight, Union, and Harmony—was "teaching the Indian children agriculture, reading, writing, and arithmetic" (Mathews, *Osages*, p. 525). Mathews believed that the agricultural and educational purposes were served at Harmony because of the presence of "two very intelligent interpreters," Noel Maugraine, who was married to White Hair's daughter, and William Shirley Williams, who was also married to an Indian and who translated the Bible into Osage (*Osages*, p. 526). Union and Harmony were active missions until 1834 or 1836; following that time, Roman Catholic missionaries worked among the Indians of the area.

38. McDermott identified this man as Samuel B. Bright, who was a farmer at Harmony Mission (*Western Journals*, p. 94, n. 17). Mathews mentioned the fact that a missionary, the Reverend Mr. Pixley, and "a Mr. Bright established a branch mission on the Neosho River ninety miles from Union and seventy miles from Harmony and called it Neosho"; this mission had very limited success and duration (*Osages*, p. 531). This person may be the same Mr. Bright whom WI mentioned.

39. This word could be "Safe."

40. William C. Requa (1795–1886), born in New York, came to Union Mission in 1821 and was the manager of the Hopefield Mission, a branch mission of Union, established by missionaries to the Osages in 1823–1824 on the west bank of the Neosho, only four or five miles above Union. Because the treaty of 1828 took from the Osages the land on which Union and Hopefield were both located, the latter was moved in 1830 to the west side of the Neosho near Cabin Creek, and by

Quartered at night with Mr Jones[41] missionary who teaches girls[.] Several Indian girls in the house[,] one about 11 very pretty—Evg prayer—examination of children on chapter of bible—Neat log house—well furnished—

40 children at Harmony

School kept by Mr Jones. Indian children good at writing[,] cyphering & geography

Monday, October 1[42]

Dinner at Mr Austins[43]—Boys at table on one side—Girls the other—comp[an]y in centre—rich beef—beautiful honey—cakes—vegetables

Osage river[44]—⟨?⟩clear Stream willow banks—navigable in part of year for Steam boats—Harmony about 500 miles from mouth

Leave Harmony at 3. O clock[—]Cavalcade. 4 waggons—Horsemen led horses—we hire a half breed called Broken hoof—Mr Choteau hires another—crossing of the osage river—group of Indians on a Knoll looking on.[45]

⟨put[?]⟩

camp after sunset in a beautiful grove at the foot of immense trees—

---

the summer of that year there were twenty Indian families and sixty pupils at New Hopefield with William C. Requa as the manager of the mission. His cousin, George Requa, who had been at Union, came with his wife to Hopefield to teach.

41. McDermott identified as Amasa Jones (1796–1870), a teacher at Harmony Mission and ordained there in 1830; his wife was Roxana Stearns (*Western Journals*, p. 94, n. 18).

42. WI wrote "Monday October 1." at the bottom of the page and began the day's entry at the top of the next page.

43. Daniel H. Austin was a mechanic and steward, who, when Harmony Mission closed, built a mill on the Osage River in 1836; John Austin was a teacher at Harmony (McDermott, *Western Journals*, p. 19).

44. The Osage River, rising in the eastern section of the Indian Territory, entered the Missouri ten miles below Jefferson City and 133 miles above the Mississippi. Flowing eastward over an extremely crooked route of 500 miles, it was the largest affluent of the Missouri in the state and moderately sized boats could ascend for 200 miles during high water; according to one report, steamboat navigation did not commence until 1837 (Gerard Schultz's report, "Steamboat Navigation on the Osage River Before the Civil War," in the *Missouri Historical Review*, 29 [April, 1935], 176, as cited in McDermott, *Western Journals*, p. 95, n. 20).

45. Latrobe wrote, "At the time of our halt [at Harmony] the settlement was surrounded by a number of strolling Indians of the Piankishaw tribe, and these excited the more interest, as they were the first of the Children of the Forest we had seen in the vicinity of their own settlements, and in their own guise. Among the men there were many fine picturesque figures; but the mixture of Indian and European costumes was strikingly grotesque" (*Rambler*, I, 155).

by a brook opposite a prarie[.] moonlight. Owl hoots, Prarie wolf howls–barking of dogs[,] bells of our horses among the trees

Supper. beef. rost ducks & prarie hens, others boiled– Fine effect of half moon among lofty trees–fire of camp with guides indians & others eating round it–dogs lying on grass. waggons–⟨Aftern⟩ Tents by fire light–groups of attendants lying at foot of trees & round fires–

Farm in neighborhood–Mr Summer[.][46] *river*–Little osage[47] ↑ugalagaklu[?]↓ *monshan*[?][48] *meaning where there is much dogwood*

Tuesday, October 2[49]

Cold but beautiful morng ⟨*illegible*⟩[50] revive the fires–dogs creeping round fire & into tent–whipped off with many a yelp–Sun breaks among pine trees–winding stream near by[.] Yesterday passed place of old[51] osage camp–near branch of osage river. Wild plum trees–beautiful prarie–river where they fought the [*blank*][52] into the Stream & killed

46. This farmer was probably Allen Summers, one of three brothers who came from Kentucky to Warren County, Missouri, in 1820, and subsequently to the Osage River area in 1829; Summers lived there until he died in 1849 (McDermott, *Western Journals*, pp. 95–96, n. 22).

47. WI could be referring to one of the three primary divisions of the Osage nation–the Little Osage (see above n. 6) to whom Mathews referred as the "U-Dse-Tsa," or the "Down-Below-People." WI could also have been noting the Little Osage River which rose in eastern Indian Territory just south of the rising of the Osage; flowing east and parallel to the Osage, the Little Osage along with two other tributaries flowed northeast and joined the Osage in Missouri between the towns called Little Osage in Bates County and Batesville.

48. These Indian words could also be "ugalagakher[?] *monsaha*"; Trent and Hellman deciphered as "*Ugatagakuge monsahn*" and wrote an apologetic note about "Irving's handwriting and the transcriber's ignorance of the Indian tongues" (*Journals of WI*, III, 121 and n. 1); McDermott used the same reading and suggested that the second word should be "mon-ca hi," which in Osage meant "dogwood" (*Western Journals*, p. 96 and n. 23).

49. WI wrote "Tuesday, Oct 2."

50. This word could be "in" or "we."

51. WI seems to have written over the *o* an *O*, or his pencil could have slipped.

52. WI could have meant to fill in this blank with any number of incidents in the late eighteenth and early nineteenth centuries in which tribes or alliances of tribes rose up against the Osages whom they feared. The name could have been many French traders who were regularly killed individually or in groups. Pike described one such incident: early in December 1804, a war party of White Hair's town plundered all traders and hunters on the Arkansas River. The following autumn a war party of Potawatomi attacked an Osage camp on the Osage River while the men were away, and many women and children were killed and sixty were taken hostage. Pike was returning forty-six of these hostages to their village, but before they arrived, a war party of Little Osage marched against the Kansa and

them with knives—The place deserted—overgrown with Sumach, hazle-nut, wild plum—prarie silent & lifeless[53]

In the course of the morning we see a Prarie wolf in the distance—Half breed Indians instantly on the qui vive—mount my Pony (I being in the waggon) general gallop across the Prarie—Henry Clay the grey-hound in full chace—Mr Choteau sends half breed boy mounted to turn the wolf, but Pourtales dashes straight forwd & makes the wolf keep ahead so as to escape—returning we start a deer, which after a run couches in a hollow & we lose him

A few miles further we see another Prarie wolf beside a ravine near the road. All set off in chace. Col Choteau & the doctor head him—come to a bare burnt patch of Prarie—the grey hound gets sight of him—fine race. Hound turns him—maneuvers & fight between wolf & hound. Horsemen[54] come up with & try to trample on him—fighting retreat of wolf. Pourtales fires one barrel of his gun, breaks wolfs leg[—]we surround & kill him— —

Beautiful sight of Hunt—Horseman galloping over green prarie—Golden ⟨au[?]⟩ sunshine—Antoine[55] towards the conclusion of chace leaves his waggon—mounts his stallion—& comes thundering along bringing up a corp de secour[56] of bull[?] dog [,] cur[?] &c[57]

———

A few miles further on pass a run of water. Here Broken Hoof visits cabin of his mother & determines to return—pay him off—just then a half breed (Joseph)[58] whom Mr Choteau had left word to follow us arrives & takes his place[.] He is accompd by an old Indian—tuer du

---

young warriors of Grand Osage had attacked whites on the Arkansas (Foreman, *Indians and Pioneers*, p. 24).

53. Through this word is drawn a diagonal line, which seems accidental.

54. WI lifted his pencil between the syllables, but he seemed to intend one word.

55. Here WI spells Antoine's name correctly, abandoning his previous spelling, "Antonio."

56. A "corps de secours," or "troupes de secours": a relieving force or company.

57. WI drew a line five-sixteenths inch long in the middle of the page to separate paragraphs.

58. In his research when preparing *Tixier's Travels*, McDermott discovered in the *Baptismal Records of the Osage Nation* that a Joseph Suisse, probably an adult, was baptized in St. Louis in 1820. On January 14, 1834, Joseph Swiss was born, the son of Joseph Swiss and Julia Mongrain (Victor Tixier, *Tixier's Travels on the Osage Prairies*, trans. Albert J. Salvan, ed. John Francis McDermott [Norman: University of Oklahoma Press, 1940], p. 153, n. 68; hereafter cited as Tixier, *Travels*). Joseph, who had been educated at Union Mission, married Julia Mongrain, the daughter of Noel Mongrain, the famous interpreter, on February 6, 1834, at the Osage Agency (McDermott, *Western Journals*, p. 98, n. 29).

Another Joseph connected with this area might be a more appropriate identifica-

village[59][–]from having, with a party he commanded[,] surprized & massacred a whole village–Indian with his bald head & single tuft of hair[.] Strings of beads hanging from the upper part of his ears–his shoul-/ders & bust bare–blanket swathed round his body–leather leggings & moccasins. Mounted on strong black horse–carries his rifle athwart–

Encamp & dine in a thicket of trees–then perform journey of 1⟨9⟩7 miles across wide naked prarie–extensive prospect from a hill–ridge beyond ridge in Smoky distance. Indian points it out.[60] pass Pawney Hill where 5 Pawneys defended them/-selves agst large party of ⟨o⟩Osages See two Prarie wolves which escape–⟨Clo⟩ White cloud of smoke from burning Prarie. Sun enters in to[61] smoke[.] Spur on to light fires–limestone country–wind by moon/-light down into wood–pass

---

tion: Joseph Maugraine (Tixier spelled "Mongrain"), the son of Noel Maugraine and Pahushan, the daughter of the first White Hair; Joseph Maugraine was also the brother of Julia Maugraine Swiss. Tixier wrote seven years later than WI, "Two half-breeds continually went from the house to the store and back. The Mongrain brothers, the sons of a Canadian and an Osage beauty, are the interpreters of the Fur Company; both speak French and the Osage language with perfect fluency. The elder, Baptiste, is fifty years old. He is tall, and his face, quite sunburnt, is darker than that of the savages. His head is covered with a dirty black scarf tied on his forehead. His very black hair hangs on the side, and is tied at the back in a small pigtail. Baptiste wears a filthy, colored shirt, *mitas*, deerskin moccasins, and a scarlet breechcloth, at the belt of which are tied his tobacco pouch, his pipe case, and scalping knife. Over all this he wears a blue blanket. Such is the physical appearance of the Chief of the Nion-Chou village.

"His younger brother, Joseph Noël, is one of the village warriors, but is still too young to be admitted to the council with the right to speak. His brother, in order to keep a greater influence, keeps him away from the fire of the braves, in spite of the right to which his proven courage entitles him. Both brothers are chiefs of lodges and each one has two legitimate Indian wives" (Tixier, *Travels*, pp. 123–24).

59. The "tueur de village": killer or slayer of the village. WI used the verb form, "tuer," rather than the noun. Latrobe called him an "old Osage warrior of the Grey Hairs' Band, whose name was 'the Destroyer of cities;' alias, 'the Burner of Wigwams' " (*Rambler*, I, 157–58).

60. According to Latrobe, this Indian is the one called the "tuer du village" by WI; he explained to the white travelers that all the land before them "was the present domain of his tribe," the members of which had left their summer location on the Neosho River and had gone either westward toward the Salt Plains for the autumn's buffalo hunt or to other hunting grounds in the territory (*Rambler*, I, 158). See also on this page, Latrobe's description of the view from the "brink of the ascent."

61. Even though WI lifted his pencil between words, he may have intended one word, "into."

thro it to bank of brook where we make fire and when joined by carriages encamp

Story of Antonio and the two Kegs of powder behind him on horse with which he dashed thro Prarie on fire

Encampt at Pawnee creek[62]—

Branch of Osage[63]

———

Old osage Indian—Killer of village—great warrior—chief—at present ambassador[64] to procure a bag of nails

Wednesday, October 3[65]

Beautiful morng Breakfast Scene—men round pans & Kettles—groups of little hounds looking on—growling & snapping of large dogs—now & then yelping from a Scourged cur

At day break Indian gets up mounts his horse & away—Osages never eat early in morning when travelling—stop about 10 or 11 for that purpose[66]

———

In the course of the morning we meet various parties of osages—men & women. ⟨hu⟩ on hunting expeditions women leading horses—with packages—skins for beds—meat corn &c[—]papposes & puppy dogs on the packages—lads with bows & rifles walking[.] Fine erect port of osage warriors—noble attitudes.[67] Meet osage interpreter[68]—with wife &

62. Pawnee Creek, one of the creeks which flowed north into the South Fork of that branch of the Osage River called the Marmiton River, in Vernon County, Kansas, south of the Great Osage Village (see Mathews, *Osages*, p. 105).

63. WI added a line five-eighths inch long to separate paragraphs.

64. Above the first letter of this word, there is a short line (one-sixteenth inch long) which could be a short underlining of the word on the line above, "great," or merely a slip of the pencil.

65. WI wrote "Wednesday Oct 3."

66. WI added a line five-sixteenths inch long to separate paragraphs.

67. Latrobe wrote, "The warrior was generally seen marching first with his firm straight step, and upright bearing, burdened with nothing but his rifle. Many of them were good specimens of the North American Indian 'brave,' and wore the head shaved, with exception of the scalp-lock on the crown, and painted vermillion. In general, they were tall, and in a certain degree martial in gait and bearing—yet though straight-limbed, too spare to be handsome. The countenances of the squaws, on the contrary, after true savage fashion, were bent towards the earth, from the burden of skins or other articles imposed upon their shoulders, and secured in its position by a strap of leather over the temples. The Indian ponies had also their burden of baskets and utensils—and the round head and glistening eyes of many a little pappoose bobbed up and down among the motley bundles, of which the load was composed . . ." (*Rambler*, I, 159).

68. Probably Baptiste Maugraine; see pp. 82–83, n. 58 above.

daughters the former a daughter of Choteau[69]—squaws riding with umbrellas

Warm day—wide treeless prarie trembling with heat.^ ↑columns of↓ Smoke hanging lazily in various direc/-tions on horizon. Kindled by Indians to drive the game to the Praries—Encamp about 11 at clear brook—↑party of↓ Indians ⟨by⟩ squaws ↑& children↓ encamp by us[.] Squaws cutting wood & dragging great branches of trees.[70]

Our dinner, surrounded by Indians—groups of Squaws & children who keep somewhat aloof—

Ride 12 miles after dinner to ⟨Nath[?]⟩[71] ↑Rev N↓ Dodges[72] house—⟨*two words illegible*⟩[73] near Osage ⟨Miss⟩ Village[74]—put up at the house. comfortable tea furnished by Mrs Dodge

Young osage couple in the Neigh/borhood, the girl well educated at^ ↑Harmony↓ Mission[75] The young man but slightly educated[—]recently married—undertaking farming—their relatives[76] come to see them. camp

69. This dash is unusually formed, curving diagonally left to right from the line; perhaps WI's pencil slipped when he was indicating a period or dash.

70. Latrobe seemed horrified by the appearance and treatment of the squaws; earlier in his narrative he described three Indians at Harmony Mission in detail and simply added, "Their squaws were hideous to behold" (*Rambler*, I, 156). He disapproved of the Indians' looking "on with listlessness and apathy at the labours of the squaws, who meanwhile were busily employed in bending the twigs of the underwood into a skeleton hut—covering them with mats and skins—making their fires, and cooking. In every thing they seem to be the drudges of the males. As to personal appearance, with very few exceptions, I can only specify three degrees,—horrible—more horrible—most horrible!" (*Rambler*, I, 159–60).

71. WI also might have written first "Mr," then flush to left edge of page, "Rev"; he apparently then crossed out both and above the line added "Rev N."

72. The Reverend Nathaniel B. Dodge (see p. 72, n. 5).

73. These words could be "a mile," "a hour," "a tea," etc.

74. Osage Village was the trading center on the right bank of the Neosho or Grand River, five miles below White Hairs' Village. Tixier described this village: "Nion-Chou, otherwise called Manrinhabotso ('The Village Which Scrapes the Sky') is the commercial capital of the Osage; it is the residence of Mr. Papin, the agent of the American Fur Company, and of the interpreters of the Government and of the Company. Nion-Chou's own chief is Baptiste Mongrain, whom we know" (Tixier, *Travels*, pp. 126–27). Mathews says that when the Frenchman Cortambert came here in 1835, he spelled it "in his phonetics 'Manrinhabatso,' which signified, he wrote, 'more or less,' that which touches the sky. The village was the trade center of the tribe, and here lived M. Melincourt Papin, representative of the American Fur Company, and the son of Noel Maugraine, Baptiste, who presented himself as 'chief' of the village. . . . Heretofore this village had been mentioned as the Osage village, since here the furs were brought to be traded" (Mathews, *Osages*, p. 592).

75. Harmony Mission (see p. 79, n. 37).

76. This word could be read as "relations."

before the door & eat them out of house & home[.] Young man cannot ⟨ke[?]⟩ help giving away provisions &c to his tribe. When we visited them we found two Indians (man & wife) lying at a fire kindled before their house.[77]

———

Indian we met today in mourng—dirt on his face—does not eat till sunset—⟨When pa⟩ The dead are painted white & other colours when buried—

A chief lately deceased was buried sitting up under a mound—.[78]

———

We spread our skin beds on the floor of room in house. Antoine &Co[?] light a fire, cook their supper & sleep under trees. Every one has his caprice said Antoine—for my part I think it much better to camp here—

Intense curiosity with which an Indian watches Dr ODwyer while he shaves

Beautiful clear ⟨*illegible*⟩[79] river[80] by Mr Dodges

Thursday, October 4[81]

Leave Mr Dodges at ¾ past 7. provided with large family loaf of bread—we have a journey of 30 miles to make over open Prarie before we can find a camping place. There being water in the interim but no wood—Pass through the village of the White Hair (osages)[.][82] Monument of chief who died lately—Mound on a hill surounded by railing—three poles with flags—trophies—a scalp—scalping Knife &c—He had

77. WI added a line one-half inch long to separate paragraphs.

78. Tixier explained the aftermath of the death of a young Osage: "As soon as he had breathed his last, his widow began to weep and to wail; she went to each lodge clapping her hands three times and uttering three cries. When she had visited every lodge in the camp she returned to her own. The dead man was then placed in a sitting position, wrapped in a blanket, in full war paint, with his weapons around him; in this position he was lowered into a grave dug in advance. A small mound was soon raised over this new tomb" (Tixier, *Travels*, p. 156). WI added a line seven-eighths inch long to separate paragraphs.

79. This illegible figure might be a dash with the pencil's having slipped; it could also be an *R*, an *L*, etc.

80. Neosho River.

81. Irving wrote "Thursday Oct 4."

82. This village, about five miles above Osage Village on the right or west bank of the Neosho River is "sometimes called White Hair's Village because the old chief lived there"; its Indian name was "No'n-Ni-O'n-Ba" meaning "Peace Pipe" (Mathews, *Osages*, p. 592). Tixier described this second village of the Great Osage tribe: "Naniompa ('The Village of the Pipe'), called thus because of a black stone good for making calumets which is found thereabouts, is composed of from forty to fifty huts. Its chief is Old White Hair, the uncle of the present Head Chief" (*Travels*, p. 127).

killed four Pawnees[83]—while looking at it an Indian approached and ⟨*illegible*⟩ stood by the tomb—a relation of the deceased—After we had rode on we saw him standing like a statue by the tomb

Passed over vast prarie where not a tree or shrub was to be seen[—] a view like that of the ocean. ⟨Mr⟩Col Choteau & Pourtales (who had left us yesterday at the dining place to go to the Agency)[84] rejoined us, with three spare horses

About 3 oclock arrive at a grove on the banks of stream & encamp—↑place called↓ *la Bete*[85]—wood entangled with rich underwood grape vines—pea vines &c Fine trees—flights of Perroquets Called la Bete or the

83. The Pawnees, a part of the Caddoan family, derived their name from the word "pariki," which meant "horn" and referred to the peculiar way they arranged the scalp lock: it was stiff, flat, and curved backward (Hodge, *Handbook of Indians*, II, 213–14). The Pawnees lived in what is now Nebraska on the Loup Fork of the Platte River and were divided into four bands. These Indians were permanent village dwellers, farmers as well as hunters, but they were excellent horsemen; they called themselves "men of men" and according to reports they were a tall, muscular people of energy, physical stamina, courage, loyalty. They were known for tribal ritual, myth, and a religion which focused on one god and which was a part of their daily lives. Friendly to the U.S. after their lands were taken over by the Louisiana Purchase, the Pawnees were the natural enemies of the Osage, and the accounts of the wars between them are many. WI would have been interested in the tribe; his nephew traveled among them the year after WI's expedition and the account was published the same year as was *Tour.* (See John Treat Irving, Jr., *Indian Sketches, Taken During an Expedition to the Pawnee Tribes [1833],* ed. John Francis McDermott [Norman: University of Oklahoma Press, 1955].)

84. Mathews told of trouble that the colonel's brother was having at the agency: "In this year of 1831, the [Osages] . . . were baiting their agent, P. L. Chouteau, in many trivial ways. They also stole his chickens and killed his hogs and came to the agency to sit with him in large numbers, frequently straining his courtesy through his attempts to honor their own old tradition of feeding anyone who came to their lodges.

"He wrote to Clark about it. He wrote that the agency was situated on a 'Barren rocky Hill in a prairie about ¾ of a mile from the Neosho and ought to be moved for that reason alone, but there was another reason as well; the government had stupidly built the agency building over an Indian burial mound the reflection of which causes unpleasant feelings'" (*Osages*, p. 550). Apparently, Colonel Chouteau and Pourtalès traveled the six miles west from the mission to the agency, which was on the right bank of the Neosho.

85. Labette Creek flowed southeast into the Neosho or Grand River just north of the Kansas-Oklahoma line. Tixier wrote that his party camped along the "river A-la-bête" on their way north to Mr. Papin's log cabin (*Travels*, p. 259), the direction from which WI's party was coming. Foreman described another excursion to settle Indian matters in 1828 during which the party came to "Riviere du Bete or 'River of Reptiles,' now called 'La Bête' or 'The Beast'"; then Foreman cited WI's account of the name-giving myth (*Indians and Pioneers*, p. 270).

Beast because the Indians saw a great and terrible animal there, the like of which they never saw before or since—

Story told by Col Choteau lying at the foot of a tree—⟨*illegible*⟩

↑*Indian[—]wagrushka e abbe* creek↓[86] Next to this creek is Nickanansa[87] a tribe of Indians ⟨Settled⟩ ↑hunting↓ on that creek ⟨left it⟩ Struck their tents to come on this. A young man who ⟨return[?]⟩ had been to St Louis returned to the Creek & came to the encampment—found it deserted—a young girl alone there, to whom he was engaged to be married, ⟨what⟩ where is the camp—it is struck—they are gone to such a place—& what are you doing here[?] waiting for you. He gave her his bundle and walked ahead according to Indian custom. ⟨Custom[?]⟩ approaching the camp the girl sat down at foot of a tree & said I will wait here, it is not proper for us to return together. He entered the town, told his sister to go after the girl—She is dead—died a few days since. His relatives surounded him weeping & confirmed the story. He returnd with them to the tree—the Girl was gone[,] the bundle lay there. The young man fell *dead*[88]

———

A little girl at White Hairs had died[.] they buried with her her play things[.] she had a favorite little horse—they killed & buried her with it.

———

An old squaw left alone when her party had gone hunting prayed the great spirit to make something to amuse her—He made the mosquito

———

Pawnee Boy At Mr Choteaus agency there is a Pawnee boy 12 years of age who is anxious to run away & return to his own ⟨cou[?]⟩ people—they fear if he did he would reveal where the horses were kept &c & all the secrets of the land ⟨where he was⟩ He has a sister with whom he is always plotting in Pawnee language—once when 7 years old he ran away with horses but was retaken. He was told if you run away again we will send 12 osage boys with bows & arrows to shoot you—Give me

86. This inserted material consists of one line which WI seemed to add later; it is flush left and above the first line. Trent and Hellman read as "Wagrathka e abbe" (*Journals of WI*, III, 126). McDermott deciphered as do we, and he reported that according to La Flesche's *Osage Dictionary*, the creek should be spelled "Wa-gthu-shka i-a bi," the Osage name for a disappearing monster (*Western Journals*, p. 101, n. 37).

87. Trent and Hellman read as "Nickanansor" (*Journals of WI*, III, 126).

88. The following paragraphs are separated by lines of seven-eighths inch, one-half inch, one-half inch, three-fourths inch, one-fourth inch, and one-half inch long.

said he 12 arrows and let your boys come & well see who has the worst of it

---

Chattering ↑& laughing↓ of the Frenchme[n] & Half breeds at their meal ⟨at foot of tree⟩ Mr Choteau laying at foot of tree & joining in—Screaming of flights of parrots—snapping & quarrelling of dogs—

Moonlight vista thro the forest—distant dewy tint of trees—Hooting of Screech owl. ⟨Mr⟩Col Choteau remarks superstition of Indians when^ ↑an↓ owl is[89] heard ⟨*illegible*⟩ several nights, they think it follows the encampment & forbodes the death of one of the party—

These creeks empty into the Neosho[90]

Friday, October 5[91]

towards morning rain & thunder—holds up about day break. An Indian visits us. encamped about a mile distant[,] attracted by the tinkling of our horse bells—Had been hunting yesterday & killed two small deer

After a while he departed to his camp from whence three Indians came & brought pieces of fresh venison. Col Choteau made them presents of Tobacco—

Leave encampt. at 10. ride all day over wide monotonous praries—cry given of a wolf at a distance—saw something seated on a ⟨Small⟩ hill. All hands on the alert. flankers sent out—turned out to be a solitary Indian who begged for food—gave him biscuit—[he] gave us the disagreeable intelligence that all the osages had departed some time since from Fort Gibson on their Buffalo hunt

↑showers in the distance—lowering sky↓[92] ⟨Pas⟩ ride after dark across gloomy plain[—]descend into thick grove ⟨& [*illegible*] showers⟩ & encamp for the night

89. The word "is" is unusually formed and may have been written over other letters, perhaps "ap."

90. WI may have intended to list some creeks which empty into the Neosho River. Foreman pointed out how important to the settlement of the West were the water-power producing rivers and tributaries and cited a report by Isaac McCoy: " 'Water privileges for machinery are found at the falls of the Verdigris, and on Ten-mile creek, Four-mile creek, Prior's creek, Rock creek, Cabin creek and Upper creek' on the west side of the Neosho; and Spring Creek, Saline Creek, Flag (Spavinaw) Creek, Honey Creek, Bayou Menard, Greenleaf Creek and Illinois River on the east side" (*Advancing the Frontier*, p. 18).

91. WI wrote "*Friday 5*" above and to the left of the first word of the paragraph.

92. These six words comprise an entire line inserted between lines, perhaps after the paragraph had been completed or after WI had crossed out the initial letters of the paragraph, "⟨Pas⟩."

⟨Enca[?]⟩ Brook of the Cabin de Planch[93]
Shang e te shenga[?][94]

Saturday, October 6[95]

Soft morning. Misty. Beautiful forest. Large trees intertwind with grape vines[96] & clambering vines[,] rich lands[?].[97] Yesterday saw prickley Pears small. Sent Joseph the Half breed on foraging party among the groves[,] brought rich store of Pawpaws[98]

———

This night horses had ⟨p[?]⟩ excellent ⟨camp[?]⟩[99] *range* [–] pea vines & cane—[100]

[*After nine lines of p. [26], Irving reversed the notebook and wrote from the back forward, from p. [34] to p. [26].*[101] *This portion of the journal is undated*[102] *and is transcribed in the order in which Irving wrote it.*]

93. Cabin de Planche Creek, also called Planche Cabin or Plank Cabin Creek, rose in the northeast corner of Oklahoma and flowed south and then east to join the Neosho or Grand River. Hopefield Mission (see pp. 79–80, n. 40) was built on the west side of the Neosho just above the mouth of the creek. Foreman wrote that the name probably commemorated "the presence of a cabin made of boards" (*Indians and Pioneers*, p. 270). WI left the first one-third of the line blank and then attempted the Osage translation of the name of the creek; Trent and Hellman did not attempt a reading of these last two lines (*Journals of WI*, III, 128), and McDermott referred to them only in a note in which he called them "almost completely undecipherable" (*Western Journals*, p. 103, n. 42).

94. The spelling could also be "shinga."

95. Irving wrote "⟨*Friday* ⟨5⟩6⟩ ↑Saturday 6↓."

96. WI did not lift his pencil between words, and although the distance between syllables suggests two words, he may have intended one word, "grapevine."

97. This word could be "undr," an abbreviation for "undergrowth"; Trent and Hellman read it as "verdure," as did McDermott (*Journals of WI*, III, 128; *Western Journals*, p. 103). By comparing the formation of the word and its context with those in the October 15 entry, we think the best reading is "land."

98. WI added a line three-eighths inch long to separate paragraphs.

99. The crossed-out word could be "range."

100. Latrobe described the usual care and feeding of the horses: each rider "unsaddles his steed, hobbles it, as the term is, by tying the two fore-feet close together, and sends it hopping into the forest like a kangaroo, crashing and scrambling through the gigantic and entangled brushwood, which rises under heavier timber" (*Rambler*, I, 150).

101. At the bottom of p. [26], the top one-third of which contains the last nine lines of the October 6 entry, three words appear upside down, "these domestic hunters"; these are the final words of the undated portion of the journal written from the back forward.

102. The next journal (number 6) begins with another October 6 entry.

Mustard
⟨mr[?]⟩ nutmeg[?]–
cups & saucers
[?some character of our camp?]

[*p. [33] blank*]

Race of dogs in the Rocky mounts. supposed to be a cross breed of the Buffalo[?] wolf.[103]

———

Old father Vail[104] addressed the Indians on the necessity of industry &c to happiness[.] An Indian replied—Father I dont under-/-stand this kind of happiness you talk of—You tell me to cut down tree—to top it—to make fence—to plough—This you call being happy—I no like such happi/-ness. when I go to S Louis, I go to see Choteau, or Clark—He says hello[105]—and negro ⟨wit[?]⟩ comes in with great plate with cake—wine &c[.] he say eat drink If he want any thing else he say hello[106][—] three, four five six negros come in & do what he want[.] that I call happy—he no plough—he no work—he no cut wood—

Ah but he has negros to do all that[.] well father—you go to our great father[,] tell him to find me one two three negros to cut wood & plough for me and Ill be ⟨cont⟩ willing to be happy like white man but for a man 50 years old to have to plough &c—Im too old—[107]

———

An agent newly arrived was preaching up as usual about their being civilized & happy—one old Indian affected to sleep. then waking up, What father—still about that word[?] happiness dont talk of that any more Ill tell you what I call happy—to have my gun—a wide range—to

103. WI added a line seven-sixteenths inch long to separate paragraphs.

104. According to Mathews, the Osages were fortunate to have men such as William F. Vaill, the Chouteaus, Clark, Lewis, Maugraine, Papin, McCoy among them, because they were men of "conscience and humanity" (*Osages*, pp. 587–88); for example, "Mr. Vaill of Union Mission wrote to the commissioners when they were counciling with the Osages in April [1833] attempting to convince them that they should move to their reservation. He wrote that there was no one to speak for the Osages, and he submitted a written argument against the efforts to remove them from their old home. He said that his argument was well received by the commissioners except. [*sic*] Rev. Schermerhorn, who was impatient with suggestions which might be in defense of the Indians" (*Osages*, p. 551; here Mathews followed very closely Foreman's account in *Advancing the Frontier*, p. 123).

105. This word could be "hollo."

106. This word could be "hollo."

107. To separate the following anecdotes, WI added lines between them of three-fourths inch, one-half inch, five-eighths inch, and nine-sixteenths inch.

hunt—to kill buffalo—to have plenty to eat—to eat & drink till full—to smoke—to lie down on our backs, beat our bosoms & sing—

Juror declines to be empanelled in a trial of an Indian for murder[.] he pointed to a scar on his head. This scar I recd. when two brothers were murdered by Indians—I cannot be an unprejudiced arbiter of them

———

Place of old Osage camp on ⟨Osage⟩ branch of Osage river—overgrown with bushes—wild plums &c

———

Backwoodmen go ahead to tread down the nettles

Mr MCoy—missionary appointed to treat with ↑Cherokee↓ Indians. A Cherokee was at Washington when he was there[.] Mr MCoy applied for his son to be appointed Doctor—another surveyor—another agent[.][108] The Cherokee returned & told his friends this man is not for God ⟨but for h⟩ nor for us but for himself. He wants to grasp every/thing—They would not make a treaty with him—

———

Farmers beyond Independence the frontier town seldom come to the village—they are content to raise food enough for themselves—get wild Honey to trade[?][109] sell for clothes &c—Lead a Lazy life in this easily cultivated & prolific country—

St Louis[110] before settling [or coming? or suffering? or ingoing?] of Yankees—young men
played pipes [prayer?] [*illegible*] wors[?] to
old people & had [ladies?] looked
on

Prarie dogs live in villages. owls & rattlesnakes live with them[.][111] Some say the latter inhabit only such holes as the dogs have deserted

108. Two of Isaac McCoy's sons were Dr. Rice McCoy, who died in June, 1832, and John Calvin McCoy, a surveyor (see pp. 73–74, n. 9).

109. This word could be "store" or "save."

110. Trent and Hellman made no attempt to decipher these five lines, not mentioning them (*Journals of WI*, III, 130); McDermott indicated that four lines are illegible (*Western Journals*, p. 104). The lead seems to have been out of Irving's pencil, but the impression on the page helps to identify some of the words by lines.

111. Flint described the prairie dog: "This animal has received its absurd name from the supposed similarity of its peculiar cry, or note, to the barking of a dog. In other respects there is little resemblance to that animal. It is of reddish brown color, interspersed with some gray and black. The color of the underside of the body is not unlike that of the skunk. It has rather a wide and large head, short ears, black whiskers, and a sharp and compressed nose. It sometimes exceeds twice the size of a common gray squirrel. . . . Like the beaver they are social and gregarious, living on the dry prairies in large communities, some of which occupy a

in consequence of the death of some relation—

—Story of Prarie dog, owl & rattlesnake who kept house together[112]

———

Indians at Mr Dodges mission—had 80 acres ⟨of [?sown soil?]⟩ & plowd & sown with corn for them—each put his horse, hobbled into his part of the patch—but as there were no divisions the whole was nearly eaten up[113]

Indians had near 200 head of cattle—oxen, cows, calves &c When the warriors went to the Buffalo hunt they left old men to guard them—after several days the old men called a council—our brothers[,][114] said he[,] are by this time in the midst of the buffalos & have meat a plenty—It is great pity that while they revel we should want—suppose we have a chace of our own ⟨Aft[?]⟩[115] so said so done—they Killed four oxen and all ate till they could scarcely crawl. A few days after[,] another council—our friends must be still among the Buffalos. sup-/-pose we have another chace—so said so done—& the 200 head of cattle melted away before these domestic hunters—[116]

———

[*inside back cover blank*]

[*back cover*]

No 5

---

circuit of miles. . . . There are several occupants, probably all of the same family, of one burrow." He says of a "species of small rattle snake" that it is numerous on the prairies and that "It is said, in the regions far to the west, to consort with prairie dogs, and to inhabit the same burrows" (*Mississippi Valley*, I, 73, 78).

112. The line separating paragraphs is one-half inch long.

113. Latrobe's account is more complete: "The Agent, who, seeing the impossibility of getting [the Indians] to do any thing when the object is not manifest and of speedy fulfilment,—incloses a large tract, sows it with maize, keeps it in his own hands till ripe, and then, summoning the band, says:—'My brethren! your village is composed of twenty lodges—here are twenty acres of ripe corn—take it and divide it justly.' The chiefs grunt their approbation—'It is all good—very good!' The satisfied Agent goes to bed, and when he gets up at sunrise the next morning, sees three hundred hobbled horses eating, fighting, and trampling the corn into the earth, one of the joint possessors having had the bright idea that by hobbling his horse and putting him into the field, the share appertaining to him might be gathered without any manual labour or mental exertion on his part; a felicitous idea, which is soon hailed and followed by the rest. This is a fact!" (*Rambler*, I, 161).

114. This word could be "brethren."

115. These letters could be "agai" or "assu."

116. WI added a line one-half inch long to conclude this undated and reversed portion of the notebook on p. [26]. Approximately two-thirds of the page is blank between this one reversed line of three words and the nine lines which are the concluding ones of the October 6 entry.

AMERICAN JOURNALS, 1832

Number 6

Cabin Creek to Fort Gibson to Red Fork River, Oklahoma

The manuscript journal is in the Seligman Collection of Irvingiana in the Manuscripts and Archives Division of the New York Public Library, where it is cataloged as #22-3300, Washington Irving Journals, Volume 27. It consists of 40 leaves, each page ruled very faintly with a double column of vertical lines on the right and a single vertical line on the left. Its 80 pages with yellow gilt edges measure $3\frac{11}{16}$ inches wide and $5\frac{11}{16}$ inches long; it is bound in a faded brown leather cover, held together with brown string tied between pages [40] and [41]. The writing is in pencil except the last half of a list on the inside front cover and two numbers written over in brown ink as well as the number "14" in dark ink in the upper left corner; on the inside front cover has been recently added in pencil the NYPL catalog indication "Journal 27" in the lower left corner. The designations of notebook number and date on the front and back covers are in ink in Irving's hand. The following pages are blank: pages [2], [4], [45], [61], [73], [75], [79], and [80]. After page [60], Irving reversed the notebook and began writing back to front from page [78] to page [62]. There are two sketches in the notebook: on page [44] there is a drawing of a river scene, and on page [67], a sketch of a camp site.

[*front cover*]

No 6 [*illegible*][1]
1832

1. To the upper right of the number "6," there seem to be two letters which are smudged beyond transcription; they are probably "th."

[*inside front cover*][2]

Mr Ellsworth	$ 7 [*illegible*]
Pd for shirts [*illegible*]	7[3] [*illegible*]
Lent me	2[4]
Pants[?]	2 37½
Shirt[?]	7 12½
pd to Frenchman[?] [*illegible*] 9 [*illegible*]	
[? Arkansaw firing?] [*two words illegible*]	
	[*illegible*]
on tour	37½
Billet–	5
Blk. man	. –50
	$ 19 37½
Postage –	2.25[5]

[*The first eleven lines of p. [1] are so nearly illegible that what can be read is meaningless.*][6]

———

[?precisely the same pretty pooch Dawson it ate sat further from me I despair not having room?]–

[*p. [2] blank, very much water stained*]

2. Except for the four items on this list in ink ("on tour," "Billet–," "Blk. man," and "Postage") and the numbers following the items, also in ink, the notes on this and the following page are extremely faded and smudged and, therefore, very difficult to decipher. The list seems to be composed of items and expenses incurred when Irving was preparing for the trip west from Fort Gibson; Ellsworth, in his account, has a similar list and says that it was on October 9 when the shopping was done (*Narrative*, pp. 7–8).

3. Written over pencil in brown ink.

4. Written over pencil in brown ink.

5. This number could be "1.25." Following the number, WI left one-fourth of the page blank. Recently, someone has added in the bottom left corner of the page in pencil, the NYPL catalog listing, "Journal 27."

6. A questioned attempt at deciphering by lines is as follows:
[? Form Space
Have you a wife Sam
Take me no wife mostly only now
& then bothersome Fancy
⟨Ha⟩ I expect her permanently
settled–horses
&c Dr [*illegible*] ↑[*two words illegible*]↓ with the
Why have we permanently settled US
infantry–Capt to be [*two words illegible*] reacting
to the army ?]

Saturday, October 6[7]

Left encampt this morning and rode through mist which gradually cleared up & shewed wide prarie—with distant line of green woody hills that looked like cultivated country. It seemed as if we could distinguish fields of grain—groves[—]pasturages—glades &c

Our Sportsmen shot two turkeys near our last nights encampt. about ½ past 11 arrived at Mr Requas establisht. on the bank of the Neosho[8] which is here a broad fine[?][9] stream, clear & with a gentle current

Mrs Requa[10] from Connecticut (Fair/field) Fine looking woman. Says when she [*blank*] first came here they ⟨have⟩ had no house. Slept under trees. was in fine health never better—

—Indian farms. Old Indian scout[?] left at home to take care of house[11]

———

our dinner, fine steaks, of venison cut from Venison ham

[*p. [4] blank, water stained*]

Leave Requas at 2—ride over Prarie—12 miles until we come in sight of the Saline—Pleasant country—Looks [*illegible*] like Park Land[.] Hill where Pawnees used to hide their effects when going hunting or to war—Holes still to be Seen[.] old Osages told Colonel of it—

Covey of Prarie Hens—Pigeons. come in sight[12] of Cols House[13]

7. In the middle of the first line WI wrote "1832" and then flush left on the second line "Oct 6."

8. For discussions of William C. Requa and Hopefield Mission on the Neosho, or New Hopefield, see pp. 79–80, n. 40. Latrobe called Requa "Mr. Riquois" (*Rambler*, I, 171).

9. This word could be "fair."

10. WI met the first Mrs. Requa; she was Susan Comstock, who came from Wilton, Fairfield County, Connecticut, to Harmony Mission in 1821 and married William C. Requa in 1822. She died here at New Hopefield Mission in June, 1833 at age thirty-seven. Requa next married the sister of the Reverend William B. Montgomery, who with Requa's assistance learned the Osage language and wrote a grammar, *The Osage First Book*; the second Mrs. Requa died at New Hopefield in October, 1835 (Foreman, *Advancing the Frontier*, p. 121, n. 12; p. 143, n. 13).

11. WI added a line one-fourth inch long to separate paragraphs.

12. Because of ink blots it is difficult to determine whether the reading is "Pigeons come in sight" or "Pigeons. come in sight."

13. Latrobe called the Saline, "an estate situated on the romantic bank of the Neosho, about fifty miles above Fort Gibson. It was the property of the Colonel, whose welcome home amid a crowd of Negroes, Indians of divers tribes and of both sexes, dogs, pigs, cats, turkies, horses, ducks, all looking fat and happy, was an extremely amusing sight" (*Rambler*, I, 171–72).

white Log house with Piazza surrounded by trees—Come to beautiful clear river Group of Indian nymphs half naked on the banks—with Horses near Arrival at House—old negro runs to open gate—mouth from ear to ear—Group of Indians round tree in court/yard, roasting venison—Horses tethered near—Negros run to shake hand & take horses[.][14] some have handkerchief round head—Half breed—squaws[—] negro girls running & giggling[—]Horses. dogs of all kind—Hens flying & cackling—Wild turkeys[—]tamed geese—Piazza with Buffalo skin thrown over railing—House[?][15] with guns[,] rifles.

Supper, venison stakes—Roast beef[—]bread cakes, coffee. waited on by half breed—sister of Mr Choteaus concubine[16]—adjourn to another room. ⟨Indians ar⟩ pass thro open Hall in which Indians are seated on floor. They come into the room—two bring in chairs, the other seats himself on the floor with his knees to his chin—⟨dog[?]⟩ another Indian glares in at the window—

House formed of logs—⟨two parts⟩ a room at each end—an open Hall with staircase in the centre Attic[17] rooms above—In the two rooms on ground floor two beds in each room ↑with curtains↓—white washed log walls—tables of various kinds. Indian [*illegible*] ornaments &c &c

Half breeds loitering about the house. dogs & cats of all kinds strolling about the Hall or sleeping among harness at one end of the piazza

In These establishments the world is turned upside down[:] the Slave the master—the master the slave. The other[18] has the idea of property[—]the latter the reality. The former owns [—] the latter enjoys it. ⟨The former has had the anxiety to gain[,] the care to keep [—] the latter the⟩

The former has to plan & ⟨the⟩ scheme and guard & economize—the latter thinks only of ⟨the⟩ living[,] enjoying[—]cares nothing how it comes or how it goes—

14. To the right of this word and extending to the line below, there is a vertical line one-half inch long in pencil.

15. This word could be "Room" or "Home"; the initial letter has been written over another.

16. According to George Foreman, Rosalie was the concubine; Masina, her sister (*Pioneer Days in the Early Southwest* [Cleveland: Arthur H. Clark Company, 1926], p. 92; hereafter cited as *Pioneer Days*). WI, in the *Tour*, mentioned that Antoine Lombard's sister was "concubine to an opulent white trader" (*Tour*, p. 31), but he identified neither the girl nor the trader. At that point in the *Tour*, the party was at the Verdigris Trading Post.

17. This word could be "other" or "to the," written together.

18. This word could be "Slave."

Sunday, October 7[19]

Breakfast—Coffee & cream. roast ↑ribs of↓ beef—venison steaks[—]wild turkey fricassed. Indians send in roast venison & beef[—]Milk that looks like cocoa nut milk—

After breakfast Mr Smith[20] who keeps school for Col Choteau calls at house[.] wears calico ⟨sui[?]⟩ surcoat after the Indian cut. Has lived many years with the Cherokees.

Ride to the Saline[21]—⟨Col⟩ Major Rogers[22] house. He & his wife cherokee half breeds. He absent at cherokee council—which has been in session 4 weeks, being discordant.

Mrs Rogers fine looking woman Her son a tall fine looking young man. married to a handsome tall half breed—⟨L⟩

19. WI wrote "Oct 7 Sunday—."

20. McDermott depended on Foreman's identification as B. H. Smith (*Western Journals*, p. 109, n. 7).

21. Saline was a salt spring about a mile from the Colonel's house; Tixier described his first impression of the Great Saline when the "sun had dispelled the mist, which from a distance looked like a large expanse of water. The Saline then appeared like a large smooth plain, nine miles wide and a great deal more in length. . . . The salt formed a crust a few *lignes* thick. . . . The salt was not crystallized in large enough amount for us to gather it pure. Therefore we filled the bags with a mixture of salt and sand with which we loaded our horses" (*Travels*, pp. 249–50). On the east bank of the Neosho, the Grand Saline was Colonel Chouteau's primary trading post in the area; it was subsequently a post office serving the Cherokees.

22. John Rogers, a Cherokee chief, was mentioned in a letter from Governor McMinn to the Secretary of War as "a white man of more than forty years residence in the Cherokee Nation [who] has removed to the Arkansas with a very numerous tribe of connections" (Foreman, *Indians and Pioneers*, p. 64, n. 3). Rogers left Tennessee in October, 1817, with thirty-one Cherokees whom he was leading to their new home on the Arkansas; they arrived in April, 1818. In 1825, a treaty assigned to some of the half-breeds in Chouteau's family the salt springs which Colonel Chouteau later sold to Sam Houston; subsequently the springs were bought by John Rogers and he called his home at the salt works the Grand Saline. He worked these mines until October, 1843, when the Cherokee Council took them (*ibid.*, p. 62). Foreman referred to Charles as "an enterprising Cherokee, son of John Rogers"; he was also the brother of Dianna, who was supposedly the Cherokee wife of Houston. When the Rogerses left Tennessee in 1817, Charles was forced to dismantle his whiskey stills, but he chose a new spot on the Spavinaw Creek, which entered the Neosho between Hopefield Mission and Chouteau's Grand Saline, where he had the water power to operate a gristmill and distillery. Having learned the business from his father, Charles supplied a large whiskey market, particularly in Fort Gibson after transporting the goods down the Neosho. WI saw soldier-laden boats looking for whiskey stills and traffic as the party descended the river from Fort Gibson (see p. 162); Ellsworth later reported to the government the extent and impunity of this trade. A great flood in June, 1833 (which partially destroyed

Log house with Piazza. Locust trees—Saline in valley. babbling[23] springs—

Ride to Hill above where Pawnee village formerly stood. Holes in the hill where the Pawnees used to hide their effects when they went hunting

In crossing the river[24] we see the same Nymphs whom we saw yesterday—They were wading across. one returned and played about in the water[25]

¼ mile from the Colls house is his race course on a beautiful little level Prarie. He has a great numbr[?] of Horses—which the blacks drive by the house in a drove[?]

Leave The Saline at 2[?][26] O clock with Mr Ellsworth in Dearborn for Fort Gibson[27]—Antoine drives the dearborn—⟨sm⟩ William the Blackboy follows in smaller Dearborn. Cross Prarie—Prarie Hens. ⟨Th⟩Heavy thunder storm on Prarie—Put down the oil skin sides of waggon. Cross swoln brooks. drive thro woods. pass river where a negro servant & horse belonging to Mr Choteau were drowned by swelling of the river—

Sun sets in clear streak—but clouds over head—arrive about ⟨½ past 6⟩—7 at Union Mission[28]—Mr Vail[29]—His wife a connecti-/cut woman—Comfortable House.—at ring of bell repair to refectory in another build-

---

Rogers' dam and still), and laws forbidding whiskey manufacture and sale terminated Charles Rogers' business; he filed a claim against the government for the loss (Foreman, *Advancing the Frontier*, pp. 27–28, especially p. 28, n. 28).

23. This word could be "bubbling."

24. WI apparently crossed the Neosho River at this point unless he called the Spavinaw Creek a river.

25. WI added a line five-eighths inch long between paragraphs.

26. This number could also be an uncharacteristically formed "7" or "9."

27. Latrobe and Pourtalès, having remained at the Saline, were not with WI and Ellsworth at this point; see p. 104, n. 47.

28. Union Mission was on the western bank of Neosho River, 25 miles north of its mouth, one mile north of Spring Creek, in Mayes County, Oklahoma. (See p. 79, n. 37 for additional information regarding Union Mission.)

29. According to Foreman, the newly arrived Creeks and Cherokees found in Union Mission a convenient school for their children, the former beginning to attend in 1829 and the latter in 1830. Along with George Requa, Abraham Redfield, and their wives, the Reverend and Mrs. Vaill conduced the school (*Advancing the Frontier*, pp. 121–23). William Fowler Vaill (1783–1865) was born in Hadlyme, Connecticut, was graduated from Yale in 1806, and was appointed missionary and superintendent of Union Mission from North Guilford, Connecticut, leaving in April, 1820, and arriving at Union in February, 1821. Vaill married the former Asenath Seldon of Hadlyme, Conn., in 1808; unable to adjust to the hardships of mission life at Union, Mrs. Vaill went insane, and in June, 1834,

ing–50–Scholars–Cherokees[,] Delawares &c[–] their ↑tribes↓ shew great anxiety for the education of their children[30]

Monday, October 8[31]

Leave the Mission after Breakfast–9 Oclock. towards noon see an Indian on a mound who mounts his horse & comes to enquire news of the Cherokees

⟨Approach the⟩

Arrive at Genl Campbells[32]–banks of the Verdigres[33]–leave luggage there for ⟨Mr⟩ Pourtales & Latrobe. ride thro woods & cane brakes to the Arkansas[34]

---

she and her husband returned to Connecticut. She declined; her husband resigned his position in September; and she died in November. Foreman reported that in "the autumn Mr. Vaill's big house at Union was unroofed and chimneys were blown down by the wind" (*ibid.*, p. 146 and n. 21).

30. Mathews noted the difference in the Osage attitude toward education and that of the Cherokee: "Mixed-blood settlers began to bring their children to the missions to be taught, chiefly because they would be an encumbrance to flight when the painted giants [Osages] should appear. The mission 'family' were given a feeling of success, but by the early part of January [1822] they had more children than they could accommodate.

"These were Cherokee mixed-blood and fullblood children thrust by their parents upon the missions in their fright. The Osages took the view that the missions were bad medicine for their children, and the few who had been given into the care of the Union Mission 'family' on the Neosho and Harmony Mission on the Osage River were called for by their bluff-frowning parents" (*Osages*, p. 486).

31. WI wrote "Monday 8."

32. John Campbell was Indian agent for Western Creeks from 1830 to 1834. The agency was on the east bank of Verdigris River, three miles above the mouth. Latrobe and Pourtalès went from the Saline "by way of Union, to the Western Creek Agency on the river Verdigris, not far distant from the Fort [Gibson]" (Latrobe, *Rambler*, I, 172). Their plans to hunt with the Osages were foiled, and Latrobe wrote that they were glad to join their companions "in overtaking, and subsequently accompanying an armed expedition to the Westward, which had been despatched a day or two previously in that direction, by the Commander of the Cantonment [Colonel Arbuckle]. An Indian runner had been sent after the body of Rangers composing it, with orders to the officers to halt till the Commissioner and his party should come up with them" (*Rambler*, I, 174).

33. The Verdigris River, rising in Kansas and flowing southward through Arkansas, joined the Arkansas River approximately fifteen miles above the mouth of the Canadian River. Navigable for 150 miles, the Verdigris flowed almost parallel to the Neosho, along which WI's party had been traveling from October 2. According to Mathews, the river's Indian name was derived from the gray-green bark of the sycamore tree (*Osages*, p. 181, n. 1).

34. The Arkansas River, also spelled by contemporaries "Arkansaw" or "Akansas," rose in the Rocky Mountains near the source of the Del Norte, and

Indian on horse back with Indian girl behind him & strapping squaw before—Arrive on banks of Arkansas—tolerably clear stream[,] neat look of white fortifications—blockhouses &c of fort Gibson[35] opposite

Cross in Scow & arrive at Gate of Garrison—Guard Cleanly dressed round the ⟨g⟩Gate—Sargeant with Irish brogue—culprits in pillory & riding the wooden Horse—⟨c[?]⟩arrive at Col Arbuckles[36] quarters—Log house[37]—⟨it[?]⟩

---

flowed eastward for several hundred miles, then southeastward to Fort Smith and finally across the state of Arkansas. Flint said of the "principal river of this territory" that it was the "next largest western tributary of the Mississippi after the Missouri"; of its approximate length of 2,100 miles, it was navigable for 1,980 miles along a broad channel with few obstructions. Flint wrote that during the summer, "it pours a broad and deep stream from the mountains upon the arid, bare, and sandy plains," and the chief tributary streams were the "Verdigris, Negracka, Canadian Fork, Grand river, Six Bull, &c" (*Mississippi Valley*, I, 279).

35. Fort Gibson was established in April, 1824, as a result of Indian unrest, particularly Osage-Cherokee conflict and a recent massacre; Colonel Arbuckle (see below, n. 36) was ordered to take his five companies from Fort Smith, which was too far from the Osage concentration to be effective, and to establish a new position at the mouth of the Vertigris (Foreman, *Indians and Pioneers*, p. 167). By June, 1824, there were 328 men on duty there, and in 1831, the entire Seventh Infantry was assigned to Fort Gibson. (See Foreman's chapter, "The Beginnings of Fort Gibson," *Advancing the Frontier*, pp. 35–48, and an 1845 map opposite p. 36.) Ellsworth described his first impression: "On the morning of the 8 of Oct, we reached the north side of Neosho or Grand River; and came in site of the numerous little log buildings, that compose Fort Gibson lying on the opposite side of the river—Although I had formed no definite idea of the Fortress, yet it did not equal my expectation—the barracks were erected in a square form 700 by 800 feet; In some instances the walls of the building & in others the stockades with port holes for musketry, form the exterior—" (*Narrative*, p. 2).

36. Colonel Matthew Arbuckle (1776–1851), formerly at New Orleans, was ordered to Fort Smith in July, 1821; in November, he left with four companies of the Seventh Infantry, but low water and disease delayed his arrival until February, 1822. Mathews wrote that Colonel Arbuckle was depressed on his arrival because of the loss of many of his men, the extent of malaria at the fort, and the disease caused by bad whiskey sold to the soldiers: however, he "apparently knew something of red man psychology" (*Osages*, p. 494), a fact which was supported by his constant attempts to make peace among the Indians, particularly the Osage and their neighbors. Ordered to establish a new position on the Neosho, Colonel Arbuckle was the commander of Fort Gibson from its beginning in 1824. Recurring poor health prompted several leaves, but his name was a dominant one in the history of this part of the West; at least three camps were designated "Arbuckle," the final one a permanent post built on the Washita River and Wild Horn Creek, named Fort Arbuckle in June, 1851, for the general who died earlier that month (see Grant Foreman's *Indians and Pioneers* and *Advancing the Frontier* for frequent references to Colonel Arbuckle).

37. Ellsworth says of the buildings that they "appear to be fast going to decay,

Tuesday, October 9[38]

Wednesday, October 10[39]

Leave Fort Gibson ↑escorted by 14 rangers[40] [&] Lt. Penticost↓[41]—ride with Col Arbuckle—Genl Houston[42] to Col Choteaus—picturesque

---

having been erected several years, and constructed of materials not durable when exposed to the weather—The only timber here is the oak . . . all the plank[s] are sawed by hand—the sides of the buildings are hewed logs, plasterd with mud in the interstices—the roofs are covered with oak staves—the inside[s] of the best houses are the square sides of the timber, sometimes white washed" (*Narrative*, p. 4). Ellsworth's assessment was accurate; Fort Gibson would soon become even more inadequate. Discipline was a problem as a result, especially leaving the fort without permission, gambling, and heavy use of illegal whiskey. The fort was rebuilt, beginning in 1845, and it was abandoned and reoccupied as a garrison twice before its final relinquishment in February, 1891.

38. WI wrote "Tuesday 9" and left the following four lines blank. That day at Fort Gibson was a busy one for WI and Ellsworth as the latter explained: "The remainder of the 9th was occupied in making arrangements—We were without horses, clothes, or provisions. We rode up to the Verdigres, to see our friends Latrobe & Pourteles to invite them to join us—but Mr. Pourteles was fixed upon the Osage trail, and could not be diverted." He went on to describe their buying horses, coats, pantaloons, shirts; hiring a guide-interpreter; packing and gathering arms for protection; and, in the evening, "writing letters to our dear friends at home" (*Narrative*, pp. 6–8). It was in one of those letters to his sister that WI explained, "I found that a mounted body of rangers, nearly a hundred, had set off two days before to make a wide tour to the West and south, through the wild hunting countries by way of protecting the friendly Indians who have gone to the Buffalo hunting and to overawe the Pawnee Indians who are the wandering arabs of the West, and continually on the maraud—Col Ellsworth and myself have determined to set off tomorrow in the track of this party—" (*Letters*, II, 727).

39. WI began this entry without indenting "Leave Fort Gibson ↑escorted by 14 rangers Lt. Penticost↓ Wednesday Oct 10 ride with Col Arbuckle. . . ."

40. Ellsworth described the fourteen rangers: "Soon after breakfast, on the 10th, the Lieutenant (Mr Penticost) was introduced to us, and informed us the escort was ready—we went to see the troops. Their countenances showed the effects of late sickness, and they appeared too feeble—but they were all *eager* to go—their costumes, were as as [*sic*] various, as the mock parades of the military in New York & Hartford" (*Narrative*, pp. 8–9).

41. Lieutenant Joseph Pentecost, the first lieutenant, was in the service until October, 1833; he did not, according to Ellsworth, possess "energy enough for the station," and worse, he and the second lieutenant "were pleased to take the execution as gentlemen, but rarely appeared as soldiers on duty & under pay" (*Narrative*, p. 8, n. 4, p. 24). Latrobe called him "an invalid Lieutenant" who was in charge of "twelve or fourteen invalid Rangers" (*Rambler*, I, 176).

42. General Samuel Houston (1793–1863), having been governor of Tennessee, came up the Arkansas River on the way to the Rocky Mountains; he disembarked

scene crossing river[43]–⟨*illegible*⟩ Creek with turban, one end hanging over blue hunting shirt–horn rifle looked like Arab

Scene at Col Choteaus on the banks of the Neosho[44]–Group of Osages [–]blankets–leather leggings & moccasins–hair cropped except ⟨lit⟩ bunch at top–Bust bare or wrapped in blanket

–Creeks–calico ^↑hunting↓ shirts– –^↑scarlet & blue &c↓ handkerchief round head–leather & scarlet leggings–

Groups of riflemen–on legs[?] or with horses–green blanket coats–Half breeds. horses & dogs–[45]

Hunters in leather shirts

Log cabbins–Stately trees about river with virginia creeper

Bustle at Blacksmiths–shoeing horses, making spoons to melt lead for t[?][46] bullets.

–Old trapper in there. Half breed boy in moccasins–light Straw cold [colored] Hunting shirt

rifleman in Calico shirt leggings &c

Negro shoeing horse

---

in March, 1829, at the mouth of the Illinois and went to the home of the Cherokee Chief Jolly, who called Houston his son, the Raven. Houston became interested in the problems of the Indians and established himself three miles north of Fort Gibson in a building he called the "Wigwam" and from which he traded. In October of the same year, the Cherokees offered him a certificate of admission to the tribe, and he lived, dressed, and married as one of them (Foreman, *Indians and Pioneers*, pp. 231–49). Foreman quoted a missionary's letter written in September, 1830: "We regard the residence of such a man as Gov. Houston among the Indians as a most injurious circumstance. He is vicious to a fearful extent, and implacably hostile to Christians and Christianity. . . . He has very considerable influence" (*Advancing the Frontier*, p. 312). His influence was not great enough to elect him to a seat in the Cherokee Council in 1831, and he was angry; he subsequently left his Indian wife and went to Texas.

43. WI could here be referring either to the Neosho (or Grand River) or to the Verdigris; Chouteau's store was on the east bank of the Verdigris River, but to get there from Fort Gibson, the party had first to cross the Neosho, then the Verdigris. From the similar description in the *Tour*, WI probably described the Verdigris (*Tour*, p. 28).

44. WI probably meant to write "Verdigris" instead of "Neosho"; Chouteau's trading post was on the west bank of the Verdigris River opposite the Western Creek Agency of which John Campbell was the agent.

45. The lines following this sentence and the next are only one-sixteenth inch long, but they apparently separated paragraphs.

46. This questioned letter could be "⟨f⟩."

tall half breed in rifle shirt–blue trousers–moccasins with pack saddles

little dog looking on at shoeing horse as if studying the art or waiting for his turn

Rifle in corner–old rifle against work bench

Leave Col Choteaus at 2 Oclock[47][–]ride thro rich entangled bottom by hamlets of Indians,[48] negros &c to [*blank*]

Encampt of rangers in circular grove–rich bottom–High trees–horses tied round–feeding on corn–brook near. trees tinted with autumn –tinkling of bells–men making messes at fires[–]some shooting at marks with rifles–parrots flying chattering through trees

We pitch our tent in the farm yard of Mr Berryhill[49]–family suffering with bloody flux–Log houses of various sizes. Skin of bullock stretched and drying–dogs–full moon pale–damp air–distant fires of rangers in grove below

Robin Hood, life & characters–Mr E–in half citizen half chasseur dress–embroidered leathern indian Pouch. Powder horn with red worsted band–

Thursday, October 11[50]

up before day–Half breed pointing out the north star & positions of 7 stars as indicating day light–

Our landlord large man with squeaking broken voice. ⟨Story of⟩ Mr Portales boots lost on the road[–]one was found–a creek Indian

47. It is interesting that WI did not mention the reunion with Latrobe and Pourtalès at Col. Chouteau's store, especially since he had written to his sister, Mrs. Paris, the previous day from Ft. Gibson, "I am uncertain whether Mr Latrobe & Pourtales will accompany me on this further tour–" (*Letters*, II, 728). Ellsworth noted that the two men and their servant were "desirous to accompany us, as far as the *Osage trail* . . ." (*Narrative*, p. 10).

48. Pourtalès was interested in this "long line of wooden huts inhabited by Creeks"; he made several observations about the Creeks, among them that they and the Cherokees were "more industrious than the other Indians . . ." (*Journal*, pp. 42–43).

49. Ellsworth wrote, "We pitched our camp in the door yard of a half breed Indian because we could here procure corn for our horses for the last time. . . . The Indian's family were mostly sick, with the bloody flux . . . some children too, had the whooping cough; and the groans & coughs kept me awake during the first part of the night" (*Narrative*, pp. 11–12).

50. WI wrote "Thursday ⟨16⟩↑11↓." Because this particular number (two straight lines) gives little clue as to handwriting, we can only assume the correction is WI's.

was seen with the lost boot on looking for the other[51]—Thats really a funny ta⟨il⟩le said our huge host with a small voice

Set off at ½ past 7—ride through deep rich bottom, by ⟨Several[?]⟩ a village of Creeks extending along a rising ground[.] pass several creeks, one with scarlet turban and plume of black feathers like a cocks tail. one with white turban & red feathers—Oriental look—like Sultans on the Stage—Some have racquets with which they have been playing ball Some with jackets & shirts but legs & thighs bare. ^ ↑middlesized↓ well made & vigorous—Yesterday one had brilliant bunch of ⟨*illegible*⟩[52] Sumach. They look like fine birds on the Prarie.

Pass house of a tall red haird lank ^ ↑lanthern-jawd↓[53] settler with one eye habitually closed when he winks—Says some of the Osages are near. They had stolen one of his horses. Says they will steal horses & then bring them home pretending to have found them and claiming a reward[54]—

Pass on to house of the last settler—the last trace of civilization[55]—⟨? in a hamlet of ?⟩ Informs Portales & Latrobe of a Camp of Osages in a swamp They determine to go there & seek guides to conduct them to the Osage Hunting party[56]—

51. Latrobe told the story in much greater detail and with his usual sense of humor (*Rambler*, I, 177); Ellsworth, who by this time was very critical of Pourtalès, used this incident to illustrate the younger man's carelessness (*Narrative*, p. 12).

52. This word may be "pass."

53. An attractive alternate reading is "lanthorn-jawd" ("lanthorn" is a British term for "lantern"; WI's subsequent use of this word supports the spelling with an *o*); another reading may be "leathern-facd." In *Tour* WI wrote "a lank lantern visage" (p. 38).

54. Neither Latrobe, Pourtalès, nor Ellsworth mentioned this man. He made quite an impression on WI, however, for in the *Tour* he called him "a tall raw boned old fellow, with red hair, a lank lantern visage, and an inveterate habit of winking with one eye, as if every thing he said was of knowing import" (*Tour*, p. 38).

55. Ellsworth misdated this event as October 12; he remembered that they "travelled all day, along the north side of the Arkansaw River and left the last settlement (Mr Hardrigers) a Creek about 10 o clock" (*Narrative*, p. 15), which is ten hours later than WI and Latrobe remembered. Williams and Simison suggested that this settler's name was Josiah Hardridge, a Creek Indian involved in the Negro slave trade (*ibid.*, p. 15, n. 2); McDermott identified him as Hardage, a man living near Choska, Wagoner County, Oklahoma (*Western Journals*, p. 113, n. 21).

56. Ellsworth attributed this information to the Osage Indian whom they met at 10 o'clock leading a horse which was not his: "This Osage informed us of a

We find ourselves off the track of Capt Deans[57] party of rangers which set off several days since & set off to find it—Said to be two miles off. Part with Latrobe and Pourtales[58]—Lose our way in a Swamp—tramp for some time through brake & briar and mud—After extricating ourselves we are ovtaken by Latrobe & Pourtales—with the old frontier man who is guiding them to the Osage camp

Just then we meet old lanthernd jawd man who had lost his horse—Had just met with Osage leading him back—who said he had wanderd to their camp

Lanthern jawd man was for tying him up & giving him a series of lashes but we interfered[59]—

Find that frontier man advised Latrobe & Pourtales not to ⟨come⟩ ↑go↓ on to Osages. They were too far to be overtaken—Pawnees were out, Osages were prepared for war &c Pourtales was not to be disuaded —He & Latrobe procured an Indian guide[60] & set off on their quest—but a young man, clerk of Mr Choteau who had set off with them from his house abandoned their enterprize & joined us[61]—Stopped ⟨to en-

---

small Osage camp, a few miles from our path, and Mr Latrobe employed him to conduct him to this camp, where the trail of the Osage hunting party began—" (*Narrative*, p. 13). The search was apparently unsuccessful.

57. Captain Dean is actually Captain Bean. WI also called him "Dean" in the October 13 entry (when WI first met the captain) and thereafter correctly identified him as Captain Bean (see below, p. 113, n. 87).

58. WI's notes are confusing here; it appears from this journal account that Pourtalès and Latrobe left the party twice during this day—the first time with a frontier settler who told them about the Osages and with whom they returned, and the second time with Chouteau's clerk, Mr. Braily, and an Indian guide whom they had hired. Braily returned immediately and Latrobe and Pourtalès, later that day. Ellsworth's account had the foreigners leaving only once—after the Osage Indian with the horse had come up to them about ten o'clock, told them of the Osage camp a few miles away, and was hired by Latrobe to guide them to it. They left at eleven o'clock and returned that evening (*Narrative*, pp. 13–15). It was generally this version, with several interesting variations from the journal and Ellsworth's account, which WI adopted for his *Tour* (pp. 44–48).

59. Ellsworth's account of this incident with the Osage and the horse varies from WI's, both here in the journal and in the *Tour*; Ellsworth wrote that the conflict was between the Osage Indian and some Cherokee Indians, the latter who claimed the horse was theirs and had been stolen and who wanted to flog the Osage (*Narrative*, p. 13).

60. Ellsworth identified this guide as the Osage Indian who would have been flogged had they not interfered (*Narrative*, p. 13).

61. This reference to Chouteau's clerk is WI's first although he had been with Latrobe and Pourtalès since October 9 when he joined them at the Verdigris Post and with the Irving party since October 10. Irving mentioned him again in the October 13 entry. Ellsworth spelled his name three ways in his account—"Mr

camp⟩ ↑about noon↓ in rich bottom, tall trees—fine *range* of Pea vines, for the horses to repose & feed for an hour—Flock of Parroquets—Beautiful transparency of ⟨V[?]⟩ the Varied autumnal leaves with the sun shining through them Horses cropping the pea vine—men lying about in the deep bed of foliage

resume our route[—]come in sight of the Arkansas river[62] and pass frequently thro rich bottom in sight of it. View beyond of beautiful country—looks as if cultivated. Groves, glades, woody upland, willowd[?] shores, Sandy—beaches—⟨fine⟩ Sunny Look of The Groves—

Pass thro ⟨old⟩ Osage ^ ↑war↓ Camp recently deserted[63]—⟨twigs⟩ cabins formed of twigs bent & rushes[—]fire in center. Council wigwam. dancing place Arrive about 3, at fine grove in rich pea vine bottom—with clear stream of water—traces of recent encampt. of Capt Dean[.] one fire still smoking—

Encamp here for the night[64][—]hobble the horses & turn them loose to graze—Latrobe & Pourtales arrive finding it impossible to get on with their slender attendance[65]—⟨*two words illegible*⟩ determine to con-

---

Brialy," "Mr Brealey," and "Mr Brailey." Ellsworth applauded Braily's good sense to leave Latrobe and Pourtalès on their fruitless search for the Osage hunting party; he was also concerned about Braily's resulting loss of provisions and Pourtalès' indignation (*Narrative*, pp. 12–14, 16).

62. The party had cut across land from the Verdigris; just before the Arkansas River is joined by the Verdigris and Neosho River, it deviates from its generally southeasterly course to flow south, then east, then northeast, then southeast again. WI's party had proceeded in a fairly direct northwesterly direction on the northeastern side of the river; therefore, this apparently was WI's first view of the Arkansas River.

63. The date of this event is uncertain; perhaps the party passed several deserted Osage war camps between October 11 and 13. WI mentioned two camps, this one and another the following day. Ellsworth's only allusion was dated October 13 when he wrote that they "passed the late camp of the Osage War party, who had been out against the Pawnees" (*Narrative*, p. 16). Pourtalès wrote in his October 12 entry, "This morning we passed several abandoned Osage camps, some of which were very large, containing from forty to eighty habitations. . . . They had been left one or two nights before" (*Journal*, pp. 43–44). WI made no correction of the date as October 11 when he included it in the *Tour* (p. 46).

64. Ellsworth said they traveled "20 miles in a north west direction" during the day (*Narrative*, p. 15).

65. Ellsworth and WI made careful distinctions between their servants and those of Latrobe and Pourtalès; the "slender attendance" numbered only two—the Osage Indian (see below, n. 66) and the Osage interpreter hired on October 9 at the Verdigris Trading Post whose name was Antoine Lumbard or Lombard. Ellsworth wrote that immediately "Mr Latrobe & Mr Pourteles found their single servt was wholly inadequate to drive 2 pack horses besides 2 Racers," but he did give the "Servant of Mr Latrobe & Co" credit for bringing in four turkeys (*Nar-*

tinue with us. Their Indian agrees to accompany them for a blanket & breech clout[.][66] Firing at mark with rifles

This day in the woods we encounter a wandering dog—He is mad cried one—he is blind cried another. He came rambling along with inflamed eyes—taking notice of no one but bewildered by the noises. The poor animal was following the traces of his master. Ill shoot him said a ranger. by no means[,] cried I[,] let the poor animal go on[.] he rambled among the horses & pursued his course[67]

———

---

rative, pp. 10–11, 36). Pourtalès referred to this "half-blood" as Antoine Lambert and credited him for successfully performing the tasks of guide (*Journal*, pp. 52–55). Latrobe was explicit: of the "half-breed, named Antoine . . . indolence seemed to be the prevailing feature. It was depicted in his heavy, sleepy, dark eye; and the Indian blood evidently predominated over the French. He was willing and active enough when excited, but it was no common occasion that would incite him to action. For an hour together he would stand at the camp-fire, with his cloak tightly twisted round his body, his arms motionless within, and gaze upon nothing with a fixed glance, in which there was neither life nor speculation. In form, he was an object of admiration to us all, and I suspect to himself no less. His body and limbs were most symmetrically moulded. His bust was that of an Antinous. Indeed, I may here observe, that the finest living models of the human figure I ever saw, were among the Indian half-breeds" (*Rambler*, I, 177–78). In the *Tour*, WI identified Antoine Lombard's origin as French and Osage, his task as "a kind of Jack-of-all-work," and his pattern as "a vehement propensity to do nothing, being one of the worthless brood engendered and brought up among the missions. He was, moreover, a little spoiled by being really a handsome young fellow, an Adonis of the frontier . . . [and] highly connected, his sister being concubine to an opulent white trader!" (p. 31).

66. The second of the "slender attendance"—"Their Indian"—was probably the new addition, the Osage Indian who had recently wandered into their midst with the horse, escaped punishment by their hand, and had been hired by Latrobe and Pourtalès to help find the Osage hunters. Latrobe did not mention this Indian, but Ellsworth wrote that when the group returned to camp on October 11, "Their Osage ser[v]t was naked, except his breech cloth—and a blanket which was sometimes on him and sometimes not—" (*Narrative*, p. 16). Pourtalès wrote, "I am enchanted by our new acquisition, Mr. Manhattan, who . . . has let himself be persuaded and now follows us on a little pony with no saddle and only a buffalo-hide strap for a bridle. He is the handsomest male Indian that I have ever seen, and, although he is only seventeen years old, his body, his size, and his proud bearing make him look twenty-five" (*Journal*, p. 44). WI's description in the *Tour* of the "young Osage"—his bearing, his dress, his manner of riding, his relationship with the Count—is full and interesting (pp. 40–43).

67. The blind dog made an equally strong impression on Ellsworth (*Narrative*, pp. 14–15); Irving included a description of the dog in the *Tour* (pp. 46–47). WI separated paragraphs with a line three-fourths inch long.

two Creeks arrive at the camp to accompany us[68]

---

n[?]

Friday, October 12[69]

This morning the two Creeks return who had carried message to Capt Deans[70] camp. Had letter to Col Arble which Mr E. opens[71]—find they are encamped in fine place on the Arkansas about 50 distant where there is plenty of game & are waiting for us

Breakfast—delicious ribs of pork—After breakfast go & wash ourselves in beautiful stream[72]—

Gaiety in camp—shots of riflemen—songs of ⟨Frenc⟩ Antoine[73] &c &c

Osage Indian[74] & His wild horse attempts to put blanket of ours on him—fine scene, figure of Indian—naked breast—blanket[—]wild piebald Horse[—]wild eyes—collar with red tuft of horsehair

Set off at half an hour after Sun/rise—ride through fine forest—⟨come out upon⟩ cross a narrow deep stream upon an old beaver dam—See

68. It is not clear from WI's account whether these Creek Indians are the same ones who brought the letter on October 12 or two additional ones; Ellsworth mistakenly suggested that the two Indians from the advanced Ranger camp arrived in the WI-Ellsworth camp on the night of October 11; Ellsworth misdated two days' entries. WI did not mention these two Indians in the *Tour*. The line between entries is three-eighths inch long.

69. WI wrote "Friday ⟨1 ⟨7⟩⟨6⟩⟨2⟩⟩↑12↓."; he redated the entry Friday 17, 16, and 12, superimposing the "7," "6," and "2," and then crossed through the numbers and above the line wrote "12."

70. This reference to Captain Bean as "Captain Dean" was WI's last before he met the captain the following day (October 13).

71. "Mr E." described receiving the letter: "at this encampment met our Cheerokee express returning from the main army with a letter to Col Arbuckle—I opened the letter—it contained a notice of the order to halt—mentioned their distance, which was about forty miles beyond us, and the pleasing intelligence that there was 'at Camp plenty of game'—" (*Narrative*, p. 15).

72. McDermott tentatively identified this stream which entered the Arkansas from the north as Coweta Creek (*Western Journals*, p. 116, n. 29).

73. Because WI crossed out *Frenc* and wrote *Antoine*, he apparently referred to Tonish (see pp. 77–78, n. 30); he called Tonish previously "our Frenchman," and this Antoine was the gay one of the servants. Antoine Lombard, from other descriptions, was neither gay nor a singer. Ellsworth and Latrobe were usually careful to distinguish between Antoine Deshetres (whom they both called Tonish) and Antoine Lombard (whom they called Antoine). Pourtalès was less careful, calling Antoine Deshetres variously Toniche and Antoine. WI in the journals seldom distinguished between the two, but in the *Tour*, he used Tonish and Antoine carefully.

74. Pourtalès' Osage, "Mr. Manhattan."

Streaming line of wild geese, squalling as they fly high over head—pass an old Osage war camp—at half past 10—Stop in forest where there is plenty of the pea vine—let the horses feed—fires made—one man runs to Spring for water—coffee prepard—groups some lying down with head on saddle—others seated at foot of tree by fire—smoke rising among the trees—horses pulling up pea vine[—]some rolling in the vine—

rangers practicing at mark with their rifles[75]—

Old ↑osage↓ Indian ⟨ha⟩ arrives at our Camp—had been out to hunt but lost his horse & was looking for it—says the rangers Camp is but 10 miles off[76]—

Half breed[77] says we shall see no Buffalo until past the Osage Hunters —they frighten every thing off like a Prarie on fire

75. Ellsworth's concern at this wastefulness was allayed by the lieutenant, who said "they fired at a hole in a large tree, and when they had finished shooting, they cut out the balls and melted them over again—" (*Narrative*, pp. 17–18).

76. Ellsworth remembered meeting an Indian dressed in skins, who begged powder and tobacco and told them that the "Rangers were only 12 miles ahead of us" (*Narrative*, p. 17).

77. From WI's almost word-for-word use of this passage in *Tour*, we can identify this person as Billet or Pierre Beatte (WI used the first name in the journals, the second in the *Tour;* other contemporary spellings of his name were Billette, Beatt, Bayatte, Beyatt, and Royotte). Ellsworth reported that at the Chouteau store at the Verdigris they hired "as guide & interpreter—a quapaw indian whose home was at Mr Riquois [at Hopefield Mission], on the Neosho . . ." (*Narrative*, p. 7). George Catlin reported that contrary to WI's appellations in the *Tour* of "Pierre" and "half-breed," Beatte's Christian name was "Alexo," and he was born of French parents who spent much time with the Osage; actually other contemporaries in the mission field called him "the Frenchman" (Foreman, *Advancing the Frontier*, p. 144, n. 14). Even though Beatte was the servant of Ellsworth and WI, Pourtalès, in his *Journal*, called him "my interpreter" and "our intrepid half-blood" (pp. 48, 52); he spoke highly of Beatte's talents in finding a ford, searching for lost horses, killing a fat doe, and in capturing a wild horse with a lasso (pp. 52–54, 63). Latrobe was most complimentary: "Beatte was the son of a French Creole, by a Quopaw mother. . . . there was something in his whole character and manner, which answered to the picture my fancy paints of Robin Hood. Wayward and distant till he become attached to our persons, we were all inclined to misjudge him at first; but before we had been a week together in the wilderness we found his value [as hunter and guide] . . . ; moreover there was that feeling about him, that he would be true to you in a strait, and stand by you either in a bear-fight or an Indian skirmish; and that was not to be undervalued. . . . In short, when the time of parting came, we all looked upon Beatte as a friend . . ." (*Rambler*, I, 178–79).

However, from the first, WI and Beatte disliked each other; for instance, in the October 17 journal entry, WI wrote, "Billet . . . talkative & forward at times taciturn & sulky at others—Brings home game—throws it down & says nothing about it"; three years after their association, WI would write in the *Tour* that even

⟨l⟩Leave the encampt. about 12—pass thro bottoms, across praries—by a lovely pool covered with water lillies[.] see distant smokes of Indians—come down to banks of Arkansas—tracks of horses down to the river side (afterwards understand to be made by Hunters who had crossed to go Buffalo hunting) ⟨g[?]⟩ let our horses drink & continue along bank, & across prarie—see smokes—fancy one to be ⟨near[?]⟩the ranger camp—follow tracks—find Horses grazing (osage Horses) arrive at Osage village on banks of the river—Old men come & shake hands[—] women & children stare & laugh[78]—Mr Ellsworth, makes speech[79]—retrace our steps[—]find rangers trail—Meet Indian & squaw, misunderstand them that the rangers camp is three miles off—push on until dark—& then encamp on the borders of ravine—drops of rain—pitch tent—Three[?][80] osages visit us & sit by our fire—give them coffee[81]

———

though Beatte "was recommended to us" as an excellent guide, interpreter, and hunter, "I confess I did not like his looks when he was first presented to me." WI did not object to the "not bad" features of this thirty-six-year-old man (who actually reminded WI of Napoleon with "high Indian cheek bones"), but his dress was irregular and soiled, his rates high and set, and he was not anxious "to secure our employ." WI remembered and described Beatte's "sullen saturnine expression" and the facts that he was "cold and laconic" and "had altogether more of the red than the white man in his composition." WI confessed that he had learned to mistrust half-breeds "as an uncertain and faithless race"; only the pressure of time prompted their hiring Beatte (*Tour*, pp. 32–33). Ironically, when WI returned to Washington, he made a plea on Beatte's behalf for back pay due him for an expedition eight years earlier, calling him "a most faithful, intelligent, & competent man.... He is a man of strong mind and good principles, and takes a deep interest in the improvement of the Osage tribe, with which he completely identifies himself" (see Foreman's long note regarding Beatte, in *Advancing the Frontier*, pp. 143–45, n. 14).

78. The difference in WI's and Ellsworth's reporting of events is revealed by comparing WI's pleasant account with Ellsworth's description of this "*dirty disgusting* set of beings," among whom some of the little boys "made water before all the women" and some squaws and men were "diseased by *vicious* indulgence" (*Narrative*, p. 18).

79. A third view is provided by Pourtalès, whose sarcastic remarks about the Commissioner suggests that their dislike was mutual (*Journal*, pp. 45–46). Interestingly, it was to this village that Pourtalès attempted to return the next day to choose a wife from among these Osage women. Ellsworth also wrote that Pourtalès wanted to take with them a Pawnee squaw held prisoner by the Osages in case they came upon Pawnees and needed an interpreter; according to the older man, Pourtalès' "opinion, had little weight" (*Narrative*, p. 19).

80. This word could be "There."

81. WI drew a line three-sixteenths inch long between paragraphs.

Scene of rangers fire. Indians, rangers—men cooking[—]eating[—] drinking

This day we made about 35 miles

After we retire to our tents the Indians lie by the fire before it and Sing a nasal low song in chorus drumming on their breasts[82]

rain towards morning—

Young Osage leaves us clandestinely in the night.[83]

Saturday, October 13[84]

Breakfast in tent[—]weather promises to hold up. give breakfast to Indians—

Mr Brailey tells of his having nearly been overtaken last year by fire on the Praries—saw it approaching & was so confused that he was hardly able to make fire & set the prarie on fire before him.

After breakfast prepare for march[—]Pourtales sets off guarded by [*blank*]—the half breed to go back to the Indian village & buy commodities.

Set off about ⟨½⟩7 ⟨pas[?]⟩ ⟨after riding ⟨on⟩two or three miles ↑or four↓ come⟩ after riding some distance pass a bee tree in the forest, recently cut down—⟨fla[?]⟩ empty flakes of Honey comb remaining—

travelling a mile or two further on we come to a bottom of woodland—See horses among the trees—recognized by the men as horses belonging to their troop—coming to the edge of a ridge the camp lies below us in beautiful ⟨grove⟩[85] ↑open wood↓ by a stream of water—undergrowth of low shrubs—blanket tents—venison hanging on sticks to smoke over

82. Even Ellsworth remembered this night with pleasure, calling it "merry enough" and describing Pourtalès' imitating the "Indian song & rub, a dub, dub, on his belly" (*Narrative*, p. 22). Pourtalès described the Osage warriors' songs in detail and called them "erotic" (*Journal*, pp. 47–48).

83. What Pourtalès did not know was that during the singing that night, the Osage visitors were talking to his young Osage "squire." Of course, Ellsworth and Pourtalès viewed the desertion differently: Ellsworth condemned what he called a common Osage practice of breaking promises (*Narrative*, pp. 22–23); Pourtalès commented, "This morning we searched in vain for my friend and protégé, Manhattan. . . . I found out later that his relatives, cousins, etc., had dissuaded him from going off with the whites; they had terrified him! I thought with tenderness of the tears a sensitive girl cousin may have shed in order to keep this gentle Telemachus from leaving. I gave up the idea of making this young Osage my groom, jockey, or page. Good-by, then, oh mighty marksman" (*Journal*, p. 48).

84. WI wrote "Saturday 13."

85. This word could be "green."

fire[–]buck skins spread– ↑–cooking at fires↓ Horses–Stacks of saddles & rifles–Congratulations of men with their companions[86]–

Capt Bean[87] about 40 years of age in leather Hunting dress & leather Stock[in]gs Dr Holt[88]–grey jacket. Linsey woolsey jacket & trousers–cloth hunting cap–old Huntsman[89] in rifle shirt of leather asks permission to go hunting–granted–men of all kinds of dress. some lying under trees–

rifles leaning agst trees ⟨&c[?]⟩ powder horns &c

86. Latrobe described in great detail the meeting of their party and the Rangers, among whom "there was an amusing variety of character"; he commented on the lack of rigid discipline and the good conduct (*Rambler*, I,180–82, 191–92). Ellsworth's enthusiasm at the meeting was evident, but he considered "the Rangers, as a case[?], almost a failure"–poorly dressed and equipped, having no force, inspiring no awe, etc. (*Narrative*, pp. 23–25).

87. Captain Jesse Bean is here named correctly by WI for the first time (earlier he had called the captain "Dean"). Bean, who was from Batesville, Independence County, Arkansas, was commissioned to raise a company of Rangers in June, 1832, for service in the Black Hawk War; being too late for action, they had been ordered to Fort Gibson, where they arrived in October. There was no room at the fort for this company and the two additional ones, and after their return from the journey with WI, they encamped in huts constructed on the Neosho seven miles above Fort Gibson. According to an *Arkansas Gazette* article in July, Bean was an excellent woodsman who knew Indian ways of war; he served gallantly in New Orleans against the British in 1814–15 and with General Jackson in Indian wars in Florida (Foreman, *Advancing the Frontier*, pp. 40, 115, n. 20). Ellsworth's assessment was that "Capt Beans is a very worthy, good natured, easy sort of a man–personally brave, and possessing the qualities of a good woods man–He is worthy of confidence, and actuated by correct motives–But he is greatly deficient in energy and more so in discipline–his army were without the least discipline . . ." (*Narrative*, p. 24). See McDermott's discussion of the raising of this company by Captain Bean, the correspondence between Colonel Arbuckle and the adjutant general, and especially the long letter of instructions from Colonel Arbuckle to Captain Bean on October 5, 1832 (*Western Journals*, pp. 28–33).

88. Latrobe's initial impression of Dr. Daniel Holt was favorable (as he contrasts him with Dr. O'Dwyer, "our scientific querulous companion in the former part of our tour"); he called Holt "a man of a thousand; of sound mind and body; and moreover an excellent marksman and fully accustomed to the life of hap-hazard and adventure we were prosecuting" (*Rambler*, I, 181). Ellsworth concurred: "The surgeon of the army, was Doct Holt, an experienced practitioner, and well calculated for his station–He does not belong to the Army, but is hired, at assistant surgeons pay, by the Commander of the Post–Doct Holt, had a compas and was Capt Beans adviser and scribe–" (*Narrative*, p. 24).

89. Although WI did not identify this man in his journals, he wrote in the *Tour*, "a veteran huntsman approached, whose whole appearance struck me. He was of the middle size, but tough and weather proved; a head partly bald and

Bee hunt[90]—led by a young fellow in a straw hat not unlike a bee hive—one without a hat following him with rifle on shoulder—Capt Dean[91] Dr Holt—Mr Latrobe ^↑Mr Brailey↓ with rifles & guns come to See first a honey comb on a bush. watch which way the bees who are at it fly—pursue the track—came to High dry ↑oak↓ tree. See the bees about a hole high up—men go to work at foot with axes.[92] By & bye down comes the tree with great crash and breaks to shivers—one man runs up with whisp of lighted ⟨str⟩ hay ⟨and smokes off the⟩ to smoke off the bees—The poor victims are pacific and suffer us to assemble round the ruin of their habitation—⟨Cut op⟩ ⟨t⟩Trunk spread open discovers stores of honey—cut open the part above &[93] combs much broken—some white clean & new, others older. take out flakes in a pail—every one with spoon & knife helps himself to the rich booty—Bees returning to their hive from abroad find the tree levelled & collect on the point of a withered branch of a neighboring tree contemp/-lating the ruin & buzzing about this[94] ⟨Fate[?] rui[?]⟩ downfall of their republic

Some strange bees arrive and begin to banquet on the honey of their ruined neighbors. Men know them by their greediness & their clean jackets

Since being at their encampt they have taken 6 or 7 Bee trees & killed 9 deer—camp abounds with honey & venison[—]15 turkies

Bees have spread into this country within a few years—

Leave much honey in the ⟨*two words unrecovered*⟩ ruin of the tree. It will be all eaten by varmints[,] said one of the men[.] what varmint—raccoons—opossums[—]skunks—Bears. ⟨the⟩

---

garnished with loose iron-grey locks, and a fine black eye, beaming with youthful spirit. . . . 'That's old Ryan,' said the Captain, when he had gone, 'there's not a better hunter in the camp; he's sure to bring in game' " (*Tour*, pp. 60–61). On August 14, John Ryan and William Ryan, both from Horsehead, enlisted in the Rangers. Ellsworth suggested that they were father and son, spelling their name "Rians" and suggesting that the son had far less ability in the woods than his father (*Narrative*, p. 52). Latrobe said that the "old man . . . was a fine specimen of that race for which the frontier has been celebrated ever since Daniel Boone led the way across the mountains" (*Rambler*, I, 192).

90. Ellsworth, too, was enthusiastic about the bee hunt and gave a very full account (*Narrative*, pp. 30–31).

91. Captain Bean; hereafter, WI named him correctly.

92. Apparently WI wrote "rifles" and then with a heavy diagonal mark from upper left to lower right crossed through the word to indicate "axes."

93. Apparently WI wrote "&" and then marked through it with a dash.

94. WI seems to have written "their" and then perhaps wrote an *s* over the last part of the word changing it to "this."

The latter will remain for days [? at a tree ?] till They make a hole & get in their paws and haul out Honey bees & all.

When queen bee is killed the hive goes to ruin

Shooting—leaping, wrestling in the camp[95]

———

dinner, venison roasted—fried &c[—]bread baked before fire—Prarie tea.[96]

Capt ⟨D⟩Bean & Latrobe go off to look after a Beaver tree—to hunt &c[97]

———

Seated with Dr Holt—man brings Kettle of honey & sets before us—from a tree just taken—the 15th. tree. ⟨The whole[?]⟩ Swarm round it like bees—getting out the rich white flakes—[98]

———

Pourtales arrives at the camp and Billet each with a turkey strung each side of his saddle. The Indian camp had moved across the river—found another camp—bought old wooden bowls & a buffalo skin &c.[99]

———

A Hunter returns to the camp on horseback with a wild turkey—He had put his leggings on the horse to protect him from the briars

Lay on the grass talking with Capt[,] Lieut[,] Doctor & others about route[100]—looking at map—tomorrow we[']ll get to the ⟨fork of the⟩ red

95. WI added a line three-sixteenths inch long to separate paragraphs; he also reduced the size of his writing.

96. Ellsworth describes the tea: "In crossing some small prairies we discovered that excellent plant the golden rod or India Tea. . . . I asked [Tonish] to gather the first he found—we tried this tea often—it is an excellent substitute for our beverage—it is *sudorific, gently stimulating* and an active diuretic—in large quantities it is laxative—Mr Irving is so much pleased with it, that he has ordered a quantity for New York . . ." (*Narrative*, p. 17). Latrobe lamented the end of the supply (*Rambler*, I, 240).

97. WI added a line one-sixteenth inch long to separate paragraphs.

98. WI added a line one-fourth inch long to separate paragraphs.

99. Pourtalès' account of his trading with the Indians is, of course, a much fuller one. He mentioned the three plates—one was Osage, one, Pawnee, and the third, Caddo (*Journal*, pp. 48–49). Ellsworth, who seldom said a positive word about Pourtalès, was delighted with the bowls "made out of knots of a tree" and went into detail about their distribution (*Narrative*, pp. 21–22).

WI separated paragraphs with a line three-sixteenths inch long.

100. Ellsworth went into tedious detail about their consideration of route and concluded that "circumstances compelled me to change the route materially as you will see; else no horses would have returned to the garrisson, and privation & hardship carried off many men—" (*Narrative*, p. 33).

fork[101]—will cross there, & then in two days will crack buffalo bones[102]
⟨? More h ?⟩

Hunter comes in with flakes of Honey—another tree found

18 trees—

Shot heard—theres a buck killed

more honey brought in. 20 trees[—]100 men in camp feasting on honey

toward. evg ⟨fire⟩ centinels posted—fires lit up in advanced posts—Horses dashing thro the camp—over fires—Capt & Doctor dine with us [—]roast leg of Venison, roast turkey, Prarie tea—Coffee[.] Owl hoots over the camp[—]⟨?⟩Has visited the camp several nights—men mock him and draw him down—is called Charleys owl because centinel coming in this morning fired gun contrary to orders and said he fired at owl because he was told it made good soup—[103]

Pourtales fires at owl—Kills it & it falls on our tent[104]

Charley is called in to eat it but declines as he did not Kill it—[105]

———

Mess at one of the tents singing psalms[106]—others whistling[.] Sit by Captains fire and hear old hunters tales.—various groups round camp fires—bells of horses[—]neighing of others—

Stories of Pawny ⟨ro[?]⟩ fights[.] ruddy[?] light in the west ⟨amon⟩ above the trees—

Thats a prarie on fire by the osage Hunters

Thats at the red fork said Billet.

It seems but three miles distant

It is perhaps twenty—[107]

———

101. The Red Fork, or Cimarron River (sometimes called the Semerone), rising in the Rocky Mountains, flowed eastward until it entered the Arkansas on its south side. The Red Fork was a rather long river (approximately 600 miles) in the Indian Territory, but it was not navigable.

102. In the *Tour*, WI combined this conversation about cracking buffalo bones with the one of the morning of October 14 in which Captain Bean and Billet (Beatte) discussed the bald hill and the Red River (see *Tour*, p. 69).

103. According to the roster in McDermott's edition of the *Western Journals*, the only Ranger listed whose name was Charles or Charlie was Private Charles Nelson, who enlisted in Captain Bean's Rangers in August, 1832, in Batesville (app. 2, p. 184).

104. Pourtalès wrote, "To finish things off, I shot down an owl whose plaintive cries filled the air directly over our heads and worked on the imagination of our superstitious half-bloods" (*Journal*, p. 50).

105. WI drew a line one-half inch long to separate paragraphs.

106. See WI's descriptions of the "most lugubrious psalm tune" and the owl incident in *Tour* (pp. 73–74).

107. WI drew a line three-sixteenths inch long between paragraphs.

About half past 8—a beautiful pale light begins to spring up in the east—precurser[?] to the moon.

sleep at foot of a tree by fire ⟨before⟩ Towards morning ⟨beautiful moon⟩ lie looking at moon & stars.

Horses straying about the camp

Sunday, October 14[108]

Bugle sounds at day break. Bustle in camp[—]catching horses—driving them in—Have you seen my horse cries one—What horse is that—broke loose over the brook—Night guard comes in—dismissed[—]fires made—Breakfast preparing[109]—some packing—blankets that have formed tents dismounted—Singing laughing joking, whooping—Saddling horses —In a little while the forest so suddenly & temporally alive and ⟨joyous⟩ animated will relapse into its ⟨for[?]⟩ primeval silence & solitude[110]

———

1 Ranger— whose wallet is this
2 " Why I guess its mine
1 " What kind of a wallet is it
2 Why its a borrowed wallet[.] I borrowed it before I started but you[?][111] know it by a bit of lead in it[.]

bugle sounds to saddle & prepare to march

Capt[—] Which way lies the red fork Have none of you hunters hunted out here[112]

Billet— You go three miles. I have only went along yonder by the edge of The Prarie You will find a bald hill, with stones on it[113]—

Capt[—] Yes ⟨the⟩ I have seen cliffs

Billet— Stones which the Osages put up. from that hill you will see the ⟨fo⟩ red fork[114]

———

108. WI wrote "Sunday—14th."

109. Ellsworth commented especially on this "excellent meal" and on the qualifications of Tonish, their cook (*Narrative*, p. 32).

110. WI drew a line three-sixteenths inch long between paragraphs.

111. WI may have written "your."

112. WI's indentation for this conversation was irregular; because he used hanging speech directives with blocked dialogue in two of the speeches, we have regularized for clarity.

113. Latrobe mentioned "the Bald Hill, a notable saddle-shaped eminence, rising from an elevated plateau . . ." (*Rambler*, I, 182).

114. WI drew a line one-eighth inch long between paragraphs.

Leave encampt at 8 o clock, ride through tangled bottoms and up and down rough broken rocky hills—Picturesque look of troop winding thro thickets & up heights. In climbing a rocky hill the girths of my horse give way and I have a fall, but am not hurt.[115] Road winds by deep brook a link of clear pools—Fine views from height, of distant praries, and of hills beyond the Arkansas. Golden day—pure delightful air. After much torturous march & climbing hills, threading narrow but romantic valleys we come upon the Arkansas[116]—broad sandy shore, lovely[?][117] —Elk, deer, buffalo, oppossum[,] turkies—Banks of Cotton tree & willow. picturesque look of troops Struggling[118] along the shore[—] some in groups among the willows—turn in through thick bushes tangled with grape & pea vines. Come to open woodland—herds of deer in all directions. The leaders of the troop start a deer—Shots of rifles— —we come to a small oak tree with marks of a bears having ^ ↑topped[119] it &↓ clambered up it ⟨after acorns⟩. About ¼ before three ^ ↑the troop↓ encamp, in in a beautiful basin under oak trees—we take our station on a rising ground overlooking the camp[120]—Hunters start in different directions to Kill game. ⟨fires⟩ horses hobbled & turned loose—fires made—men silent—no whooping as in the morning—all busy or reposing—this day we made about 14 miles

Huntsman brings in buck hanging across his horse—Shots heard from time to time—concert of bells of all tones among the horses

115. WI did not mention his accident in the *Tour*. Neither Latrobe nor Pourtalès found it worthy of comment, but Ellsworth's concern prompted an account: "In our travelling today Mr Irving . . . was thrown from the horse upon the sharp flinty ground—the horse somewhat frightened sprang forward, and left the rider covered up by the saddle port-manteau blanket. . . . He fell upon his hip, and received little injury, except a general shock, to the whole system— . . . when our factotum *Tonish* came up, he mended the best girth which was broken, and we pursued our journey—" (*Narrative*, p. 35).

116. The group had traveled about twelve miles from the previous night's camp when they reached the Arkansas, which Pourtalès said looked "exactly like crayfish soup" (*Journal*, p. 51). Latrobe wrote that "about three o'clock in the afternoon, [we] struck the Arkansas again. Its hue was here of a deep red, and the stream apparently about half a mile in breadth, flowed with a rapid whirling current among shoals and sand-bars" (*Rambler*, I, 182).

117. Beginning on the line above, going through this word, and extending to the line below is a broad brown ink smudge, which prevents a clear reading of the questioned word; it also may be crossed out. Alternate readings could be "banks of," "rocky—," "herds of," "Forests—," "Tracks of."

118. This word could be "Straggling."

119. This word could be "toppld," "tipped," or "tapped."

120. Both Ellsworth and Pourtalès described this particular camp site with enthusiasm (*Narrative*, pp. 35–36; *Journal*, p. 51).

Mode of roasting bread by twisting dough round a stick & standing it endways before a fire—

⟨?⟩Beverage of corn just ripe but not quite fit for grinding—parched before slow fire[—]pounded—sifted[—]a couple of spoonsful to ½ pint of water[—]sweetened with sugar[121]

Captain Bean returns from hunt unsuccessful. Had seen track of Buffalo in the bottom since the last rain—& of an elk that had walked out in the bar and then reentered the woods above—If we had shot him we should have all feasted this evening[122]—Had seen traces of a bear

Lad comes in with doe round his shoulders—companion follows him—A laugh round at him for shooting in partnership[123]

———

Clamour in camp—a young fellow McLellan has shot an Elk for the first time & brought home some ribs as a specimen.[124] He is hoisted on the shoulders of his companions. Groups round fire examining the spoil.

Bee hunters on the track of a hive

This day after leaving the Arkansas we came thro a bottom where there was a great quantity of persimmons[125]

———

⟨Thought at first the Panther might be an owl⟩

Monday, October 15[126]

↑before↓ Day break—howling of wolves[—]at Daybreak—↑imitations of↓ cocks crowing[,] hens cackling among the youngsters of the camp—⟨breakfast⟩—Horses driven in—breakfast—whistling singing dancing hallowing after horses joking laughing—Scampering after horses

121. Ellsworth told his wife that this "most *agreeable beverage*" cures "the deliterious effects of bad water" and provides great sustenance for a long journey (*Narrative*, p. 36).

122. Even though Captain Bean, the inveterate hunter, was unsuccessful, Ellsworth reported that "Antoine Lumbard the Servant of Mr Latrobe & Co went a hunting for us, and brought in 4 Turkeys—there were several deer killed at this camp . . ." (*Narrative*, pp. 36–37).

123. WI drew a line one-half inch long to separate paragraphs.

124. Shooting the elk was a memorable event; Ellsworth said that a Ranger "had killed a fine *elk*—as this was the first Elk killed, great joy was manifested throughout . . . for the Elk was about the size of a two year old steer . . ." (*Narrative*, p. 37). In surveying the roster of Bean's Rangers, the only name which might identify the successful elk hunter is Private Willis McClenden, who enlisted in the Rangers on July 30, 1832, in Batesville (*Western Journals*, p. 184).

125. WI drew a line nine-sixteenths inch long to separate paragraphs.

126. WI wrote "Monday 15th."

⟨Ca[?]⟩Troop detained for party which went out at day break in quest of the elk which was killed[127]–⟨They are said to have⟩ to bring in the meat–They are said to have got on the trail of the other Elk–

———

Story of Uncle Sams gun[128]–

———

Bugle sounds to march. Capt leaves guard to await return of hunters–after some[?] mile or two come upon Indian ↑or buffalo↓ trail[–]view of red ↑fork↓ ⟨river⟩ from high hill ↑rolling & bloody[?][129] stream↓–grove & intervals of various trees & tints–rocky ridges–lines of heights –then down through rich bottom of land–affair of Billet with a Skunk[130] –traces of deer–of a bear–marks of bears on the [? trunk of ?] oak trees–come to a halt–capt & Billet looking out for a ford of the arkansas[131][–]we are about ¼ of mile above the fork–river narrower than below & deeper–current strong–banks crumbling and abrupt–no crossing–Billet is sent to look above at a Sand bar

127. Ellsworth suggested that the game killed the day before was protected from wild animals by hanging it on a limb and spreading powder or urine near it (*Narrative*, pp. 38–39).

128. Latrobe identified this gun as the double-barreled gun which Ellsworth had "brought away" from a government agent on the Missouri; *U. S.* was marked on the gun, probably on the stock. Latrobe went on in a playful way to describe this "piece of respectably ancient mould and fabric" which was "in a most ridiculous state of repletion"; he concluded that they put it "into some kind of trim . . . and you shall not fail to hear of 'Uncle Sam's' further adventures" (*Rambler*, I, 206–8). True to his word, Latrobe continued his mock epic (*ibid.*, I, 220).

WI set off his reference to the gun with lines above and below, each three-eighths inch long.

129. These words which WI inserted above the line are difficult to decipher. Latrobe's description of the river at this point as "a turbid bright red stream" (*Rambler*, I, 184), supports the reading "bloody." Trent and Hellman and McDermott read as "–rolling of bear by stream–" (*Journals of WI*, III, 146; *Western Journals*, p. 125). An alternate reading is "rolling & sandy."

130. Ellsworth suggested animostity between WI and Billet during the killing and disposing of the "pole cat" (*Narrative*, p. 47), while Latrobe in a humorous retelling of the incident remembered the "sly twinkle" of WI's eye and the "restlessness about the muscles of the lips, whenever the subject was mentioned" (*Rambler*, I, 184–85). Both confessed that later when the stock of food was low, they, as well as WI, enjoyed eating skunk (*Rambler*, I, 185; *Narrative*, pp. 47, 109).

131. Pourtalès remembered pleasantly this search for a ford (*Journal*, pp. 51–52). Latrobe wrote that Captain Bean's direct orders included the point at which the party was to ford the Arkansas, "near its point of junction with the Red Fork"; however, they found the river here "extremely turbid and deep" and were forced to "ascend higher in search of a ford" (*Rambler*, I, 183–84).

Resume our route—about a mile distant come to ford pointed out by Billet who strips & wades nearly across. Council—Capt Determines to make rafts & cross—troops return to bottom of Pea vines—our Frenchmen[132] lead our horses to bank & prepare to make a raft of Buffalo Hide[133]

Pile luggage in center of ⟨raft⟩ Hide draw up the sides by the loop holes & tie the strings across—

Launch it upon[?] river & the Frenchmen & half breeds conduct it across yelping like Indians.[134] Some of the ⟨par⟩ troop headed by Lieut Penticost cross 1½ miles up the river—fording a long oblique distance—Others seeing this abandon the construction of their rafts and set off to ⟨for[?]⟩ follow their trail[135]—

I cross in the Buffalo skin, seated on a quantity of baggage[?], with a double barreld gun and rifle ⟨which I⟩ saluted by Col Penticost & two rangers who had crossed. return their salute by discharge of carabine—Land safely & dryly—at 2 O clock—*[136]

———

*Billet who went before had a towing line & when he came to where he had to swim he held the cord between his teeth—Antoine[137] followed the boat[?][138]—

Arkansas at this place beautifully diversified by high bluffs of wood & rock—long willowed reaches—rich bottoms—and embowered promontories, On the west bank where I landed tracks of elk, dear, bears, raccoons[,] waterfowls—woods tinted with autum[?]—

This morning in rich bottom passed a stately peccan tree—

132. WI often called Tonish (Antoine Deshetres) "our Frenchman" or "the Frenchman."

133. The accounts of the decision to build rafts vary only slightly (Ellsworth, *Narrative*, pp. 39–40; Latrobe, *Rambler*, I, 185–86; Pourtalès, *Journal*, p. 52).

134. This tradition also impressed the other travelers (Ellsworth, *Narrative*, p. 40; Latrobe, *Rambler*, I, 186; Pourtalès, *Journal*, p. 52).

135. Ellsworth (*Narrative*, pp. 40–41) and Latrobe (*Rambler*, I, 187) describe from two points of view this division of the party.

136. WI's asterisk indicates a footnote, which for the convenience of the reader is transcribed as the following paragraph. In the manuscript it appears at the bottom of p. [42] following the paragraph which begins "This morning"; WI's line setting off the note from the text extends from paper edge to binding edge.

137. Tonish, not Antoine Lumbard. Ellsworth said Billet and Tonish placed WI in the raft and "plunged in" the river (*Narrative*, p. 41). In the *Tour*, WI wrote that Beatte took the cord in his teeth and went ahead and Tonish followed the bark, steadying and propelling it (*Tour*, p. 86).

138. This word could be "bark," a reading suggested by that in the *Tour* (p. 86).

Capt & Dr Holt form raft of logs & cross—Long line of troops crossing at distance from point to point

Break our way through thick under/wood to the camp which is in a small wild rocky dell ⟨*illegible*⟩ in the narrow and which is like a cul de sac—encampt in green grassy bottom of the dell—ridges of lime-stone rocks above, lofty trees[139]—

My Horse & pony missing—fearful that they have not crossed. Mr Ellsworth & Billet set off in quest of them—

Fires lit in dell—Looks like a robbers retreat. Groups of men round fires—Rifles, powder horns &c leaning agst trees ⟨acr[?]⟩ beside them—Horses grazing around with bells tinkling—baggage—blankets &c hang-ing on ⟨? lines to ?⟩ horizontal poles to dry—

⟨Set out in search of my horses⟩

no account of my horse—walk with the Doctor to the head of the hill—Splendid view of the Arkan/-sas, with picturesque bluffs of tinted woodlands—bottoms of further[?] green—long reaches of distant hills—blue lines of untrodden[?] countrie[?] ⟨the⟩ gleam of the red fork among hills—beautiful sunset. See[140]

[*p. [44] is a sketch of a tree-lined river with a boat crossing at the right and an encampment on the left, dated "14 Oct 1832" at the bottom of the drawing. The journal has been turned clockwise one-quarter revo-lution; before turning the journal, Irving wrote "Smoke from t" at the top left corner.*]

[*p. [45] blank*]

Smoke from the low dell of our encampmt. See two laggards[?] of the troop rafting over[141]—Shots among the forests on the other side—distant smoke of praries on the horizon—

Return to camp—a deer and five turkeys brought in—Sup on excellent venison steaks & coffee—Repair to captains fire—After dark see Glow of fires in Western heavens—Capt. ⟨They⟩ If they are on this side the

139. The camp was described by Pourtalès (*Journal*, p. 53), by Ellsworth, who called it "Bears den" (*Narrative*, p. 43), and by Latrobe, who remembered their calling it "Bear's Glen" (*Rambler*, I, 187).

140. At the top of the next page [44] of this journal, WI wrote "Smoke from t"; apparently, he decided to draw a scene. After two pages, WI resumed his sen-tence with the words "Smoke from the low dell."

141. Ellsworth wrote, "in the morning we sent across the river for 3 of our horses, and found several Rangers who could not swim and whose horse[s] had swam acros, making a raft to transport themselves" (*Narrative*, p. 43).

Fig. 7. Sketch on notebook p. [44] of tree-lined river with a boat crossing at the right and an encampment on the left, dated Oct. 14, 1832.

arkansas they must be Pawnee fires—No osages dare hunt there—Antoine thinks them osage fires on the other side of the ArKansas.

Capt. We must now look out[.] I must issue written orders—no man hunts without leave or fires off ^ ↑a↓ guns on pain of riding a wooden horse with a sharp back—

It will be difficult to teach our young fellows caution—they are in the land of a silent, watchful crafty people.[142]

———

One man says—where[?] I go my gun goes.—I never like to leave it behind—theres no one will take such care of it as me, And there is nothing that will take such care of me—

———

Capt & others determining our position. Do you see that blazing star[143] ⟨another⟩ ↑thats↓ the evening star[.] *another*[—]thats the planet Venus that looks down into our camp

———

A band of hunters are still out on the other side of the river

Capt[144][—]I should send to look after them but old Ryans with them and he knows how to take care of himself & them—If it were not for him I would not give much for the rest—Hes quite at home— —never lost in the woods—It will be four to keep watch & one to tend the fire—

———

Story of the Sargeant[:][145]

I was once belated[?] in passing thro a Hammock in Alabama near the Tombigbe[146]—Heard wolves howl—My horse came crowd-/-ing near me—drove him off but he returnd & stood looking at me & the fire &

142. WI separated the following four anecdotes with lines of one-fourth inch, one-fourth inch, a looping mark, and three-eighths inch.

143. Following this word, there is a long pencil mark which extends downward through five lines.

144. WI apparently wrote this word in the left margin after completing the paragraph; therefore, we used blocked dialogue.

145. McDermott identified the sergeant as Isaac Bean, the captain's brother (*Western Journals*, p. 128, n. 53). WI mentioned Sergeant Bean in the October 17 entry, but there is no internal evidence to connect this story definitely with him.

146. Trent and Hellman and McDermott transcribed similarly as follows: "'I was once belated in passing thro' a [forest] near the Tombigbee . . .'" (*Journals of WI*, III, 149; *Western Journals*, p. 128). Both editions omit the two words following the word "forest"; although WI's pencil lead was diminishing here, indentation in the paper reveals "in Alabama" as the two words.

WI's account of this story in the *Tour* is almost a word-for-word retelling from

dozing & nodding & loitering[?] on his ⟨feet[?]⟩[147] fore feet for he was powerful tired—By & by I heard a Panther cry ↑thought at first it might be an owl↓—felt awkward[—]had no weapon but double bladed pen Knife, prepared to defend myself—*[148]

*(I prepared for defence. piled up small brands of ⟨*illegible*⟩[149] fire to pepper him with)

The company of my horse seemd a comfort—He laid down close beside me and fell asleep being so tired—In the morning I found the track of a Panther within 60 paces—⟨He⟩ they were large as my two fists—He had evidently been walking backward and forward trying to make up his mind to attack me—

Wild look of dell with fires glaring here & there among the rocks & trees

Fine spring of water at the head of it—This day we made about 4 miles besides crossing the river

Tuesday, October 16[150]

Awake before day.[151] Fine night[—]Moon shining feebly down into the camp—↑checquered light↓ fires nearly extinguished[—]men lying about their fires—light clouds drifting across the moon. At daybreak Billet Sets off ⟨&[?]⟩to cross the river in search of my horses[152]—

---

the journal, and at this point he wrote, "I was belated in passing through a tract of wood, near the Tombigbee river . . ." (*Tour*, p. 97). His journal synonym for "tract of wood" was "Hammock"; a less likely alternative reading could be "Hurricane."

147. This reading could be "⟨front⟩."

148. WI's asterisk indicates an insertion following this paragraph; he also drew a line from the asterisk in the middle of the first line of page [49] down the left margin and then, apparently without lifting his pencil, encircled the note in the middle of the page, then enclosed it in parentheses.

149. This reading could be "⟨coa⟩."

150. WI wrote "Tuesday 16th. Oct."

151. WI did not mention here or in the *Tour* that early this particular morning he complained "much of a swelling of the eye-lids and an erruption about the wrists . . ."; Dr. Holt administered "a wash of the sugar of lead but salt water was his greatest relief." WI thought he was poisoned, but, according to Ellsworth, the problem was the diet of highly salted meat and almost no "vegitables" (*Narrative*, pp. 43–44).

152. Pourtalès said that a "detail composed of Billet and Antoine Lambert" went across the river to get the horses (*Journal*, p. 53); Beatte (Billet) returned soon with them. WI corrected his own mistake later in this day's entry and in the *Tour* (p. 98).

Returns about 8 oclock with all three—Bustle of preparation—some men sent back over the river in quest of guns left behind—⟨Ryan & hunting party not yet arrived⟩ Demand for tall horses to stem the current—Intend to make a raft & return—

Yellow[153] Leaves showering around us—⟨sigh⟩ signs of autumn[154]

———

At meal times great borrowing of frying pans—Kettles &c. When about to get off—loud demands who has a frying pan from the mess—Who has seen my horse &c &c &c[155]

———

Capt resolves to start & leave a rear guard to bring up Stragglers

Bugle Sounds. troop files off[—]we remain as our packing is not complete—Antoine[156] who accompd Billet to look after the horses the other side of the river got on false trail & has not yet returnd

Rear guard in groups some seated round their fires—others lying on ground lazily talking—their horses unsaddled[157] stand dozing by—one takes the occasion to shave—

Some distant mounted—among the trees, with guns over shoulders—quiet of the grove except low talk of lazy groups, or a pensive whistle of some solitary laggard

We leave the encampt at ½ past 9[158]—our route lies over a rolling country of oak clearings[159]—Grand distant prospects like cultivated country. Our route at first is by mistake about NW but we alter it to W.[160] Crossing a beautiful range of open hills four deer are descried grazing on side of ⟨an opposite⟩ ↑a↓ ⟨m[?]⟩hill—one of the rangers gets

153. WI apparently began the paragraph with the word "Leaves," then added the word "Yellow" beginning flush left.

154. After this word, WI made a false start, "⟨B[?]⟩," then drew a line seven-sixteenths inch long between paragraphs.

155. WI drew a line five-sixteenths inch long between paragraphs.

156. Antoine Lombard, not knowing of Beatte's finding the horses, did not return until the next day after finding lost Rangers, killing a bear, and guiding the Rangers back to the main camp (Ellsworth, *Narrative*, pp. 44–45, 48; Latrobe, *Rambler*, I, 188–89).

157. WI first wrote "saddled," then added the prefix flush left.

158. Ellsworth indicated that the departure time was "½ past 8" (*Narrative*, p. 44); the discrepancy might be explained by the fact that when they were in camp, the party was divided into Mess No. 1 and Mess No. 2, the Rangers camping each night apart from the Ellsworth party (Latrobe, *Rambler*, I, 189, 191). The two groups may have filed off separately.

159. An alternate reading is "openings."

160. There is a difference in the account of the initial route of the party that morning: Ellsworth wrote that their course was "too northerly"; they corrected the course south, and the day's travel to the Red Fork netted only six or seven

permission of Capt and started off for an intervening wood The troop halted & watched—bang went the gun—One deer fell. The Rangers were starting forth but Capt. withheld them. Let the man have another shot. (the surviving deer having stopped) The deer started & ran. The whole line broke, Horse/-men galloping in every direction. Antoine[161] who had been skirting the forest on white horse ⟨found he⟩ came in sight but had no chance[.] The deer got off.

⟨Get in an old⟩

Found an old Indian camp some thought Pawnee—⟨some⟩ but Dr said it is some bold Delawares[162] who have hunted here—$_\wedge$ ↑old↓ Skull of a Stag by the encampt—Fine stream close by[—]Immediately after[,] we come on an old well beaten trail of either Indians or buffalo[163]

———

miles (*Narrative*, p. 44). Pourtalès said that they did not wait for Billet and Antoine but left traveling west (*Journal*, p. 53).

161. Tonish (Antoine Deshetres).

162. The Delawares, of the Algonquian speaking group, were formerly located in the lower Hudson and the entire Delaware River basins (from New Jersey to southeastern New York and southwestern Connecticut). These Indians called themselves "Lenápe" or "Leni-lenápe," which meant "our man," "real man," "original people," or "men of our nation"; the English called them "Delaware" after the river; the French called them "Loups" or "wolves"; and the other Indians called them "grandfathers" or "Wapanachki," which meant "eastern or people of dawn." When the early Dutch explorers discovered them, these Indians were an outstanding fishing, farming, or hunting people, depending on their geographical location. They were village dwellers, particularly in longhouses, and they were a matrilineal people (descent through the women, with living arrangements according to matriclans). With their movement west, they changed to a more warlike, wild people. At the beginning of the Revolutionary War, they were neutral but later, very pro-British. Many participated in the defeat of St. Clair; some followed Tecumseh and his brother and some moved to Canada after the War of 1812. The Delawares remaining in the east joined the Oneidas and Senecas, going with them by 1810 to their respective reservations in Green Bay and Oklahoma. The main body of Delawares went from Indiana to southern Missouri in 1815; when their reservation was established by treaty in 1829, they proceeded to the fork of the Kansas and Missouri Rivers in eastern Kansas. Many of the Delawares were hired as drivers, guides, and scouts when Independence became a center of trade. The Delawares were allies of the western Cherokees against the Osages; part of the Cherokee Country was even called the Delaware District by their brothers, and their histories are intertwined. When the Delaware reservation was abandoned in 1854, most Delawares settled with the Cherokees and Creeks (see Hodge, *Handbook of Indians*, I, 385–87; Wright, *Indians of Oklahoma*, pp. 145–55; *Dictionary of Indian Tribes*, II, 122–34).

163. WI drew a line one-fourth inch to separate paragraphs.

—After leaving the place soon[?] we had the first affair with deer[—] we came in sight of others on a hill Hunters sent forward—shoot but miss—a fine buck starts up from ↑side of↓ a stream & escapes—Several other deer seen. ⟨*illegible*⟩[164]

We proceed—passing side of a hill we see two horsemen on the bald ridge of a distant hill who appear to be reconnoitering[?] us—Pawnees cry some—Capt & others regard them—Portales brings his opera glass—They prove to be two of our men who had remained behind & ⟨were com[?]⟩ ↑had↓ lost their way—

Antoine[165] points[?] up a fine buck. Shoots but misses him

Cross the dividing ridge of Red fork & Arkansas. In[?] the former making a great bend—push on and encamp ‸ ↑about ½ past 3↓ on a beautiful peninsula made by a deep, clear but almost motionless brook. The Huntsmen start off immediately—our man Billet among the first—

This day we made about 15 miles[—]we are about 102 Miles from Fort Gibson.

Delightful mode of life. Exercise on horse-/back all the fore part of the day diversified by hunting incidents—then about 3 oclock encamping in some beautiful place & with full appetite for repose, ⟨lie[?]⟩ lying on the grass under green trees. in genial weather with a blue cloudless sky—Then so sweet sleeping at night in the open air & when awake seeing the moon & stars through the tree tops— —Such zest for the hardy, simple but savory meals the product of the chase. Venison roasted on spits or broiled on the coals—Turkeys fresh from the thicket—Honey from the tree—coffee—or delightful Prarie tea

The weather is in its perfection Golden sunshine, not oppressive but animating—Skies without a cloud—&[?] if there be clouds, of feathery texture and lovely tints—air pure, bland, exhilerating—an atmosphere of perfect transparency—and the whole country having the mellow tint of autumn. How exciting to think that we are breaking thro a country hitherto untrod/-den by whiteman, except perchance the solitary trapper. A glorious world spread around us without an inhabitant[166]

———

Young man comes into camp who has killed a deer—Has made a sack of the hide—filled it with meat & slung it on his shoulders

———

164. Pourtalès described this comedy of hunting errors (*Journal*, pp. 53–54). The illegible word could be deciphered "<herds>."

165. Tonish.

166. The following three anecdotes are set off by lines of three-eighths inch, five-sixteenths inch, and one-fourth inch.

Capt returns—has seen a gang of 60 Elk—followed & refrained from shooting in hopes of getting a[?] shot of[167] a large buck ⟨& doe⟩ at length wounded one but lost it—

———

Billet returns with fat doe on his horse—Skinnd—In a little while some ribs are roasted & furnish a delicious treat—Such is hunters life—feasting and fasting—we had just before made a meal of remnants of turkey & salt pork[168]—

Wind changes—driving clouds—threatens rain hot[?][169]—moon breaks out about midnight—

Wednesday, October 17[170]

Cloudy morng threatg rain. ⟨pre⟩ halted for the day—preparations for hunting[171]—Hunters summoned—charged to go to river & below—but not to go up the brook— —To bring all their spoil into the camp & lay it down by the Capts fire that it may be ⟨divided⟩ portioned out—

Hearty breakfast of ribs of Venison & coffee with cakes baked in pan before the fire—

Set off with Capt Bean[,] his brother Sergeant Bean & Lieut Penticost & accompd. by two men on foot who are to bring home a doe killed by the Sargeant last evg.[172] Soon come to the doe lying on hillside disem-/ bowelled & leave the footmen to cut it up & carry it to camp—Come upon Elk trail—deep prints like a cows—Elk beds where they laid the night before last—Go quietly Indian file—come to where Capt shot the Elk last night—⟨foll⟩ See ⟨sta[?]⟩ blood on shrubs & grass on the trail for some time when it ceases ^ ↑See a deer or two scampering in the forest↓—Capt looks for separate trail of wounded Elk—Thinks it must be some-/ -where about the neighborhood of Some Buzzards hovering in the air. Regain the trail of the Elks—carrys us thro open oak ⟨woo[?]⟩ forested hills—until we come to a ⟨b⟩Bend of the red river where the elk had forded[.] It is probable they did not stop for ten miles last night—Give up the pursuit and turn[?] our course to creek ⟨of⟩ on which is the

167. WI wrote the word "of" when he apparently intended "at."

168. The feasting-fasting pattern was praised by Pourtalès (*Journal*, pp. 55–56), accepted by Latrobe (*Rambler*, I, 180), and lamented by Ellsworth (*Narrative*, pp. 46–47).

169. This word could be "but."

170. WI wrote "Wednesday. 17th. Oct."

171. Ellsworth and Pourtalès attributed the delay to the fact that many of the men had measles and fever and needed the rest (*Narrative*, p. 46; *Journal*, p. 54).

172. Ellsworth remembered that WI "begged to accompany the Capt today, not only to look for the stricken Elk but to kill more—" (*Narrative*, p. 49).

encampt. Sargeant & Lieut take one side of the creek—Capt & myself the other—⟨after a[?]⟩ Pass old Buffalo trail, or road—come up with two hunters on foot who had wounded an elk but lost him—& had found the elk killed by capt last night

They conduct us to it, about 1½ miles from where it was shot. It had abandoned the trail of its Sound ↑unhurt↓ companions and had turned off to die alone*[173]

———

*The Elk when mortally wounded always leaves the trail & turns aside to die

—Lay ⟨among⟩ ^ ↑in open↓ oaks wood on ⟨hill⟩ side of a slope—⟨Capt &⟩ already began to spoil—Capt & men go to work to cut it up—Flesh tainted inside—Capt & men Skin it & cut Collops off of the ribs—& the outside ⟨of[?]⟩ generally—

Buzzard soaring in the air waiting to banquet on the spoil—Capt forms sack of the hide—gathered up through holes in the edges by thongs cut from the same—↑⟨leaves it on the spot to be sent for⟩↓ puts it on his horse & sets off for camp—foot/men pursue their sport

Return to camp. ⟨Antoinio⟩ Antoine the half breed returned with a bear which he killed near our old camp[174]—Old Ryan & his party had met with Antoine and learned of the ford—& crossed the river with him. Picturesque scene of the camp—Some roasting bear meat & venison. others stretching & dressing skins—some lying on skins in the shade—Horses feeding—Hunters coming in with game—turkeys &c. Groupes relating the mornings exploits—clothes hanging to dry—tent pitched—fine luncheon—

Latrobe has caught a mess of small fish in the brook[175]

One hunter brings in an otter The rest return without success—Game frightened from the neighborhood.

Dinner—Bear meat roasted—excellent[—]The rest of bears meat & venison is roasted to take with us.

Venison & Bears meat jerked at Capts fire

Camp nearly surrounded by deep glens with quiet clear pools at

173. WI's asterisk in the middle of line 5 of page [59] indicates a footnote; before the two-line note at the bottom of the page, WI drew a line from binding edge to right margin.

174. Ellsworth described Antoine Lombard's excursion on October 16–17 and said that he returned to camp at 1:00 P.M. (*Narrative*, pp. 44–45, 48).

175. Ellsworth said that Latrobe caught "Roache or sun fish" (*Narrative*, p. 49).

the bottom—In which the autumnal glory[?][176] & mellow evg skies are beautifully reflected

[*p. [61] blank*]

[*At this point, Irving completed the dated portion of the journal; he reversed the notebook and wrote from page [78] forward to page [62]. These undated miscellaneous notes are transcribed in the order in which Irving wrote them.*][177]

Carandolet—or *Vuide Poche*[178]—a few miles below St Louis—
A traveler from New Orleans nearly out of provisions stopped his canoe there and asked for food—no beef—no mutton—no bread—all sick with fever & ague[—]turned[?] upon him & asked what he had[.] Nothing but a few ⟨crusts⟩ fragments of biscuit in a pouch—Begged them—Shook them out and gave him the empty bag to travel on with—Thence the place took the name of Vuide Poche or empty pouch[179]

———

Capt Courtois[180]—old round[?][181] dried fellow[—]looked like Don Quixote—could not read & write—but study French afternoons—[*three unrecovered words*][182] Duke under the Spanish Govt—and had title of commandant—with small pay—when asked when was Caran/dolet founded—replied de tante temps[.][183] when the province was transferred he was recommended to govt & was made capt of militia with which he was well pleased—[? In genl ?] training having no silk sash he made one of red silk Hkf[184]—Invited Gov Lewis Genl Clark[185] &

176. This word could be "groves."

177. The following six pages are badly water-stained; transcription is especially difficult on pages [78] and [77].

178. See p. 66, n. 140; WI discussed "Vaide Poche" in his September 14 entry.

179. WI drew a line three-fourths inch long to separate paragraphs.

180. McDermott offered as a possible identification Louis Courtois, the son of Joseph Courtois and Marguerite Perthuis, who was married at St. Geneviève in 1770 and died in 1815 at age 71. Other possibilities may be Lieutenant J. M. Courtois, Captain Louis Courtois, and his son Lieutenant Louis Courtois—all in the military in the War of 1812 (*Western Journals*, pp. 133–34, n. 59).

181. This word could be "burned."

182. These words may be "cleard[?] & made."

183. These words may be deciphered as "de tante tempo"; WI may have been referring to the French idiom, "de temps en temps" or "from time to time." The French words could also be "de toute temps" which may have been WI's attempt at "en tout temps" meaning "at any time."

184. WI's abbreviation for "handkerchief."

185. Meriweather Lewis and William Clark (see p. 60, n. 108).

others to dine with him at Vuide Poche Militia drawn out—ordered to fire at each toast—then asked permission for them to come & drink to healths of the party—Shouldrd their arms[,] entered, drank & returned to their Stations like statues After transfer of govt he retained[?] his living[186] in the village—Old people looked up to him. Settled all abuses—his word was law He was good farmer. Kept a small shop & was well to do in the world.

Capt Courtois wore old fashioned cocked Hat when on Militia duty—

He was once put on a jury, which was a new institution in the country & quite strange to him. When asked he observed[?][187][—]my mind is made up on the subject—and what is it Capt Courtois—why if the man is guilty, he should be punished—and if he is innocent he should be set at liberty & no harm done him—Aye but Capt Courtois that is not the thing—you must say is he guilty or not guilty. I tell you my mind is ⟨fix⟩ made up. if he is guilty &c

There was no getting any other answer from old Capt Courtois & the jury had to be dismissed.

[*p. [75] blank*]

Chief cook of Osage[188] Village—a great dignitary—combining grand chamberlain[,] minister of State, master of ceremonies & town crier. Has under cooks. He tastes broth &c. When strangers arrive he goes about the village & makes proclamation—Great white man[—]Great Chief arrived—warriors turn out & prepare to receive him properly—

Chief lodge prepared for reception—mats placed &c.—

In the course of our journey from Independence we met with camp[189] of Osages hunting deer[190]—The Cook a tall man painted—head decoratd with feather—Had an old great Coat, with a wolfs ⟨*illegible*⟩ tail ⟨sta⟩ dangling below

[*p. [73] blank*]

In the Chilhowee Mountains of NCarolina[191] is a rock called the garden rock. Indian superstitn so strong concerning it that ⟨the⟩ no one

186. These words may be "remained here living."
187. This word could be "descried," "declared," or "allowed."
188. WI apparently first wrote "Osages," then enlarged the *e* to form the singular.
189. This word could be "compy" (the "of" becomes the *y*).
190. This word could be "men."
191. The Chilhowee Mountains, located in Blount County, Tennessee, between the Tennessee River and Little River, were approximately parallel to the Great

dared to approach it—Supernatural being inhabited it—Gigantic—one eye—⟨Hunters⟩ not seen by men but the wandering hunter now & then had a glance[?] of his eye[192]—

⟨He fell in love⟩

near the mountain lived an old woman & daughter—⟨?⟩He fell in love with and gaind her—Mother & no one ever saw her—Mother watched[—] surprized her in the lodge with him—He disappeared and has never been seen since[—]the hunters say he still inhabits the mountain, which is in the [*blank*][193] reservation in NCarolina

Col. Choteaus comparison of two half breeds . . . This one has been twice as long at the mission as the other and therefore is twice as good for nothing[194]—

———

The choctaws, Col Arbuckle says are very good honest fellows—[195]

———

The[196] Cherokees are sly, bargaining avaricious. They have become civilized enough to know the value of property—They are factious—Electioneering—chiefs try to get adherents & make parties

Old trapper at Blacksmiths[197]

———

Capt—"What are ↑is↓ you doing at Sante Fe
trapping bears
Theres none to trap there[—]only here & there
Whats become of your party
Scatterd—some gone to California—some down Columbia river
Some—

———

Smoky Mountains of North Carolina and just north of that range. (See W. P. Cumming, *North Carolina in Maps* [Raleigh: State Department of Archives and History, 1966], plate 13, U.S. Coast Survey, 1865.)

192. For another version of this myth, see pp. 156–57.

193. WI apparently intended to add the word "Cherokee."

194. The following six lines between anecdotes are 1⅛ inch long, one-eighth inch long, three-eighths inch long, 3¼ inches long, one-half inch long, and one-eighth inch long.

195. This dash could be a slightly out-of-place comma in the line above, after the word "says."

196. WI may have crossed his uppercase *T*; he repeated this unusual formation at the beginning of the next sentence with the word "They."

197. See WI's description of this scene in the October 10 entry when they were at Colonel Chouteau's trading post on the Verdigris River.

This flour is bad enough to kill a Snake—theres lumps in it as big as terrapins[198]

———

The Osages are true[?] Indians—Hunters—full of ceremonies & superstitions—We are poor people say they—we cannot farm & our hunting is failing us—The pride of the Osages is broken—

They steal horses.

Give you a grand ceremony & then perhaps follow you and Steal your horse

———

⟨Horses if they smell⟩

Wild horses—tell you by their smell if the wind sets from you & run off—otherwise come near & gaze at you[.] Stallions prance round and snuff at mares

Horses if they smell mares[?] make off

Wild horses in distinctly[?][199] one[200] colour—some black some brown

One gang will be good—

another bad

Best horses cannot be taken

Buffalos. When the cows have calves the Bulls keep scatterd round the prarie, keeping guard ags wolves—charge furiously on any that approach

[*Following this one paragraph on p. [67], Irving turned the notebook clockwise one-quarter rotation and sketched three figures sitting and one standing before a tent, the outline of which overlaps the last three lines of the paragraph.*]

⟨Saline near the Washita[201] which used to ↑& is still↓ be a great fighting ground of the Osages—& Pawnees. Their sculls & bones may be seen blanching there—⟩[202]

———

198. In his account of the night of October 10, Ellsworth described the flour: "awful stuff—musty and a little sour," so bad that some of the soldiers who said their flour contained terrapins purchased corn and kept an iron mill in the camp in constant use (*Narrative*, p. 12).

199. This could be two words—"droves of."

200. There is a mark on the page above the *e* which suggests the reading, "uni."

201. In the middle of page [66] above the first line and the word "Washita," there is writing resembling "—Riv," "— 2" or "—In."

202. WI struck out this paragraph with a large *X* and set the following anecdote off with lines of seven-sixteenth inch and one-half inch.

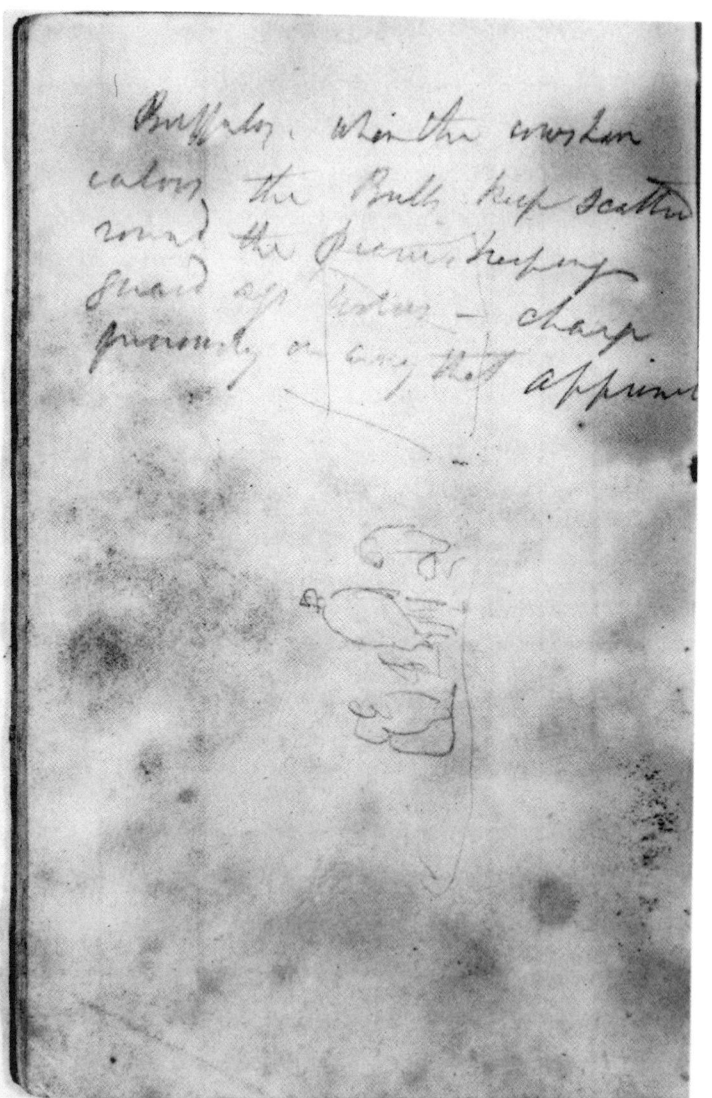

Fig. 8. Sketch on notebook p. [67] of three figures sitting and one standing before a tent, the outline of which overlaps the last three lines of the paragraph.

A grey horse has been noted for six or seven years on the Praries and the hunters have in vain tried to catch him. He prances on rocks[?] and outstrips the fastest horse

———

⟨Six men, a ⟨party⟩ ↑detacht↓ from a large force came upon what they thought to be wild horses. They approached them and found they were tame—thought to take them—but perceived Indians near a lodge. Supposed them Osages and came near them when they discovered they were Pawnees—They ⟨spran[?]⟩ turnd & fled—Pawnees sprang on their[203] horses & pursued them—one badly mounted fell behind—a Pawnees gained on him. one lanched arrow & missed him[—]lanched another arrow—the man dodged it—his stirrup gave way[—]he fell—turned & shot Pawnee between the shoulders with his rifle The other Pawnees turned to cry over their friend—the man escaped—Pawnees horse followed the whitemen to their camp and was taken—⟩

Story of young lady carried off by Indians—[*blank*] Young man by name of Philips followed her with a band. came upon track of Indians on a ⟨poin⟩ prarie. saw they must come near a point of wood—made a circuit and got into the wood. Young ⟨m⟩lady saw them & fell behind ⟨companio⟩ Indians—Philips seeing they could not come within ⟨*illegible*⟩ certain distance of wood called forth—Young lady ran toward him[—] Indian pursued her. ⟨Phil[?] *illegible*⟩ gained on her[—]began to strike at her with his ⟨hatchet⟩ tomahawk—Philips says his horse seemed to stand still tho at utmost speed—within [*blank*] yards young lady stumbled over log & fell partly thro loss of blood—Indian was just going to tomahawk her when Philips shot him thro head[204]—Narrator had the story from Philips brother

Indians when they have killed game & cannot bring it home, leave a blanket or some other garment by it[,] the smell of which keeps off wolves.

A rag with powder rubbed on it is said to do the same[205]

———

Billet—I want to know what way[?][206] he go any how—

———

203. Page [66] ends with this word; WI struck out this portion of the paragraph with a large *X*, and he used the same method on the remainder of the paragraph on the following page.

204. This word could be "hand."

205. WI set off the following three anecdotes with lines of one-sixteenth inch, one-half inch, and three-sixteenths inch.

206. This word could be "why."

Charley the hero of the owl camp[,] a Kind of butt in the camp[207]–

———

Billet[208]–half frenchman–half Indian–talkative & forward at times taciturn & sulky at others–Brings home game–throws it down & says nothing about it

Antoine[209] thorough frenchman–vaunts exults sings, boasts.

⟨r⟩*Ring*[210] *fires.* Made by Indians on Praries, to drive game to a point. A few men ⟨swift⟩ will run from point to point and make ⟨?⟩a range of fires for Miles

[*pp. [79–80] blank*]

[*inside back cover contains what seems to be a list of ten lines*][211]

[*back cover*][212]

No. 6.

207. See WI's entry for October 13 for a description of this incident.

208. Billet, or Beatte.

209. Antoine Deshetres, or Tonish.

210. Apparently WI began the word with an *r* as and then over it wrote *R*; therefore, the initial letter resembles a *B*.

211. As nearly as it can be deciphered, the list on the inside back cover is as follows:

Looking glass
Knife
Dearskin
[*illegible*] coat
Coonskin[?]
Supper [*illegible*]
[*two lines illegible*]
[*illegible*] Evg[?]
Put [*two words illegible*]

212. The notebook was reversed; in the middle of the back cover approximately one-eighth of the page from the top is a "7" and what appears to be the left half of the number "0"; then a line was drawn and what seem to be additional numbers follow.

AMERICAN JOURNALS, 1832

Number 8

Little River to Fort Gibson to Verdigris River

The manuscript journal is in the Seligman Collection of Irvingiana in the Manuscripts and Archives Division of the New York Public Library, where is it cataloged as #22–3300, Washington Irving Journals, Volume 27–A. It consists of 16 leaves of unlined, off-white paper, each page ruled with a double column of vertical lines on the left (the right line of the pair is actually two lines closely approximate), and a single vertical line on the right, plus one unlined, unruled leaf at the front and one at the back, making a total of 18 leaves. Its 36 pages measuring $3\frac{13}{16}$ inches wide and $5\frac{11}{16}$ inches long are held together with a string between pages [18] and [19]; the edges have faded, barely discernible gilt, and the notebook is bound in faded brown leather. Pages [2], [36], and the inside back cover are blank; the inside front cover is blank except for the number *15* written in pencil in the upper left corner. Also written in pencil are pages [1], [3–25], the upper half of [26], the top 2½ lines (when the journal is reversed) of page [31], the lines crossing out pages [29–31, 33–34], and the writing on pages [32–34], and [36]. The bottom half of page [26] and pages [27–31] are in brown ink; the notebook number and date are also in ink and in Irving's hand, but the date seems to have been added later or gone over with fresh ink; the back cover is also in light brown ink. After page [28], Irving apparently reversed the notebook and began writing back to front from page [34] to [29].

[*front cover*]

No 8
1832

[*inside front cover is blank except for the number "15" added in someone else's hand*]

chilowy Inds[1] N Carolina & Tennesse
Nashville,[2] Knoxville[3] to the right

[*p. [2] blank*]

Wednesday, October 31[4]
Encampt. ⟨bank⟩ on the little river[5]–Canadian[6]–⟨Yankees[?]⟩ In[7] a

1. Chilowy Indians, or the Chilhowee, were formerly an important Cherokee settlement on the Tellico River, which is a branch of the Tennessee River, in Monroe County, Tennessee, near the North Carolina border. The spelling of this branch of the Cherokee Indians varied: William Bartram in 1792 spelled it "Chelowe"; others wrote "Chilhowee," "Chillhoway," and "Chilhowey." John Swanton also says of the "Over-the-Hills and Valley Settlements or Overhill Settlements" that the Chilhowee was one of three dialect groups of the Cherokee Indians (*The Indian Tribes of North America,* Smithsonian Institution Bureau of American Ethnology Bulletin, no. 145 [Washington, D.C.: Smithsonian Institution Press, 1971], p. 217; hereafter cited as Swanton, *Indian Tribes*).

2. Nashville, Tennessee, the capital of Davidson County and of the state, was on the left bank of the Cumberland and enjoyed steamboat navigation from New Orleans. Founded in 1784 and named for General Nash, who was killed in the Battle of Germantown, Nashville's population in 1832 was 5,566; it was then Tennessee's leading city culturally, a place of active trade and manufacture, and the home of the University of Tennessee founded in 1806. Baird enthusiastically reported in 1832 that "there is not only wealth here, but there is intelligence, refinement, benevolence and hospitality, to an almost unrivalled extent" (Baird, *View*, pp. 193–94).

3. Knoxville, Tennessee, the most important town in east Tennessee, was the capital of Knox County and formerly the capital of the state; located 199 miles east of Nashville on the west or right bank of the Holston River, four miles below the confluence with the French Broad River, and 22 miles above its conjunction with the Tennessee River. It became the state capital the year it was laid out (1794) and remained so until 1817. Its population in 1832 was approximately 3,000; its hilly location gave it a beautiful view of the river and of the thirty-miles-distant mountains of Chilhowee. In Knoxville was the University of East Tennessee which was founded in 1807 as East Tennessee College.

4. WI wrote "1832. Oct. 31 ↑Wednesday↓."

5. Little River is in central Oklahoma, rising southeast of what is now Oklahoma City and flowing ninety miles southeast to the Canadian River which it entered from the north.

6. The Canadian River, sometimes called the Rio Colorado, rose in the Guadalupe Mountains in New Mexico and was the Arkansas' great southwestern branch. It flowed 900 miles southerly then easterly across the northern part of Texas and the southern part of the Indian Territory; of its two branches, the larger was the North Fork which flowed for 600 miles almost parallel to, and entered, the main stream about 100 miles west of Fort Smith and then entered the Arkansas River approximately 500 miles from its mouth. This river was explored and described by Major Long.

7. This word could be "for."

day or two past discontent in the camp as among the children of Israel in the wilderness[8]—want of bread—for a week past the troops have been out of flour. a corporal last night was put under arrest for mutinous talk on the subject—determined that we start from here direct for the garrison.[9] Capt & Drs. Horses & the horse of a ranger had strayed yesterday & ⟨before⟩ men had been sent back to the camp in search of them. Capt & one man set off this morning on their trail. We made every preparation for starting—Horses of troops all saddled[10] 10 O clock & Capt not returned ⟨we⟩ Mr Ellsworth determines to start on ahead & let Capt ⟨?⟩& troops over/ take us[11]—We set off with[12] escort of 14 men under Lieut Penticost—at 10 Oclock. Scout[13] the Prarie—See white

8. Numbers 11:1–15 records the discontent of the Israelites: "And the people complained in the hearing of the Lord about their misfortunes. . . . Now the rabble that was among them had a strong craving; and the people of Israel also wept again, and said, 'O that we had meat to eat! We remember the fish we ate in Egypt for nothing, the cucumbers, the melons, the leeks, the onions, and the garlic; but now our strength is dried up, and there is nothing at all but this manna to look at' " (*Holy Bible*, Revised Standard Version).

9. The garrison was Fort Gibson. Apparently the WI party had intended to proceed farther south through the Indian Territory before going back to the fort, but this decision changed their direction to northeast. Latrobe wrote that they were "now to set out on [their] return home," and in the approaching "eight days' uninterrupted march to the N.NE." they would discover that the distance and difficulty in getting to the fort were greatly underestimated on this last day of October (*Rambler*, I, 238–39).

10. This word is smudged, barely legible.

11. Ellsworth said that because he did not know how long the captain's delay could be, and because the "Commissioners would be anxious for my return," he requested a twenty-man detachment to accompany him to the garrison (*Narrative*, p. 129).

12. This word is badly smudged, but the best reading seems to be "with."

13. This word could be "skirt" although it appears to be "scout"; Ellsworth wrote that the party "travelled on the prairie southeasterly parralel to the Canadian river, which gave us an excellent opportunity to see the face of the country on both sides of this large stream—Praries of great extent were seen up and down the river—especially, at the West the prarie was boundless—On the opposite side of the Canadian the praries exceeded those on the north, and we beheld many Buffaloe and wild horses at a great distance feeding on the wild pastures with perfect unconcern" (*Narrative*, p. 129).

14. The name "Tonish" seems to be written over an illegible word, or perhaps, it is marked through; however, Ellsworth's reading confirms ours: when they saw a "large drove" of wild horses, "Tonish Billet & Antoine all fixed their Lariats and set off full speed—One never is satiated with the sight of a fine race—the zeal the rider, & the object are always among the most interesting out-door scenes" (*Narrative*, p. 133).

wolves—deer &c. ⟨keep⟩ See Buffalo & wild Horses. Billet Tonish[14] & Antoine set off in pursuit of horses but in vain—Portales shoots at Buffalo.[15] Keep a S. course & then turn South east in old osage ↑war track.↓[16] terrible brush wood, thickets, deep ravines—See deer, fine bucks &c—Buffalo—encamp ⟨at⟩ 5 minutes before 3—in a small valley—near pools of water. Made this day 14 miles or thereabout[17] Form our little camp—Set guard make fires—Sup on Stewed Buffalo—roast venison—begnets[18]—tea without sugar— —Spread our ⟨beds⟩ skins under trees ⟨& sleep⟩ old Mr Sawyer[19] Sits at foot of my bed & gossips until I fall asleep—Large bear seen in neighborhood of our camp—but escaped the huntsmen—Fine star light night—shooting stars—

Thursday, November 1[20]

beautiful day break—camp cherful[21] in good spirits with prospects of soon being at home & getting bread—notes of quails— —⟨*illegible*⟩

15. Ellsworth said that none of the men felt compelled to shoot at the buffalo they passed that day because they had enough meat and had "fully gratified" their hunting instinct; "Mr Pourteles had however not killed *his* Buffaloe—he had no *tongue* as trophy—he pursued 3 bulls quite a distance, but directed his fire to the rump of the animal which is bomb proof, against bullets or arrows—" (*Narrative*, p. 133).

16. Ellsworth disagreed with WI in this detail: "We had expected to find an Osage trail from this prarie, but we did not and were compelled to break a new road which impeded us very much—" (*Narrative*, p. 131).

17. Ellsworth expressed disappointment at this distance as they expected to travel 25 miles that day (*Narrative*, p. 133).

18. This word is apparently a misspelling of "beignets," a French word for fritters. In the November 3 entry, WI wrote that "Tonish is cooking flour fritters in Buffalo fat for us." According to Ellsworth, this dish was one of their primary staples, as long as the flour lasted; he explained to his wife that "when pork is plenty, a little of that is fried, and in the fat is boiled some fritters—i e small pan-cakes" (*Narrative*, p. 28).

19. In his October 18 entry, Ellsworth mentioned hearing gun fire and, upon investigation, discovering "the lost man Mr Sawyer[?] firing for help . . . [he] was found bearing his course directly from us—It was cloudy and he mistook the points of compass—" (*Narrative*, p. 50). Latrobe called him "a comical old fellow, the butt of the troop," "one of those strange mixtures of simplicity and shrewdness," a person whom Nature seems to have "made up of scraps and leavings," and who "was celebrated for losing himself" (*Rambler*, I, 195–96). Latrobe discussed a loquacious visit on the evening of October 26 by "old Sawyer . . . to sound the intentions of the Commissioner" (see *Rambler*, I, 217–18, for this account).

20. WI wrote "*Thursday November 1.*"

21. This word could possibly have another *e* if the *h* is read differently, but it looks more like "cherful."

Billet[22] singing indian nasal song—prepare for marching but detained by the wandering of one of Latrobes horses—at length (it being found) we set off at 8. Fatiguing march over ⟨de⟩ Hills & through deep ravines of ⟨po[?]⟩ parched dwarf oaks with flesh tearing twigs[—]through tangled ⟨&c⟩ thickets &c. Billet Kills a fat doe[23]—Latrobe a fine turkey.—⟨Get⟩ arrive at the valley of the Grand Bayou on [24] little river—Wander about in a labarynth of swamps thickets, inundated lands—tangled with grapevines thorny vines &c which almost pull us off our horses[25]—⟨One[?]⟩ nearly mired in a deep creek[.] one of the pack ⟨ponies[?]⟩ horses falls on his side & ⟨damages⟩ ↑wets↓ his lading.[26] tracks of bears, wolves, buffalo, wild horses, turkeys, ducks &c ⟨*illegible*⟩[27] try several times to find fording place of Bayou which is deep & miry with steep [*two unrecovered words*][28] banks—at length succeed—all get over girth deep and Stop to rest the horses in a meadow—about ½ past 11 having made about 10 miles Spread wet baggage to dry—Hang up the two shirts which I washed yesterday

22. The letters crossed out could be "na" or "in" or "mr." The word "Billet" is slightly misformed by the pen's apparently catching below WI's usual *l*, so that it appears to be "Bilyet."

23. Ellsworth mentioned Billet's "fine doe" but added that "the rangers neglected to bring him to the camp and only a little was brought by Billet to our Mess" (*Narrative*, p. 135).

24. The preposition could be "in."

25. Latrobe described this long march; the first four days (October 31–November 3) were "employed in breaking a painful pathway with many a tear, scratch, and grumble, through the Cross Timbers. Before we reached the vicinity of the Arkansas River we had to recross the Grand Bayou, though much lower down than before . . ." (*Rambler*, I, 239). Ellsworth added, "Billet several times attempted to ford the Bayou or Swamp—his horse one time sunk into the mire so as to be just discernable, and the rider jumping off into the water drew him out . . ." (*Narrative*, p. 134). Gregg wrote that this terrain through which WI was traveling was "so matted in many places with grapevines, green-briars, etc., as to form almost impenetrable 'rough,' which serve as hiding places for wild beasts, as well as wild Indians . . ." (for a detailed description of what he called the "celebrated Cross Timbers," see Gregg, *Commerce of the Prairies*, II, 283–84).

26. Ellsworth said that "the horse that fell was [Latrobe's] Gumbo, the poor old black horse, that looked as though he would sink every moment and give out—" (*Narrative*, p. 134). According to WI's November 4 entry, Gumbo did "give out."

27. This crossed-out word could be "at" or "we."

28. The unrecovered words could be "to the"; some clue might be derived from Ellsworth's description: "The Banks were p[r]ecipitous and almost perpendicular & the bottom was miry—I saw two or three horses in the slough and determined not to ford mine over—" (*Narrative*, p. 134). WI might have written "with slough to the banks," but what seems to be a crossed *t* suggests "steep" rather than "slough" as the reading of the word before the unrecovered words.

Resume our march ¼ before 1—excessively fatiguing to man and horse —a broken hilly country covered with Scrub oaks, with interlacing limbs as hard as iron, & intersected by deep ravines of red clay, down which the horses fairly slide; & then scramble up the other side like cats. The oaks are all ⟨wit⟩[29] brown & dried as if a Simoom[30] had passed across—a ⟨dr[?]⟩ miserable sterile dreary country at this season of the year. Here & there is a bottom where there are cotton & elm trees which give a transient variety and absolute thickets of Persimmons laden with rich fruit.[31] In a meadow of one of these bottoms we see a fine wild black Horse[.] Billet approaches horse riding on a mare & whinnies to attract him. Horse prances round her at a distance. Billet dismounts[,] aims with his rifle over the back of his mare & fires hoping to cress[32] the horse, but he escapes—about ½ past 3 we[33] encamp near a brook on a pleasant meadow, though the herbage is much parched and offers but indifferent food for our jaded horses[34]— —

29. This crossed-out word is probably the beginning of "withered," or perhaps "bak," the first three letters of "baked."

30. A "simoom" is a violent, hot, sandy wind in the deserts of Africa and Asia.

31. Flint wrote that the "persimon," or *dyospyros Virginiana*, was "the size of a common horse plumb. When green, it is astonishly astringent. It is only ripened by the frost of winter. There are varieties in its size, from low shrubs to considerable trees. When the small blue persimon is thoroughly ripened, it is even sweeter than the fig, and is a delicious fruit" (*Mississippi Valley*, II, 48).

32. There is a mark which resembles a circumflex over the word "cress." Ellsworth gave a detailed description of Billet's attempt to capture this "fine horse feeding alone" (*Narrative*, pp. 134–35). Gregg objected to "the cruel expedient of 'creasing,' which consists in shooting [the mustang] through the upper *crease* of the neck, above the cervical vertebræ; when, the ball cutting a principal nerve, he falls as suddenly as if shot in the brain, and remains senseless for a few minutes . . ."; the horse was tied, recovered, and was easily tamed. However, many horses were killed by accident (*Commerce*, II, 288–89).

33. In McDermott's edition of the *Western Journals*, he omitted two pages of manuscript (pp. [8–9]) following WI's phrase, "about ½ past 3 we" at the bottom of p. [7]. Page [8], which naturally begins with the predicate, "encamp near a brook on a pleasant meadow," is the verso of the leaf containing pages [7–8]. Page [9], which ends with the phrase, "not having found their horses," is the recto of the following leaf. McDermott's version continued with p. [10] of the manuscript, which begins "resume our march about one." The editor even indicated in a note that there was no November 2 entry and referred to WI's *Tour* and Ellsworth's *Narrative* to fill in the missing information (*Western Journals*, p. 143, n. 12). Trent and Hellman made the same omission (*Journals of WI*, III, 161).

34. Latrobe mentioned the fact that "the poor animals had nothing to eat,—the grass was dead or burnt, and we met with no cane before we reached the Arkansas" (*Rambler*, II, 240).

Beautiful evening. Western horizon a clear apple colour[35] then above a delicate lake[36] then a deep purple blue[37]—not a cloud—Steady chorus of Insects blended into one note—tinkling of horse bells--low murmering talk of tired rangers round their fires. Supper—Stewed turkey & Bufalo meat—Begnets[38]— —

Sleep under tree—beautiful moonlight for the first half of the night—then fine star light—

⟨Billet says⟩

At ¼ past 3—old Sawyer who is one of the centinels is impatient to be relieved—If the stars dont delude[39] me it is near day break.

Billet—I hear the owl

I[—]does that hoot towards day.

Billet—Just like the Cock.[40]

Friday, November 2[41]

⟨Beautif⟩ Cool—morning light mist in the valley which is dispelled by the rising sun—

Breakfast before sun rise & then make preparations for departure—

March at ½ past 7—this morng march thro a more easy country[42]—Post oak risings & small praries—see deer & turkies—at length come out upon extensive praries & see north fork[43] about ⟨4[?]⟩6 miles to our left. ⟨encamp⟩ ↑Halt↓ at 11[44] beside a small brook on the edge of a prarie

35. From the more detailed description in the *Tour*, the apple color which WI saw was a shade of green (*Tour*, p. 255).

36. The reading of this word, "lake," seems illogical in context; however, in WI's *Tour* account of this evening he used the word "lake"; he changed his journal account of a cloudless night to read in the *Tour*, "One narrow streak of cloud, of a mahogany colour, edged with amber and gold, floated in the west, and just beneath it was the evening star, shining with the pure brilliancy of a diamond" (*Tour*, p. 255).

37. This word could be "Hue."

38. At this point in the journey, flour became a valuable item; Ellsworth said that their escort begged and was given some which "was musty & had been wet" (*Narrative*, p. 135).

39. This word could be "deceive."

40. See WI's account of this conversation with Billet (Beatte) and with Sawyer, whom he called "the oldest man in the troop" (*Tour*, p. 257).

41. WI wrote, "Friday Nov 2."

42. Ellsworth said that their direction was northeast and that the post oak and walnut trees "suceeded to the cast iron black jack"; he added that they "found land better" (*Narrative*, pp. 135–36).

43. The North Fork of the Canadian River (see p. 137, n. 6).

44. Ellsworth remembered "½ past 11 having travelled 10 miles—" (*Narrative*, p. 136).

⟨by⟩ ↑at↓ an old ↑Creek↓ Indian encampment. figure drawn on ⟨ba[?]⟩ tree with charcoal of Indian & squaw with hieroglyphic sign that the Indians were on their way homeward[45]—while resting at the encampt. Capt Bean & his men arrive.[46] Left the encampt. at [*blank*] ⟨?⟩Yesterday. Have travelled 36 miles in two days. Capt & Dr most of the way on foot not having found their horses

resume our march about one ⟨pass⟩ keeping Easterly, ⟨making a⟩ approaching the North fork obliquely—⟨f⟩ difficulty in finding a place to encamp where there is water—pass over a burnt prarie[47] at length about ¼ after 4—encamp in a small bottom near the burnt Prairie & not far from the North fork[48]—good range for the horses

make my bed ⟨among⟩ under a dry tree on a hillock among long dry Prarie grass,—a perfect couch—Sleep soundly & sweetly & warmly tho a heavy dew fell—Starlight—watch the stars on the prarie as at Sea— Lightning in the east a sign of ⟨com⟩ approachg bad weather—clouds about the horizon—flocks of wild ducks show cold weather at hand—

Camp short of provisions. improvidence of men who left piles of Buffalo meat at their camp the day before yesterday[49]

Saturday, November 3[50]

Breakfasted early on coffee & the last of Buffalo meat—[51] march ¼ ⟨before⟩ after 7—⟨*illegible*⟩ weather clouds up ‸↑low rumbling of thun-

45. Ellsworth was offended by the Creek's "*very indecent* manner of making pictures on the trees. The wood is first cut off, and with paints they represent the warrior in such attituds of amorous feeling in going or returning as may be indicative of their true sensations, but very abhorrent to every principle of modesty or virtue—I forbear giving details—" (*Narrative*, p. 136).

46. Ellsworth explained the rapid travel of Captain Bean and Dr. Holt, who, even though on foot most of the way, had traveled 36 miles in two days: the "path was broken for them, and their anxiety to return with us, induced them to ride early & late to join our party—" (*Narrative*, p. 136).

47. Prairie fires which were then burning all around them left "very painful [stubble] for the horses feet—not only thatch, but small bushes, are burnt even with the ground; and as soon as the horse presses his weight upon them, they too frequently run into the fray and make him lame—" (Ellsworth, *Narrative*, p. 137).

48. They traveled 28 miles that day (Ellsworth, *Narrative*, p. 136).

49. This comment is interesting in light of Ellsworth's earlier criticism, "I was surprised to find Mr Irving opposed to any restrictions and ridi[c]ule the idea of taking thought for tomorrow—" (*Narrative*, p. 46). Leaving the meat behind this time was contrary to Captain Bean's orders (*ibid.*, p. 135), and Latrobe commented that because the men did not dry surplus meat and even threw it away to avoid carrying it, it was "always a feast or a fast" (*Rambler*, I, 240).

50. WI wrote "Saturday Nov 3."

51. This dash is actually a long extension of the *t*.

der↓ wind veers to NE & it begins to rain—cross praries & pass thro open ⟨land⟩ oak forests See deer but not within shot[—]several flocks of wild turkeys—men on the alert, eager for a dinner a few days since they dispised such small game & I have seen dead turkeys left behind on marching—

Cross the North Fork about ½ past 9—quite fordable—ride through rich well timbered bottom—cross small branches and 7 minutes before 1 ⟨rain[?]⟩ encamp in an oak forest beside a ⟨sma⟩ brook[52]—rain holds up until we ⟨pitch our tent⟩ make fires, pitch tent[,] dry[?] our clothes &c Hunters are gone out & Billet among the number in quest of food, for a great Scarcity reigns in the camp Some of the men have not had any thing since yesterday morng—Tonish is cooking flour fritters in Buffalo fat for us, to take with coffee, without milk or sugar—

Billet returns with two turkeys—10 Turkeys killed in this camp

This part of country has good bottoms along the rivers—some good pasture land in the praries & good mast[53] in the forests—Might make good land to raise stock on

Billet had said the wind would lie[54] to the north—this morning a flight of brandt[55] flew from the north over our heads—there comes the wind said Billet—and in fact the wind soon veerd—

Night cold gusty with freaks[56] of rain—Large log fire before our tent—

In the night wild geese fly over making crackling in the air—

Sunday, November 4[57]

Raw cloudy gloomy morning—three men sent out from each mess to hunt for the horses, Very[58] apprehensive that many of them have made for the fort—for horses have an instinctive[59] knowledge ⟨wh⟩ of their

52. Ellsworth said they "rode to day 20 miles" (*Narrative*, p. 137).

53. Mast, forest tree nuts which have accumulated on the ground, was considered good food for swine.

54. This word could be read "be." In *Tour*, WI said, "Beatte prognosticated rain, and that the wind would veer to the north" (*Tour*, p. 259).

55. Of the genus *Branta*, there are several kinds of brant or wild geese which breed in the Arctic; the most common has a black neck and head. Flint wrote the "noise of their countless flocks, as they journey through the air in the spring, to the sources of the great rivers and lakes, and in autumn, to the Gulf of Mexico, is one of the most familiar sounds to the ear of an inhabitant of the West . . ." (*Mississippi Valley*, I, 76–77).

56. This word became "flurries" in the *Tour* (p. 259); here it could end in "ing" or "ly," but "freaks" seems to be the best reading.

57. WI wrote "Sunday Nov 4."

58. This word could be "Many."

59. This word could be read as "intuitive"; the reading "instinctive" seems to be a better one even though the *c* is barely legible.

approach to home and can make a straight course for it As they graze every step they take is towards home.

Set out on the march ¼ before 8–After marching an hour ⟨[? we fi ?]⟩ or so we strike a Creek trail, leading directly on our course, which enables us to go on briskly though very irregularly, many of the horses being almost knocked up[60]–Land improves–fine praries like park scenery, ⟨ri[?]⟩ now mellowed by the sober tints of autumn. A young buck springs up on our right & dashes ahead but ⟨is brought down [*illegible*]⟩[61] Childers[62] a young ranger who had accidentally alighted from his horse fires & breaks his neck & the buck tumbles[63] head over heels Tonish flanked us on the left & killed a fat doe. another ranger killed a buck. Mr Latrobe kills a polecat which is treasured up by the men. several turkeys killed–Noble prospect from a hill over richly tinted woodlands, praries &c and long lines of distant hills

about 3, we encamp in grove ↑in a hollow↓–on the bank of a branch, after a march of about 26 miles–The horses come straggling up, but many remain behind & some it is feared will give out

–our course this day a little to the northward of east–

Billet arrives late (we had to send a horse back for him). ⟨his black poney mare tired⟩–Poor Gumbo gave out nine miles off–& Billets blk poney mare not long after & had to be abandoned–[64]

Supper–Stewed venison ribs & turkey made into a rich soup–

comes on to rain about 9. Heavy rain in the night–

This afternoon we saw a round hill or mound 15 or 20 miles off said to be within 8 miles of the garrison. still I fear some of the horses will

60. Ellsworth reported that because of horse distemper and fatigue, he "requested Capt to tell the rangers that they must walk to relieve their animals–for Government would not pay for horses worried down so near the garrison if the men were able to walk–"; as a result, "many were seen footing it all day" (*Narrative*, p. 138).

61. The first letters of this word could be "Yo," *M*, *r* or *w*, among other choices.

62. McDermott listed in the roster of Bean's Rangers an Alexander C. Childers, who had enlisted on August 25 in Batesville, Arkansas; he was a bugler (*Western Journals*, p. 182 and n. 7).

63. Because WI often crossed a *t* within the word without lifting his pen, as he did here, an *s* resembles a *d*; however, it seems apparent that the tense here is present.

64. According to Ellsworth, Billet's pony mare was kicked by one of the horses, and as a result she lost her colt and on this day "gave out" as did old Gumbo, the pack horse, and a wild colt which Tonish had caught (*Narrative*, p. 138). Latrobe listed the additional horses which had been "left to their fate": "Pourtales' Crop, Mr. Irving's generous bay, and my own gallant hunter . . . and the horses which still accompanied us were so emaciated, that, at last, we could not think of riding them" (*Rambler*, I, 240–41).

give out before we reach there—"If we pass any house where there are fat cattle or fowls they will have to lock them up" said one of the hungry rangers—

Monday, November 5[65]

Cloudy dismal morng, after a rainy night. Camp before daylight sounds with imitations of cock crowing—owls hooting—The poor fellows had supper last night & are cheerful again.

I had prepared my bed in the open air last night—when it began to rain—crept into the tent—Sound of the axe in all quarters[—]men cutting poles to make booths of blankets &c

Capt & troop start before us—Billet ⟨brings up⟩ goes back for his mare & brings her to camp together with Portales colt—has to leave his mare, which is like to die. The ⟨m[?]⟩ wild mare lost her foal last night and had to be abandoned in the camp—we set off about 8—Cold ⟨mor⟩ ⟨m[?]⟩ gloomy morng. overtake the Capts. troop—Capt misses the trail & makes a circuit towards the NW around a rocky hill—we leave the troop & guided by Billet strike NE[66]—send word to capt, who has to follow us—wretched travelling among rocks, quicksands &c—at length come out upon Prarie—& after riding couple of miles we stop beside a brook to rest the horses. Capt & most of the troop go on. Some[67] ↑two↓ of our horses lie down with fatigue & sickness.[68]

Some of the men set the Prarie on fire, but it is too damp to burn to any extent

resume our march after ¾ of an hour. traverse[?] praries—a long scatterd line stretching 3 or 4 miles over hill & dale—encamp ↑in a wood↓ beside the deep fork,[69] about 4 oclock having made about 20 miles. Cold windy night. wind sounding through the forest & whirling about

65. WI wrote "Monday Nov 5—."

66. Ellsworth wrote, "The capt went off without Billet, and mistook the path [—]I was confident he was out of the way, and trying the compass found him going *West* whereas our true course was *N East*—I send a corporal to tell him he was wrong and directed Billet to take us in the right course—" (*Narrative*, pp.138–39).

67. The word "Some" may be struck through; the line is barely legible.

68. WI wrote "down with fatigue & sickness" between the lines, as if they were added after he began the next paragraph.

69. Ellsworth, like WI in this journal, called the river the "Deep fork" (*Narrative*, p. 139); however, in the *Tour*, WI called it "the Little North Fork, or Deep Creek" (*Tour*, p. 263). Latrobe discussed this river as the "Deep Creek, which seems to identify itseslf with the Little North Fork of the Canadian. It was by far the most serious impediment in our course, as its great depth and swiftness precluded all idea of fording" (*Rambler*, I, 239). Ellsworth, in retrospect, criti-

the dry leaves—Long logs cut for firing—making long fires, before which men cook and gossip—Antoine arrives pretty late bringing up the tired horses—⟨we⟩ ↑our party↓‸[70] send all our horses across the stream as it is rising—

Tuesday, November 6[71]

⟨raw gusty w⟩ cold windy morng—all the men have leave to go out ⟨shooting &⟩ huntg till 12. to supply the camp with food[72][—]great firing at turkeys with which the bottom abounds. Billet brings home six. Preparations for crossing the stream—trees felled to serve for bridges, but fall rather short. our men carry across the baggage on a felled tree, part of which is two feet under the water—[73]

Capt & others pass afterward over trees felled from each side to meet each other

Grove of Peccan trees—Latrobe kills two prarie hens[.] Mr Ellsworth & I, pass across felled tree, holding by a stretched cord & aided by Billet—

Several of the horses too weak to cross stream—Leave them with a guard of 12 men & leave two of our tired horses with them[74]

Leave the camp ¼ after 1[75]—cross rough stoney woody hills—have a fine prospect of woodlands, hills & Praries towards the Arkansas—

flocks of Prarie Hens

---

cized the captain's decision to pitch the camp on the south bank of the river: "The rains were swelling the stream every moment, and it was then just fordable—" (*Narrative*, p. 139).

70. The inserted words are divided by the end of the line.

71. WI wrote "Tuesday Nov 6."

72. Ellsworth remembered slightly differently that the "Capt gave a certain number permission to hunt till 12 oclock" (*Narrative*, p. 139).

73. The three accounts vary regarding this crossing. Latrobe positively described the obstacle's being overcome after several hours (*Rambler*, I, 239). Ellsworth recalled a much more difficult crossing; with the water rising and flowing at such speed (five knots an hour), Billet urged immediate crossing. It was Ellsworth's idea to stretch the ropes across the creek; he described removing everything but his shirt and stockings, entering the extremely cold water, and crossing waist deep "circumspectly as my foundation was a *teetering log* 3½ feet under the water—a few inches mistep would inevitably throw me into the current." WI, Latrobe, and Pourtalès crossed similarly, and the "servants have been faithful and daring—they must have extra pay, or reward from us respectively—" (*Narrative*, pp. 139–40).

74. The two horses were Ellsworth's and Latrobe's; a detail of twenty fatigued men remained (Ellsworth, *Narrative*, p. 140).

75. Ellsworth disagreed with WI's time; according to the commissioner, the party left "this side of deep creek at 2 PM" (*Narrative*, p. 140).

Capt & Billet wound a buck on a small Prarie to our left but it escapes—[76]

walk the whole way & lead or drive my horse—most of the rangers do the same. after marching ab[out][77] ⟨8⟩6 or 7 miles encamp in a good bottom among lofty sycamores on the banks of a small Stream[78]—Yesterday found out by examining maps that we were about fifty miles from the fort—

To day in course of the march Billet climbed a tree on a hill and saw the forests along the Arkansas[79]

Towards the end of our march we saw smoke along a ^↑woody↓ glen about 3 or 4 miles off[,] made no doubt by Indian hunters—

some of the rangers met a Creek Indian who told them the fort was but about 15 miles off—(he must be mistaken) Said he lived about 3 miles off—& had meat & corn—Rangers elated with the news.

This day weather cleared up sunny

Wednesday, November 7[80]

Last night a fine moonlight, but windy & cool[—]lay at the foot of a tree—This morning cloudy, but likelihood[81] of clearing up[.] preparation for early start—our flour all out[—]pepper also—salt nearly gone—we live on soup & stewd game

two of the men (Lieut[?][82] Penticost) lost their horses—have to remain to Search[?] them

Leave camp ½ past 7. Cross ⟨*illegible*⟩ rough hilly, stony country—

76. Ellsworth added that Billet did kill at least three "pole cats, alias skunks"; he then admiringly explained Billet's method of killing turkeys: Billet imitating their "gobble & clucking—they flock around him & he shoots them down—" (*Narrative*, p. 141).

77. The last three[?] letters of this word are difficult to read, being faded.

78. WI's revised estimate agreed with Ellsworth's; the camp was probably beside a tributary to the north of the Canadian's Deep Fork.

79. According to Ellsworth, Billet and Tonish were both sick, with Billet's having such violent pains in his side that he requested the doctor to bleed him. Because the doctor's eyesight at night was not good, "Captain Beans" bled Billet (*Narrative*, p. 140).

80. Before beginning this day's entry, WI skipped two lines, then wrote "Wednesday Novr 7—"; the *r*, which is an unusual addition to WI's abbreviation of November, could be the result of his pen's slipping.

81. The second *i* in "Likelihood" is barely legible.

82. McDermott read this word as "Lane" (*Western Journals*, p. 148); Ellsworth offered little assistance in identifying the other ranger when he said, "Pentecost and one or two others lost their horses during the night, and they were left behind to pick them up if they could—" (*Narrative*, p. 141).

⟨from⟩ ↑meet 5 Creeks–↓ from[83] Brow of hill have a fair look over wide praries–Billet sees Hill about 20 miles of[f] within 8 miles of fort[84]–Set off with fresh spirits–Cold march across burnt Praries, where Indians had lately hunted–See smoke of Indian Hunters at distance–Straggling march of 50 men in clusters or singly–deep muddy ravines & brooks[?][85]–Stop about mid day for an hour to rest horses & warm ourselves[86][–]sharp NW wind sweeping prarie– –weather cloudy. resume our march & ⟨at⟩ just at dusk arrive at creek[87] which empties into the Arkansas. Encamp in grove where several trees have been prostrated by Tornado[88]–huge fires soon ⟨spark⟩ blazing & sparkling–make supper of Stewed venison (Billet having killed a deer this morning). Fine moonlight night–sleep round camp fire–[89]

This day we made from 20 to 25 miles–NE. & by E.

Clear moonlight frosty night–A cup of water standing by the head of my bed froze ½ inch–

Thursday, November 8[90]

Cold bright morning–Make breakfast on the reliques of our provisions –remnant of venison. Turkey. Polecat. ⟨St⟩ Some roasted–some stewed

83. WI apparently added the words above the line after he marked out the word "from" in the previous line; he then added "from" in the margin to the left of the word "Brow."

84. Fort Gibson.

85. This word could be "brushes," "brooks," or "branches"; in *Tour*, WI wrote, "Part of the way was over stony hills, part across wide prairies, rendered spongy and miry by the recent rain, and cut up by brooks swollen into torrents. Our poor horses were so feeble, that it was with difficulty we could get them across the deep ravines and turbulent streams" (*Tour*, p. 266).

86. Ellsworth said that after traveling fifteen miles they stopped at one o'clock (*Narrative*, p. 141).

87. McDermott identified this creek as Pecan Creek; it entered the Arkansas about ten miles above the Verdigris (*Western Journals*, p. 148, n. 24).

88. In *Tour*, WI described the damage done to the forest by the hurricane (pp. 267–68); Latrobe also called the storm a hurricane and remembered that it "had passed and levelled many a noble tree, about twenty miles from the Arkansas" (*Rambler*, I, 240).

89. Ellsworth remembered this one as an "unpleasant" evening which found ground and trees wet, the fire difficult to start, and the supper late–a meal made up of "a piece of a boiled turkey–without coffee flour or salt . . . Several around us, poor fellows! had nothing but *water*. Some cooked the *heads* of *Turkeys* and the bones of the legs by burning them in the fire & then scraping them–This was truely hard times" (*Narrative*, pp. 141–42).

90. WI wrote "Thursday Nov 8–."

without salt[–]a[91] little coffee–with a remaining & long treasured lump of sugar–[92] Rub each morsel of meat on the salt bag–

Set off at ½ past 7 in high spirits for the ford of the Arkansas which we were told by Billet was about 13 miles off (Some of the men this morng [? were seen ?] to stew turkey ⟨bones⟩ ↑heads↓ & to rasp the bones for breakfast). March briskly ⟨over pa[?]⟩ through thickets across ⟨ri[?]⟩[93] branches over hills & praries–Portales horse Crop mires in a branch & is extricated with difficulty–From a hill see mounts beyond the fort. We are told the ford is about 9[94] miles off–on we go[–]the miles stretch–the horses tire[–]we dismount, having[95] fatigue ourselves [–]mount again–the horses stagger[,] lag behind–Crop Stops,[96] Portales flogs him on–at length he gives out–& the wild colt likewise[97]–Smoke of fires ⟨at⟩ on Praries–Get on tracks of Indians–at length to our joy come in sight of habitations of men–Creek Indians log houses among trees[98] –push on. horse ⟨tires[?]⟩[99] fagged–arrive at log house owned by White man with black fat wife[100]–delightful sight of hogs, poultry–crowing

91. It is difficult to determine whether this mark is the letter *a*, an "&," a heavy dash, or a crossing out of the beginning letter of a word.

92. An unusually long horizontal extension of the letter *r* suggests that it doubles as a dash; it also comes at the end of the line.

93. These letters could be "ra" or "ro."

94. This number is not clearly formed; it could be transcribed as "6" or "4," but the best reading seems to be "9."

95. This word could be "being."

96. This word could be read "flags."

97. Latrobe and Ellsworth mentioned Crop's "giving out"; Ellsworth added that the horse was a "fine racing horse (cost $150)" and was left in the open prairie along with another wild colt (Ellsworth, *Narrative*, p. 142; Latrobe, *Rambler*, I, 240). When WI related this detail in *Tour*, he called Pourtalès' horse a "prime hunter that had taken the lead of every thing in the chase of the wild horses" (*Tour*, pp. 269–70).

98. Latrobe wrote that "the sight of the first frontier 'clearing' on the Arkansas, about six miles above the Western Creek Agency, was cheering to both animals and men. We reached it about noon on the 10th of November. The Rangers and their officers resolved to proceed no further, but commenced a fearful slaughter among the pigs, hens, and geese, with which they as usual found the log-hut of the backwoodman surrounded . . ." (*Rambler*, I, 241–42). The date varies from that of Ellsworth and WI.

99. This word might be "lame" or "tires." Later in his account, Ellsworth said that he "hired two rangers to go and look for Mr Irvings horse which was left Lame on this side of th[e] Arkansaw about 87 miles distant" (*Narrative*, p. 147).

100. After WI's party had by-passed the Creek Indian Settlement in order to push on to the Agency by night, the men became increasingly determined to stop at the next place where food was available for men and horses. Two miles later, they "found such a place–it was a negro house Madam *Bradleys*–her man, was

of cocks &c. horse pricks his ears–⟨Mr[?]⟩ Stop at the door, Capt & others[101] eating at a table–huge Iron pot with beef & turnips–put in for a share–fat negress gives a plate heaping with beef & turnips[,] Corn bread & butter–apologizes for giving it in such poor style!–

Capt determines to camp there– –I push on with Mr Ellsworth to the ford where our companions were[102]–Corn cribs on banks of river[103][–] Give corn to horses–ravenous appetite for it–Scene with canoe. crossing baggage[104]–↑Cotton tree barks[105]–↓ ‸Stream swift–drive horses in–Mr Latrobes & mine get entangled in dry trees and return–⟨Ca[?]⟩ other horses swim in line, ⟨C[?]⟩Get to footing & land safely–canoe returns–we all get in & lead two horses, who send large wave into boat.–land safe–⟨*illegible*⟩[106] Set off thro woods for Choteaus agency–Horse seems renovated by the [? idea of getting ?] among corn, pricks ear, raises head trots &c Arrive at agency[107] Supper at Nannys[?].[108] Newspapers–Moonlight on Verd[i]gres river

---

a white one & absent at this time"; Ellsworth described with obvious delight the meal that followed (his memory of the menu varying slightly from WI's): "boiled turnips potatoes pork and Corn bread & butter"; he said that for all he cheerfully paid "one bit 12½ cents" and added that "Mr Irving relished the meal quite as much as I did and will have a good story to tell in his sketch book about Madame Bradleys entertainment" (*Narrative*, p. 143).

101. This word might be a shortened version of "officers"; however, Ellsworth remembered that there were four men at the table when they arrived, "Capt Beans & three others" (*Narrative*, p. 143). WI mentioned the "Captain of the rangers and his officers, round a three legged table" (*Tour*, p. 271).

102. Antoine came to their table and warned them that if they did not hurry, they would not be able to cross the river that night (Ellsworth, *Narrative*, p. 143).

103. Arkansas River. Ellsworth said that at the ferry stood a large corn crib and they gave each horse four ears of corn (*Narrative*, p. 143).

104. Ellsworth added that they put their plunder in the first load of the log canoe and that one horse was led by the paddler in the stern with the others following (*Narrative*, p. 143).

105. "Bark" is probably plural; the top of the S immediately below the word makes it difficult to decipher. The bark which WI described was a hollowed-out log canoe which Ellsworth called "perogues" and which he disparaged as "tott[er]ing." The craft was rather large; eight men sat in the bottom as they "passed over" the river. Unfortunately, the canoe was lost later that night when it pulled loose from its moorings (*Narrative*, pp. 143–44).

106. WI may have written one or two letters and then crossed them out to make another dash.

107. Colonel Chouteau's Verdigris Agency.

108. McDermott called this word illegible (*Western Journals*, p. 150); Trent and Hellman transcribed it as "Nanny's" (*Journals of WI*, III, 168). Ellsworth did not help to any significant degree in reading this word, saying only that they "heard the supper horn of Mr Chouteaus boarding house–"; they slept in "Col

Friday November 9[109]

Leave my horse at the agency & set off after breakfast, for the garrison ⟨where are Mr⟩ with Mr Latrobe & Mr Ellsworth–and resume our quarters at Col Arbuckles[110]

At night ⟨wi⟩ serenade of the widow by the quartermaster & one or two other old Bachelors[111]

In the fort is the widow Nix; a plump buxom dame, whose husband was 50 years of age when he married her. amassed 20 000 $ as Sutler to the Garrison, which functions he discharged from the first establishment of the fort. The widow came to the fort a short time since & is the object of desires of all the men.[112] The ghastly Qr Master–Capt Clark.[113] The old Col[114] himself–all aspire to her favor.[115] ⟨She⟩ A Lawyer with the Militia title of Major Lewis has just made his appearance at the fortress[116] as aspirant, & occasions some jealousy among the military men who all unite agst. the intrusion of the black coat. The Serenade

---

Chouteaus store in a small room, with a large fire." WI did not mention, as did Ellsworth, that their "rest was very poor–both were too hot–and we longed for morning which came slowly along–" (*Narrative*, pp. 144–45); in fact, in the *Tour*, WI said, "Here we passed the night comfortably quartered . . ." (*Tour*, p. 244).

109. WI wrote "Friday Nov 9th."

110. According to Latrobe's account, he and Pourtalès stayed at the Verdigris Agency; the "Commissioner and Mr. Irving repaired to the Fort on the Neosho, six miles east of the Agency" (*Rambler*, I, 243–44).

111. At this point, WI shifted from pencil to brown ink and began to write a smaller and more legible hand, evidence of his return to "civilization."

112. General John Nicks, who had been postmaster and sutler at Fort Gibson, was made a brigadier general of the Arkansas Militia in 1828; when an important Creek and Osage treaty was signed May, 1831, General Nicks was one of the men who witnessed it (Foreman, *Indians and Pioneers*, p. 165, n. 47; *Advancing the Frontier*, p. 109). In an extensive note, McDermott pointed out that Nicks was a North Carolinian, first a captain in the Third Infantry in 1808 and advancing to the rank he held when he died at Fort Gibson in December, 1831. He had been owner with John Rogers of trading posts at Fort Gibson and Fort Smith, and when he died he left his widow, Sally, $10,000 worth of goods to dispose of as the newly appointed sutler (*Western Journals*, p. 151, n. 31).

113. McDermott identified the quartermaster as Captain Isaac Clark, Jr., from Vermont (*Western Journals*, p. 151, n. 32). The word "ghastly" could be read "ghostly."

114. Colonel Matthew Arbuckle (see above, p. 101, n. 36).

115. Through the word "favor" there is an ellipse drawn in pencil and looping diagonally down into the two lines below, through the words "militia, made," and back up through the words "his" and "title." It is impossible to determine whether this mark was made by WI.

116. The line crossing out the words "the fortress" seems to be simply an extended crossing of the *t*'s in both words and not an elimination of the words.

of the widow was a horrible chorse voice[117] that broke the sleep of man[,] woman & dog throughout the fortress.

Saturday, November 10[118]

Breakfasted at Dr Pitcher.[119] ⟨Take⟩ ↑engage↓ my passage in the Steam boat Little Rock, ⟨[*illegible*] f⟩ which arrived last night & leaves today[120] for the mouth of the river.[121]

Visited the theater a building erected for Indian Council house——The Soldiers get up plays—No Negroes admitted.

Sail at about 2 oclock. Col & officers accompany me to the vessel.[122] We go down Grand river[123] & turn up the Verdigres to take in cargo, of Skins at the agency. Take tea with Latrobe & Pourtales at the agency with Mr [*blank*] & Col Lane[?][124]

117. Alternate readings for these two words are "chorse aria," "choric aria," and "chorse voce."

118. WI wrote "Saturday Nov 10."

119. McDermott identified the post surgeon at Fort Gibson as Dr. Zina Pitcher (1797–1873) (*Western Journals*, p. 151, n. 33).

120. This decision signaled a change in plans for WI; Ellsworth said they had planned to rest at Fort Gibson for eight or ten days in their "batchelors-hall—But alas! in the night the sound of *steam* was heard a steam boat had arrived! the first this season—the water was falling and she must return tomorrow—The opportunity was too good to be lost—Mr Irving must go—he left me a power of attorney to dispose of his little effects, and a request to settle some trifling demands" (*Narrative*, p. 145). Latrobe, too, was sorry to see WI "resolve to take advantage of [the small steamboat's arrival], to commence his return to the East . . ." (*Rambler*, I, 244).

121. The Arkansas River.

122. WI's casual leave-taking contrasted with Ellsworth's, who wrote, "I parted with him with great reluctance—We had shared much together, and I trust formed a mutual attachment to last during life." Williams and Simison found no record of any later relationship (*Narrative*, p. 145, n. 3). Ellsworth also gave WI a note expressing great feeling and hoping that "when our journey (though by different paths) through the cross-timbers and praries of life, is completed, we may meet, to enjoy together the *Paradise* which lies beyond." He signed his note to WI, "Very affectionately & respectfully farewell—" (*Narrative*, p. 146).

123. Grand River, or Neosho.

124. The first letter of this name is *L*, and the second may be an *o* rather than an *a*. Latrobe mentioned the "agreeable society" of the officers at the Verdigris Agency (*Rambler*, I, 244); Ellsworth said that when he and WI spent the night at that agency on the way to Fort Gibson, "A Mr Dudding & a young Doct. took one bed and the other was left for Mr Irving & myself" (*Narrative*, p. 144). These may have been the men with whom WI, Pourtalès, and Latrobe had tea two days later.

⟨*illegible*⟩[125] picturesque ⟨Sce⟩ groupes of[126] Creek Indians crossing ferry in canoe with horses—others lying about the banks—led horses &c

I am now writing on board the steam boat which lies about a mile below the agency. Close by one of the sandy banks of the ⟨r[?]⟩ Verdigres— —beautiful embowered stream—Gleam of Sky along the water between the lines of trees which fringe each bank. Moon rising among the Groves[127]

[*At this point the chronological narrative ends, and the notebook reverses, with Irving writing from p. [34] to p. [29]. For the convenience of the reader, the transcription is in the order Irving wrote the notes, not in the natural page order.*]

Mr E.—Spurs without rowels—When we met the 8 Osages [he] charged them not to make war & then ⟨spoke of⟩ told Billet[128] to tell them of Skunk[129]—

Uncle Sams gun three Inches in breech 1 in muzzle—

Corn diminishes as his warlike propensities increase[130]

⟨Pawnees always on horseback—Their dwellings of mats & skins. Here today[—]tomorrow 100 miles hence—

125. An ink smudge here makes the words—perhaps two or three—illegible. A diagonal smudge then precedes the following word, "picturesque."

126. A meaningless mark resembling an S appears between the words "of" and "Creek."

127. In the blank space at the bottom of the page are ink blots and faded-through ink from the previous page.

128. WI's formation of the name resembles "Bilyet."

129. At the end of journal number 6 (October 6–October 17, 1832), WI mentioned that on their journey from Independence they met a camp of Osage hunters (see p. 131); Ellsworth dated this meeting with the Osages October 26. He wrote that at eleven that morning when one Indian armed with bow and arrow approached and was well received, six others sprang out from hiding and told the party through interpreters that they were out "on a *stealing party* to get Pawnee horses"; at that announcement, Ellsworth said that he "urged the Indians to a pacific course; after being introduced to them as a big man come from their father the President. . . ." Ellsworth also commented that "Mr. Irving has added a little here to make a good story, and says the Osages listened with attention to what I said, but remarked 'they go and steal some horses before peace was made as they must not steal any afterwards'—but this is certainly by way of addenda" (*Narrative*, p. 114). Ellsworth also said that he killed a pole cat with " 'uncle Sam' and pointed them to the place as they are fond of that animal" (*ibid.*, p. 115).

130. WI crossed out the following paragraph with a large *X*.

Sometimes dash upon you 40 or 50—look like a troop of wild horses [—]only a leg hanging over to hold on by—⟩[131]

⟨⟨B⟩Tonish says when he was about 15 years of age he ⟨saw⟩ was one day hunting in his neighborhood & he saw a white deer—after a little while another white deer got up & so to the number of Seven. He fired but missed—fired again & missed—⟨fired⟩ could not hit the deer [*blank*] went home & told the circumstance to [*blank*] an old hunter or halfbreed—Theyre hard to hit says he & can only be shot by a particular bullet—He cast balls but would not let Tonish see how he cast them—went out—shot[,] missed—but at length killed one—⟨from⟩ the rest ran off & were never seen again⟩[132]

This vast extent of country without human habitation—visited only by wandering hordes who make an irruption[,] pull out a ⟨pie[?]⟩ few pieces of its rich game & then retreat to their homes[133]—

———

My gun is so powerful dirty—My horse goes quite peart[134]—

———

Kentucky originally one of the finest hunting grounds in the west[?][135] —the fertile soil, deep bottoms—prairies & other ranges affording sustanance to the richest game. ^ ↑Salt licks↓ The Indians lived[136] in it—some had their permanent villages in the South on the Tennessee waters[,] others north in Ohio. Nearest town the[?] [*blank*] came into the country to hunt & then fight—Called therefore the ⟨field⟩ land of blood—⟨the⟩ traces of deep buffalo tracks, where the soil is worn away by the travel[137] of ages—near Licking river[138] &c

———

131. After this word, one-fourth of the page is blank except for a squiggle in the left margin.

132. WI crossed out this long passage with a large *X*. He later used this story in the October 28 entry of *Tour*, in which he made Tonish fourteen and the old hunter became an "old Osage hunter" (pp. 213–14).

133. The following anecdotes are separated by lines of one-fourth inch, one-half inch, and three-fourths inch.

134. WI's interest in the language is apparent here, as he jotted down expressions he heard as he traveled.

135. The last letter of this word seems to be a *d*; however, there are not enough loops for the word to be "world." We have transcribed the word as "west," interpreting the last sweep of the pencil as the crossing of the *t*.

136. This word could be "herd."

137. There is a large smudge above the word "travel," apparently where WI crossed the *t*.

138. It is difficult from the context to determine whether WI referred to the Licking River in Ohio or the one in Kentucky. The former rose in central Ohio,

⟨Sawa cully[139]—the Spirit of the mountain—Gigantic—one eye perpen/dicularly opening in forehead—projected so that he could see in every direction—His mountain guarded by snakes—He stepped from mountain top to mountain top—where his steps had been all was clear & smooth—old Indian shewed a clear place to Rogers[?].[140] Sawacully has been here last night. If you throw fire brands & ashes here today you will find all clear tomorrow—

In the neighborhood lived an old man & wife with one beautiful daughter sought by all young warriors & hunters— —Her father said I will appoint a day for hunting—the best hunter on that day shall[141] have my daughter—day came. Hunters assembled—went off at dawn—A[142] young man made his appearance (describe him) sat down to breakfast tranquilly—no hurry—went forth—hunted—brought in load of game[—]laid it down[—]said nothing[—]smoked his pipe—went out again [—]brought in more—laid it down—other hunters had not come in—dined—went out again—brought in another load—When the other hunters came in & saw his great pile of game they gave up to him & he recd. the ⟨pr[?]⟩ bride

Lived with her a year—⟨asked her if⟩ said he must go[143] to his land to see his people—she might go with him if ⟨*illegible*⟩ she pleased—she agreed[—]they went off—Crossed a river at foot of mountain—their footsteps were seen on the Sand on other side but no more seen or heard of them—Years rolled away—⟨f⟩Father of bride set out in quest

---

flowed southeast, and entered the Muskingum River opposite Zanesville. The larger Licking rose in eastern Kentucky in Floyd County, flowed northwest across the state for approximately 200 miles, and entered the Ohio opposite Cincinnati.

139. After writing "Sawa cully" (which we have been unable to identify further) in pencil, WI used light brown ink for the remainder of this page and the following two pages (pp. [31–29]). Each page is crossed out with a large X.

140. In the undated notes at the end of the journal dated October 6–October 17, 1832, WI mentioned this myth, locating the giant and the Indians in the Chilhowee Mountains of North Carolina (see pp. 131–32, n. 191). This expanded version of the same story was being told to WI by someone, probably the person whose name is questioned. The name seems to be "Rogers," except that there is a decided dot over one of the last three loops in the word (the name could be read "Rojers," "Requs," or "Rojier"). On October 7, WI and his party were in the home of Major and Mrs. Rogers, who, as WI reported, were both Cherokee half-breeds (see pp. 98–99, n. 22).

141. Just below the word "hunting" and above the words "day shall," there is a large ink smudge.

142. In the series of three crossed-out pages relating this story, this word marks the end of the first page.

143. Preceding the word "go" is a mark which may be a single quotation mark.

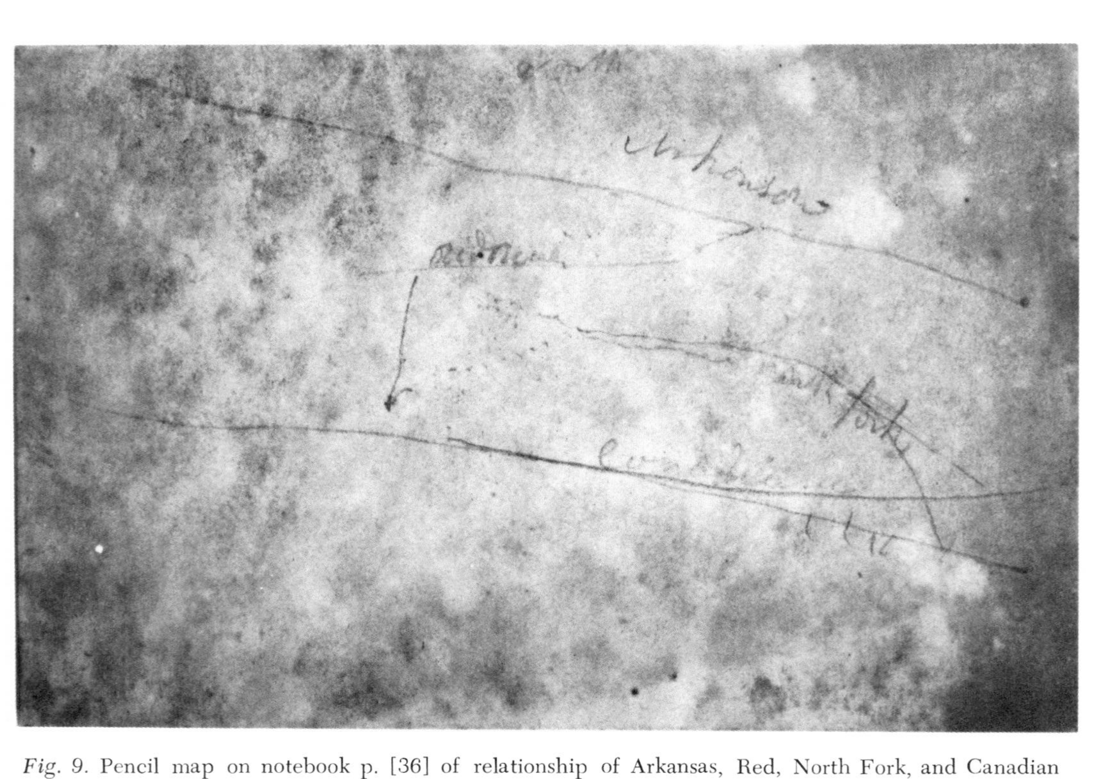

Fig. 9. Pencil map on notebook p. [36] of relationship of Arkansas, Red, North Fork, and Canadian rivers.

of her—took the direction of footsteps—went[144] to mountain—found snakes in abundance, proceeded, found his daughter in a wig wam. great rattle-snake lying beside her—

How is this my daughter. Why do you not kill that snake.

It is my husband—gave me my choice—Snake by day—man by night—Such are all the snakes of this mountain, who are subjects of Sawa cully—old man remains at night[—]finds his son in law a[145] young man—remains in the mountain—⟨When[?]⟩ Conjures[146] when they want game, conjure & let it out from a cave—⟩

[*p. [35] blank*]

[*p. [36] contains a pencil map of the relationship of the rivers mentioned in this journal: the "Arkansas," "Red River," "North Fork," and the "Canadian." The notebook is turned counterclockwise ("North" appears at the top of the map and just below the binding). The line representing the Canadian River meets at the left edge of the map what appears to be "West."*]

[*inside back cover blank*]

[*back cover*]

No 8

144. Here ends the second crossed-out page of the story.

145. There seems to be an ink smudge between the words "law" and *a*. A problem in transcription arises here because the words are written together as "lawa" and the smudge could be read as an apostrophe, the *a* as an *s*, as "son in law's." There also seems to be an ink blot at the beginning of the next line.

146. This word could be "conjurer."

AMERICAN JOURNALS, 1832

Number 9

Verdigris River to Mississippi River--Stack Island

The manuscript journal is in the Seligman Collection of Irvingiana in the Manuscripts and Archives Division of the New York Public Library, cataloged as #22–3300, Washington Irving Journals, Volume 27–B. Its eighteen off-white leaves with extremely faded gilt edges, measuring $3\frac{11}{16}$ inches wide and $5\frac{11}{16}$ inches long, are covered in faded brown leather, torn on opposite lower corners, and held together with a light brown string tied between pages [18] and [19]. The front and back fly leaves are unruled and the remaining sixteen leaves are ruled with a single vertical line at the left margin and double vertical lines (the left line of this pair is actually two very close lines) approximately one-half inch apart at the right margin. Irving reversed the journal after page [15], writing back to front from pages [34] to [16]. The inside front cover and pages [1–2], [33], and [35–36] are blank; the inside back cover is blank except for the number "16" in pencil in the upper left corner (when the notebook is reversed) and the NYPL catalog indication, "Journal 27B," in pencil and added recently in the lower left corner (also when the notebook is reversed). Pages [3–7], [10], [17–22], [26–32], and [34] are written in brown ink. The remaining seven pages are written in a combination of brown ink and pencil as follows: page [8] is in ink with one word ("county") in line 14 and the last five lines in pencil; page [9] is in pencil with the last five lines in ink; page [11] is in ink for the first twelve lines and in pencil for the remaining nine lines; page [16] is in ink with the last five lines in pencil (top and bottom are designations in Irving's reversed order of pages, [34–16]); page [23] is in ink except the first three lines which are in pencil; page [24] has the first nine lines in pencil and the last eleven lines in ink; page [25] is in pencil except for the first three lines in ink.

[*front cover*][1]

No 9.

1832

[*inside front cover blank*]

[*pp. [1–2] blank*]

Sunday, November 11[2]

On board[?][3] of the Steam boat Little Rock—⟨r⟩River Verdigris—Get under way about 6 Oclock from ⟨*two words illegible*⟩ about a mile below the osage agency. Verdigris river—beautiful dawn—while yet twilight past a fire on the shore. Indians around it—canoe fastened close by. Streaming flights of wild ducks. Pigeons in clouds,[4] some rising from the sand bar where they go to drink & to peck[5] gravel; others flying in successive clouds over the trees—Banks of river with growth of cottonwood—.

River of moderate breadth, finely wooded banks. Land Mr Brown[,][6] Creek Indian & trader at his place opposite the mouth of the Illinois.[7]

1. There are several black ink blots in the lower quarter and center of the leather cover; the inside front cover is water-stained; and there are heavy ink blots on p. [2], particularly those matching the last line of the following page.

2. WI wrote "Sunday. Nov. 11. 1832."

3. The *d* is irregularly formed, and the word order is unusual.

4. A mark above the comma may be interpreted as a dash, but it may be a slip of the pen.

5. There is a dot in the manuscript above the *e*, which suggested to McDermott and Trent and Hellman the reading "pick" (*Western Journals*, p. 155; *Journals of WI*, III, 173).

6. Although McDermott suggested David Brown, a Cherokee and half-brother of the successful merchant Walter Webber, WI may have referred to Captain John Brown. Foreman wrote that David Brown was educated at Cornwall and Andover and became a zealous missionary among his Cherokee brothers (*Indians and Pioneers*, pp. 227–28, n. 31). In 1830, Webber, along with Sam Houston (dressed as an Indian) and John Brown, a Cherokee chief, went to Washington to make charges against the Indian agents (*ibid.*, p. 247). Captain Arbuckle reported that in the summer of 1832, John Brown, an "educated and respected half-breed Cherokee merchant," led a revenge party of 100 Cherokees and some Delawares against the Pawnees who had attacked a hunting party outfitted and joined by Brown; the outcome resulted in tension between the Creeks and the Cherokees (Foreman, *Advancing the Frontier*, p. 113). Later, when the Cherokees, Choctaws, Chickasaws, and Creeks refused to support the 1836 bill to create the Indian Territory, the National Council of the Cherokee Nation met at Chief Jolly's home at the mouth of the Illinois to hear Agent Stokes' explanation. John Brown was one of the four signers of a subsequent letter to the agent confirming their negative decision (*ibid.*, p. 186). This Mr. Brown may have been the man WI met.

7. The Illinois, called by the Osage Indians a name meaning "Medicine Stone Creek" (Foreman, *Indians and Pioneers*, p. 228, n. 32), rose in the northwest corner

Cross the river & stop[8] to get wood. go ashore & shoot pigeons

As the ⟨Sun⟩ day advances the ⟨weather⟩ temperature grows[9] warm & genial—The forests ⟨*illegible*⟩[10] very much stripped of leaves. Young cotton wood groves. grey branches. light tinge of green in tops—Golden sunshine—loneliness & stillness of the Scene—the Sabbath of the woods[11]

———

⟨Passengers⟩ ↑Persons↓ in Steam boat—

Mr Gregory—clerk.

Dr Cunningham:[12] Editor sub rosa of a paper at Little Rock[13]—⟨was[?]⟩ originally of Philada. then NYork—

---

of Arkansas, flowed south-southwest, and entered the Arkansas River four miles above the mouth of the Canadian. Near the Illinois' mouth were salt springs.

8. This word is badly smudged, and the smudge extends to the next line to word, "shoot."

9. The smudged ink in the middle of this word extends to the line below.

10. The crossed-out letters seem to be "you[ng]."

11. WI drew a line 2⅝ inches to separate paragraphs or to underline "the Sabbath of the woods."

12. Dr. Matthew Cunningham (1782–1854) was Little Rock's first physician; born in Philadelphia, graduated from the University of Pennsylvania School of Medicine, he came to Arkansas Territory by way of New York and St. Louis. In 1820, he "built the second house in Little Rock, a log cabin, a short distance away from the 'little rock,' and in a dense forest . . ." (Work Projects Administration, *Arkansas: A Guide to the State* [1941; reprint ed., St. Clair Shores, Mich.: Scholarly Press, 1976], p. 172; hereafter cited as *WPA's Arkansas*). When the legislature decided that the capital would be moved from Arkansas Post to Little Rock, it was reported that "Mrs. Matthew Cunningham, wife of the physcian, in 'a good two horse wagon . . . ,' was already on her way down from Missouri to the same point . . ."; she was always hailed as Little Rock's first woman resident (John Gould Fletcher, *Arkansas* [Chapel Hill: University of North Carolina Press, 1947], pp. 71, 73; hereafter cited as Fletcher, *Arkansas*). Dr. Cunningham had married Eliza Bertrand, a widow, in 1808[?]; their daughters were Henrietta and Matilda (McDermott, *Western Journals*, p. 156, nn. 2, 5).

13. WI's casual reference to a Little Rock newspaper and "sub rosa" management belied the journalistic war involving some of Arkansas' earliest and most influential citizens. William Woodruff (1795–1885), born in New Jersey and trained as a printer, set out from the East in 1819 for Arkansas Post to found the first newspaper. In March, 1819, President Monroe acted on a bill to establish the Territory in July; on November 20, 1819, Woodruff published the first issue of the *Arkansas Gazette*, for years an unchallenged Democratic voice in Arkansas; when the seat of Territorial government was moved from the Post to Little Rock in 1821, Woodruff also moved the paper. President Monroe appointed as the first governor General James Miller (1776–1851), born in New Hampshire and hero of the War of 1812, when he said "I'll try, sir!" then completed the dangerous mission successfully. Setting out from Pittsburg in a splendidly outfitted keelboat in September, 1819, Miller arrived on December 26 to find that the territorial secretary, Robert Crittenden (1797–1834), a young and ambitious Kentuckian, had already called into session

Lieut—[*blank*] ⟨*two words illegible*⟩[14] educated at WPoint—

One bank of the Arkansas settled by Cherokees, the other by Choctaws—Log houses along the river—

Touch at Fort Smith.[15] Right bank of river on rocky Bluff—ruinous

---

the legislature (composed of three judges and Crittenden). Apparently Governor Miller, who played by rules in a lawless land, was virtually ineffective, and Crittenden was Arkansas' real power from 1819; Foreman and other writers referred to him as "Acting-Gov." from 1821. Miller's successor, Governor George Izard (1776–1828), died suddenly in November, and President Jackson appointed John Pope as the third governor. Crittenden, after ten years suddenly deprived of position and power, was bitter and sought revenge. Two years earlier, he had killed in a duel a political rival and popular congressman, Henry Conway; that man's family—along with Governor Pope, Chester Ashley (a "Yankee" and, some said, unscrupulous lawyer who came to Little Rock in 1820), and Woodruff's *Arkansas Gazette*—formed a powerful coalition against Crittenden. In 1830, Crittenden persuaded his brother-in-law, Charles P. Bertrand, to come from New York to begin a Whig paper, the *Arkansas Advocate*. In 1831, Crittenden lost a race for Congress against the Conway-Woodruff candidate, as well as having become embroiled in a bitter political battle over the building of the state capitol. By the time WI met Cunningham, identified by McDermott as *Advocate* editor Bertrand's stepfather, the Crittenden faction included C. F. M. Noland and Albert Pike, associated with the paper, and the war was on. In the summer of 1833, knifings, duels, brawls, fellow churchmen refusing to take communion together, and especially journalistic diatribes were the norm. Crittenden lost his battle and died the following year a broken man, and Governor Pope's nephew died as a result of a duel with Noland, who had written anonymous and scurrilous letters to the *Gazette* about the governor (see Fletcher, *Arkansas*, pp. 52–55, 90–98; *WPA's Arkansas*, p. 93; Foreman, *Indians and Pioneers*, pp. 98, 173, 220).

14. The first word may be "from"; the second seems to have six or seven letters.

15. Indian tension, particularly between Osage and Cherokee, prompted General Jackson's order in September, 1817, to Major William Bradford and Major Stephen Long to select a site on the Arkansas River and the Osage line to garrison one company. In October, Long went from Arkansas Post upriver to the mouth of the Verdigris and then back to the mouth of the Pouteau on the western border of Arkansas Territory; the Indians called this site the "Belle Point" and the army called it Cantonment Smith (later Fort Smith) in honor of General Thomas A. Smith. Actually it was too far from Indian action, and in April, 1824, it was abandoned in favor of Fort Gibson (see p. 101, n. 35). In 1826, Major McClellan was ordered to establish his Choctaw agency at the abandoned fort, but he found it to be in bad repair and built the agency fifteen miles above Fort Smith. Troops were not garrisoned there until 1833, when a political controversy regarding protection from the Indians on the Arkansas border resulted in President Jackson's ordering the 7th Infantry to the abandoned fort. In 1836, Captain John Rogers, the former sutler at Fort Smith and owner of much of the land there, sold a large tract of land to the government, and in 1838 Fort Smith was rebuilt and Fort Coffee dismantled in its favor; additions and rebuilding occurred in 1845 and 1850, and the fort was abandoned finally in 1858 (see Foreman's *Advancing the Frontier* and *Indians and Pioneers* for references to Fort Smith throughout).

old wooden buildings &–[16] block house–a number of the inhabitants come down among whom I was introduced to Mr Rogers,[17] formerly[18] of western part of State of NYork who owns a great part of Fort Smith– and Mr Cairns[19] a mercht.

a daughter of Dr Cunningham comes on board–. cross the line & enter upon the Territory[20]–Log houses occupied by White Men–Groupes of negroes in Sunday dresses along the shore–Songs and choruses of our Negro fire men.

Pass Devils elbow[21] a great sandy bend in the river

In the course of the day pass by ⟨th⟩ a red boat bearing US. troops on an expedition to destroy whiskey stills.[22]

Stop at Van Buren[23] to take passengers two men in fur caps with rifles, ⟨boat[?]⟩[24] & bedding. Van B. an embrio town at present 4 or 5 triffling[?][25] log huts.

about dusk stop ⟨at⟩ to take in wood, having made about 100 miles since daybreak.

16. Above the dash is a dot of red sealing wax.

17. See n. 15 above.

18. The ink blot above this word matches a blot on the verso; this condition persists throughout the page.

19. Perhaps Peter A. Carnes, of Duval and Carnes (McDermott, *Western Journals*, p. 156, n. 4).

20. Arkansas Territory.

21. Between Fort Smith and Van Buren, the Arkansas flowed sharply north, then east, and finally south making a great bend.

22. See above, pp. 98–99, n. 22; Foreman commented, "Through some strange conception of the fitness of things, the patrol boat was painted red, thus distinguishing it for a long distance from other river craft and aiding violators of the law in eluding it" (*Advancing the Frontier*, p. 29; see pp. 25–31 for discussion of problems involving whiskey sale to Indians).

23. Van Buren, which would become the county town of Crawford County, Arkansas, was not listed in contemporary guidebooks or on maps, even though settlers were living here as early as 1818. The fact that WI called the "embrio town" Van Buren, rather than its previous name, Phillips Landing, suggests an earlier renaming than most sources: *WPA's Arkansas* indicated that in 1838 two promoters bought the site and renamed it for the president (p. 253); Foreman wrote that during the battle in Congress over maintaining a fort on the western border of Arkansas, one of the two sites approved in 1838 was here where Van Buren was later built (*Advancing the Frontier*, p. 52). The town was laid out in 1841 on the left, or north, bank of the Arkansas, five miles east of the Indian Territory and 160 miles northwest of Little Rock; it gained early distinction as the place which "furnished more whiskey to the Indians than any other . . ." (*ibid.*, p. 25).

24. This crossed-out word may be the place-name "VanB."

25. Trent and Hellman and McDermott read as "straggling" (*Journals of WI*, III, 174; *Western Journals*, p. 157); however, the first letter is a crossed *t*.

This day, (in boatmans slang) we overtook the rise. I.E. we came to where the river was at the highest of its late temporary swelling—having commenced falling ⟨bel[?]⟩ above—

Monday, November 12[26]

The fog which fell[27] last night contind until late this morning so that we did not get under way until about 9 oclock.

Immense flock of pigeons on Sand bar in the river—

Banks delicately wooded with cotton wood & willows—Grey tints mingled with Slight[28] green—Now & then, at long intervals, come by settlement—Log house—cattle[29] standing along shore in the sun shine—deep Bayous—running in among wild forests that shoot their branches and half prostrate trunks athwart

In some[30] places as we skirt the shore the cattle gaze for a time in astonisht & then gallop into the woods—

Stop at Crawford Court House[31] a few log houses on high bank Justice runs wild in this part of the country—She uses the[32] sword more than the scales

Find at Crawford Court House a keel boat with freight belonging to Mr Mapes,[33] of NYork—one of the proprietors of the Steam boat—

26. WI wrote "Monday 12th."

27. Following this word is an ink smudge.

28. Trent and Hellman and McDermott read as "light" (*Journals of WI*, III, 174; *Western Journals*, p. 157); however, there is a letter preceding the *l*, which we decipher as S.

29. The *t* and *l* are smudged by the opposite page.

30. Above the *e*, there is an ink blot from the word "stop" on the opposite page; above the words "a time" in the next line is another blot matching the word "agency" opposite.

31. Crawford County was created in 1820, and after a short time, the county seat was moved from Fort Smith to Billingsley's Settlement, about twenty miles downstream (Foreman, *Indians and Pioneers*, pp. 144–45 and n. 25) and on the right, or south, bank of the Arkansas approximately 136 miles northwest of Little Rock. The settlement, which became known as Crawford's Court House, did not fulfill Baird's 1832 prediction that the villages springing up around each county's courthouse along the rivers in Arkansas "will at some future day become important places" (*View*, p. 244); the county seat was moved to Van Buren, and this town disappeared.

32. Above the *t* there is an ink blot corresponding to two letters in the word "Monday" on the previous page. On this page there are six distinct ink blots, all matching words or letters on the previous page.

33. The first two letters could be "Ph," but WI wrote clearly "Mapes" below; McDermott identified as Charles Mapes, the postmaster at the mouth of the Arkansas in 1832 (*Western Journals*, p. 157, n. 10).

Stop about 3[?][34] hours to take it on board. Mr Mapes embarks also & Mr Nolan,[35] & his horse. Genl Montgomery,[36] his negro servants & a half grown bear[?]—

Mrs Trimble[37] & two other ladies of the place dine on board.

resume our course about 2 OClock & go on till dark when we stop at[38] Clarkes Agency.

Tuesday, Novemebr 13[39]

Set off about day break—Pass high broken ridge of rock, coloured with Iron &c Called the Dardanells.[40] Here Pension[?] Braily[41] lives—

34. The number could be a "5" or a "9."

35. Charles Fenton Mercer Noland (ca. 1810–1858) was a soldier in the Arkansas journalistic wars of this period, being allied with Charles Bertrand's newspaper, the *Arkansas Advocate*, becoming its coeditor (see pp. 160–61, n. 13 above). Noland was the author of the letters maligning the governor which were published in the *Advocate* and signed only "Devereaux." Fletcher called him "a bold young gamecock from Kentucky who had an itch for writing and . . . under the name of 'Pete Whetstone,' [was] Arkansas's pioneer humorist in the backwoods style later to be immortalized by Mark Twain" (*Arkansas*, p. 94). William Porter wrote of him in 1845, "Col. N. is a son of the old Dominion, was educated at West Point, was an officer in the U.S. Dragoons, and since his resignation has been a resident of Arkansas, where his time is about equally divided between courts of law, land offices, and the legislature" (Franklin J. Meine, ed., *Tall Tales of the Southwest* [New York: Alfred A. Knopf, 1930], p. 453).

36. General William Montgomery (1790–1835), born in Tennessee, settled in Arkansas at Arkansas Post in 1818, then moved to the mouth of the White River at a point which took his name; President Jackson appointed him a brigadier general of the Arkansas militia (McDermott, *Western Journals*, p. 158, n. 10).

37. Mrs. Trimble could have been the wife of one of the territorial Judges, William Trimble, who was appointed in 1825 and represented Hempstead County in the 1831 legislature (McDermott, *Western Journals*, p. 158, n. 11).

38. There is a smudge between the words "stop" and "at."

39. WI wrote "Tuesday—Novr 13."

40. Bishop Davenport wrote in 1832, "Dardanelles, a place in Cadron, Arkansas Territory, on Arkansas river, where the Agent of the Cherokee Indians resides. Two rocky ridges here border the river for some distance, whence originated the name" (*Gazetteer*, p. 250). Although the town was not laid out until 1842, explorers as early as 1819 found a Cherokee trading post at this point on the right, or south, bank of the Arkansas in Crawford County about 72 miles northwest of Little Rock. Dardanelle Rock, a part of this chain of the Ozarks which gives the terrain its sublimity, rose 280 feet above the river. Latrobe discovered this "most picturesque scene" along the Arkansas a month after WI saw it (*Rambler*, I, 265).

41. According to Foreman, on May 1, 1820, Colonel David Brearley was appointed the "Indian Agent on the Arkansas," dealing especially with Cherokee and Quapaw (*Indians and Pioneers*, p. 42, n. 59). In 1826, Congress passed an act to sell Lovely's Purchase, and Colonel Brearly was appointed agent for the McIntosh Creeks; his important role in the selection and purchase of the Creek Agency on

Great gambling place formerly[42] It used to be said If a dollar could get by the Dardanelles there was some chance of your carrying it up the river.[43]

Between 11 & 12 pass along mounts. of Petit Jean.[44]

½ past 12 Stop at Louisburgh[45] to take in wood—Seat of Justice of the county[46] Hard work for Justice to get seated as the seat has been changed^ ↑⟨by leg[?]⟩↓ every ^ ↑session of the↓ Legislature.[47]

Stop after dusk at Little rock[48]— —In the Evg. Capt Brown[49] agent

---

the Verdigris in 1827 and in the complicated relocation of the Creeks during 1828 is discussed by Foreman (*ibid.*, pp. 250–61).

42. The mark below this word is apparently the end of an unclearly formed *y*.

43. The period is actually an extension of the final *r*.

44. The Petit Jean River, or Creek, rose in the western part of Arkansas and flowed eastward, entering the Arkansas approximately halfway between Dardanelle and Lewisburg. Petit Jean Mountain, cut by a canyon with a waterfall of 75 feet, rose 1,100 feet and was one of three outstanding peaks in the Arkansas River valley, actually a part of its southern valley wall; it was apparently named for a Frenchman, Jean la Caze, who escaped the revolution and settled with his family in this area (*WPA's Arkansas*, pp. 7, 246).

45. Lewisburg was a small post-village on the left, or north, bank of the Arkansas, the county town of Conway County, approximately 40 miles above Little Rock; it was replaced as county town by Springfield (interestingly, Flint listed Harrisonburg as county town of Conway County, in *Mississippi Valley*, p. 276).

46. WI added the word "county" in pencil (the page is written in brown ink); he probably intended to add the name of the county, "Conway."

47. WI added two marks indicating writing above the line. Because of his method of crossing out words, it is difficult to determine the order in which he wrote and crossed out this line; another interpretation is "has been changed every ↑⟨by leg[?]⟩ session of the↓ ^ Legislature."

48. Little Rock, or Acropolis, as it was still called by many at this time, was the county town of Pulaski County, the capital of Arkansas Territory, and was situated on the right, or south, bank of the Arkansas "on a very high stone bluff," which, Flint said, was "ludicrously called Little Rock, from the prodigious masses of stone about it" (*Mississippi Valley*, I, 285). The first hut was built in 1812 by a hunter, William Lewis; in 1819, William Russell bought the Lewis tract for $40; settlement began in 1820, and by 1821 a town was staked out and the seat of government moved from Arkansas Post upriver approximately 300 miles. Even though steamboat travel began in 1822 (with the *Eagle's* arrival) and the town was well located on the river and the Great Southwest Trail, it grew slowly; it was not formally chartered until 1831, had a population of fewer than 500, and was even then known as a "boisterous frontier village" (*WPA's Arkansas*, p. 172). Baird wrote in 1832, "It is a small but pleasant town, and has some fine society. It was a few years ago, as all this country was, often a scene of shocking violence and fatal rencontres between hostile individuals and parties. But at present, the morals of this place and of the whole territory are improving" (*View*, p. 243).

49. Captain Jacob Brown was, according to Foreman, the "dispursing agent of

for settling the Indians comes on board—also Mr [*blank*][50] editor of the ⟨?⟩Gazette—

Wednesday, November 14[51]

Went on shore to the printing office of the Gazette—Breakfasted with Dr Cunningham[52] called on Dr Fulton,[53] Gov Pope[,][54] met with Dr Ritchie who begged to be remd to Mr Peale[?][55] of Missouri—Has a brother in Phila.

⟨M[?]⟩Dr Fulton desired to be remd. to Presdt[,][56] Gov Cass[57] &

---

annuities, stationed at Little Rock" in 1835 (*Advancing the Frontier*, p. 302). He had been a member of the 6th Infantry, Jefferson Barracks, then in September, 1831, was appointed the superintendent for removal of Indians here at Little Rock (McDermott, *Western Journals*, p. 159, n. 17).

50. William Woodruff was founder and editor of the *Arkansas Gazette*, the first newspaper published west of the Mississippi and still published in Little Rock; see pp. 160–61, n. 13 for discussion of Woodruff's place in the history of this section.

51. WI wrote "Wednesday 14th."

52. See p. 160, n. 12 for discussion of Dr. Matthew Cunningham.

53. McDermott identified as Dr. John T. Fulton, who was the assistant agent for the removal of the Choctaw and brother of William S. Fulton, the governor of Arkansas Territory from 1835 until 1841 (*Western Journals*, p. 159, n. 17). Fulton had replaced Crittenden as territorial secretary in 1829 (see pp. 160–61, n. 13).

54. Governor John Pope, who was third territorial governor of Arkansas from 1828 until 1835 (see pp. 160–61, n. 13). Foreman discussed the actions taken by the "humane Governor Pope" on behalf of the starving Quapaw Indians including sending corn and reporting in a June 22, 1829, letter to the Secretary of War (*Indians and Pioneers*, 182–83).

55. Among the artists who were gathering in the St. Louis area in the early 1820's was Titian Ramsay Peale (1800–1885), who along with Samuel Seymour, a landscape artist and engraver from Philadelphia, accompanied Major Stephen Long on his expedition up the Missouri (Work Projects Administration, *Missouri: A Guide to the "Show Me" State* (New York: Duell, Sloan and Pearce, 1941), p. 168; hereafter cited as *WPA's Missouri*).

56. Andrew Jackson (1767–1845), the seventh president of the United States, was elected in 1828 and served for eight years.

57. Lewis Cass (1782–1866), born in New Hampshire and educated for the military, resigned his commission as major in 1800 and moved to the Ohio valley, first to Marietta, then to Zanesville. He practiced law and, in 1807, was appointed by President Jefferson as the U.S. marshal of Ohio, serving until 1813 when he entered the War of 1812. President Madison appointed him governor of Michigan in October, 1813. Governor Cass was particularly interested in the Indians and was successful in dealing with them and gaining their respect; he was a member of Schoolcraft's expedition, and he played a major role in the Black Hawk War, as he had been appointed secretary of war by President Jackson in 1831. From 1836 until 1842, he was the U.S. ambassador to France (see p. 221, n. 139), and he was active in Democratic party politics until his death.

Mr McLane[58]–

Judge [*blank*][59] & family come on board–Leave Little Rock near 1 Oclock

Several ladies dine on board & accompany us a few miles to a farm[?][60]–

Stop at night on account of snags &c

Thursday, November 15[61]

resume our course at day break. Pass cotton plantations. Cotton here of fine long staple. Equal to new orleans.[62]

Pass Quawpaw settlements[63] (tenant at ⟨*illegible*⟩ will–)[64] See groupes in a fine lofty grove

58. Louis McLane (1786–1857), born in Delaware, was at this time the secretary of the treasury (1831–1833), but he had been a U.S. senator from 1827 to 1829 and the minister to England from 1829 until 1831, during which time WI had served as the secretary of the legation (see Introduction, pp. xlvi–xlvii). McLane was a close friend of WI. When McLane's political views came into conflict with those of the president he was serving as secretary of state, WI urged him to remain in the cabinet; however, McLane resigned in 1834, and, except for a brief return as minister to England in 1845, retired from public life (STW, II, 61–62).

59. Baird wrote that there were four judges holding circuit courts throughout the Arkansas Territory, by presidential appointment and Senate consent, with a salary of $1,500 each (*View*, p. 142).

60. WI wrote over one letter in forming another or the ink is smudged; the resulting word resembles "afarm."

61. WI wrote "*Thursday, Nov. 15.*"

62. Flint wrote that along the Arkansas, "cotton of the same staple and luxuriance as those of Red river" was produced; he also compared the cultivated belt below the Post, called "the coast," with New Orleans and added that there was "a great extent of cotton lands of the first quality in the country along the river, above the Post in the 'Quawpaw purchase'" (*Mississippi Valley*, I, 282–83).

63. The Quapaw take their name from a tribal word meaning "downstream people," for this branch of the Siouan linguistic family followed the Mississippi and then the Arkansas (the other branch, the Omaha group went upstream on the Missouri). This tribe actually gave the Arkansas its name as the French explorers called them "Akansea" and found them to be peace-loving farmers, potters, and mound builders. Several families lived in each long house covered by bark and a dome roof (see Hodge, *Handbook of Indians*, II, 333–36; Wright, *Indians of Oklahoma*, pp. 218–22).

64. WI's use of the legal term, "tenant at will," is interesting in light of the definition: "One who holds possession of premises by permission of owner or landlord, but without fixed term. . . . In this case the lessee is called 'tenant at will,' because he hath no certain nor sure estate, for the lessor may put him out at what time it pleaseth him" (Henry Campbell Black, *Black's Law Dictionary*, 4th ed., rev. [St. Paul, Minn.: West Publishing Co., 1968], p. 1635). According to Foreman, the Quapaws had ceded to the U.S. in an 1818 treaty all land lying

Pass Quawpaw hunting camps on woody banks of the river—
Put Lieut Dawson[65] on shore at Col Deshas[66] cotton plantation.
Evg about sun set stop at the Post of Arkansas.[67] ⟨take[?]⟩ to land Mr & Mrs Cumming[68] & to take in freight

Friday, November 16[69]

get under way at day break. at 9 oclock enter the cut leading to White river—In a few miles enter White river[70]—Clear water with yellow turbid stream of the Arkansas boiling up in it. After some miles,

---

west of the Mississippi between the Red and Arkansas rivers and the Canadian, except for a tract on the south bank of the Arkansas between Little Rock and Arkansas Post; six years later they gave up the remainder of their land, receiving a total of 83¢ for 1,000 acres (which was valued in a simultaneous deal at $6.00 an acre). Furthermore, the Quapaw were to be removed to the Red River area to become a part of the Caddo tribe. Disaster followed: the Caddo refused to accept them; floods destroyed their land; many of the tribe starved; and the government was indifferent to their plight. After 1827, many Quapaw drifted back to their ancestral land; a plan was devised by General Clark to merge them with the Osage, who agreed if some of the land taken from the Quapaw be given to them (Foreman, *Indians and Pioneers*, pp. 180–83).

65. Lieutenant James Low Dawson, from Maryland, was appointed second lieutenant in the 7th Infantry in 1821, made first lieutenant in 1824 and captain in 1833; he resigned from the army in 1835 (McDermott, *Western Journals*, p. 160, n. 18).

66. Trent and Hellman and McDermott rendered as "Dallas" (*Journals of WI*, III, 176; *Western Journals*, p. 160). "Desha" seems to be a better reading in light of what appears to be an *h* added over the original spelling. Colonel Ben Desha came to Arkansas in 1824 and died there in 1835 (McDermott, *Western Journals*, p. 167, n. 33).

67. Arkansas Post, or as it was variously called in contemporary works, the "Post of Arkansas," the "Post," or "Arkansas," was the county town of Arkansas County; an "ancient" settlement, Latrobe wrote that De Soto's followers lived here as early as 1540 (Rambler, I, 271), but the more common theory was that the French settled this place in the 1680's. In 1832, the population was about 600 people largely of French descent. Located on the north bank of the Arkansas only 50 miles from its mouth, it was the original seat of the territorial government (1819–1821); because it lacked a central location, it yielded to Little Rock, 114 miles northwest by land. Flint commented on the poor soil, the overflow of the White River which almost reached the Arkansas, and the resulting swamps which could be seen from the court house; he also mentioned the unusual columns of clay rising out of the bayou (*Mississippi Valley*, I, 285).

68. William and Francine Cummins, a Little Rock lawyer and his wife, who was the daughter of Colonel Frederick Notrebe of Arkansas Post (McDermott, *Western Journals*, p. 160, n. 19).

69. WI wrote "Friday. Nov 16." An ink smudge follows the period.

70. The main branch of the White River rose in the Ozark or Black Mtns. in northern Arkansas and flowed northeast, then southeast, until it joined the other

with cypress & cotton wood groves on each side—come to the Mississippi. Sweep round a large island & go up to Montgomerys point.[71]

Pass the day at the point shifting cargo[.] Point—naked table of land with woods in rear. three or four disconsolate houses[—]negroes—half breeds—oxen[—]dogs—Bear tied to Stake—turkies[?][72]—Boatmen

Leave the point about 4—Stop at mouth of Arkansas after dark & leave Mr Mapes[73]—Sail all night

Saturday, November 17[74]

Last night ran repeatedly agst drift wood—

This morng, 8 oclock, passed thro Stack island[.] reach a beautiful broad & long reach of the river—

Here about 20 years since was a formidable gang of river pirates, 30 or 40 in number. Kept on an island under the eastern shore called Stack island & sometimes Robbers Harbour—Ring leader named Mason.[75] The band consisted of outcast Kentucky/ians—Spaniards—French—&c &c &c well armed—resolute—had boats on the river—horses on the main/land—boarded arks & defenceless boats—noted the cargo—took whatever they wanted—no resisting them. Some of the Keelboats & barges had crews of 40 men well armed—these the robbers dared not attack The robbers have often been seen by these barges lurking about their island.

---

main branch, the Black River, which rose in southern Missouri and flowed south; after these branches united, the White River flowed south 120 miles to join the Mississippi 30 miles above the mouth of the Arkansas. The White River, navigable above the junction of its branches in high water, was a twisting 350 miles long; its spring-fed tributaries suggested its name to the Indians, because its clear water contrasted starkly with the Arkansas and the Mississippi. Latrobe described "the singular natural canal or bayou [of six miles] called the Grand Cut," an effective flood control between the Arkansas and White rivers (*Rambler*, I, 271).

71. Montgomery's Point, in the "delta" of the White and Mississippi, named for General William Montgomery (see above p. 164, n. 36) and called by some "notorious," was not favorably described by Latrobe, who a month later was detained there for two days: it "did not . . . rank either in fact or in courtesy above a small hamlet, and was apparently merely of importance as the point where goods might be deposited . . ." (*Rambler*, I, 272). This entrance into the Mississippi, at this point approximately 600 miles above New Orleans, was WI's second on his tour.

72. Trent and Hellman and McDermott read as "drinkers" (*Journals of WI*, III, 176; *Western Journals*, p. 160). The word could also be read "darkies."

73. See the November 12 entry.

74. WI wrote "Saturday, Nov 17."

75. McDermott referred the reader interested in the career of Samuel Mason to Otto A. Rothert, *The Outlaws of Cave-in-Rock* (Cleveland: Arthur H. Clark, 1924), pp. 157–266; and Thomas Nuttall, *A Journal of Travels into the Arkansa Territory, during the Year 1819* (Philadelphia: Thos. H. Palmer, 1821), pp. 227–28.

They could descry boats at a great distance both up & down the river—⟨When⟩ They had spies in New Orleans. ⟨when they knew a party of boatmen was⟩ The boatmen & traders had to return by land, by an Indian trail thro the Country of the Choctaw nation[76]—several hundred miles—Had to cash their merchandize & carry the money on pack horses—The robbers had trails leading to the ⟨Indian⟩ great Indian trail—They would way lay the traders & rob them. Seldom killed them unless they fought in defence of their goods. Sometimes when they surprized poor travellers thro mistake they would give them money—

The terror of these robbers spread far & wide. In those days people looked upon an expedition down the Mississippi & Ohio as a fearful undertaking—Country wild & unsettled—little known—Indians, River pirates, alligators &c &c &c Long voyage—required Hardy and enterprizing men—& then the long ⟨road⟩ journey back thro savage tribes & robber hordes—

—At length the Authorities offered a large reward for Masons head. He wished to divide his spoil—He had a rival ring leader—they quarrelled about division of Spoil. The rival killed him—carried his head to Natchez & claimed reward.

—⟨He was⟩ A man present who had been robbed on the Indian trail, recognized his buttons on the coat of the robber—& recognized the latter for one of those who had robbed him. The robber was ⟨cap⟩ siezed, tried & hung and the band was broken up—

The very island has since been washed away by the floods of the river & no trace of the robbers remains, but the pilot who told me this story said he had no doubt that thousands of dollars of the robbers money lay buried about the shore and on the old Indian trail and would be digged up as the country became settled & cultivated—[77]

———

⟨At⟩ Just below this reach we begin[78] to see neat white painted houses—and a look of some advanced civiliza/-tion—Cotton plantation

———

[*With page [15] of the manuscript, the dated portion ends, and the notebook is reversed. For the convenience of the reader, this portion of the journal, which contains miscellaneous notes, is transcribed in the order it was written by Irving, from page [34] to page [16].*]

76. Trent and Hellman and McDermott read as "natives" (*Journals of WI*, III, 177; *Western Journals*, p. 161).

77. WI set off the following paragraph with lines of one-half inch.

78. Above and to the left of the *b*, there are two ink blots, one a dot and the other larger.

Clermont–a ⟨chie⟩ late chief of the Osages[79]–shrewd, intelligent, wary: difficult to be brought to a point. He & Col Arbuckle[80] had a great regard for each other, but often disputed about Indian matters; both were prone to beat round the bush. One Evening he & the Col had a long talk in which Clermont played sly [81] as usual. At length Col Arble got out of patience–Well, said he[,] You have talked now for two hours and have said nothing–Brother[,] replied Clermont[,] you have talked about as much and said about as little, so as i⟨s⟩t is growing late, I think (wrapping himself in his blanket) Ill go home–

[*p. [33] blank except for the numerous ink blots from the bottom quarter of p. [32]*]

Gen. Houston,[82] ↑tall↓[83] large, well formed fresh looking man. low crowned[?] large ⟨*illegible*⟩ brimmed white beaver–boots with ↑brass[?]↓ eagle[?][84] spurs–Given to grand eloquence. ⟨ex[?]⟩A large & mili-/-tary mode of expressing himself[:]

79. See above, the September 26 entry and notes (pp. 72–73, nn. 6 and 7). When Clermont died in May, 1828, the Union Mission people lamented his death and the *Arkansas Gazette* eulogized him (Mathews, *Osages*, p. 548); in an August, 1828, letter between Union Mission friends, Clermont was remembered as a "man of manly countenance, stately figure, robust constitution, and great intellectual powers" and a "jealous, thoughtful, fox-eyed observer, of all that was going on around him, that most eloquent speaker, and managing, intrigueing politician . . ." (Foreman, *Indians and Pioneers*, p. 136).

80. See p. 101, n. 36 above. For an account of one confrontation between Arbuckle and Clermont following an 1823 Indian attack and decapitation of an American major, see Mathews, *Osages*, pp. 504–11.

81. The second letter may be an *h*, but the context suggests our reading.

82. Trent and Hellman and McDermott deciphered as "Gov. Hunter" (*Journals of WI*, III, 178; *Western Journals*, p. 162), a possible reading; however, neither Governor Robert Hunter, colonial governor of New York from 1710 to 1719, nor Governor William Hunter, elected governor of Rhode Island in 1811, fits WI's description. Other evidence supports "Gen. Houston" as the correct reading: WI's reference to the style of dress and speech; the fact that Houston and General Nicks were connected as recently as 1830 by controversy regarding the position of sutler of Fort Gibson (see Foreman, *Indians and Pioneers*, pp. 247–48), and Nicks is the next person WI mentioned; also, following the *n* of "Gen," WI's pen moved upward in what may have been the beginning of an *l*, completing the abbreviation "Genl."

83. This word could be read "late."

84. Trent and Hellman did not transcribe the word above the line (*Journals of WI*, III, 178), and McDermott indicated that word as illegible (*Western Journals*, p. 163); actually several readings, in addition to the one in the text, are possible: "brass angle spurs," "Cross angle spurs," and "Cross eagle spurs."

–I encamped last night at –––[85] for, I slept last night–[86]

–––

Old Genl Nix[87] used to say God made him two drinks scant

–––

Little ∧ ↑thick, shortlegged[?]↓[88] dutchman at Little Rock great coward–at time when he was held up as candidate used to go with three pistols & two dirks belted round him–one of the pistols being long[,] used to get the muzzle filled with dirt.–A swaggering[?] man called at his house & abused him all to naught–His wife who had been widow of a very spirited fellow exclaimed[,] Ah if my first husband was alive you would not dare to do so in my house

–ah then I had a husband[89]

–––

Tour of two old Dutch Burghers thro [*unrecovered*]–&c to look for names of old Sturdies[?]–find 60–⟨[? though th ?]⟩ consoled themselves that there is [? some salt yet in sturdies ?].

Give names & histories of the old Sturdies they met with–[90]

Choctaws[91]–much attached to the Whites–Boast that they have never

85. WI left this place-name blank, apparently not intending to fill it in as the line is a heavy one approximately one-half inch long and above the line; the point is the manner of speaking, not the name of the place.

86. WI set off the following sentence with lines of five-eighths inch and one-eighth inch.

87. See p. 152, n. 112 for reference to General John Nicks.

88. This word could also be read "thicklegged."

89. WI drew a line three-fourths inch long to separate paragraphs.

90. This paragraph is an extremely difficult one to decipher; Trent and Hellman omitted many words, phrases, and even lines, reducing the reading to three lines (*Journals of WI*, III, 179). McDermott indicated that two words are illegible and several words later that one line is illegible, when in fact he omitted more than two lines (*Western Journals*, p. 163). In addition to the usual problems, the paragraph is badly smudged with ink blots throughout.

91. The Choctaw Indians, the first of the "Five Civilized Tribes" discussed by Grant Foreman, were an important branch of the Muskhogean linguistic family which also included the Chickasaw and Huma. Found initially by De Soto, they may have derived their name from the Spanish word "chato," meaning "flat," from the Choctaw custom of the artificial flattening of the head (the name could have come from the Creek word "cate" which meant "red" from their original location in the southeastern U.S.). When the French began to settle in the lower Mississippi valley, they found the Choctaw friendly people, excellent farmers, and reluctant warriors, usually fighting only in defense; they became early allies of the French in their wars against other Indians, especially the Natchez and Chickasaw. Choctaw loyalties were divided when English interests superseded French in the area; many served under several American generals in the Revolutionary War as well as under General Jackson in the War of 1812. Theirs was the language of trade in the region.

killed a white man. Call the Whites [*blank*] (S E[?])[92] the Beloved, Supposing them to ⟨super⟩[93] be peculiar favorites of the deity—The choctaws are the most honest of Indians—

Chickasaws,[94] amalgamated with the choctaws, their language nearly the[95] same. Their women handsome. They came from the upper parts of the Missouri—Their tradition is that they followed a chief who had a pole of supernatural virtues—⟨Wh⟩ He set it up occasionally and as long as it remained perpendicular they remained in that place. When it

---

Part of their ritual included picking clean the bones of the dead before burial, and it was their legend (as well as that of the Chickasaw) which recounted migration by sacred pole to the great mound in Mississippi which they called "Nanih Waya"; their last council was held there in 1828 before their removal to the Indian Territory. By a treaty of 1820, the Choctaw were the first of the southeastern tribes assigned land in the Territory—a large tract in southern Oklahoma, southwestern Arkansas, and eastern New Mexico; also, they were the first whole tribe to be removed by the government, by a treaty signed in 1830. The removal lasted three years, and the tribe suffered extreme hardship (see Grant Foreman, *The Five Civilized Tribes: Cherokee, Chickasaw, Choctaw, Creek, Seminole* (Norman: University of Oklahoma Press, 1934), pp. 17–94; hereafter cited as *Five Civilized Tribes*; Hodge, *Handbook of Indians*, I, 288–90; Wright, *Indians of Oklahoma*, pp. 97–118).

92. This notation could be an attempt at Indian symbols, or it could be a poorly formed "IE" which WI intended to complete later with the Indian word for "Beloved."

93. These letters or word could be "be fav" or "be par."

94. The Chickasaw were named "Chikasha" by their close relatives of the Muskhogean linguistic family, the Choctaw, with whom they shared language (except for a few dialect differences), religion, and the tradition of migrating to northeastern Mississippi by following a leader with a magic pole. They were also one of the "Five Civilized Tribes" studied by Foreman (pp. 97–144); however, even though a relatively small tribe, the Chickasaw were known for their warlike nature, established when they attacked and routed De Soto's men after the Spaniard had demanded 200 Chickasaw as servants. This warring continued as they were friends of the English and in conflict with almost all other Indian tribes, including the Shawnee, Caddo, Cherokee, Creek, Illinois, Kickapoo, Osage, Quapaw, and especially, the Choctaw. The Chickasaw were accused of precipitating the Natchez rebellion against the French in 1729, and they were successful in significant battles against the French. Three government treaties with the Chickasaw in 1786, 1818, and 1832 ceded their lands north of the Ohio, north of the southern boundary of Tennessee, and east of the Mississippi. There were constant questions about relocation, even as late as 1837, because they had no definite, separate tract and were assigned land with other tribes (especially the Choctaw, their traditional enemies), and there were stipulations about sale of former lands. Finally, they came into the Territory in 1837–1838 at Fort Coffee (near the Choctaw Agency) and near Fort Towson. Unrest continued for years (see Hodge, *Handbook of Indians*, I, 260–62; Wright, *Indians of Oklahoma*, pp. 84–97).

95. Ink blots around this word resemble quotation marks; at the beginning of the two following lines are smudges from a crossed-out word on the preceding page.

inclined they travelled in the direction it inclined. In this way they travelled from place to place until they came to their present residence

The Quipaws[96] a small remnant of a tribe below little rock—They once sold out & removed to Texas but ⟨*illegible*⟩ were drawn back by their love to their native place.[97]

⟨The bravest & finest race is the Delawares.[98] They are ⟨said to be na⟩ called the *fathers*. all the others give them preference. They used to war with the Osages who stand in awe of their fearlessness, Look at these delawares say the osages ⟨the[?]⟩ dey got short legs—no can run, must stand & fight a great heap—" [(] ⟨The o⟩ The Delawares really are short legged—& the osages long—)

Delawares [—] all their equipments of the best—Their camp Kettles of brass. They are clean neat, civil generous, obliging, light hearted gay, fearless. Go to the Rocky mountains in bands of 20 men. have frequent skirmishes. Excellent hunters—when they go out to kill a deer you may be sure of their succeeding.⟩

⟨Pawnees[99]—When they attack in the Praries it is necessary to tie your horses head to head in circle. They come round you, with feathers ⟨blankets⟩ mantles &c fluttering—with whoops & yells, that strike a panic into the horses.⟩[100]

⟨Pawnees keep in the Praries—will not follow into the thickets.⟩

Old osage looked at our Steamboat at the agency with wonder, came aboard, gazed at machinery &c Said God must have helped to make it.

Ralph Izard[101] & another toper fell asleep on a bed in an Inn where there was a ball & supper—woke after the company had gone—called lustily for Supper. waiter told them it was over—"we paid 3$ for ball & supper & must have it. 'Impossible—none in the house." well, give us a candle

96. For a discussion of the Quapaw, see p. 167, n. 63.

97. WI crossed out the following two paragraphs with two long diagonal lines.

98. For a discussion of the Delaware, see p. 126, n. 162.

99. WI crossed out this paragraph with one diagonal line in pencil from left to right. For a discussion of the Pawnee, see p. 87, n. 83.

100. To set off the following three anecdotes, WI drew between them lines of one-eighth inch, one-half inch, and three-fourths inch; he crossed out the first of these with parallel diagonal lines from left to right.

101. Ralph Izard (1741–1804) was born near Charleston, South Carolina, educated in England, and known as an outstanding patriot and politician; he was the father of George Izard, second governor of the Arkansas Territory.

& we will go home—" Waiter gave them a Spermaceti[?][102] light—They sallied forth—the night was rainy. They were too tipsy to keep their legs—Sat down in public square. Stuck the ⟨can⟩ light on end between them. thot themselves still at table—The day broke & shewd them still seated toe to toe,[103] with the light burning between them—

Arkansas. Continual succes-/-sion of gentle fertile wooded Scenery. Graceful ⟨gr⟩ woods thickets—embowerd shores— —Islands—long receding Bayous—willowed banks. Yellow sands.—cattle feeding peacefully ⟨bes[?]⟩ along the shore—every thing ⟨gentle⟩ peaceful but man—Land of the *bloody hand*[104]—

Petit Jean Mountains[105] on the Arkansas—a picturesque line of winding highlands, ⟨ro⟩ of mingld[106] rock & cliff & wood; with fine[107] bottom below—opposite these rich peccan bottoms, with hills beyond—river winds among groves, yellow sand bars &c Mounts. with the autumnal tint & smoky haze—log house[108] among groves with children[?][109] about it—Long vistas of river between woody points—Wild geese on sand bars[110]

When ⟨th⟩ Sarazin[,][111] chief of the Qua⟨p⟩wpaws returnd ⟨from the⟩

102. Trent and Hellman read as "sperm-light" (*Journals of WI*, III, 181); McDermott added, "sperm [part of word illegible] light" (*Western Journals*, p. 165). The dictionary definition of "spermaceti" is a white, waxy substance derived from the head of the sperm whale and used in making candles, among other things.

103. What appears to be a colon after "toe" is actually an ink blot combined with WI's comma; on this page, there are numerous blots from the ink of the opposite page.

104. This underlining may be WI's line to separate paragraphs.

105. See p. 165, n. 44; WI was at this point on November 13 between 11:00 A.M. and noon.

106. Because of the heavy ink flow and resulting smudge, it is impossible to determine whether the participle has an *e*.

107. Below this word are two dots of red sealing wax.

108. The position of the word at the right edge of the page makes it difficult to determine whether the word is plural or singular; Trent and Hellman read as "Ev[enin]g house" (*Journals of WI*, III, 181).

109. The reading is difficult because of an ink blot over the initial two letters, a blank space between the syllables, and an almost indistinct and poorly formed *r*.

110. WI set off the following three anecdotes with lines of three-eighths inch, one-half inch, three-eighths inch, and one-half inch.

111. Foreman quoted a June 22, 1829, letter to the secretary of war from Governor Pope, who said that the chief of the Quapaw, Saracen, vowed that his people had never shed the blood of whites and that they desired to live in peace in the Arkansas Territory. Pope added that these Indians were "a kind of inoffensive people and aid the Whites in picking out their cotton and furnishing them with game" (*Indians and Pioneers*, p. 183).

with his tribe from their abode at Cadeau[112] called on Gov Pope ⟨pro[?]⟩ spread a white deer skin under his feet & another on his shoulder—as emblem that they had never shed the blood of a white man The old man made a speech about their ⟨goin[g][?]⟩ ⟨exile⟩ removal He had lost a son & when he told of his wrath[113] the tears streamed down his cheeks When I went to that country said he the sun did not seem to shine—every thing was strange & forlorn—but when I returnd to this[114] ↑our[?]↓ country of my youth where are the tombs of our fathers the sun shone bright and every thing was again cheerful[115]

———

Arkansas—Settlers like to live apart where they can have good range[,] raise corn for bread—Cattle which feed on prarie on pea vine or cane-brake Hogs which find mast in plenty—depend on their rifle occasionally work one day out of seven

———

Quawpaws. Much intermarried with the French. ⟨?⟩A great part of them half breeds. Honest—liked & helped by the whites—

———

In general the frontier men seem to think themselves imposed upon by the Indians, because the latter having lost nearly all their property seek to hold on to what is left—

They have got the Indians[116] coat; & now begrudge him the fringe.

Post of the Arkansas—about here the speculator[?] Law[117] founded his colony

Old Spanish & French[118] settlers—retain their characteristics—

They were accustomed to be ⟨under⟩ governd by Commandants whose will was law. One who was capricious would exact all kinds of services ⟨and⟩ from those under him & bother them in a thousand ways—Another who was avaricious would squeeze them—Tho' the govt is now changed & they have equal rights with their meddlesome, quarrelsom litigious electioneering ⟨citizens⟩ fellow citizens of the US. they retain their old

112. Usually spelled "Caddo"; WI used the French spelling.

113. This word could be "death," with an irregularly formed *d*.

114. WI may have crossed out "this" before adding "our"[?] or "my"[?] above the line; there is a mark going through the *h* and *i*. The phrase would be as follows: "to ⟨this⟩ ↑our[?]↓ country. . . ."

115. In this sentence, there are extensive ink blots which make deciphering difficult: for instance, the word "shone" may be "shine."

116. Ink blots may have affected the punctuation of this sentence; WI may have intended an apostrophe here and the semicolon may be a comma.

117. Trent and Hellman omitted the first three faded and difficult lines of this page, beginning "Post of the Arkansas" (*Journals of WI*, III, 182).

118. WI wrote these words, beginning with "Old," in pencil and over them in ink.

passive acquiescence in the ⟨aff⟩ disposition of public affairs.[119] Do not intermeddle or distress themselves in Elections or worry themselves about public affairs—Have not the entrprize[120] of the Yankees. Nor their eagerness for gain & conquest. If an Ameri-/-can cultivates 20 acres & has 40 uncultivated the next year he cultivates 10 more. If he has 3 Negroes gets 6 and so with his stock The old Spanish & French Cultivate the same number of acres, have the same number of negros &c &c year in & year out. Content to live within their income & not eager to increase it. Simple in appearance & habits. remarkably honest & punctual. Kind & neghborly[121] among themselves. more civil & courteous than the Americans. Dress in their best on Sundays—dance—sing, [*illegible*][122] polite to the women. Never quarrel but with the tongue—[123]

When one has been absent[124] and returns; great rejoicing embra/cing —throughout the family.

Qu—How do they treat their negroes.

A. Work them hard; feed & clothe them poorly. It is proverbial in this part of the country that a Frenchman is ⟨*illegible*⟩ hard upon his horse & his negro.

Qu. do they wear old dresses—white[?] night cap—pipe—

Songs?

There are but two or three families at present at the fort—Most of them are at a settlement below fronting[?][125] on river where they retain French language. Keep apart from americans.

They have nothing of the public spirit that makes itself uneasy & unhappy about public men and public[126] measures & sucks in Sorrow[127]

119. Trent and Hellman and McDermott read as "despotism of public affairs" (*Journals of WI*, III, 183; *Western Journals*, p. 166).

120. Heavy ink flow may have obscured the second *e*.

121. Heavy ink flow may have obscured the *i*.

122. This word may be crossed out; the smudge makes it difficult to read, but it may be "always."

123. The smudge on the first of the next line may be a crossed-out word.

124. Trent and Hellman and McDermott read as "about" (*Journals of WI*, III, 183; *Western Journals*, p. 167).

125. Trent and Hellman and McDermott read as "frontier" (*Journals of WI*, III, 183; *Western Journals*, p. 167); however, the word ends with a *g*.

126. Written over the final letter of this word is a puzzling letter resembling a *g*.

127. Trent and Hellman read as "public manners and sinks in sorrow" (*Journals of WI*, III, 184); McDermott only changed the "and" to "&" (*Western Journals*, p. 167). However, the first noun seems clearly to be "measures" and the verb "sucks" rather than "sinks." Perhaps WI had in mind the expression that Jacques used in Shakespeare's *As You Like It*: "More, I prithee, more. I can suck melancholy out of a song, as a weasel sucks eggs" (II, v, 12–14).

through the newspapers. Nothing of that spirit that sets up two newspapers in the little village of little Rock, & sets ⟨fri⟩ neighbors by the ears calling each other hard names and reviling each other because they differ on abstract points[128]

They have given up competing with the Ams. who have too much enter-/-prize and industry for them.

A few old fellows exert a patriarchal sway over the community. Their word & opinion is law.

very fond of holy days—they dance & pass their time merrily.

All vote for Col Desha[129]—

They do not[,] like Ams.[,] trouble them-/-selves with cares beyond their horizon & import sorrow, thro newspapers, from every[?] point of compass

Mr Cumming[130]—married daughter of Mons[131] [*blank*] the great man of the place. worth 40 or 50000$. She ⟨*illegible*⟩[132] inherits french vivacity of tempermt & it is said rules her husband with the slipper. She is a pretty, dark, black eyed woman. Her father when he travels affects the Don. On board Steamboat has his own servt. His own wine. Cannot drink Steamboat wine.—[133]

(Judge [*blank*] very official[134]—Over[?] mindful of dignity of his office. rather slow, but upright and amiable.)

At the Post—Old fashioned French[135] looking houses.[136]

———

Abundance of dogs[—]whenever you hear of poor people ∧ ↑in this part of country↓ you may be sure to find abundance of dogs

Old negro with a long good humoured horse face and a Straw hat mashed[137] back from it like a mandarin cap

128. For a discussion of this war between the *Arkansas Gazette* and the *Arkansas Advocate*, see pp. 160–61, n. 13.

129. For a reference to Colonel Desha, see p. 168, n. 66.

130. For a reference to Mr. Cummins, see p. 168, n. 68.

131. WI's abbreviation for "Monsieur."

132. WI may not have crossed out the word; a large ink blot obscures what may be the word "has" or the two words may be read "The Mrs."

133. This dash may be ink blots from the opposite page.

134. The miscellaneous undated notes follow in loose chronological order the dated portion of the journal; WI's reference here to the unnamed judge was apparently to the Little Rock judge mentioned in the November 14 entry.

135. This smudged word could be "Spanish"; WI mentioned earlier and will mention again that both French and Spanish influence was seen in the architecture of Arkansas Post.

136. WI drew a line one-fourth inch long to separate ideas.

137. Trent and Hellman and McDermott read as "smashed" (*Journals of WI*,

⟨This day pass Quawpaw hunting camp on the border of the river After S

Put ⟨Col⟩ Lieut Dawson on shore at Col Deshas[138] Cotton plantation ↑After↓ ⟨about⟩ Sunset stop at the⟩ Post of the Arkansas—a century old. Originally a Spanish post—then French. A decayed ruinous place. old Spanish wooden building, with piazza—out houses—French buildings, with casements. Piazzas—remains of Stockade, at present surrounds garden & house of Monsr [*blank*] the principal mercht Near the old Spanish House are two large ruins—neglected kitchen garden Town stands on the abrupt end of a flat Prarie that extends 70 miles.

French town & american town, the former on the site of the Spanish post The latter two or three hundred yards off—Melancholy silent deserted look of the place. Commands a bend and winding of the river. Old French mercht. ⟨wit[?]⟩ large strong built man with Strong features —Tall Sons.—French jabberd about the place. Young men[139] in Blanket surtouts[140]—

———

German Mercht. at Little rock who ⟨had arrived[?]⟩ came there a Pedlar—Set up Store *for cash* at 25 pr Cent under the others—never trusted except to sure people—⟨[? made a ?]⟩ In 5 years has made a little fortune—chuckles at it—Ask him how he uses it.—oh—most proke—tinks I must puy a Steam bote—

———

choctaws[141] believe in witches—one choctaw set up for a Doctor. His father, mother & other relatives died. It was suspected he was a wizard & had practiced spells on them. Several of the old men who were not wizards held a council upon it & determined he was a wizard—He heard it and cleared out. His own brother set off in pursuit of him. tracked him for two days and killed him with a rifle—In such cases they do not attempt to resist or to defend themselves when overtaken

———

III, 185; *Western Journals*, p. 168). The word could also be "masked," although the context discourages that reading.

138. WI mentioned this disembarkation in the November 15 entry in almost these same words.

139. Trent and Hellman and McDermott transcribed as "mons[ieur]" (*Journals of WI*, III, 185; *Western Journals*, p. 169); however, there are not enough letters for that reading. The word could also be "man" or "mon."

140. WI sets off the following three anecdotes with lines of three-eighths inch, three-fourths inch, and one-half inch.

141. For a discussion of the Choctaw, see pp. 172–73, n. 91.

A small burg flourishing village which published two rival newspapers had 3 hotels & the usual number of Judges Generals & Colonels, not to speak of lawyers & Doctors—[142]

[*pp. [35–36] blank*]

[*inside back cover blank*]

[*back cover*]

No 9.

142. WI wrote this paragraph, which seems to be about Little Rock, in pencil.

AMERICAN JOURNALS, 1833

Travels in the United States - The Dutch Tour

This manuscript journal is in the Seligman Collection of Irvingiana in the Manuscripts and Archives Division of the New York Public Library, where it is cataloged as Washington Irving Journals, Volume 28. It apparently originally consisted of 34 leaves of off-white, unlined paper, and its pages measure 3⅞ x 6 inches. It is bound in an unlined tan cardboard cover and tied with an off-white string between pages [34] and [35], or leaves 17 and 18. Except for the first three lines of the front cover, the journal is written throughout in pencil. Blank are the inside front cover, pages [2], [6], [34], [44–50], [57–62], and [67]; torn out of the notebook or partially torn out are leaves 11, 14–15, 20, 26–28, 32; loose is leaf 9. On page [13] is a drawing of a house. The last eight lines of page [1] and the three lines of page [66] are written with the notebook reversed.

[*front cover*]

Esopus &c
Dutch tour[1]
1833.
From Albany to Com-/munipaw

[*inside front cover blank except number "12," top flush left*]

Measure of rooms for carpets
& fireplace for ⟨g⟩Grate
Globe for 2 or 3 inches

1. In an October 28 letter to his brother Peter, WI briefly described this two-week trip, from September 10 to 25, "visiting old scenes about the Hudson. I made a delightful journey with Mr. Van Buren in an open carriage from Kinderhook to Poughkeepsie, then crossing the river to the country about the foot of the Catskill Mountains, and so from Esopus, by Goshen, Haverstraw, Tappan, Hackensack, to Communipaw . . . in the course of which we visited curious old Dutch places and Dutch families" (*Letters*, II, 779).

[*remainder of writing on p. [1] is upside down*]
Gemoenepa[2]—Manings[?] Article 1751
Comonapa 1713
1⟨8⟩710 *Communipaw*[3] made one by Govt

———

Comonopa
1668 Carteret[4]
Comounepaw[?]

[*p. [2] blank; in the top quarter of the page, approximately in the middle of the page, is a torn portion, five-eighths inch wide.*]

Tuesday, September 10[5]
Leave Albany with Mr Van Buren[6] & John Van Buren[7] for Kinder Hook[8]

———

Near Albany—Kiddsholes where it is said Kidd buried money[9]—Not

2. Apparently, WI was making notes on the evolution of the name "Communipaw," the principal village of the Hackensack Indians, whose land was in the valley of the Hackensack and Passaic rivers in New Jersey. "Gamoenapa" was the original Dutch spelling; other spellings in seventeenth-century documents were "Gamoenepa," "Gamonepa," and "Gemoenepaen" (Hodge, *Handbook of Indians*, I, 333–34).

3. WI used triple underlining and drew a line one-fourth inch long between items.

4. In 1664, James, duke of York, granted a large tract of land to two court favorites, Lord John Berkeley and Sir George Carteret; New Jersey was named in honor of Carteret's defense of the Isle of Jersey in the English Civil Wars. In 1665, government powers were added to the grant. (See Michael Kammen, *Colonial New York: A History* [New York: Charles Scribner's Sons, 1975], pp. 74–127; hereafter cited as Kammen, *Colonial New York.*)

5. With this initial entry, WI began misdating; he wrote "1833. ↑Tuesday↓ Sept 11." He may have been using an old calendar, because in 1832, September 11 was on Tuesday; at any rate, he misdated the following entry, corrected the succeeding dates until September 23, when he misdated again.

6. At this time Martin Van Buren (1782–1862) was vice-president and powerful in New York politics; from 1833 until 1840, WI advised him. Van Buren and WI had long been friends (see Introduction, p. xlvi), and in the winter of 1831, when they were in England, the Van Burens—father and son—were introduced by WI to country life and an English Christmas as they all traveled together and spent the season at Barlborough Hall (see *Letters*, II, 669, n. 17, 676, 680–81). Perhaps the Van Burens were returning the favor.

7. John Van Buren (1810–1866), the son remembered by WI in 1831 as "a young gentleman about 23" (*Letters*, II, 676), was outstanding in his own right as a lawyer and later attorney general of the state of New York.

8. WI set off the Albany section with lines of one-eighth inch and one-fourth inch.

9. According to Maud W. Goodwin, the career of "Captain William Kidd, Gentleman" (1650–1701), respected New York sea captain turned pirate, "so impressed

far below about 1 mile is a rough rocky Hill with old brick house. Here fortunes have been spent seeking for copper

13 Miles below Albany we pass Barren Island—a rocky island ⟨near⟩ round backed—commanding a pass of the river.[10]

Kinderhook[11]—Brom Van Alstyne[12] a helter skelter wag[?][13]—
woodchuck
visit Jesse Marvin[14]—trees loaded with fruit about the house

Wednesday, September 11[15]

Beautiful view along the valley of the Kinderhook hill from Wyncoops[16] house.

---

the popular imagination that a host of legends sprang up concerning him . . ." (*Dutch and English on the Hudson* [New Haven: Yale University Press, 1921], 178). The folklore included much buried treasure along the Hudson. WI collected "copious particulars about Kidd" from Colonel Aspinwall in 1824 (*Letters*, II, 50), which he incorporated into "Kidd the Pirate" in *Tales of a Traveller*, published in Philadelphia, London, and Paris in 1824.

10. At Barren Island, which is about fourteen miles south of Albany, agents of Kiliaen Van Rensselaer, one of the early seventeenth-century patroons, exacted payment from the passing skippers or they were fired upon (Work Projects Administration, *New York: A Guide to the Empire State* [New York: Oxford University Press, 1940], p. 614; hereafter cited as *WPA's New York*). The island was fortified in 1644.

11. Kinderhook, meaning "children's corner" in Dutch, was on the east side of the Hudson, approximately 20 miles below Albany and ten miles above the town of Hudson; it was a town of 2,706 people in Columbia County. Three miles east of Kinderhook, or Kinderhook Landing as some guides called it, was the birthplace and home of Martin Van Buren.

12. There were several families of Van Alstynes or Van Alstines living in Kinderhook; Brom Van Alstyne has been identified as the model for WI's Brom Bones in "The Legend of Sleepy Hollow." He was a local character who lived in Kinderhook when WI visited there in 1809 (STW, I, 430, n. 91).

13. This word could be "waif."

14. Jesse Merwin (1784–1852) was a local schoolmaster whom WI immortalized as Ichabod Crane. In May, 1809, WI went to Kinderhook to recover from the shock of Matilda Hoffman's death on April 27; he wrote to Henry Brevoort from the Van Ness estate: "The only Country acquaintance I have made, is a schoolmaster who teaches the neighbouring children—a pleasant good natured fellow, with much native, unimproved shrewdness and considerable humour—as he is a kind of inmate at Van Ness's we have become very great friends, and I have found much entertainment in his conversation" (*Letters*, I, 263). WI consistently misspelled his name.

15. WI misdated as "Wednesday 12 Sept."

16. "Wyncoop," or "Wynkoop" as it was spelled in the 1790 Census of New York, was an outstanding family name; Dirck Wyncoop was a member of the Provincial Congress and the first Ulster County Court judge in 1788 (E. Wilder Spaulding, *New York in the Critical Period: 1783–1789* [Port Washington, N.Y.: Ira J. Friedman,

Breakfast at Dr Beekmans.[17]

Training day at Kinderhook[—]legions of cake carts—Men in old cocked hats & particoloured Calico trousers selling cake.

Old Crash[?] Lymes[?] ⟨wh⟩ 70 years old Has been drunk the last 50—contracts to work and employs black men under him whom he never pays.

Frank who had lived with Mr Van Ness[18] & recollects my shooting the Crow 25 years since.

Abundance of Dinner at the training—

worthies of Kinderhook

Brom Van Alstyne

Meet at breakfast Dr Clark[—]father to Mrs Beekman

leave at ½ past 11. drive by the village. fine view of Kinderhook with catskill mounts. behind

Valley of the Kline[?] Kill where the good men lived—rich valley—catskill at distance

Hudson[19]—South ⟨lay⟩ bay with romantic promontory forming over Hdsn[?]. Catskill mounts opposite

[*p. [6] blank*]

Hollan[?]

Race of men inhabit side of Hill ⟨just⟩ near Hudson—⟨half⟩ Indian Habits —Huntsmen—fishermen—used to come to Hudson Indian file[?]—thought their lawyers cheated them—Van Buren plead their cause[20]

1963], p. 233; hereafter cited as Spaulding, *Critical Period*). There were two Wynkoops listed in 1790 as heads of households in Kinderhook: John and Peter.

17. The Beekman House, built in 1736 on Broad Street, still stands (*WPA's New York*, p. 565).

18. WI spent his month in Kinderhook twenty-four years earlier at the home of Judge William P. Van Ness (1778–1826); ironically, it was to this same place he went with Van Buren, who had studied law with Van Ness and bought his estate, Lindenwald.

19. Hudson, on the east side of the river and 29 miles below Albany, was the county town of Columbia County; its population in 1830 was 5,392. Situated on a plain 60 feet above the water, it commanded a fine westward view of the river, the village of Athens on the opposite shore, and the Catskill Mountains.

20. WI may have referred here to the patroon system of landholding and the resulting problems of the "rootless rural proletariat" in the Hudson River Valley which began to emerge in the 1730's and continued as a major controversy involving land grants, rents, migrations, etc., and resulting often in riots and unsettled legal questions. For instance, the Wappinger Indians had claims on some of the manor land, and when they petitioned the government in 1767, no lawyer would take the

Sunday, September 15[21]
Serene ⟨Sunny⟩ day—Golden sunshine—Shimmer of the landscape—universal note of the crickets—
Evg walk to the Hills

Monday, September 16[22]
Leaves Staatsburg[23] 10 OClock[—]Ride into interior—Crum elbow[24]—pleasant valley[25]—9 peartrees—nut trees—Sycamore—Farms[?], woods[26] ⟨meadows⟩ ⟨plain[?]⟩ fertile little valleys—
arrive at Pokeepsie[27] about 2—put at[28] at Hatchs—
See—Gilbert Livingston
Judge Emmett
Mr Theron[?] Rudd[29]

---

case. The government rejected their claim (Kammen, *Colonial New York*, pp. 294–304).

21. WI wrote "Sunday Sept 15."

22. WI wrote "Monday—16."

23. Staatsburg, village in Clinton, Dutchess County, on the east bank of the Hudson, was ten miles north of Poughkeepsie. The village was named for Dr. Samuel Staats and Dirck Van der Burgh, early settlers (*WPA's New York*, p. 571). WI was driving east away from the river.

24. Just north of Poughkeepsie, the river bends to the west; this bend was called Crum Elbow. In the vicinity of Hyde Park, just south of Staatsburg, is the Roosevelt estate; in 1866, James Roosevelt acquired the place originally built in 1826 by Ephraim Holbrock and renamed it Crum Elbow. In 1882, his son Franklin Delano Roosevelt was born there (*WPA's New York*, pp. 573–74).

25. Perhaps WI was simply describing the landscape; Pleasant Valley was also a small flourishing village in Clinton, Dutchess County, seven miles east of Poughkeepsie. Population in 1830 was 2,419.

26. The words "Farms" and "woods" were written over illegible words and, therefore, difficult to decipher.

27. Poughkeepsie, approximately equidistant from Albany and New York, was the county town of Dutchess County, with a population in 1830 of 7,222. There were five landings along the township's ten-mile length, but the main village was situated on a plain a mile east of the river and was at this time flourishing and handsome.

28. WI intended to write "up."

29. Gilbert Livingston was the descendant of the great landholding family of Robert Livingston (1654–1728), who immigrated to America in 1673, accumulated 160,000 acres along the Hudson's east side, and in 1686 was made first lord of the manor of Livingston. From the beginning the Livingstons were active in New York politics and commerce, and Robert was secretary of Indian affairs from 1676 to 1721. His fourth son was Gilbert; in 1790, at the death of Robert, third lord of the manor, the manor was divided by law among eight heirs. (See *Burke's American Families with British Ancestry* [Baltimore: Genealogical Publishing Co., 1975], pp. 2792–93; *WPA's New York*, pp. 607–10; Dixon Ryan Fox, *The Decline of Aristocracy in the Politics of New York: 1801–1840*, ed. Robert V. Remini [1919;

Tuesday, September 17[30]

cross Ferry. High banks.—drive up road ⟨thro⟩ among Hills.

Paltz[31]—in rich valley between range of mounts—Head winds, rocks & trees—Stream runs thro valley—Budds tavern—neat rooms old fashioned ⟨fr⟩—

Smoak[?] in the ↑Shawangot[?]↓ mountains[32]

Catskill mounts in the distance—Hazy—

—Shawangunk mounts woody with rocky headlands

⟨This morng⟩

Trees of the country—oak Black wall nut &c

—Paltz—Stone houses

Mr Budd—little stout man with red nose

Old Fort 1705[33]—large old Stone house— ∧ ↑small↓ casement ↓windows↑

[*Along the left margin approximately three-fourths down the page are*

---

reprint., New York: Harper Torchbooks, 1965]; hereafter cited as Fox, *Decline.*) Appleton's travel guide pointed in 1846 to the country seat of William Emmet on the east side of the river as striking; perhaps this was the place WI visited (*Handbook*, p. 74).

The top edge of this leaf (pp. [10–11]) has been torn off to one-fourth inch at the widest point of the tear; however, there seems to be no writing missing.

30. WI wrote "Tuesday 17."

31. New Paltz Landing was a village on the west side of the Hudson in Ulster County, opposite Poughkeepsie and fifteen miles below Kingston Landing; New Paltz, also in Ulster County, approximately seven miles west-northwest of the Landing, was on the west bank of the Wallkill River. It was a French Huguenot town settled in 1677 after an Esopus Indian attack on Kingston; the land was purchased by twelve patentees from the Indians, and in 1678, twelve families made their way here; the population in 1830 was 4,973.

32. The Shawangunk Mountains, approximately 25 miles west of the lower Hudson, ranged about 2,000 feet above and between the Rondout and Wallkill rivers; a part of the Appalachians, these mountains extended through Ulster, Orange, and Sullivan counties, New York, and took their name from the Indian word meaning "pile of white rock," the formation's being of white and pink sandstone (*WPA's New York*, pp. 36, 403).

33. New Paltz, named by the Huguenots in memory of their refuge, "Rheinish Pfalz," is today one of two "museums of early eighteenth-century stone work . . ." (*WPA's New York*, p. 21); Kammen wrote that many of the fine houses built in the early 1700's are still called "forts" because of the architectural precautions taken against Indian attack; one example he gave was "The Old Fort" or Daniel DuBois house, built in New Paltz in 1705 "to supplant a log palisade, fulfilled one of the terms of the Huguenots' patent, which required that they build 'a place of Retreat and Safeguard upon Occasion' " (Kammen, *Colonial New York*, p. 147). Two-feet thick walls were constructed of native limestone and fieldstone.

two words, "ch Yard"[?], written after the journal was turned clockwise a quarter turn; these words seem to refer to the following list.]

—Andros Dubois[34]
Elting
Le fevre
Hasbrouk
Dayo[35]

———

1731 Oct 7
A D Bois
SVRVIVER of 12 Patentees[36]

———

rude old square grave stone rudely engraven

Noah Elting & Jacomintje[?] his spouse

Rich valley on plain with woods, groves, orchards—meadows[—]river winding through—⟨Hills⟩ Sharp[?] mount with farms[—]woods—uplands—

Rocky point on headland where there is a deep lake 1 mile long ⟨&⟩ with fort on it.

Van Wagoner[?][37]

Mr Dewitt[—]milliner

34. WI may have been copying names of some of the twelve original patentees from tombstones; a Dutch Reformed Church was built here in 1839, but there had been three previous buildings as the congregation dated from 1683. WI's initial entry may represent two family names, or the Dubois's given name was Andros. Colonel Edmund Andros was the colonial governor of New York from 1674 until 1781, following the third Dutch War and subsequent treaty in which the Dutch relinquished to England any claim to New Netherland. It was Louis DuBois who located the land for the Huguenot settlement and organized its purchase in 1677 (see n. 31 above). Louis Bevier, also a patentee, built his house in 1699, and his son added to it in 1735; Captain Josiah Elting bought it in 1765; twelve Le Fevers were listed in the 1790 census as heads of families in New Paltz; Abraham Hasbrouck and his brother John, both patentees, built houses on this ridge during the years 1694 to 1712; and Pierre Deyo, one of the original twelve patentees, built his house during this period, but it underwent structural alterations during the next century (*WPA's New York*, pp. 402–3; Kammen, *Colonial New York*, pp. 145–46).

35. The second letter of this name, an *a* or *u*, was written over another letter, perhaps an *e*, which would have been the correct spelling, "Deyo." Following this list of names is WI's version of a tombstone inscription with a half-square drawn around it; we have set off the epitaph with lines above and below it.

36. See above, n. 34.

37. There were several spellings of this name listed in the 1790 Census, any of which WI may have written: "Van Waganer," "Van Wagenen," "Van Wagener"; the more usual spelling of "Dewitt" was "De Witt," and there were seven De Witts listed in the 1790 census as heads of families in Kingston.

[p. [13] consists of a page-sized drawing of a house, apparently of three stories and with three gables and a chimney. The journal has been turned counterclockwise a quarter turn, and at the top of the drawing Irving has labeled as follows: "Old ⟨fort⟩ ↑house↓ of Stone used as fort in Indian wars."]

Tuesday and Wednesday, September 17–18[38]

at Kingston—[39]

Mr Sudams coachman, liberated Several years since—Goes to NYork[,] Albany, comes back—says he was never a slave until now[40]

———

Kingston—at the west end of the village was the fort where DeWitt built a mill—

———

Rich plain—old DeWitt Frenchman—

Farms of Wynkoops and Ten Eycks—rich old names

Dutch consider it a disgrace to let their farms go out of their families—Have retaind them from Generation to Generation

Corner of orchard where Esopus—the old sachem[41] was buried negroes buried near by.

Spooks run there and in a blue storm

Old peoples in village believe in witches, ghosts &c

Old Blk woman at Elmendorfs[—]strong believer

Brink—a Doctor who cures by Charms—Witch Doctor

Witches of the Rondout[42] bewitch cattle &c—

Miss Wyncoop—old maid—goes from home to home—visiting—⟨great⟩ Skilled in pastry &c &c visited wherever there are preparations for a feast—a great gossip

Old Dutch houses every room on a different level[—]Steps to go up & down.[43]

———

38. WI wrote "Tuesday 17. Wednesday 18" at the top of the page, the remainder of which is blank.

39. Kingston, formerly Esopus, was the county town of Ulster County; it was situated on Esopus Creek three miles west of the Hudson River and Kingston Landing, 100 miles above New York, and 65 miles below Albany. Its population in 1832 was 4,170, and its fine courthouse was built at a cost of $40,000.

40. WI set off the following note with lines of one-half inch.

41. Indian word meaning "leader."

42. Rondout Creek, rising in Ulster County and flowing northeast, entered the Hudson just below Kingston Landing; near the mouth of the creek was a thriving town, also called Rondout.

43. WI separated the following four anecdotes with lines of one-fourth inch, one-eighth inch, one-half inch, and one-half inch.

Fig. 10. From the Dutch Tour p. [13], a drawing of a house of three stories with three gables and a chimney.

↑⟨Juliet[?]⟩↓ Jacobs[44] valley—brook running thro it—old Indian Spring—Considered as haunted—

———

Mr Elmendorfs brother went sparking—Dutch lass seated on his lap [—]broke his pipe to pieces—returng home thot he heard something in the spook ground—ran—heard the rattling of his pipe—thot it the rattling of chains—scamperd home[—]forced open door in spite of latches & pitched head foremost on the floor

———

Hunting in the mounts[—]bear—deer—lakes in the mountain where deer are hunted in canoes by torch light—

———

⟨Great⟩
Old Dutch house with great Sycamore tree—under which an old Dutchman used to sit and read ⟨the⟩ a dutch bible in a chanting tone—

Friday, September 20[45]
Call on Mr Snyder[,] County clerk.[46] inspect old treaties in Dutch & English with Indians[—]tied by Wampum belt—Records &c Kept in great [*unrecovered*][47] chest with curious, cumbersm[?] old dutch ⟨lock⟩ steel lock.

Snyder, a genial spoken good humoured man
among the records are accounts of trials &c in what was concernd[—] Hildyonda Van Sleghenhorst[?][—]She once kept a Store—was summoned to appear in court ⟨told⟩ asked if ready for trial[—]yes if Judge would swear & kiss the book that he would decide rightly between all parties; said he had sworn so when he had entered upon office—well she thot he could have no objection to swearing again by way of refresh-/ing his memory—
She Sues a boy for breaking her window with a pebble Stone
appears to ⟨be⟩ have been a Shrew

[*pp. [21–22], or leaf 11, torn out of journal*][48]

44. WI simply may have made a false start on one line and then dropped to the next.

45. WI wrote "Friday 20."

46. Ulster County.

47. This word resembles "deal."

48. The stub is approximately three-sixteenths inch wide at its maximum.

after leaving Kingston ½ past 10 drive through Hurley[49]—then to Marbletown[50]—enter into beautiful valleys between Shawgu[?][51] mounts & alleghanys—former cultivated in some places to summits. Hamlets gleaming on sides—

Clouds rolled off to Catskill or Blue mounts.—

vast sloping sides of Shawgu[?] Mounts—richly wooded with opening of farms &c

Throughout the country solid Stone farm houses. Dutch a rural aristocracy—

Dutch farm houses with good barns—fruits—Sycamore[,] Elm & willow trees

Valleys with enormous fruit trees—rich meadows—winding Streams

Rochester[52]—Scatterd hamlet or village in rich valley—with the broad ⟨slo⟩ wooded slopes of the Shawangunk mounts. descendg to it—Noise of stream from mountain &c &c[—]training day

Beautiful variegated side of soft sloping Shawangunk—

distant blue Summits of the Catskills

Training—picturesque groupes on border of ⟨the⟩ a pastoral stream (The Rondout).

—Militia training—in rich meadow—with magnificent mount-/-ain scenery in the background

—Horses galloping about the meadow[—]some with two men on it—

Beautiful drive through rich valleys with rondout ⟨curv[?]⟩ winding through—Alleghanys to right—Shawangunk to left—

dine at Widow Hournbecks[?][53]—Ham & Eggs—

Waggon loads of the train bands arrive—Heavy shower

set off about 6 Oclock—⟨for⟩

after a time a heavy shower comes on with thunder—dark[,] dark—only see our road by flashes of lightning—arrive safe at Ellenville[54] where we ⟨find[?]⟩ put up for the night at very indifferent Inn kept by [*blank*]

49. Hurley, approximately three miles southwest of Kingston and also on the east bank of the Esopus, was another town created splendidly from stone; its population in 1830 was 1,408.

50. Marbletown was named for the ledge of limestone from which much of the stone for houses in surrounding towns was quarried; it was also on the east bank of the Esopus, in Ulster County, approximately ten miles southwest from Kingston with a population in 1830 of 3,223.

51. WI's abbreviation, probably for "Shawangunk."

52. Rochester, a town in Ulster County, had a population in 1830 of 2,420; the Shawangunk Mountains were in the southeastern part of town.

53. WI may have written "Hovenbeck"; there were many Hornbecks in this area.

54. "Ellensville," as it was spelled in several guides, was a village in the southern

Property of Dutch dignitaries
Dutch proud[55]

———

↑⟨at⟩↓ Leave Ellenville at 6 oclock[.] Drive along the Hollow which narrows to Wurtzburg[56]—at Mr Nevins—good house—See Judge Demick—

—Leave Wurtzburg at 10—cross the Shawangunk Mounts—Splendid view ⟨on⟩from the Summit of the mountains

[pp. [27–30], or leaves 14 and 15, torn out][57]

looking towards Highlands[58]—

—Surveying the ⟨rich &⟩ varied valley of the Catskill[?]—and a rich broken country of vast extent watered by various Streams winding their way to bear their tributes to the Hudson—

distant line of blue mountains across the country ⟨Through the⟩ with the gap or entrance to the Highlands through which the Hudson enters[59]

———

Scenery of all these parts like the Italian scenery bordering on the Apennines[60]

Sunday, September 22[61]

At Goshen[62] ^↑Edsels[?] Hotel↓—Hear good sermon from the Episcopal preacher Mr Clark of Brooklyn.

---

part of Ulster County; it was on the left bank of Rondout Creek and on the Delaware and Hudson Canal, 80 miles southwest of Albany.

55. WI drew a line three-eighths inch long to separate thoughts.

56. Approximately ten miles south-southwest of Ellensville, Wurtsborough was a small village in Sullivan County, on the Delaware and Hudson Canal.

57. The stub of leaf 14 varies in width from one-half to 2½ inches; leaf 15 is only a small triangular fragment, three-eighths inch at its widest point, at the top of the notebook. Apparently, these leaves were torn before WI wrote in the book.

58. WI was looking west across the Wallkill River and toward the Highlands of the Hudson, "a pre-Cambrian area of granite and granite-injected crystalline rocks," through which the Hudson flowed for eighteen miles and which provided a foundation for later New York buildings (*WPA's New York*, p. 27); the highest peaks of the range included St. Anthony's Nose, Sugarloaf, Butter Hill, and Breakneck Hill.

59. WI drew a line one-fourth inch between paragraphs.

60. The Apennines extended through the entire Italian peninsula and were composed primarily of granite and limestone; except for the Po, the rivers of Italy rose in the Apennines.

61. WI misdated as "Sunday 21—."

62. WI was traveling southwest toward New York from Middletown to Goshen, named by the early settlers because of the fertile soil; at this time, Goshen was

Dine at Genl Wyckham–meet Mr Van Duyer[?][63] there–

People in this neighborhood well off–⟨&⟩ rich–⟨fr⟩ live frugally & put out their money on land & mortgage

pass the Evg. at Mr Van Dyck Editor of the Jackson paper[64]–His mother Mrs Van Dyck of Kinderhook

Monday, September 23[65]

Leave Goshen a little after 6–

–Breakfast at Munro[66]

This was the head quarters of Claudius Smith[67]–head of a gang of Skinners during the revolution[–]he had a cave in this neighborhood & one back of Goshen. was taken & hanged at Goshen

Ramapough Mountain & river at Iron works[68]

Scunnenonk Mountain between Goshen & the river mounts

[*p. [34] blank*]

Haverstraw[69]–Smiths house on a hill where Andre & Arnold had an interview–Stone house (white)–Arnold came down in boat with Smith

---

the half-shire (sharing the county seat with Newburgh) of Orange County, New York; its population was 3,361; it was twenty miles from West Point and 63 miles from New York.

63. WI may have written "Van Duzer."

64. The *Goshen Democrat* (1834–1845) continued the *Orange County Patriot*, published from 1809 until 1833; the primary Jacksonian paper at this time was the *Albany Argus* (1813–1856), which had always been supportive of the Albany Regency (see p. 7, n. 35) and had vowed neutrality. However, with the September 27, 1827, issue, the *Argus* came out as a Jackson paper (Fox, *Decline*, p. 315, n. 2).

65. WI misdated as "Monday 22." above the word "Goshen" on the first line.

66. Monroe was a town in Orange County, nineteen miles south-southwest of Newburgh and 50 miles northwest of New York; its population in 1830 was 3,671.

67. Claudius Smith's two caves at the edge of the Highlands southeast of Goshen (just east of what is now Tuxedo) housed men and stabled horses; Smith was a notorious Tory highwayman, ruthless and hated, who stole horses from the Patriots and sold them to the English (*WPA's New York*, pp. 385, 398).

68. WI was traveling south at this point; Ramapaugh (sometimes spelled "Ramapo") River rose in Rockland County, New York, flowed south into New Jersey, and joined the Long Pond and Pequanock rivers to form the Pompton. The iron works were on the river in Rockland County, 35 miles north of New York.

69. WI had traveled northeast to Haverstraw, a town in Rockland County, on the west side of the Hudson, forty miles north of New York; its population in 1830 was 2,306. At the back of the town were the high hills where Major John André hid; General Benedict Arnold had been giving information through André to Sir Henry Clinton for a year before Arnold's defection on September 25, 1780; the meeting WI described occurred five nights earlier (*WPA's New York*, pp. 606–07, 618–20).

[—]landed on shore [*unrecovered*] Vulture[70]—sent Smith on board to see Andre. They had interview on shore till day light ⟨affeared to go on board lest people should see—pulled up to⟩ affeared to send Andre back to the ship lest people should see it—pulled up along shore two miles and then went to Smiths house[—]remained there a day or two—Smith disguised Andre and crossed the river with him—left him near Tarry town

Smith was taken—confined in Goshen Gaol—His wife came to see him[—]exchanged dresses with him—He got off—rode behind a friend—Got to NYork—went to England—after the peace returned to NYork—Came up here, but could not stand the Scorn of the people—died soon. The Smiths once owned much land hereabout—a place called Smiths Clove[71]—⟨property⟩ mostly Lawyers. The property has slipped out of the hands of the family—There is a lawyer a nephew of Smith of Haverstraw

Tuesday, September 24[72]

Leave Haverstraw about ½ past 8. drive along river 1 mile & up close —pass thro ridge of mounts into an open Country—Snug stone farm houses. Waggon breaks down close by a farmers of the name of Herring[?][73] who assists us. Waggoner named Girand aids us & takes our trunks in his waggon. Go on for 2 miles to Nyack post office at Clarkston[74] kept by Oblines[?]—Get the[?] waggon mended—dine there

Rockland County. Hilly. ⟨dro[?]⟩ diversified—Snug brown stone farm houses perched on hillock & commandg fine views[75]

Autumnal day. Maple[76] trees tint the forest. noise of crickets & treetoad

Drive from Oblines[?] to Nyack[77][—]fine view[?] through the opening

70. The Sloop of War *Vulture* was lying in Haverstraw Bay; it was to this ship which Arnold fled when he learned of André's capture on September 23 with Arnold's drawings of West Point in his pocket.

71. The place Smith took André to meet Arnold was called Long Clove, the foot of a mountain on the west side of the Hudson. The word conceivably could be "Close."

72. WI misdated and included the date as follows: "Leave Haverstraw about ½ past 8. Tuesday—23. drive. . . ."

73. This word also could be "Horning."

74. Clarkston, the county town of Rockland County, was 122 miles south of Albany, on the west side of the Hudson, with a population in 1830 of 2,298. The post office WI mentioned may have been Nyack Turnpike which was also in Rockland County.

75. WI drew a line five-eighths inch long between thoughts.

76. The *M* is written over an illegible letter.

77. Nyack, on the west side of the Hudson in Rockland County, 28 miles north

of the trees & Hills over Tappan bay to the opposite shore— —Snug Stone Cottages of Nyack—Bold bluffs to the left advancing into the Hudson. ⟨Long Pall[?]⟩ romantic coast to the

[*pp. [39–40], or leaf 20, torn out*][78]

South—Range of rocky heights embracing the [*unrecovered*]—

Fine drive along the coast to Tappan—road near the river, with belt of trees & shrubs & rocks below it—

Drive up Tappan sloat[?][79]—number of Dutch waggons returning from the Landing—

Women with Dutch Sun bonnets—people talk dutch— —⟨p[?]⟩ neatness of houses—grass plots &c. open upon pleasant rural country with belt of woody hills to the left; the line that terminates in the pallisades

Stop at Judge [*blank*] formerly member of assembly ⟨8⟩70 years of age. His brother 80 & their two wives taking tea in the little hall of the farm house

Grand daughter of 13 years of age with uncommonly fine large black eyes.

Farm stands at some distance from the road, with ⟨tree⟩ meadows between—Old mans son & grand/son come in—

⟨F⟩See from the house the hill where André was hanged.

Drive through Tappan—Still quiet little village. Old Church where André was confined[?][80]—quiet church yard with old Dutch & French names—Inn where Court marshall was held—pleasant rural country around—

Leaving Tappan we pass thro Harington[81]—very neat Dutch stone Cottages—ask an old lady who is out is this road to where such & such belong—we find our room[?] here[?][—]compliment her on its neatness—quite a picture—

Arrive about 8 oclock at Hackensack[82]

---

of New York, was at this time a village with a beautiful view of the Palisades to the north and Tappan Bay, approximately five miles wide, to the east.

78. Only a small triangular fragment remains of the leaf; it was torn out before WI wrote, because the sentence continues without interruption.

79. This word could be "slant," "slint," or "slont." Tappan's Landing, or Piermont, was 24 miles north of New York, on the west side of the Hudson; the village of Tappan, or Tappantown, was three miles west of the Landing. Major André was hanged there on October 2, 1780.

80. This word could be "confirmed."

81. Harrington, a town in Bergen County, New Jersey, had a population of 2,581 in 1830.

82. Hackensack, the county town of Bergen County, New Jersey, largely of stone

Wednesday, September 25[83]

[*blank*] Met[?] [? Domine Ransqus ?][84] at Hackensack

Leave Hackensack—drive thro English[?] neghborhood to Communipaw[85][—]old Van Horn[?] ⟨say⟩ Saw NYork burnt—wanted to see trinity steeple fall, but turned away his head & when looked again it was down

[*pp. [44–50] blank; pp. [51–52], or leaf 26, missing; pp. [53–54], or leaf 27, torn out; pp. [55–56], or leaf 28, partially torn out; pp. [57–62] blank; pp. [63–64], or leaf 32, partially torn out; p. [65] blank. On p. [66], Irving reversed the notebook and wrote three lines.*]
Barren Island—Hamlet[?] just above on west shore[?]—
Slant[?]—

[*p. [67] blank*]

Marbletown { [*two words unrecovered*][86]
Aleghaney &
Shawangung }

Rochester beyond the Church[?][—]water Horses & after Rochester come to Wawasing[87]—

[*inside back cover*]
Hildajonda Van Slegtenhorst
Shawongonck 1709[88]

———

Indians Burying Ground
Near Warwasing

[*back cover*]

1833[89]

---

houses and twenty miles northwest of New York, was on the Hackensack River; its population was 2,200. The Hackensack Indians, whose name means "the stream that unites with another in low level ground," lived in the valleys of the Hackensack and Passaic (Hodge, *Handbook of Indians*, I, 519).

83. WI wrote "Wednesday."; it may be read "Wed midday."

84. This name could be "Renequs."

85. Communipaw was a village in Bergen County, New Jersey, on the west shore of New York Bay; largely a Dutch settlement, it was made famous in Book II of WI's *A History of New York* by Diedrich Knickerbocker.

86. The first word may be "Ann"; apparently WI was listing mountain ranges near Marbletown. The bracket is his.

87. Wawasing, on the road between Marbletown and Ellensville, was in Ulster County and had a population in 1830 of 2,738.

88. WI drew a line one inch long to separate items.

89. The date, in WI's handwriting, is in the center top of the cover.

JOURNAL, 1842

Travels from the United States to Bayonne

This manuscript journal is in the Seligman Collection of Irvingiana in the Manuscripts and Archives Division of the New York Public Library, where it is cataloged as #22–3300, Washington Irving Journals, Volume 30. The journal apparently originally consisted of 44 leaves; its 84 pages of off-white paper, each with 23 very faded blue lines, measure 4 7/16 x 7 1/16 inches. The scratched red leather cover is not attached to the journal's pages; there is a white string between pages [44] and [45]. Leaf 1 (pages [1–2]) is loose, and the last leaf (pages [87–88]) is missing. Leaf 43 (pages [85–86]) is torn out approximately three-fourths inch from the binding; on the part of page [86] which remains is the word "footman" in ink as well as some illegible letters on the next line. In black ink is the front cover, and in brown ink are pages [2–14], the first thirteen lines of [15], [22], the first three lines of [23], [28–41], the name "Delphine Gay" on line 9 of [44], and the back cover; in pencil are the last two lines of page [15], pages [16–21], the last sixteen lines of [23], [24–27], the name "Pierre" on line 10 of [35], [42–44], [47–51], and the inside back cover. Blank are pages [1–2] and [45–46].

[*front cover*]

1
New York to Bayonne
⟨W I[?]⟩ from April 10th.
to July 20th. 1842

[*inside front cover blank except number "23" top flush left and the catalog indication "Journal 30" bottom flush left*]

[*pp. [1–2] blank*]

Sunday, April 10[1]

Drive down to White Hall in Carriage with Abm. Schermerhorn.[2] Embark on board Steam Ferry boat to be taken on board of Liverpool Packet Ship Independence Cap Holdridge. Accompanied to Ship by Eben Irving[3] & his son Washington.[4] J Treat Irving.[5] Irving Paris.[6] Henry Brevoort.[7] Charles Augustus Davis.[8]

1. WI wrote "April 1842" in the center of the first line and then wrote "10th. Sunday." at the beginning of the second line flush left; we have indented the paragraph.

2. Abraham Schermerhorn (1783–1850) was a wealthy merchant and leading citizen of New York; Philip Hone mentioned in his February 14, 1835, diary entry that he met with a "large and exceedingly respectable" group to form a regular Knickerbocker Society; included were, among others, the Irvings, Moores, Schermerhorns, and Brinkerhoffs. WI was elected secretary, and Schermerhorn and Judge Irving were members of a committee appointed to write a constitution (*The Diary of Philip Hone, 1828–1851*, ed. Allan Nevins [1927; reprint ed., New York: Kraus Reprint Co., 1969], I, 148–49; hereafter cited as Hone, *Diary*). In a May, 1835, letter, WI referred to Schermerhorn as "my particular friend" (*Letters*, II, 822), and in June, 1838, WI's nephew John Treat Irving married Helen Schermerhorn (1820–1893), Abraham's daughter.

3. Ebenezer Irving (1776–1868) was the brother whom WI called "the Bramin" (see p. 37, n. 231).

4. Washington Ebenezer Irving (1822–1894), WI's nephew, was the twelfth of Ebenezer's thirteen children and his youngest son.

5. John Treat Irving, Jr. (1812–1906), author of *Indian Sketches* (1835), was WI's nephew, the son of John Treat Irving, who had died in 1838.

6. Irving Paris (1816–1879), WI's nephew, was the youngest son of his sister Catharine Irving Paris and the younger brother of WI's beloved niece, Sarah Paris Storrow.

7. Henry Brevoort (1782–1848), one of the "Nine Worthies" of the "Lads of Kilkenny" (see STW, I, 76–78), was one of WI's oldest and closest friends; their correspondence is voluminous. From an old New York family, Henry once worked for John Jacob Astor; a large inheritance (particularly valuable New York City property) and good business sense contributed to Henry's becoming a millionaire by the mid-1840's. Philip Hone described the new Brevoort mansion at Ninth Street and Fifth Avenue and later, the highlight of the 1840 social season, "Mrs. Brevoort's *bal costumé, costumé à la rigueur*," for 500 guests on February 27 (Hone, *Diary*, I, 373–74, 461–65). Henry's son, James Carson Brevoort (1818–1887), was to join WI in Paris and proceed with him to Spain as one of two attachés to the American Legation at Madrid.

8. Charles Augustus Davis (1795–1867) was a successful New York businessman and sometime satirist who imitated Seba Smith and made famous the character Major Jack Downing, letter-writing critic of President Jackson (see particularly *Letters of J. Downing, Major, Downingville Militia . . . to Mr. Dwight of the New York Daily Advertiser* (1834), a collection of a series of letters run by the newspaper the year before). Davis was a friend of WI, one of those constantly in attendance

Arrived on board and Set sail before 12. OClock with a fair wind.

Passengers. Henry Lee Jr[9] of Boston. Hector Ames.[10] Mr and Mrs Patterson of Boston. Mr Little of d[itt]o. Two sons

Had an easy pleasant voyage, without any incident of moment excepting the losing of a boy overboard: a fine lad who ⟨had⟩ was making his first voyage. Ship was going at the rate of 9 or 10 miles an hour. Hove to & lowered boat, but it was too late to save him. On 28, we were in the Channel with a head wind: when, a Steamer coming in sight most of the passengers, myself among the number got on board and were landed next day in the evening at Bristol.[11] Put up there for the night at the [*blank*] Hotel–

Sunday, May 1[12]

Set off with Hector Ames, Mr Lee & Mr Little in Rail road cars for London, where we arrived in about 4 Hours. Mr Lee, Hector Ames & myself took lodgings at Thomas Hotel[,] Berkeley Square. Walked about the West end of the ⟨park⟩ town. The Parks &c with Lee & Ames. Lovely weather. Parks crowded with groupes of populace, men women & children on the grass. Great parade of carriages in St James Park. Felt singularly low Spirited. Dreaded to throw myself once more into this ⟨great⟩

---

when WI returned from Europe; his New York home was a gathering place for the fashionable writers of the day, and he was one of the signers of the invitation to the dinner for Dickens on February 18, 1842.

9. In a May, 1842, letter to Catharine Paris, WI mentioned "a Mr Lee of Boston a connexion of the Storrows"; the editors identified him as Henry Lee, Jr. (1817–1898), who was the son of the economist and merchant Henry Lee (1782–1867) (*Letters*, III, 220, 222, n. 31). There had been a Mr. Lee, never referred to by given name, with whom WI associated in Paris in 1823 and 1824 and in London in 1824, usually at the Storrows' home; in October, 1823, after seeing Lee twice, WI wrote, "Mr Lee called on me with introduction from Van Wart," and in a later entry, WI wrote that he was "a hearty, hard, business looking young man" from "N York" (*Journals and Notebooks*, III, 233, 300).

10. According to PMI, Hector Ames was the son of Barrett Ames of New York City (III, 182), and in 1839, Hector's sister Sarah had married WI's nephew Irving Van Wart, a match of which WI approved as Miss Ames was "a perfect little lady in mind, manners and person" (*Letters*, II, 943, 944, n. 3). WI was pleased with his choice of Hector as one of the two attachés to accompany him to Spain, for he was "an amiable, intelligent, quiet little fellow" (*Letters*, III, 221); however, STW referred to him as "the taciturn Hector Ames" when he departed the Legation on June 13, 1843 (II, 378, n. 62).

11. Bristol, in southwest Gloucester, had by the twelfth century become a major port; located at the confluence of the Avon and the Frome rivers, it is only six miles from Bristol Channel and 115 miles west of London. One of the first transatlantic steamships had recently been built at Bristol (1838).

12. WI wrote "May 1. ↑Sunday↓."

↑turbulent↓ Stream of life and to encounter the harrassing parade and dissipation of the great world.

Monday, May 2[13]

Called on Mr Everett.[14] Mrs Bates[15] ⟨sho[?]⟩ ordered clothes at Stultz. Preston.[16] Evg went out to Leslies,[17] he was not at home. Returned home fatigued & dispirited.

13. WI wrote "May 2."

14. Edward Everett (1794–1865), one of the first Americans to study at a German university (STW, II, 363, n. 151) and subsequently a professor of Greek at Harvard, was American minister to England from 1841 until 1845. The controversial issue of British detention of American ships suspected of participating in slave trade, among other tension-producing issues, had reached a crisis when Everett took office. Fortunately, more reasonable heads prevailed (including Lord Aberdeen, who replaced Lord Palmerston as English foreign minister, and Daniel Webster, who replaced John Forsyth as American secretary of state), and agreement was reached in the Webster-Ashburton Treaty of 1842. (For a helpful discussion of this issue and Everett's part in it, see "Trouble on the North American Frontier," in Paul A. Varg's *United States Foreign Relations, 1820–1860* [East Lansing: Michigan State University Press, 1979], 94–117; hereafter cited as Varg, *Foreign Relations.*) Edward Everett edited the *North American Review* from 1820–1823, and his brother, Alexander Hill Everett (1790–1847), was one of WI's close friends in his earlier European period.

15. Mrs. Bates was probably the wife of Joshua Bates (1788–1864), an American who was a leading member of the House of Baring in London and who helped negotiate investments in the United States (Varg, *Foreign Relations*, p. 25). WI knew members of the Baring family in Paris in 1824–1825 (see entries in *Journals and Notebooks*, III), and Alexander Baring, first Baron Ashburton (1774–1848), whose wife was American and whose business and personal attitude toward America was positive, was the British negotiator in the important Webster-Ashburton Treaty of 1842. (See Ralph W. Hidy, *The House of Baring in American Trade and Finance: English Merchant Bankers at Work, 1763–1861* [Cambridge: Harvard University Press, 1949]; hereafter cited as Hidy, *The House of Baring*).

16. William C. Preston (1794–1860), a U.S. senator from South Carolina, was at this time in London; Preston had traveled in England and Scotland with WI in 1817. Despite their political differences, WI and Preston remained friends: like most Southerners, Preston was in favor of Nullification, and in 1832 on his return from the West, WI wrote from Columbia, South Carolina, that it was "really lamentable to see so fine a set of gallant fellows . . . so sadly in the wrong" (*Letters*, II, 736). In a July 13, 1852, letter from Sunnyside, WI asked his old friend repeatedly, "Do you reccollect . . . ," and then described one adventure after another as they rambled about Wales and Scotland thirty-five years earlier (*Letters*, IV, 312–13).

17. Charles Robert Leslie (1794–1859), an artist and an intimate friend of WI during his former London period, had also recently been in the United States as a professor of drawing at West Point, a position he accepted in the fall of 1833 and held for six months when his yearning for the London culture prompted his resignation. On May 7, 1842, WI wrote his sister Catharine Paris that his meetings

Tuesday, May 3[18]

Called with Everett on Lord Aberdeen[19] met with cordial reception. Talked about affairs of Spain. Called on Bandinel[20]—Evening at Opera. Lucia de Lammermoor[21]—But tolerably performed. Called ⟨at⟩ this day ⟨to⟩ at Murrays.[22] My heart was in my throat on finding myself in the drawing room the Scene of many an interesting literary meeting at the early period of my London Career. Kindly received by Murray and his family, promised to dine with them on my return to town.

---

with Mr. Rogers (see n. 24 below) and Leslie were among his "most gratifying meetings with old friends during my brief sojourn in London . . ." (*Letters*, III, 217–18). Leslie's 1820 portrait of WI hangs in the New York Public Library.

18. WI wrote "–3–."

19. George Hamilton Gordon, fourth earl of Aberdeen (1784–1860), had been English foreign minister in Wellington's cabinet in 1828–1830 and, therefore, associated with McLane and WI in those years. The choice of "the conciliatory Aberdeen," as H. C. Allen described him, to replace Palmerston as foreign secretary in 1841 was as fortunate for the British as was the American choice of Everett as minister to the Court of St. James; each was kindly disposed to the other's country, which, of course improved then-strained Anglo-American relationships (see H. C. Allen, *Great Britain and the United States* [New York: St Martin's Press, 1955], pp. 383, 389–404; hereafter cited as Allen, *Britain and the U.S.*).

20. James Bandinel (1783–1849), a clerk in the British Foreign Office, was also a friend from WI's former sojourn in England. On May 7, 1842, WI accepted his friend's invitation to share his "bachelors hall," and two days later he wrote from the Little Cloisters, Westminster Abbey, that Bandinel was "a peculiar character; a capital scholar a man variously and curiously informed; of great worth, kindness, and hospitality" and that his quarters were "a perfect 'old curiosity shop' " (*Letters*, III, 218; see also STW, II, 119, 365, n. 12).

21. *Lucia di Lammermoor*, an opera by Gaetano Donizetti, with Libretto by Salvatore Cammarano, was based on Sir Walter Scott's novel *The Bride of Lammermoor*; it was first performed in Naples on September 26, 1835, with Fanny Tacchinardi Persiani (1812–1867), for whom it was composed, in the lead role (see David Ewen, *Encyclopedia of the Opera*, 2d ed. [New York: Hill and Wang, 1963], 273–75). In later letters from Madrid, WI often mentioned attending the Italian Opera, being delighted by Persiani's singing and enjoying particularly this opera with its "delicious music," which was "a great resource to me," "my delight," "my passion," and "my favorite" (*Letters*, III; see IV, index).

22. It was natural that WI should be anxious about this meeting; his once-intimate relationship with John Murray II (1778–1843) and his son John Murray III (1808–1892), who had assumed leadership of the publishing firm, had been strained when WI left England; this visit to 50 Albemarle Street was WI's first since September 18, 1831. The Murrays embraced WI and held a dinner in his honor on May 10, 1842, then convinced him to attend the Literary Fund Dinner the following evening (see McClary, ed., *WI and the House of Murray*, pp. 179–81).

Wednesday, May 4[23]

Dined at Everetts. Met there with Rogers.[24] accompanied him in the evening to Lady Hollands,[25] in West Street.[26] In the house formerly occupied by her mother Lady Affleck[27]–⟨Met here⟩ Here Lady Holland keeps up a Kind of Holland house on a small scale. Here was her prime minister Allen.[28] Here opposite to her was seated Lady Seymour,[29] the

23. WI wrote "Wednesday 4."

24. Samuel Rogers (1763–1855), a banker-poet whose substantial inheritance enabled him to collect art, promote culture, and help friends, had been a friend of WI since their meeting twenty years earlier. WI had dedicated his "edition" of Bryant's poems to Rogers in 1832 and had drunk toasts to him as "The friend of American genius" at the Booksellers' Dinner in New York in March, 1837 (STW, II, 53), a dinner which Philip Hone said was the "greatest dinner I was ever at, with the exception perhaps of that given to Washington Irving on his return from Europe" (*Diary*, I, 251). WI's description of their reunion, therefore, is not surprising: "Mr Rogers was quite affected on meeting with me. . . . The old man took me in his arms quite in a paternal manner" (*Letters*, III, 218). Rogers' home was a cultural center in his day.

25. Elizabeth Vassall Fox, Lady Holland (1770–1845), whose drawing room was the scene of many gatherings of the literary and social lights of her day, had entertained WI often in his earlier time in London and Paris; pleased to be introduced in 1820 to the coterie at Holland House, WI wrote in a journal entry that "Society is selected there for its amusing qualities no matter what are politics &c" (*Journals and Notebooks*, III, 253). Emily Foster reported WI's later opinion of Lady Holland, the more commonly held one: "She seems by a sort of spell to collect wit, & talent for the purpose of blasting it—He has heard good stories, anecdotes, jokes, wither away under her haughty glance, she gave Irving the most fascinating smile woman ever *wore*, but he took care she have no opportunity of withdrawing her sunshine by keeping strange. Singular tyranny, to escape it it must be *defied*, kindness & yielding temper she tramples down & domineers over with her *uncomfortable* eye—" (from the *Journal of Emily Foster*, as quoted in STW, I, 436, n. 54).

26. The original Holland House was at 33 South Street.

27. Trent and Hellman transcribed as "Coffrich" (*Journals of WI*, III, 198).

28. Dr. John Allen (1771–1843), physician and writer on subjects historical and political, was born and educated in Edinburgh. After setting up practice there in 1791, translating scientific works into English, and working for political reform in Scotland, Allen was selected by Lord Holland to accompany him to Spain in 1801. When they returned in 1805, Allen became a regular member of the household at Holland House, occupying his own room, working with Lord Holland on his Parliament speeches, and carving his meat "at table." He accompanied Lord Holland again to Spain in 1808 and became interested in Spanish history, writing several articles on that subject. His primary work was *Inquiry into the Rise and Growth of the Royal Prerogative in England* (1830).

29. Lady Jane Georgiana Seymour, youngest daughter of Thomas Sheridan and granddaughter of Richard Brinsley Sheridan, was married in June, 1830, to Edward Adolphus Seymour, twelfth duke of Somersett (1804–1885). In 1835, her husband fought a duel with Sir Colquhoun Grant, whose daughter had eloped with Lady

⟨Goddess⟩ ↑Queen↓ of beauty, dressed in black and looking very beautiful. Here was the Bishop of [*blank*] ⟨a[?]⟩ very lively & conversable. Col Charles Fox [30] grown Stout and grey—

Thursday, May 5[31]

Accompanied Mr Everett to the house. In antechamber was introduced to the diplomatic corps. [*blank*] St Aulaire[,] the French Ambassador. [*blank*] The Russian.[32]

Cordial meeting with Sir R Peel,[33] who invited me to dine with him

---

Seymour's brother, a plot she had aided without her husband's knowledge. In August, 1839, Lady Jane Seymour reigned as Queen of Beauty at an extravagant tournament at the castle of Lord Eglinton, one of the most popular noblemen in Scotland.

30. Charles Richard Fox (1796–1873) was born the year before his mother's first marriage was dissolved on the grounds of adultery with Henry Richard Vassall Fox, third Baron Holland (1775–1840); his parents were married three days after the divorce. Charles Fox served in the British Navy from 1809 to 1813 and joined the Grenadier Guards in 1815; WI had been pleased with his initial acquaintance in Liverpool in 1817 with "this fine young fellow," then an ensign with the 85th Regiment: "a Son of Lord Holland, he has a noble frankness and ingenuousness of disposition & a degree of enthusiasm that I do not often find in the English character. He has been particularly civil to me & has repeatedly expressed a wish that I would take introductory letters to his father & friends when I go to London" (*Letters*, I, 474). Fox became the surveyor-general in 1832, a member of Parliament in 1835, a colonel in 1837, and a general in 1863; he was an avid coin collector, a great wit, and a fine host.

31. WI began misdating the entries with this one, which he indicated as "6th. Thursday."; perhaps he referred to an 1841 calendar. He misdated subsequent entries until Saturday, June 4, 1842.

32. The French ambassador was Count de St. Aulaire and the Russian ambassador, Baron Brunow. It was particularly important for WI to meet members of the Prussian and Russian delegations; as Edward Everett wrote in his official dispatch of May 6, 1842, that when he and WI were at the Foreign Office, "Lord Aberdeen observed that Prussia and Russia had left the question of recognising the present order of things in Spain, to be decided by Austria; and that Prince Metternich took the ground that the Government of Queen Isabella II was not yet sufficiently settled to be recognised. Lord Aberdeen said that since he had been in office, nothing had engaged more of his attention than this subject, and that his efforts had been unwearied to induce Austria and her allies to recognise the present government, believing that their refusing to do so was one great cause of the continuance of the disorders in Spain" (William R. Manning, ed., *Diplomatic Correspondence of the United States: Inter-American Affairs 1831–1860*, vol. 7: *Great Britain, Documents 2672–3127* [Washington: Carnegie Endowment for International Peace, 1936], p. 244; hereafter cited as *England: Dip. Corresp.*).

33. Sir Robert Peel (1788–1850), a Tory, served in the British Home Office from 1822 until 1827; in an 1827 letter, WI wrote, "My friend in London . . . is no other than *Mr Peel*" (*Letters*, II, 258). Peel was prime minister of England in 1834–1835

on the follow[in]g Saturday, but ⟨was⟩ declined as I am going out of town. Made acquaintance with Lord Stanley,[34] Duke of Buccheugh[35] &c

Queen pleasing in her appearance, acquits herself with grace and ease. Prince Albert tall, well formed a ⟨pr⟩ bland prepossessing countenance & demeanour.[36]

Friday, May 6[37]

Set off at 8½ Oclock in Rail road cars for Birmingham,[38] where I

---

and again from 1841 until 1846; WI was grateful on his return to London for the cordial "recognitions" of Lord Aberdeen and Sir Robert Peel, who "seemed to be in high good humor at having, themselves, got once more into office" (*Letters*, III, 217). The prime minister was an attractive, popular national figure, who promoted legal reform and free trade; he is credited with creating the police force and Scotland Yard (the English "Bobby" was named in his honor).

34. Edward George Geoffrey Smith Stanley, fourteenth earl of Derby (1799–1869), was elected as a Whig to Parliament in 1822, traveled in Canada and America in 1824, and was a close ally of Lord Canning, in whose ministry of 1827, Stanley was the undersecretary of the colonies. Once again in Parliament in 1831, Stanley spoke brilliantly in favor of the Reform Bill, worked effectively for reform in Ireland (especially in matters of education and navigation), and joined Peel's ministry in 1841 as colonial secretary. Even though he became Lord Stanley in 1834 at the death of his grandfather, he remained in the House of Commons until 1844, when he became a member of the House of Lords. When his father died in 1851, he succeeded to the earldom, and as Lord Derby formed a ministry of short life in 1852. Lord Derby continued to be a dominant figure in politics, was a patron of literature and sport, and from 1852 was chancellor of the University of Oxford.

35. Walter Francis Scott, fifth duke of Buccleuch and seventh duke of Queensberry (1806–1884), carried the gold stick at the coronations of William IV and Queen Victoria. He was created a privy councillor in 1842 and was Lord Privy Seal in Peel's ministry from February, 1842, until June, 1846. He was honored by degrees from the Universities of Oxford, Cambridge, Edinburgh, and Glasgow, and was president of the Highland Agricultural Society.

36. Queen Victoria (1819–1901), granddaughter of George III, was crowned in 1838 succeeding her uncle, William IV, who had reigned from 1830 until 1837. WI was presented to her on Wednesday, May 4, 1842, and acknowledging his sister Catharine's "great interest . . . in the young Queen," WI wrote that Victoria was "quite low in stature, but well formed and well rounded. Her countenance, though not decidedly handsome is agreeable and intelligent. Her eyes light blue, with light eye lashes, and her mouth generally a little open, so that you can see her teeth. She acquits herself in her receptions with great grace and even with dignity. Prince Albert stood beside her; a tall, elegantly formed young man, with a handsome prepossessing countenance. He is said to be frank, manly, intelligent and accomplished; to be fond of his little wife, who in turn is strongly attached to him. It is rare to see such a union of pure affection on a throne" (*Letters*, III, 217). On February 10, 1840, Queen Victoria had married her first cousin, Prince Albert of Saxe-Coburg-Gotha (1819–1861).

37. WI misdated as "7 Friday."

38. Birmingham, in Warwick and 110 miles northwest of London, was a major

arrived about 2 oclock[—]Found Sister Sarah[39] and her daughter Marianne[40] at home—

Saturday, May 7[41]

Returned to town in the afternoon train. Took up my quarters with Mr James Bandinel in the little Cloisters, Westminster Abbey:[42] where I was joined in the evening by Hector Ames. Dined at Mr Rogers. Lord

---

metal manufacturing town since the sixteenth century. The Reform Act of 1832 enfranchised the city, and it soon grew into an industrial center ultimately the second largest city of England.

39. The S is unusually formed and resembles WI's *L*; however, WI had written to another sister Catharine only three days earlier from London that he was worried "extremely to be thus detained from seeing sister Sarah, and I fear she will be grieved at my delay" (PMI, III, 194). WI's youngest sister, Sarah Irving (1780–1849), married Henry Van Wart (1783–1873) about 1804, and with one brief interruption, lived in Birmingham, England, where Van Wart was outstanding in business and politics and where WI was an integral member of the household when he was in England (STW, I, 146).

40. Marianne Van Wart (ca. 1814–1887), fifth of six Van Wart children and the younger girl, was described by WI in a July, 1815, letter to his mother as "a little morsel of a creature, but promising to be very pretty & delicate" (*Letters*, I, 395). Of this 1842 meeting, WI wrote to his sister Catharine Paris that she "would be much pleased with [Marianne]. She has a charming intelligent countenance, and is a noble hearted, disinterested and most companionable little being"; two years later, his good opinion was enhanced by Marianne's devotion to her mother, who at that time was ill (*Letters*, III, 216, 815).

41. WI misdated as "8 Saturday—."

42. The letter *A* was written over an illegible letter. See n. 20 above for reference to Bandinel and WI's lodgings with him.

John Russel & Lady there.[43] Lord Prudhoe.[44] Leslie– –Evg[45] with Rogers to Marquis of Northamptons[46] Soiree–See Young, Milnes[?].[47]

43. Lord John Russell, first Earl Russell (1792–1878), was a statesman and close friend of Thomas Moore, both of whom WI met in Paris in 1820–1821. WI wrote in a December, 1823, journal entry, that he had "Dined Tete a tete with Lord John Russell–at his lodgings Bains de Tivoli"; he commented later in the entry that "Lord John is not affraid of [Lady Holland]–has been accustomed to her from infancy–& indeed is a kind of pet" (*Journals and Notebooks*, III, 252–53). Having entered Parliament in 1813, Lord Russell made his reputation as an advocate of parliamentary reform and introduced and worked tirelessly toward passage of the Reform Bill of 1832. WI worried in an August, 1831, letter that "Lord John is almost knocked up by the fatigues and perplexities he has undergone; not understanding very clearly, it is insinuated, the nature of the mighty egg he has been employed to hatch" (*Letters*, I, 647). Lord Russell was prime minister (1846–1852, 1865–1866), foreign minister (1852–1853, 1859–1865), and Whig leader in the House of Commons. Among his writings were *Memoirs of Affairs of Europe* (1824–1829), *Memoirs of Thomas Moore* (1853–1856), and the *Life and Times of Charles James Fox* (1859–1860).

44. Algernon Percy, fourth duke of Northumberland (1792–1865), joined the navy in 1805, commanded his own ship in 1814, and rose in the service to admiral in 1862. In 1816, Percy was created a peer with the title Baron Prudhoe; his name was known abroad because of his explorations in the East in the 1820's and his support of explorations to the Cape of Good Hope and other places in the 1830's. He was also interested in science and language and was awarded an honorary degree from Oxford in 1841. Beginning in 1842, Lord Prudhoe financed for twenty years the research in Egypt and the publication of Edward William Lane's *Arabic Lexicon*. In 1847, Lord Prudhoe became a duke, and when he died with no children, his dukedom passed to a cousin and the barony became extinct.

45. The following two lines, from the phrase "Evg with Rogers" to the word "Hallam," were added, perhaps later, between lines in much smaller handwriting.

46. Spencer Joshua Alwyne Compton, second marquis of Northampton (1790–1851), was a member of Parliament from 1812 to 1820 when he removed to Italy. He became marquis in 1828 and returned to London in 1830 when his father died. From that time until his death, he was active in Parliament and a patron of the arts, literature, and science. In 1837, the marquis of Northampton edited and published *The Tribute*, a volume of poems which included a few of his own and those of some of the best poets of the day. Active in the Geological Society and the Archæological Association, he was president of the Royal Society from 1838 until 1849.

47. WI may have referred here to Richard Monckton Milnes, first Baron Houghton (1809–1885); while he was at Trinity College, Cambridge, Milnes formed close friendships with Tennyson, Thackeray, and Arthur Henry Hallam (1811–1833), son of Henry Hallam, who was a friend of WI. Milnes was active in politics; he was one of the earliest admirers of John Keats (his *Life of Keats* was published in 1848) and was a poet himself (*Poetical Works* was published in 1876).

Galley Knight.[48] Hallam.[49]

Sunday, May 8[50]

Lee breakfasted with us. Attended morning service in the Abbey. Sat in the Stalls of the prebendaries. Sermon by Mr Freres[?].[51] Service beautifully chaunted.

Dined with Mr Bandinel. Lee and Hector Ames at Mr Annandales[–] 3. Great Queen St.[–]where we met Mr McCulloch.[52] Mr and Mrs

48. After traveling in 1810–1811 to Spain, Greece, Egypt, Palestine, etc., Henry Gally Knight (1786–1846) began his career as a poet of Oriental verse; early works included *Ilderim: A Syrian Tale* (1816) and *Eastern Sketches, in Verse* (2d ed., 1819). Despite Byron's praise of his poetry, Knight began in 1831 to study and write about architecture, particularly Norman; his works included *An Architectural Tour in Normandy* (1838), *The Normans in Sicily* (1838), and *The Ecclesiastical Architecture of Italy from . . . Constantine to the 15th Century*, 2 vols. (1842–1846). A beloved landlord, Gally Knight was a member of Parliament for four periods of time, beginning in 1824 representing Aldborough and finally representing North Nottinghamshire from 1837 until his death. He was a member of the Commission of the Advancement of Fine Arts, and at the Literary Fund Dinner which WI attended, Gally Knight offered the toast to England's dramatists (see the *London Times*, Thursday, May 12, 1842, p. 5).

49. Henry Hallam (1777–1859), the historian, was a friend of WI from his former days in England; when WI was honored in 1830 with a medal from the Royal Society of Literature, he was especially pleased "that the other medal is voted to Hallam, the author of the Middle Ages" (*Letters*, II, 518). Among Hallam's works were *A View of the State of Europe during the Middle Ages* (1818), the *Constitutional History of England from Henry IV's Accession to the Death of George II* (1827), and an *Introduction to the Literature of Europe during the Fifteenth, Sixteenth and Seventeenth Centuries* (1837–1839).

50. WI misdated as "9–Sunday."

51. WI may have heard James Hatley Frere (1779–1866), whose voluminous writings on the prophecies were lauded by his contemporaries. Over the years, his works, from *A Combined View of the Prophecies of Daniel, Esdras, and St John* (1815) to a *Grammar for the Blind* (1851), explored his dual interests. The name of this preacher may also be spelled "Furnes."

52. WI may have met John Ramsay McCulloch (1789–1864), Scottish political economist, who began his prolific career with an eight-volume "Essay" on the national debt (1816), continued it with 76 articles in the *Edinburgh Review* (1818–1837), typified it with a popular edition of *Wealth of Nations* (1828), and culminated it with his most important work, *A Dictionary . . . of Commerce and Commercial Navigation* (1832). In 1841, McCulloch published in London *A Dictionary, Geographical, Statistical, and Historical, of the Various Countries*; the first of two volumes of "Mr. M'Culloch's Geographical Dictionary" had been favorably reviewed with particular attention paid to the maps of the world and British possessions in America, its "handsome appearance," and its promise "to be very complete, and a great improvement on our common gazetteers" (*London Times*, Thursday, January 28, 1841, p. 5).

[*blank*] ⟨The⟩ who recently were three years in UStates about which Mr [*blank*] has published a very good humored work.

Evening at Mr Everetts, where I met Miss Rogers. Dr & Mrs Booth[.][53] Mr Romaine Dillon[.] Mr Broadhead,[54] employed in researches concerning early hist. of New York.

Monday, May 9[55]

Mr Broadhead breakfasted with us. Gave me some documents concerning New York.

Dined at home. Compton,[56] Charles Mills, Frank Mills,[57] Lord Canning[58] (son of George Canning) Mr Lee, Leslie

53. Dr. Booth may be James Booth (1806–1878), an Irish mathematician who published widely in his field and who came to England in 1840 to become principal of Bristol College; he was awarded an L.L.D. in 1842 and was ordained the same year at Bristol.

54. John Romeyn Brodhead (1814–1873), whose *History of the State of New York* was published in two volumes (New York: Harper & Brothers, 1853–1871), originally planned a work in three volumes, to cover the beginnings through 1789. The two-volume work is a detailed study of New York history until 1691, and apparently Brodhead did his "researches" well; this history is cited by many modern historians as the standard account for the study of seventeenth-century New York. In a July, 1842, letter to New York Governor William H. Seward, WI excitedly discussed Brodhead's project and the necessity of New York's providing funds for its completion (*Letters*, III, 245–46).

55. WI misdated as "10. Monday."

56. WI had visited H. C. Compton the week of June 7–14, 1824, at his "Manor house. Stoney Cross near Southampton in the new forest" and described him as "tall, manly & handsome about 36. find him at some chemical experiment" (*Journals and Notebooks*, III, 343). In a letter to his brother Peter, WI wrote that Compton, Frank Mills' brother-in-law, was "a complete specimen of an English country gentleman" (*Letters*, II, 54).

57. Francis Mills (1794–1854), a fellow of Merton College from 1816 until 1846, was a close friend of WI during his earlier European sojourn (*Letters*, II, 54, n. 1); it was with Frank Mills that WI went from Paris to Compton's Manor House in June, 1824. In March, 1832, WI wrote that he and Mills had "brightened the chain of old friendship" and that his friend had "caught a dramatic mania, and aided in cooking up the piece for Drury Lane. He wrote the songs . . ." (*ibid.*, pp. 696–97). On June 1, 1824, Frank introduced WI to his brother Charles, "a neat genteel man, with the quiet, sensible english manner" (*Journals and Notebooks*, III, 339; for a description of WI's association with Frank Mills, "a companionable pseudo-dramatist," and Compton, see STW, I, 260–61).

58. Charles John Canning, Earl Canning (1812–1862), the third son of statesman George Canning (1770–1827), entered Parliament in 1836 and the peerage in 1837. A follower of Peel, Lord Canning was under-secretary for foreign affairs (1841–1846), postmaster general (1853–1856), then governor general of India (1856 until his death). Perhaps WI had met Lord Canning twenty years earlier; in a letter to Brevoort from Paris in March, 1821, WI wrote that George Canning, who with

Tuesday, May 10[59]

Had at breakfast Mr de Gayangos[60] an arabic scholar. Consul to Tunis —Has pub-/-lished "Arabic Dynasties in Spain." Mr Romaine Dillon, & Mr [*blank*] Moore ⟨*illegible*⟩ of NY. lately from Madrid.[61]

Dined at Murrays. met there Moore[62] and Lockhart[63] & Leslie. Moore looks thinner than when I last saw him. Has had trouble in his family.[64]

---

his family was then in Paris, had been "very polite in his attentions to me," in fact praising WI's works and inviting him to dinner at his home (*Letters*, I, 615).

59. WI misdated as "11. Tuesday."

60. Pascual de Gayangos (1808–1897), born in Seville, wrote a favorable review of William H. Prescott's *History of the Reign of Ferdinand and Isabella* (1838) in the *Edinburgh Review* (January, 1839); soon thereafter, Prescott contacted the critic who would become his scholar-scribe (see C. Harvey Gardiner, "Prescott's Most Indispensable Aide: Pascual de Gayangos," in *William Hickling Prescott: A Memorial*, ed. Howard F. Cline, C. Harvey Gardiner, and Charles Gibson [Durham: Duke University Press, 1959], pp. 81–115; also reprinted in this volume are the review [pp. 138–41] and Prescott's initial letter to Gayangos [p. 142]). In 1838, WI not only yielded to Prescott the "American subject" of Mexico, but also helped Gayangos with his research for Prescott during WI's years as minister to Spain. Gayangos became professor of Arabic at the University of Madrid (1843–1881), then minister of public instruction until his death (STW, II, 365, n. 17).

61. The *M* was written over another letter, perhaps an *a*.

62. Thomas Moore (1779–1852), Irish poet, had become WI's intimate friend after their meeting in Paris in December, 1820; earlier, WI had satirized Moore's poem, "Lalla Rookh" in *Salmagundi*, but three months after they met, WI wrote to Brevoort, "Scarce a day passes without our seeing each other & he has made me acquainted with many of his friends here. He is a charming joyous fellow—full of frank, generous, manly feeling. . . . His acquaintance is one of the most gratifying things I have met with for some time . . ." (*Letters*, I, 615). Moore was a lyrist (*Irish Melodies*, 1807–1835), a satirist (*The Twopenny Post Bag*, 1813), a novelist (*The Epicurean*, 1827), a biographer (*Sheridan*, 1825; *Lord Byron*, 1830; *Lord Edward Fitzgerald*, 1831), and an historian (*History of Ireland*, 1846). In his diary entry of May 10, 1842, Moore revealed his excitement at Murray's "Asking me to meet at dinner, *to-day*, the man of all others I wanted to shake hands with once more—Washington Irving" (PMI, III, 199).

63. John Gibson Lockhart (1794–1854) earned a reputation as a harsh critic after joining *Blackwood's Magazine* in 1817, but he reviewed favorably WI's *History of New York* in February, 1820 (McClary, ed., *WI and the House of Murray*, p. 25, n. 4). In 1820, Lockhart married Sophia Scott, Sir Walter Scott's daughter; in 1823, he wrote an anonymous novel, *Reginald Dalton*, about an Oxford student. The comments about some of the intimates of Holland House, including Samuel Rogers, Henry Hallam, and Isaac D'Israeli, among others, created a commotion (*ibid.*, pp. 60–61, n. 17); however, it was this novel which was the last thing PMI read to his uncle before his death (PMI, IV, 314). Lockhart was the editor of the *Quarterly Review* from 1825 until just before his death, and he promoted the careers of his countrymen by writing biographies of Burns (1829) and Scott (1839).

64. Thomas Moore's dejection regarding his sons was well founded: both John

His son Russel has returned from the army broken in health and threatened with consumption. Tom has been somewhat wild; has got into scrapes by his amours; ⟨threat[?]⟩ had to go to India to escape prosecution. Last news of him he had sold out and was returning home. Moore speaks despondingly as if he fears he shall eventually have to come upon the Literary Fund.

Murray looks as well as when I parted with him about 10 years since. His son John who is a Steady worthy fellow, mainly conducts the business and manages both that and his father.

⟨12 Wednesday⟩

Wednesday, May 11[65]

Drove down into the City. Visited Aspinwall[66] at his office.

Called on the Rothschilds[67] and drew for my Quarters Salary. Two or three of the Young Rothschilds in their office: Jew looking gentlemen, Stout and greasy: invited me to dine with them on Sunday but I declind, as I should be out of town.

Morn[?].[68] This morning I breakfasted with Miss Rogers[69] where I met Wordsworth,[70] Rogers—The Miss Stanleys daughters of Lord (once Sir John) Stanley.[71] [*blank*] Lockhart—Leslie.

Russell Moore (1823–1842) and Thomas Lansdowne Moore (1818–1846) died within four years of this journal entry (*Letters*, III, 222, n. 20).

65. WI misdated as "12. Wednesday."

66. Colonel Thomas Aspinwall (1786–1876), after losing an arm in the War of 1812, was U.S. consul to London from 1815 until 1853. By October, 1819, WI wrote Brevoort that for Colonel Aspinwall he felt "the highest friendship and esteem" (*Letters*, I, 566); in 1824, the Aspinwalls were living in a cottage in Versailles, France, when WI was there, and from that year, Aspinwall was WI's literary agent in London.

67. The house of N. M. Rothschild & Sons had entered the American market in 1833, which cut into the business of the House of Baring; in January, 1835, Rothschild assumed from Baring the account of the U.S. Department of State, and by June of that year, had branches in Boston, New York, Philadelphia, and Baltimore (Hidy, *The House of Baring*, p. 195).

68. This word could be "Mon"; the context suggests our reading.

69. WI met Miss Rogers the previous Sunday evening at the Everetts.

70. William Wordsworth (1770–1850) lived at Rydal Mount, Grasmere; even though he was in the autumn of his career at this time, his reputation in the late 1830's began to flourish in England and abroad. In 1842, Wordsworth resigned his position in the Stamp Office, which he had held since 1813, and published his last volume of poems, *Poems Chiefly of Early and Late Years*. In 1843, he succeeded Southey as England's Poet Laureate. WI and Wordsworth harbored a career-long dislike; neither appreciated the other's best work.

71. Sir John Thomas Stanley (1766–1860) had welcomed WI to his London home

after breakfast accompanied Rogers &c to Leslies, to look at his picture of the christening.[72]

Dined at the Anniversary of the Literary Fund.[73] Prince Albert presided. ⟨Sat⟩ I sat between Moore & Hallam. Bishop of Glou-/-cester[74] opposite & Mr Everett. Met Lockhart, Lord Mahon,[75] Lord Lands-

---

in June, 1824, exacting a promise for a subsequent visit to the country (*Journals and Notebooks*, III, 342); during WI's absence from England, Sir John had become the first baron of Alderley in 1839.

72. Describing to his sister Catharine this meeting with Leslie, WI wrote that his friend was "occupied in painting a picture of the Royal christening. His picture of the Coronation has been the making of him. He has more orders for paintings than he can execute" (*Letters*, III, 218). The editors explained that Leslie began in 1841 his *Christening of the Princess Royal*; his subject was Victoria Adelaide Mary Louise, born in 1840; the other painting WI mentioned was *The Queen Receiving the Sacrament after the Coronation, June 28, 1838* (*ibid.*, p. 221, nn. 14–15).

73. Thomas Moore wrote that when he learned that morning that he was to be seated between Hallam and WI, he was pleased, and he recounted in his diary the effort he and the Murrays had exerted the evening before to convince WI to attend; "he told me his mind was made up on the point; that the drinking his health, and the speech he would have to make in return, were more than he durst encounter: that he had broken down at the Dickens dinner . . ." (PMI, III, 200). Moore argued that others would respond to the toasts at too great length, and WI would endear himself if he would but thank his hosts briefly. WI attended with this plan in mind, but as he wrote to his sister, "the very idea of being singled out, and obliged to get on my legs and return thanks, made me nervous throughout the evening" (*ibid.*, p. 199). His pleasure at being warmly received was obvious, however.

74. James Henry Monk (1784–1856) was an outstanding student at Trinity College, Oxford, and became a fellow in 1805, assistant tutor in 1807, and professor of Greek from 1809 until 1823. He published extensively, such as a translation of Euripides' *Hippolytus* (1811) and the *Life of Richard Bentley* (1830). He was a close friend of Henry Hallam; eight volumes of their correspondence were published in 1844. Ordained in 1809, Monk became bishop of Gloucester in 1830, and in 1836 when that see was combined with Bristol, he became the bishop of Gloucester and Bristol.

75. Philip Henry Stanhope, Viscount Mahon (1805–1875), viscount from 1816 until he became fifth Earl Stanhope in 1855, was an outstanding historian, member of Parliament, and patron of the arts. In and out of Parliament from 1827, he served without interruption from 1835 until 1852; a follower of Peel, he was the under-secretary for foreign affairs in Peel's first ministry (1834–1835). Only one month before this Literary Fund dinner, Lord Mahon had delivered a brilliant speech in Paliament promoting the extension of the copyright law, and a compromise bill was passed. He was also responsible for the creation of the National Portrait Gallery, which opened in 1859. Among his works are *The History of the War of Succession in Spain* (1832), *History of England from the Peace of Utrecht to the Peace of Versailles*, 17 vols. (1836–1853), and the *Memoirs of Sir Robert Peel* (1856–1857). WI had known Lord Mahon in Spain in 1827–1828; in 1844, the historian wrote to WI suggesting that he write a book about the manners and customs of Spain (STW, I, 335–336, 486, n. 70).

downe[76]–Marquis of Northampton. Mr James.[77] Mr Milnes &c
⟨Sat[?] in⟩ Very nerovus throughout the dinner knowing my health was to be drunk.

Sir Robert H Inglis[78] introduced it with a very kind & complimentary speech. It was cheered in the warmest manner which con-/-tributed to embarrass[?] me. Rose, ⟨expressed⟩ ↑declared↓ my want of talent for public speaking and returned thanks. After dinner James came up and shook hands with me cordially by way of renewing old acquaintance

At this dinner Campbell[79] was deputed to give Hallams health. He made an introduct-/-ory speech, but, having drunk too much wine, became so prozy and maudlin that he was absolutely clamored down.

76. Henry Petty-Fitzmaurice, third marquis of Lansdowne (1780–1863), from the beginning of his long career in 1802 in Parliament, was interested in financial issues; he became chancellor of the exchequer in 1806. An active Whig and constantly attempting to help unify the party, he was president of the Privy Council during three periods: 1830–1834, 1835–1841, and 1846–1852. Lord Lansdowne agreed with Lord Russell's complaint that he lacked the personal ambition and self-love necessary in politics, but all agreed that Lord Lansdowne was a generous patron of literature. WI was presented to him by one of his beneficiaries, Thomas Moore, in November, 1823, in Paris, and they subsequently visited his London home and his estate near Bath (*Journals and Notebooks*, III, 247).

77. George Payne Rainsford James (1799–1860), prolific writer of melodramatic historical romances, was influenced by Sir Walter Scott and encouraged by him and by WI, who once described him as "my friend James, the novelist" (PMI, III, 163). WI saw James in Bordeaux in 1825 when the latter was writing his first novel, *Richelieu* (1829), which was followed by nearly 100 novels, approximately one every nine weeks for eighteen years. In addition, he wrote numerous magazine articles, tracts on political issues, poems, plays, and histories; William IV appointed him historiographer royal. In about 1850, he was made British consul for Massachusetts and in 1852, for Virginia; in 1856, he was consul-general in Venice. James married an American, and his last novel, *The Cavalier* (1859), was published in America. A popular writer in his day, his work was parodied by Thackeray as "*Barbazure*, by G. P. R. Jeames."

78. Even though he was called to the bar in 1818, Sir Robert Harry Inglis (1786–1855) never practiced law; instead, he kept alive the voice of the old-line country gentlemen Tories in Parliament from the early 1820's, publishing many of his speeches. Inglis defeated Peel to represent the University of Oxford and held that seat from 1829 until 1854; he was on several commissions to study debts and public records. Inglis was a Fellow of the Society of Antiquaries and the Royal Society, Antiquary of the Royal Academy, and president of the Literary Club.

79. Thomas Campbell (1777–1844) was a Scottish poet, of whom WI wrote a sketch in *The Poetical Works of Thomas Campbell* (1810) and an expanded version in the *Analectic Magazine* (March, 1815). Other volumes of Campbell's poems include the *Pleasures of Hope* (1799), *Theodric and Other Poems* (1824), and *Pilgrim of Glencoe and Other Poems* (1842). WI and Campbell had been friends for more than twenty-five years.

Thursday, May 12[80]

Breakfasted with Hallam. met there with Wordsworth, ⟨Milnes⟩, Everett.

Dined with Rogers. met there Lord Prudhoe. ⟨Sir⟩ Lord John & Lady Russell, Leslie—

Evening accompanied Mr Mrs & Miss Everett to the Queens Fancy Ball[81]

Friday, May 13[82]

Breakfasted at Sir Robert H Inglis. met there Wordsworth, Milnes, young Wordsworth,[83] Everett. Bandinel

After breakfast. ⟨called⟩ ↑went↓ with Bandinel to Egyptian Halls. British Museum—Called at Millers.[84] Accompanied Miller to See Mrs Miller and John Miller beyond Knightsbridge.[85]

Dined at home, went with Bandinel to the German Opera[—]Covent-garden[86][—]Don Juan miserably performed.[87]

80. WI misdated as "13. Thursday."

81. The following day, WI described to his sister Catharine Paris this event, "which surpassed, in splendor and picturesque effect, any courtly assemblage that I ever witnessed, or could imagine. . . . There were at least two thousand persons present, all arrayed in historical, poetical, or fanciful costumes, or in rich military or court uniforms" (PMI, III, 201). The *London Times* reporter was equally enthusiastic about "Her Majesty's Dress Ball," naming the guests by position and title and describing in detail many of the costumes (Friday, May 13, 1842, p. 6).

82. WI misdated as "14. Friday."

83. WI probably met William Wordsworth (1810–1883), Wordsworth's youngest son, who succeeded him in the position in the Stamp Office in 1842. There were two other sons by his wife, Mary Hutchinson (m. October, 1802): John (1803–1875) and Thomas (b. 1806).

84. John Miller was a London bookseller, whom WI had met at Murray's in August, 1817 (STW, I, 421, n. 72). Miller risked the publication of the first volume of *The Sketch Book* (February, 1820) after Murray turned it down; because of Miller's bankruptcy and the book's initial success, Murray took over the publication of the second volume (July) and subsequent editions. From 1818 until 1861, Miller was associated on a commission basis with WI's Philadelphia publisher, Carey, to find new works; in an 1822 letter, WI described Miller to Brevoort as "a most deserving & meritorious little man—indefatigable in the discharge of any commission entrusted to him; and moderate & conscientious in his charges. He devotes himself almost exclusively to American business" (*Letters*, I, 679).

85. Knightsbridge was a hamlet in Chelsea, Kensington, and St. Margaret's; it enjoyed a reputation as a haven for holiday makers. It is now in central London, just southwest of Hyde Park, home of the Victoria and Albert Museum.

86. WI may have intended two words; he failed to lift his pen, but the *g* is slightly larger than his usual lowercase *g*.

87. WI's disappointment was understandable; Friday's *Times* announced "Mozart's grand opera of *Don Juan*" with Herr Millinger in the leading role (*London Times*,

Saturday, May 14[88]

Lee breakfasted with us—called on Catlin.[89] Lady Strafford (Miss Caton) whom I found grown rather plump, but looking well, and as usual full of good sense and good humour.[90] Called on Charles Bristed,[91] and invited him to breakfast tomorrow—

Dined at Lord Stanleys. Present Mr & Mrs Everett. Lord & Lady Mahon. Lord and Lady Canning

Evening at Mrs Bates with Mrs Everett.

May 13, 1842, p. 5). From February, London opera enthusiasts had anticipated the German Opera, the "popular entertainment supported by the most celebrated singers of Germany . . . this season at Covent Garden Theatre" (*ibid.*, Monday, February 21, 1842, p. 5). On May 2, the season had opened, as it did each year, with Carl von Weber's overwhelmingly successful *Der Freischütz*, and the reviews of each subsequent opera presented had been favorable. The 1842 German Opera season was cut short because of low receipts, and the company left London after the July 2 performance.

88. WI misdated as "15th. Saturday."

89. WI probably visited George Catlin (1796–1872), the American portrait painter whose more than 600 portraits of Indians, pictures of village life and customs, etc., painted from 1829 until 1838, were regularly exhibited by him in America and Europe from 1837 until 1852. Catlin had also recently published at his own expense in London his two-volume *Letters and Notes on the Manners, Customs, and Conditions of the North American Indians* (also published in 1841 in New York by Wiley and Putnam). Readers of the *London Times* review learned that in spite of "Being an American, and native of Wyoming, nursed, therefore, in a prejudice against the Indian character . . . Catlin draws a highly favourable portrait of the Indian character, when unadulterated by the white man's vices" (Thursday, October 14, 1841, p. 3). Catlin also painted many other portraits (including a group portrait of 115 members of the Constitutional Convention at Richmond in 1829–1830), and he published in London in 1848 *Catlin's Notes of Eight Years' Travels and Residence in Europe* and *Catlin's Notes for the Emigrant to America.*

90. Elizabeth Caton was one of the beautiful daughters of Baltimore native Richard Caton. In a July, 1816, letter to Brevoort, WI wrote, "I shall make a point of cultivating the acquaintance of Betsey Caton should I meet with her & she be disposed to be sociable" (*Letters*, I, 451). In November, 1825, he asked to be remembered to Elizabeth in a letter to her sister Marianne, who in 1825 had married Robert Colley Wellesley, second earl of Wellesley. Elizabeth, however, also married an English aristocrat, Sir George William Stafford Jerningham, Baron Stafford, in May, 1836 (*ibid.*, II, 150, 151, nn. 3–4).

91. Charles Astor Bristed (1820–1874), the grandson of John Jacob Astor, II, was an outstanding student, first at Yale, and then from 1840 until 1845, at Trinity College, Cambridge, where he won three classical prizes and the University Latin Essay Prize. In January, 1847, he married Laura Brevoort, the daughter of WI's close friend, Henry. Bristed was an author, sometimes using the pen name Carl Benson; he was a member of the American Philological Association and a trustee of the Astor Library.

Sunday, May 15[92]

Charles Bristed took an early breakfast with us. Set off at 9¾ Oclock in Rail road cars for Birmingham, where I arrived at ½ past 2.

Dined at home–Evening the Goddards[?] &c came in.

Tuesday, May 17[93]

dined at William Van Warts,[94] with the family.

Wednesday, May 18[95]

Passed the day at home. Capt Holdridge[96] came up from Liverpool to dine with us–Mr Church[97] dined here also. Evg. Mr Goddards[?] family. Miss Kell[?][98] &c.

92. WI misdated as "16 Sunday."

93. WI misdated as "18 Tuesday."

94. Never one to hide his preferences among family members, WI described his nephew William Van Wart, third child of his sister Sarah Van Wart of Birmingham, as "my delight [who] is I think, the flower of the flock. Full of life, activity, good spirits and good humour; combining the good qualities of both his parents. He is the life of the house whenever he enters it." Even William's wife, Rosalinda, was "a most intelligent cultivated woman," whose drawings and paintings "would not discredit a regular artist," and his children were "fine," "handsome," "charming," etc. (*Letters*, III, 216–17).

95. WI misdated as "19. Wednesday."

96. WI had known Captain Holdridge and his wife in Paris in October, 1823. WI advised his ill nephew William S. Irving to go to Hyères, and on October 12, he wrote to William's companion, "You will meet there with Capt Holdridge, of the Fulton packet ship & his wife, who intended wintering there for the benefit of her health" (*Letters*, II, 11). WI hoped that "Capt. Holdrege & his wife & several other Americans" would provide "a kind of family circle" around William; however, he died on November 15 on the way to Nice, and WI asked "Captain Holdredge . . . to have a tomb[stone] placed over poor Williams grave" (*ibid.*, p. 21). WI saw and corresponded with the captain during the following year.

97. This guest may have been Edward Church, with whom WI was associated in Paris in 1823 when Church was the American consul at Lorient and who was a principal, along with WI's friend Reuben Beasley, in the unfortunate Seine Steamboat Company venture in which WI and his brother Peter lost money (*Journals and Notebooks*, III, 244 and n. 297; STW, I, 195–97). In a February, 1841, letter to Sarah Van Wart, WI expressed his relief that her son Irving had put aside a project which "originated with Dr. Church (Dousterswivel, as your son William used to call him) of Steam Carriage memory" (*Letters*, III, 78).

98. This name is smudged, but it resembles "Kell" or "Kehl"; it seems rather strange that WI should refer to his married niece, Matilda Van Wart Kell (see May 19 entry below), as "Miss Kell." Matilda, of whom WI thought highly, was, according to STW, the fourth child and older daughter of his sister Sarah Van Wart (STW, II, chart opp. p. 255). In a May, 1840, letter, WI reacted to the happy news of her engagement to Charles Aylett Kell (*Letters*, III, 52, 53, n. 2), and

Thursday, May 19[99]

At home. afternoon Mr Lee and Hector Ames arrived. Evg at Matilda Kells

Friday, May 20[100]

Leave Birmingham at 12 O Clock in Rail road car (London line) in company with Mr Lee and Hector Ames. Stop at Weedon Station, Northamptonshire.[101] Take post chaise for Sulgrave[,][102] natal place of the Washington ⟨f⟩Family from whence John & Laurence Washington emigrated to America in Cromwells time. John[—]great grand father of George Washington. We drove by cross roads checked by numerous gates across the country[.] Rich looking though low country—huge trees overgrown hedges—Old grey Stone villages, with ⟨t⟩Tudor style of architecture Stone shafted windows with water tables—moss grown wea/ther[?] Stained—Old grey Gothic churches with towers wrapped in ⟨I⟩ ivy—⟨The⟩ Some of the oldest looking villages I have seen in England. Large rambling Gothic mansions—Gardens with Yew trees of formal[?] cut[103]

at Lichborough[104] a large picturesque Tudor mansion, various[?] Gables Stone Shafted windows—Escutcheons in relief—one with three coronets[?]—

---

by this 1842 visit, she was "living most happily" with her husband, with whom WI was "much pleased," and with her two small children, the older a son, Robert Henry Van Wart, and the recently born Rosalind (*ibid.*, 216, 816, n. 1).

99. WI misdated as "20."

100. WI misdated as "21. Friday—."

101. Of the three Weedons in the general area, the village with the railroad station was actually Weedon Bec or Weedon Beck, 41 miles southeast of Birmingham, four miles southeast of Daventry, and 69 miles northwest of London.

102. The post chaise ride from Weedon to Sulgrave Manor was approximately ten miles in a southwestern direction; Sulgrave Manor, in Northamptonshire, was 7½ miles east of Banbury. It was the home of the Washington family beginning in 1539 when the first Laurence Washington (predating George Washington by seven generations) bought the manor and rebuilt it; in 1626, the family removed to Brington, and in the churchyard of Great Brington are buried the brothers who left Sulgrave. For WI's published account of his visit to Sulgrave Manor, see his *Life of George Washington*, ed. Allen Guttmann and James A. Sappenfield (Boston: Twayne Publishers, 1982), I, 10, n.; hereafter cited as WI, *Life of Washington*. In his note, WI rather sadly reported that a "part only of the manor house remained, and was inhabited by a farmer"; he would be pleased that in 1914, the farmhouse and surrounding acres were bought by the British Peace Centenary Committee and restored as Sulgrave Manor and Washington Museum.

103. These words may be "funeral cast."

104. Litchborough, Northamptonshire, still noted for its manor house, was five miles northwest of Towester.

Canons Ashby[105]—Old Gothic mansion by road[?] side, at present owned by Sir—[*blank*] Immense trees—Elms &c—some over run with ivy—

arrive at Sulgrave a little after four. Stop at vicarage. ⟨Rob⟩ Rev Mr Harden[?]. Send in Card—follow it—Find Mr Harden & Mrs Harden and Mr Clark—clergyman of neighboring parish. Neat parsonage—Little lawn in front ∧ ↑with↓ rustic Seats—Shrubs &c. ∧ ↑Polite reception—wine & biscuit↓ Mr Harden knew of the monument of Washington family—He & Mr Clark accompd. me to church. It is a grey gothic church[—] Square tower. Has been repaired[?] in simple Gothic style—Singular green mound near the church called Castle Close. It appears to have been surrounded by a ditch[.] May have been part of fortress or Keep in old times. Mr Clark says there are several what are called Roman & Danish Mounds in this part of the country—& remains of Roman camps near Daventry—Charleton near Brackley—Deddington[106] &c Rural Scenery round church. Parsonage in distance with Shrubbery—Low grey thatched Stone houses of village with casements. Rich green meadows with rough hedges—numerous cattle—

Church Simple—Old oak pews, with seats ⟨on aisle[?]⟩ that let down on hinges on aisl[?] for poor[?]. Tomb of Washingtons: flat Stone on pavement[?],[107] close by the pulpit. Inscription in block[108] letter[:]

> Here lyeth buried ye[109] bodies of Laurence Wasshington Gent
> and Anne his Wyff by whome he had issue [*unrecovered*][110]
> Sons and vij[?] daughter iv Laurence died Anno (obliterated)
> and Anne deceased 6 day of October ano 1564

above the inscription is an escutcheon bearing the Washington Armes below are brass ⟨engraved⟩ plates on which are engraved effigies of the

105. Canons Ashby, a village in south Northamptonshire, was 7½ miles south of Daventry and 4½ miles north of Sulgrave; it was the sixteenth-century seat of the Drydens.

106. Daventry, Northamptonshire, the northernmost of the three villages, was four miles west of Weedon on the railroad line between Birmingham and London; among several Charletons, WI specified this one in Northamptonshire, four miles southwest of Brackley and approximately seventeen miles south of Daventry; Deddington, in Oxfordshire, was six miles south of Banbury and approximately twenty miles south of Daventry. The Charleton site is called Rainsborough Camp on one modern map of this area.

107. This word may be "parament"; the two words may be "as monument."

108. This word may be "black."

109. The *e* is a superscript.

110. This configuration contains four upward strokes; Trent and Hellman transcribed as the numeral "IIII" and the following figure "vij"[?] as "VII," and they omitted the figure preceding "Laurence" at the beginning of WI's fourth line (*Journals of WI*, III, 204).

Sons & daughters—also an[?] effigie on brass ↑plate↓ of a female probably Anne—the ⟨rest of the⟩ effigy of Laurence obliterated. ⟨The⟩ Mr Harden said the remains of this monument should be carefully preserved.

Walked to the old Manor house—Now much delapidated: old grey stone & plasture house, with Great grey stone Stables & outhouses. Has been purchased not long since by Colonel Hutchinson, who resides a few miles distant.—It is farmed by a Mr Lotz[?][111] a hale sturdy farmer. Were Shown about the house by a plump country lass. House has never had much pretension to grandeur: though there are the remains on a Gable End, of Escutcheon of arms with Supporters[?] Lion & Dragon Rampant—and Escutcheons on border of old Gothic window of Dairy—The rooms are low & panelled—Old oaken stair case—The remains of a hall flagged with blk stone—Large fire place—wooden ⟨Ciell⟩ joists of cieling—a portion of the hall is ⟨turn[?]⟩ divided off into a dairy—Great pans of cream (they have 17 cows)—Gothic window—on the walls in rude relief the Family Supporters—Lion and Green Dragon. Old plain fire places up stairs. ⟨There⟩ The family arms were formerly emblazond in Coloured glass in one of the windows—but we were told Colonel Hutchinson had removd them to his room at his residence—Little garden surrounded by low Stone wall—formerly probably a terrace. On the Gable End near the arms[?][112] is a primitive Sun dial such as we see in the old country houses in this part of the country—Lofty old Elms about the building—Rooks sailing about—Every/thing has an ⟨old⟩ ancient air—which indeed[?] pervades this part of the country—literally a piece of Old England—a country little hackneyed—mere cross roads, little traveld—Farmer came home while we were looking about the house. Tall, stout, fresh complexion[—]Coat ⟨with⟩ square with deep pockets—Breeches, gaiters—very respectful. The house is to undergo repairs which will probably obliterate some of its peculiarities—It is visited occasionally. Mr Harden says there are enquiries made now & then about Washington. It is ⟨said⟩ a tradition that Que. Elizabeth, before queen, was at Sulgrave—It is recorded that she was in a retired[?] part of Northampton[113] shire—Primitive manners[?] of Country people—Mr Clark gave an enter-/-tainment to about 1000 country people[.] They danced on the green. ⟨Not⟩ very orderly. Not a rude or profane word spoken

Mr Harden wished us to dine with him—we declined. While Post horses were putting to[,] we took a snug dinner of cold beef and ham, with home brewed ale at a decent little village ale house—number of

111. Trent and Hellman read as "Lets" (*Journals of WI*, III, 204).

112. Trent and Hellman transcribed as "acorns" (*ibid.*, p. 205).

113. The *N* was written over an illegible letter.

country lads smoking in outer room. Landlady tidy, short little woman. we were waited upon by her daughter a very pretty girl with fair complexion and fair hair.—Every thing neat and good. Excellent bread, and nice butter—Left Sulgrave about ¼ past 5. Returned through the old grey moss grown village with escutcheon over the doors &c reached Weedon about 7—and at 8 ∧ ↑Hector & myself↓ Set off in cars for London where ⟨Hector &⟩ we arrived at 11 & put up at Victoria Hotel. Lee returned to Birmingham

Saturday, May 21[114]

Breakfasted at Victoria Hotel. Drove in Hackney Coach to Southampton rail road station Set off at 11-oclock A M. arrive at Southampton[115] a little before 3 having been delayed nearly an hour on road—rainy day. Put trunks on board ⟨rail r⟩ ↑steam↓ boat Grand Turk. Call on the Aspinwalls[116][—]find them all at home ⟨Mr⟩Col & Mrs A[,] Eliza and [*blank*] Take dinner of cold meat. Col. accompanys us to Steam boat[.] Set sail at 5 OClock. pass the night on Sofa in cabin. Quiet voyage

Sunday, May 22[117]

arrive at Havre[118] 6 OClock Send for Mr Taylor[119]—Get our luggage passed at customs house without examina/-tion. Mr Beasley[120] drives

114. WI misdated as "22 Saturday)." At the top left edge of the page is a line drawn in pencil through the word "Saturday" and diagonally to the right through five lines; it does not appear that WI intended the paragraph to be crossed out.

115. Southampton, in southern Hampshire, was approximately 75 miles southwest of London; an ancient city, Southampton's location on a peninsula between the Test and Itchen rivers and at the head of Southampton Water with the protection of the Isle of Wight made it one of the best natural harbors in England.

116. In addition to his friendship with Aspinwall, WI was a great favorite of "Madame and all the young fry"; in earlier years, Aspinwall's children called WI the "chocolate merchant," and his wife and children anticipated WI's visits to Highgate (PMI, II, 379). Eliza was the second of seven children, five girls and two boys (*Letters*, II, 83, n. 2).

117. WI misdated as "23 Sunday."

118. Le Havre, 110 miles west-northwest of Paris, was founded in 1516 as Havre de Grâce. Because of its location on the English Channel at the mouth of the Seine River on its right bank, Napoleon made it a primary naval harbor, and from the beginning of transatlantic travel, it has been a primary European port.

119. WI first referred to Mr. Taylor in a September 24, 1823, journal entry as the "chancellor" of Reuben Beasley (see n. below); Taylor had "just retd from Engd" (*Journals and Notebooks*, III, 224). WI subsequently mentioned him several times in 1823 accounts of Paris dinners, as well as in 1825 Paris and Le Havre entries.

120. Reuben G. Beasley was confirmed as U.S. consul at Le Havre on January 2, 1817, and served in that position until he died in 1847; STW called Beasley "a wealthy hospitable magnate, a shareholder in many European businesses" (I, 195).

to town in his [*ink blot*] carriage to meet us. Takes us out to his country retreat Justemilieu[121]—where we breakfast. Mr Fareish[?][122] of NYork there. ⟨D⟩Mr Winslow[123] ⟨comes⟩ pays us a visit. Drive out in Cote[?]. ⟨meet⟩ call on Mr Winslow. See his wife daughter and niece & youngest daughter.

Dine at home at Beasleys. Mr Fareish[?] & Mr Taylor there. Retire to bed at 9 OClock[124]

———

Monday, May 23[125]

Set off at ¼ past 5 in Steam/boat for ⟨Paris⟩ Rouen. In the course of our voyage we pass a vessel which had ran on a sand ⟨bank⟩ ↑bar↓ and been upset by the violence of the Current. 9 men on the Sides making frantic signals of distress and crying Sauvez nous! Sauvez nous—put out our yawl—Several boats put off also from the shore to their assistance, but they cannot get to her on account of the violence of the current. The distress of the poor [*ink blot*] fellows immense[?][126] Sympathy[127] of ladies on board of our boat who ⟨implore⟩ weep[?] and implore the captain to aid these poor people. The Capt puts Steam/boat about—passes wreck—tows the boat up to her & gets off the men[—]One boy had been drowned—Land the men on shore, all but one who was wounded—a Subscription was made for him and 15 dollars collected on board[128]—

He was a devoted friend and often host of WI and Peter Irving from 1820, their friendship withstanding a disastrous business relationship in the Seine Steamboat Company (*ibid.*, pp. 195–97); in addition, through Beasley's marriage to Jennie-Adelaide Guestier, WI became an intimate of the household of Bordeaux wine merchant M. Daniel Guestier (see below, n. 254).

121. The name of Beasley's country estate at the mouth of the Seine translates as the "Golden Mean." WI wrote his sister Sarah Van Wart that he arrived early Sunday morning, then "passed the day at the delightful little half-rural retreat of my friend Beasley, which is situated in a garden on the descent of the hill overlooking Havre"; however, WI was deeply saddened by the memories of Peter and the happy times they had spent together there (PMI, III, 203).

122. Trent and Hellman transcribed as "Forceth" (*Journals of WI*, III, 206).

123. WI mentioned in a Paris journal that on two successive days in January, 1824, a "Mr Winslow" called on them and played chess with Peter; Beasley was in Paris at the time, and the following evening, he sat "some time with us" (*Journals and Notebooks*, III, 265–66).

124. WI drew a line one-sixteenth inch long to separate entries.

125. WI "corrected" to the misdating "2⟨3⟩4 Monday."

126. Trent and Hellman transcribed as "increases" (*Journals of WI*, III, 207).

127. WI's spelling resembles "Symaphy."

128. See WI's account book entry (p. 479) regarding this collection.

Arrive at Rouen[129] ½ past 1 & put up at the Grand Hotel D'Angleterre—visit Cathedral[—]Tomb of Long sword[130]—

Tomb & monument of Duke [*blank*][131] In one part of monument he is represented as an infant in nurses arms—In another as a warrior in complete armour and mounted on horseback—below on Sarcophagus is his Emaciated body in winding Sheet

⟨e⟩Evg at Theatre[—]Play ["]Il y'a seize ans["]

Tuesday, May 24[132]

Leave Rouen at 5 OClock in Steam boat for Paris—Breakfast and dine on board, where we have an excellent restaurant—Arrive at St Germain[133] at ¼ past 7. depart in Rail road cars at 8. Arrive in Paris where I am met by Mr Storrow[134] and conducted to his house

129. To Rouen, on the right bank of the Seine approximately 56 miles east-southeast of Le Havre, was an eighty-mile trip by river; even so, the river is tidal to Rouen, and it was the primary seaport of Paris. William the Conqueror died in Rouen (1087), and Joan of Arc was condemned and burned there (1431); the ancient city boasts three of the finest Gothic churches in France: the Cathedral (Notre Dame de Rouen) begun in 1201; the "Gothique flambyant" Church of St. Maclou (1437–1521); and the Abbey Church of St. Ouen begun in the fourteenth century. It was the little garden behind St. Ouen which had been Peter Irving's "favorite resort during his solitary residence" in Rouen, and here in 1842 WI wrote that he "felt my heart completely give way. . . . My dear, dear brother! As I write, the tears are gushing from my eyes" (PMI, III, 204).

130. On the south side of the nave of the cathedral was a chapel in which WI visited the tomb of William Longsword, second duke of Normandy (d. 943) and the son of Rollo (see n. below). Richard the Lion-Hearted and Henry II of England were also buried in the cathedral. (See Francis Miltoun, *The Cathedrals of Northern France* [Boston: L. C. Page, 1903], pp. 79–90; hereafter cited as Miltoun, *Cathedrals.*)

131. WI probably was in the ambulatory on the south side of the cathedral where there was an effigy of Duke Rollo (d. 930), the Norse pirate who established the duchy of Normandy in 911 and who was the ancestor of William the Conqueror. Rollo enlarged the cathedral at Rouen and began the "dynasty which fostered the development of theology and the arts in a manner previously unknown" (Miltoun, *Cathedrals*, pp. 82–83; see also L. Russell Muirhead, ed., *North-Western France*, 3d ed. [London: Ernest Benn, 1958], pp. 41–43; hereafter cited as Muirhead, *North-Western France*).

132. WI misdated as "25 Tuesday."

133. WI had now entered the old district of "Ile de France"; St. Germain-en-Laye was between Mantes and Paris, approximately eighteen miles west-northwest of Paris.

134. Thomas Wentworth Storrow, Jr. (1805–1865), was the son of WI's old friend Thomas Storrow in whose household WI had been an intimate in his earlier days in Paris and Versailles. (See Stanley T. Williams, ed., *Washington Irving and the Storrows: Letters from England and the Continent, 1821–1828* [Cambridge, Mass.: Harvard University Press, 1933].) Young Storrow had married WI's favorite niece Sarah Paris (1813–1855) on March 31, 1841, and they left Sunnyside for Paris the

Sunday, May 29[135]

Drive out with Mr & Mrs Storrow & Hector Ames to Meudon,[136] thence to St Cloud[137] where we dine—return in Evg.

Tuesday, May 31[138]

Evg. go with ⟨L⟩Genl Cass[139] to Mr Guisots[140]—Minister of Foreign Affaires—Mr Guisot, small thin dark man with grey hair. Speaks very fair English—

---

following May. WI's pleasure at this reunion with the Storrows was heightened by a recently arrived great-niece, Catharine, born in Paris on March 12, 1842. WI wrote to Sarah's mother on May 29 that "since my arrival in Paris, I have been living very quietly, avoiding all engagements, that I might pass my time as much as possible with Sarah" (*Letters*, III, 232).

135. WI misdated as "30 Sunday."

136. Meudon was one of the many picturesque suburbs in the "environs of Paris," approximately 7½ miles southwest of the city and six miles east of Versailles; immediately south on the south bank of the Seine was the Forêt de Meudon, which occupied more than 2,600 acres and in WI's day was a wild and popular escape from Paris.

137. St. Cloud, also a suburb 7½ miles west of Paris and three miles northwest of Meudon, had been the retreat of many members of the French royalty and the scene of the founding of the First Empire in 1804 and the relinquishing of the crown by Charles X in 1830; it had also earlier been a favorite spot of WI, particularly the park of St. Cloud, with its 970 acres and beautiful view of the Seine, and the nearby country seat of Villamil which Moore rented and WI visited (see PMI, II, 46, for the May 16, 1821, journal entry).

138. WI wrote "Tuesday."

139. General Lewis Cass (1782–1866) was U.S. minister to France, serving from 1836 until he was recalled in 1842. A Democrat, Cass had been a member of the Ohio legislature, governor of the Michigan Territory, and secretary of war in Jackson's cabinet; later he served as a member of the U.S. Senate from Michigan. During the sensitive Ashburton-Webster negotiations in 1842, Cass had worked against a concurrent French-British treaty which provided the right to search ships, maintaining that the treaty was a British ploy to dominate the seas (see n. 143 below). When Cass openly attacked his own government's position in the Ashburton-Webster treaty because it did not deny the British the right to search, he was recalled as minister to France (Varg, *Foreign Relations*, pp. 113–14).

140. Following the "July Revolution" in 1830 which deposed Charles X as king of France, François Pierre Guillaume Guizot (1787–1874), historian, statesman, and orator, was appointed provisional commissary of education; the following month, King Louis Philippe made him minister of home affairs and subsequently minister of public instruction. The first decade of the king's reign saw political differences between these men, but in 1840, Louis Philippe called on Guizot to form a ministry. As prime minister and minister of foreign affairs, Guizot faithfully promoted for eight years the king's conservatism at home and his pacific policies abroad. (For an excellent discussion of their relationship, see Emile Bourgeois, "Louis Philippe and Guizot," in *History of Modern France: 1815–1913* [New York: Octagon Books,

Introduced there to the Prince [*blank*] formerly head of Polish nation,[141] an elderly man—with a pale, somewhat melancholy countenance; amiable in his deportment and manners. Spoke with much interest of Spain, though he had never been there—

Mr Dupin[142] came up to Genl Cass—After a friendly salutation, well said Genl C. alluding to the question of the right of search—C'est une affaire finie—

nette! replied Dupin with ⟨a bra[?]⟩ an expressive gesture— ⟨As[?]⟩ Then Speaking of the English pretext of Philanthropy[143]—he snapped his fingers—bah! its a mere thing in the air: while at bottom there are the most interested motives— —'Speaking the other day in the Chambers on the ⟨right of Sear⟩ ↑signing of the↓ treaty by the French Ministry—It would be a matter, not of *censure*, said he, but of *impeachment*

Dupin has a remarkably shrewd penetrating look, and a concise tren-/chant mode of expressing himself—

—Greek Envoy [*blank*] a large, good humored man. Had not much conversation with him.[144]

1972], I, 228–88; hereafter cited as Bourgeois, *Modern France.*) Most popular among Guizot's many works was *Histoire de France* (1870–1875); the edition to which I have referred is *The History of France from the Earliest Times to 1848*, trans. Robert Black, 8 vols. (New York: John B. Alden, 1885); hereafter cited as Guizot, *History of France.*

141. Louis Philippe refused to give aid to Polish and Italian patriots, and the many Polish exiles in Paris during this time became heroes to French liberals (Paul A. Gagnon, *France Since 1789* [New York: Harper & Row, 1964], p. 128).

142. André Marie Jean Jacques Dupin (1783–1865), statesman and jurist, whom some historians call "Dupin, the elder" to distinguish him from François-Pierre Charles Dupin (1784–1873), was from 1817 "conseiller et ami de la famille d'Orléans." After the duc d'Orléans became King Louis Philippe in August, 1830, André Dupin was in charge of the bill to revise the Charter of 1815 under which the king would rule; loyal to the king, he was an Orléanist and a colleague of Guizot (Bourgeois, *Modern France*, I, 119). Charles Dupin ("the younger"), made baron by Louis XVIII in 1824, was a councillor of state in Louis Philippe's government, but became in the mid-1830's a member of the Opposition within the majority in the Chamber, a Republican or member of the "tiers parti," more loyal to the king's son, the duc d'Orléans, than to the king; this group opposed the colonization of Northern Africa and for three days in November, 1834, formed an unsuccessful ministry.

143. The French-British treaty against which Cass had worked (see n. 139 above) was supposedly not "political" but supportive of the "noble and holy cause" against slave trade; however, many Europeans, especially the French, saw the treaty as providing "England with a pretext for exercising a superior right of police at sea." The treaty, supported by Guizot, received a slim majority vote in the French ministry on February 22, 1842, but because of the overwhelmingly negative public outcry after the announcement of the vote to Parliament, Guizot was not able to get the treaty ratified by the Chamber (Bourgeois, *Modern France*, I, 245–46).

144. Louis Philippe "did his own diplomacy, his favourite pursuit, receiving

The Saloon ⟨of the⟩ large, square, with Somewhat of a vaulted ceiling–⟨Walls⟩ dingy & smoked–⟨Ha Bra[?]⟩ Furniture &c bear evidence of having been much used As is ⟨this⟩ generally the case in public establishments of the kind[.] Returned home before 10 O Clock–

–The question of the right of search has roused all France, and is producing an effect throughout the continent–

When the question of the ratification of the treaty was in suspense the Duke of O[145]–went to the King and observed, it was an affair ⟨of⟩ not of a *ministry*, but of a *dynasty*

Friday, June 3[146]

Visit the Invalids in company with Sarah[147] and Hector Ames.

Napoleons remains, in a Chapel Ardent[148]–hung with purple, wrought with bees[?][149] ⟨Two⟩ On each side of the entrance to the Chapel was seated a veteran invalid in uniform holding a tricolored Standard planted in the ground. Another veteran patrolled about the entrance. ⟨*illegible*⟩ Through a grille we had a full view of the interior. Napoleons body is in a Sarcophagus of some dark kind of wood richly wrought. His imperial mantle was spread over it, upon it were deposed[150] his crowns. At foot of the Sarcophagus and much lower was a richly wrought and gilt box containing his heart. On top of it was his Sword, and under a Glass case

---

the ambassadors in person, and settling with them the peace of Europe" (Bourgeois, *Modern France*, I, 196); one of his recent diplomatic successes had been to help in "consolidating the liberty of Greece" by supporting the new king, Otho of Bavaria (*ibid.*, pp. 197–98).

145. Ferdinand Philippe Louis Charles Henri, the duc d'Orléans, was King Louis Philippe's oldest son and active in the military affairs of the present ministry of Comte Molé. The duke was beloved among the French, and the nation was saddened by his death in a carriage accident at Neuilly on July 14, 1842 (see WI's July 15, 1842, journal entry below).

146. WI wrote "June ⟨4⟩3."

147. Sarah Paris Storrow, WI's niece.

148. One of the political moves of Louis Philippe was to recapture some of the romance of the Empire by bringing Napoleon I's body from Longwood at St. Helena where he had died and was buried in May, 1821, to the banks of the Seine to be buried "amid those French people I have loved so well." Louis Philippe's own sailor-son, the prince de Joinville, accomplished this mission, presenting the coffin to his father in the Chapelle ardente at the Hôtel des Invalides in December, 1840. (For a detailed description of the journey, the condition of the body, the funeral procession and ceremony, see Elizabeth Wormeley Latimer, *France in the Nineteenth Century: 1830–1890* [Chicago: A. C. McClurg, 1896], pp. 87–92; hereafter cited as Latimer, *France in the Nineteenth Century.*)

149. This word could be "bas," "lius," "lea[f]," etc.

150. WI probably meant to write "deposited."

his famous little Cocked hat. Around the Sarcophagus lay quantities of wreaths or chaplets of *immorteles*; votive[?] offerings, from time to time, at his shrine.

[p. [29] blank except for the following: "⟨June⟩ ↑Saturday↓ June 4"][151]

Saturday, June 4[152]

at 8 o clock in the evening drive out with Genl Cass to Neuilly[153] to be presented to the King. Pleasant drive through the park. Guards about, here & there. At the Entrance to the Court yard of Chateau a lancer mounted on each side, a sign always, of the presence of the King. Went through suite of rooms. Found the company assembled in an interior saloon

Queen[154] & Madame Elizabeth,[155] with various ladies, among whom were Madame Soult[156] and The Countess of Monjoie[157] (Dame d'Hon-

151. This date at the top left of the page is the first correct association of day and date since Thursday, May 5.

152. WI wrote "June 4 Saturday."

153. The royal country residence at Neuilly-sur-Seine, built by Louis XV, was the favorite of several country retreats and the home of the family of Louis Philippe; it was destroyed during the Revolution of 1848; and its beautiful "English park" was divided into lots for building. Neuilly is now a residential suburb of Paris, on the right bank of the Seine, just four miles west-northwest of the Notre Dame Cathedral.

154. Queen Marie Amélie Thérèse (1782–1866), born in Naples, was the granddaughter of Maria Theresa and niece of Marie Antoinette; she married Louis Philippe in 1809, reared seven children, and was by WI's report "a devoted wife and mother" (PMI, III, 208) and by all reports a generous and beloved queen. For a discussion of "Louis Philippe and His Family," see Latimer, *France in the Nineteenth Century*, pp. 34–57.

155. In a June 10 letter, WI described this meeting in greater detail and accuracy; for instance, regarding the king's sister Eugénie Adélaide Louise (1777–1847), Mademoiselle d'Orléans, often called Madame Adélaide, WI wrote that she had "more force of character" than the queen and "possesses vigorous good sense and great ambition. She is said to take great interest in public affairs, and in the stability of her brother's throne" (*Letters*, III, 236–37). In fact, it was she who helped Talleyrand persuade Louis Philippe to "accept" the position of the lieutenancy general of the Kingdom on July 30, 1830 (Bourgeois, *Modern France*, I, 113).

156. Madame Soult was probably the wife of Marshal Soult, the duc de Dalmatia, one of the survivors of the era of the Empire whom Louis Philippe restored to position; Soult was president of the Council in 1832 and 1840 and a primary spokesman for Guizot's ministry (Albert Guérard, *France: A Modern History* [Ann Arbor: University of Michigan Press, 1959], pp. 293–95; hereafter cited as Guérard, *France*).

157. If this person is the countess of Montijo, whose younger daughter Eugénie would later marry Louis Napoleon and become the empress of the French, it is not altogether surprising that WI misspelled her name. In 1827, WI had known the countess' father, William Kirkpatrick, American consul at Malaga; that same year

neur) Seated at a Round table ⟨on which⟩ with needle work &c before them. Company around the Room. King, [158] dressed in black, with Shoes & Stockings, conversing with Mr Bulwer[159] British Secy of Legation. I was presented to the queen, who excused herself from Speaking English & conversed with me in French. She is thin & rather pale, an amiable counte/-nance—blue eyes, light, or grey hair[.] Madame Elizabeth, Sister to the King; a very frank, cordial manner; a countenance indicative of good nature and good sense. I had a very cordial reception from the King: who in conversation; shewed himself well informed of all the passing ⟨aff⟩ events in America. The affairs of Mexico & Texas &c &c[.]

---

he also visited in the home of Count Teba, also the marquis de Montijo, meeting his little daughters but not his beautiful wife. It was not until after WI was in Madrid as ambassador to Spain that he was invited to a ball given by the countess de Montijo, who welcomed him as an old friend of her husband and subsequently included him in her circle (PMI, IV, 133–34). George Ticknor of Boston described the countess as "the most cultivated and interesting woman in Spain," among other superlatives, and Walter Savage Landor called her a "lode-star of her sex" (Latimer, *France in the Nineteenth Century*, pp. 167–68).

158. WI remembered his first glimpse of the king eighteen years earlier when he was "the Duke of Orleans, in hussar uniform, mounted on a superb horse, in a public procession, the admiration of every eye. Still he is a fine-looking man for his years . . ." (*Letters*, III, 236). Louis Philippe (1773–1850), from the Orléans branch of the Bourbons and therefore not in the direct line of succession to the throne, was duke of Valois, duke of Chartres, and duke of Orléans. Although Louis Philippe supported the Revolution, he was a moderate (unlike his father who was guillotined), refusing to participate in the Terror or to fight against Republican France and escaping to Austria; Louis XVIII restored his titles and by the time he became the lieutenant of the Kingdom following the July 1830 Revolution, he was a wealthy man. Brought to power by moderate liberals, he walked the thin line between enlightened bourgeoisie and the landed plutocracy. His reign as the "Citizen King" of the French from August 7, 1830, until he abdicated on February 24, 1848, was marked by a mixture of the instability of toppling ministries and steady progress in diplomacy and democracy. After 1840, with Guizot firmly in place, Louis Philippe's conservatism ultimately stifled politics and progress and resulted in his downfall.

159. William Henry Lytton Earle Bulwer (1801–1872), Baron Dalling and Bulwer, was the older brother of novelist Bulwer-Lytton. Sir Henry Bulwer began his diplomatic career in 1826 in Greece, and from 1827 he held posts in Berlin, Vienna, the Hague, and Brussels before coming to Paris as secretary of the British embassy. At this meeting with WI, Bulwer was the chargé d'affaires, and from 1843 until 1848 he would serve as the English ambassador to the Court of Isabella in Madrid. In 1846 he was embroiled in the controversy surrounding the selection of a husband for the young queen; Bulwer's contingent lost to Guizot's. Honored in 1848 as a knight commander of the Bath and in 1851 with the Grand Cross, Bulwer was the English minister to Washington from 1849 until 1851 and to Florence, Italy, from 1852 until his retirement in 1855.

Had some conversation with Countess of Monjoie[,] Mr Chabaunais[?],[160] who reminded me of our having met in 1829 at the house of the Duke de Caze,[161] with Mr[162] Bulwer, with Genel ⟨Addi[?]⟩ Aid de Camp to the King, &c &c

I am told the King is extremely annoyed ⟨at⟩ in taking his rides about the park, to find himself continually in sight of Centinels placed here and there for his security since the repeated attacks upon him. He says it ⟨is as bad as⟩ is almost as bad as the case of Napoleon at Long wood: who could never find himself out of sight of a centinel.[163]

Sunday, June 5[164]

Dined with Col Thorn,[165] to witness the contract of marriage of his daughter with the Baron [*blank*][166] Thorn lives in the Hotel Monaco,

160. Trent and Hellman transcribed as "Chabannes" (*Journals of WI*, III, 210).

161. At the beginning of the Second Restoration in 1815, one of the strongest voices for moderation was that of Élie Décazes (1780–1860), the minister of police and favorite of Louis XVIII. A Doctrinaire, he supported the Charter and the Restoration, but "studied the interests of the *bourgeoisie*" (Latimer, *France in the Ninteenth Century*, p. 11). To implement his goal to "royalise the nation, nationalise the crown," he introduced the Franchise Bill, which, with Guizot's help, passed in January, 1817 (Bourgeois, *Modern France*, I, 10). In 1818, Décazes was minister of home affairs, and in 1819 he became the president of the Chamber. Several factors—among them Décazes' influence over the king, Richelieu's resignation from the government over the question of the power of the gentry, and the murder of the beloved duc de Berry in February, 1820—consolidated the Ultras against the king's favorite. Décazes resigned that same month to spare Louis XVIII controversy; the king immediately made him a duke and appointed him the French ambassador to London where he served until Villèle's ministry began in 1821 (see Guizot, *History of France*, VIII, 227–37). Décazes returned to France to sit in the Chamber of Peers and subsequently to support the July Monarchy. WI was later to speak highly of the duke's son, Louis Charles Élie Décazes, the duc de Glücksbery, who was at this time the French chargé d'affaires in Madrid (*Letters*, III, 284).

162. The letters "Mr" were written over two illegible letters.

163. The king's protectors were motivated by many threats and at least thirteen attempts at regicide, the most spectacular having been on July 28, 1835, when a Corsican named Fieschi shot at the king and three of his sons with a 25-barrel gun, killing numerous soldiers and bystanders and injuring the duc d'Orléans and the prince de Joinville (for an account of the incident and the trial and execution of the five "conspirators," see Latimer, *France in the Nineteenth Century*, pp. 49–53).

164. WI wrote "Sunday June 5."

165. PMI identified as Colonel Herman Thorn; in the long June, 1842, letter to his sister Catharine Paris, WI reminded her of the American colonel's "history . . . and the stand he has taken among the old French noblesse by dint of his wealth" (PMI, III, 209).

166. In his June 7 entry, WI added the name "Pierre," but still left blank the family name.

Rue de Varennes, Faubg St Germain[–]a noble mansion, ⟨with⟩ entre Cour et Jardin. The latter of great extent: ⟨but⟩ looks like a morsel of an ⟨e⟩English park. Fine lawn ⟨of⟩ with noble trees (Horse Chestnut & others) on each side. broad terrace back of the Hotel. At Dinner we had the Prince & Princess de Bethune,[167] the Duchess de Montmorency[168] &c.

The prince is head of the house of Sully[,] a somewhat dandyish old gentleman: with his Scanty white hairs brought from behind so as to partially cover the top of his head, and white whiskers that reach to the corners of his mouth: good humoured, but light and somewhat faddy. The princess is a woman of good sense, knowledge of the world and excellent manners. Sat at dinner between Mrs Thorn & Mrs. Channey[,][169] her daughter in law. The latter, German by birth, speaks English very well. ⟨*illegible*⟩ Her conversation was full of intelligence and talent.

⟨In [*illegible*]⟩ After dinner company began to arrive and in the course of the evening the assemblage became quite numerous; composed of the old noblesse, the high aristocracy of the Faubourg St Germain. Genl Cass came in the Evening. The company all signed as witnesses, the contract of marriage. The bride elect a very pretty, becoming girl, with a frank amiable expression of countenance.

167. Approximately 85 miles south of Paris is Sully-sur-Loire, elevated to a duchy in the early seventeenth century when Henry IV's famous minister, Maximilien de Béthune, Baron de Rosny (1559–1641), bought the lordship and became the duc de Sully. The person WI met here may have figured in the constitutional battles of 1848 relating to the abdication of Louis Philippe and the election of Louis Napoleon and including massive efforts through petitions; for example, "dans le Loiret, une pétition recueille 213 signatures dans la commune de Sully, la première est celle de M. de Béthune-Sully . . ." (André-Jean Tudesq, *Les Grands Notables en France [1840–1849]* [Paris: Presses Universitaires de France, 1964], II, 1207; hereafter cited as Tudesq, *Grands Notables*).

168. WI probably met the wife of Anne-Charles-François, the duc de Montmorency (1767–1846), who had early entered government service in the "gardes du corps," advanced rapidly, emigrated to Switzerland and Belgium, then returned to France in 1800 after the death of his father, Anne-Léon II, and resumed his participation in municipal affairs. In 1813, Napoleon made him count of the Empire, and the next year, he became a major general in the national guard of Paris and a member of the Chamber of Peers. The duke's son, Anne-Louis-Victor-Raoul (1790–1862), was aide-de-camp to the duc d'Orléans from 1815 until 1820; it is not surprising that the duke returned to Louis Phillipe's July government. Throughout his career, he was a friend of the unfortunate and a patron of the arts and sciences; the duc and duchesse de Montmorency were mentioned several times by Tudesq as "grand Notables" in France in the 1840's, once regarding the duchess' being hostile toward the fortifications being built in Paris between 1841 and 1845 (I, 531; see Ludovic Lalanne, *Dictionnaire Historique de la France* [1877; New York: Burt Franklin, 1968], II, 1313).

169. Trent and Hellman transcribed as "Chauncy" (*Journals of WI*, III, 211).

Understanding from Genl Cass that the Marquis of Brignolle,[170] Sardinian Ambassador, was present. I told Gen Cass that I had an idea I had seen him play the part of Orosmin in a translation of Voltaires Zaire,[171] at the country palace of his mother at Sestre di Ponente near Genoa,[172] in 1804 or 5, when he was about ⟨19 years⟩ 19 or 20 years of age. Genl Cass offered to introduce me to him but I first wished to ascer-/-tain whether ⟨he⟩it was the same. We went into an adjoining saloon ⟨where⟩ to look for him. Genl Cass told me to point out the gentleman present whom I should suppose to be him. I examined the countenances and pointed to a tall grey headed person, who was seated conversing with the Neapolitan Ambassador. I was not mistaken[.] It was indeed the once young and elegant Brignolli, who thirty seven years before I had seen playing the hero of the drama with a grace and talent that captivated all the ladies present; and who I believe made a serious impression on the beautiful representative of Zaire, ⟨Madame Rivarolla⟩. Genl Cass introduced me to him and I recalled the ⟨scene I have just⟩ circumstance just mentioned. He remembered having played the part and Set me right as to the name of the representative of Zaire, which I had supposed to be Madame Novara [*blank*] but which he told me was Rivarolla[173] ⟨I found that[?]⟩ ⟨He expressed[?]⟩ He paid me some

170. In a letter written almost thirty-eight years earlier, WI described Antonio Brignole Sale (1786–1863) as "the eldest Son of Madame B. about 18 years old, tall and well made" (*Letters*, I, 129). According to Nathalia Wright, young Brignole Sale became an able statesman and the marchese de Groppoli (*Journals and Notebooks*, I, 123, n. 266).

171. While visiting England in 1726, François Marie Arouet Voltaire (1694–1778) discovered Shakespeare and was inspired by *Othello* to write *Zaïre* (1732); one of his best plays, it presents Orosmane, generous sultan turned jealous lover and ultimately murderer of the fair Christian captive girl Zaïre. WI mentioned that the play had been translated into Italian, and the editors of WI's letters suggested the version by Francese da Giovambatista Richeri, published in Genoa in 1748 (*Letters*, I, 162, n. 9).

172. Sestri Ponente was a village six miles west of Genoa which WI first visited on October 26, 1804, and to which he usually referred as "Sestri di Ponenti" or "Sestri" (*Journals and Notebooks*, I, 117 and index). For descriptions of the estate of Anna Maria Gasparda Vincenza Pieri, Marchesa Brignole Sale (1765–1815), and the particular evening he spent with the Genoese beau monde, see WI's November 8, 1804, journal entry and his long December 25, 1804, letter to William Irving (*ibid.*, pp. 121–24; *Letters*, I, 127–29).

173. In his earlier versions, WI spelled the "leading lady's" name "Reverolle"; Wright suggested that she was Anna Cicopero, Marchesa Rivarola (*Journals and Notebooks*, I, 123, n. 265).

civil compliments[174] upon my Life of Columbus, a subject so interesting to the people of Genoa.

Monday, June 6[175]

At 12 Oclock drove out with Sarah to Mrs Welles,[176] at Suresne.[177] Took St Cloud in our way and passed some time in the park. Mrs Welles in a maison de campagne beautifully situated on the banks of the Seine; with fine Shrubbery, walks, garden &c. 40 acres. returned through Bois de Bologne[178]

Tuesday, June 7[179]

at 12 Oclock attended at the church of St Roque[180] to witness the marriage ceremony of Miss Thorn to the Baron Pierre [*blank*] After the ceremony the numerous company adjourned to Thornes Hotel, where a breakfast was served at 2 Oclock to about 36 persons. The repast was in a noble saloon ⟨to[?]⟩ in one wing of the Chateau looking out upon a noble avenue of trees under which a grand military band performed various pieces of music. I was seated nex[t] to Madame de Varenne[?], ⟨an⟩ a very intelligent old lady, with fine black eyes, and hair almost entirely white—I found afterwards she was the person who planned the escape of Lavalette[181]—

174. WI may have written "complement"; although the *i* of "compliment" is not dotted, WI has been given the benefit of the doubt.

175. WI wrote "Monday June 6th."

176. During WI's Paris days in the 1820's, Samuel Welles (1778–1841) was in charge of the Paris branch of the outstanding Boston banking firm W. Welles and Company (see *Letters*, II, 172, n. 1). From 1820 when he used the Welles address as his own, WI was an intimate in their home, often dining "en famille with Mr & Mrs Welles," attending social events with them, and seeing through them members of the international banking families, such as the Barings and the Wigginses (see *Journals and Notebooks*, III, index). Although WI wrote of this visit that he and the Storrows "passed the evening delightfully" with Mrs. Welles (*Letters*, III, 237), he must have been saddened that yet another old friend had died only the year before.

177. Suresnes was a small town two miles north of St. Cloud, with only the Seine and the Bois de Boulogne separating it from Paris to the east.

178. The Bois de Boulogne, one of the beautiful woods or forests in the environs of Paris, was approximately 2½ miles long and 1½ miles wide; it was situated between Neuilly-sur-Seine to the north and Boulogne to the south, with the Seine to the west and Paris proper to the east.

179. WI wrote "Tuesday 7th."

180. WI's spelling may be "Rogue." The Church of St. Roch on the Rue St. Honore was built from 1653 until 1754, and its shot-marked walls resulted from an October, 1795, skirmish between Napoleon and the Royalists.

181. Lavalette was Napoleon's aide-de-camp. Guizot included in his description

The loveliest woman present was the Princess Demidoff daughter of Jerome Bonaparte.[182] She had somewhat of the Bonapartian countenance, and one of the most delicious fascinating smiles I have ever seen. I was presented to her after Breakfast just as she and her hus-/-band were on the point of getting into their carriage to proceed on a journey.

In the course of the morning I was introduced to the Marquis de la Grange,[183] a member of the Chamber, and an exceedingly intelligent man. He told me he was occupied writing the History of his ancestor [*blank*] De la Force—connected with the history of Spain.

⟨If[?]⟩ Thought ⟨the[?]⟩ Charles V presented a fine subject for the

---

of the frenzied year of 1815 the fact that when Louis XVIII was restored to power, he did not take the opportunity to "place clemency by the side of justice," giving as examples the execution of Marshal Ney in September and the king's rejection of Lavalette's appeal several days later, even though the latter "had not betrayed an oath in serving the Emperor Napoleon." When even the petition by the duchess d'Angoulême and the last request of Lavalette to die by bullet rather than scaffold were rejected, Lavalette's friends plotted his escape from prison, accomplished by disguise on December 20, 1815, and completed when he was smuggled out of France by Sir Robert Wilson, friend of political prisoners (Guizot, *History of France*, VIII, 221–25; reprint of "Escape of Lavalette," opp. p. 215).

182. Mathilde Laetitia Wilhelmine (1820–1904) was the third child and only daughter by a second marriage of her father Jérôme (1784–1860), Napoleon's younger brother. According to the writers of *Burke's Royal Families*, Mathilde inherited the beauty, talent, and fortitude of the Bonaparte women (I, p. 98). There were early tentative plans for a marriage to her first cousin, Louis Napoleon; however, in 1840, she married a Russian banker, Anatole Nikoliaevitch Demidoff, Principe de San Donato (1813–1870). They were separated in 1843, and when Louis Napoleon returned to France to become the president of the French Republic in 1848, he asked his cousin to preside at the Élysée (Latimer, *France in the Nineteenth Century*, p. 166). He later married Eugénie de Montijo, another beauty (see n. 157).

183. Adélaïde-Édouard le Lièvre de La Grange, Marquis de La Grange et de Fourilles (1796–1876), entered diplomatic life in 1821, but after the Revolution of 1830, he "retired" to scholarly pursuits in archaeology and literature; in 1837, he reentered political life when he was elected "des légitimistes" deputy from Blaye and became embroiled in the key issues of the day, usually in opposition to Thiers. One of his many political pamphlets attacked Guizot's ministry in 1842. The work which WI discussed with La Grange was published in four volumes in 1843, *Mémoires du maréchal duc de La Force et de ses deux fils, les marquis de Castelnaut et de Montpouillan*, a work for which he was honored by membership in 1846 in the Académie des Inscriptions et Belles-Lettres. During the 1840's, his was a voice in the Chamber against anarchy; when faced with the decision, he preferred "la domination d'un homme à un despotisme collectif," and he contributed to the election of Louis Napoleon in December, 1848. He was subsequently elected senator in the Legislative Assembly in 1849 and continued to write and publish (Tudesq, *Grands Notables*, I, 174; see also *Nouvelle Biographie Universelle*, XXVIII, 845–47).

histoire pen: Thought Robertsons history,[184] though a beautiful[?][185] composition was not satisfactory.

Dined with Mr Bulwer, in a ∧ ↑curious↓ little mansion made up of irregular saloons & pavillions, with garden behind it, which formerly belonged to the Princess Pauline[186] and was a kind of Maison de Plaisance. At dinner we had Genl Cass, Col. Charles Fox, a monsr ⟨Walewsky⟩ who is engaged ⟨o⟩in a history of the Moriscoes[187]—and Mr Walewsky,[188] a pole, said to be a Son of Napoleon. He has the Bonaparte stamp in his countenance. A Handsome man about 35—Speaks English very well—very intelligent and agreeable—conversation turned upon travellers

184. William Robertson (1721–1793), Scottish preacher, principal of Edinburgh University, was one of the great British historians of the eighteenth century. His first work, the two-volume *History of Scotland during the Reigns of Queen Mary and King James VI* (1759), surprised and pleased the contemporary literati, especially Hume, Burke, Gibbon, and Walpole, who wrote enthusiastically of Robertson's language and knowledge; Lord Chesterfield compared his style favorably with Livy's. Robertson's *History of the Reign of the Emperor Charles the Fifth with a view of the Progress of Society from the subversion of the Roman Empire to the beginning of the sixteenth century,* was published in three volumes in 1769 and contained an introduction which set the standard for articulating general ideas in history based on carefully researched details. For this history, Robertson received an unusually large sum (£4,500), an international reputation, and the praise of such diverse critics as Voltaire, Catherine II of Russia, Hallam, and Thomas Carlyle. Many subsequent scholars criticized some of Robertson's assumptions, especially regarding the Middle Ages, but as late as 1857, Prescott published a new edition, appending his own more accurate account of Charles V's life after his abdication. Among Robertson's many other works was the extremely popular two-volume *History of America* (1777), which account of Columbus was used by WI in his own research; he commented in 1828 that the English view of Columbus had come from Robertson's history, which "though admirably executed is but a general outline" (*Letters*, II, 305; see the long essay on Robertson in the *Dictionary of National Biography* (1896), XLVIII, 425–30).

185. If this word is "beautiful," WI omitted the *i*; the word may be "truthful."

186. Marie Pauline (1780–1825), another of the beautiful Bonaparte women and sister of Napoleon, was the fifth of six daughters of Charles Marie Bonaparte (1746–1836). Pauline's second marriage in 1803 was to Don Camillo Filippo Luigi Borghese, and she lived and died in the Borghese Palace near Florence.

187. WI's version resembles "Morriscoes."

188. Alexandre Florian, Comte Colonna-Walewski (1810–1868) was the natural son of Napoleon by the "famous Marie Walewska" (1786–1817) (*Burke's Royal Families*, p. 109). An able statesman and conservative Catholic, Count Walewski was the French agent in Cairo in 1840 during Louis Philippe's reign, but it was during the Second Empire as one of the two most trusted and capable advisers of his cousin, Louis Napoleon, that he became the popular French ambassador to England, then French minister of foreign affairs (Latimer, *France in the Nineteenth Century*, pp. 177–78; Bourgeois, *Modern France*, p. 232).

in the East. La Martine[189] was shewn up as being excessively *poetical*[190] in his mode of viewing and relating things, False & exaggerated as to landscape[,] people, facts &c. Cass spoke of his interview with Lady Hester Stanhope and of her indignation against La Martine who she declared, *lied* abominably. She mentioned various circumstances concerning herself which he had stated which were totally false. Lady Hester Stanhope was much considered and honored in the country as long as she ⟨ha⟩ could spend money freely but when her means became Straitend, as they latterly did, ⟨she⟩ the prestige vanished and she fell into neglect.

Sir William Gell[191] in one of his first works gives a fanciful and false account of the Island of [*blank*] and the ruins of the palace of [*blank*] When the English took possession of the island all was found to be false. He was asked how he came to fabricate such fables—"Why" Said he—I never dreamt that we were to gain possession of the Island"—He supposed there would be no travellers after him to detect his misrepresentations. His subsequent writings about$_\wedge$ ↑well known↓ countries are of quite a different character as to veracity.

189. Alphonse Marie Louis de Prat de Lamartine (1790–1869) was one of the leading Romantic poets in nineteenth-century France, considered among many contemporaries equal to Victor Hugo, Alfred de Vigny, and Alfred de Musset. Moved to poetry by the death of his first love, he published the immediately popular *Méditations, poétiques et religieuses* (1820), reminding many of Byron. In the decade which followed, he published four more volumes and began a diplomatic career in 1823 as secretary of the French legation at Florence. Earlier a royalist, he began to romanticize the Revolution and left the government with the July Revolution. He traveled in Palestine, Greece, and Syria, where he visited Lady Hester Stanhope (1776–1839), the eccentric daughter of the third Earl Stanhope; based on those travels was *Souvenirs, Impressions, Pensées et Paysages pendant un voyage en Orient* (1835). From 1833, he was an eloquent member of the Chamber and a prolific writer, but his romantic account of even the terror of the Revolution in *Histoire des Girondins* (1847) and his eloquent speeches elevated him to leadership in the Revolution of 1848; his cometlike influence which rose "above parliamentary factions" helped keep France stable and lasted approximately one year (Guérard, *France*, p. 296; see Latimer, "Lamartine and the Second Republic," in *France in the Nineteenth Century*, pp. 125–49, particularly her use of Mrs. Oliphant's article on Lamartine in *Blackwood's Magazine*).

190. WI may have written "pastoral."

191. Following a diplomatic mission to the Ionian Islands, William Gell (1777–1836) was knighted in 1803 and began his career as a classical archaeologist; the locations of his topographical subjects rendered in detailed drawings of ruins and other places of interest to the English traveler were Rome, Troy, Ithaca, Greece, and Morea; his most famous work was *Pompeiana: The Topography, Edifices and Ornaments of Pompeii* (1817–1823). Relatively short on scholarship and long on society, Sir William was nevertheless honored by learned organizations at home and abroad, including membership in the Royal Society and the Institute of France.

Speaking of Mad. La Norman[192] the famous fortune teller, Bulwer said he had once been to see her—found her ingenious—prone to put questions and draw hints[193] and conclusions from the replies—

⟨The Pole⟩ ^ ↑Walewsky↓ told of his having some years since called upon her, knowing that a beautiful, woman with whom he had some liason, was about to call on her. Mad. Le Norman began to talk to him in the usual way but he repeatedly interrupted her telling her he had no occasion for her Science, but had come to aid it. ⟨Such a lady is⟩ ↑He described the lady who was↓ coming ⟨here⟩ to consult ⟨you said he.⟩ ↑her.↓ ⟨Such and such things you may tell her.⟩ He related many striking facts concerning her—He stated what might be said to her as to the future—I do not ⟨t⟩ advise you to tell all these things said he, I counsel[194] nothing: you may do as you please, but here are six Louis, for you. so saying he took his leave—

The lady's fortune ^ ↑past and future↓ was told in a manner to astonish her, and greatly to the advantage[?] of ⟨the Pole⟩ Mr Walewsky

Charles Fox told us of a singular ↑train of↓ coincidences which had happened to his father Lord Holland. When a boy he was nearly drowned in the Thames, and brought to shore perfectly insensible

On another occasion in [*blank*] he met with another accident of great danger [*one line blank*] and another time in Lisbon he ⟨f[?]⟩[195]

In the Evening I accompanied Bulwer to the Duchess of [*blank*] niece of Talleyrand[196] ⟨Foun[?]⟩ Met there with Lady Rancliff,[197] whom I

192. Trent and Hellman identified as Marie-Anne Lenormand (1772–1843), who had advised the Empress Josephine as well as other members of French society (*Journals of WI*, III, 215, n. 1).

193. This word may be "points."

194. This word may be "conceal" or "council."

195. WI left the remaining three-fourths of the page blank, apparently intending to add the stories regarding Lord Holland, a task never completed.

196. Trent and Hellman identified as Dorothée de Courland, Duchesse de Dino (1792–1862), wife of Count Alexandre de Périgord, Talleyrand's nephew (*Journals of WI*, III, 216, n. 1). Earlier in his career, Charles Maurice de Talleyrand-Périgord, Prince de Benevento (1754–1838), had been excommunicated, and later he had betrayed several French leaders, whom he supposedly was serving. In 1830, when Louis Philippe sent Talleyrand to England, many felt it was a wise political move; however, in a September, 1830, letter to Louis McLane, WI wrote that the appointment was "little relished" and unworthy of Louis Philippe: "The policy is of the dissolute, heartless kind of the old school; the trickery and intrigue of cabinets and saloons; not the policy suited to a free country and a frank and popular government. . . . As to Talleyrand, he cares for nobody and nothing" (*Letters*, II, 548). WI was proved wrong in part, as Talleyrand negotiated important treaties in London which promoted Louis Philippe's pacific policy.

197. Elizabeth Mary Forbes, Lady Rancliffe, was the oldest daughter of George

had not seen for ⟨many⟩ ↑16↓ years. She was looking very well ⟨though⟩ grown plump. Introduced to a very handsome girl. Mademoiselle de Navalles[?][198] grand daughter of Lafayette.

Met the Marquise de Brignolle, and was introduced to her sister in law Madame. [*blank*]

Old Lady Aldborough[199] present—⟨abo⟩ nearly 90 years of age, but fashionably dressed ∧ ↑animated↓ & full of conversation.

Monday, June 13[200]

Dined at Lord Cowleys[201] (British Ambassador) present Ld & Lady Cowley—Miss Wellesley[202]—Lord & Lady Throgmorton,[203] Marquis and Marchioness Durazzo—Lady Rancliffe[,] Mr Bulwer, Mr McTavish[204] &c

---

Forbes, sixth earl of Granard (1760–1837), and the wife of George Augustus Parkyns, second Baron Rancliffe (1785–1850). In November, 1823, in Paris, WI had been swept into the active social circle of Lord Granard and his daughter; in journal entries from November 10, 1823, until August 28, 1825, WI frequently mentioned Lady Rancliffe's telling him stories, introducing him to her friends, discussing objects d'art in Paris, etc. (*Journals and Notebooks*, III, 241, n. 281, and index).

198. Trent and Hellman transcribed as "Noailles" (*Journals of WI*, III, 216; see n. 224 below).

199. WI probably referred to the widow of John Stratford (d. 1823), who became third earl of Aldborough in 1801 when his brother died without issue. In 1777, he had married Elizabeth, whom the *Gentlemen's Magazine* later called the toast of Ireland and one of her country's best horsewomen; Lady Aldborough died in January, 1846, at her hotel in Paris.

200. WI wrote "Monday June [13]"; the brackets are WI's.

201. In a June, 1842, letter to his sister, WI "complained" at getting "launched into society" and mentioned this dinner at the home of Lord Cowley, "brother to the Duke of Wellington . . ." (*Letters*, III, 237). Henry Wellesley, first Baron Cowley (1773–1847), began a long diplomatic career in 1792 as secretary to the British legation in Stockholm. He subsequently served one brother in India as adviser; was for a short time a member of Parliament and the Privy Council; was secretary of the legation in Spain (1809–1811); and then was ambassador to Spain from 1811 until 1822 and ambassador to Vienna from 1823 until 1831. Having been ambassador to France for a time in 1835 during a short Tory government, he served again in that position from 1841 until 1846.

202. Lord Cowley was married twice and by each wife had a daughter; this Miss Wellesley was probably Georgiana Charlotte Mary, who was the only child by his second wife, Georgiana Charlotte Augusta (d. 1860), and who later married William Henry Lytton Earle Bulwer (see above n. 159).

203. WI may have met Robert George Throckmorton, eighth Baron Throckmorton (b. 1800), who married in 1829 Elizabeth Acton (d. 1850) and who served in Parliament from 1831 until 1835. His daughter was Dame de la Crois étoilée, lady in waiting to the empress of Austria.

204. Other people at this dinner, whom WI did not mention in this journal entry

Evg to Thornes—Grand fete—Gardens illuminated.[205] Introduced to Eugene Sue[206] ⟨Strong[?]⟩ Stout man about 36 Strong[?] black beard. Spoke with great approbation of Coopers writings[207]

Tuesday, June 14[208]

Dined with Col & Lady Mary Fox—present Mr Dumas,[209] Bulwer, Mr [*blank*]

---

but did include in a letter to his sister, were General Cass and "Mr. Rumpf, son-in-law to Mr. Astor, besides other persons of my acquaintance" (*Letters*, III, 237). Perhaps one of these persons was John McTavish, whose fur trading company had been associated with Astor's and whose partnership with WI's good friend Henry Brevoort was often discussed in their letters of 1816; WI called McTavish "certainly a charming Companion" who seemed likely to marry one of the beautiful Caton sisters (*Letters*, I, 451–52).

205. In a June 14, 1842, continuation of a letter to his sister Catharine Paris, WI described the "magnificent fête given by our countryman, Colonel Thorn," trying not to enjoy too much the brilliantly lit hotel, the "extensive gardens fancifully illuminated," the strolling musicians and singers—"one of those fairy scenes that would have enchanted me in my greener years of inexperience and romance; but I have grown too wise to be duped by such delusions . . ." (*Letters*, III, 237).

206. Like our own Cooper, the French novelist Marie Joseph (Eugène) Sue (1804–1875) wrote novels of the sea based on his own experience: *Plik et Plok* (1831) and *La Vigie de Koatven* (1833). By the time WI met him in 1842, Sue had published *Arthur* (1838), *Mathilde* (1841), and *Le Morne au diable* (1842); his pictures of street life combined with social consciousness brought him success in this era of the Citizen King. Among his works were *Les Mysteres de Paris* (1842–1843) and *Les Sept Peches capitaux* (1847–1849).

207. By the time Eugène Sue applauded James Fenimore Cooper (1789–1851), this prolific American novelist had completed the Leatherstocking series (1823–1841), many novels of manners, of the sea, of intrigue, and of social commentary, as well as his major and often defensive treatises lauding or condemning his countrymen. While he was American consul at Lyons (1826–1833), Cooper was a part of the international literary scene and joined WI as the first American writers to be highly praised abroad. Cooper and WI harbored political and literary enmity until Cooper's death, when, ironically, WI was on the committee to plan Cooper's memorial service on February 24, 1852.

208. WI wrote "⟨Th⟩ Tuesday June [14]"; the brackets are WI's.

209. Although STW suggested (II, 366, n. 45) that WI met Alexandre Dumas the younger (1824–1895), it seems more likely that the writer was Alexandre Davy de la Pailleterie Dumas, or Dumas *père* (1802–1870), who was at this time at the height of his career as dramatist and had begun to write historical novels. In 1823, Dumas *père* was employed as a clerk in the house of the duc d'Orléans, which position he resigned when he began his own writing; his first dramatic piece was a collaboration, *La Chasse et l'amour* (1825), but it was *Henri III et sa cour* (1829), produced by the Comédie Français, which established him as a leader in the French romantic movement. Even though Dumas lost favor with Louis Philippe in the mid 1830's, he remained on affectionate terms with the young duc d'Orléans until the latter's death

Wednesday, June 15 [210]

Dined with Mr & Mrs Greene.[211] Present Mr & Mrs Storrow[,] Mr & Mrs Ledyard[212]–⟨Col Fo⟩ Genl Cass[,] Dr Randolph of Phila. Mr Ray[,] The Miss Greens–

Thursday, June 16[213]

⟨drove⟩ ↑Went↓ out to Versailles in Rail road cars with Mr & Mrs Storrow & the child & Mr Ames[–]took up quarters in the Reservoir Hotel[214]

–Evg drove to Viroflay[215] to Bois Repos[es] dined with Mr & Mrs Ellis.[216] Met there Lady Ryal, Genl Cass, Ledyard–a Mr Wilkinson &c After dinner walked in wood of Meudon, visited Mr Wilkinsons country

---

(see above, n. 145). After this meeting with WI, Dumas *père* wrote the novels for which he is most famous, including *Le Comte de Monte-Cristo* (1844), *Les Trois Mousquetaires* (1844), and his 22-volume *Mes Mémoires*; his works comprise 103 volumes in the Calmann-Levy edition. Although Dumas acknowledged his illegitimate son in 1831, subsequently filing for custody, it was not until 1847 that Dumas *fils* published his first work, a book of poems, and the following year, his first novel, *La Dame aux camélias*, brought him fame.

210. WI wrote "Wednesday June [*blank*]"; he apparently intended to add the date.

211. WI first mentioned calling on Mr. Greene in Le Havre on September 24, 1823; later in Paris and Versailles entries, he recalled social engagements with Mr. and Mrs. Greene, and once, with their child; this association lasted at least until July, 1825 (see *Journals and Notebooks*, III, index).

212. WI probably met on this day, and the one following, New York-born Henry Ledyard (1812–1880), a lawyer, who in 1839 became secretary of the American legation in France and married General Cass' daughter, Mathilda; in 1842, when Cass fell out of favor (see above, n. 139), Ledyard was made chargé d'affaires *ad interim* in Paris from November, 1842, until June, 1844. He returned to America (Detroit), became active in local and state politics, and joined Cass in Washington when the latter became secretary of state. In a July, 1843, letter to Sarah Paris Storrow in Paris, WI sent "kind regards to Miss Ledyard, and the young Ledyards" (PMI, III, 287), and on August 21, 1844, the Ledyards embarked with WI for England from Le Havre.

213. WI wrote "Thursday June [*blank*]."

214. Versailles was approximately eleven miles west of Paris; it was only a village when Louis XIII built a retreat there; it was Louis XIV who added the main attraction, the château (1661–1682), and Louis Philippe who made it a national monument. There was an active American community in Versailles when WI was earlier in France, including the Storrows, and WI visited there often, once mentioning dining at the Hotel de la Reservoir in August, 1824 (*Journals and Notebooks*, III, 385 and index).

215. Viroflay was a village just east of Versailles.

216. After meeting Mr. Ellis on January 9, 1824, and his wife the following January 24, WI reported that he saw, called on, and dined with them often until February 3, 1825 (*Journals and Notebooks*, III, index).

retreat His wife a pretty French woman. two daughters are very handsome

Monday, June 27[217]

accompanied Mrs & the Misses Wheaton[218] to Soiree of Duchess De Caze.

Wednesday, June 29[219]

–Dined with Baron Rothschild[220]–at his villa at Bologne.[221] Present Duke de Caze, Marquis de Salvandy[222]–Madam de Girardin[,] for-/ -merly Delphine Gay[223][–]Mr Bulwer &c Evening Company. Duke &

217. WI wrote "Monday 27 June."

218. WI probably escorted the wife and daughters of Henry Wheaton (1785–1848), lawyer, journalist, diplomat, and scholar, who was at this time the American minister in Berlin (serving there from 1837 until 1847). After practicing law for five years in Rhode Island, Wheaton was the reporter of the U.S. Supreme Court (1810–1827), then was appointed the American chargé d'affaires in Denmark in 1827. When his family arrived in London in 1831 on its way to Copenhagen, WI intervened to get their luggage through customs duty-free (*Letters*, II, 620–21). After mastering Scandinavian languages, Wheaton wrote *History of the Northmen* (1831); he was an outstanding student of international law: among his works were *Elements of International Law* (1836) and *History of the Law of Nations in Europe and America* (1841). When Polk demanded Wheaton's resignation, the diplomatic world was shocked; after returning home in 1847, he lectured at Harvard.

219. WI wrote "Wednesday–29 June."

220. Baron James de Rothschild (1792–1868), youngest son of the founder of the Rothschild international banking empire, was responsible for establishing the House of Rothschild in Paris after the Restoration in 1814. His success was aided by loans to the government, and he lost heavily in the Revolution of 1848 even though the "great bankers, Rothschild at their head, subscribed to the relief of those wounded in February" (Bourgeois, *Modern France*, I, 316).

221. Boulogne, not to be confused with Boulogne-sur-Mer to the north, was in WI's day just west of Paris, on the west bank of the winding Seine, east of St. Cloud and south of Neuilly-sur-Seine; it is now a part of the city.

222. Probably Marquis Narcissé Achille, the count de Salvandy (1795–1856); one of the liberal followers of Guizot, he was named minister of public instruction in 1844, a concession to the Catholics who supported him (Bourgeois, *Modern France*, I, 260–62).

223. The name "Delphine" was written in ink in contrast to the page in pencil; apparently WI added it later and wrote over the last name "Gay" in ink. As a young woman, Delphine Gay (1804–1855) was the heroine of the Romantic coteries in Paris, equally for her poetry, beauty, and wit. She contributed to the journal *La Muse française* and published volumes of poetry, *Essais poétiques* (1824) and *Nouveaux Essais poétiques* (1825). In 1831, she married Émile de Girardin (1806–1881), newspaperman and founder in 1836 of *La Presse*; from 1836 until 1839, Madame de Girardin wrote for her husband's newspaper a successful gossip column under a nom de plume. She also wrote comedies and short novels.

Duchess of Grammont.[224] M. de Kaunitz[?][225]—minister of Saxony his wife & daughter (Madam Bernstorff[?]—wife of Prussian charge d affaires &c &c—

[pp. [45–46] blank]

Monday, July 11[226]

Leave Paris at 11 Oclock in carriage & four horses—for Bordeaux accompanied by Alex Hamilton Jr.[227] Carson Brevoort & Hector Ames—Benjamin Gowien[228] Domestic—Fine weather—

224. STW said that Colonel Thorn (see above, nn. 165, 205) was disappointed that WI did not pursue an acquaintance with the duchess of Gramont (II, 366, n. 48). Regarding this matter, a bemused WI reported to Henry Brevoort that during a party, after the duchess had "held me for some time in very amiable conversation," Colonel Thorn "took me aside and implored me to leave a card the next day for the Duchess and at the same time read me a most affectionate lecture on my neglect of this piece of etiquette with respect to various other persons of rank." WI admitted that it was not modesty, as Colonel Thorn supposed, but boredom that prompted his inaction (*Letters*, III, 242). The editors identified the subject of this letter as Rosalie de Noailles (1767–1852), widow of Théodule, marquis de Grammont (*ibid.*, p. 243, n. 2).

225. Trent and Hellman transcribed as "Kenevitz"; the word could be "Kenritz" (*Journals of WI*, III, 217).

226. WI wrote "Ju⟨ne⟩ly 11."

227. Alexander Hamilton, Jr. (1816–1889), was the grandson of Alexander Hamilton (1757–1804), and the son of WI's friend and neighbor James Alexander Hamilton (1788–1878), who had early been an editor of the *New York American*, a periodical always friendly to WI. When Joseph G. Cogswell (1786–1871) declined the nomination as secretary of the legation in Madrid, WI's second choice was young Hamilton, a man whom Hone called "exceedingly bright and talented" (*Diary*, II, 597). President Tyler's initial political reservations gave way to his judgment regarding Hamilton's ability, and WI told Mrs. Hamilton that having her son with him in Madrid "will be like taking a bit of home with me . . ." (PMI, III, 182). He joined WI and Brevoort in Paris.

228. WI described in more detail to his sister Catharine Paris this fortunate acquisition: "a Mulatto named Benjamin Gowien, native of South Carolina, who came out with Mr Middleton, when he went Minister to Russia, remained with him ten or twelve years, and has been travelling about Europe in various capacities for twenty four years past. He speaks most of the European languages fluently; is a capital travelling servant, and indeed a valuable servant at all points. Steady, quiet, respectful and trustworthy. . . . he has already been three times [at Madrid] and made himself well acquainted with the language and with the customs of the country" (*Letters*, III, 252).

arrive at Orleans[229] at 9½[230] OClock[—]put up at La Boule d'Or a very neat clean hotel

Tuesday, July 12[231]

Leave Orleans at 8 Oclock[—]Stop about 1 oclock at Blois[232] and visit the old castle where the Duke de Guise was assassinated[233]

Fine cool day having had showers last night—arrive a little after 7 oclock at Tours.[234] Put up at the Hotel de Londres[?]—Good—

229. The ancient city of Orléans, on the right bank of the Loire River at its northernmost point, was approximately 72 miles southwest of Paris. It was the ancestral duchy of Louis Philippe and the town into which Joan of Arc entered in April, 1429; the subsequent nine-day siege delivered it from the English and is celebrated annually on May 8.

230. The 9 was written over an illegible number.

231. WI wrote "Ju⟨ne⟩ly 12."

232. From Orléans to Blois, WI followed the scenic route of approximately 35 miles in a southwesterly direction along the right or north bank of the Loire. From feudal times, Blois was a duchy, then a seat of favorite resort of kings; a picturesque town rising from the river with steep and narrow streets and an infamous castle towering above it, Blois was, and is, a convenient point of departure to the Châteaux country.

233. The oldest part of the castle dates from the thirteenth century and has immense historical significance, but during the Religious Wars of 1560–1593, which Guérard said might have been called the War of the Guises and Bourbons, the castle earned the infamy to which WI referred (*France*, pp. 150–54). The struggle for power culminated in the final war when Henri de Loraine, the duc de Guise (1550–1588), the hero of the Catholics, entered Paris in May, 1588, and with the populace besieged Henry III in the Louvre; as the duke attempted to calm the crowd, the king escaped to Blois, called into session the States General, and ordered the duke to attend. Counting on Henry's weakness and ignoring his own friends' warnings that the king planned to kill him, the duc de Guise and his brother, the cardinal, went to the castle and were assassinated by Henry III's bodyguards on December 23, 1588. Dumas' play *Henri et sa cour* included this incident (see above, n. 209).

234. WI traveled approximately 37 miles from Blois to Tours, ancient capital of Touraine and center of learning in the Middle Ages; long contested by the French and English, the town was ceded permanently to France by a treaty in 1242. On the south bank of the Loire River, Tours was earlier a center for the manufacture of silk and a favorite seat of kings, but it was devastated by the Religious Wars. It is now a great rail and road center, manufacturer of wines, and doorway to the Châteaux country.

Wednesday, July 13[235]

Rise early, visit Cathedral[236] &c—

leave Tours at 8 Oclock drive through Monbaizon[237]—ruins of castle—fertile country round it—gardens—Small river

Pass thro fertile green country—ridges of low hills with Chateaux & vineyards

Pass through Chate⟨a⟩llerault[238]—beset by knife merchants. arrive at Poittiers[239] about 5. Picturesque approach to the town—limestone crags[?] on one hand[,] Small river on the other—Put up at Hotel de France—Good—take bath[—]walk in public promenade built partly on walls of old town Enchanting view below the walls small rich valley with the Vienne[240] gliding thro it

Visit Cathedral[241]—very spacious aisle. Side aisles nearly as wide as the nave

Thursday, July 14[242]

Walk before breakfast with Mr Brevoort visit Cathedral—Church of S. [*blank*] Saxon architecture[243]—Columns with very high reliefs Leave Poitiers at 8 Oclock—.

235. WI wrote "July 13."

236. WI actually wrote "Cathredal," but his intention is clear. The St. Gatien Cathedral, which took nearly 400 years to build, represents each stage of French Gothic architecture from 1220, as well as early Renaissance; the two towers, dissimilar in design and height, are topped by Renaissance cupolas.

237. Almost eight miles directly south of Tours, Montbazon was on the left bank of the Indre River, a branch of the Loire. On a hill rising from the river were the ruins of the castle which included an enormous square keep dating from the eleventh century.

238. Approximately 27 miles south-southwest of Montbazon and on the east bank of the Vienne River, another branch of the Loire, Châtellerault was known for its recently built arsenal (1829), its ancient local manufacture of cutlery dating from the fourteenth century, and its splendid Renaissance Henry IV Bridge, which surpassed the Pont Neuf in Paris in width.

239. Leaving Châtellerault, WI probably crossed the Vienne, then followed the left bank of the Clain River past the Forêt de Châtellerault for approximately 21 miles to Poitiers. The valley of the Clain narrowed with rugged cliffs filled with caves leading to the historically rich town of Poitiers, with its fine Romanesque buildings, its ancient university (founded in 1431), and its famous residents, including St. Hillary, Eleanor of Aquitaine, and Joan of Arc.

240. Poitiers was actually on the west or north bank of the curving Clain River, a branch of the Vienne which joined that river just south of Châtellerault.

241. WI probably visited the Notre Dame la Grande, which was, in France, one of the four or five best Romanesque churches with a particularly fine sculptured west façade.

242. WI wrote "14."

243. Another outstanding cathedral in Poitiers was St. Pierre's, built from 1166

Weather this day very hot—dusty[—]pass through country of vineyards. Straight road—monotonous. See at a distance the chateau of the Rochefoucaulds[244]

arrive about 7 Oclock at Angouleme[245]—have to wind up hill through the town, put up at Hotel de la Port—walk out about boulevards along the crest of the hill looking over rich extent of country with the [*blank*][246] gleaming through parts of it—We are in the country of truffles[,] Pateés[247] &c

Friday, July 15[248]

Leave Angouleme at 7 oclock. beauti/ful walks made ⟨along⟩ ↑around↓ the place on the boulevards &c—

a hot dusty days drive—about 3 posts[249] before reaching Bordeaux hear of the death of the Duke of Orleans.[250]

Pass over magnificent hanging bridge over the Dordogne[251]—arrive at Bordeaux[252]—about 6 Oclock put up at Hotel de Paris.

---

until 1271, described as having a façade "too broad for its height," but overall, a "well-planned structure whose fine proportions are rendered yet more imposing by a slight decrease in height and narrowing of the nave towards the choir" (Muirhead, ed., *North-western France*, p. 355). From the south door of St. Pierre's Cathedral, a lane led to the baptistry of St. Jean, the oldest Christian structure in France, which was built in the mid-fourth century, enlarged in the seventh century with apses and reused Roman columns and in the eleventh century with a porch, and restored beginning in 1834.

244. The three letters following the *R* were written over other letters, perhaps "eau." La Rochefoucauld, a beautiful château dating from the twelfth century, was northeast of Angoulême approximately eight miles east of the road on which WI was traveling. The journey from Poitiers to Angoulême was approximately 62 miles primarily in a southerly direction. The Charente River, which rose at a mid-point, occasionally meandered close to WI's route, once crossing it.

245. The walled town of Angoulême, on the south bank of the Charente River, was built primarily of stone on a plateau approximately 235 feet above the river.

246. The Charente River, which at Angoulême changed from a basically north-to-south direction to a northwestward flow, entered the Atlantic just west of Rochefort.

247. WI's spelling could also have been "Paties" or "Pattés," but not "pâtés," as Trent and Hellman transcribed (*Journals of WI*, III, 218).

248. WI wrote "15."

249. WI traveled approximately 70 miles from Angoulême to Bordeaux in a southwest direction.

250. Duc d'Orléans, favorite son of King Louis Philippe (see p. 223, n. 145).

251. The bridge over the Dordogne was approximately ten miles north of Bordeaux.

252. Bordeaux, 300 miles south-southwest of Paris and an ancient city favorably located for trade, was on the left or west bank of the Garonne River, approximately 20 miles above its confluence with the Dordogne. The city was alternately destroyed and rebuilt in the third and tenth centuries by Germans and Vikings; it passed to English control with the marriage of Eleanor of Aquitaine and Henry II in 1152 and

Saturday, July 16[253]

Keep at home all day on account of the heat Drive out in the evening to Floirac, to visit the Guestiers—Mr Guestier[254] absent: ⟨f[?]⟩ Find Mrs G[255] at home with her Son in Law Wash[.] Phelan[256] who married her daughter Minna—and Mr [*blank*] who married her niece Miss Lawton[.][257] Nu-/-merous family—four born since I was here—Accompd. in this drive by Hamilton & Brevoort—Fine drive home by moonlight

---

was not restored to the French until 1453. During the eighteenth century it became a great port trading heavily with the West Indies and Africa; it gained distinction with buildings by Victor Louis and other noted architects of the day, and after suffering much at the hand of the Revolution, it was enjoying a resurgence under Louis Philippe. For WI, this entrance was a "coming home," for his first European tour began in Bordeaux on June 30, 1804 (see *Letters*, I, 8–52, for his impressions from that date until August 5, 1805, when he departed for Switzerland); he spent time in Bordeaux in later years, particularly in 1825.

253. WI wrote "16 July."

254. WI first mentioned meeting Pierre François Guestier (1793–1874) in Paris in an August 16, 1823, journal entry; he had called on Mrs. Reuben Beasley, Guestier's sister, and found him there visiting. In the months following, WI often was in their home; and during his long stay in Bordeaux in 1825, WI was an intimate of the entire family, including Pierre's father, wine merchant Daniel Guestier (1755–1847). It was Pierre's estate, "La Cruz," just beyond Floirac on the right bank of the Garonne four miles above Bordeaux, to which WI returned on his first day in Bordeaux (for his initial description of this estate in 1825, see *Journals and Notebooks*, III, 536–37; for the detailed and enthusiastic account of his return to this "place of places," see the July 19, 1842, letter to his niece in *Letters*, III, 249–51).

255. In 1818, Pierre François Guestier married Anna Elizabeth Johnston (1801–1873), the oldest daughter of William Johnston (1770–1821). Following their meeting, WI seemed to enjoy the company of "Mrs G" in Paris as much as that of her husband, for she "plays & sings delightfully," "tells anecdotes of her grandfather—and his escapes from Guilotine during revolution," etc. (*Journals and Notebooks*, III, 216, 254); he was pleased to find "my dear Mrs Guestier in excellent health, and looking very much as when I left her, between sixteen and seventeen years since. Time certainly has not dealt roughly with her" (*Letters*, III, 250).

256. Among WI's Bordeaux friends in 1825 was the family of Bernard Phelan; born in Ireland in 1770, he settled in Bordeaux in the early 1800's and married in 1806 one of Daniel Guestier's daughters, Marie-Elisabeth (1789–1870) (*Journals and Notebooks*, III, 528, n. 164). Their son Pierre-François-Jean Scott, called Washington by his parents because of their devotion to WI, had only recently (April, 1842) married Wilhelmina-Anna-Nathaline ("Minna"), the daughter of Pierre Guestier (see *Letters*, III, 251, nn. 4–5; the editors cite John P. Young's University of Bordeaux 1947 dissertation, "Washington Irving à Bordeaux").

257. Trent and Hellman transcribed as "Lorton" (*Journals of WI*, III, 219), but the editors of *Letters*, III, confirm my reading (p. 251, n. 4); this niece was probably the daughter of Ann Suzanne Guestier Lawton, who was one of the daughters of

Sunday, July 17[258]

Drive out about 12 Oclock to Lescure, countryseat of Mr Nathl Johnson.[259] Found him at home & Mrs N Johnson Mr. J just recovering from some[260] illness—After a while old Mrs Johnson[261] returned from Church accompd by her daughter Georgina[?][262] & her husband Mr Deluz—passed an hour there very agreably In afternoon Hamliton[,] Brevoort & myself drove out to Floirac where we dined en famille with the Guestiers Mr Guestier[263] had returned and greeted me cordially on my arrival. about 20 persons sat down to table—Mrs Phelan[264] was there—Doctor [*blank*]—Passed a very pleasant evening—

Monday, July 18[265]

Paid morning visits to Mrs Deluz[,] Mrs Nath Barton[,][266] Mrs Phelan

---

Daniel Guestier and the wife of Jean Edouard Lawton (1791–1863), Bordeaux wine exporter (see *Journals and Notebooks*, III, 529, n. 177).

258. WI wrote "Sunday 17."

259. On October 8, 1825, WI first mentioned meeting Mrs. Pierre François Guestier's uncle, Nathaniel Johnston (1776–1842), who was by that time head of the firm Nathaniel Johnston et fils (he the "fils"); from that time until February 8, 1826, WI made constant journal references to members of this family (see *Journals and Notebooks*, III, index), among them young Nathaniel ("Nat") Johnston (1804–1870), Mrs. Guestier's brother, to whom WI here referred. In fact, in his July 19, 1842, letter to Sarah Storrow, WI wrote that Lescure "is now kept up" by old Mrs. Johnston's "son Nathl Johnson" (*Letters*, III, 250).

260. Trent and Hellman transcribed as "severe," a possible reading (*Journals of WI*, III, 219).

261. In 1797, William Johnston (1770–1821) married Suzanne Gledstanes (1773–1853), to whom WI referred in his July 19, 1842, letter as "My excellent friend old Mrs Johnson, who always showed such a regard for my dear brother Peter, received me with a warmth and kindness that melted my very heart" (*Letters*, III, 249, n. 11, 250).

262. Trent and Hellman read as "Georgiana" (*Journals of WI*, III, 219); she was the sister of Mrs. Pierre François Guestier and Nat Johnston.

263. In his July 16, 1842, letter to Sarah Storrow, WI complained that only the day before, Reuben Beasley had gone with Daniel Guestier to the latter's château in Medoc for a week and that Pierre Guestier was also away from Bordeaux "somewhere in the interior" (*Letters*, III, 248); WI's pleasure that "Mr Guestier returned from his country tour" is obvious (*ibid.*, p. 249).

264. Mrs. Phelan, also mentioned in the following day's entry, was probably Marie-Elisabeth Guestier Phelan, sister of Pierre François Guestier (see above, nn. 254, 256).

265. WI wrote "18—."

266. Mary Susanne Scott, daughter of the British consul to Bordeaux, Henry Scott (1773–1832), married Nathaniel Barton, another first cousin of Mrs. Pierre François Guestier; "Nat" was the son of Mrs. Guestier's aunt Anna Johnston (1771–1842), who married Hugh Barton (1766–1854), a partner of Daniel Guestier (*Journals and

& Mr Grigsby[267] of Virginia, American Consul. Dined at Lescure—At table Old Mrs Johnson, Mr & Mrs N Johnson[,] Mr & Mrs Deluz—Mr & Mrs N Barton and Mr Scott,[268] British Consul Returnd in Evg in carriage with Mr & Mrs Deluz

Tuesday, July 19[269]

Leave Bordeaux at 4 OClock P M in dilligence for Bayonne—⟨travel⟩ hot dusty journey in the afternoon—travel all night

Wednesday, July 20[270]

Day cooler. there have been showers to lay the dust. arrive at Bayonne[271] at 4 OClock ⟨Rec[?]⟩ At Diligence office find Mr [? Souller Tulaze ?][272] who conducts us to Hotel St Etienne—Take bath. Stroll about the town

[*pp. [42–84] blank*]

[*Of pp. [85–86], approximately three-fourths inch remains; on p. [86] is the word "footman" and several illegible letters.*]

[*pp. [87–88] missing*]

[*inside back cover blank*]

[*back cover*]

1

Notebooks, III, 528, n. 165). After meeting "Mr Nat Barton" on October 13, 1825, WI mentioned him frequently in his Bordeaux journal, as well as his parents, brother, and wife (see *ibid.*, index).

267. John Warren Grigsby was confirmed as American consul at Bordeaux on February 23, 1841, and served in that position from May 28, 1842, until October 29, 1849.

268. In 1832, Thomas Brand Graham Scott succeeded his father Henry Scott as British consul to Bordeaux; WI had known the Scotts in Bordeaux in 1825.

269. WI wrote "19."

270. WI wrote "20."

271. The distance from Bordeaux to Bayonne was approximately 100 miles; in a July 20, 1842, letter to his sister, WI called Bayonne "the frontier town of France with the Pyrenees in view" (*Letters*, III, 252).

272. Trent and Hellman transcribed as one word, "Lucaze" (*Journals of WI*, III, 220).

AMERICAN NOTEBOOKS, 1833

Number 1

Notes Concerning the Far West

This manuscript notebook is in the Seligman Collection of Irvingiana in the Manuscripts and Archives Division of the New York Public Library, where it is cataloged as #22–1576, Washington Irving Notebooks, Volume 7. Four notebooks, three in this series concerning the Far West and one, "Notes on the Indians"[1] (also titled by Irving, "Notes for Astoria, 1835"), are in a grey cardboard slipcase measuring 3⅝ x 5⅞ x 7/16 inches. Notebook number 1 consists of eight leaves of off-white paper, lined vertically with four very faded red lines, the middle line of the page actually being two closely approximate lines. Its sixteen pages measure 3 7/16 x 5 13/16 inches and are bound in red and white mottled cardboard held together with a brown string between leaves 4 and 5. Pages [4–5], [13], [16], and the inside back cover are blank; the writing throughout is in brown ink; on the front cover are two blotches of blue ink in the middle of the page, and on the lower right quarter of the back cover is another blue ink blot. The notebook number and title are in brown ink in Irving's hand on the front cover, and on the back cover the information is on a piece of paper pasted to the notebook. On the upper left third of the inside back cover is a leather bookplate of gold leaf with the words "Ex Libris Robert Hoe."

[*front cover*]

Notes concerning the
Far West
1

1. This notebook has been published in *Astoria, or Anecdotes of an Enterprize Beyond the Rocky Mountains*, ed. Richard Dilworth Rust (Boston: Twayne Publishers, 1976), pp. 492–94.

[*inside front cover*]
Wild horses called *Mustangs*[2]
—*mustang girls*

"Canst thou bind the sweet influences of the Pleiades, or loose the bands of Orion?"

Job.[3]

———

Even in the occupations of hunting & fishing, by which the Savage provided for his wants, he must have recognized his dependence on the luminaries of heaven & in the nightly excursions to which he was impelled either by hunger or revenge, he must have watched with anxiety for the returning moon to light him to his prey.

Encyclopedia[4]

———

Memoranda by
Washington Irving
of
Sunnyside

[*p. [1]*]
Prarie Grass[5]—tall, coarse & full of seeds at the top: & when ripe is rather too wiry for fodder. If it were cut early before it has lost its succulence & tenderness, it would, probably, be excellent fodder.

Flint[6]

———

2. These wild horses were particularly identified with the American prairies and were descended from those horses brought to these shores by the Spaniards; the word is related to the Spanish "mestrenco," or "strayer, wild with no master."

3. WI quoted exactly this verse, Job 38:31, which is one of a series of questions or challenges put to Job by God to convince Job of the relative weakness and greatness of the two.

WI set off the following encyclopedia information with lines of one-eighth inch and 2¼ inches long.

4. Although this quotation has not been identified, it may refer to the *Encyclopædia Americana . . . on the Basis of the Seventh Edition of the German Conversations-Lexicon*, ed. Francis Lieber, 13 vols. (Philadelphia: Carey and Lea, 1829–1833).

5. WI used double underlining.

6. WI quoted in this notebook primarily from Timothy Flint's *The History and Geography of the Mississippi Valley*; the third edition was published in two volumes in 1833 (see "Note on Sources," p. lxvii). Page references to Flint in this volume are to the 1833 edition; the first is I, 54–55, a very close rendering with only a few omitted words. Following this passage, and throughout the notebook, WI separated quoted or paraphrased passages by skipping lines or drawing lines of

Blue Grass Yields a fine soft sward, & is not unlike the common spear grass[7] of NEngland. We are not satisfied whether it be indigenous, or not. We have constantly observed it growing about deserted houses & Indian villages. On the upper praries of Illinois it is said in many places to be displacing the prarie grass. It seems, like the robin red ↑[*illegible*]↓ breast attached to the abode of civilized man.

idem[8]

Grape Vines—Hanging like cordage from the trees.[9]

Pawpaw. The prince of wild fruit bearing shrubs.—Stem straight, white & of unrivalled beauty. We have seen no culti-/-vated shrub so ornamental & graceful as the pawpaw—A pawpaw shrub hanging full of fruits, of a size and weight so disproportioned to the Stem, and from under long rich looking leaves of the same yellow with the ripened fruit, & of an African luxuriance of growth, is to us one of the richest spectacles we have ever contemplated in the array of the woods.

Flint[10]

Michaux[11] says our trees are larger, taller and more of them useful for timber than those of Europe

---

one-half, three-sixteenths, one-half, three-eighths, seven-sixteenths, nine-sixteenths, and three-eighths inch.

7. The final letters resemble "ll."

8. Flint, *Mississippi Valley*, I, 55.

9. Flint discussed grape vines in his book on pp. 50–51; although the exact words have not been located, WI could have been paraphrasing the passage beginning, "Nothing is so familiar to the eye of a traveller in this country . . . as to see vines, often of a prodigious size . . ." (I, 50).

10. *Ibid.*, p. 48.

11. WI continued to quote Flint, who here referred to another writer of travel literature, André Michaux (1746–1802). Michaux was a French scientist, who with his young son, François André, traveled and studied in America from 1785 until 1796; in 1793 he went to Kentucky with a French delegation to settle political problems of navigation on the Mississippi. Michaux's interests were primarily botanical; his son carried on his work and in Philadelphia in 1824 presented to the American Philosophical Society the valuable travel diary of his father. The younger Michaux's own journals were popular in America and reveal an enthusiastic and observant traveler. (See an edition of André Michaux's *Journal of Travels into Kentucky; July 15, 1793–April 11, 1796* and François André Michaux's *Travels to the West of the Alleghany Mountains in the States of Ohio, Kentucky, and Tennessea, and Back to Charleston, by the Upper Carolines . . . Undertaken, in the Year 1802* [1805] in *Early Western Travels, 1748–1846,* vol. 3, ed. Reuben Gold Thwaites [Cleveland: Arthur H. Clark, 1904], pp. 27–104, 107–306. Information regarding Michaux is from the Preface to that volume, pp. 11–20.)

The forest has a general physiog-/nomy an aspect of luxuriance which discriminates it to the most superficial observer, from that on the other side of the mountain. We may add that to us the varieties of trees of the same class appear to be more numerous Trees of the same class here are inferior to those that are there, for the same uses as timber. They are less tough, elastic and durable.[12]

Panocco[13] Nymphia nelumbo—a magnificent kind of pond lily—have their home in dead lakes in the centre of cypress swamps. Mus-/-quitoes swarm above—Obscene birds wheel their flight over them. Alligators swim among their roots & moccasin snakes bask on their leaves. In such lonely & repulsive situations[,] under such circumstances and for such spectators, is arrayed the most gaudy & brilliant display of flowers in the creation. In the capsule are embedded from 4 to 6 acorn shaped seeds which the Indians roast & eat when green, or they are dried and eaten as nuts, or are pulvarized into meal & form a kind of bread.[14]

———

[*pp. [4–5] blank*]

Flowers.[15] The friable soil of the Western country does not naturally cover itself with the fine sward of the northern Atlantic country. It is the region of coarse grass, tall flowering plants with gaudy flowers; & to an unpractised eye presents a flora of great variety.[16]

———

Garden flowers. Jessamines white, cape Armenian & yellow. Sensitive plants Spanish dagger. Primrose. Jonquils white & yellow Iris—↑blue & yellow↓ touch me not Violets, lilies Roses monthly perpetual, moss scarlet, white—damascus, multiflora. bell, honey-/suckle. Woodbine. flowering pomgranate Bamboo. Myrtle, Altheas, Crape myrtle. Daffodil.[17]

Buffalo Easily domesticated & the animals springing from a mixture of the breeds are said to unite the desirable[18] properties of both. Their beef is generally preferred to that of the domestic ox. The whites wage upon them a gratuitous war of extermination and these innocent useful & noble animals instinctively fly their footsteps. They remain in the

12. Flint, *Mississippi Valley*, I, 49–50.
13. WI used double underlining.
14. Flint, *Mississippi Valley*, I, 64.
15. WI used double underlining.
16. Flint, *Mississippi Valley*, I, 65–66.
17. *Ibid.*, p. 66.
18. WI changed Flint's adjective, "valuable."

vicinity of the savages, who destroy no more of them, than subsistence or profit requires. The⟨ir⟩y still range from Red River of the north to the populous regions of mexico, but let the smallest set-/tlement of whites be fixed in their vicinity & the animals soon draw a line of a hundred leagues of demarcation between them & their enemies.

Flint[19]

Beaver-Trappers To these lonely and sequestered regions repair hundreds of white hunters who hunt for subsistence and trap for gain. They make their way in companies of armed partnerships, fitted out as a kind of guerillas—Sometimes a pair of Sworn friends hunt together—There are not a few who repair alone to these solitary streams and mount-/ains. Outlawry, avarice, necessity, and appetite for lawless & unrestrained & unwitnessed roving, constant exposure and danger, the absolute necessity of relying alone upon their own personal strength and resources, create a very singular compound of astonishing quickness of perception & a reckless confidence in their own prowess. We have seen more than one hunter of this cast incurably attached to a solitude of labor & danger compared with which Robinson Crusoes sojourn on his island was but a pastoral experiment—A lonely hunter cast upon the elements, with nothing but praries & mountains in view, without bread ∧↑or↓ ⟨&⟩ salt & every hour in jeopardy from beasts & savages ⟨amidst scenery & dangers⟩ trusting to no divinity but his knife & gun building all his plans for the future on his traps, regarding the footstep of man imprinted in the sand an object of calculating apprehension, and almost equally dreading the face of the white man & the savage, in situations thus ∧↑lonely &↓ exposed, braves the heat of summer & the ices of winter, the grizzly bear & robbers of his own race and the savages for years. When he has collected a sufficient number of packs of beaver he fells a hollow tree, slides it into some full mountain stream & paddles down the thousand leagues of the missouri & is seen bustling about the streets of St Louis to make bargains for his furs.

Flint[20]

Prarie Wolf. Gray. Sharp nose form somewhat resembling the fox Bold, fierce, cunning, mischievous—In their bark & howl resemble the domestic dog. Sometimes travel in packs—When they bark at night the house dogs retreat to the cabin door—whine & paw for admittance[21]

19. Flint, *Mississippi Valley*, I, 68–69.

20. *Ibid.*, pp. 69–70.

21. *Ibid.*, p. 71.

Prairie dog—Sometimes twice the size of a gray squirrel—have well beaten highways from which every impediment is carefully removed. In mild weather ⟨the⟩ sport about the mouths of their habitations having much of the sprightliness, activity & Spirit of defiance of the squirrel.

When overtaken, away from its home, this little animal shows all the impotent fierceness of a small cur. But when taken it easily domesticates, & becomes gentle and affectionate.

Flint[22]

Birds It is remarked in the more populous & cultivated districts of the west that in proportion as the wilderness disappears & is replaced by apple, pear, peach & plumb trees and fruit gardens, the birds which cheered the infancy of the immigrants, and whose notes are associated with the recollec-/-tion of the charms of youthful existence, & the tender remembrances of the natal Spot, and a distant and forsaken country, are found among the recent orchards.[23]

———

Nightingale Sparrow pours from its little throat a powerful song, like that of the nightingale. In the southern regions of the Mississippi valley like the mockingbird, it sings through the warm nights of Summer, only during the darkness & the dawn of morning.[24]

Owls. ‸↑many varieties↓ Their hooting & screaming in every variety of tone & sound, often imitating the cry of human distress & laughter & sometimes the shrieks of a babe, are heard over all this valley in the deep forests & bottoms. We have heard forty at a time on the lower courses of the Mississippi.[25]

———

Swan—their noise on the wing is like the distant sound of a trumpet.[26]

The noise of countless flocks of Swans Geese & Ducks as they journey through the air in the Spring, to the sources of the great rivers & lakes and in autumn, to the Gulf of Mexico, is one of the most familiar sounds to the ear of an Inhabitant of the West, and one of his pleasantest associations with Spring & autumn.[27]

[*p. [13] blank*]

22. *Ibid.*, p. 74.
23. *Ibid.*
24. *Ibid.*, p. 76.
25. *Ibid.*
26. *Ibid.*, p. 77.
27. *Ibid.*, pp. 76–77.

Lenape tribe[28]—about the Shawungunk mountains[29]

Points & Islands of timber—the wooded projections & scattered stumps of trees are called, which give the plains the appearance of vast parks with ornamental trees artificially arranged to beautify the prospect. Nothing can exceed the beauty of these vast natural meadows in the Spring & summer season.

[*unrecovered*] Holly[30]

Texas—The surface is beautifully & often fancifully diversified[?] with prarie & woodland, presenting to the enterprizing farmer large and fertile fields already cleared by the hand of nature & waiting, as it were, to receive the plough.

Idem.

North of this mountain range & on the extreme head waters of the Brazos river, the country becomes level again & presents to the view interminable praries. These stretch away to the N & NW beyond Red & Arkansaw river and are finally lost in the vast ocean of Prarie that terminates at the foot of the Rocky Mountains

idem

The inland trade now passes in large caravans from St Louis in Missouri to St Fe in NMexico, then a wilderness infested with Indians.

Comanches on horseback—bow & arrows—long spear with a sword blade for point—dart forwd in columns like lightning—divide into two squadrons one half to right the other half to left—& surround their prey.

idem

28. See p. 126, n. 162 for a discussion of the Delaware, or Lenápe Indians.
29. See p. 186, n. 32 for a discussion of the Shawangunk Mountains.
30. The initial name of the author of this source could be "Mrs," "Thos," "Wm," or "Mry"; the writer whom WI cited may be Mary Austin Holley, a cousin and the fiancée of Stephen Fuller Austin (1793–1836), the Father of Texas. By 1831, when Mary Holley visited Texas, there were 5,600 Anglo-Americans in the colony which was initiated only a decade earlier; interest in the Texas question was heightened in 1833 when Austin went to Mexico to present a state constitution and was imprisoned and held for two years. Also, by this time, General Sam Houston had removed to Texas. Mary Austin Holley wrote the first history of Texas in English, and her small book of impressions was published as *Texas: Observations, Historical, Geographical and Descriptive, in a Series of Letters* (Baltimore: Armstrong & Plaskitt, 1833); an enlarged version was published as *Texas* (Lexington, Ky.: J. Clark & Co., 1836).

[*p. [16] and inside back cover blank*]

[*back cover*]

no 1
Notes concerning
the Far West
1833

AMERICAN NOTEBOOKS, 1833

Number 2

Notes Concerning the Far West

This manuscript notebook is in the Seligman Collection of Irvingiana in the Manuscripts and Archives Division of the New York Public Library, where it is cataloged as #22–1576, Washington Irving Notebooks, Volume 7, one of four notebooks boxed together. Its cover, a rust, yellow and off-white mottled cardboard is of a slightly different design from the other three notebooks in this series. Its sixteen pages measure 3⁷⁄₁₆ x 5¹³⁄₁₆ inches; it is tied between leaves 4 and 5 with off-white string. The writing throughout is in brown ink; the inside back cover and the back cover are blank. On the front cover is pasted a piece of off-white paper containing notebook number, title, and the year. The inside front cover has, in addition to handwritten information, a leather bookplate of gold leaf with the words "Ex Libris Robert Hoe."

[*front cover*]

West
2
No 2.
Notes Concerning
the Far West
1833[1]

[*inside front cover*]

Memoranda by
Washington Irving
of
Sunnyside

———

1. WI wrote "18⟨2[?]⟩33." The four lines, beginning with "No 2.," are written on a piece of paper pasted to the cover.

Tour of the Prairies[2]

———

[*p. [1]*]

The Horse between the Rocky Mounts & Pacific are of an excellent race, lofty, elegantly formed, active and durable. Many of them appear like fine English ⟨Hunters⟩ Coursers Some are pied with large Spots of white irregularly Scattered and intermixed with a dark brown bey the greater part, however, are of an uniform colour, marked with Stars and white feet, and resembling in fleetness & bottom, as well as in form and colour, the best blooded horses of Virginia

Lewis & Clark[3]

Buzzard as we label the largest bird of North America—Seen by Lewis & Clark on the Columbia River.[4]

———

The Love of Gain is the Indians ruling passion & the fear of pun-/-ishment must form the corrective.

The native justice of the Indian mind will always give way to his impatience for the possession of the goods of the defenceless merchant and he will plunder him unless[5] prevented by the fear of punishment.[6]

The Osages are among the largest and best formed Indians and are said to possess fine military capacities, but residing as they do in villages and having made considerable advance in agriculture, they seem less addicted to war than their northern neigh-/-bors, to whom the use of rifles gives a great superiority.

According to universal belief the founder of the nation was a snail passing a quiet existence along the banks of the Osage till a high flood

2. WI set off this line with lines $2\frac{9}{16}$ inches and 1⅞ inches long; following the second line is a bookplate.

3. In this notebook, WI copied closely from the Lewis and Clark journals (see the September 13, 1832, journal entry for WI's meeting with General Clark). Because WI noted only the authors of his source, giving neither volume nor page numbers, it is impossible to determine which edition of the journals he used; in identifying the references, we have used Elliott Coues' edition of the *History of the Expedition under the Command of Lewis and Clark* (see p. 60, n. 108 for earlier citation). This initial passage regarding horses is from Coues, ed., *Lewis and Clark*, III, 840.

4. *Ibid.*, II, 679. Throughout this notebook, WI separated passages by skipping lines or drawing lines (in order) of one-half, seven-sixteenths, nine-sixteenths, one-fourth, three-fourths, seven-eighths, one-half, three-eighths, 1⅞, and three-fourths inches long.

5. There is an ink blot above and to the right of "unless."

6. Coues, ed., *Lewis and Clark*, III, 1238, 1239.

swept him down to the Missouri & left him exposed on the shore. The heat of the sun at length ripened him into a man, but with the change of his nature he had not forgotten his native seat on the Osage towards which he immediately bent his way. He was, however, Soon ove[r]taken by hunger & fatigue, when happily the Great Spirit appeared and giving him a bow and arrow, Shewed him how to kill and cook deer, and cover himself with the skin. He then proceeded to his original residence, but as he approached the river, he was met by a beaver, who inquired haughtily who he was, and by what authority he came to disturb his possession. The Osage replied that the river was his own, for he had once lived on its borders. As they stood disputing the daughter of the beaver came and having by her entreaties reconciled her father to this young stranger, it was proposed that the osage should marry the young beaver, and share with her family the enjoyment of the river. The Osage readily consented, and from this happy union there soon came the village ⟨of⟩ & nation of the Wasbasha, or Osages, who have ever since preserved a pious reverence for their ancestors, abstaining from the chase of the beaver, because, in killing that animal they killed a brother of the osage[.] Of late years, however, since the trade with the whites has rendered beaver skins more valuable, the sanctity of these maternal relatives has visibly reduced, and the poor animals have nearly lost all the privileges of kindred.

Lewis & Clarke.[7]

Pawnees.[8] This people were among the most numerous of the Missouri Indians but have gradually been dispersed & broken & even since the year 1797 have undergone some sensible changes.

4 bands. One on the Platte river 500 men to whom of late years have been added the 2d band[—]Republican Pawnees from having lived on the Republican branch of the Kansas. 250 men.

3d Pawnee Loups residing on the Wolf fork of the Platte about 90 miles from the principal pawnees 280 men.

4th band resided on the Kansas and Arkansaw, but were so often defeated by the osages that they at last retired to their present position on the Red River where they form a tribe of 400 men. All these tribes live in villages & raise corn, but during the intervals of culture rove in the plains in quest of the Buffalo.

L & Clarke[9]

---

7. *Ibid.*, I, 12–13.
8. WI used double underlining.
9. Coues, ed., *Lewis and Clark*, I, 55–57.

Mountain of little people, or Little Spirits near White Stone river little devils in human form 18 inches long with remarkably large heads[—] they are armed with sharp arrows with which they are very skillful and are always on the watch to kill those who have the hardihood to approach their dwelling.—Many have suffered from these little evil spirits, and among others, three Maha Indians fell a Sacrifice to them a few years since. They have inspired all the neighboring nations[—]Sioux, Mahas, and Ottoes, with such terror that no consideration could tempt them to visit the hill.

L & Clark[10]

Prarie dog One of them dislodged by 5 barrels of water poured in their hole.

We discovered two frogs in one hole and near it a dark rattlesnake which had swallowed a small prarie dog.[11]

Antelope Wonderfully fleet. Shy timid, generally repose on ridges which command a view of all the approches of an enemy. Acuteness of their sight distinguishes the most distant danger[—]the delicate sensibility of their smell defeats the precautions of concealment & when alarmed their rapid career seems more like the flight of birds than the movements of an earthly being.[12]

wolves hurl them into the water

Rocky Mounts—Their general course is from S East to the north of NW. & they seem to consist of several ranges which successively rise above each other till the most distant mingles with the clouds.[13]

at present Covd. with snow.

Gates of the Rocky Mounts. For five & ¾ miles these rocks rise per-/ pendicularly from the waters edge to the height of near 1200 feet. Black granite near the base & lighter above—upper part appears to be flint of a yellowish brown & cream colour. nothing can be imagined more tremendous than the frowning darkness of these rocks, which project over the river & menace us with distruction[.] River 150 yards in width Seems to have forced its channel down this solid mass, but so reluctantly has it given way that during the whole distance the water is

10. *Ibid.*, p. 86.
11. *Ibid.*, p. 111.
12. *Ibid.*, p. 120.
13. Although not using the exact words of Lewis and Clark, WI may have been referring to the July 14, 1804, entry (Coues, ed., *Lewis and Clark,* II, 412).

deep even at the edges & for the first three miles there is not a Spot except one of a few yards in which a man could stand between the water and the towering perpendicular of the ⟨water⟩ mountain. at the outlet there are vast columns of rock torn from the mountain, which are strewn on both sides of the river[—]the trophies as it were of the victory.[14]

Submission Lewis ove[r]taking three ⟨f⟩ Indian females in a deep ravine one of them a young woman immedi-/-ately took to flight, the other two an elderly woman and a little girl seeing we were too near for them to escape, sat down on the ground, and, holding down their heads, seemed as if reconciled to the death which they supposed awaited them. The same habit of holding down the head and inviting the enemy to strike, when all chance of escape is gone, is preserved in Egypt to this day.

"[15]

Ringing the antelope. About 20 Indians mounted on fine horses, & armed with bows & arrows, ⟨left the⟩ separated into little squads of two or three & formed a scattered circle round a herd of antelopes for 5 or 6 miles keeping at a wary distance. Having gaind their position a small party rode towards the herd & with wonderful dexterity the huntsman preserved his seat, & the horse his footing, as he ran at full Speed over the hills & down the Steep ravines & along the borders of the precipices. They were soon outstripped by the antelopes which on gaining the other extremity of the circle were driven back and pursued by fresh hunters—They turned and flew rather than ran in another direction, but there, too, they found new enemies. In this way they were alternately pursued backwards and forwards, &c—[16]

Shoshone Shield—a circular piece of buffalo hide, about two feet four or five inches in diameter, ornamented with feathers & a fringe round it of dressed leather, and adorned or deformed with paintings of strange figures. The buffalo hide is proof against any arrow, but in the minds of the Sho-/-shonees, its power to protect them is chiefly derived from virtue commu-/-nicated to it by the old men & jugglers

To make a shield is one of their most important ceremonies and begins by a feast to which all the warriors, old men & jugglers are

14. *Ibid.*, pp. 425–426. The concluding four lines of this page are difficult to read because the ink from the following page has blotted on this one.

15. *Ibid.*, pp. 488–89. WI used a ditto mark here, varying from his pattern of "idem."

16. *Ibid.*, p. 496. WI did not go on to report that the antelope finally escaped.

invited– –operation of dressing it continues several days after which the old men & jugglers declare it proof against the arrows & sometimes even the bullets of the enemy.[17]

———

Indian Horse—Halter of several strands of buffalo hair plaited or twisted together about the size of a mans finger & of great strength, or merely a thong of rawhide made pliant by pounding & rubbing. Halter very long—never taken from the neck of the horse when in constant use. one and two round the neck in a ⟨noose[?]⟩ knot & then brought down under the jaw, round which it is formed into a simple noose passing through the mouth; it is then drawn upon the right side & held by the rider in his left hand, while the rest trails on the ground. This cord remains round the neck when the horse is turned loose to graze

The horse becomes an object of attacht[—]a favorite is frequently painted & his ears cut into various shapes. the mane & tail, which are never drawn nor trimmed are decorated with feathers of birds & sometimes a warrior suspends on the breast of his horse the finest ornaments he possesses.[18]

———

The Antelope This fleet and quick sighted animal is generally the victim of its curiosity; when they first see the hunters they run with great velocity; if he lies down on the ground and lifts up his arms, his hat, or his foot, the antelope returns on a light trot to look at the object, & sometimes goes and returns two or three times, till they ap-/-proach within reach of the rifle; so too they sometimes leave their flock to go and look at the wolves who crouch down & if the antelope be frightened at first repeat the same maneuvre, and sometimes relieve each other till they decoy it from the party, when they seize it. But generally the wolves take them as they are crossing the rivers—for although swift of foot they are not good swimmers

Idem[19]

———

Snowy mountains. They glisten with great beauty when the sun shines on them in a particular direction, & most probably from this glittering appearance have derived the name of the Shining Mountains.[20]

———

Noise in the Mountains Since our arrival at the falls we have repeat-

17. *Ibid.,* pp. 560–61.
18. *Ibid.,* pp. 562–63.
19. *Ibid.,* I, 291.
20. *Ibid.,* II, 401.

edly heard a strange noize coming from the mountains in a direction a little to the north of west. It is heard at different periods of the day and night, sometimes when the air is perfectly Still & without a cloud & consists of one stroke only, or of five or six discharges in quick succession, It is loud and resembles precisely the sound of a Six pound piece[?] of advance[?] at the distance of three miles. The Minatarees frequently mentioned this noise like thunder which they said the mountains made; but we had paid no attention to it, believing it to have been some superstition, or perhaps a falsehood. The watermen[?] also of the party say that the Pawnees & Ricaras give the same acount of a noise heard in the Black Mountains to the westward of them. They attribute it to the breathing[?] of the rich mines of silver confined within the bosom of the mountain.[21]

The Mandans believe in one Great Spirit presiding over their destinies. This being must be in the nature of a Good genius since it is associated with the healing art, and the great spirit is synonymous with great medicine a name also applied to every thing which they do not comprehend. Each individual selects for himself the particular object of his devotion, which is considered his medicine, and is either some invisible being or more commonly some animal, which thenceforth becomes his protector or his intercessor with the Great Spirit, to propitiate whom every attention is lavished and every personal consideration is sacrificed. "I was lately owner of seventeen horses" said a Mandan to us one day "but I have offered them all up to my medicine and am now poor." He had in reality taken all his wealth, his horses, into the plain and turning them loose committed them to the care of his medicine and abandoned them forever. The horses, less religious, took care of themselves, and the pious votary travelled home on foot.[22]

White Mountains [*unrecovered*][23] Indian name Agivcochook[?]. There is a curious tradition preserved in [*unrecovered*][24] New England of the veneration of the Indians for the summits of these mountains. They considered them as the dwelling places of invisible beings & never ventured to ascend them. They had also a tradition that the whole country was once drowned with all its inhabitants except one Indian with his

21. *Ibid.*, pp. 402–03.
22. *Ibid.*, I, 207–08.
23. There may be two unrecovered words.
24. This word seems to begin with the letters "poccal."

wife, who foreseeing the flood, fled to these mountains, were preserved & afterwards repeopled the country.

Note to Thatcher[?][25]

Indian [*unrecovered*][26]
A wonderous night! for [? 'ore his gear ice ?]
with brandled[?] wolves, all harnessed[?] then[?] & ⟨*illegible*⟩ there
High seated on a Sledge, made in a triar[?]
On[?] Mount Agivcochook, of hickory,
He lashed & realed & sung right jollily;
And once[?] upon a car of flaming fire.
The dreadful Indian shook with fear to see
The King of Panacook, his chief, his sire
Ride flaming up towards heaven, than any mountain higher.*[27]

* See F and M. His Coll.

[*inside back cover and back cover blank*]

25. This source has not been identified; WI may have referred to James Thacher (1754–1844), a physician and author born in Massachusetts, and a patriot who witnessed the execution of Major John André (see p. 192, n. 69); Thacher kept a journal from 1775 until 1783 which was published in 1824, and among his books on medicine and history was *Essay on Demonology, Ghosts and Apparitions,* published in 1831.

26. These two underlined words seem to be the title of a nine-line poem, of which many of the words are unrecovered, illegible, or questioned; therefore, the poem is unintelligible.

27. The asterisk is WI's; it refers to the note on the line below in which he cited his, as yet unidentified, source.

AMERICAN NOTEBOOKS, 1833

Number 3

Notes Concerning the Far West

This manuscript notebook is in the Seligman Collection of Irvingiana in the Manuscripts and Archives Division of the New York Public Library, where is it cataloged as #22–1576, Washington Irving Notebooks, Volume 7, one of four notebooks boxed together.[1] The sixteen pages of notebook 3 measure 3⁷⁄₁₆ x 5¹³⁄₁₆ inches and are written throughout in brown ink; the back cover is blank. On the front cover is pasted a piece of off-white paper containing the notebook number, title, and year. The inside front cover has, in addition to handwritten information, a leather bookplate of gold leaf with the words "Ex Libris Robert Hoe."

[*front cover*]

West
3
No 3
Notes Concerning
the Far West,
1833[2]

[*inside front cover*]

Memoranda by
Washington Irving
of
Sunnyside

———

Tour of the Prairies[3]

———

1. See description of notebook 1. Notebooks 1, 3, and "Notes on Indians" are identical regarding cover, size, color, and arrangement of lines of the paper.

2. Beginning with "No 3," these four lines are written on a piece of paper pasted to the cover.

3. WI set off this portion of the title by lines of 2⁵⁄₁₆ inches above and below; in the middle of the page is the bookplate.

[*p. [1]*]
That imaginary region of happiness & contentment, which, like the "town of the brave and generous Spirits," the expected heaven of the aboriginal American, lies always "beyond the place where the sun goes down."

Long. Vol. 1. P 17[4]

The Occidental Plane tree (Syca-/more) is, perhaps, the grandest of the American forest trees, and little inferior in any respect to the boasted Plane tree of the Levant The Platanus Orientales attains a diameter of from 10 to 16 feet An American Plane tree on the Ohio measured 14 feet in diameter[5]

Indian Mounds.

The Survey of these productions of human industry[,] these monuments without inscription, commemorating the existence of a people once numerous and powerful but no longer known and remembered, never fails, though often repeated, to produce an impression of sadness. As we stand upon these mouldering piles, many of them now nearly obliterated we cannot but compare their aspect of decay with the

4. In this notebook, WI quoted or very closely paraphrased Edwin James, *Account of an Expedition from Pittsburgh to the Rocky Mountains, performed in the Years 1819, 1820 . . . under the Command of Maj. S. H. Long*, originally published in three volumes in London (Longman, Hurst, Rees, Orme, and Brown, 1823) and in the same year in Philadelphia. The account of Major Stephen Harriman Long is included in four volumes of Reuben Gold Thwaites, ed., *Early Western Travels 1748–1846* (Cleveland: Arthur H. Clark, 1905), vols. 14–17. The page numbers which WI sometimes cited apparently refer to the American edition of Long, as they do not coincide with the pages in brackets in Thwaite's edition which refer to the London edition. Stephen Harriman Long (1784–1864), born in New Hampshire, was a career military officer; he joined the U.S. Army Corps of Engineers in 1814, was an assistant professor of mathematics at West Point, and spent the major portion of his professional life in the Topographical Engineers (from 1818 until his retirement in 1863 after he had attained the rank of colonel). In addition to this expedition to the Rocky Mountains, he led another in 1823–1824 to discover the sources of the Mississippi River; he also surveyed the routes of the Baltimore and Ohio Railroad and the Western and Atlantic Railroad in Georgia. In *Col. Long's Report to the Estillville Convention* (July 16, 1831) were the findings of a survey "of a route for a road leading across the entire range of the Alleghany Mountains. . . ."

This initial passage from Long regarding the village of Olean down the Alleghany and Ohio Rivers is found in Thwaites, ed., *Long*, XIV, 59 (London, I, 15); subsequent references to Long in this edition of WI's notebook will be to the Thwaites edition; in parentheses, will be cited volume and page numbers in the London edition of Long.

5. Thwaites, ed., *Long*, XIV, 68–69 (London, I, 21).

freshness of the wide field of nature, which we see reviving around us, their insig-/-nificance with the majestic and imperishable features of the landscape.

Long. V.1.P ⟨*illegible*⟩↓66[?]↑[6]

White hunters. A party of white hunters were encamped on the Missouri. In the rudeness of their deportment and dress they appeared to us to surpass the savages themselves. They are usually the most abandoned and worthless among the whites, who adopt the life of wandering hunters; frequently they are men whose crimes have excluded them from society.

Long. V 1. P 110[7]

Thunder. When a man is killed in battle the thunder is supposed to take him up, they "do not know where. In going to battle each man traces an imaginary figure ⟨of the thunder on the Soil and he who represents it incorrectly is Killed by the thunder. A person saw this thunder one day on the ground with a beautiful moccasin on each side of it; having much need of a pair he took them and went his way; but on his return by the same spot the thunder took him off and he has not since been heard of⟩

Long. V 1.[8]

⟨State of the dead⟩

Future state Thinking the deceased has far to travel they bury with his body mockasins some articles of food &c to support him on the journey.[9]

Ghosts. Many persons they ⟨think⟩ believe, have become reanimated, who had been, during their apparent death, in Strange Villages, but as the inhabitants used them ill they returned. They say they have never seen the *Master of Life* and therefore cannot pretend to personify him, but they have often heard him speak in the thunder.[10]

---

6. *Ibid.*, pp. 120–21 (London, I, 59–60); the illegible number, obscured by an ink blot, could be "110," "60," "66," "40," or some other number.

7. *Ibid.*, p. 174 (London, I, 102).

8. *Ibid.*, p. 194 (London, I, 117). WI used a large *X* to cross out the passage; following this passage, and throughout the notebook, WI separated topics by skipping lines or drawing lines (in their order) of five-sixteenths, five-sixteenths, one-half, one-half, three-fourths, five-eighths, eleven-sixteenths, one-fourth, three-eighths, one-fourth, eleven-sixteenths, and one-fourth inches long.

9. Thwaites, ed., *Long*, XIV, 195 (London, I, 117–18).

10. *Ibid.* (London, I, 118).

Smoke from burning[11] *praries.* It some-/times affected our vision painfully, and so far intercepted the rays of the sun that the disk of that luminary appeared of a blood red and the eye could repose upon it uninjured.[12]

The celebrated ⟨chief⟩ Omawhaw chief Blackbird was (agreeably to his orders) interred in a Sitting pos-/ture, on his favorite horse, upon the Summit of a high bluff of the Missouri, thus he might continue to see the White people ascending the river to trade with his nation. A mound was raised over his remains on which food was regularly placed for many years afterwards; but this rite has been discontinued, and the staff that on its summit supported a white flag, has no longer exis-/tence.

Long, V. 1. 226[13]

Town of brave & generous Spirits: ⟨the⟩ or ⟨*illegible*⟩ Wanoch-a-te. Here those are received after death who have conducted themselves properly—by Killing enemies—Stealing horses or doing acts of generosity—but those who have done otherwise, go to the town of poor and useless Spirits[14]

Wahconda, a great Spirit, appears in different Shapes—Grizzly ⟨bear[?]⟩ bison[?] beaver—owl &c all who see & converse with him become Medicine men or magicians—[15]

The Sioux pretend[16] that a hill near Whitestone River is inhabited by a small and dangerous race of people about 18 inches high with remarkably large heads, who having killed three Omahaws a few years since, have inspired all the neighbouring Indians with a superstitious dread. Lewis & Clark visited the haunted hill but were happy enough to escape the vengeance of its Lilliputian inhabitan[t]s

Long. P 275 V1.[17]

The Minnatarees believe that they formerly lived underground. "Two boys" say they "strayed away from them and absented themselves sev-

11. The initial letter of "burning" may be written over another, perhaps a *c*; in Long, the word is "conflagrated."
12. Thwaites, ed., *Long*, XIV, 263 (London, I, 160).
13. *Ibid.*, pp. 317–18 (London, I, 204–05).
14. *Ibid.*, XV, 51–52 (London, I, 246).
15. *Ibid.*, p. 52 (London, I, 247).
16. The original reading is "have a belief"; WI's paraphrase changed the meaning.
17. The "5" of "275" is written over an illegible number. Thwaites, ed., *Long*, XV, 60 (London, I, 254).

eral days. At length they returned and informed the nation that they had discovered another world, situate above their present residence where all was beautiful and light. They saw the Sun the ⟨Moon⟩ earth the Missouri and the Bison. This account so delighted the people that they immediately abandoned their Subterranean dwelling and, led by the boys, arrived on the surface of the earth at the spot which their villages now occupy & where they have dwelt ever since.

idem.[18]

Cook what meat you have says the Omawhaw to his squaw, for the Wahconda will give us more tomorrow, and if not tomorrow, next day, and if never, let us eat what we have got.—

Long[19]

Their geographical knowledge of the country over which they roam is remarkably exact. They know ever[?][20] river, inlet & creek, together with their courses & distances

Altho remarkably accurate in their knowledge of the proper direction in which to travel yet they are often lost during foggy days & during heavy Snow Storms[21]

The Indians are cruel horse masters perhaps in a great measure through necessity. The backs of their horses often sore from friction of rude saddle fashioned after the Spanish manner—Ride well[—]make great use of whip & heel. The former attached to wrist by a broad band passing thro a hole perforated towards the end of the handle—Lash two thongs of bison skin plaited or interlaced[22]

Dogs—mixed breed, between ours & a native breed with ears erect[23]

The Pawnee Loups make propitia-/-tory offerings of human victims to Venus, the Great Star—performed annually previous to their horti-/-cultural operations—abolished by their present chief.[24]

18. *Ibid.*, p. 64 (London, I, 258–59).
19. *Ibid.*, p. 72 (London, II, 6).
20. The original read, "intimately every river and creek in the vicinity . . ." (Thwaites, ed., *Long*, XV, 75 [London, II, 9]).
21. *Ibid.*, p. 76 (London, II, 10).
22. *Ibid.*, pp. 78–79 (London, II, 12–13).
23. *Ibid.*, 79 (London, II, 13); the dogs to which Long referred were those of the Konzas.
24. *Ibid.*, pp. 151–53 (London, II, 80–82); this Indian chief was Latelesha, or the Knife Chief, reported to be "mild and humane."

Coquimbo or burrowing owl—of a Social disposition, does not retire from the light of the sun but endures ⟨the⟩ ↑its↓ strongest mid day glare and is in all respects a diurnal bird. It stands high upon its legs and flies with the rapidity of the hawk. Have a note like that of the Prarie dog—Supposed that the dog is tutor to the young owl— —rather vice versa[25]

Wild horses The most timorous & ⟨most[?]⟩ watchful of the inhabitants of the wilderness. Attached to each others society though the males are occasionally found at a distance from the herd.[26]

———

Village of prarie dogs. area of a mile square—herd of buffalo grazing —wild horses—deer—Marmots sporting about—as we approached they perched themselves in their burrows & gave the note of alarm.[27]

———

Bees rarely if ever seen more than 250 miles in advance of white Settlements.[28]

Cottonwood tree—so called[29] from downy appendage to the seed which floats in the air in may & June The branches of the tree not ⟨very⟩[30] numerous & have less tendency to pyramidal form than those of almost any other tree[31]

———

We recd. blows & bruises from the canes & had our ↑sweaty↓ hands & faces scratched by rough leaves—our feet entangled by flexible & spiny stalks of green briar[32]

———

Shiennes or Shawneys have no permanent town but rove in pursuit of the herds of bisons in the vicinity of the Platte Arkansa and Red river. They are habitually at war with all the nations of the Missouri.[33]

———

25. *Ibid.*, XVI, 27–29 (London, II, 226–27).
26. *Ibid.*, p. 130 (London, II, 313).
27. *Ibid.*, pp. 158–59 (London, III, 10–11).
28. *Ibid.*, p. 160 (London, III, 12).
29. WI failed to lift his pen between these words; he may have intended one or two words or a hyphenated word.
30. This crossed-out word could be "many"; an ink blot obscures it.
31. WI here quoted from a note written by Edwin James (Thwaites, ed., *Long*, XVI, 177, n. 84 [London, III, 27, n.]).
32. *Ibid.*, p. 182 (London, III, 30–31).
33. *Ibid.*, p. 211 (London, III, 53).

Wild[34] Horse—readily distin-/guishes the native from the white man by his accute sense of Smelling.[35]

———

Owl—the burrows they inhabited appeared fallen in[,] delapidated[,] like ruins[—]fit abodes for serpents lizards & owls[36]

———

The harsh & guttural noise of the bison, shrill bark & scream of Prarie wolf & howl of white wolf.[37]

Not a human being to be perceived. It seemed for a moment that our little cavalcade alone was endowed with the vital principle & that the vegetable world held a ^↑Solitary &↓ Silent dominion[38]

———

Osage Vespers—National lamen-/tations—[39]

———

It is remarked by hunters that the most remote & elevated sources of all the rivers of this region are in & near extensive woodless plains.[40]

———

Prevailing timber. Cotton wood Willow Sycamore blk walnut peccan Coffee tree, Sweet & sour black gum red & water elm, ash linden yellow & white poplar—catalpa—blk & honey locust—buck eye—bur oak white & blk oak mulberry, white & sugar maple red oak hickory Iron wood—white dogwood—box[,] elder.[41]

[*inside back cover*]
Kaskaia indians, with leather lodges—roam throughout the range of the Rocky Mountains[—]warfare[?] bow & arrow lance war club & shield—fight on horseback.[42]

———

The condition of the savages constant alarm & apprehension. In times of profound peace whether at their villages or on hunting expeditions

34. An ink blot from the previous page makes the word appear crossed out, which does not appear to have been WI's intention.
35. Thwaites, ed., *Long*, XVI, 215 (London, III, 57).
36. *Ibid.*, p. 223 (London, III, 64).
37. *Ibid.*, p. 224 (London, III, 65).
38. *Ibid.*, p. 260 (London, III, 96).
39. *Ibid.*, p. 267 (London, III, 102–03).
40. *Ibid.*, XVII, 52 (London, III, 155).
41. *Ibid.*, pp. 115–16 (London, III, 208).
42. *Ibid.*, pp. 157–58 (London, III, 246).

continually on the alert—by day scouts patrol for a considerable distance around them—at night centinels are posted.[43]

[*back cover blank*]

43. *Ibid.*, p. 166 (London, III, 253[?]).

CONSULAR INFORMATION

Notes on Correspondence Regarding Trade U. S., Spain (1842)

This manuscript notebook is in the Arents Collection of the New York Public Library where it is cataloged by title as "Consular Information, Orig. MS, W. Irving [ca. 1842]"; by accession number as 4377; and by catalog number as 1450–A. Its sixteen leaves have no cover, and it is held together with a thin blue ribbon tied between leaves 8 and 9; it is enclosed in a red cardboard folder in three sections which then fits into a red cardboard slip case with a red leather spine. Its off-white, gilt-edged pages measure 4 7/16 x 7 1/4 inches; there is a stamped impression in the upper left corner of leaves 1–5: "SUPERFINE" and a figure within an oval. With only one exception, Irving has written only on the verso; therefore, blank are pages [2], [6], [8], [10], [12], [14], [16], [18], [20], [22], [24], [26], [28], [30], and [32]; the writing throughout is in brown ink.

[*p. 1*][1]

Consular information[2]
letters *of Geo Read Am. Consul*[3]—Feb. 7 } 1842
23 }

1. WI numbered this page in the top right corner "1."
2. WI used double underlining (the pen tip may have divided under pressure). WI had been commissioned on February 10, 1842, as envoy extraordinary and minister plenipotentiary to Spain; he accepted by letter on February 18, and Secretary of State Daniel Webster's initial full letter of instructions was sent to him on March 19. (For this letter and ten of WI's diplomatic letters from Spain from March 10, 1843 [no. 17], until July 18, 1846 [no. 83], see William R. Manning, ed., *Diplomatic Correspondence of the United States: Inter-American Affairs, 1831–1860*, vol. 11, *Spain: Documents 5033–5678* [Washington: Carnegie Endowment for International Peace, 1939], pp. 25–26, 331–58; hereafter cited as Manning, ed., *Spain: Dip. Corresp.*) WI "took leave" from the legation on July 29, 1846 (*ibid.*, p. 25, n. 5).
3. George Read, from Pennsylvania, was confirmed as U.S. consul in Málaga, Spain, on January 18, 1839, and served until about 1852 (the next consul was con-

Malaga The Spanish vessels which have gone hence to the US. principally belong to Catalonia & come here having on board parts of Cargo the produce of that province, completing their lading with productions of Andalusia & trade entirely with the Southern ports. The return trade ⟨of⟩ ↑for↓ these vessels cannot be made from the UStates with our produce and these vessels almost never come back direct to this port. They dispose[?] of their outward adventures & then go to Cuba or Perto[4] Rico for the produce of these islands or for cotton which may have been conveyed there in Am: bottoms, & so home to the manufactures of Catalonia. When such is the disad-/-vantage under which the national flag labors that it cannot return home ⟨fr[?]⟩ with produce of the country that consumes her productions, how much more so must it be for that of the U.S.

[*p. [2] blank*][5]

It will be seen that only [*blank*] Spanish vessels have brought home the produce of the US. during the last four years to this port. There is scarcely a nation on Earth, China perhaps excepted, in which there exists so little reciprocity in its commercial intercourse with other nations. ⟨and as regards the U S. this is palpably evident from inspection of the ⟨*illegible*⟩ returns⟩ Spain has always presented an Exclusive policy from the earliest periods. Exclusive in her religion, Exclusive ⟨in⟩[6] Commerce. She drove out the Moors. She banished the Jews and she would not allow a foreigner to set foot in her Colonies without ⟨a[?]⟩ royal decree[?] & as to Americans ⟨who to⟩ ↑at↓ this day, who are residing more or less among other nations, you will not find two of them resident in Spain unconnected with official employment from their own Government. say so little inducement have they to fix a residence here that even the Consulary[7] appoint/-ments are held in two instances only by Am: Citizens in all the Peninsula.

---

firmed on May 16, 1852). (See *Lists of U.S. Consular Officers, 1789–1939*, National Archives Microfilm Publications, no. 587, in 21 vols.)

4. This word could be "Porta," WI's usual spelling.

5. WI numbered the recto of the following leaf, actually p. [3] and the second with writing, with a "2" in the upper right corner.

6. This word may be blotted out rather than crossed out.

7. This word may be "Consulars."

Tobacco of US. landed at Gibraltar[8]

	Hhds.	Bales	Kegs	boxes
1838.	5816.	3414	862–	346
1839.	6896	1957	406	1481
1840	4395	2193	964	495
	17,107	7564	2232.	2322
Am. Average	5702[9]	2521	744	774

[*p. [5]*][10]

Exports from Malaga direct to US.
in four years prior to 1842.
in Spanish produce—nearly } $4,800,000

Recd. in same port from US.
in produce $387,885
" Specie. 433,854 821,739

The Tobacco sold at Gibraltar goes very materially to pay for the produce of this part of the country sent to the U.S.

Only a Small part of the cotton consumed in Catalonia is for returns exported hence in Spanish vessels from N Orleans; it is the greater part the proceeds of produce carried to Cuba from other provinces of Spain, & may be, even of other countries; as ⟨Am: vessels⟩ for instance ~~Jerked beef taken to Cuba from the river Plate[?] by vessels that may~~ have taken out cargoes in that direction. Am: vessels cannot carry their own cotton to Spain in consequence of high discriminating duties; an extra bonus being allowed to the national ⟨*unrecovered*⟩ flag on this & other articles coming thro' the deposit Stores of Cuba & Porto Rico. The new tariff has not touched the articles of cotton, raw or manufactured.

[*p. [6] blank*][11]

The prohibitory & protective System adopted so universally by Spain proves a total barrier to the introduction of articles the growth & produce

8. Apparently, WI added the following information after he had completed the Read letter; this page [4] is the only verso in the notebook with writing, and WI did not number it. Between the columns of figures, WI drew a squiggled vertical line; he used double underlining for the final figure in each column.

9. WI dropped the fraction "⅓" in this and the following average.

10. WI numbered the following page "3" in the upper right corner.

11. WI numbered the following recto page "4" in the upper right corner.

of U.S. excepting Staves. There has been a reduction in the import duty on this article by the late tariff from about $3.85. to $1.44 pr 1000 Staves American, Roman &c—All sizes now ⟨being⟩ ‸↑having↓ the same duty. Hamburg staves pay double the duty of American; but they are 3 or 4 times the size of an Am: pipe Stave & 6 times the wood of a barrel Stave, generally speaking.

On *Rice* the duty is $3.49 ‸↑pr 100 lbs↓ under national flag & ⟨4⟩$.4.61. under foreign. Equal or more than fixd cost & amounting to an entire prohibition

On Naval Stores the duties are small—& of course the discrimg. amount to very little Tar & pitch may be brought but the consump-/tion is small & it is a disadvantage to these articles to remain lying any length of time in a warm climate.[12]

———

Unless the fundamental principles of protection & prohibition be done away with I see no change that can benefit Am. Am: No doubt the 20 pr ct[13] duty imposed on fruit & wines will have

[*p. [8] blank*][14]

a prejudicial effect on this province & indeed it *has* been *severely* felt, this last vintage, not so much by any restriction of consumption, but by reducing the prices on the growers[?] hands & what has greatly tended to produce the effect has been the great abundance of production. So that notwithstanding the duty, the con-/-sumption of fruit has been unusually great in the US. at prices under those of other years when there was no duty. Malaga wines were once in great vogue in US. Consumptn lessens & the prices continually decline. Duty has caused no advance. If Malaga were deprived of the markets of US. the injury would be [*unrecovered*][15] to their wine districts. The great impulse given to them within the last six years is entirely owing to the large consumption of fruits in US. formerly 400 000 Boxes of Raisins was a large crop. This year US has taken 700,000 & had the Southern & Westn States been less embarrassed perhaps more would have gone.

The port charges at Malaga not unreasonable excepting the item for "Cleaning the Mole"[16] which never is cleaned. Within ten years the

12. WI drew a line one-fourth inch long in the left margin to separate paragraphs.
13. The superscript "ct" is not WI's usual *t*.
14. WI numbered the following recto page "5" in the upper right corner.
15. This word may be "worsened."
16. The mole was built in water, a kind of barrier of stone to protect against the waves.

Am Ships have paid upwards of $10,000 on this object without any equivalent.

[p. [10] blank][17]

Bilbao:[18] *Letters—M D. Aguirre 14 Jan, 1842*[19]

Up to the French war in 1808 the ^↑Am↓ trade with this port[?] was very considerable[:] in 1806—79 AM Ships 8,299 tons fully loaded & discharged here

The Am. ^↑carrying[?]↓ trade important during the wars ⟨between⟩ ↑of↓ Spain ^↑with↓ ⟨&⟩ Engd.

In 1818 The importation of Fish (a bulky article) emplo⟨yed⟩ing a good many US.. Ships began to cease & has altogether disappeared from our market—

All other Staple & Colonl. produce contind to be imported, altho on a reduced scale till 1821 when the Custom House was established here & the Am: trade nearly annihilated. In 1823. The priviledges were restored to Biscay & the trade with US. began to revive a little[.] The exports of merino wool had acquired some importance when the heavy import duties laid upon this article in the US. stopped the trade & in consequence the importg[?][20] of whale oil which had become considerable[,] declined almost to nothing

In 1832 the year previous to the civil war 10 vessels only entered from US—7 Am 2 Span 1 foreign. During the war the trade dwindled

[p. [12] blank][21]

to nothing

By the new tariff Colonial produce cannot be imported from foreign countries & therefore Sugars, Cocoas, Hides & other articles formerly

17. WI numbered the recto of the following leaf "6" in the upper right corner.

18. WI used double underlining.

19. The abbreviation for the month may be "Jun." Although Máximo de Aguirre was a Spanish native, he was confirmed as U.S. consul in Bilbao, Spain, on February 10, 1834, and resigned on December 27, 1856 (Manning, ed., *Spain: Dip. Corresp.*, p. 337, n. 1; *Lists of U.S. Consular Officers*). Williams called him "troublesome Máximo Aguirre," a problem WI inherited from the previous consul, Aaron Vail; when Aguirre was fined by his government, he sought and was refused official refuge as a member of the U.S. diplomatic corps. One of the results was some of WI's "best official writing. These well-reasoned and sarcastic letters" are on file in the American embassy in Madrid (STW, II, 136, 383, n. 1).

20. This word may be "exportg."

21. WI numbered the recto of the following leaf "7" in the upper right corner.

imported from the US. are to be erased from the list of the Am: trade. of the Staple articles of US. Fish, oils Rice & Tobacco, The first has been driven completely out of the market by the English & Norwegian Fish. Oils will have to pay 6 Rlba.[?] pr. Arroba[22] & doubtful if it can support competition with Sardinian Oil manufactured in Gallicia. Rice will be excluded by duty of 40 pr Ct. upon the value of $6 pr 100 lb[?][23] of the new tariff. Tobacco is the only remaining article, but this branch precarious—as Govt may confiscate the privilege to farm it out as in rest of Spain

Number of Am: Ships arriving in Billbao

			value of am produce		
1831.	1.	of 144 Tons	Tobacco.	$14,000	None took away cargoes
1839.	2.	– 272	Tobacco & Staves	22 575	
1840.	1.	– 199.	do	25 490	
1841	5	– 748.	" Cod oil Whale oil Tobacco	42 600	

Three Span Ships during the same period—

[p. [14] blank].[24]

Letters from Pablo Anguera 14 Jan 1842[25]

Barcelona No Am. vessel for several years past

Spanish vessels load at N Orleans and other ports of US. call at Havanna or Porto Rico & arrive here as coming from one of the two last ports; bringing a certificate from the Collector of Customs of the intermediate touching[26] port, legalized by the Am. Consul—Stating that nothing had been discharged—

22. An arroba is a unit of liquid measure in Spanish equaling 17.04 quarts of wine and 13.28 quarts of oil.

23. This abbreviation may be "th" or "ct."

24. WI numbered the recto of the following leaf "⟨7⟩8" in the upper right corner.

25. Pablo Anguera, apparently born in New York, was from Catalonia, Spain; he was not confirmed as U.S. consul in Barcelona until August 30, 1850, and served in that position until 1857. In a note dated March 23, 1842, WI added his own name to an official pamphlet which listed consular personnel; at that time the U.S. consul in Barcelona was "A. B. Leonard" (STW, II, 371, n. 119). The *Lists of U.S. Consular Officers* includes J. A. Leonard, confirmed in July, 1840, but sending no dispatches; Paul Pou, confirmed in September, 1842, and served until his death in October, 1846; and Justus Pou, brother of Paul, confirmed in January, 1847, and served until his death in January, 1850.

26. Below this word is a line three-eighths inch long with no apparent significance.

Spanish vessels clearing from ⟨Spanish⟩ ↑this↓ ports only take on[27] here some AM[?]: red wine of very little value, as Ballast & proceed to load at Malaga fruits.

The duty on Cott ‸↑from US↓ (by the new tariff) into this province has been suspended by order of Span Govt. & the old charges are still in full force.

[p. [16] blank][28]

Barccelona

				Produce US.
1838.	15.	Spanish Vessels.		
	3481.	Bales Cot.	8000 Staves 1,302 Hides	$181,457
1839.	2 vessels.	540 Bales Cot.		27,000
1840.	1 "	319 "		15,950

Tarragono

from 1 Jan 1838 to 1 Jan. 1842	
4 Am Ships—Dollars & Staves	$ 20,650
Took away in wine, Brandy & paper	16 000
1 Span Vessel in 1839 wine almonds, nuts	2,700

[p. [18] blank][29]

Alicant letter Arthur M Culloch Consul.[30]

9 March 1842

By the Consular register of 1810 to 1820 I observe large importations of Tobacco, Staves, Fish, Nankeen, Rum, Spice, Flour, Butter, Coffee, Rice, Pepper, Cocoa, Salmon, Cheese, Dye Woods, Tar—Sperm Candles—At present in consequence of the New tariff & differential duties on goods imported in Span & Forgn Bottoms fish & Staves are the only articles of commerce here

27. This word could be "in."
28. WI numbered the recto of the following leaf "9" in the upper right corner.
29. WI numbered the recto of the following leaf "1⟨9⟩0—" in the upper right corner.
30. Benjamin Renshaw was appointed consul in Alicante, Spain, in January, 1835; he did not go but was appointed consul at another post in March. Arthur McCulloch, of Alicante, was appointed acting vice-consul at Alicante by the consul at Barcelona on June 2, 1837, a post he apparently held until August, 1849[?]. The following consul did not receive the archives until May, 1853 (*Lists of U.S. Consular Officers*).

The Expts. were Wines, Brandies, Barilla, Almonds, Raisins, Salt Liquorice, Saffron, Anniseed, Grass Matts, Olive oil, Raw Silk &c These are now reduced to a small quantity of Wine[,] almonds, Grass Matts & liquorice. Many of the other articles are now more abundant in Malaga.

If there were no differential duties the US. would send many articles to Spain which are at present excluded by excessive duties arising from the "Beneficio de Bandera"

Tobacco may be said the only article of importance recd. from US. in Spain & this being a Govt monopoly leaves no advantage to the Merc: community in genl & purchases by Contractors are frequently made in London the great Depot of Tobacco.

[p. [20] blank][31]

⟨T⟩N B.[?] by new Tariff. Oak Staves pay less duty than Roman ^↑oak↓ Staves but the amt of this is trifling[.] Codfish cannot compete in our market with that of the Eng factories & is worth at least 50 cents pr Quintal less than the latter & still pays the same duty [This has been attended to][32]

AM Ships arrived in Alicant

1838.	
–2–478 tons Salt & Staves }	$2673.71
1839.	
3–Staves, Log wood Ballast }	4320[33]
1840	
1–Codfish & Staves	"3076.36[34]
	150
1841	
2. Ballast, Tobacco for Govt Const[?].	68000
	78220. 7[35]

Am Sh. laded in Alicant ^↑for US↓ in same time 7 Ships Wine Matts, Raisins liquorice &c }	$29,237.99/
Only 1 Spanish Ship for US. in that time. Wine. Matts liquorice	6496.24/

31. WI numbered the recto of the following leaf "1⟨0⟩1" and underlined with a quarter circle in the upper right corner.

32. These are WI's brackets written over parentheses.

33. WI actually wrote "$⟨4⟨*illegible*⟩6⟨9⟩20⟩↑4320↓."

34. WI used a ditto mark to indicate the "$"; the numbers "076" were written over illegible numbers.

The trade of this city & province with the US. once more extensive than with any other is now dwindled into insignificance both in imports & exports

[p. [22] blank][36]

⟨*Cadiz.*[37] *Letter* of Alex Burton Consul[38]

31 Jan. 1842

1838.	American Ships with Am prod.	
26.	1492 thousand Staves $80 pr m.	$119 360
1839		
56[?].	Staves. 331 Hhds Tobacco (Sp Gov)	300 860
1840		
21.	Staves	102,160
1841		
32	Staves. 510 Hds Tobacco Sp Gov.	196,760⟩

Other Am Ships, Same year

Am Ships—entered in Cadiz

1838.				
76.	Am prod.	119 360.	Foreign	50,000
1839				
81		300,860		51,000
1840				
70		102,160.	↑many in↓ Ballast	
1841		196,760		54. –
		$719,140		$155 000
		115,000		
		–834,140[39]		

35. WI actually wrote "782⟨7⟩2⟨*illegible*⟩0.[0]7."

36. WI numbered the recto of the following leaf "12" and underlined with a quarter circle in the upper right corner.

37. Beginning with this word, WI crossed out with large looping marks the top half of the page; apparently he wished the retained material to begin with the words "Am Ships—entered in Cadiz."

38. Alexander Burton had spent long hours in conversation with WI when the latter was doing research for the *Conquest of Granada* (1829) in Cádiz in 1828–1829 (STW, I, 333). Burton was confirmed as U.S. consul in Cádiz on April 2, 1824, and resigned on November 28, 1855; he died in Cádiz in 1860.

Am. produce. Staves & some tobacco for Governt Contract.
Foreign produce. Hides from Uruguay
Copper ore–Peru
Cocoa & Cott. Guayaquil
Dye wood–

[*p. [24] blank*][40]

Number of Staves laden in Am Ships is generally about 25 thousand per 100 Tons. price of sale at Cadiz averages about 80$[–]on this the former Statement is founded

From 1838 to present time (Spring of 1842) 3 Swedish & ⟨ab⟩ an equal numbr of Austrian vessels, took in cargoes of Salt & some wine for US. & retd thence with Staves

No Spanish Ships within same time have cleared for the US. or arrived from same Except one[41] ship did 1841 with 167 Hhds Tobacco for Gov Contract

Within the last 12 Years but one Am ⟨Ship⟩ vessel has entd port of St Lucar (in 1839) came from NY. 60,000 Staves carried back Salt, small amt wool, ⟨oils⟩ olive oils &c–

⟨The⟩ Ships come to Cadiz in ballast for Salt–having brought Cotton to ports in Europe average 300 tons–4 men pr 100 tons which is 1/3 less than in Brit. Vessels ⟨in same t⟩

Many of the vessels which bring Staves take the proceeds to Malaga for returns in fruit & wine.

proceeds of wines sent to US are usually retd. to shippers here by bills in Engd.

This part of Spain does not afford market for

[*p. [26] blank*][42]

Am: Codfish. Bilbao & Alicant were formerly ⟨the⟩ resorted to with codfish–The Brit N Fd ld.[43] catch of Fish is preferred in Spain, being cured as taken from day to day on their coast, & is therefore less salt

39. WI used a hyphen or dash before the figure to indicate the dollar sign.

40. WI numbered the recto of the following leaf "1⟨2⟩3." and underlined with a quarter circle in the upper right corner.

41. WI's indenting the word "one" was apparently without significance; therefore, we have not indicated a new paragraph.

42. WI numbered the recto of the following leaf "1⟨3⟩4" in the upper right corner.

43. These letters seem to be WI's abbreviation for Newfoundland.

than that caught in US. vessels on board of which it remains until their fare is completed & they return to the US.

Am[?][44] Commerce with Spain has become limited & declining. It is reduced in this port to the exchg of a few Staves for Salt. both articles of little ⟨*illegible*⟩ value. Span. wools, olive oils & Sherrywines too high priced for our markets—they obtain wines of lower qualities from other countries

· The New Spanish Tariff is considered even more unfavorable to Foreign commerce than the last Tariff while the shackles & vexations of the licit trade are increased almost all the principal articles of the produce of our country continue as before excluded our Tobacco, Breadstuffs, Manufactures of Cotton, leather, wood &c are either prohibited or taxed with duties that amount to Exclusion If the latter were moderated & the prohibitions taken off the merchandize now sent from US to Gibraltar would come direct to Cadiz & Malaga

[*p. [28] blank*][45]

In short, if something is not done in favor of commerce at Cadiz, this beautiful city and port, perhaps the best situated for foreign trade of any in Europe, will ere long, be reduced to a mere fortress and the port will serve only as a naval station for foreign Ships of war.

Let. Alex Burton. Am Consul
31 Jan 1842

Teneriffe[46]

44. This word could be "our."
45. WI numbered the recto of the following leaf "1⟨4⟩5" in the upper right corner.
46. WI used double underlining.

No Am. vessels entering ports of the Canary islands

		imports	exports
1838.			
24	*Am. V.*	47,369.92/.	$159 371.12/
1839			
15	Am V.	38 366.	139 819.43/
5	foreign vessels.	4,500	40 108.25
	with cargoes from & to US.		
1841[?][47]			
19.	Am. V.	29 465.86	120 915 52
3	Foreign.		25 866 66
1840			
17	Am. V.	15 690.96	101 193 5
3	foreign	1 500	7 950
		$136,892.74	$595,224. 3[48]
			136 892.74
			$458,331.29

[p. [30] blank][49]

Cargoes from US. made up generally of *Staves*[50]—*Whale oil*[51]—*lumber*—Herrings—a little rice—leather, &c—Sundries—

Exports from Teneriff
Wine[52] *Barilla*[53]—almonds Potatoes & onions

The United States has been the best Market for the Sales of the produce of these islands ∧↑(wine & Barilla)↓ for many years past but business is Stagnant at present

Let. Joseph Cullen. Consul[54]
20th. Jan. 1842.

[p. [32] blank]

47. Either WI dated "184⟨0⟩1" with the year out of sequence, or he dated "184⟨1⟩0" with two entries for that year.
48. The "4" was written over an illegible number; following the sum is a line with no apparent significance which we have omitted.
49. WI numbered the recto of the following leaf "1⟨5⟩6."
50. WI used triple underlining.
51. WI used double underlining.
52. WI used heavy triple underlining.
53. WI used triple underlining.
54. Joseph Cullen was confirmed as U.S. consul in Teneriffe, Canary Islands, on January 26, 1836, serving in that position until about 1847 (he was replaced on March 3, 1847).

CONSULAR INFORMATION

Notes on American Trade with Spain and Cuba, Undated[1]

This manuscript notebook is in the Seligman Collection of the Manuscripts and Archives Division of the New York Public Library, where it is cataloged as Washington Irving Notebooks, Volume 9. It is unbound, and its ten leaves are held together with navy blue ribbon tied between pages [10] and [11]; its pages measure 4⅝ x 7¼ inches, and the paper is pale blue. The notebook is kept in a green (with white streaks) cardboard folder; when its four flaps are closed it measures 4¾ x 7¾ inches. The writing is in brown ink except the black ink in the middle of page 5. Blank are pages [8], [10], [12], [14], [16], [18], and [20]. Several leaves have a watermark with the numerals "1840," presumably a date.

[*p. 1*][2]

Am: Trade with Spain

Am policy of Commercial ⟨restrictions⟩ prohibitions as a system exhibited in Spain, "possessing a genial climate, an active population, a soil of bounteous fertility, a sea coast of great extent, numerous harbours, the noblest colonies ever enjoyed by any nation and boundless treasures of

1. The New York Public Library has dated the notebook 1844 from a letter dated December 7, 1844, written from Madrid to William R. King, in which WI requested data on U.S. trade with Spain. On March 10, 1845, WI wrote a long letter to Ramón María Narváez, Spanish minister of war and president of the Council, regarding the discrepancies in the amount of duty on flour imported to Cuba from America and from Spain (Manning, ed., *Spain: Dip. Corresp.*, pp. 343–46). In addition, as he pointed out in a subsequent letter to Secretary of State John C. Calhoun, WI used the subject for "reiterating our general policy with respect to the Island of Cuba" (*ibid.*, p. 347). WI may have copied into this notebook background information in 1844–1845. The watermark, "1840," only suggests that date as the early limit, and WI may have done this research in 1842 in preparation for his departure to Spain.

2. WI wrote "1" in the upper right corner of the page; in the upper left corner in someone else's hand and in pencil are the letters "t v ie."

the precious metals, she has been for years the least prosperous of any of the powers of the old world

Digest. V 2. 271[3]

The prohibition of Tobacco was adopted for the purpose of encouraging the growth of that article in the Spanish Colonies; but as these possessions are now so greatly reduced in extent it can scarcely be an object to persevere in the policy and if tobacco were freely admitted and the whole trade placed on a more liberal basis, there can be no doubt that it would be much enlarged, and to mutual benefit

The Provinces of Spain in the Mediter-/ranian are not able to supply bread Stuffs adequate to the consumption of[4] the country, & have to import—If a mere revenue duty were ⟨proh⟩ substituted for the prohibitory import, large supplies might be drawn from the US. & paid for in wine, brandy, barilla[5] & the Silks of Valencia[.] These articles, with fruit, olive oil, and salt, all of which might be furnished by Spain under an open trade, are now obtd. by the US. from France, Portugal & Italy—

Idem 273

Average importations of Spain in 1827–29	$20,972,450
Exportations	$13,745,900
at this day, 1836, Her imports	16,000,000

idem[6]

———

3. Three notations in the notebook suggest that WI was using a document printed in 1836: after the words "at this day" is the date "1836"; after the words "In the last thirty years," WI added, in parentheses, "before 1836"; regarding population growth, the second number is preceded by "now," and WI added above the line, in parentheses, the date "1836." It seems certain that WI was copying from the second volume of *Digest of Existing Commercial Regulations of Foreign Countries, with which the United States have intercourse* (Washington, D.C.: Blair & Rives, 1836). The first volume was printed by Francis Preston Blair in 1833, and the third and final volume was printed by Blair & Rives in 1836. To the left of the citation in pencil is the fraction $\frac{5479}{4.}$

4. At this point p. 1 ends; WI numbered the verso of this leaf "2," but he continued the quoted material on the recto of the following leaf, numbering it "3" in the upper right corner. This pattern continues through p. 7, with pages 1, 3, 5, and 7 containing notes from the *Digest* and pages 2, 4, and 6 containing notes which WI may have added later; for the convenience of the reader, we have transcribed in this order, and we will indicate the end of each page in the notes.

5. Barilla is a variety of saltwort, the source of soda ash; it is a product native of Spain.

6. From the left margin, WI drew a line three-sixteenths inch long to separate items.

Population of Spain has doubled in 111 years[—]its greatest progress has taken place during the present century.

idem.

In the last thirty years (before 1836) her agricultural products have increased more than ⅓, Shewing that her industry has made some advance. The loss of her colonies ap-/-pears to have the beneficial ⟨effect⟩ influence[7] on her people, rousing them from their inactive dependence on their possessions abroad and forcing them to rely on their own labor for the Supply of their wants. Having ↓⟨Idem⟩↑ no longer the gold and silver of the New World wherewith to purchase their supplies of foreign commodities, as in former days, they now pay for them in the products of their own fertile soil or by the avails of their manufactures—

But with all her advantages ⟨who⟩ her whole annual imports exceed but little the annual imports of the US. from her own possessions alone[8]

———

⟨Ex⟩Imports of Spain in 1826		15,361,020
Exports		7 790,264
Chief imports	exports thru her colonies	1,343,212
	Elsewhere	6,447,015
Cotton Manufacture		2,064,384
Lemon[?] do		1 069,776
Salt fish		962 688
woods		804 288
Cotton wood		801 456
Hemp & flax		795,648
⟨F⟩ Rice		490,896
Wheat		38 928

[*in the left margin, written after the notebook has been turned clockwise a quarter revolution*]

of the Imports 3,457,428 from her Colonies
11 903,592—Elsewhere[9]

7. At this point, page 3 ends, and WI went to page 5 which he numbered "⟨4⟩5."

8. WI drew a line from the left margin three-sixteenths inch long to separate sections.

9. At this point, page 5 ends, and WI continued the *Digest* material on the recto of the following leaf, which he numbered "⟨6⟩7" in the upper right corner.

Exports–(principal)

Silk manufactures	1,408,896[10]
⟨Indigo[?]⟩ Lead[?]	1,033,728
Wool	775,920
Wine	909,832
Fruits	738,000
Brandy	580,240
Quick Silver	318,240
Barilla	380,592
Digest	P 279–80

⟨Articles prohibited in 1820⟩

1820 Raw Cotton–product of foreign country prohibited–excepting (for the present) raw cotton from Pernambuio[?] and Asia Minor. Subject to a duty of 15 pr Ct in Spanish vessels[–]20 pr Ct in foreign. & from Foreign pass[eng]ers[?] in East Indies Duty 9 pr [c]t Span.[–] 12 foreign–

Digest–292[11]

Stock & Codfish–foreign 48 pr Ct Span 74 pr.

---

1 March 1821. Tobacco admitted–4 real for[?] pr Ct duty.

Foreign Salt prohibited[12]

[*p.* 2]
Average price of Tobacco in US. from 1826 to 1835 as Seen by report of the Select Committee on the Tobacco trade was $5 1[?]/8 pr ⟨Cent⟩ hundred pounds.

In 1837, exports of tobacco from US to Spain ↑about↓ 1,729 Hhds. Same year Exportd from Engd 1837, about 1,150 Hhd am tobac

10. The numbers "408" have been written over three other numbers, perhaps "349"; the last number in the sum, "6," has been written over what appears to be a "7."

11. WI separated the following items with lines from the left margin or gutter of one-half inch, one-half inch, one-fourth inch, and one-eighth inch.

12. At this point p. 7 ends; after leaving p. [8] blank, WI seems to have begun using a different section of the *Digest*. Accordingly, we are inserting at this point the notes on the previous verso pages 2, 4, and 6, numbered by WI in the upper left corner of each page.

In France the duties on Tobacco greatly diminish the use of it.

⅝ of Tobacco used in Spain is am. Tobacco

[*p. 4*]

Mr Dodges observations to the Zoll Verein[13][:] The advantages ↑to the Zoll Verein↓ of diminishing duties on Raw Tobacco—Their manufacturer would con-/-tinue to put a great and encreasing market in the US.

Low duties would bring an increased consumption of the article ⟨&⟩ to US[—]would have more money to expend in Encreas[?] objects of traffic[?][14]

———

In Prussia by reducing duties on Rice they have increased the consumption & obtained [*unrecovered*][15] out of revenue

[*p. 6*]

Expenses of Monopoly ⟨*two letters unrecovered*⟩

Resguardia[?] or armed force

———

Multiplicity of Custom house officers

———

Costs of fabrication

———

Costs of Employor[?]—

———

Costs of prosecution of Smugglers

———

Costs of Sustaining the same in prison

———

Amount of labor lost to the country in men ⟨empl⟩ occupied as Smugglers and in men employed to ⟨detect⟩ Suppress Smuggling.

———

[*p. [8] blank*][16]

13. The Zoll-Verein, a union of the German states to promote a uniform system of customs, was formed in 1819 and lasted until late 1870 when the new confederation became the German Empire or Deutsches Reich.

14. WI drew a line from the left margin five-sixteenths inch long; on the following page there are seven lines drawn from the left margin varying in length from one-eighth inch to one inch.

15. The letters of the word resemble "guale," "grinle," or "puerte."

16. WI numbered only the recto of leaves 5–10 as pages 8–13 in the upper right corner. For the convenience of the reader, we have indicated the blank pages either in the notes or in the text, depending on clarity.

1834 every 1000 of foreign Staves of whatever wood or dimensions, dry, dressed or undressed, pay 30 reals in a foreign 20 reals in Spanish vessel for the duty of General Rents[?]" and 30 pr Ct. for duty of "puertas–"

Empty casks, new or old, tho' not dischargd from the vessel, 20rs foreign 15 for the frst. duty in Span, 5 for 2d duty–

Digest, P 411[17]

———

Grain rice flour & vegetables were absolutely prohibited in 1826 to secure monopoly of grain of Castile[?] & flour of Lowlands

Idem 412

———

To encourage the growth of Cot in the Kingdom, Egypt Cot prohibited. 33 pr Ct on all other

Idem 412

———

29 April 1832 discriminatory duties revoked & am: vessels subjected to the same duties as those of other nations

———

[*p. [10] blank*][18]

Cuba.

Since the opening of the Spanish Colonies in 1809 to foreign intrusion there has been a very great increase in the population & products of Cuba[:] ⟨Prior⟩ ↑Before↓ the population 300,000[–] now ↑(1836)↓ 1,000,000 Sugar risen from 80,000 000 to 200,000 000 lbs

———

Nett rent or income answers to 7 pr Ct of the representative Capital of the Estate, & is almost equal to half of the produce

Digest 423

———

⟨Each five pe⟩

In respect to population each five persons appears to have a value on the gross product of 120 Dolls. & of nett rent 53 Dolls

These great resources enable Cuba to promote an extensive and lucrative trade & bring in to the treasury a very conside-/-rable revenue–

17. To separate the seven items on these two pages, WI drew from the left margin lines of three-sixteenths inch, one-eighth inch, one-eighth inch, three-sixteenths inch, three-sixteenths inch, and one-eighth inch.

18. WI numbered the recto of the following leaf "9" in the upper right corner.

The trade, however would be greatly increased were the restrictions on foreign vessels removed. These provoke counter/-vailing restrictions—

Repeated but unavailing representations had been made by the U.S. to the Spanish Govt. of the injustice of its course in imposing the duties of discrimination in tonnage and imports in favor of Spanish bottoms[19] and against foreign navigation; but all negotiation[?] failing retaliation has been adopted. Spanish vessels & cargoes coming into & departing from Am: ports ⟨ha⟩ are placed in same conditions with respect to duties of all Sorts that Am: Ships are Subjected to in Colonies of Spain. ⟨Customs[?]⟩ This system was adopted at earnest solicitations of those citizens most interested in trade with Cuba & Porto Rico. US the best customers these islands possess. Draw from them an immense amt of their productions & furnish at the lowest rates, all the bread stuff & other provisions which may be wanted. ⟨Relief⟩ ↑Supplies↓ from other sources are precarious[—]from US certain—

An uninterrupted commerce between these parties unfettered by discriminating duties could not fail to animate the industry of the islands and to augment their wealth It would, too, afford great profits ↑[*from proximity*]↓[20] as is the case in all trade where the returns are made at Short periods.

In report of Com. of Commerce, 1834, says the trade with Cuba as now carried on operates almost entirely to the benefit of Spanish Ship owners, to the exclusion and injury of our[21] own. Am: vessels are now constrained to go to Cuba in ballast, and for the tender of these sources[?],[22] on bringing the produce of that island to the US. our Ship owners are taxed not less than $300,000 annually in the shape of tonnage money. Am. produce & merch: all in Am Vessels subjected to dis-/-criminating duties amounting to the enormous average of nearly 80 pr Ct ad val[ore]m. tho the duties imposed by our Govt upon the products of Spanish Colonies scarcely average 20 pr Ct. ad valorem & will even be reduced to 15 pr Ct by the new tariff.

Committee advise a bill to collect ‸↑tonnage↓ duties on Span vessels equivalent to discrim. duties This Bill became a Law 30 June 1834[23]

19. At this point, WI's page 9 ends; the verso of leaf 6 is blank, and WI continued the passage on the recto of the following leaf which he numbered "10" in the upper right corner.

20. The brackets and underlining are WI's.

21. At this point, p. 10 ends, and the verso of leaf 7 is blank; WI continued the passage on the recto of leaf 8 which he numbered "11" in the upper right corner.

22. This word may be "sundries."

23. WI drew a line from the left margin of one-fourth inch between paragraphs.

———

Laws by which Cuba is govd. are for the most part those of Spain—"Ordinances of Bilbao—" those of "Catalonia," "Law of Indies", "Royal decrees" forming voluminous code—but since the admission of ⟨*unrecovered*⟩ foreigners Commerce & collectn of resources are regulated by Special ↑ordinances↓ of the local Govt.

[*p. [16] blank*][24]

1835. Genl Tariff for collect of Import & export duties in Cuba

Goods or merchandize not comprehended in this tariff will be subject to a valuation & will indiscriminately pay the 27¼ per Ct. Duties as established thereon, excepting therefrom utensils or ⟨manufactures⟩ ma[c]hinery for agricultural purposes which are subjected to a duty of 21¼ pr Ct.

Spanish flour (accordg to regulations of royal ordinance of 1834) imported under the Spanish flag, fixed duty of 16 reals per Bbl[—]under a foreign flag 48 reals beside the balanza & foreign flour under foreign flag 68 reals & balanza duty—

If deposited in the warehouses of Casa Blanca pay 1 pr Ct. on the estimated value of 100 reals pr Bb. on submg[?][25] for deposit & 1 pr Ct on taking out[26]

———

Tonnage duty
12 reals [*unrecovered*][27] pr ton foreign
5 national

Balanza duty 1 pr Ct on total amt of customs duties & tonnage duties—

[*p. [18] blank*][28]

Countervailing act
30 June 1834

—Spanish vessels from Cuba & Porto Rico to pay ⟨net[?]⟩ ↑additional↓ tonnage duty equivalent to the amt of discriminating duty that would

24. WI numbered the recto of the following leaf "12—" in the upper right corner.
25. This word may be "entering."
26. WI drew a line from the left margin one-eighth inch long.
27. This word may be "puerte" or "puerta."
28. WI numbered the recto of the following leaf "13" in the upper right corner.

have been imposed on cargoes if exported from Havan[?] in am bottoms
P 552–

Such vessel clearing out for such ports with a cargo directly or indirectly intendd for Said islands shall pay such further tonnage duty as shall be equivalent to the amt of discriminating duty that would be payable for the time being upon the Cargo if imported into Havana in Am. bottoms

Spanish vessels clearing out ^↑for other ports↓ shall give bonds ⟨that⟩ in security of dbl ↑[? or trple ?] &↓ amt of Cargo but no part of cargo is to be landed in these islands.

These duties to be regulated from time to time by those imposed in Cuba &c and to cease when they cease–

[*p. [20] blank*]

COMMONPLACE BOOKS

Concerning Will Wizard, the Courts, Government, etc., Undated[1]

This manuscript notebook is in the Manuscripts and Archives Division of the New York Public Library where it is cataloged as Washington Irving Papers, Notebooks, Volume 16. Its 28 leaves are bound in a badly worn red cardboard cover; the front cover is double, resembling an envelope which opens along the side and has a small flap, the inside of which is of a black and off-white design. Each page measures 4⅛ x 6⁹⁄₁₆ inches, and the paper is off-white, thick, and with tiny vertical and six horizonal lines in the grain. In leaf 5 is a watermark which has a foot on a ball, below which is a bar and figures which resemble the letters "VDL"; in leaves 6, 7, and 21 is a watermark picturing what seems to be a nymph standing, reaching out. The notebook is tied with brown string between leaves 4 and 5, 14 and 15, and 24 and 25; there are no loose leaves. The writing throughout is in pencil except for the number "76" on the inside front cover in someone else's hand; blank are the front and back covers, pages [17–22], [29–34], and [41–56].

[*front cover blank*]

[*inside front cover blank except for the number "76" in ink in the center and one-fourth from the top a horizontal line 2⅜ inches long in pencil; the designations "(40 M 36)" and "Case 26/0" at the bottom of the page in pencil; and "Wormser 3 June 1740 [1940]" written in pencil along the inside margin after the notebook had been turned one-quarter revolution clockwise*]

These people but little better than our slaves. They are completely subjucated by the tyrany of opinion—and the slang whangers[2] may be considered as so many slave drivers.

1. It is possible that this commonplace book can be dated as early as 1806. See the Introduction, pp. liv–lv, for a discussion of dating.

2. In his April 4, 1807, letter to Asem Hacchem, the "principal slave-driver to

Ovid says the golden age possessed no gold and was for that reason called the golden age—that in the happy or fortunate epoch[?][3] the evils produced by the precious metals (such as increase of wants, avarice, envy) were not known. In the iron age there was abundance of Gold—but it was called the iron age on that account because the sorrows accompanied by gold made it hard & laborious—[4]

In the tempests & whirlwinds it is the towns, the temples & the lofty palaces ⟨that have⟩ and not the cottages that have to tremble

⟨The poor animals[?]⟩

Will Wizard[5]—believes fortune to be nothing but superiority of talents, foresight & bravery—Cicero recommended Pompey to the Roman Senate because he was vigilant, brave & fortunate—"Let a man be brave persevring & I'll engage says Will he will be fortunate—"And were I a monarch—should a general or an admiral be unfortunate as it is always termed I should at once decline his services—in compliance with the world, I would if I found no other fault, dismiss him from my employ for want of *fortune*[6]

Will a great stickler for the ‸↑Episcopal↓ church ⟨of England⟩—believes in the divinity of its origins—⟨and⟩ compares it to a noble river

---

his highness the Bashaw of Tripoli," Mustapha Rub-a-dub Keli Khan said that in the battle of words, the country is defended "*vi et lingua,* that is to say, by *force of tongues*" and that the knight-errants "denominated editors or SLANG-WHANGERS are appointed in every town, village and district. . . ." He went on to say that if Hacchem should "witness the enormities sometimes committed by these tremendous slang-whangers, [his] very turban would rise with horror and astonishment" (Granger and Hartzog, eds., *Salmagundi,* no. 7, p. 143). Slang-whangers are mentioned in other Mustapha letters (see for example, no. 9, pp. 171–72).

3. This word could be "period."

4. At the end of the word "laborious," there is a loop which is characteristic of the ending of some of WI's final *s*'s in this notebook, a habit he changed by the 1830's.

5. PMI wrote that James Kirke Paulding, William Irving and WI "made up the trio, Launcelot Langstaff, Anthony Evergreen, and William Wizard" (PMI, I, 176). In the first number of *Salmagundi,* Launcelot Langstaff, Esq., explained the various responsibilities of the three as they attempted "to instruct the young, reform the old, correct the town and castigate the age." "William Wizard, esq. has undertaken to preside" in "the territory of criticism" even though he "has not had the advantage of an education at Oxford, or Cambridge, or even at Edinburgh, or Aberdeen, and though he is but little versed in hebrew" he is "fully competent"; his "qualifications" follow (Granger and Hartzog, eds., *Salmagundi,* no. 1, pp. 67, 71). Williams said that Will Wizard tried to be witty but was often flippant (STW, I, 81).

6. To set off the following five sections, WI drew lines in the middle of the page of three-sixteenths inch, three-sixteenths inch, one-eighth inch, one-fourth inch, one-fourth inch, and five-sixteenths inch.

which he says the devil has for a long time been trying to ⟨cut up⟩ ↑divide↓ into narrow[7] shallow channels that are fordable at pleasure.

The [*unrecovered*][8] of a priviledged corps Others enter it to enjoy their advantages viz:—When punished by whipping they are striped on the back instead of the soals of the feet—when put to death the[y] suffer the bow-string instead of being ⟨burnt alive⟩ impaled alive.

Will Wizard hates winter—every thing looks like death—The world appears in its winding sheet—and the trees fill him with melancholy ideas—they appear like so many skeletons.

Thus have I seen all my air with castles one after another vanish ⟨away⟩. The earth, ⟨nature⟩ still wears the same aspect I so often contemplated with fond delight when I was a boy, excepting ⟨a little⟩ that the ↑lustre of the↓ sunshine ⟨of it⟩ appears a little dimmed ⟨of its lustre⟩—owing no doubt to the disappearance of these[9] fairy ⟨air built castles⟩ prospects.

⟨But all these visions have passed away—nature appears now in her true &[?]⟩ I have learned to know the true character of what we term the world—and ⟨like many of those I have known⟩—it has not improved upon ‸↑⟨my⟩↓ acquaintance.—In fact the Landscapes of fancy—are now formed of barren-rocky heaths and I am insensibly extending[10] my views beyond them—to another country which appears more inviting in the distance—and In[11] which I am well convinced my expectations shall suffer no disappointments

---

We embark on the river of life, at first but a scanty stream[12]—but we are wafted forward—the river enlarging and accelerating in current—until we exchange our ⟨bark⟩ worn out bark to set[13] sail on the broad ocean of Eternity.

Magnanimity—a word of which it is im/possible these people can have any true idea.

7. The word "narrow" was written over an illegible word.
8. This unrecovered word seems to end in the letters "gring."
9. The word "these" was written over another word which apparently ended in *y*.
10. The *t* was written over an illegible letter, perhaps a *p*.
11. The *n* is slightly below the line.
12. The letters "am" were written over an illegible letter.
13. The word "set" was written over the word "sail."

Everything of a speculative nature in a country takes its character from the ⟨nature of ⟨our[?]⟩ ↑the↓⟩ government—Magnani-/-mity with us thou knowest—is ‸↑on the one hand↓ that noble independence of soul—⟨wch. con-/-[*unrecovered*] the groveling paths of the herd, and the sordid selfishness of vul-/garity—nobly aspires to render service [*unrecovered*] the paths⟩[14] which conscious of its own worth—contemns the groveling paths ⟨of the⟩ and the sordid selfishness of the common herd it nobly[?] aspires by a gene-/-rous ambition,—to render public services and to acquire immortal harmony—& on the other hand it is [? that artist ?][15] in the princes or government wch. ⟨[*unrecovered*][16] their services⟩—perceiving these services—publickly ⟨rewards⟩ ‸↑acknowl-edges↓ and munificently rewards them.—

Alas alas! in this country the whole bent of the government is to make *six penny* savings—instead of boasting of how many great men it has fostered and brought into the world—it is eter-/-nally bragging of how many *good* & *great men* it has done without, and as if jealous of talent and worth no sooner does a public officer be-/-come remarkable for his talent or his bravery—than he is in some sly way by the government or some villanous dirty manner by the mob displaced from office.

This was remarkably the case in the ⟨military⟩ naval commander who thun-/-dered against tripoli and even ⟨made⟩ occassioned a panic in the bosom of his highness himself—the people here was enraptured[?] with the office and the Bashaw[17] magnanimously re-/-called him and buried him in obscu-/rity. He however has retired from [*two unrecovered words*][18] service, and has entered in the employ under a master who will reward his faithful services—in a country where ⟨he can⟩ [*blank*] and slang whang-/-ers cease to [*unrecovered*].[19]—

This country blessed with men of noble souls and brave spirits, some of the officers of their *infant Navy* such as would do honor to this or any country—but there lies before them no road to glory—every effort is made to cramp their spirits—poverty and *abuse* are the only recom-/

14. WI crossed out this passage with five large *X*'s across the page.

15. These questioned words may be "right to sit."

16. This word is hyphenated; it may begin with the letters "pal" and end on the next line with the letters "ging."

17. In addition to "slang-whanger," another frequently used term in the Mustapha letters was "bashaw"; Mustapha wrote regarding the government, "This empire is governed by a grand and most puissant bashaw, whom they dignify with the title of President" (Granger and Hartzog, eds., *Salmagundi*, no. 3, p. 92).

18. The words fall at the end of one line and at the beginning of the next; therefore, they may be one hyphenated word. The first word may be "naval."

19. This unrecovered word resembles "amoroy."

-pense they receive while their tempers are warm—with the prospect of neglect and ignominy when their spirits are worn out.—

But what is to be expected from a nation of ⟨pedlars⟩ shop keepers and pedlars—and from a gov-/-ernment who barters the best spirits of their country—and ‸↑on↓ whom they would have to depend in the hour of adversity for the beggarly saving of 20 dollars pr month.

Our readers must long ere this have formed some accurate idea of our friend & colleague William Wizzard[20] Esquire. In fact a lady ⟨of my ac-/quaintance⟩ of a bright mind, not *blest* with his acquaintance, and who has never been favoured to her knowledge with a sight of his eccentric person or phiz—gave me an account of him agreeably to the representation she had formed in *her minds eye* from the various sketches she has discovered in some of this work.[21] And had honest Will sat for his likeness it could never have been represented truer. It is however impossible yet for the reader to have formed an accurate opinion of the qualities of his mind—which is so curious a compound of excellence and adding[?] of brilliance and quaintness that his ⟨*two unrecovered words*⟩[22] intimates ⟨acquaintances ↑friends↓⟩[23] are every day discovering something to admire and to laugh at.

His life and opinions are an ever/lasting source of instruction and ⟨a⟩of amusement to his friends.

Will like all old bachelors has [*unrecovered*][24] in an invisible attachment to every thing that belonged to the days of his boyhood—those happy times when he figured as an Adonis in the beau monde—not only to the manners and customs of those times but even to the very [*unrecovered*][25] and cut of a coat—indeed in this particu-/-lar he gives constant testimony, for as he was formerly a dashing ⟨and⟩ beau⟨s⟩ and prides himself vastly on his appearance—He had ⟨at⟩ provided himself with a most as-/-tonishing wardrobe which has con-/-tinued to supply him with his [*four unrecovered words*][26] ever since. So that he is constantly ⟨displaying⟩ ↑sporting↓, some old fashioned brocaded vest—broad backed coat or tight small clothes, to ⟨great[?]⟩ the great amusement of his

20. In this notebook, WI usually spelled Will's last name "Wizard," as it is spelled in *Salmagundi*.

21. Apparently WI referred to *Salmagundi*.

22. The second word may be "mask."

23. WI first wrote "intimate acquaintances" and then apparently struck "acquaintances" and above that wrote "friends"; he then struck "friends" and added the *s* to "intimate."

24. The word may be "lucked" or "locked."

25. The word may be "dashes," "designs," "daper," etc.

26. The first unrecovered word was hyphenated and may begin with a *q* and end with "el."

friends who rally him on his grotesque appearance but Will is immoveable—⟨and⟩ humou-/-rously styling himself *the representative on earth of the last century.*[27]

He is apt to support these trifling partialities, with all the force, which is only worthily brought forward in ⟨objects⟩ favour of objects of much greater importance—this is one of his ec-/-centricities that he supports an old coat with the same ardor that he exhibits in favour of an old friend—and as he has laid it down as an honourable principle never to forget or despise the persons of his early attachments he also carries the same principle to his old clothes. besides "I know my self in these clothes, says Will. I am the same man I was twenty years ago, standing on my old character and ^↑the↓ merits with which I started in ⟨*unrecovered*⟩ the world, ⟨and⟩ were I to change my dress I ought also to change my principles ⟨to⟩ ↑[*two unrecovered words*]↓ to[28] the fashion of the day—and should then be lost in the crowd of new comers—those changelings who like camelions are forever assu-/-ming the colour of the thing nearest and become confounded in the common surrounding mass. I would not be known from the up-/start of yesterday

One great cause of his attachment to the Chinese—is their stability in the article of dress—while we are forever jumping from fashion to fashion says he, and imitating in turn every people under the sun—so that one generation ⟨is⟩ from their costume is hardly to be recognized as the descendant of the other, the Chinese are invariably & ⟨forever⟩ ↑eternally↓ the same, "yesterday, today and forever" Chin-long the em-/-peror of China is the identical Chin-/Long he was 40 years ago—⟨*unrecovered*⟩ while our very President has been the laughing stock of his people and has been nearly driven from his throne on account of the *crime* of wearing the very *red breeches*[29] that were fashionable in his ⟨youth⟩ early day.

In fact Will has got a complete set of opinions and principles for every

27. For one description of Will Wizard's "picturesque costume," see *Salmagundi*, no. 5 (Granger and Hartzog, eds., p. 124). Will's affection for things Chinese was emphasized throughout *Salmagundi*, beginning with no. 1, in which the reader learns that Will's tastes had been improved by his living in Canton, his seeing the "tragedians of China," and his being "a great connoisseur in mandarine dresses, and porcelaine" (*ibid.*, no. 1, p. 71). In no. 5, he prided himself above all "upon his waistcoat of China silk, which might almost have served a good housewife for a short gown" and then "dilated most copiously on his silver sprigged Dicky, which . . . was quite the rage among the dashing young mandarins of Canton" (*ibid.*, no. 5, p. 124).

28. After crossing out the word "to" and adding the two unrecovered words, WI added "to" in the left margin of the next line.

29. Initially Mustapha thought that the reason the people of the higher classes

thing laid down and established with the most mathematical precision—and reason & comfort are often obliged to submit to his established rules of ↑[*unrecovered*]↓[30] times and seasons. Will is a ⟨confessed⟩ true Darwinian with respect to the use of flannels[31]—He scouts the idea of a young persons wearing ⟨fl⟩ it next the skin, urging as an irresistible argument that if flannell shirts are necessary to the young, blanket ones must certainly be wanting in old age. In fact he has changed in his principle here—for he first maintained that flannell was un-/-ncessary all together—and insisted that if it was necessary God would have provided man with fur like a bear—In support of this hypothesis he never wore flannel himself nor made any material alterations in his dress between summer and winter—A severe ⟨winter⟩ rheu-/-matism however, some winters ago broke in upon Will's philosophy & so far altered his opinions as to in-/-duce him to allow that flannell was necessary after a person has arrived at 40 years—but nothing can make him pardon the use of it previous to that age.

As for himself he puts on his flannels on the first day of November and lays them off on the first day of June. ⟨His friends laugh at⟩ ⟨t⟩This chronological arrangement ⟨for his flannels, often⟩ has several times made him suffer inconvenience—for neither heat can make him forsake nor cold ressume[?] his flannels before the stated periods[32]—and tho' his friends have laughed at these whimsicalities, Will insists, that he has in this made a proper distribution of the seasons—and if the weather is not comfortable to the arrangement, it is none of his fault—He is too independent—in his principles to think of accomodating himself to the weather—No the weather must accomodate itself to him—It often refuses compliance and over-/rules[?] the correctness of his ⟨Will[?]⟩ rules—but not his establishment. He consoles himself that he is no weather cock—driven about by every wind that blows.

[*pp. [17–22] blank*]

Courts of Law

The verbosity and the eternal propensity to prattle of this people is nowhere more dis-/-coverable than in their courts of justice

---

were attempting to dethrone the bashaw was that he wore "red breeches," everyone's detesting that color because of the dispute with the "barbarian" British twenty years earlier, but he found that was not the explanation for the bashaw's being in disfavor (Granger and Hartzog, eds., *Salmagundi*, no. 7, pp. 143–44).

30. The unrecovered word may be "Good."

31. The final letter may be either *l* or *s*.

32. The *r* in "periods" was written over an illegible letter.

Every thing there seems to be nothing but wind—for in this department of the ⟨gov⟩ Logocracy,[33] there is absolutely an ⟨much[?]⟩[34] astonishing quantity of gentry who are appointed *public prattlers* and are considered on that account priviledged officers of the court.

Justice in trifling[?] offences are not conducted here in the summary way in which it is with us—where the Cadi[35] hears the cause, determines on its out-/come, and orders the offender to the bas-/-tinado; but the most trifling out-/rage of law here—occassions some/times the chattering of a month.

The great cause which was agitating the court at the time I was at present[?] was ⟨this⟩ simply thi⟨ng⟩s,[36] a young girl of 16 years of age had thrown a cup of cold water in the face of another of the same age—The offence was dreadful—the laws of the country Was infringed—and the people rose in their majesty to punish the offence. The attorney for the People stated the offence and stated ⟨much heroically⟩ that She the defendant, Margaret Elisabeth Muckinfush, not having the fear of God before her eyes, did on the 24th day of August [? Such fact ?], in such and such a place make an assault upon the body of [*blank*] & then and there did wound, beat and other/wise greatly misuse—by throwing a cup of cold water in the face of the said [*blank*] ‸↑to the great injury of the said [*unrecovered*]↓ so that her life was dispaired of and to the great injury of the peace of the people of New York & their dignity

Instead of endeavouring to admi-/-nister justice—it appeared to me as if the great object was to bewilder the Evidence so as to prevent the attaining truth and by that means to defeat it.

Instead of the offender it seemed rather the trial of each of the witnesses & their characters were over hauled by the chattering officers and their reputations were torn to tatters to very rags—

I was astonished, that a judge could sit calmly on a bench and see

33. When Mustapha complained that the people here had difficulty identifying their form of government—perhaps aristocracy, pure democracy, or mobocracy—he explained that it was "a pure unadulterated LOGOCRACY or *government of words*" in which the pen was the most devastating weapon (Granger and Hartzog, eds., *Salmagundi*, no. 7, pp. 142–43). The present bashaw was well suited for his position for he was "a man of superlative ventosity" uttering speeches and proclamations at every turn and resembling a "bladder of wind" (*ibid.*, p. 147). Logocracy was a favorite subject of Mustapha (see for example no. 9, p. 171; no. 11, p. 193; no. 14, pp. 231–32).

34. This word may be "most."

35. Cadi is an Arabian word meaning "judge."

36. The ending of this word may be simply an *s*; WI often wrote the *s* with a flourish below the line; the reading would be "this."

the poor witnesses who had come to prove the offence worried & baited like so many [*blank*] ⟨I was however⟩

I was however informed that it is the universal practice in the courts of this barbarous country and thru th⟨eir⟩is ⟨lawyers⟩ constituting the priviledg⟨ed⟩es of these lawyers who are the only privileged order in the country—Every scurvy scoundrel who practices[?] has been raised on a dunghill—the moment he is admitted in this class, he is permitted in court to be insolent and insulting to his betters.

I am sorry to add that even this shameful practice is indulged by the better sort of their Lawyers. Men who in their private walks are considered polished amiable and ⟨agreeable⟩ ↑intelligent↓—It shows strongly, however, the inherent nature of these poor infidels—Let them only be placed in some situation where the restraints imposed on their dispositions by the rules of civilized life can be a moment thrown off—and immediately their barbarous nature, shines thro the thin polish of politeness—they become insolent, and in fact in some measure blackguards

This ⟨departure from⟩ conduct ⟨from th⟩ is the more surprizing, when you Know that it has no avail with their hearcy[?][37]—that the thing is properly understood—they are considered as having a right to say any thing—and that none but fools be-/-lieve what they say—So that their departure from the character of gentle-/-men in this instance serves no other purpose than to expose the depravity of their own hearts—and that they are ⟨naturl⟩ notwithstanding the little civili-/zation they have undergone—naturally barbarians—

I cannot help here reminding them of the conduct of his highness the bashaw ‸↑in a like situation[?]↓ to mere[?] mumble one of the fudgi[?] or assistant deputize[38] to one of the officers of the res effendi, who having made rather free with His highnesses name in one of his speeches—the bashaw sent for him and interrogated him on the subject—poor *Meli* endeavoured to excuse himself by assuring the bashaw that he did not mean nor believe what he said—↑had no Intention of injury to his feelings↓ that his ob-/-servations were merely sportive, and he sincerely hoped his Highness would think no more of it—The bashaw im/-mediately ordered an officer in waiting to favor Mali with fifty stripes on the soles of his feet—and when it was acc-/-omplished while the miserable Mali was ‸↑still↓ smarting and roaring with pain he waggishly shook him by the hand informed him he had no intention of wounding his feelings—that his lashes were merely sportive and he sincerely hoped that the fudgi would think no more of it.

37. WI may have intended the word "herecy" or "heresy."

38. WI's spelling may be "deputys."

Quere[:] would it not be good for these people if some of their lawyers could be served just so?

[*pp. [29–34] blank*]

To hear the various opinions of the ^↑magi or↓ [*unrecovered*][39] as they are termed, of this ⟨country⟩ people ^↑one↓ would ⟨indeed⟩ conclude that they were ↑indeed↓ in their infancy and had profited nothing by the experience of all those who ha⟨d⟩ve gone before them.

They tickle themselves with the idea of restoring again the golden age, and introducing once more the gentle order of things which our arabian [*unrecovered*] tell us existed in the primitive times.

Their customs pursuits and their principles are even at variance with each other. While avariciously extending their com-/-merce with all the world—becoming the rivals and competing with the most powerful nations under the sun, and consequently exposing themselves[40] through the jealousy of others, to be injured and insulted abroad—they are at home in their public spirits[?][41] ⟨deprecating every⟩ despising every thing that looks like[?][42] adding to their military strength, and prating about nothing but cultiva-/-ting the arts of peace.

This language is to be observed from their president (an honest chicken/hearted philosopher) down through all his satilites and partizans. They are forever talking about na-/-tional character, national rights and national privileges—until their nation has neither character, right or priviledge remaining—and at the very moment that one necessity is forcing them to see the falacy of all their empty [*unrecovered*] calculations— they are in the [*unrecovered*][43] of all this—snarling at the only means of preserving themselves from utter ruin—there is an army & navy to defend their ports and [*unrecovered*] after they shall be driven from the ocean.

For my own part I have found man to be—man in every part of the world where I have met with him— —the same head/strong erring, wilful wild beast[?] that nature originally formed him. The laws of civil Society may in some measure curb his propencities or restrain his excesses—but his nature re-/-mains radically the same. And so long as his nature remains so long will his evil dispositions lead him to commit excesses and to in-/-trude on the rights and comforts of his neighbours—

39. The unrecovered word could be "Lagis."

40. WI added the second syllable below the line.

41. This word could also be "prints."

42. There seems to be material missing between the last word on p. [35], "like," and the first word on p. [36], "adding"; the word "like" may be "alien."

43. The word could be "face."

and so long will it be necessary for his neighbours practicing in the law of self de-/-fence, ⟨at time⟩ to be at all times on his guard—and some times to be under the necessity of using[?] himself to repel injustice. What happens to individuals happens also to nations—however pacific and well disposed a government in itself may be to practice peace and to preserve unbroken its harmonious connections with other countries—other governments not existing on the same plans, nor excited by the same mild wishes will interrupt its gentle prospects and will either force it into a state of warfare or vassel/-age.

No wisdom or philosophy is requi-/-site to discover this—the dunce who turns over the page of history will find that it ever has been the case since the world began.

But yet the rulers[44] of this people are preposterously hoping to settle the nation down to the simple habits con-/-formable only with the shepherd state and to reproduce the same, in fact never found, but in the eutopian dreams of the poets.

If man ever was the happy animal thus represented—it was owing to the introduction of the arts & sciences when they were settled down in small pastoral communities—comprehending a narrow tribe, of relatives and friends living in a perfect equality of conditions—when, as Ovid observes of his golden age—the luxur⟨y⟩ies[45] & the convenience of Gold was unknown

Oh my friend it would tickle the ⟨to witt[?]⟩—to see the continual per-/-plexities this government is undergoing between its principles and its practices and to see[46] it when ever its [*unrecovered*][47] children are insulted or thrashed[?][48] by a naughty neighbour—like an indignant mother, when her young ones come home complaining stand vociferously scolding from the door of her hovel[49]—making a mighty bustle in her own yard—pacifying her little brats by a show of resentment that nobody cares for without and then quickly[50] forgetting the insult[51]

———

[*pp. [41–56] blank*]

44. The *l* of "rulers" was written over an illegible letter.
45. WI may have written the *y* over the "ies," changing to singular.
46. The word "see" was written over an illegible word.
47. The two parts of the unrecovered word are on two lines and hyphenated; the second syllable is "ling."
48. This word may be "threatened."
49. WI inverted the order of the following two participipial phrases in this sentence by a long serpentine line from line 1 to line 4; his intended order is given here without notation for the convenience of the reader.
50. This word could be "quietly."
51. WI drew a line one-fourth inch long following this entry.

[*inside back cover*][52]

101	103	46
14	14	6½
87	89[53]	39½
1.10	1.7	1.9
87	89	39
72.6	44.6	19.6
159.6	7.3	9.9
7.19.6	2	1
2	142.9	69.3
8. 1.6	7.2.9	3.9.3
		10½
Brailey[?][54]	*Hunter*	3.10.1½
		Davis

[*back cover blank*]

52. WI made the following calculations in these three columns of numbers: the first process is subtraction; the second process yields the same number except for dropping the fractions; the third process is addition; the fourth process is conversion from shillings to pounds; the fifth process (in columns 1 and 3) is addition. Just below the name "Davis," the top layer of cardboard is torn away, approximately one inch inward from flush right.

53. WI wrote "8⟨7⟩9."

54. The name may be "Beasley"; it may also begin with *C*, *G*, or *O*.

COMMONPLACE BOOK

Notes on Reading and Observations regarding Manners, American Character, Economics, Navy, etc., (1825?)[1]

This manuscript notebook is in the Berg Collection of the New York Public Library, where it is cataloged as Commonplace of Washington Irving. Its 48 leaves are covered back and front with a stiff, mottled blue cardboard, badly cracked and worn, and tied with an off-white string between leaves 24 and 25. There are no loose leaves. The notebook is housed in a green silk-covered cardboard folder which folds twice into thirds and which slips into a green leather case which breaks horizontally around the middle. The 96 pages measuring 4 x 6 inches are off-white, heavy paper with numerous tiny horizontal lines and four vertical lines within the design of the paper itself; there is a watermark of unidentified design on most of the leaves. Blank are the front and back covers, pages [12], [18], [34], and [42]. In pencil are pages [10], [20], [24], [30–33], [40–41], [43–46], [51–56], [58–60], [64–65], [68–76], [78], and [83]; in various colors of ink (brown and black) are pages [1–8], [11], [13–17], [19], [21–23], [25–29], [36], [38], [57], [61], [77], [86–91], [93], and the inside back cover. In a combination of ink and pencil, often with only a few lines in one and the remainder in the other, are the inside front cover and pages [9], [35], [37], [39], [47–50], [62–63], [66–67], [79–82], [84–85], [92], and [94–96].

[*front cover blank. At the bottom, slightly to the left of center, is a blob of red sealing wax; at the top of the cover, almost at its center, is a round, white spot left exposed below the cardboard's blue surface, perhaps as the result of wax's being at some time pulled off. There is writing in this soft, white layer of cardboard.*]

1. There is strong evidence to suggest that WI copied these passages into this notebook in 1825. See Introduction, pp. lvii–lix, for a discussion of dating.

[*inside front cover*]

Memoranda by
Washington Irving
of
Sunnyside[2]

[*at the bottom of the inside front cover, upside down*]

Highlands[–]cold Spring–mockingbird causes consternation among the Irish men of the ⟨farm[?]⟩ neighborhood–one reports that I said plant your potatoes in the full of the moon–They ⟨cast⟩ fire at it & drive it away–[*erasure*] cast silver bullets

---

[*p. [1]*]

Dr Cudworth[3] says Truth is the most unbending[?] & uncompliable, the most necessary firm, immutable & adamantine thing in the world"

An ugly woman ‸↑ostentatious in her dress but↓ who was ⟨ugg⟩ uglier the finer she dressed: made you wonder how a bird could be so ugly with such fine plumage

Ella Virginia Hobart
New York City
1894.[4]

Dirty man spilling[?][5] &c. makes a dirty little world around him, and reigns monarch of the little dirty world.

Chesterfield speaking of the manner in which his son should get[6] into the confidence & secrets of court, says

2. Following the title, WI drew an uneven line approximately 2½ inches long and skipped one-fourth page before reversing the notebook. Throughout this commonplace book, WI continued his habit of separating passages by skipping lines or drawing a line (or both) between them; the skipped lines vary from one or two to three-fourths of the page, and the drawn lines vary in length from one-eighth inch to a line from margin to margin. Sometimes the lines are double, sometimes drawn from the left margin (more often in a single line in the middle of the page); we have regularized with notation only if there is something significant about WI's configuration.

3. WI may have been referring to Ralph Cudworth, the author of *The True Intellectual System of the Universe* (London, 1678); Williams cited this work as a major source of the first two chapters of WI's *A History of New York* (STW, II, 273).

4. These three lines are not in WI's hand; below the date is a line 1¼ inches long with two short vertical marks in the center.

5. The word could be "spelling."

6. WI wrote the word "get" over two words, "go in."

Upon my word I am not sayg too much when I say that Superior good breeding, insinuating manners and genteel address are half your business. Your Knowledge will have but very little influence upon the mind, if your manners prejudice the heart against you; but, on the other hand, how easily ⟨to⟩ ↑will you↓ *dupe* the understanding where you have first engaged the heart! and hearts are, by no means, to be gained by that mere common civility which every body practices. Bowing again to those who bow to you, answering dryly those who speak to you, and saying nothing offensive to any body, is such negative good breeding that it is only not being a brute. * * *[7] It is an active, cheerful, officious, seducing good breeding, that must gain you the good will and find ⟨the⟩ sentiments of the men and the affections of the women.[8]

The penetration of Princes seldom goes deeper than the surface. It is the exterior that always engages their hearts. Princes in general (I mean those Porphyrogenets who are born & bred in purple) are about the pitch of women; bred up like them, and are to be addressed and gained in the same manner. They always see, they seldom weigh. Your lustre, not your solidity must take them—

Chesterfd.[9]

estoy en persuasion ‸↑de↓ que la Urbanidad solida y brillante, tiene mucho mas de natural, que de adquirida. Un espiritu bien complexionado, desembarazado con discrecion, apacible sin baxeza inclinado por genio y por dictamen a complacer en quanto no se oponga a la razon, acompañado de un entendimiento claro, o prudencia nativa que le dicte como se ha de hablar, u obrar, segun las diferentes circumstancias, en que se halla, Sin mas escuela parecera general-/-mente bien en el trato

7. These asterisks are WI's to indicate an omitted clause in this sentence about personal cleanliness.

8. WI omitted the final two sentences in this paragraph and approximately a page of the following paragraph before resuming his transcription.

9. WI has quoted from the fourth earl of Chesterfield's *Letters to His Son*, the first edition of which was published by Philip Stanhope's widow in 1774. In the two letters preceding this one, Chesterfield had concentrated on providing his illegitimate son with advice on the importance of good breeding in climbing the ladder of social success, and in the second of those letters, he urged Philip not to break the chain at all courts "which connects the prince or the minister with the page of the back stairs" (Letters LXXXIX, November 14, O.S. 1749). The letter from which WI copied is Letter XC, undated, but written between November 14 and November 24 (Oliver H. G. Leigh, ed., *Letters to His Son on the Art of Becoming a Man of the World and a Gentleman by the Earl of Chesterfield* [New York: Chesterfield Press, 1917], I, 239–44; hereafter cited as Chesterfield's *Letters to His Son*).

comun Es verdad que ignorara aquellos modos, modas ceremonias y formal-/-idades, que principalmente se estudian en las cortes, y que el capricho de los hombres altera a cada paso; pero lo primero las ventajas naturales las quales siempre tienen una estimabiledad intrinseca que con ninguna, precaucion se borra, supliran para la comun aceptacion el defecto de este estudio lo segundo, una modestia, y despejada preven-/-cion a los circumstante de esa misma ignorancia de los ritos Politicos, motivada con el naci-/-miento, y educacion en Provincia, donde no se practican, sera una galante escusa de la transgresion de los estilos, que parecerá mas bien a la gente razonable que la mas escrupu-/-losa observancia de ellos.

Fijoo Teatro Universal
Discurso 10–
Sec[?] ⟨*unrecovered*⟩6–[10]

⟨"⟩Chesterfield says "your Conversation with women should always be respectful; but at the same time, enjené, and always addressed to their vanity. Every thing you say or do should convince them of the regard[11] you have (whether you have it or not) for their beauty, their wit, or their merit."[12] What worthless doctrine–On the contrary I would recommend as far as I have observed[?]–perfect sincerity. A manner characterised by that kindness and tenderness which every man of proper feeling must have towards that lovely sex, which addresses itself in every way to the[?] heart. When we consider our relations with woman ⟨as sis[?]⟩ as mother, wife, daughter, sister, or friend all her charms on our heart of such a sweet & gentle ↑nature↓ ⟨kind⟩, such a perpetual

10. WI here quoted Don Fray Benito Geronymo Feijóo, *Theatro Critico Universal, o Discursos Varios en Todo Genero de Materias, Para Desengaño De Errores Comunes*, vol. 7 (Madrid: En la Imprenta de Don Eugenio Bieco, 1745), pp. 249–50; hereafter cited as Feijóo, *Theatro Critico Universal.* Discurso Decimo, entitled "Verdadera, y Falsa Urbanidad," is divided into 21 numbered sections and two titled sections; all of the passages which WI quoted came from section 6, pp. 249–52. In some editions, Geronymo is spelled "Jerónimo" in Feijóo's name.

11. This word could be "respect."

12. This idea about women is repeated often in Chesterfield's advice to his son, and it was probably to several passages that WI reacted negatively: in Letter XVII (October 16, O.S. 1747) Chesterfield wrote, "Women have, in general, but one object, which is their beauty; upon which, scarce any flattery is too gross for them to swallow" (Chesterfield's *Letters to His Son*, I, 28). He enlarged on this theme in Letter XLIX, maintaining that women "are only children of a larger growth" who have "entertaining tattle, and sometimes wit" but no "solid reasoning.... No flattery is either too high or too low for them. They will greedily swallow the highest, and gratefully accept of the lowest..." (*ibid.*, I, 107).

law[?][13] of kindness, such a constant ministry of blind[?][14] and cheering office amid[15] the rude cares of this disastrous life, that we cannot think of her other than with affection; as the soother of our cares—Woman is by nature the comforter as man is the protector—

It is ⟨s⟩ absurd to suppose that womans heart is to be won merely by flattery and deception. The sexes like each other for the real attributes of each others sex. And though the necessity of loving something may often ⟨turn the⟩ ⟨enclose[?]⟩ ↑open↓ the soft heart of a female to an unworthy occupant, though she may be pleased with the gay & frivolous for want of something better, yet she will never fail to appreciate that frank⟨ness &⟩ sincerity which[16] is the true attribute of man—

Do not fear to acknowledge ignorance; but dread to expose it. When a man confesses he knows nothing on a subject ⟨⟨we credit him⟩ for his modesty and think he knows something but when he pretends to know a vast deal and we discover ⟨that⟩ the contrary, we are apt to believe all his knowledge pretension⟩[17] he at least gets credit for modesty—& we are apt to believe he knows something, but when he pretends to know every thing, and we discover him deficient, we are apt to believe ⟨him⟩ it all pretension.

———

I never ⟨yet⟩ knew a man who spoke lightly of the sex & doubted[?] female virtue in general who was not a man of cold or vitiated heart or limited understanding.

It is wonderful the continual forbearance and fortitude & self command that woman is obliged to exert & which in general she does exert. Nothing requires greater fortitude than the command of the passions. Man prides himself on giving way to them—⟨with him in[?]⟩ he makes a boast[?][18] of his self indulgence. Let any man consider how few gratifications he ⟨*unrecovered*⟩[19] denies himself & how few he is capable of denying himself and then he will wonder at the ⟨strength of the feeble⟩ miraculous forbearance & fortitude of this feeble being woman whose whole life is a continual triumph over the passions.[20]

13. This word could be read "case" or "care."
14. This word could be "Kind."
15. There is an ink blot above the word "amid" from the opposite page.
16. The ink blot below this word has faded through from the recto.
17. After WI crossed out the last three words of the line, "we credit him," he used two slanting strokes to cross out the subsequent four lines.
18. This word could be "bawd."
19. The unrecovered word seems to end in the letters "dies."
20. The remaining three-fourths of the page is blank, except an ink blot faded through from the recto.

⟨Take care⟩ "Beware says Epictetus not to play the part of a dunce for it is a mischievous[21] cha-/-racter ⟨that⟩ and a fals step that will make the fall usually into low and vulgar manners & lose[?] the respect of others—[22]

Do not laugh long, nor often, nor violently

Epictet.[23]

On no occasion call yourself a philosopher nor launch out fine maxims before the ignorant, but *do* what these maxims teach

For example, at a feast do not say how one ought to eat, but eat as one ought.

"[24]

If any one reproaches thee with knowing nothing and thou are not offended ↑piqued↓ with this reproach, know that from that moment you ⟨comm[?]⟩ begin to be a Philosopher.

[*p. [12] blank*]

Of Seeking popularity by flattering the people &c.[25]

Of the ruinous passion for office. The dependence of mind—the uncertainty of habit ⟨with⟩ which it produces.

21. WI's spelling could be "mischevious" or "mischeivous."

22. WI was studying Latin at this time: in journal entries of February 25 and March 6, 1825, he mentioned writing Latin exercises (*Journals and Notebooks*, III, 459, 462). Therefore, he could have been translating Epictetus or using an English version. One of the best Latin editions of this first-century Stoic philosopher's works, faithfully taken down by his pupil Arrian in eight books as *Epicteteae Philosophiae Monumenta*, was a six-volume work edited by J. Schweighäuser (Leipzig, 1799–1800); the English edition which WI may have used was Elizabeth Carter, ed., *All the Works of Epictetus, which are Now Extant* (Dublin: Hulton Bradley, 1759) or the same translation published in London (S. Richardson, 1758).

23. To the left of the name is an ink blot which could be a crossed-out word.

24. WI usually used "idem" rather than ditto marks, as he did here, to indicate that he cited the same source as above.

25. This series of six titles or topics probably related to WI's proposed "American Essays"; for a discussion of the list of topics as well as the "reconstruction" of nineteen essays, see Richard D. Rust's article on this subject, cited above (p. lix, n. 137). WI's paragraphing here is irregular, sometimes overhanging, sometimes indenting, sometimes writing the second line even with the first; between the second and third topics, WI skipped a line and drew a line in the space, and between all except two of the titles he left some space; therefore, we have regularized for clarity.

Of probity in dealing—of the old maxim Honesty is the best policy.

Of moderation in luxuries—of vulgar display of wealth.

Of affectation of Knowledge

Of respect to religion. Of respect to the clergy, who ⟨are in our⟩ form in our busy country the deposition of truth & knowledge—The veneration of Society is a ⟨ho⟩ tie upon them—they must conform to the expectation of the world—The real respectability of our clergy—the devoutness of our religious services.

———

Los establecimientos de ceremonias urbanas solo se hicieron para los genios medianos y infimos, como un ⟨suplimiento⟩ Suplemento de aquella discrecion superior a la suya, que por si sola dicta, y regla el porte, que se debe tener asia los demas hombres

Hay hombres que naturalmente y sin estudio son ayrosos en todos[26] los movi-/-mientos materiales; que muevan las manos, que los pies &c[27] todo sale con una gracia nativa, que a todos ena-/-mora; que es lo que cantaba Tibulo de Sulpicia: Illam quidquid agit, quo quó vestigia flectu, componit furtim, subse-/-quiturque decor.

Guardense los preceptos, y reglas para los que son naturalmente desayrados, si es que puede enmendar el Arte este defecto de la Naturaleza

Feyjoo D. 10 ¶ 6[28]

No life so laborious as that of a Knaves. He does ten times the work of an honest man with the risk of being punished for his industry. ([*unrecovered*][29] & industry) One half the pains that it costs him ⟨to keep clear of the gallows⟩ ⟨to get⟩ [? to secure a favor ?] he might build a palace, and the same hazards & ingenuity that conducts him to a gallows might have placed him on a throne.

———

26. After the word, "todos," WI omitted the word "ellos," went back to the previous sentence to copy the next three words, then resumed quoting the passage with the word "que."

27. WI omitted eighteen words.

28. Feijóo, "Discurso Decimo," *Theatro Critico Universal*, sec. 6, p. 251. WI began this passage with the fifth word of the first sentence of the fourth paragraph in section 6; he omitted one sentence at the end of his first paragraph and began a new paragraph where Feijóo did not.

29. The unrecovered word may begin with a "ch"; perhaps it is an abbreviated version of "character."

Solo respectivamente a dos clases de personas nadie esta exempto de guardar el ceremonial, que son los[30] principes y las Mugeres[31]

Plutarch speaking of Agesclaus[?] says that in virtue of his urbanity, although small & of a contemptible appearance he was even in his old age more amiable than all other men however handsome

Quintilian says that with this condiment the same sentence, the same speech sounds better in the mouth of one person than of another.

to keep his soul unspotted by this world.

Cicero calls it the colour of Urbanity
⟨Et tu⟩

Et Brutus, quis est, inquit, tandem[?] urbanitatis color? Nascio, inquam; tantum esse quandam[?] scis.

Dialog ⟨et [*unrecovered*]⟩
de Claris Oratoribus

Of Sincerity in Friendship

Let your friendship be with those of your own standing rather than with those elevated by ⟨fortune or⟩ rank or fortune—There is greater sympathy between men who concured[?] in habits & situations. It is not so much the assistance of the purse that we should look for or the consolation of ⟨good⟩ the heart. Kind looks, encouraging words, endearing express-/-ions, these give us comfort far beyond the ⟨aid of⟩ purse[?] of business[?] and used, in the very many troubles of this our mortal life, are sources of the Sweetest consolation.

[*p. [18] blank*]

Duelling. There is a false fierce kind of courage often manifested among young men which is mistaken for Gallantry of Soul.—

Against the blustering manner sometimes mistaken for Spirit—Mildness always praised as one of the attributes of the brave. The forbearance that ought to be manifested towards each other in a republic where each has his equal rights. The Jealousy with which one should maintain the laws, as a fabric which he has adjusted to build.

30. The *l* is written over another letter, perhaps a *c* or a *t*.

31. Feijóo, "Discurso Decimo," *Theatro Critico Universal*, sec. 6, p. 251.

Quarrellsome man of war; quarrelling with his comrades, with his Govt. Like an illmade gun that is apt to burst in ones hand.

———

When you do not know what to do do nothing—Its easier to supply a deficiency than repair an evil

———

Of Liberty—⟨mans [*unrecovered*]⟩ The temperate en-/-joyment of it—I have noticed that those who arrive in Am: from Europe particularly from Ireland, have confused notions of liberty as an absense from all restraint. They run riot on it—Like ⟨men⟩ ↑strangers—↓ in a wine country who get drunk with wine—Natives are sober

In Europe men are struggling for liberty[—]in Amer. enjoying it. They have ⟨a⟩ romantic enthusiastic[?] notions concerning it—we have stripped it of its romance but enjoy it rationally. Liberty is with them a mistress, with us a wife—A man may sometimes appear to treat his wife with coldness, but he will die to defend her—She is a part of himself.

Courage is in a man what chastity is in a woman—we always ⟨give him credit for it unless⟩ ↑he is always presumed to possess it until↓ he gives proof to the contrary—A swaggering fellow therefore who makes great boast of his valor inclines us to doubt its being genuine—as we should doubt the virtue of a woman who was continually boasting of it.

Inflammable courage soon burns out, like a brushheap in ablaze

There are cases in which a gent may be compelled to fight even against his wishes, as a kind of self defence against the prejudices of society

Never part with a friend in anger—it makes awkward meeting again—If you have disputed endeavor before parting to say some thing general—to make some ⟨rema[?]⟩ indifft remark—it will serve as a link on which to hold your next meeting.

Religion—General feeling of it

toleration of it in a country which countenances all sects & beliefs

Levity on religious subjects a proof of a low or trivial mind. Subject too exalted to be treated lightly—we may doubt[?], but we must doubt with awe. A Subject that fills the mind—⟨The sou⟩

———

People ⟨from⟩ ↑in↓ the country send their sons to the cities; on the contrary those of the cities shd. send theirs to the country— Perhaps an exchg would be good. The sons of country people come to city with frugal habits & frugal notions[?][32]—⟨th⟩ are brot up simply—have not idle connexion[?]—generally begin moderately & rise—⟨Sons in⟩ Young men in cities brot up in the idle plea-/-surable & dissipated habits[?]—expensive[?]—indolent proud—extensive acquaintances—idle away their youth[—]Shift away[?] after life—Send them early to learn agriculture ⟨& [*illegible*]⟩ Get a knowledge of lands &c You then send[?] good breeding into the country—they get health—a rich father can position[?][33] them out on good farms—neither riske of trade nor the capital nor credit necessary

There are two kinds of injustice, says Cicero. ⟨Of the one⟩ The inflicting an injury—and the neglecting to defend others from injury

Of Distinctions in Society—We may talk as much as we please about equality—There is an equality of rights in nature, but none of conditions. Strength, talents, &c &c give ⟨one[?]⟩ continual superiority—as in the trees of the forest—

⟨With us⟩ We have no hereditary distinctions, but we have classes of society arising from talents, manners, wealth &c. This is a natural aristocracy—Wealth is respectable as implying talents in ↑its↓ acquisition. The rich man is important in society as having great means of usefulness—

The mere vanity of wealth is contemptible.

There is one dignity which a man will be sure to grow into ⟨b⟩ if he conduct himself worthily. the dignity of a ⟨respe⟩ venerable old age—

Always suspect the morality of an act when concealment & mystery is required—and always the policy of it

Every trader is bound to extend his views beyond his own instrument[?][34] & not only to pursue it according to the strict rules of integrity but to direct it to such objects as ↑shall↓ advance the comforts[?], prosperity[,] the intellectual moral and religious imprint[?][35] of his [? de-

32. This word could be "actions."
33. This word could be "portion."
34. This word could be "involvement."
35. This word could be "impact."

fends rights ?] [*unrecovered*][36] & if his line of life enables him, of foreign nations, even in the remotest corners of the globe

[? C Johnson ?]

Has to contend with competitor Let his competition be open, fair, amicable;[37] not trickery ungenerous, & malevolent—Displayd not in depricating [*unrecovered*][38] a character of rival, but by strivg to surpass him in knowledge diligence [*unrecovered*]—always put yourself in place of the person you bargain with & draw your rule of ⟨right⟩ equity & kindness.

Govt.[?][39]

Never be grasping—be content with moderate profits.

Frugality the duty of a trader—He risks the property of others & has more than small temptations to expense[?] from the continual shower[?] of ready money passg thro his hands—T

Substance[?] *of Govt*[?][40]

Men are apt to proportion their expenses to their business rather than to their capital & the habit of ⟨hav⟩ turng great sums, tho' the property of others, makes them negligent of small sums.

Shun all unnecessary concealments. There are cunning men who always walk in mystery! are always doubted—we connect an idea of Knavery with cunning—& we attribute to them faults of which they are not guilty—

Always doubt the credit of an ostentatious man

Foundations of a traders credit are propriety[,] integrity, punctuality, industry, prudence, firmness of dealing[,] freedom from Extravagance from wild spirit of Speculation & from vice.

———

Clear accounts—be able to look into your acct. at all times & with a Eagle glance

———

36. The unrecovered word seems to begin with a *C* and end with an abbreviation, perhaps "gn."

37. There is an ink blot to the right of the semicolon.

38. The unrecovered word could be "shile," "thik," "chile," etc.

39. The source is unidentified; perhaps it is "Govt," "Gest," or "Gent."

40. The source seems to be the same as above; at the left margin there is a dash and a *T* which seem to have no significance.

A young man destined for trade should nevertheless be well educated to keep his mind from becoming contracted & illiterat[?][41]

We were not born for ourselves alone says Plato, our Country & our friends have Separate claims upon us.

—Men say the stories were designed for the service of men by being made able to communi-/-cate reciprocal benefits to each other

---

Well do they advise who forbid every action the justice of which appears doubtful, for equity is clear of itself & hesitation marks a purpose of inquiry[42]

Cic l 1

Great gains dangerous as well as great losses—when I hear that a man has made great sum by spoil I should look warily at him. It tempts to adventuring & creates confidence in luck or chance or fortune Whenever a man boasts of being lucky have a care of him[.] Losses make a man prudent & if he has any/thing left it is [? safer dealing ?] with him [? soon after ?]

Great fortune & a permanent [? sum are ?][43] seldom made by sudden run of luck—Behold how great men are made

[*The last six lines on p. [31] are difficult to decipher; the number of unrecovered words renders the passage meaningless.*][44]

Nothing so ominous as a time of *unexampled prosperity*—Notice[?] [*four unrecovered words*] & [*unrecovered*]

It is Difficult for the poor to ⟨let⟩ live on terms of intimacy with the rich. jealousies on the one part[;] want of sympathies on the other

41. This word could be "illiberal."

42. This word may be "injury."

43. These questioned words, "sum are," could be one word separated by end-line hyphenation, perhaps "em/pire."

44. An attempt at the reading is as follows: "Behold how great [? men are made ?] by [? little rills ?] & the [? Smale their fly [*two words unrecovered*] little fountain ?] & run [? pitiously then?] collecting the little [*unrecovered*]—[? sudden burst distinct then overflows makes courage useless ?]."

Do not depend too much upon friendship nor the assistance of others—Think how little you care for others or are agitated[?][45] by their misfortunes

---

Do not think your ⟨spa[?] imp⟩ are important to the worlds happenings The world soon gets reconciled to every loss See how many great men go down & the waves close over them—Napoleon

[p. [34] blank]

There is no cover large enough to ↑conceal↓ cover itself—⟨A knave may⟩ a crafty man may overreach himself in individual transaction but estab/-lishes a general character as a Knave.

Polignotus[46]—Greek painter,

Ornamented a Portico of Athens with paintings representing the principal events of Troy. They were precious for their grace & for the expression of the figures. ⟨The⟩ Refused all recompense. The Ampligelinear[?][47] Council passed a Solemn[?] decree to thank him and ordered that when he travelled he should be lodged & entertained in any city at the public expense—

Extract.

All new laws which it may be prepared[?][48] to introduce should bear reference to the state of circum-/-stances in which the people may cite it, time be actually placed; to the nature of the Govt. already established to the climate[?]; the character of the soil; the extent & local situation of the territory; the manner of life of the inhabitants, as consisting in agricult communt. & other pursuits, their customs, prejudices[,] superstitions—we ought not to attempt a direct change by violent enactments—this is a species of tyrany. Followg rather the example of Salem[?] legislators should impose such laws only as the people are fit to receive, not just as are most benefit in the abstract: since it is better to leave

45. This word possibly may be "afe[c]ted."

46. Polygnotus, who flourished in mid-fifth century B.C., was praised by Aristotle for his large murals with many figures at Delphi and at Athens which gave new life to mythological subjects, especially Odysseus' descent into hell and the capture and destruction of Troy.

47. There was a religious association which met at Delphi on alternate years called the Amphictyonic League; WI's word could begin with "Amphyel" or "Amphgel."

48. This word may be "proposed."

disorder altogether untouched than to ordain laws which will be either imperfectly[49] obeyed, or altogether neglected; & thus the whole body of the law ⟨for⟩ [*unrecovered*][50] disrespect—

Encyclopedia

———

It is the law & not men who ought to rule. This constitutes the essential difference between a free and an arbitrary Govt. "Law" says Plutarch "is queen over mortals & immortals"

Idem

———

Of young Ams. travelling—what they ought to regard—what to bring home.[51]

———

"Je m'efforçais de considerer toute chose au monde avec une sagesse toute vulgaire, la sagesse des cyniques."

[? S. Pelliso ?][52]

———

⟨*two unrecovered words*⟩
Disorderly life and profligate pleasures really deplorable

Alors on s'imagine être en paix; mais cette paix, ell[e] est mauvaise, elle est impie; un sourire sauvage, sans charite, sans dignite, un amour du desordre, de [l']ivresse, de la raillerie, voila tout—

[? S. Pelliso ?]

Le peu de jours que j'avais vecu dans le cynisme m'avaient etrangement souille.

Toutes les fois que l'homme se laisse aller un moment à avilir son intelligence, a considerer les oeuvres de Dieu avec la langue infamante de la raillerie ⟨*unrecovered*⟩ le ravage[53] qui se fait dans sa raison le destine[?] a de faciles[?] rechutes.

49. At this point the page ends; WI continued this encyclopedia article on the following page after drawing a line across the page to set off a short note on traveling which he had written earlier. For the continuity of the passage, we have moved the note to the end of the two encyclopedia passages.

50. This word could be "merits," "earns," "wins," etc.

51. This passage is out of order; see n. 49 above.

52. This source has not been identified; the first initial could be an *L* or a *T*, and the last name could be "Pellias," "Pillias," "Pilliso," "Pillies," "Pellies," etc.

53. With this word, the page ends; WI may have begun a sentence with "la ravage" without using the uppercase, then continued the quoted passage on the following page in very small letters. He does not cite the source here, but we assume it is the same as the two above.

It is a trite ⟨matt⟩ subject of jest with foreigners travelling among us that men of ordinary appearance & in ordinary situations of life have the titles of Judge—General &c—but this ⟨should⟩ ↑is↓ rather a ⟨matter⟩ testimony in favor of the intelligence of our ordinary people that men among the ordinary ranks of life can execute such offices. It is certain that they are filled suff[icient]ly well for all our purposes but to make judges & generals of Inn Keepers & farmers in Engd. would be ⟨negligent⟩ sad blundering[?]. It is natural too that we should be vain of these titles because they really imply merit. A man cannot be appointed to any office military or civil without the concurrence or voice of his neighbors It is therefore a proof of merit in himself and in a country where merit gives[?] distinction it is reasonably a ⟨matter of worth⟩ ⟨being proud of⟩ to be vain of the title which designates[?] it.

In a sea voyage it is not he who ↑always↓ spreads ↑or passes[?]↓ most Sail that is always most fortunate & expeditious. He is liable to a thousd accidents—to carry away[?] spare rigging—to lose in one day what he has gained in five

Tis the wary mariner who incessantly[?] Evaluates[?] the change & caprices of the breeze & aspect of the sea & sky—now puts out sail to catch the light breeze—now hoists the top galleon[?] sail—now takes in when the breeze freshens—Gets all Sails[?] stowd away when the storms blow—sends aside[?] close riggd topsail[?]—& waits a faun[?] sky to spread her sail again.

Americans—abroad—generally noticed for their quiet accommodating disposition—civility to servants—The result of our equality at home.

———

Civility to Servts. the least we can render them in return for the hardness of their lot—Doomed by fortune to ⟨be⟩ administer to the wants & be subject to the caprice of others—We might have been in their situation—there is no law of nature why a footman should have been born to stand behind ⟨his⟩ a ⟨coach⟩ carriage instead of sitting in it—His ⟨fo[?]⟩ nature may be superior to his masters[.] Chance—fortune has thrown him on a difft. lot in life—Let us then while we enjoy our superior lot, do nothing to render his harder one more grubbing[?][54]

[*p. [42] blank*]

54. An alternative reading is "galling."

Wit—a dangerous weapon[—]like the small sword used in old times—A man was ready to draw it on all occasions & frequently put his friend to death.

Age gradually loosens our hold on life[,] quenches the brightest eye, blanches[?] the ruddiest cheek and calms the hardiest blood—the days draw on when we say there is no pleasure in them—We die by degrees ⟨& the death bed is but⟩ one faculty after another gives out and we are half extinguished while we yet move upon the earth—The ↑sickest[?]↓ sick bed in youth performs rapidly the process of old age in extinguishing the faculties. The desire for life languishes with the decline of our ⟨health⟩ vigour ⟨& at⟩ and we sink purposely[?][55] into the sleep of death like weary children who after the sport & fatigue of the day is over, sink into the maternal bosom

Credit—paper currency—a whole system built upon promises—A community prom-/-ising each other great sums, multiplying the aggregate Myths[?][56] & fancying themselves rich. The Banks great manufacturers of promises where they promise by wholesale & buy & sell promises—But if a time comes to cash those promises then one fails after another & the failure of one promise authorizes the forfeiture of another—

Words coined into cash—and every one knows how inexhaustable the coinage of words is. ⟨? Yet a ?⟩[57] This may be called a land of promises—

Honesty made easy.

Nothing is easier than ⟨to act honestly⟩ the path of honesty—Tho apparently it is difficult— —A thousand difficulties conjured[?] into its path by the imagi-/-nation—but the honest man, like the [*unrecovered*][58] Knight finds all these phantoms vanish as he advances.

the Speculative & the ignorant [*unrecovered*]
—It is a good thing when imagination enters into business
Speculation is the romance of trade—it turns it all into poetry

55. An alternative reading is "profoundly."
56. An alternative reading is "together."
57. The crossed-out words may be "If at a" or "If it is."
58. This word may be "noblest," "venerable," "modest," etc.

Every man carries about him, says ⟨*unrecovered*⟩[59] ↑Locke↓ a touchstone, if he will make use of it, to distinguish substantial gold from superficial glitterings, truth from appearances. And indeed the use & benefit of this touchstone which is ⟨reason⟩ natural reason, is spoiled and lost only by assuming prejudices, overweening presumption & narrowing our minds. The want of exercising it, in the full extent of things intelligible, is that which weakens and extinguishes this noble faculty in us.

Of the understanding one may most truly say, that its force is greater generally than it thinks, till it is put to it.

Proverb. Use less & have less.

Locke[60]

Equal distribution of providence–gives meat to one and appetite to another–

Truth[–]its rarity like pure water

History[?] what it consists of

We are the first born of the Am. fam. of nations

Foreigners find fault with our roughness–we have not the polish of old coun-/-tries in the given[?][61] manner that a new country has not the polish of an old one. I should be sorry to see the smooth worldliness of the old countries manners unfit to a complaisance to ours. It is indeed says Moore with the advanced age of free states &c (vide 293/vol 2d.

It is with the advanced age of free States as with that of individuals, they improve in the theory of their existence as they grow unfit for the practice of it, till, at last, deceiving themselves with the semblance of rights gone by, and refining upon the forms of their institutions after

59. The word begins with a *B*, and the first letters could be "Bur" or "Bro"; the name may be "Burns."

60. John Locke's *Essay Concerning Human Understanding* was first published in 1690; WI quoted here from "Of the Conduct of the Understanding," perhaps from the first collected edition: John Churchill, ed., *The Works of John Locke* (London, 1714). WI may have used the 12th edition published in nine volumes in London, 1824, or the one to which we have referred: *An Essay Concerning Human Understanding*, 2 vols. (New York: Valentine Seaman, 1824). Appended in volume 2 of this edition is "Of the Conduct of the Understanding"; the passage WI quoted is on p. 261. (This essay is hereafter cited as Locke, "Conduct of the Understanding," *Human Understanding*.)

61. An alternate reading is "same."

they have lost the substance, they smoothly sink into slavery, with the lessons of ⟨slavery⟩ liberty on their lips.

Moores ‸↑Memoirs↓ ⟨life⟩ of Sheridan
vol 2*d.*[62]

A man to be valued for what he has in him & not what he has above[?][63] him

General observations drawn from par-/-ticulars are the jewels of knowledge, comprehending great store in a little room.

Locke[64]

The mind once jaded by an attempt above its power is either disabld for the future, or else checks at any vigorous undertaking ever after

vide His article on *practice*[65]

A set of opinions that a man gets by inheritance—as our Dutch—who inherit the opinions & garments of their ancestors

I[66]

How few men know what they believe

I

They imbibe, says Locke, at the first the allowed opinions of their country & party and so never questioning their truth, not one of an hundred ever examines. They are applauded for presuming they are in the right. He that considers is a foe to orthodoxy, because possibly he may deviate from some of the received doctrines there. And thus men without any industry or acquisition of their own, inherit local truths & are inured to assent without evidence This influences farther than

62. In the first paragraph, WI referred to Moore's biography of Sheridan by page and volume; in the second, by author, title, and volume. Thomas Moore's *Memoirs of the Life of Right Hon Richard Brinsley Sheridan* was published in 1825 in London in a two-volume edition, in Paris in a two-volume edition, and in Philadelphia in a one-volume edition. WI mentioned in several journal entries the fact that in November, 1825, he was reading Moore's biography (see *Journals and Notebooks*, III, 545–46, the November 19, 20, and 23 entries, in particular).

63. This word may be "about."

64. Locke, "Conduct of the Understanding," *Human Understanding*, II, 290.

65. *Ibid.*, 292. Paragraph 28 in the essay is subtitled "Practice."

66. In this and the following excerpt, WI abbreviated "idem" with *I*.

⟨Locke⟩[67] is thought, for what one of a hundred of the zealous bigots in all parties ever examined the tenets he is so stiff in; or ever thought it his business or duty ⟨to do so⟩ so to do? It is suspected of luke/-warmness to suppose it necessary, and a tendency to apostacy to go about it. And if a man can bring his mind once to be positive & fierce for positions, whose evidence he has never once examined, and that in matters of greatest concernment to him; what shall keep him from this short & easy way of being right in ⟨matters⟩ ↑cases↓ of less moment. Thus we are taught to clothe our minds as ^↑we do↓ our bodies, after the fashion in vogue, and it is accounted fantasticalness or something worse, not to do so.[68]

Mems. What we Americans need not see & remember.—not to bring home french dishes—[? nor dances ?]—

I recollect an youngster[?] who retd home scandalized his whole family by a naked Venus, at which was [*unrecovered*][69] to his bed room. He always ⟨affected[?]⟩ a smiled[?] ⟨of⟩ with self satisfaction at his superior virtue and the homebred squeamishness of his worthy family— [*blank*] who threw a worthy family into a panic by the [*unrecovered*][70] of a naked Venus.

Another had the fat coach horses condemned that he might drive a new pair[?] in style & [*five unrecovered words*][71] new horses—& Third scandalized his old father grievously by talking about [? P⟨a⟩oll Verona ?] & [? Julie Ramegar ?] which the ⟨other⟩ good old gent took to be some foreign acquaintance of his son, [*unrecovered*][72] than they [? should be ?]

I really dont See the propriety of sending our young men abroad to study foreign follies and foreign fopperies—none ought to be sent who are self satisfied[?]—idle—dissipated—volatile—

They ought not to [*three[?] unrecovered words*][73] on a great ⟨*unre-*

67. Apparently WI completed the portion of the passage he wished to quote, wrote the source, then decided to add more from the passage and simply crossed out the author's name.

68. Locke, "Conduct of the Understanding," *Human Understanding*, II, 300. Paragraph 34 of this essay is subtitled "Indifferency."

69. This word could be "launched."

70. This unrecovered word might be "indiscretion"; it also may begin with the letters "under."

71. These five words may be "made the house Servt mount."

72. The word may be "which" or two words, "no talk" or "not all."

73. The words may be "pick to get."

covered⟩[74] extent of ground merely to say that they have travelled—Travellg generalizes a young mans mind—enlarges his ideas

[*unrecovered*][75] of foreign minister [*blank*] haunted by the ghost of any deportd[?] dollar

Smoking[76] No man should be selfish enough to indulge a habit that offends & distresses his neighbors—He should be wary how he contracts such a habit.

Agst despondency. There are always good events turning up as well as bad.—Evils are great in the distance, but dwindle as we approach. We see them thro the medium of the imagination which refracts & enlarges.

Some good always springs up aside of the evil ⟨which self⟩ which we do not forsee

The capacity of the heart to digest misery. If the evils are not averted[?] we get accustomed to them—⟨Strife[?] [*unrecovered*]⟩ It is hard to starve hope—it finds herbage in the most sterile situation. It is like the camel of the desert

Poverty a mere comparative evil

Distress which softens the heart makes it susceptible to small pleasures.[77] They derive a zest from surrounding desolation—A melancholy & unfortunate person finds a thousand small comforts and solaces which in prosperity he would not have regarded. They are like the green spots and little fountains in the desert, which are inexpress-/ably gratified[?][78] & refreshing from surrounding sterility. There is no day so dark that has not its casual gleams of light and clearing[?].[79]

A stout heart carries us thro[—]keep our spirit together, to seize hold mercifully[?][80] of the least[?] turn of luck—

⟨We are[?]⟩ By ⟨fashion[?] we⟩

An anxious mind takes ⟨on⟩ misery in to nurse & uses[?] sources not its own.

74. The crossed-out word may be a false start at the end of the line.

75. This word may be "Flag," "Rag," "Bag," "Say," etc.

76. The overhanging paragraphing has been regularized.

77. See WI's journal entry of November 26, 1825, in which he discussed these same ideas in very similar terms (*Journals and Notebooks*, III, 696).

78. This word could be "grateful."

79. This word could be "cheering" (see *Journals and Notebooks*, III, 696).

80. This word could be "manfully."

An evil can happen but one way, but in apprehension we suffer it a thousand ways.—

We inflict ideal[?] miseries on us which hover[?] [? never sent ?]—

Suppose the evil never happens. ⟨how⟩ We have already suffered its sharpness by anticipation

Employ the mind

There is nothing like getting first in the field. The Mississippi was first known to the Settlers and gave its name to the whole body of waters which flows to New Orleans, though the Missouri ⟨enters[?]⟩ which flows into it is a vast deal more grand

Truth like oil will ever rise to the surface

WB.[81]

A good bargain is that where both parties are Satisfied.

A hard bargain is mean and ungenerous

A sharp bargain is Knavish.[82]

I have little opinion of his honour ⟨or generosity⟩ who boasts of a bargain whereby his ⟨own[?]⟩ neighbor lost thro his simplicity—nor of his generosity when he boasts of his neighbor losing thro his necessities

Avoid yielding to Surmises & suspicions. Check such a disposition if you find it in yourself Weed out these suspicions which are the tares and nettles of the mind (heart)

These suspicions often lay at the bottom of an otherwise gentle nature and ⟨sur⟩ Sour it—

Do not suspect snakes in the grass Your offices are not of sufficient importance to others that they should trouble themselves to combine agst you.

Better to be unsuspicious even tho' it lies you open to ⟨S⟩deception. You can but be cheated once or in one way—but the suspicious man is cheated in spirit a thousand times & a thousand ways and above all he is cheated out of his quiet

An unsuspicious man may have an enemy but a suspicious one cannot have a friend—at least he can not enjoy him, for there is no enjyt. in fr[ie]ndship when there is suspicion

81. We have been unable to identify "WB"; during 1824–1825, WI mentioned in journal entries several people whose initials are "W.B.": Sir William Bagshawe, William Becher, the Reverend William L. Bowles, William Brockedon, Walter Buchanan, Sir William Brabazon, etc. (see *Journals and Notebooks*, III).

82. WI's paragraphing is very irregular on this page; we have followed what seems to be his intention and intended with each new thought.

Agst ⟨resentment⟩ or revenge

The [? Christn Notion ?] of forgiveness & there cannot be better rules for a happy life

As long as we kepp[83] ⟨out⟩ alive the determi-/-nation of revenge we keep the ⟨*unrecovered*⟩ injury ⟨sharp⟩ burning in our bosom—otherwise we let it go out.

Story of Indians revenge

Notice the Am: Ch[aracter]: as exemplified in our revo-/-lution—⟨*illegible*⟩ suffering—persevering—

The ⟨bloodless⟩ ↑quiet↓ nature of the revolution—

The character of Washtgn as impressed on our Constitution & nation.

—Independence & self dependence traits of Am: character—To be cultivated & encouraged—have others help others ⟨take care⟩ ↑look to↓ of[84] yourself for help Our backwoodsman throwing himself into the wilderness—building a canoe—travelling on the waters

Young Ams. to learn much by travelling in their own country—a good school of pubes-/cence[?]

Am: does not despond—not so subject to despondence—accustomed to privations by travelling[?][85]

———

Agst Wastefulness—

Agst wastefulness of trees

———

A system of manners must gradually grow up moulded to our govt. & circumstances—⟨manners in a country—are always the mode[?] of Old⟩ all manners imported into a country are forced—Climate has a great effect. The heats[?] of our country prevent the close buttond up habits of an Englishm. The ⟨fa⟩ equality of ranks and ⟨independ constant inter-/changing of⟩ vivacity of intercourse prevents their reserve.

No national prejudices—treat all foreigners with kindness & courtesy—Let the name of a Stranger be Sacred in our land remembrg. our gnfathers were all strangers & sojourners—

Endeavor to get what is good of their customs, manners, &c of all countries.

———

83. WI apparently intended to write the word "keep."

84. WI inadvertently failed to cross out the "of" along with the other two words.

85. This word may be "burthens."

Great respect for teachers—in a country where knowledge is power the teachers are all important—⟨Some of the⟩

The office of teacher so respectable some of our greatest & best men have risen from teachers.

—At[86] universities be respectful. do not imitate the customs[?] of other countries—⟨we⟩ Here we have not many years to give to education & those all important

We should make our country *the Strangers home*

Navy[87]—The importance of our ships[—]detached Sov[erei]gnties—the safety of the country delegated to them They carry our character in safety to every part of the world

Commanders not aiming at their own sanguine[?] exploits—they must think of the dignity & ⟨safet⟩ interests[?] of the nation. Young officers may be bold & boiling—commanders mush be cool[,] discreet.

Our officers calm, courteous—not picking[?] quarrels—the brute part of courage. We hate the dg that is always shewg his teeth but we cherish the noble animal whose courage is sheathd in gentleness

———

feisty temper could not be tried[?] like guns—& swords. How much anger he can contain without bursting.

They[?] might have been palliatd[?] when we were questiond as warriors[?] There is not a question of our courage now, but there is of our courtesy—Let our officers be noted for their urbanity.

Fierceness may please the mob but generosity pleases every body

———

⟨Shall[?]⟩ Let your courage be sheathed in Courtesy.

———

The best ⟨*unrecovered*⟩[88] blade is the most pliant—It yields to circumstance but always comes back to its straightness—The finest temper bends before it breaks

———

a quarrelsome Soldier is a gun that kicks, & bursts in our hands—Like a bursting gun, does more mischief to friends than foes

86. The line to the left of the word "At" may be a dash or it may be the line to separate paragraphs.

87. WI wrote the *N* over an illegible letter.

88. This word may be "steel" or "shiel."

⟨fr⟩ Economy

Pay in cash for what you want & then youl[l] be likely to buy nothing but what you want

We feel the weight of a ⟨coin⟩ ↑dollar↓ in hand—but a dollar on credit is always light in our estimation.

Goods bought for future pay appear like goods ⟨bought⟩ got for nothing—but money paid for goods enjoyed appears like money lost—

To get goods on credit appears to some like getting them for nothing—but the pay day arrives & then we seem to be paying away money for nothing.

The longer the credit the harder will seem the payt—as it is for an enjoyment so long past by

"pawn the future for the present"—but if we live the future will become the present & then we will have to ⟨soon pay the present⟩ sacrifice the present to pay off the debts[?] of the past

We feel the weight of a dollar cash more than a guinea debt—

———

Navy. officers not brawlers in foreign taverns. Box lobby swaggerers. Recollect the high standg they have at home—they are to bear the character of Govt. Inform themselves concerning the countries—read their hists.[—]learn languages—make their cabins cells of Study.

———

We take the lead of republics—we are of importance[—]our example diffused[?] over america The elder republic

———

Their superiority be seen in the trim of the ships—In foreign ports I have felt a pride in seeing the flag of my country The ship always a picture

———

Commanders more noted for courtesy—. What I have heard of Danbridge[?] for his courtesy[89]

Men make a fuss about loving their country yet as a matter of course, wd. you praise a man for loving his mother—

———

Man who is bad to his family but pretends to general philanthropy—He

89. Because WI failed to lift his pen between words, the first letter of the unidentified name may be *B*.

takes the candle that should illumine his dwelling & puts it on the house top to illumine all the world.

———

Each man has his little sphere of usefulness & if he cultivates & gladdens that he does his duty—then bit by bit the whole world would be made a garden

———

Dont leave your own concerns to run abroad on schemes of public utility. There are large heads[?] enough at work for that

———

Moderation in language—our intemperate language with respect to persons in authority react on the Nat. char: After all the abuse heaped on them. See what pure unsullied characters our late presidents maintain

Man

———

Weakest part of our community the fashionable of Atlantic Cities—less national character, more vulgarity

———

Young men sons of wealthy men frivolous[?]—Ephemeral copies of Europeans

———

Never estimate a mans means by his expenses. It is what he saves, not what he spends that makes him rich

He that makes the most display is often the poorest—as the broad brook ⟨is the shallowest & the soonest⟩ makes the most show by bubbling but is shallowest & soonest dried. The narrow brook runs deep & quiet and is full in the driest weather

We do not judge of a tree by the broadness of the bows but the depth of its roots

———

Small showers fill the mill pond & keep the mill going & the miller rich but great floods [? sweep a way[90] ?] the mill dam, mill & miller

———

Do not be studious of petty comforts & petty indulgences—a little negli-/gence on these points is manly—Be not curious which of dishes [*unrecovered*][91] wines—nor make parade of such knowledge. ⟨Eating is⟩ Never make a business of eating—nor an amusement even—but a

90. WI seems to have written the word "way" over the word "mill."
91. This word may be "use" or "nor."

necessary refreshment—The table is a place for conversation not for mere eating. The prolonging of repasts may be good for the head but it is fatal to the stomach—If we could Sit & talk without insensibly eating & drinking too much

Never stretch so far as to lose your balance

A mans position is Secure according to what he stands on[,] not to what he leans on—

———

A rich mans sons are taught how to spend money—a poor mans how to save it. The cons-/equence is the former[92] are poor, the latter rich.

———

Omlet Soufflee—pierce it—then wind escapes & down it Sinks to a pancake

Dont make fine thinkers or fine writers or fine painters[?] or fine talkers of your children. teach them mathematics & make sensible practical men of them— [? heap on ?] comn. sense ⟨it⟩ an ounce of com: sense is worth a pound of sensibility—Strengthen the judgement—⟨*unrecovered*⟩ Econ on the imagination

———

We are the elder born of a new family of empires

~~I profess no false enthusiasm as concerning my country[—]I know~~ her faults & imperfections but I know from all that I have seen of this land that she has within her the most munificent & magnificent place for human Sucesses[?][93]

———

our bgn
[? no anteced[ent] ?]—
[? This is ?] Country[94] a great hive[?] of nations
Valour bristling up like the quills of a porcupine

Agst. affected contempt for the world & defiance of public opinion

No good man can dispise the opinion of the good. If a man ‸↑is↓ really indift to good opinion we lose the highest bond of good conduct

Men ⟨ap[?]⟩ are apt to defy the world when they want to do wrong.

92. The word "former" was written over an illegible word.

93. This word could be "affairs," "traffic," or possibly the abbreviation "oppor."

94. The *C* seems to overlap another letter, perhaps an *R*.

[*In the middle of p. [74] are four unrecovered words, apparently a French idiom.*][95]

a man should distrust the praises of the world & should not be led away by its caresses nor surprised at its caprices, but he should persist in ⟨doing⟩ deserving the good opinion & [*one letter unrecovered*] in doing right

———

No animal but man is conscious of the beauty of other animals—They are indiscriminate in their affection to each other[—]not led by beauty or merit—They attach themselves to man without preference to good looks or good qualities[—] the beggars dog think[s] he[']s much [? better t[ha]n ?][96] a king

Do not be rigid about any kind of study nor discountenance poetry & fiction

We are curiously compounded—less[?] & strong. These things softn & sweeten our nature

———

Reading is good—but reading with reflection[—]reflection is the digestion of readg

One of the Am charistcs.[—]versatility—

Has to depend upon ingenuity. ⟨We have had to d⟩ The way in which great part of nation here lives in country far from convenience has made them shrewd at expedients, quick at using their own reserves[?][97] —Born to [*unrecovered*][98] resources—make the most of talent—talents convertible—whatever he possesses he can turn to acct & bring into action —His ingenuity like the indians[?] Knife—

An american therefore not despondent when ⟨? out cast ?⟩[99] baffled on one point[?][100] immediately thinks of another.

Mother wit does everything.

He is a proteus[?]—an Am: goes thro so many changes—⟨one tim[e]⟩

95. The key words seem to be "fais," "bien," and "rien" (the third word resembles "crasse"); the idiom, "Cela ne fait rien," may offer a clue to these words.

96. These two words may be one unrecovered word; WI did not lift his pen between words or syllables, the final one which may end in a *y*.

97. This word may be "resources."

98. This word seems to begin with a *p* and may be "preserve"; it also may be two words with no space between, perhaps "see all."

99. These words may be "at mast" or "at most."

100. A possible alternative reading for the three words may be "in one pursuit."

Hear of the same man at various times of his life & youd thouht you heard of so many difft. men: Schoolmate Lawyer, judge, mercht manufacturer[?] Land surveyer—wherever he is thrown he feels at home

This keeps him from being dispondent

Vulgarity of our cities[—]Gentility of the country—notice the natural gentleman I saw on the black river[?] country

Excellence of character in our country—virtue of our women—

⟨Spe⟩ the improvg state of our country keeps up a speculation in rural life—shifting of Jobs[?] when a man speculates on his home & sells his household gods

---

Endeavour to keep up a freshness of character.

When a young man has lost that ⟨th⟩ one of the greatest charms of youth is gone.

like the dew on the flower—like the fragrance to the flower—like the blue[?] on the plum[?]

Do not ⟨be vain⟩ seek distinction by excentricities[?][—]by [? affected neglect of dress ?]

Senecas Epistles to Lucilium[101]

---

*A young country like young man is the better for advice & rebuke even tho it stings & humiliates[102]

Cleanliness costs nothing and it is no[103] near a virtue that in many countries it has been made a part of religion

---

Like the sun of my own country let me sink suddenly to rest, when all my light & heat is over, not slowly ⟨be extinguished in the⟩ expire thru the long twilight of a lingering old age

---

⟨It is not the⟩ We may learn much from foreigners that will be beneficial but much that is disadvanta-/-geous—Foreign manners are not suited to our country. We should avoid the aristocratical manner of the higher and the servile habits of the lower classes. There is a general

101. WI's source was *Seneca ad Lucilium Epistulae Morales*; see WI's 1823 notebook, "Extracts &c," into which he copied a passage from this same source, Epistle 99 (*Journals and Notebooks*, III, 610 and n. 7).

102. The asterisk is WI's and is actually an *X* to the left of the letter *A*.

103. WI probably intended to write "so."

taint of ostentation & pride in foreigners ⟨all would be that⟩ The existence of a noble ⟨rank⟩ class puts every man as lesser[?].[104] All are wanting to appear better than they really are, instead of standing firmly on their feet

---

*There is a superscilliousness—an aiming at privilege—distinction. We have caught it—we would form exclusive classes—Ridiculous attempt where fortune is so precarious—where does one of our exclusive circles ⟨remain[?]⟩ ⟨exist⟩ maintain their ⟨height and are⟩ standing for a doz years. The ⟨*unrecovered*⟩ transient aristocracy of a handful of years. What has become of the aristocracy of the revolution—[105]

Wines, madiera is not suited to our great families—⟨the family does not⟩ it takes too long to ripen. French wines are better, a man may then stand a chance to maintain his standing until his wine grows drinkable

---

[? Bad plea ?] that luxury encourages trade & industry.

If it introduces business[,] at our expense.

If it gives one opportunity to make money[,] teaches two to spend it

Ceux qui mettent leur sagesse a s'indinger[,] à se plaindre[,] à denigrer, traitent de folie, la pitie, l'amour et le besoin de se consoler avec de nobles illusions qui honorent l'humanite et son [*unrecovered*][106]

[? S. Pelliso ?]

Shd learn foreign languages at an early age so as to be acquainted with idioms. In this way we get a knowledge of foreign nations & can judge of them without having their ideas[?] filtered thro the Eng language & tinged with english idioms. We should see them with our naked eye, not thro Eng spectacles—

We should get knowledge & improvt[107] as direct ⟨*illegible*⟩ from any country as we Get their merchan-/-dize—not imported thro England as

104. Another reading may be "lessor," but there seems to be a *t* in the final syllable, as in "Captor."

105. The asterisk at the beginning of the passage is WI's; it is actually a large *X* in the margin to the left of the paragraph with a small semicircle setting it off.

106. The letters of this word resemble "anteur" or "antim"; the unidentified author is the same one from whom WI quoted three passages earlier in this notebook (see n. 52 above). We have followed WI's rendition as closely as possible, including omitting accent marks throughout and including the misplaced comma following "folie."

107. This word may be "imports," "imprints," or "impart."

a depot—We are so placed as to have direct intercourse with all the world.

———

⟨Na⟩ Equality in Nature—child knows nothing of diffs of each. a Beggars brat makes as much ⟨noise as⟩ racket as if it were a rich mans child & had a right ⟨to make a noise in the world⟩ ↑⟨to give trouble to⟩↓ to give trouble & make a noise in the world

Of a national name

We have no designation—we are confounded among other nations—It may do among ourselves to call ourselves Amerns but the moment we leave our shores

In Europe an Am: is thot to be a Creole We ⟨lost⟩ neglected the choice Columbus

———

Of naming towns—rivers &c

———

Old [*unrecovered*][108] will be superseded by new. We shall have neghboring powers[?] to draw off our attachmt[?] from Europe

A prospect into futurity in America says our late President Adams, is like contemplating the heavens through the telescopes of Herschell: objects, stupendous in their magnitudes and motions strike us from all quarters, and fill us [with] amazement.

———

A profligate American youth, says the venerable Presdt Adams, must be profligate indeed, and richly merits the scorn of all mankind—

Of ⟨Loyalty⟩—Love of Constitution[109]

We have no throne as in Engd[—]Must attach ourselves[?] to a mere abstraction[.] The union should be [*unrecovered*][110] A love & reverence for it next to love of God[.] What sh[oul]d we say to hearg[?] on slightest clash of interests a talk of death of the King yet a talk of severance of union not less mons/trous[?].

Rash light men who use[?] it—think only of selfish interests & persl interest dont see how ⟨they⟩ their own interest is sinister[?][111] What

108. The last syllable of this word seems to be "ships" or "ness"; one possible reading is an abbreviation, "relatships."

109. The paragraphing on this page is irregular; we have attempted to follow what seems to be WI's intention.

110. This word may be "insulated."

111. This word may be "involved."

would Georgia be separated—We sh[oul]d make a country of petty powers like Germany.

Union our band of greatness[—]gives us the first place among Republics—This gone we sink beneath neighboring republics, who are growg up around us

———

⟨The ⟨To⟩ show of public [*unrecovered*]⟩

Of popular eloquence: 4 July orator—no vauntg[112]

Of Vauntg[113] hyperbolical language in oration, writings & conversation

4t of July a kind of intoxication of the mind.

———

Of Elections. not quick to change men in office. Country badly served by men who are unacquaintd with offic[e][—]do not execute their offices quietly—sounds busy with election[?]

Clergy fulfil their function best[—]been apart from politics & not changed

———

"Truth is simple & uniform & ever attended with a happy coincidence of all its parts, whereas error is infinite."

[? Essay on Freedom & holdg ⟨of⟩ up Public Office ?]

[*The first eight lines on p. [85] concerning "A Man in travelling" and the "crack of the postillion whip" are difficult to decipher; the number of unrecovered words renders the passage meaningless.*][114]

———

—men[?] who according to Burton brag inwardly & find themselves fat with self conceit

———

Libertas non est licentia—Tacitus

112. The paragraphing of these three lines varies; we have regularized.

113. This word may be "correct &," but the context and its similarity to the word above it, "vauntg," suggest our reading.

114. An attempt at deciphering this passage is as follows: "A man in travelling comes [? undeniably under ?] the sphere of little fame[?] [*two unrecovered words*] little systems of fancying[?] themselves [*three unrecovered words*] a few cracks of the postillion whip & ⟨? the he tend ?⟩ then grows ⟨fond[?]⟩ begins to favor/-ing crack of the whip. [? they bend ?], and he [? comes within the range ?] of another [? gent genius ?]."

We are apt to imagine that great stations imply great talents whereas I have occas-/-sionally found the talents of a great statesman employed in regulating a coblers state and on the other hand a cobler conducting the affairs of an cabinet

Population, riches, true religion virtue, magnani-/-mity, arts, sciences & learning are the necessary effects and productions of liberty; & an extensive trade navigation, & naval power entirely flow from the same source: in this case, if natural advantages & encouragements are wanting, art, expense, and violence[?] are lost & thrown away. Nothing is more certain than that trade cannot be forced; she is a coy & humorous dame, who must be won by flattery & allurements, and always flies force and power[?]; she is not confined to nations sects or climates, but travels & wanders about the earth, till she fixes her residence where she finds the best ⟨and⟩ welcome and kindest reception; her contexture is so nice and delicate that she cannot breathe in a tyranical air; evill & pleasure are so opposite to her nature, that, but touch her with the sword & she dies: but if you give her gentle & kind entertain/-ment she is a grateful & beautiful mistress; she will turn deserts into fruitful fields, villages into great cities, cottages into palaces, beggars into princes, convert cowards into heroes, ⟨blout[?]⟩ blockheads into philosophers, will change the covering of little women into the richest brocades, the fleece of harmless sheep into the pride & ornaments of Kings; by a further metamorphosis will transmute them again into armed hosts & haughty fleets.[115]

* * * * *

Trade cannot long subsist much less flourish in arbitrary govts.; there is so close & inseparable an connexion between that & naval power that I dare boldly affirm that the latter can never arrive at any formidable height & continue long in that situation under such a state. When there is an extensive trade great numbers of able-bodied and courageous sailors, men bred to fatigues, hardships, and[?] & hazards and consequently soldiers by profession are kept in a constant pay; not only without any charge to the government but greatly to its benefit, not only by daily adding to its wealth and power, but by puting[?] & employing abroad to their countrys honour & safety, these turbulent & unruly spirits that would be fuel for factions & the tools & instruments of ambitious or discontented great men at home. These men are always ready at their countrys call to defend the profession they live by, & with it the public

115. WI indicated omitted material by inserting five small *x*'s in the middle of a skipped line.

happiness; they are & ever must be in the public interest, with which their own is so closely united; for they subsist by exporting the productions of the peoples industry, which they constantly increase by so doing; they receive their pay from the merchts. a sort of men always in the interests of liberty, from which ⟨they⟩ alone they can receive protection and encouragement, and as this race of men contribute vastly to the public security & wealth, so they take nothing from it; they are not quartered up & down their native country like the bands of despotic princes to oppress their subjects, interrupt their industry, debauch their wives & daughters, insult their persons, to be examples of lewdness & ⟨profligacy⟩ prodigality, & to be always ready at hand to execute the bloody commands of a Tyrant.

No monarch was ever yet powerful enough to keep as many seamen in constant pay at his own ex-/-pense, as single cities have been able to do without any at all: the pay of a sailor, with his provision is equal to that of a trooper[116] in arbitrary govts.; nor can they learn the trade by taking sea air for a few summer months, & wafting about the coasts of their own country: they gain experience & boldness by various & difficult voyages, and by being constantly inured to hardships & dangers: nor is it possible for single princes, with all their power & vigilence, to have such regular supplies of naval provision as trading countries must always have in store."

The above is quoted in a tract en-/-titled Continued corruption, Standg armies &c considered—& as quoted as from a judicious & excellent author

---

The blood of England, with her constitution has been enriched by the Britons, Romans, Saxons, Angles, Danes & Normans, with other natures[?],[117] & they also in scorn call [? her poor ?] mongrels do not consider that all the royal families in Europe are the same

from the same tract.

From the treaty of Utrecht to the war begun in 1744 due care not being taken of British American by our ministers[—]the French sowed the seeds of war ⟨*illegible*⟩ on the sea coast & in the interiour parts, which so far increased[?], that, if the vigilance & public spirit of the generous & public Massachusett Bay had not prevented, the French would have gotten such firm hold of the key of North America that our ministers in my opinion would never have recovered it out of their hands.

idem.

116. This word may be "trouper."
117. This word may be "nations" or "natives."

Philip de Comines[?] observes When people whose interest binds them together divide and forsake one another, it is a certain sign of destruction, not only for towns & little states but for princes & great potentates—"*Concordia res* ⟨*parvu*⟩ *pervæ crescunt; descordia maxumæ dilabuntus*"

Wealth.

Advice given by Micaenas to Augustus. *Magnæ opis non tam multa capiendo quam hand perdendo quærantur.* Great riches are acquired rather by frugal expenses than by plentiful receipts.

The gods only know, says Cicero, the plenteous fruits of economy.

["]Precedents," says the author of Free Briton "tho' subversion of principles ⟨&⟩ made on the spur[?] of present occasions, will not sleep"—a tenet[?] to those who rashly legislate for some party or private interest.[118]

An ancient & excellent maxim on Govt—a public minister who injures one threatens all & therefore he is to be opposed by all.

Honor & virtue are the principles of the English govt. & fear the principle of despotic govt.

idem.

^↑Lord Clarendon says↓" "The chearfulness of subjection is the strength of it"[119]

The proper remedy of all our maladies & dangers is the free, uncorrupt & proper use of the right of election. Incorruption is as necessary to its beneficial use as freedom is to its existence; for an attempt might as well be made to erect a permanent palace for a prince on the top of

118. Sir Francis Walsingham (1530[?]–1590) wrote *The Free Briton Extraordinary* (London: J. Peele, 1730), in response to a pamphlet, "A Short View," regarding the Treaty of Seville (1729).

119. The magnum opus of Edward Hyde, the first earl of Clarendon (1609–1674), was *The History of the Rebellion and Civil Wars in England*, 3 vols. (Oxford, 1704); probably, WI copied from what seems to be the 4th edition of this work, published in 3 vols. in Oxford, 1704–1707; in this particular edition was "bound up the 'Free Briton,' No. 106. By F. Walsingham, in relation to the History." It is not surprising that WI was interested in the *History*; reissued in its 11th ed. in 1819 and in its 12th ed. in 8 vols. in 1826, it was obviously popular at the time WI copied into his commonplace book.

Mount Vesuvius, or to graft a flourishing tree on a rotten stock, as to prevent the fall of a free state daily undermined by corruption."

idem

"Truth will sooner or later swim uppermost"

idem

The persons much concerned in planting the colony were certainly men of great accomplishments, tho the monuments of their wisdom have been neglected by several of their Successors, So that Ralegh, Bacon & Popham with several others, have great reason to complain of the treatment they have recd. Besides the universal knowledge of history Raleghs talents for policy & war made Spain tremble, & her cabinet council could not sleep in quiet until they had prevailed on King James, who had not in his breast one spark of etherial fire, to put them to death contrary to law. Bacon, when sitting on an eminence with all the learning of the earth before him, marked its ⟨effects⟩ defects & gave the outline of its augmentation, & ⟨Judge[?]⟩ Popham's law & judgt were sufft to recommend him to the great Elizabeth; yet we ⟨see⟩ every day see persons far less qualified, censoring in effect the institutions devised by these & other men esteemed for their law, learning &[120] history.

idem

No wise man was ever obstinate, & the confession of an error is in its nature the declaration that the mind is better informed than when it was committed; whereas the perse-/-verance in it, without [*unrecovered*][121] it by foe[?] and friend[?], is in effect the daily repetition of it.

idem

St Bernard told More the Doge of Venice that the Republic would last as long as the custom contd of doing Justice. Which father Paul in his advice to that republic says was a maxim no less politic than holy, because under this short rubric are contained so many good advices that were they all faithfully observed we might justly expect thereby to perpetuate the dominion of the Commonwealth to all ages—Afterwards he says, on all occasions whenever the public faith is engaged, it is necessary to observe it inviolably, without being amused by any

120. The ampersand could be the word "of."

121. The word could be "acessing," "inquiring," "informing," etc.

profit that may accrue to the republic by the[122] breach[?] of it. And it is fit to consider that the benefit reaped by breaking it is momentary, but the damage that follows upon the not observing it is perpetual."

Tract. contd. Corruption[?].[123]

Polybius speaking of Rome & Carthage says In all things that regard the organization of wealth, the manners ⟨&⟩ also & the customs of the Romans are greatly preferable to those of the Carthaginians[—]among the latter nothing is reputed infamous that is joined with gain: but among the former nothing is held ⟨base⟩ more base than to be corrupted by gifts, or to want[?][124] an increase of wealth by means that are unjust; for as much as they esteem the possess-/ion of honest riches to be fair & honourable, so much on the other hand, all those that are amassed by unlawful acts are viewed by them with horror & reproach. The truth of this fact is clearly Seen in the following instance[:] Among the Carthagns money is openly employed to obtain the deputies[?] of the state; but all Such proceeding is a capital crime in Rome."

idem

Rome—Its liberties were long preserved by putting the sword into the hands of the citizens who returned from military service to their private stations, & by taking care that armies should not be employed in their civil affairs.

"[125]

Dionysius of Halicarnassus to the pantheon[?] of the Romans says that the harmony arising from the constitution of Romulus was so firmly

122. At this point, p. [91] ends, and after the first two-thirds of the following page which contains almost unrecoverable pencil jottings, perhaps made earlier, WI drew a line across the page and continued in ink the quoted passage below the line; we have transcribed in WI's intended order for the convenience of the reader.

The first seven lines of p. [92] contain many unrecovered, questioned, and crossed-out words as follows: "Reader hast thou ever in travelling in [? summer on some ?] cross country road remarked some old [? inn mile away. tavern. Old chalice ?] ⟨In such a one⟩ perhaps not for the [? peculiar past ?] of traveller know little[?] of Yours[?] off of the high road—[? In rest in former ?] times had [*unrecovered*]—." The next two lines, which appear to be the second paragraph, seem to be, "Reads[?] fairy tales—fancys every thing [? about her ?] of the kinds[?]." WI then drew a line from flush left slightly downward and wrote four lines: "Necessity for a nat: name[—] Bad names of Towns[,] Rivers[—]New York, New London"; finally, he added the name "Lady Clinton."

123. The final word of the citation may be "Compton."

124. This word may be "merit" or "covet."

125. The ditto marks are WI's abbreviation for "idem."

establishd among them that tho' as it often happens in all cities both great & small, many great political contests have arisen between the people & their magistrates, they never, within the course of 620 years proceeded to bloodshed & mutual slaughter but by persuading & informing one another; by submitting in some things & necessary or voluntary submission in others, they put an end to their disputes in such a manner as became fellow citizens.

"

Ship—a floating sovereignty—more importt than a frontier post as that is in want[?][126] of advice & superiors and has but one kind of neghbor to deal with—But a ship is continly changing place country [*unrecovered*][127] —coming in contact with new neighbors—people—laws—manners—prejudices languages—What caution ought to be[?][128] here exerted: & with rival champions of the deep

———

Avoid all useless bravadoes—all boasts of superiority. Let your character depend upon your deeds—not words.

A pound of self praise never outweighed an ounce of courage

[*Upside down at the bottom of p. [94]*]
A little man who had dried away from his whiskers—So that he looked like an exceeding small man in a great bush[?] of hair. His whiskers had thrived to great bushes, but had exhausted the face in which they had taken root.[129]

It is incredible the mischief that some hot blooded men do in a scene[?] —They ⟨get the no⟩ dazzle the minds of the young men—get charable[?] for spirit—Set example and give rise to a whole ⟨st[?]⟩ tribe of duellrs

———

In affairs of honor take advice from older men—cool calm men—Never take advice of a dueller or a man who has fought a duel

———

He who tampers with legislation poisons the fountains from which the public is Supplied

126. This word may be "reach."
127. This word may be "cus[to]m" or "closer," but the context is confusing.
128. Because WI did not lift his pencil, these two words could be "better."
129. The reversed portion ends here.

Criticism[?] in Ameri–we begin to clip[?] & train[?] & read too soon let them [? be free from growth first ?]

The Courtesy of Bayard oftener mentioned than his valor[130]
Francis &c at Clerk of Govt[?][131]

Wine like poetry grows in the midst of poverty–
from a Steward [*unrecovered*][132]

The most precious[?] Wines produced from the poorest soils–soils that can produce nothing else produce wine

---

I dont want to hear of my countrymen as Speculative

[*inside back cover*]
In business never reach farther than you can stand firm, stretch your arm[133]

[*back cover blank*]

130. WI mentioned in a December 5, 1824, journal entry that William Brockedon, the painter, told him of Bayard's Castle and its beautiful location (*Journals and Notebooks*, III, 433); he also copied into his 1819–1823 "Extracts &c" from Bayard's *La très joyeuse, plaisante et récréative histoire* (*ibid.*, 568–69, n. 11). Professor Reichart identified this early sixteenth-century "knight without fear or blame" as Pierre du Terrail, seigneur de Bayard (ca. 1474–1524), who was born near Grenoble (*ibid.*, 433, n. 109).

131. WI identified Francis as one of Thomas W. Storrow's clerks, whom WI saw on Christmas day, 1824 (*Journals and Notebooks*, III, 440).

132. The letters could be "Lrnd" (i.e., Learned).

133. After the notebook was turned a quarter rotation clockwise, someone wrote along the gutter, "Wreden 9/2/60."

COMMONPLACE BOOK

Passages from Elizabethan and Jacobean Plays (1817?)[1]

This manuscript notebook is in the Folger Shakespeare Library, Washington, D.C., where it is cataloged as "D.a.2"; it is titled and described as follows: "Commonplace book. Ca. 1810. Extracts from old plays—all Elizabethan except one, Tuke's *Adventures of Five Hours*, and many by obscure dramatists. No Shakespeare extracts are included. Some of the extracts later supplied chapter headings for The Sketch Book." There were originally 46 leaves in the notebook; leaves 1–7 are missing, having been cut out (perhaps by Irving), and on the recto of the stubs of leaves 1, 3–4, and 7 there are ink marks as if there might have been writing on these pages. The last seven leaves (40–46) are loose but clearly in order as all have at least a part of a matching stub. The 78 pages measuring 4⅞6 x 7¾6 inches are no longer attached to the rust leather cover but are held to it by a thin white string tied between pages [46] and [47]. The notebook is housed in a brown, rust, black, and white mottled cardboard slipcase with green spine and green flaps and tied with a white string. The paper is off-white with five vertical lines and numerous closely approximate horizontal lines in the texture of the paper. In leaves 8–11 at an angle in the corner of the page is a watermark of a half crown of fleur-de-lis resting on a design; leaves 36–41 contain more of the crown. In leaves 12–17 is a watermark with line drawing of loops and half fleurs-de-lis, and leaves 30–35 contain a mirror-image. In leaves 18–21 and 23 at the bottom binding corner of the verso is the watermark number "09" upside down, and in leaves 24–29 in the bottom binding corner of the recto is the number "18" upside down; therefore, when the notebook is reversed, between the middle leaves (23 and 24) at the top edge is the watermark "1809." Leaves 43, 44, and 46 contain

1. The watermark, "1809," suggests that as the earliest possible date of composition; the fact that WI used some of the quotations in *The Sketch Book* suggests 1819 as the latest possible date. The Folger dates the notebook about 1810. See Introduction, pp. lv–lvii, and note below for further discussion of dating.

the watermark letter "A" in the bottom binding corner. In black ink (occasionally, brown ink) are the front cover, the back cover, and pages [17–88]; in pencil are page [15] and the inside back cover and the Folger leaf numbers "10," "20," and "30" in the upper-right corner of pages [35], [55], and [75]. Blank are pages [16], and [89–92].

[*front cover*]

Extracts from
Old Plays[2]

O Plays[3]

[*inside front cover*][4]

Col Briket[?]
Newton
Hon Mr Chapman[5]

2. WI apparently copied from the first two volumes of Charles Wentworth Dilke's edition of *Old English Plays; Being a Selection from the Early Dramatic Writers*, 6 vols. (London: Printed by Whittingham and Rowland for John Martin, 1814–1816). The first four plays from which WI took notes (pp. [17–33] in the notebook) were in volumes 1–2 in Dilke's collection. Volume 6 of this series had the title *Old Plays: Being a Continuation of Dodsley's Collection*, and another printing of Dilke published by Rodwell from 1815–1816 in six volumes had that same title (with the exception of volume 4 which had as its subtitle, *Being a Selection from the Early Dramatic Writers*). Still a third printing of Dilke published in 1816 in six volumes (London: Rodwell and Martin) was also titled *Old Plays: Being a Continuation of Dodsley's Collection.* WI wrote on the cover of this commonplace book "Extracts from Old Plays"; he could have used any of these versions of Dilke. After the first four plays in the notebook which were in Dilke, WI apparently began using one of the later editions of Robert Dodsley's *A Select Collection of Old Plays*, first published for Dodsley in twelve volumes in London in 1744. It seems likely that WI used an 1810 edition (London: Printed for W. Miller, by J. Ballantyne and Co., Edinburgh, 1810). Plays were deleted, added, reincorporated, etc., with each of the versions of 1780, 1810, 1825–1827, and 1874–1876; as far as we can determine from the prefaces of these editions, each of the next eight plays from which WI copied is in the 1810 version. Excerpts from the subsequent fourteen plays are from another source, one of them from Lamb's *Specimens*; among them are four plays by Middleton and three by Jonson.

3. This line may not be in WI's hand; the *O* is heavy, as if the writer drew over it several times. On the back cover are the letters *O P.*

4. Unrecovered at the top flush left are some numbers or letters in brown ink, an initial number "9" and two of what seem to be three concluding numbers, "5" and "6." Also there are two small ink blots in the top fifth of the inside front cover flush left and one larger ink blot about two-thirds down the page flush left.

5. These names are in the upper right corner in pencil; in the list of subscribers of the first edition of Robert Dodsley's *A Select Collection of Old Plays* (1744) are Robert Bricknil, Esq., Thomas Chapman, Esq., and Mr. Norton.

[pp. [1–14] torn out and missing]

[p. [15] in someone else's hand reads "MS. by Washington Irving, representing his reading of old plays in notes to supply chapter headings for his own books. In Sketch Book *some verses from this commonplace book will be found used."]*

[p. [16] blank]

[p. [17]]

From Lusts Dominion.
Marlow[6]

———

Hah! banish me! S'foot, why say they do,
↑There's↓[7] Portugal a good air, & France a fine country,
Or Barbury rich, & has Moors; the Turk
Pure devil, & allows enough to fat[8]
The sides of Villany, good living there;
I can live there, & there, & there;
Troth tis a villain can live any where.
But, say I go from hence, I leave behind me
A cardinal that will laugh; I leave behind me
A Philip that will clap his hands for joy,
And dance 1 voltoes through the Castile court;
But the deep⟨e⟩'st[9] wound of all is this, I leave

6. In the fourth edition of Dodsley's collection, W. Carew Hazlitt said that *Lust's Dominion* was added to the collection for the first time; he pointed out that the play was printed in 1657 and 1661 with Marlowe as author. Hazlitt added that the play was no longer attributed to Marlowe, but that Dilke persisted in this "error" (W. Carew Hazlitt, ed., *A Select Collection of Old English Plays: Originally Published by Robert Dodsley in the Year 1744,* 4th ed., vol. 14 [London: Reeves and Turner, 1875], p. 95). Dilke gave the subtitle and author as "The Lascivious Queen: a Tragedy. By Christopher Marlowe" (*Old English Plays*, I, [89]) and compared the play favorably to *Faustus.* To separate speeches and to indicate when he skipped lines in this play, WI drew 21 lines varying in length from one-eighth inch to 1½ inches; we have regularized without further notation.

7. WI wrote above an ink blot which extended into the left margin.

8. WI wrote the words, "the sides of Villany," at the end of the line, then crossed out and rewrote the words in the pattern of his source. WI often used the ampersand and other abbreviations or varied punctuation or capitalizations; we shall transcribe what he wrote, commenting only on significant deviations from the text.

9. In Dilke's edition, the abbreviation was used; apparently WI first wrote the *e* and then followed his source.

My wrongs, dishonours & my discontents,
Oh! unrevenged–[10]

Eleazer, in Lusts'[11] Dominion
by Marlowe

———

Eleazar⟨s⟩–Who Spurns the moor
Were better set his foot upon the devil
Do spurn me, & this confounding arm of wrath
Shall, like a thunderbolt breaking the clouds
Divide his body from ⟨th⟩his soul! Stand back.
Spurn Eleazar![12]

———

–make m⟨y⟩e lay by
Hostile intendments–[13]

———

Eleazar. Away then, work with boldness & with speed
On greatest actions greatest dangers feed.[14]

———

The Boy is proud, Ambitious, he woos greatness
He takes up Spanish hearts on trust, to pay them
When he shall finger Castiles crown–[15]

———

But love me & Ill kneel & sue to thee
And circle this white forehead with the crown
Of Castile, Portugal and Arragon
And all those petty kingdoms which do bow
Their tributary knees to Philips heir–[16]

———

10. *Lust's Dominion*, I, iv, 15–28. Because editions of Renaissance plays number lines variously, we shall identify subsequent passages copied by WI by author, play, act, and scene. WI did not copy the remaining 8½ lines of this speech of Eleazar to his wife, Maria.

11. The mark is on the line, but WI seems to have intended an apostrophe.

12. *Lust's Dominion*, II, i. WI skipped 81 lines of text before copying the next line.

13. *Ibid.*, II, i. WI skipped 4½ lines at the beginning of this aside of Mendoza and 1½ lines at the end.

14. *Ibid.*, II, ii.

15. *Ibid.*, II, iii. WI omitted the last two words of this line and the final two lines of this speech of the Queen Mother.

16. *Ibid.*, III, ii. WI began this speech of the King to Maria in the eighth line.

Maria, dying—
Heaven ope your windows, that my spotless soul
Riding upon the wings of innocence
May enter Paradise—[17]

———

Eleazar
Now by the proud complexion of my cheeks
Ta'en from the kisses of the amorous sun
Were he ten thousand kings that slew my love
Thus should my hand, plumed with revenges wings
Requite mine own honour & her death—
(Stabs the King.)[18]

———

In his breast
That dares but dart a finger at the door
Ill bury this sharp steel—[19]

———

—Oh misery
When Indian slaves thirst after empery—[20]

———

Eleazar
By heavens great star, which Indians do adore
But that I hate to hear the giddy world &c[21]

———

Cry all, arm, arm,
Prince Philip & the Cardinal do ride
Like Jove in thunder; in a storm we'll meet them[22]

———

Eleazar
I rush'd among[23] the thickest of their crowds
And with a countenance majestical
Like the imperious sun dispersed their clouds

17. *Ibid.*, III, iii. WI noted that this is Maria's last speech before she dies; he omitted the final 1½ lines of her speech.
18. *Ibid.*, III, iv.
19. *Ibid.* WI omitted the final three words of the line in the speech by Eleazar.
20. *Ibid.* WI skipped the initial five words in this line of the speech by the Queen Mother.
21. *Ibid.*
22. *Ibid.* WI omitted the first 8½ lines of this speech by Eleazar.
23. WI first indicated tense by "ed," then, apparently to follow his original, he wrote a *d* over the *e* and added an apostrophe between the *h* and *d*; in the 1814 edition of Dilke, the preposition was spelled "amongst."

I have perfumed the rankness of their breath
And by the magic of true eloquence
Transformed this many headed Cerberus
This pyed camelion, this beast multitude
Whose power consists in number, pride in threats,
Yet melt like snow when majesty shines forth
This wolf I held[24] by th'ears & made him tame
And made him tremble at the Moors Great name—[25]

Your desperate arm
Hath almost thrust quite through the heart of hope
Our fortunes lie a bleeding by your rash
And violent onset.[26]

———

Ambition plumes the ⟨m⟩Moor, whilst black despair,
Offering to tear from him the diadem
Which he usurps, makes him to cry at all,
And to act deeds beyond astonishment.[27]

———

Zarack. Oh, fly my lords! fly for the day is lost!
Eleaz. There are three hundred & odd days in ⟨the⟩ ↑a↓[28] year
And cannot we lose one of them? come, fight.[29]

———

By all those mourning lines which thou hast sent
Weeping in black to tell thy languishment[30]

———

—to beat down his usurpation
I have thrown about this thunder—[31]

———

24. This word may be "hold."

25. *Lust's Dominion*, III, vi. WI skipped a scene and fifteen lines in the following scene before beginning to copy from the text.

26. *Ibid.*, IV, ii. This speech is by the Cardinal.

27. *Ibid.* WI skipped the initial five and final four lines of this speech by Philip.

28. Beneath the crossed-out word is a mark which resembles a single quotation mark; WI probably intended a caret.

29. *Lust's Dominion*, IV, iii.

30. *Ibid.*, IV, iv. WI omitted the initial three lines of this scene and speech by the Queen Mother.

31. *Ibid.* WI omitted the initial four lines and first word of the fifth line of this speech by Eleazar.

Thou hast a lean face and a carrion heart[32]

———

To have this head,[33]
Thy face, & all thy body stuck with scars
Why tis a sight more glorious than to see
A lady hung with diamonds—⟨*illegible*⟩[34]
A mangled, lame, true soldier is a gem
Worth Casars empire, though fools spurn at them.[35]

Philip—
I thought I should have had a tomb hung round
With tatterd colours, broken spears; I thought
My body should have fallen down full of wounds
But one can kill an Emperor, fool, then why
Wouldst thou have many? curse, be mad and die.[36]

———

Eleazar
Kings indeed are deities
And who'd not, as the sun, in brightness shine?
To be the greatest is to be divine.
Who among millions would not be the mightiest?
To sit in godlike state; to have all eyes
Dazzled with admiration and all tongues
Shouting loud prayers; to rob every heart
Of Love; to have the strength of every arm;
A Sovereigns name, why tis a sovereigns charm
I have stood upon the top of fortunes wheel,
And backward turnd the iron screw of fate.
The destinies have spun a silken thread
About my life—[37]

———

32. *Ibid.*, IV, v. After he quoted a portion of Philip's speech in line 18 of this scene, WI skipped approximately 1½ pages in the text.

33. Following this word, there is an ink blot.

34. Following the word "diamonds," WI omitted the beginning of the next sentence, "If thou lose," and skipped the following two lines in this speech by Philip before beginning again. Probably the illegible marks are WI's "& & &c."

35. *Lust's Dominion*, IV, v.

36. *Ibid.* Apparently, WI first drew a line after the question mark in the last line, then wrote the word "curse" through it. After he wrote the first line of the following speech, he added the underlined word "Eleazar" in smaller letters above the word "indeed"; we have regularized.

37. *Ibid.*, V, i. WI omitted the first three words of line 18 of this speech. At this

There were a lady for Ferraras duke: one of great blood,[38] firm age, undoubted honour; above her sex most modestly artful, though naturally modest; too excellent to be left unmatched Though few worthy to match her—

This last from Marstons Parasitas[ter][39]

From Parasitaster or the fawn
by ‸↑Jno↓ Marston[40]

———

Why in your steadier age, in strength of life
An⟨&⟩d[41] firmest wit of time &c—[42]

———

In very sighing sadness—[43]

———

⟨Clean linen is the first thing our life craves and the⟩

Hercules—[44]

'Fore heaven you are blest with three rare Graces, fine linen clean linings, a sanguine complexion & I am sure, an excellent wit, for you are a gentleman born—

Herod—Thank thee dear ⟨f⟩Fawn, but why is clean linen such a grace, I prithee?

---

point he finished taking notes from *Lust's Dominion*; around the following passage, which is the last on the page, he drew a semicircle to the left and top of the passage to set it off.

38. WI may have written "blood" over another word, causing a smudge.

39. Volume 2 of Dilke's collection of *Old English Plays* contained John Lyly's *Endymion* and three of John Marston's plays: *Antonio and Mellida* (from which WI also quoted in this notebook), *What You Will*, and *Parasitaster*.

40. This passage is from *Parasitaster*, III, i; it is, therefore, out of order. To separate speeches and to indicate when he skipped lines in this play, WI drew twelve lines varying in length from one-fourth to one inch long; we have regularized without notation unless there exists an unusual characteristic.

41. Apparently WI first used a large ampersand to begin the line and then wrote the word "And" through it (beginning flush left).

42. *Parasitaster*, I, i. Following these words of Renaldo, WI drew a double line (his pen point could have separated as he wrote causing the double line).

43. *Ibid.*, I, ii. WI began in the middle of this line spoken by Nymphadoro.

44. Apparently WI inserted the speaker's name in smaller letters after he had copied the speech.

Herc. Oh my excellent, & inward dearly approved friend—Clean linen is the first thing our life craves, & the last our death enjoys—[45]

———

Ill maintain that wisdom in a woman is a most foolish quality. A lady of a good complexion, naturally well witted, perfectly bred & well exercised in the discourse of the best men shall make fools of a thousand of these book thinking creatures. I speak it by way of justification. I tell thee I am truly learned for I protest ignorance; & wise for I love myself & virtuous enough for a lady of fifteen—[46]

———

Constancy?—Constancy and patience are virtues in no living creatures but Centinels and anglers—[47]

———

This Granuffo is a right wise good lord, a man of excellent discourse & never speaks: His signs to me & men of profound reach instruct abundantly; he begs suit with signs, gives thanks with signs, puts off his hat leisurely, maintains his beard learnedly, keeps his lust privately makes a nodding leg courtly & lives happily.[48]

———

Woman.

"Thou last and only rareness of heavens works
From best of man, made model of the Gods,
Divinest woman! thou perfection
Of all proportions beauty, made when Jove was blithe
With well filld nectar & full friends with man.
Thou dear as air, necessary as sleep,
To careful man, Woman; Oh who can sin so deeply
As to be curséd[49] from knowing of the pleasures
Thy soft society, modest amorousness
Yields to our tedious life?[50]

———

I have vowed to loathe thee; the Irishman shall hate aqua vitae, the Welshman cheese the Dutchman[51] shall loathe salt butter before I relove thee—Does the babe pule? ⟨Though⟩ thou shouldst ⟨have⟩ ha'

45. *Parasitaster*, II, i.
46. *Ibid.*, III, i. This speech and the one following are by Dulcimel.
47. *Ibid.*
48. *Ibid.* This speech is by Gonzago.
49. WI indicated tense with "ed," then to follow the original, he added the apostrophe without crossing out the *e*.
50. *Parasitaster*, III, i. This speech is by Tiberio.
51. Apparently WI wrote "Du⟨c⟩t⟨t⟩chman."

cried before–tis too late now; no; the Spring trees in Autumn shall sooner call back the spring with shedding of their leaves than thou reverse my just irrevocable hatred with thy tears; away! go! vaunt!–[52]

———

Wretched ⟨beyond⟩ above expression! that snoredst over a beauty which thousands desired; neglectedst her bed for whose enjoying a very saint would have sued–[53]

———

I will now begin to sigh, read poets, look pale, go neatly, & be most apparently in love:–[54]

Triumphant Cupid, that sleeps on the soft cheek
Of rarest beauty, whose throne is ladies eyes[55]

———

Drunkenness! Oh 'tis a most fluent & swelling virtue; sure the most just of ↑all↓ virtues, tis justice itself, for if it chance to oppress & take too much it presently restores all again; it makes the King & the peasant both equal; for if they are both drunk alike, they are both beasts alike: as for that most precious light of heaven Truth, if time be the father of her I am sure drunkenness is oftentimes the mother of her & brings her forth. Drunkenness brings all out, for it brings all the drink out of the pot all the wit out of the pate & all the money out of the purse.[56]

———

From Mother Bombie
by John Lyly.[57]

———

⟨I see it through your brains, your⟩
^↑Dromio↓ Ah, master I smell your device, it will be excellent

52. *Parasitaster*, IV, i. This speech is by Zuccone.

53. *Ibid.* This speech is by Nymphadoro.

54. *Ibid.* WI used this speech by Tiberio as a headnote for "Love-Symptoms" in *Bracebridge Hall* (Smith, ed., *Bracebridge Hall*, p. 71).

55. *Ibid.*, V, i. This speech and the one following are by Hercules.

56. *Ibid.*

57. This play is in volume 1 of Dilke's *Old English Plays*, following *Lust's Dominion*. Its title in that collection is *A Pleasant Conceited Comedy; Called Mother Bombie*, by John Lyly (although Dilke noted that the name could be spelled "Lilly" and "Lily"). The other plays in volume 1 of Dilke's collection are Marlowe's *The Tragical History of the Life and Death of Doctor Faustus* and Lyly's *Midas*. To separate passages from this play, WI drew four lines of three-fourths inch, one-half inch, 1⅛ inches, and one inch.

Memphio Thou canst not know it till I tell it

Drom. I see it through your brains; your hair is so thin & your skull[58] so transparent, I may sooner see it than hear⟨e⟩ it—[59]

Ill make repentance reap what wantoness hath sown[60]

A tavern is the rendezvous, the Exchange the Staple of good fellows. I have heard my great grandfather tell, how his great great grandfather should say, that it was an old proverb when his great grandfather was a child, that it was a good wind that blew a man to the wine—[61]

Lucio's Dream

In the dawning of the day, for about that time by my starting out of my sleep, I found it to be, methought I saw a stately piece of beef, with a cape cloak of cabbage, embroiderd with pepper, having two honourable pages with hats of mustard on their heads, himself ⟨sitting⟩ in great pomp sitting on a cushion of white brewish, lined with brown bread; methought being powderd, he was much troubled with the salt rheum; and therefore there stood by him two great flagons of wine and beer, the one to dry up his rheum & the other to quench his choler: I as one envying his ambition, hungering and thirsting after his honour, began to pull his cushion from under him, hoping by that means to give him a fall; and with putting out my hand I awaked & found nothing in all this dream about me but the salt rheum—[62]

Halfpennys Dream

Nay, then, let me come in with a dream short but sweet, that my mouth waters ever since I waked. Methought there sat upon a shelf three Damask prunes in velvet caps & prest satin gowns like Judges; and that there were a whole handful of currants to be arraigned of riot because

58. In the 1814 edition of Dilke, this word is spelled "scull."

59. *Mother Bombie*, I, i. WI began quoting approximately half through the first scene of this prose play, then went on to one of the last speeches in scene 3.

60. *Ibid.*, I, iii. This sentence is part of a speech by Sperantus.

61. *Ibid.*, II, v. WI used this speech by Stellio as a headnote for "The Boar's Head Tavern, Eastcheap" in *The Sketch Book.* According to Dilke, this speech was "probably intended as a sneer at the Popish doctrine of oral tradition; and perhaps Swift had it in his eye when he wrote that passage in his 'Tale of a Tub,' in which Lord Peter proves their right to wear gold lace" (Dilke, *Old English Plays*, I, 234, n.).

62. *Ibid.*, III, iv. WI copied the entire speeches of Lucio and Halfpenny describing their dreams; the "titles" are WI's, separated from the text by lines transcribed here as underlining.

they clung together in such clusters; twelve raisins of the sun were impanneld in a jury; and as a leaf of whole mace, which was bailiff was carrying the quest to consult, methought there came an angry cook & gelded the Jury of their stones & swept both Judges jurors, rebels & bailiff into a porridge pot: whereat I being melancholy, fetched a deep sigh that waked myself & my bedfellow[63]

———

Antonio & Mellida.

John Marston—[64]

———

Your honour with a paugh? 'Slid, now every Jackanapes loads his back with the golden coat of honour; every ass puts on the Lion Skin and roars his honour: upon Your honour. By my ladys pantable I f⟨a⟩ear I shall live to hear a vintners boy cry, 'tis neat canary, upon my honour[65]

———

Oh, music, thou distill'st
More sweetness in us than this jarring world;
Both time & measure from thy strains do breathe,
Whilst from the channel of this dirt doth flow
Nothing but timeless grief unmeasured woe[66]

———

Feliche
—Oh, calm, hush'd, rich content
Is there a blessedness without thee?
How soft thou down'st the couch where thou dost rest
Nectar to life, thou sweet ambrosian feast[67]

———

F⟨s⟩eliche
Why, man, I have been borne upon the spirits wings
The souls swift pegasus, the Phantasy;
And from the height of contemplation,
Have viewed the feeble joints men totter on.

63. *Ibid.*

64. *Antonio and Mellida: A Tragedy* is in volume 2 of Dilke's collection; it is not in Dodsley's. Harvey says that this play aided Ben Jonson's satire of Marston in *The Poetaster* (Sir Paul Harvey, *The Oxford Companion to English Literature*, 2d ed. [Oxford: Clarendon Press, 1946], p. 31). To separate passages in this play, WI drew eleven lines varying in length from one-fourth inch to two inches long; we have regularized without notation.

65. *Antonio and Mellida*, II, i. This speech is by Catzo.

66. *Ibid.* This speech is by Mellida.

67. *Ibid.*, III, ii.

I envy none; but hate or pity all
For when I view, with an attentive thought,
That creature fair, but proud; him rich but sot;
The other witty, but unmeasurd arrogant;
Him great yet boundless in ambition;
Him highborn, but of base life; t'other fear'd.
Yet feared fears, & fears most to be most loved;
Him wise, but made a fool for public use;
The other learn'd, but self opinionate.
When I discourse all these, & see myself
Nor fair, nor rich, nor witty, great nor feard;
Yet amply suited with all full content;
Lord how I clap my hands & smooth my brow,
Rubbing my quiet bosom, tossing up
A grateful spirit to omnipotence.[68]

Castilio. Ha ha, but if thou knewst my happiness
Thou wouldst even grate away thy soul to dust,
In envy of my sweet beatitude:
I cannot sleep for kisses; I cannot rest
For ladys letters, that importune me
With such unused vehemence of love,
Straight to solicit them, that—[69]

Fel. Confusion seize me, but I think thou liest.
Why should I not be sought to them as well?
'S foot Methinks I am as like a man.
Troth, I have a good head of hair, a cheek
Not as yet waned, a leg[70] faith in the full:
I have not a red beard, take not tobacco much;
And—'Slid for other parts of manliness—[71]

———

Cast—Pew waw—you neer accorted them in pomp
Put your good parts in presence graciously.
Ha, ⟨and⟩ as[?] you had, why they would have come off, sprung
To your arms, and su'd and prayed, and vowd
And opened all their sweetness to your love—

68. *Ibid.*
69. *Ibid.*
70. WI apparently began with the letters "li," then wrote *e* over the *i*.
71. *Antonio and Mellida*, III, ii.

Fel. There are a number of such things as thou
Have often urged me to such loose belief:
But 'slid you all do lie, you all do lie.
I have put on good clothes, & smuggd my face,
Struck a fair wench with a smart speaking eye;
Courted in all sorts blunt & passionate;
Had opportunity, put them to the ah:
And by this light I find them wondrous chaste,
Impregnable: perchance a kiss or so,
But for the rest, oh most inexorable.[72]

———

(⟨after⟩ brating[?] Castilio)

Fel. Honest musk-cod take that; & that, (striking him) & belie no ladies love; swear no more by Jesu this madam, that lady: hence, go forswear the presence, travail three years to bury this bastinado & avoid! puffpaste, avoid!—[73]

Most Mighty, valiant & high towering heart.[74]

———

Sweet precious issue of most honourd blood
Rich hope, ripe virtue! Oh untimely loss.[75]

———

Oh that my spirit in a sigh could mount
Into the sphere where thy sweet soul dost rest.[76]

———

As having clasped a rose
Within my palm, the rose being taen away,
My hand retains a little breath of sweet;
So may mans trunk, his spirit slipped ↑away↓[77]
Holds still a faint perfume of his sweet ↓guest—↑
Tis so; for when discursive powers fly out,
And roam in progress through the bounds of heaven,

72. *Ibid.*

73. *Ibid.* WI skipped much of the play before beginning to copy at the top of the next page.

74. *Ibid.*, V, ii. This line is by Piero.

75. *Ibid.* These are Andrugio's lines.

76. *Ibid.* Following this speech by Mellida, WI went back to earlier acts in the play and copied speeches, an unusual pattern.

77. After WI wrote the word "away" in this line and "guest" in the next line, a large drop of ink fell on the space between the words and was smudged through the words; he then rewrote above and below the lines.

The soul itself gallops along with them,
As chieftain of this winged troop of thought,
Whilst the dull lodge of spirit standeth waste
Until the soul return—[78]

———

Dildo—Ay, but master, you have one little fault: you sleep open mouthed.
Balurdo—Pew, thou jestest. In good sadness Ill have a looking glass nailed to the testern of the bed that I may see when I sleep whether tis so or not; take heed you lie not; go to, take heed you lie not—[79]

'Tis not the bared pate, the bended knees
Gilt tipstaves, tyrian purple, chairs of state,
Troops of pied butterflies, that flutter still
In greatness summer, that confirm a prince:
Tis not the unsavory breath of multitudes
Shouting & clapping with confused din,
That makes a prince. No, Lucio, he's a king
A true right king, that dares do aught, save wrong,
Fears nothing mortal, but to be unjust;
Who is not blown up with flattering puffs
Of spongy sycophants; who stands unmoved,
Despite the justling of opinion:
Who can enjoy himself, maugre the throng
That strive to press his quiet out of him:
Who sits upon Joves footstool as I do,
Adoring, not affecting, majesty;
Whose brow is wreathed with the silver crown
Of clear content; this Lucio is a King.
And of this empire, every mans possessed,
Thats worth his soul—[80]

———

Avoid him, for he hath a dwindled ⟨ga⟩ leg,
A low forehead, a thin coal-black beard
And will be jealous too, believe it, sweet,
For his chin sweats, and hath a gander neck,
A thin lip and a little monkish eye:
'Precious, what a slender waist he hath!

78. *Antonio and Mellida,* IV, i. This is Antonio's speech.
79. *Ibid.,* III, ii.
80. *Ibid.,* IV, i. This speech is by Andrugio.

He looks like a maypole, or a notched stick;
He'll snap in two at every little strain,
Give me a husband that will fill mine arms
Of steady judgement, quick & nimble sense
Fools relish not a ladies excellence.[81]

The Antiquary
By Shakerly Marmion 1641.[82]

Petrucio
I have calculated by all the rules of reason & art, that I shall be a great man; for what singular quality concurs to perfection and advancement that is defective in me? Take my feature ⟨of⟩& proportion, have they not a kind of Sweetness & harmony to attract the eyes of the beholders? ⟨t⟩The confirmation of which many authentical judgements of ladies have sealed & subscribed to.[83]

Petrucio
I feel of late, a strong and witty genius growing upon me; and I begin, I know not how, to be in love with this foolish sin of poetry.[84]

False friends

They walk like spirits; not to be discern'd;
Subtle & soft like air, have oily balm
Swimming o'er their words and actions;
But below it a flood of gall—[85]

Petrucio
See the abundant ignorance of this age! he cites my father for a precedent: alas, he is a good old man, and no more; there he stands,

81. *Ibid.*, I, i. This speech by Rosaline (in much smaller than usual writing) ends the page.

82. This play was not in Dilke's collection of *Old English Plays*; it appeared in volume 7 of the 1744 edition of Dodsley's collection as "*The Antiquary: a Comedy.* By Shakerly Marmion, Esq." In the 1780 and 1825–1827 editions of Dodsley, it was in volume 10; in the 4th ed., published in 1874–1876 and edited by W. Carew Hazlitt, it was in volume 13. To separate passages from this play, WI drew nineteen lines varying in length from one-half inch to 1½ inches long; we have regularized without notation.

83. *The Antiquary,* I, i.

84. *Ibid.* WI omitted the first half of this speech.

85. *Ibid.* Earlier in this conversation, Lionel explained to Petrucio what a "faithful, not a ceremonious friend" is.

he has not been abroad, nor known the world; therefore, I hope, will not be so foolishly peremptory to compare with me for judgement, that have travel'd, seen fashions, and been a man of intelligence.[86]

———

Petrucio
Therefore I have chose honour for my mistress, upon whose wings I will mount up to the heavens; where I will fix myself a constellation, for all this under world of mortals to wonder at me.[87]

———

the Antiquary

⟨They say⟩
He is grown obsolete,
And tis time he were out of date. They say he sits
All day in contemplation of a statue
With ne'er a nose, and doats on the decays
With greater love than the selflovd Narcissus
Did on his beauty—[88]

Old Man in Love

———

By'r Lady it shows
Great haughtiness of courage; a man of his years
That dares to venture on a wife.[89]

Mocinigo—A man of my years! I feel
My limbs as able as the best of them;
And in all places else except my hair,
As green as a bay tree; and for the whiteness
Upon my head, although it now lie hid,
What does it signify, but like a tree that blossoms
Before the fruit come forth? And, I hope, a tree
That blossoms, is neither dry nor wither'd.[90]

———

86. *Ibid.*

87. *Ibid.*

88. *Ibid.* This speech is by Lionel.

89. *Ibid.* WI added a title to these lines by Lorenzo; after indenting, he wrote the abbreviation, "Mocin," in the second blank line, then smeared it, and rewrote the name in full on the next line.

90. *Ibid.*

For shame—away
The rosy Morning blushes at thy baseness—[91]

———

Antiquary. Why, Sir, and you know again, that 'tis an old custom, (which thing I will no way transgress) for a rich man not to look upon any as his kinsman in distress.[92]

———

What use! did not the signory build a state chamber for antiquities? and tis the best thing that e'er they did: they are the registers, the chronicles of the age they were made in & speak the truth of history better than a hundred of your printed commentaries.[93]

Look farther & tell me what you find better or more honourable than age. Is not wisdom entaild upon it? take the preheminence of it in every thing; in an old friend, in old wine, in an old pedigree—[94]

———

I wonder what black leaf in the book of fate has decreed that misery upon man, to be in love, it transforms him into a worse monster than e'er calypsos cup did; a country gentleman among courtiers, or their wives among the ladies, a clown among citizens—nay an ass among apes, is not half so ridiculous as that makes us.[95]

———

Bravo—What will this age come to? Where be those stirring humours that were wont to trouble the world? Peace, I think will oerspread them all like a gangrene, and men will die with a lethargy: theres no malice extant, no jealousies, no employment to set wicked-/-ness awork; tis never a dead time with me but when theres nobody to kill[96]

———

I'll resolve you something: there is ‸↑as↓ ⟨a⟩ great a mystery in the acquisition of knowledge as of wealth; have you not a citizen will grow rich in a moment, and why not he ingenious? Besides who knows but he might have digged for it, & so found out some concealed treasure of understanding.[97]

———

91. *Ibid.*, II, i. This rejection is by Lucretia.
92. *Ibid.*
93. *Ibid.* This speech by the Antiquary ends the page.
94. *Ibid.* This speech is by the Antiquary.
95. *Ibid.* This speech is by Aurelio.
96. *Ibid.*, III, i. WI underlined "Bravo" twice.
97. *Ibid.* This speech is by the Duke.

—The multiplicity of learning does but distract a man; I am all for your modern humours, and when I list to express a passion, it flows from me with that spring of amorous conceits, that a true lover may hang his head over and read in it the very phys'nomy of his affection—[98]

———

And when my head labours with the pangs of delivery by chance comes up a countess's waiting woman, at whose sight, as at the remembrance of a mistress my pen falls out of my hand; and then do I read to her half a dozen lines, whereat we both sit together and melt into tears—[99]

———

Tut! I leave your Helicons and your pale Pirenes, to such as will look after them; for my own part, I follow the instigation of my brain, and scorn other helps ⟨*illegible letter*⟩.[100]

———

⟨The⟩An antiquary
Printed bookes he contemnes, as a novelty of this latter age; but a manu-/ script he pores on everlastingly, espe-/-cially if the cover be all moth-eaten, and the dust make a parenthesis between every syllable—
(from Micro-cosmographie—or a
piece of the world discovered—1628)[101]

———

Too young! I like you the better. There is a price
Due to the early cherry. The ⟨fruits[?]⟩ first apples
Deserve more grace: the budding rose is set by;
But stale, & fully blown, is left for vulgars
To rub their sweaty fingers on. Too Young!
As well you may affirm the tender tree
Too young to graft upon; or you may say
The rising suns too young to court the day.[102]

There is no wrong
Like to the breach of wedlock; those injuries

98. *Ibid.* This speech is by Petrucio. There is a vertical squiggle flush left connecting the last and first lines of the passages.
99. *Ibid.* This speech is by Petrucio; in the first line of the passage, WI inverted the words "up comes." Following the speech, WI drew a double line.
100. *Ibid.* This speech is by Petrucio.
101. *Ibid.*, note. WI here copied a footnote in which Dodsley drew from the "character of an Antiquary" in *Micro-cosmographie* to explain what makes a manuscript interesting. WI used this quoted passage as a headnote of "A Literary Antiquary," in *Bracebridge Hall* (Smith, ed., p. 61).
102. *Ibid.*, IV, i. This speech and the one following are by Aemilia.

Art writ in marble time shall ne'er raze out.
The hearts of such, if they be once divided
Will ne'er grow one again: sooner you may
Call the spent day, or bid the stream return,
That long since slid beside you—[103]

———

Antiquary Will you believe me, gentlemen upon my credit?
Leonardo— Yes, Sir, any thing.
Antiquary Do you see these breeches then?
Leon— Ay, what of them?
Ant These were Pompeys breeches I assure you—
Duke ⟨Is it⟩ ∧↑Is't↓ possible?
Ant He had his denomination from them; he was called Pompey the Great, from wearing these great Breeches[104]

———

——— Give him a pair
Of Velvet Breeches from our grandsires wardrobe[105]

From the Goblins

by *Sir John Suckling*[106]

———

Orsabrin Now have I forgot which side I'm on!
No matter: I'll help the weakest:
Theres some justice in that.[107]

———

Welcome, Welcome, mortal wight,
To the mansion of the night.
Good or bad, thy life discover;
Truly all thy deeds declare;

103. *Ibid.*

104. *Ibid.* WI underlined the speakers' names with double lines (we have regularized the paragraphs); following this conversation, WI drew a triple line.

105. *Ibid.*, V, i. Rather than writing Lionel's name, WI began copying this speech with a line.

106. This play, *The Goblins: a Comedy*, was in volume 7 of the 1744 edition of Dodsley following *The Antiquary*; in the 1780 and 1825–1827 editions, it was printed in volume 10 following *The Antiquary* and preceding both *The Ordinary* and *The Jovial Crew*, the order in which WI copied these plays in the commonplace book. The play was not in the 1874 version edited by Hazlitt. To separate passages from this play, WI drew eight lines varying in length from five-eighths to one inch; we have regularized without notation.

107. *The Goblins*, I, i. WI underlined the speaker's name with a double line.

For about thee spirits hover,
That can tell, tell what they are
Pinch him if he speak not true;
Pinch him, pinch him, black & blue.[108]

———

'Twould be
Like throwing a dead fly into an aunts nest,
There would be such tearing & pulling,
& getting up upon him[109]

———

'Sfoot theyll apprehend the head of the bass viol
As soon as thee, thou art so like it;
Only I must confess, that has a little the better face—[110]

I'm[111] a rogue if I do not think
I was designed for the helm of State:
I am so full of nimble stratagems,
That I should have ordered affairs and
Carried it against the stream of a faction,
With as much ease as a skipper
Would laver against the wind[112]

———

Oh thou kind innocence!
Witness all that can punish falsehood,
That I could live with thee,
Even in this dark and narrow prison:
And think all happiness confined within the walls[113]

———

'Tis a rare wench she i' th' blue stockings
What a complexion she had,[114] when she was warm!
'Tis a hard question of these country wenches,
Which are simpler: their beauties or themselves.

108. *Ibid.*, III, i. This speech and the one following are by Peridor.

109. *Ibid.*

110. *Ibid.*, IV, i. This speech by Nassurat ends the page.

111. WI wrote the *I* slightly to the right of another letter which he probably crossed out.

112. *The Goblins*, IV, i. WI used this speech by Nassurat as a headnote for "A Village Politician," in *Bracebridge Hall* (Smith, ed., p. 187), but he changed it to a prose version.

113. *Ibid.* This speech is by Orsabrin.

114. WI may have first written "ha' " and then added the "th" and the *d* following the *a*.

Theres as much difference betwixt
A town lady & one of these,
As there is between a wild pheasant & a tame—

Pellern[?]. right!—
There goes such essencing, washing, perfuming,
And daubing to th' other, that they are
The least part of themselves. Indeed
Theres so much sauce a man cannot taste the meat—[115]

Nassaurat By this light, I hate a woman drest up to her height,
Worse than I do sugar with muscadine:
It leaves no room for me to imagine
I could improve her, if she were mine.[116]

Come do not weep my girl
Forget him, pretty pensiveness; there will
Come others, every day, as good as he—[117]

Of all ways of destroying mankind, the judges
Have the easiest; they sleep & do it.[118]

From *The Ordinary.*
by Wm Cartwright
1651.[119]

That thing of wealth, that worm
Bred out of Splendid muck that Citizen—[120]

---

115. *The Goblins,* IV, i. Following the conversation between Nassurat and Pellegrin, WI went to the next passage, underlining the name twice.

116. *Ibid.*

117. *Ibid.* WI used this advice by Tamoren to Reginella as a headnote for "Love-Charms," in *Bracebridge Hall* (Smith, ed., p. 95), changing some punctuation.

118. *Ibid.*, V, i. This speech is by Nassurat.

119. *The Ordinary: a Comedy,* by William Cartwright, was printed in volume 10, the last volume in the 1744 edition of Dodsley's collection; in the 1780 and 1825–1827 (and we assume the 1810) editions it was moved to the tenth of twelve volumes in the order followed by WI in copying. To separate passages from this play, WI drew seventeen lines varying in length from one-half inch to 1½ inches; we have regularized without notation.

120. *The Ordinary,* I, i. These lines are from a long speech by Meanwell.

How bright it flames! put out your nose good lady;
You burn day light—[121]

———

Sure the surveyor
Of the highways will have to do with her
For not keeping her countenance passable.[122]

———

—There is one
Although I speak it to his face, that can
Write a geography by his own conquests;
H' hath fought o'er Strabo, Ptolemy, & Stafford;
Travell'd as far in arms as Lithgoe naked;
Borne weapons wither Coriat durst not
Carry a shirt or shoes. Jack Mandeville
Ne'er saild so far as he hath steerd by land
Using his colours both for mast & sail—[123]

———

Slicer
I've worn some leather out abroad; let out
A heathen soul or two; fed this good sword
With the black blood of pagan Christians;
Converted a few infidels with it.
But let that pass—[124]

———

One drums his table, the other is his music;
His swords his knife; his colours are his napkins
Carves nourishing horse, as he is us'd to do
The hostile pagan, or we venison: eats
Gunpowder with his meat, instead of pepper,
Then drinks oer all his bandoleers, & fights—[125]

———

a mizer

———

He knows t'a crum how much
Loss is in twenty dozen of bread, between
That which is broke by th'hand & that is cut.

121. *Ibid.*, I, ii. This speech and the one following are by Shape.
122. *Ibid.* WI drew a double line.
123. *Ibid.*, I, iv. The line at the beginning of this passage indicates the omitted initial part of the line, "But for your deeds of valour," in this speech by Hearsay.
124. *Ibid.* WI used this speech by Slicer as a headnote for "An Old Soldier," in *Bracebridge Hall* (Smith, ed., p. 30), but he changed it to a prose version.
125. *Ibid.* This speech is by Hearsay.

Which way best keeps his candles, bran or straw
What tallows lost in putting of them out
By spittle, what by foot, what by the puff,
What by holding downwards & what by
The extinguisher.[126]

That old Eremite thing, that like
An image in a German clock doth move
Not walk—[127]

—Where a sullen
Pair of brown loaves darkend the dirty table
Shadows of bread, not bread.—[128]

Can I lie hid no where securely from
The throng & press of men? must every place
Become a theatre, where I seek shelter?
And solitudes become markets, 'cause I'm there?[129]

Saint Francis & Saint Benedight,
Blesse this house from wicked wight;
From the night mare & the goblin,
That is hight, Good fellow Robin;
Keep it from all evil spirits
Fairies, weazels, rats, & ferrets:
From curfew time
To the next prime.[130]

⟨By Woden, God of Saxons,
From whence comes Woensday, that is Wodensday;
Truth is a thing that ever I will keep,
Unto thylke day in which I creep into
My sepulchre; Ill be as faithful to thee,
As Chaunticleer to Madame Partelot—⟩[131]

---

126. *Ibid.* Following this speech by Slicer, WI drew a double line and turned back a page to copy the next speech by Hearsay.

127. *Ibid.*

128. *Ibid.*, II, i. This speech is by Slicer.

129. *Ibid.*, II, iii. This speech is by Hearsay.

130. *Ibid.*, III, i. Following this speech by Moth, WI drew a double line.

I'll sow
One ground or other every month with pease
And so I will have green ones all the year
These yeomen have no policy i' th' world—[132]

Lets keep these two
In desperate hope of understanding us.
Riddles & clouds are very lights of speech.
Ill veil my careless anxious thoughts, as t'were
In a perspicuous cloud, that I may
Whisper in a loud voice, & evn be silent
When I do utter words. Words did I call them?
My words shall be no words; my voice no voice;
My noise no noise; my very language silence.
(*Sir Christopher the Curate*)[133]

—'tis merely froth & barm
The ye[a]st that makes your thin small sermons work—[134]

Theres nothing so ridiculous as the hungry
A fasting man is a good jest at any time—[135]

Thou son of parchment, got between the standish
And the stiff buckram bag; thou that mayst call
The pen thy father, & the ink thy mother,
The sand thy brother, & the wax thy sister
And the good pillory thy cousin removed;
I say learn reverence to thy betters[136]

Sir Christopher
I do beseech you shew
Merciful cruelty, & as it were a kind
Of pitiful hard heartedness.[137]

---

131. *Ibid.* This crossed-out speech is by Moth.

132. *Ibid.*, III, ii. WI initially wrote the "I'll" to the left, but he rewrote it to the right because he omitted the first sentence of the line. These words are by Credulous.

133. *Ibid.*, III, v. WI wrote what seems to be the word "the," then over it, "Sir"; he did not underline the final word.

134. *Ibid.* This speech is by Bagshot.

135. *Ibid.* This speech is by Vicar Catchmey.

136. *Ibid.* This speech is by Sir Christopher.

137. *Ibid.*, IV, v.

Sir Thomas Bitefig. (Sick–)
Because lifes
Frail & uncertain, let me counsel thee
Tis good to be beforehand still. First then,
I charge thee lend no money; next–serve God;
If ever thou hast children, teach them thrift;
They'l learn religion fast enough themselves.
Nay do not weep, but hearken. When heaven ‸↑shall↓
Please to call in this weary soul of mine,
Be n't idle in expense about my burial;
Buy me a shroud, any old sheet will serve
To clothe corruption; I can rot without
Fine linen; 'tis but to enrich the grave,
And adorn stench, no reverence to the dead,
To make them crumble more luxuriously.
One torch will be sufficient to direct
The footsteps of my bearers. If there be
Any so kind as to accompany
My body to the earth, let them not want
For entertainment: pr'ythee let them have
A sprig of rosemary, dip'd in common ‸↑water↓
To smell to as they walk along the streets.
Eatings & drinkings are no obsequies.
Raise no oppressing pile to load my ashes;
But if thou'lt needs b'at ⟨the⟩ charges of a tomb
Five or six foot of common stone, engrav'd
With a good hopeful word; or else a couple
Of Capital letters filled up with pitch,
Such as I set upon my sheep, will serve;
State is not meet for those that dwell in dust.[138]

From The Jovial Crew or the Merry Beggars
Richard Brome 1652[139]

———

138. *Ibid.*, V, i. Before this act's initial speech, of which WI omitted the initial 2⅔ lines and the final five lines, the characters are listed as "Sir Thomas Bitefig *as sick*, Jane."

139. *The Jovial Crew, or the Merry Beggars: A Comedy* by Richard Brome was published in volume 6 in the first edition of Dodsley's collection in 1744; in the 1780 and 1825–1827 (and we assume, in the 1810) editions, it was published in volume 10 following *The Ordinary*, the previous play from which WI copied. This play was omitted by Hazlitt from the 1874 edition. To separate passages from this

Springlove
'tis the season of the year that calls me.
What moves her notes, provokes my disposition,
By a more absolute power of ⟨n⟩Nature, than
Philosophy can render an account for.[140]

Old rent.
Can there ⟨be[?]⟩ ↑no↓ means be found to preserve life
In thee, but wandering like a vagabond?
Does not the sun as comfortably shine
Upon my gardens, as ⟨others far remote?⟩ ↑the open fields?↓
Or[141] on my fields as others far remote?
Are not my walks & greens as delectable
As the highways & commons? Are the shades
Of sycamore & bowers of Eglantine
Less pleasing, than of bramble, or thorn hedges?
Or of my groves & thickets than wild woods?
Are not my fountain waters fresher than
The troubled streams, where every beast does drink.
Do not the birds sing here as sweet & lively
As any other where?—[142]

———

Beggars! they are the only people can boast the benefit of a free state in the full enjoyment of liberty, mirth & ease; having all things in common & nothing wanting to natures whole provision within the reach of their desires.[143]

—Whats that to absolute freedom; such as the very beggars have; to feast & revel here today, & yonder tomorrow; next day where they please, and so on still the whole country or Kingdom over? Theres liberty! the birds of the air can take no more[144]

———

play, WI drew ten lines varying in length from one-half inch to 1⅛ inches; we have regularized without notation.

140. *The Jovial Crew*, I, i. WI underlined the next speaker's name twice.

141. WI apparently dropped down a line and began to copy the word "are," then in the left margin wrote the word "Or" and reshaped "on" over the "ar."

142. *The Jovial Crew*, I, i. The dash indicates omitted material at the end of the line.

143. *Ibid.*, II, i. This speech is by Hilliard.

144. *Ibid.* WI used this speech by Meriel (in which she contrasts the beggar's freedom to her own as Oldrents' daughter) as a headnote for "Gipsies," in *Bracebridge Hall* (Smith, ed., p. 170).

Nay, When a man meets with bad tidings, why
May he not then compel his mind to mirth,
As well as puling stomachs are made strong
By eating against appetite.[145]

———

That your virtue & valour may lead you to the most honourable actions; and that the love of all exquisite ladies may arm you.[146]

———

Old rents

Oh mine ears! What was that, a sigh? and in my house? look, has it not split my walls? if not, make vent for it; let it out; I shall be stifled else–

Ods my life! he sighs again & means to blow me out of my house. To horse again heres no dwelling for me[147]

———

Old rents–My house is for no business but the belly business; you find me not so uncivil, sir, as to ask you from whence you came, who you are, or whats your business; I ask you no questions, and can you be so discourteous as to tell me or my friend any thing like business; if you come to be merry with me you are welcome; if you have any business, forget it: you forget where you are else; and so to dinner–[148]

———

Beggars

With them there is no grievance or perplexity
No fear of war or state disturbances,
No alterations in a commonwealth,
Or innovation, shakes a thought of theirs[149]

———

I love a misers feast dearly; to see how thin & scattering the dishes stood as if they feared quarrelling–

And how the bottles to escape breaking one another were brought up by one at a time.[150]

———

145. *Ibid.*, II, i. This speech is by Hearty.

146. *Ibid.*, III, i. Following this speech by Rachel, WI drew a double line, then underlined twice "Old rents."

147. *Ibid.*, IV, i. Following these speeches by Oldrents, WI drew a double line; he began the next page by underlining twice the speaker's name.

148. *Ibid.* WI drew a double line, then apparently added his title after he copied the next line.

149. *Ibid.*, IV, ii. This speech is by Vincent.

150. *Ibid.*, V, i. This conversation is between Oldrents and Hearty (whose line begins "And how the bottles . . .").

How one of the Serving men ⟨unused⟩ ↑untrained↓ to wait spilt the white broth[151]

From *The City Night Cap*
Thos Davenport 1661[152]

—She that is lip-holy,
Is many times heart-hollow.[153]

---

a ⟨silent⟩ *faithful* wife

She's modest, but not sullen, and loves silence;
Not that she wants apt words, (for when she speaks,
She inflames love with wonder) but because
She calls wise silence the souls harmony.
She's truly chaste; yet such a foe to coyness,
The poorest call her courteous; & which is excellent,
(Though fair & young) she shuns to expose herself
To the opinion of strange eyes. She either seldom
Or never walks abroad but in your company
And then with such sweet bashfulness, as if
She were venturing on crack'd ice; & takes delight
To step into the print your foot hath made,
And will follow you whole fields; so will she drive
Tediousness out of time with her sweet character.[154]

151. *Ibid.* This line is by Oldrents. WI drew a double line before copying from the next play.

152. *The City Night-Cap: A Comedy* by Robert Davenport was published in volume 9 of the 1744 edition of Dodsley's collection; it was published in volume 11 of the 1780 and 1825–1827 (and we assume in the 1810) editions of Dodsley which also contained the play from which WI subsequently copied. *The City Night-Cap* was also included in volume 13 of Hazlitt's 1874 edition of Dodsley. WI underlined only the words "The City" in the title and he wrote "Thos" rather than the correct first name of the author. To separate passages from this play, WI drew ten lines varying in length from one-half inch to one inch with the exception of the one immediately preceding the next play, that a triple line varying in length from three-fourths inch to 3⅜ inches; we have regularized without notation.

153. *The City Night-Cap*, I. This play is divided only into acts; following this line by Lorenzo early in the play, WI drew a double line and went back to a speech earlier in the act; after he copied it he apparently added his title, underlining "faithful" twice.

154. *Ibid.* WI quoted in full this speech by Philippo (in which he praises Abstemia to her husband Lorenzo) in "Wives," in *Bracebridge Hall* (Smith, ed., p. 44).

a patient wife— *Abstemia*—

—Hast thou not seen me
Bear all his injuries, as the ocean suffers
The angry bark to plough thorough her bosom,
And yet is presently so smooth, the eye
Cannot perceive where the wide wound was made.[155]

———

By the unblemish'd faith⟨,⟩ then⟨,⟩ of a gentleman;[156]

———

—by the sweet
Excellent blush of virtue, there is in you
Plenty of truth & goodness.[157]

———

An honest man is still an unmoved rock,
Wash'd whiter, but not shaken by the shock.[158]

———

Abstemia—on being cast off by her husband—

———

Farewell Lorenzo,
Whom my soul doth love: if you e'er marry,
May you meet a good wife, so good, that you
May not suspect her, nor may she be worthy
Of your suspicion: and if you hear hereafter[159]
That I am dead, enquire but my last words,
And you shall know that to the last I lov'd you;
And when you walk forth with your second choice,
Into the pleasant fields, & by chance talk of me,
Imagine that you see me lean and pale,
Strewing your paths with flowers; & when in bed
You cast your arms about her happy side,
Think you see me stand with a patient look
Crying, all hail, you lovers, live & prosper:
But may she never live to pay my debts: (weeps)
If but in thought she wrong you, may she die
In the conception of the injury.

155. *Ibid.* WI quoted this speech by Abstemia in "Wives," in *Bracebridge Hall* (Smith, ed., p. 44).

156. *Ibid.* These words and the following two speeches are by Phillipo.

157. *Ibid.*

158. *Ibid.*, II. In the following passage, WI underlined "Abstemia" twice.

159. The first syllable of the word is smudged; it appears that WI first wrote "hear," then changed it to "here."

Pray make me wealthy with one kiss: farewell, ^↑sir:↓
Let it not grieve you when you shall remember
That I was innocent: not this forget,
Though innocence here suffer, sigh & groan
She walks but through thorns to find a throne[160]

———

Break up the court; & cousin, learn this reed;
Who stabs truths bosom, makes an angel bleed.[161]

———

Lorenzos conviction of her chastity

———

Oh⟨!⟩, Abstemia!
How lovely thou lookest now! now thou appearest
Chaster than is the mornings modesty,
That rises with a blush, over whose bosom
The western wind creeps softly: now I remember,
⟨*illegible*⟩ ↑How,↓ when she sat at table, her obedient eye
⟨How⟩ would dwell on mine, as if it were not well,
Unless it looked where I look'd: oh how proud
She was, when she could cross herself to please me!
But where now is this fair soul? like a silver cloud,
She hath wept herself, I fear, into th' dead sea,
And will be found no more.[162]

Lorenzo
Thou wealth worth more than kingdoms, I am now
Confirm'd past all suspicion, thou art far
Sweeter in thy sincere truth, than a sacrifice
Deck'd up for death with garlands. The Indian winds,
That blow from off the coast, & cheer the sailor
With the sweet savour of their spices, want
The delight flows in thee—[163]

———

160. *The City Night-Cap*, II. WI quoted this speech by Abstemia, omitting only "& when in bed . . . prosper" (lines 11–14 of the passage), in "Wives," in *Bracebridge Hall* (Smith, ed., p. 45). WI drew a double line.

161. *Ibid.* This speech is by the Duke of Verona; WI added the title before copying the next passage.

162. *Ibid.*, V. WI quoted in full this speech by Abstemia in "Wives," in *Bracebridge Hall* (Smith, ed., pp. 45–46).

163. *Ibid.* WI quoted in full this speech by Lorenzo (on having his wife restored to him) in "Wives," in *Bracebridge Hall* (Smith, ed., p. 46).

From Grim the Collier of Croydon
author unknown
1662[164]

In lovely London are we here arrived.
Where, as I hear, the earl hath a fair daughter
So full of virtue, & soft modesty,
That she ne'er gave a man a foul word.[165]

⟨? Hark har ?⟩
Now shall your lordships see a Spaniards Skill
Who from the plains of new America
Can find out sacred simples of esteem
To bind & unbind natures strongest powers.[166]

Grim. In wisdom I am appeas'd, but in anger I broil as it were a rasher upon the coals.[167]

Grim. If I love thee! dost thou doubt of that?, nay, rip me up & look into my heart, & thou shalt see thy own face pictured there as plainly as in the proudest looking glass in all Croydon; if I love thee! then tears gush out, & shew my love.[168]

---

164. *Grim the Collier of Croydon, or the Devil and his Dam; with the Devil and St. Dunstan,* by J. T., appeared in volume 5 of the 1744 edition of Dodsley's collection. It was in volume 11 of the 1780 and 1825–1827 (and we assume in the 1810) editions. The date of printing was given as 1662, although Collier, the editor of the 1825–1827 edition of Dodsley, wrote that anyone who reads the play will recognize that it was written much earlier. Dodsley, in his introduction to the play retained by Collier and Hazlitt in their editions, wrote that the "initial letters J. T. are placed before this play as those belonging to the author of it. What his name was, or what his condition, are alike unknown" (Hazlitt, ed., *A Select Collection of Old English Plays*, 4th ed. [1874], VIII, 387). WI quoted two of these excerpted passages in *Bracebridge Hall*; in his edition of that work, Herbert F. Smith says that the text of this play by William Haughton may also be found in *Anonymous Plays*, ed. John S. Farmer (London, 1908) (*Bracebridge Hall*, p. 331, n. 163.2–3). To separate passages from this play, WI drew seven lines varying in length from one-half to three-fourths inch with the exception of the one preceding the next play which is 2¼ inches long; we have regularized without notation.

165. *Grim the Collier of Croydon*, I, iii. This speech is by Belphegor.

166. *Ibid.*, II, i. This speech is by Castiliano.

167. *Ibid.* WI underlined "Grim" twice in this passage and the one following.

168. *Ibid.*

Ill live a private, pensive, single life[169]

Grim—Nay, I tell you, I am so well beloved in our town, that not the worst dog in the street will hurt my little finger.[170]

From *The Widow*
By Ben Jonson, Fletcher & Middleton[171]

Twas her voice sure,
Or my soul takes ⟨such⟩ delight to think it was,
And makes a sound like hers[172]

From fire, from water, & all things amiss
Deliver the house of an honest justice.[173]

'Tis gone again, Since such are all lifes pleasures,
No sooner known but lost, he that enjoys ⟨them⟩ ↑'em↓
The length of life has but a longer dream;
He wakes to this i' th' end, & sees all nothing[174]

That light in yonder window,
That was my only comfort in the woods,
Which oft a trembling leaf would lose me,
Has brought me thus far. Yet I cannot hope
For succour in this plight, the worlds so pitiless,
And every one will fear & doubt me now.

169. *Ibid.*, IV, i. WI quoted this line by Musgrave as a headnote for "A Bachelor's Confessions," in *Bracebridge Hall* (Smith, ed., p. 163).

170. *Ibid.*, V, i. WI quoted this boast by Grim as a headnote for "Village Worthies," in *Bracebridge Hall* (Smith, ed., p. 178). WI underlined "Grim" twice.

171. *The Widow: A Comedy*, by Ben Jonson, John Fletcher, and Thomas Middleton was published in volume 6 of the 1744 edition of Dodsley's collection; it appeared in volume 12 in the 1780 and 1825–1827 (and we assume in the 1810) editions. Volume 12 also contained the next play from which WI copied. *The Widow* was omitted from Hazlitt's 1874 edition of Dodsley. WI underlined the title twice, and to separate passages from this play, he drew thirteen lines varying in length from one-half to one inch with the exception of an additional line from margin to margin preceding the next play's title; we have regularized without notation.

172. *The Widow*, I, i. This speech is by Francisco.

173. *Ibid.* WI quoted this speech by Martino as the headnote for "The Culprit," in *Bracebridge Hall* (Smith, ed., p. 234). WI drew a double line.

174. *Ibid.* This speech is by Francisco.

To knock will be too bold; I'll to the gate,
And listen if I can hear any stirring.[175]

———

Was ever man so crossd? No, tis but sweat, sure
Or the dew dropping from the leaves above me[176]

———

⟨*unrecovered*⟩ arresting, in what kind soever,
Is a most gentleman-like affliction[177]

———

Fancied Spectre

⟨'Light[?]⟩[178] What should that be? a prodigious thing
Stands just as I should enter, in that shape too
Which always appears terrible.
Whateer it be, it is made strong against me
By my ill purpose: for tis mans own sins
That[179] put on armour upon all his evils,
And give them strength to strike him. were it less
Than what it is, my guilt would make it serve;
A wicked mans own shadow has distracted him.

x x x x x x x x

———

And what does fond man venture all these ills ^↑for↓
That may so sweetly rest in honest peace?
For that which being obtain'd, is as he was
To his own natural sense, but removed nearer still
To death eternal. What delight has man
Now at this present, for his pleasant sin
Of yesterdays committing? Alas, tis vanished
And nothing but the sting remains with him.[180]

———

175. *Ibid.*, III, ii. This speech is by Martia.

176. *Ibid.* This speech and the one following are by Francisco. WI drew a triple line and made two false beginnings (one the letter *A* above the crossed-out word).

177. *Ibid.* The unrecovered word could be "admit," "arest," etc.

178. The crossed-out word could also be " 'S'foot."

179. To the left of this word in the margin is an ink blot.

180. *The Widow*, III, ii. In the middle of this long speech by Francisco, WI omitted lines, and in the space drew a double line and above it inserted eight *x*'s.

A distrest man's flatteries
Are like vows made in drink, or bonds in prison,
Theres poor assurance in them—[181]

———

In my opinion now, this young mans likeliest
To keep his word; he's modest, wise & courteous;
He has the language of an honest soul in him:
A womans[182] reputation may lie safe there,
I'm much deceived else; h'as a faithful eye.[183]

———

Give me fortune, give me health
Give me freedom, I'll get wealth.
Who complains his fate's amiss
When he has the wide world his.
In every hamlet, town & city,
He has lands that was born witty.[184]

———

O pagan!
This fellow will be ston'd to death with pipkins;
Your women in the suburbs will so maul him
With broken cruises, & pitchers without ears;
He will never die alive, thats my opinion.[185]

Methinks theres somewhat whispers in my soul
This hour I must begin my acquaintance
With honest love, & banish all loose thoughts;
My fate speaks to me from the modest eye
Of yon sweet gentlewoman.[186]

———

—Ever since I knew what malice was
I always held it sweeter to sow mischief,
Than to receive money; 'tis the finer pleasure[187]

———

181. *Ibid.*, III, iii. This speech is by Philippo. WI drew a double line.

182. WI may have first written the letters "A ma," and then to the left in heavier ink he wrote *A*, and over the "ma," he began the word "woman."

183. *The Widow*, III, iii. This speech is by Philippo.

184. *Ibid.*, IV, ii. WI centered this speech by Latrocinio.

185. *Ibid.*, V, i. This speech is by Martino.

186. *Ibid.* Following this speech by Francisco, WI drew a double line.

187. *Ibid.* This speech is by the Second Suiter.

From The Adventures of five hours
Sir Samuel Tuke
1664[188]

Antonio's discription of Camilla, fainting—

At the first sight, I did believe her dead;
Yet in that state so awful she appear'd,
That I approached her with as much respect,
As if the soul had animated still
That body, which, though dead, scarce mortal seemd.
But as, the sun from our horizon gone,
His beams do leave a tincture on the skies,
Which shews it was not long since he withdrew;
So in her lovely face there still appear'd
Some scatter'd streaks of those vermillion beams,
Which us'd t'irradiate that bright firmament.

x x x x x x

My admiration did suspend my aid,
Till passion join'd to pity made me bold;
I kneeld and took her in my arms, then bow'd
Her body gently forward; at which instant,
A sigh stole from her; oh the ravishing sound!
Which being a symptom of remaining life,
Made me forget that 'twas a sign of grief.
At length she faintly opens her bright eyes;
So breaks the day; & so do all the creatures
Rejoice, as I did, at the new born light:
⟨But as the Indians, who adore the sun,
Are scorch'd by's beam, e're half his race be run;
So I who did adore her rising eyes
Found myself wounded by those deities.⟩[189]

---

188. *The Adventures of Five Hours: A Tragi-Comedy*, by Sir Samuel Tuke, was published in volume 12 of the 1744 edition of Dodsley; it was also in volume 12 of the 1780 and 1825–1827 (and we assume in the 1810) editions, and in volume 15 of Hazlitt's 1874 edition. The play is divided into acts, but not into scenes. To separate passages in this play, WI drew thirteen lines, several of them double, varying in length from three-eighths inch to 1½ inches; to indicate some omitted lines, he used three sets of *x*'s, the first of six and the others of three *x*'s. We have regularized without notation.

189. *The Adventures of Five Hours*, II. For no apparent reason WI crossed out with three large *X*'s the final four lines of Don Antonio's speech.

If I must needs be killed, unless it were
Behind my back, I'd have it i' the dark;
For I hate to be kill'd in my own presence[190]

———

—Amongst all the curses, there is none
So wounds the spirit as privation:
For 'tis not where we lie, but whence we fell;
The loss of heaven's the greatest pain in hell.[191]

———

Don Octavio
We shall still live, though 'tis by others breath,
By our good fame, which is secured by Death.
Diego
But we shall catch such colds, sir, under ground,
That we shall never hear fames trumpet sound.[192]

Either we sleep & dream extravagantly
Or else the fairies govern this house[193]

———

Peace; slave; he is my noble friend, of noble blood,
Whose fame's above the level of those tongues
That bark by custom at the brightest virtues,
As dogs do at the moon.[194]

———

Im now upon the frontiers of this life
There's but one step to immortality.

x x x

Look down, ye spirits above; for if there be
A sight ⟨of⟩ on earth worthy of you to see
'Tis a brave man, pursu'd by unjust hate,
Bravely contending with his adverse fate[195]

———

190. *Ibid.*, V. This speech is by Diego.

191. *Ibid.* This speech is by Don Octavio.

192. *Ibid.* WI underlined twice both names.

193. *Ibid.* In the upper right corner of this page, WI wrote and crossed out words which resemble "Had dice & bath"; the last word could be "Hate" or "&fate." These lines are by Diego.

194. *Ibid.* This speech is by Don Octavio.

195. *Ibid.* This speech and the one following are by Don Octavio.

—Sir, tis not my custom to receive
An obligation, but with a purpose,
And within the power of my return.
Friendship, Antonio is reciprocal,
He that will only give, and not receive
Enslaves the person whom he would relieve.[196]

———

Faith, Sir, I never pain myself for love,
Or fame, or riches; nor do I pretend
To that great subtilty of sense, to feel
Before Im hurt; and for the most part
I keep myself out of harms way.[197]

How happy are the men of easy phlegm!
Born on the confines of indifference,
Holding from nature the securest tenure,
The peaceful empire o'er themselves; which we,
Th' unhappy men of fire, without the aids
Of mighty reason or almighty Grace
Are all our lives contending for in vain.[198]

———

I have observ'd the signs of smotherd grief;
I've seen those lovely eyes much swoln,
Those are true tears, Camilla which are stolen.[199]

———

↑I↓[200] Dare boldly say there lives not in the world
A more valiant man than I, whilst danger
Keeps its distance; but when saucily
It presses on, then (I confess) 'tis true,
I have a certain tenderness for life,
Which checks my ardour, & inclines my prudence
Timely to withdraw

x x x

196. *Ibid.* WI turned to earlier passages to copy the remaining five excerpts from this play.

197. *Ibid.* This speech is by Diego.

198. *Ibid.*, I. This speech is by Don Henrique.

199. *Ibid.* This speech is by Porcia.

200. The *I* on the line above is the final word of the line, "Sir, you may call it what you please; but I"; WI needed it to complete the sentence he was quoting, but he apparently did not want to alter the line to insert it.

—I have such a piercing sight, that I
Discover perils out of others' ken;
Which they not seeing soon enough to shun,
Are forc'd t'encounter; & then their struggling
Is, by th' unwary world, taken for courage.[201]

———

(from—The *Witch*
Middleton
Supposed 1604[?].[202]

Though the fates have endued me with a pretty kind of lightness, that I can laugh at the world in a corner on't; and can make myself merry on fasting nights to rub out a supper, (which were ^↑a↓ precious quality in a young formal student) yet let the world know there is some difference betw⟨een⟩ixt my jovial condition and the lunary state of madness. I am not quite out of my wits.[203]

used { The treasures of the deep are not so precious
As are the conceal'd comforts of a man
Lock'd up in womans love. I scent the air
Of blessings, when I come but near the house.
What a delicious breath marriage sends forth,
The violet beds not sweeter![204] Honest wedlock
Is like a banqueting house built in a garden,
On which the springs chaste flowers take delight
To cast their modest odours: ———
——— Now for a welcome

201. *The Adventures of Five Hours*, II.

202. With Thomas Middleton's play, *The Witch* (first printed in 1778, 151 years after Middleton's death), WI began using another source, unidentified at this point. The excerpts from the fourteen remaining plays are shorter than those from the previous plays collected by Dilke and Dodsley; it seems probable that WI used a work which also excerpted passages. To separate passages, his own titles, and plays, and to indicate omitted material in the following pages, WI drew 32 lines (occasionally double lines) varying in length from one-eighth inch to two inches, with the exception of one line of 2⅞ inches and another from margin to margin; there are also three sets of four *x*'s to indicate omitted material. Unless there is something unusual about these markers, we have regularized without notation.

203. *The Witch*, V, i. This speech is by Almachildes.

204. To the left of these six lines, WI drew in the margin a vertical squiggle, and to the left of that, he wrote the word "used." He used lines 1–6 of this excerpt as a headnote in *The Sketch Book* for the essay "The Wife."

Able to draw man's envies upon man;
A Kiss, now, that will hang upon my lip
As sweet as morning dew upon a rose,
And full as long.

Middletons, "Women beware Wom[em]."[205]

———

Love crossed.

———

From Middletons Blurt Master Constable.[206]

used { ———I never heard
Of any true affection but 'twas nipt
With care, that, like the caterpillar, eats
The leaves off the spring's sweetest book, the rose.[207] }

———

—He that truly loves
Burns out the Day in idle fantasies.[208]

———

Loves eye the jewel of sleep, oh, seldom wears!

x x x x

But say, a golden slumber chance to tie,
With silken strings the cover of love's eye,
Then dreams magician like, mocking present
Pleasures, whose fading, leaves more discontent.[209]

From Websters Dutchess of Malfy

Delio. Yond's the cardinals window. This fortification
Grew from the ruins of an ancient abbey;
And to yond side o' th' river lies a wall,
Piece of a cloister, which in my opinion
Gives the best echo that you ever heard;

205. *Women beware Women,* II, i; this play by Thomas Middleton was not printed until 1657. The dashes in lines 9–10 are actually lines of 1¼ and ¾ inches and indicate omitted material.

206. WI added this line after he had written his "title" and copied from the text.

207. Thomas Middleton, *Blurt, Master-Constable. Or the Spaniards Night-walke* (1602), III, i. WI used this speech by Fontinelle as a headnote in *The Sketch Book* for the essay "The Broken Heart."

208. *Ibid.* This speech is by Camillo.

209. *Ibid.*

So hollow & so dismal, and withal
So plain in the distinction of our words,
That many have supposed it is a Spirit
That answers.
Antonio. I do love these ancient ruins:
We never tread upon them but we set
Our foot upon some reverend history;
And, questionless, here in this open court,
Which now lies naked to the injuries
Of stormy weather, some men lie interr'd
Lov'd the church so well, & gave so largely to't,
They thought it should have canopied their bones
Till doomsday. But all things have their end:
Churches & cities, which have diseases like to men,
Must have like death that we have.[210]

———

From a play calld *Adrasta*

Damon. Come, hands to work! It is the festival
Of our Sylvanus, we must round entrench
The fittest place for dancing.
Laur[inda]. And strew the banks
On which the summer Lord & Lady sit
To see the sports, with those rich spoils of May.
Armin[o] Our shepherds will be frolic then, and lose
No ceremony of their ancient mirth.
Damon I ⟨seek⟩ like them well: the curious preciseness,
And all-pretended gravity, of those
That seek to banish hence those harmless sports,
Have thrust away much ancient honesty.[211]

———

Ben Johnsons Sad Shepherd.

———

^↑*Aeglamour.*↓ Here she was wont to go! and here! and here!
Just where those daisies, pinks and violets grow:
The world may find the spring by following her;
For other print her airy steps neer left.

210. John Webster, *The Duchess of Malfi* (1623), V, iii. WI quoted lines 3–9 of the copied speech by Delio ("yond side . . . That answers") in "Hawking," in *Bracebridge Hall* (Smith, ed., p. 78). Here he underlined twice the speakers' names.
211. WI quoted from John Jones' *Adrasta: or The Women's Spleene and Love's Conquest* (1635), IV, i. He underlined twice the title and Damon's name.

Her treading would not bend a blade of grass,
Or shake the downy ⟨f[?]⟩ blow-ball from his stalk!
But like the soft west wind she shot along,
And where she went, the flowers took thickest root,
As she had sow'd them with her odorous foot.[212]

———

⟨from[?]⟩ Imitation by *Goff*[?] in his *Careless shepherdess*—

This was her wonted place—nor can she be
Far from the spring she has left behind; that rose
I saw not yesterday, nor did that pink
Then court my eye; she must be here, or else
That graceful mary gold would sure have closed
Its beauty in its wither'd leaves, that violet
Would too have hung its velvet head, to mourn
The absense of her eyes.[213]

———

‸↑Aeglamour.↓—You are goodly friends! right charitable men!
Nay, keep your way and leave me; make your toys,
Your tales, your posies, that you talk⟨e⟩'d of; all
Your entertainments: you not injure me.
Only if I may enjoy my cypress wreath,
And you will let me weep, tis all I ask.[214]

No sun or moon, or other cheerful star
Look'd out of heaven, but all the cope was dark,
As it were hung so for her exequies!
And not a voice or sound to ring her knell;
But of that dismal pair, the screeching owl,
And buzzing hornet! Hark! hark! hark! the ⟨fowl⟩ ‸↑foul↓
Bird! how she flutters with her wicker wings!
Peace! you shall hear her screech.[215]

———

Song.

Though I am young and cannot tell
Either what Death or Love is well,

212. WI quoted from Ben Jonson's *The Sad Shepherd*, I, i. He apparently added and underlined twice the speaker's name after he had started quoting.

213. Apparently, WI copied from a satire of the passage above; it is likely that the edition from which he quoted included this "Imitation," perhaps in a footnote.

214. *The Sad Shepherd*, I, ii. This speech and the one following are by Aeglamour.

215. *Ibid.*

Yet I have heard they both ⟨have[?]⟩ bear darts
And both do aim at human hearts:
And then again, I have been told,
Love wounds with heat, & death with cold;
So that I fear they do but bring
Extremes to touch, & mean one thing.

As in a ruin w⟨ee⟩e it call
One thing to be blown up, or fall;
Or to our end, like way may have
By flash of lightning or a ⟨grave⟩ wave:
So loves inflamed shaft or brand
May kill as soon as death's cold hand
Except Loves fires the virtues have
To fright the frost out of the grave.[216]

Lorels description of his cottage &c

An hundred udders for the pail I have
That give me milk and curds, that make me cheese
To cloy the markets! twenty swarm of bees,
Whilk all the summer hum about the hive,
And bring me wax and honey in bilive. (Ie. freely ↓actively↑)
An aged oak, the king of all the field,
With a broad breech there grows before my dur,
That mickle mast unto the ferm doth yield.
A chestnut, whilk hath larded mony a swine,
Whose skins I wear to fend me fra' the cold;
A poplar green, and with a kerved seat,
Under whose shade I solace in the heat;
And thence can see gang out and in my neat.
Twa trilland brooks, each, from his spring doth meet,
And make a river to refresh my feet;
In which, each morning, ere the sun doth rise,
I look myself, and clear my pleasant eyes,
Before I pipe———[217]

---

216. *Ibid.* This song is by Karolin.
217. *Ibid.*, II, i.

∧↑*Amie*↓ How often when the sun, heavens brightest birth,
Hath with his burning fervour cleft the earth,
Under a spreading elm or oak, hard by
A cool clear fountain, could I sleeping lie
Safe from the heat! but now no shady tree,
Nor purling brook can my refreshing be.[218]

———

I grant the linet, lark and bullfinch sing,
But best the dear good angel of the spring,
The nightingale.[219]

———

a witch.

Within a gloomy dimble she doth dwell,
Down in a pit, oergrown with brakes & briars
Close by the ruins of a shaken abbey,
Torn with an earthquake down unto the ground,
'Mongst graves and grots, near an old charnel house,
Where you shall find her sitting in her fourm,
As fearful and as melancholic as that
She is about; with catterpillars kells,
And knotty cob-webs, rounded in with spells.
Thence she steals forth to relief in the fogs,
And rotten mists, upon the fens & bogs,
Down to the drowned lands of Lincolnshire;
To make ewes cast their lambs, swine eat their farrow,
The housewi⟨f⟩ves tun not work, nor the milk churn!
Writhe childrens wrists, & suck their breath in sleep,
Get vials of their blood! and where the sea
Casts up his slimy ooze, search for a weed
To open Locks with, and to rivet charms,
Planted about her in the wicked feat
Of all her mischiefs, which are manifold.[220]

———

George. Ay, this gud learned man
Can speak her ⟨rightly⟩ right.

Scarlet. He knows her shifts & haunts.

218. *Ibid.*, II, ii.
219. *Ibid.* This speech is also by Amie.
220. *Ibid.* This long speech is by Alken.

Alken. And all her wiles & turns. The venomd plants
Wherewith she kills! where the sad mandrake grows,
Whose groans are deathful; the dead-numbing night/-shade,
The stupifying hemlock, adder's tongue,
And ⟨illegible⟩ martagan: the shrieks of luckless owls
We hear, and croaking night crows in the air!
Green bellied snakes, blue fire drakes in the sky,
And giddy flitter mice with leather wings!
The scaly beetles, with their ⟨hum[?]⟩ habergeons,
That make a humming murmur as they fly!
There in the stocks of trees, white faies do dwell,
And span long elves that dance about a pool,
With each a little changeling in their arms!
The airy spirits play with falling stars,
And mount the sphere of fire to kiss the moon!
While she sits reading by the glow worms light,
Or rotten wood, oer which the worm hath crept
The baneful schedule of her nocent charms,
And binding characters, through which she wounds
Her puppets, the sigilla of her witchcraft.[221]

———

But you must wait occasions, and obey them:
Sail in an eggshell, make a straw your mast,
A cobweb all your cloth, and pass unseen
Till you have 'scaped the rocks that are about you.[222]

———

—Witches in the Mask of Queens[223]

———

Hag. Sisters stay, we want our Dame;
Call upon her by her name,
And the charm we use to say;
That she quickly anoint & come away.
1. Charm. Dame, dame! the watch is set:
Quickly come, we all are met.—
From the lakes and from the fens,
From the rocks & from the dens,
From the church & from the caves

221. *Ibid.*

222. *Ibid.*, III, ii. This speech is by Puck-Hairy.

223. For the next three manuscript pages, WI copied from Ben Jonson's *The Masque of Queens* (1609), titling the section.

From the church yards, from the graves,
From the dungeon, from the tree
That they die on, here are we!
Comes she not yet?
Strike another heat.[224]

2. Charm The weather is fair, the wind is good,
Up, dame, on your horse of wood:
Or else tuck up your gray frock,
And saddle your goat, or your green cock,
And make his bridle a bottom of thread,
To roll up how many miles you have rid.
Quickly come away:
For we all stay
Nor yet! nay, then,
We'll try her again.

3. Charm. The owl is abroad, the bat, & the toad,
And so is the Cat-a-mountain,
The ant and the mole sit both in a hole,
And the frog peeps out o' the fountain;
The dogs they do bay, and the timbrels play,
And the spindle is now a turning;
The moon it is red, and the stars are fled,
But all the sky is a burning:
The ditch is made, and one nails the spade,
With pictures full, of wax and of wool;
Their livers I stick with needles quick,
There lacks but the blood to make up the flood.
Quickly dame then bring your part in
Spur, Spur your little martin
Merrily, merrily, make him fail,
A worm in his mouth and a thorn in his ∧↑tail,↓
Fire above and fire below,
With a whip in your hand, to make him go.
Oh now shes come!
Let all be dumb.[225]

———

224. WI wrote these two lines of the first charm to the left of the indented margin, but he used a double indentation for the other two underlined passages; we have regularized.

225. This third charm, from *The Masque of Queens*, is the last on the manuscript page; WI began the next page with the fifth charm.

Flow water and blow wind.
Rouncy is over, Robble is under,
A flash of light and a clap of thunder,
A[226] storm of rain, another of hail.
We all must home in the egg-shell sail;
The mast is made of a great pin,
The tackle of cob web, the sail as thin
And if we go through & not fall in—[227]

———

About, about and about,
Till the mist arise, & the lights fly out,
The images neither be seen, nor felt;
The woollen burn and the waxen melt:
Sprinkle your liquors upon the ground,
And into the air; around, around.
    Around, around,
    Around, around,
    Till a musick sound
    And the pace be found
    To which we may dance,
    And our charms advance[228]

———

from a Song in the Gipsies Metamorphosis[229]

———

Cocklorrel would needs have the Devil his guest
    And bade him into the peak to dinner
Where never the fiend had such a ⟨guest⟩ feast
    Provided him yet at the charge of a Sinner.

His stomach was queasy, (he came thither coacht)
    The jogging had made some crudities rise
To help it he call'd for a puritan poacht
    That us'd to turn up the eggs of his eyes.

x x x x

Six pickled ta⟨y⟩ilors sliced & cut,
    Sempsters & tirewomen, fit for his palate;
With feathermen and perfumers put
    Some twelve in a charger to make a grand sallet.

x x x x

226. The *A* is covered with an ink blot.
227. *The Masque of Queens*; WI went to the ninth charm in the next passage.
228. *Ibid.*
229. WI referred to Ben Jonson's *The Gipsies Metamorphosed* (1621).

The jowl of a jailor serv'd for a fish,
    A constable sous'd with vinegar by;
Two aldermen lobsters asleep in a dish.
    A deputy tart, a churchwarden pye.[230]

———

An excellent song, & a sweet songster, and would have done rarely in a cage with a dish of water and hempseed![231]

———When the years at hottest,
And that the dogstar foams, & the Stream boils,
And curls, and works, & swells ready to sparkle.[232]

———

Robin.———mix with us
  In all the preferr'd solace of the Spring.
Aeglamour. A Spring, now she is dead! of what? of thorns,
  Briars and brambles? thistles, burs and docks?
  Cold hemlock, yew? the mandrake, or the box?
  These may grow still; but what can spring beside?
  Did not the whole earth sicken when she died?
  As if there since did fall one drop of dew,
  But what was wept for her! or any stalk
  Did bear a flower, or any branch a bloom,
  After her wreath was made![233]

———

Clay. I take the town to concord, where I dwell,
  All Kilborn be my witness, if I were not
  Begot in bashfulness, brought up in shamefacedness.
  Let 'un bring a dog but to my vace that can
  Zay I have beat 'un, & without a vault;
  Or but a cat will swear upon a book,
  I have as much as zet a vire her tail,
  And I'll give him or her a crown for 'mends.

a *Tale of a Tub*[234]

From ⟨D⟩Thos Dekkers Fortunatus[235]

230. *Ibid.* WI indicated omitted material between two stanzas of the song.

231. *Ibid.* This speech is by Pup.

232. Here, WI went back to Jonson's *The Sad Shepherd*, copying two passages. The first one, spoken by Aeglamour, is in act 1, scene 2.

233. *Ibid.*, I, ii. WI underlined twice the second speaker's name.

234. As WI indicated, this speech is from Ben Jonson's *A Tale of a Tub* (acted 1633, printed 1640), III, i.

235. There is a long ink blot from the first line of the previous page which appears to be crossing out the name of the play.

———long life
Is a long journey in December gone,
Tedious and full of tribulation.

Fortunatus[236]

———

I'm not enamour'd of this painted idol
This strumpet world; for her most beauteous ⟨locks[?]⟩[237] ^↑looks↓
Are poison'd baits, hung upon golden hooks.
When fools do swim in wealth, her Cynthian beams
Will wantonly dance on the silver streams;
But when this squintey'd age sees virtue poor,
And by a little spark set shivering,
Begging of all, reliev'd at no man's door,
She smiles on her as the sun shines on fire,
To kill that little heat.

Dekker.[238]

———

Ford.

Oh no more, no more! too late
Sighs are spent; the burning tapers
Of a life as chaste as fate,
Pure as are unwritten papers,
Are burnt out; no heat, no light
Now remains; 'tis ever night.
Love is dead; let lovers eyes,
Lock'd in endless dreams,
Th' extremes of all extremes
Open no more, for now love dies;
Now love dies, implying
Love's Martyrs must be ever, ever dying.

Song in The Broken heart.[239]

236. WI quoted from Thomas Dekker's *The Pleasant Comedie of Old Fortunatus* (1600), I, i; he underlined twice the speaker's name.

237. This word could be "hooks."

238. *Old Fortunatus*, I, ii. This speech is by Ampedo.

239. WI copied three passages from John Ford's *The Broken Heart* (acted c. 1629, printed 1633), the first from act 4, scene 3.

Org[ilus]. A horrid Stillness
Succeeds this deathful air. Lets know the reason:
Tread softly; there is mystery in mourning.[240]

———

———Oh, my lords,
I but deceived your eyes with antick gesture,
When one news strait came huddling on another,
Of death, and death, and death; still I dancd forward,
But it struck home, and here, and in an instant.
Be such mere women, who, with shrieks & outcries,
Can vow a present end to all their ⟨pleasures⟩ sorrows,
Yet live to vow new pleasures, and out live them:
They are the silent griefs ⟨that⟩ which cut the heart strings
Let me die smiling.

Broken heart[241]

Glories, pleasures, pomps, delights & ease
    Can but please
Outward senses, when the mind
Is not troubled, or by peace refin'd.
Crowns may flourish & decay,
Beauties shine, but fade away.
Youth may revel, yet it must
Lie down in a bed of dust.
Earthly honours flow and waste,
Time alone doth change and last.
Sorrows mingled with contents, prepare
    Rest for care;
Love only reigns in death: though art
Can find no comfort for a Broken Heart.

Idem[242]

Thierry. Suppose it death[243]

Ordella. I do.

240. *Ibid*., IV, iii.
241. *Ibid*., V, iii. This speech is by Calantha.
242. *Ibid*.
243. WI quoted a conversation from John Fletcher's *Thierry and Theodoret* (acted c. 1617, printed 1621), IV, i; this excerpt is in Lamb's *Specimens*, from which WI could have copied. He underlined twice the first three speakers' names.

Thi[erry]. And endless parting
With all we can call ours, with all our sweetness,
With youth, strength, pleasure, people, time, nay reason!
For in the silent grave, no conversation,
No joyful tread of friends, no voice of lovers,
No careful father's counsel, nothing's heard,
For nothing is, but all oblivion,
Lust and an endless darkness: and dare you woman
Desire this place?

Ord[ella]. 'Tis of all sleeps the sweetest:
Children begin it to us, strong men seek it,
And kings from height of all their painted glories
Fall, like spent exhaltations, to this centre:
And those are fools that fear it, or imagine
A few unhandsome pleasures, or lifes profits,
Can recompense this place; & mad that stay it,
'Till age blow out their lights, or rotten humours
Bring[244] them dispers'd to th' earth.

Thierry & Theodoret[245]

—a commanding majesty of chaste
And humbly glorious virtue—

Spanish Gipsey.
by Middleton & Rowley[246]

— —

We'll entertain no mounty-banking stroll,
No piper, fiddler, tumbler through small hoops,
No ape carrier, baboon bearer;
We must have nothing stale, trivial, or base:
Am I your Major Domo, your Teniente,
Your captain, your Commander.

idem[247]

———

If one city cannot maintain us, away to another; our horses must have wings; does Madrid yield no money? Seville shall; is Seville close fisted?

244. To the left and above this word is an ink blot from the following page.
245. WI varied his pattern by giving the title last.
246. WI quoted three passages from Thomas Middleton and William Rowley's *The Spanish Gipsie* (acted 1623, printed 1653); this speech by Roderigo is in act 5. WI underlined the first word of the title and "by Middleton."
247. *Ibid.*, II, i. This speech and the one following are by Alvarez.

Valladolid is open; so Cordova, so Toledo: Do not our Spanish wines please us? Italian can then, French can; ⟨pre-/-ferments[?]⟩

Idem.[248]

Wincot.—Now whence come you?

Clown. Who, I, Sir? from a lodging of largess a house of hospitality, and a palace of plenty; where theres feeding like horses, and drinking like fishes; where for pints, we're served in pottles; and instead of pottle pots, in pails; instead of Silver tankards, we drink of water tankards; claret runs as freely as the Cocks; and canary, like the conduits of a Coronation day; where there's nothing but feeding and frolicking, carving and kissing, drinking and dancing, music and madding, fiddling and feasting.

English Traveller—*Heywood*[249]

Riotous Supper of Young Lionel & his com-/-panions—
English Traveller
Heywood.[250]

In the height of their carousing, all their brains,
Warmd with the heat of wine, discourse was offerd
Of ships, & storms at sea: when suddenly,
Out of his giddy wildness, one conceives
The room wherein they quaffd to be a pinnace,
Moving & floating;[251] & the confused noise
To be the murmuring winds, gusts, &[252] mariners;
That their unsteadfast footing did proceed
From rocking of the vessel: this conceiv'd,
Each one begins to apprehend the danger,
And to look out for safety. Fly, saith one,
Up to the main top, & discover: he
Climbs by the bed post, to the tester, there,
Reports a turbulent sea & tempest towards;

248. *Ibid.*

249. WI quoted from Thomas Heywood's *The English Traveller* (1633), II, i. He underlined twice the names of the speakers and the author.

250. WI gave his title for the excerpt, repeated the title and author of the play, then copied Young Geraldine's description of the feast at Lionel's house in act 2, scene 1.

251. WI wrote "&flo^↑a↓ting."

252. To the left of the ampersand is a vertical ink mark.

And wills them, if theyll save their ship & lives,
To cast their lading overboard. At this
All fall to work, & hoist into the street,
As to the sea what next come to their hand,
Stools, tables, tressels, trenchers, bedsteds, cups,
Pots, plates, & glasses: here a fellow whistles;
They take him for the boatswain; one lies struggling
Upon the floor, as if he swam for life:
A third takes the bass viol for the Cock-boat,
Sits in the belly on't, labours, & rows;
His oar, the stick with which the fiddler playd:
A fourth bestrides his fellows, thinking to scape
As did Arion, on the dolphins back,
Still fumbling on a gittern

Clown. Excellent Sport!

Wincot—But what was the conclusion?

Y. *Geraldine.*[253] The rude multitude
Watching without, & gaping for the spoil
Cast from the windows, went by the ears about it;
The Constable is called to atone the broil,
Which done, & hearing such a noise within,
Of imminent Shipwreck, enters the house, and finds them
In this confusion: they adore his staff,
And think it Neptunes trident; and that he,
Came with his Tritons (so they call'd his watch)
To calm the tempest, & appease the waves
And at this point we left them.
(the above is in Lambs Specimen)[254]

Therefore 'tis fitter I should reverence
The thatched houses, where the Britons dwell

253. WI indented "Clown" and underlined twice the names of the speakers; we have regularized. He also added a short triple line above the word "rude" as if he stopped copying, then decided to complete the passage.

254. WI's note suggests that he may have copied the passage from Lamb's *Specimens*; however, included in WI's quotation are the interruptions by the clown and Wincott, which Lamb omitted in his version with a long line. WI may have used another source and later noticed the passage was also in Lamb's work; the previous passage from Heywood's work is not in *Specimens*.

In careless mirth; where the bless'd household ↓gods↑
See naught but chaste & simple purity.
'Tis not high power that makes a place divine,
Nor that the men from gods derive their line;
But sacred thoughts, in holy bosoms stor⟨d⟩ed,
Make people noble, & the place adored.
Bonduca[255]

I see as fair as day, that thou wantst drink.
Did I not find thee gaping, like an oyster
For a new tide? Thy very thoughts lie bare,
Like a low ebb; thy soul, that rid in sack,
Lies moor'd for want of liquor. Do but see
Into thyself; for, by the gods, I do;
For all thy bodys chappd. & crack'd like timber,
For want of moisture.—
Bonduca.[256]

———

Duchess—Do we grow fantastical in our death-bed?
Do we affect fashion in the grave?

Bos[ola] Most ambitiously: princes images on their tombs
Do not lie, as they were wont, seeming to pray,
Up to heaven; but with their hands under their cheeks
(as if they died of the tooth ache); they are not carved
With their eyes fixed ⟨on⟩ ‸↑upon↓ the Stars; but as
Their minds were wholly bent upon the world,
The self same way they seem to turn their faces.
Webster—Duchess Malfy.[257]

[*pp. [89–92 blank*]

[*inside back cover not in Irving's hand*]

[*back cover*]

O P

255. WI quoted from John Fletcher's *Bonduca* (acted c. 1616, printed 1647), IV, i; this speech is by Bonduca.

256. *Ibid.* WI underlined twice the title of the play.

257. WI quoted from John Webster's *The Duchess of Malfy*, as it is spelled in Lamb's *Specimens*, where this passage is printed. WI's version varies from Lamb's which reproduces Bosola's speech in prose; the earlier passage from this play which WI copied is not in *Specimens*.

MISCELLANEOUS MATERIALS

Notes for Life of Washington

Commonplace Book Fragment,[1] *Notes for* Life of Washington, *Undated*[2]

This manuscript fragment is in the Clifton Waller Barrett Library of the University of Virginia where it is cataloged as #6256–a and housed in a folder. It is described as "Ams (fragment) A Trip Through the West." There are four leaves torn from a notebook at the top; leaves 1, 3, and 4 measure 3½ x 4⁷⁄₁₆ inches, and leaf 2 measures 3½ x 4⅜ inches. The writing in black ink is from binding to bottom edge of each of the eight

1. The description of this fragment in the Clifton Waller Barrett Library catalogue is misleading: "406. Irving, Washington. Autograph Manuscript of a portion of *A Trip Through the West*, unsigned, 8 pp., 32 no, about 850 words. With some corrections in Irving's hand. An exceedingly interesting item containing Irving's notes, Oct. 31 to May 1, of his trip through the West during which he gathered material for 'Astoria.' On the first of May, Irving records '*he shot Buffaloe.*'" Several clues raise suspicions: the dates and days do not coincide with the trip WI made to the West; even though most of the narrative is in first person, there are several lapses into third person; on p. [2], WI wrote that "after Gists back was turned . . . called him a big Knife." Also in a letter in the control folder to Mr. Portis of the University of Virginia library, Wayne Kime from New College, University of Toronto, suggested that WI was copying from Christopher Gist's account of a trip in 1749, which WI "describes in his Life of Washington, I, chapter V." WI was indeed taking notes from Christopher Gist's *Journal, 1750–1751* which was published in Philadelphia in 1776; Gist began his journal, "1750.–In Complyance with my Instructions from the Committee of the OHIO COMPANY bearing Date the 11th Day of September 1750," and on the next line, at which point WI began his notes, "Wednesday Octr 31.–Set out from Colo Thomas Cresap's at the old Town on Potomack River in Maryland . . ." (because the earlier edition of Gist is not readily available, we have cited from William M. Darlington, *Christopher Gist's Journals* [Pittsburgh: J. R. Weldin, 1893], pp. 31–32; hereafter cited as Darlington, ed., *Gist's Journals*). In the eight pages of WI's notes which follow, he varied from sketchy jottings, skipping days at a time, to almost word-for-word renderings of paragraphs at a time. To observe how WI used this material, see Washington Irving's *Life of George Washington*, I, 32–36.

2. Because writing a biography of George Washington was an active interest of WI for most of his adult life, it is difficult to date this particular fragment of

pages.[3] The paper is yellowed white and, like stationery, is lined in the texture of the paper with five horizontal and many closely approximate vertical lines. There is an unusual watermark at the binding edges of leaves 3 and 4, a line drawing design with loops and fleur-de-lis.

[*p. 1*][4]

Oct 31

Cresap[5] by pottamac creek[6] To Juniatta[7] abt 14 m.[8]
beyond Wills creek cross Allegany ridge on 5th

12 Cross a ⟨fork[?]⟩ a great Laurel Mt–
14 Loyalhannan on Kiskominetas[9]
19 Shannopin[10] just above it Vasqueses[?][11]

The land in genl from Potomac to this place mean stony & broken with here & there good spots upon the creeks & branches but no body of it[12]

---

his research. From letters, journal entries, and biographical data, we may infer that WI's most intense periods of work were in 1825 (when in eighteen May entries in his journal, he mentioned reading John Marshall's biography), 1828, late 1829, 1841, 1843, 1847, 1849, and particularly 1851 until the end of his life.

3. WI may have torn out the pages before he wrote because the writing on the verso of each leaf begins at the binding edge; he would have turned the notebook around with each new page if the leaves had been attached. His pattern in writing in notebooks with the binding at the top of the page was to write on the recto from binding to bottom edge, then flip the leaf up and on the verso to write from bottom to binding edge.

4. Without identifying the source, WI began taking notes by numbering the page in the upper right corner. In the *Life of Washington*, WI identified Christopher Gist as "a hardy pioneer, experienced in woodcraft and Indian life, who had his home on the banks of the Yadkin, near the boundary line of Virginia and North Carolina" (I, 32).

5. Colonel Thomas Cresap was "the earliest permanent settler in Western Maryland," having come from England about 1720 and then having settled at Old Town in 1742 or 1743. Cresap was an agent and member of the Ohio Company. His name or "Cresap's" is on many early maps of the area (Darlington, ed., *Gist's Journals*, pp. 90, 202–03).

6. It seems strange that WI should write "creek" rather than "river," as did Gist.

7. Gist identified as "a large Branch of Susquehannah" (p. 32).

8. WI may have added later the phrase "To . . . 14 m." between lines.

9. Gist spelled this creek "Kiscominatis."

10. The place Gist called Shannopini Town or Shannopin, a Town of the Delawares, is now Pittsburgh.

11. This place was not mentioned in Gist's account; Venango was in a northerly direction from Shannopin.

12. This line is a close rendering of the original (November 20–23). WI added a line three-sixteenths inch long beginning in the margin.

---

24 Set out from Shannopin Swam horses across the Ohio[13] went down along the river, land good bottoms not broad

25 To Loggs town lands rich bottoms above a mile wide hills High & steep

Loggs town—reprobate traders[14]
writes to Croghan[15] by one of them tho unwell preferred the woods to such compy.

on the way from Beaver Creek to Muskingum killed & dressd [*unrecovered*][16] turkeys

Tho 11 in company plenty of provisions.[17]

Dec 5 Elks Eye Creek—town of Ottawas

Mark Coonce an old French man married to squaw of 6 Nations—civil but after Gists back was turned, Judg he was from Virginia called him a big Knife.

14 Muskingum Saw English Col[our]s on Kings house & ⟨E⟩Crogans, asked the reason Informed that the French[18] had taken several Eng traders and Croghan had ordered all the white men to come into this town & sent expresses to the traders of the lower towns—& the Inds had sent to their people to have a meeting about it.

17—News that 2 more of Croghans people had been taken[19] with 7 horse loads of skins & carried to a new Fort the French were building on one of the branches of Lk Erie.

13. This head branch of the Ohio River was called the Ohio by the Senecas and Alleghany by the Delawares; on the map attached to "Washington Journal of 1753–4, London, 1754," this river was designated "The Ohio or Allegheny River" and the main river, "The Ohio or the Fair River" (Darlington, ed., *Gist's Journals*, p. 94).

14. Gist wrote that he found "scarce any Body but a Parcel of reprobate Indian Traders" (p. 34); WI used the final three-word phrase (*Life of Washington*, I, 33).

15. Darlington said that the "history of George Croghan, the Indians' friend and generous protector, is the history of the Indians of Pennsylvania . . ." (*Gist's Journals*, p. 190).

16. WI seems to have written "20" and then marked over it with "&"; Gist wrote that "one of Curran's Men & myself killed 12 Turkeys" on "Friday 30" (p. 35).

17. On November 29, Gist was "in Want of Provision," so on that day he killed a deer and on the next, twelve turkeys; on December 4, he killed "three fine fat Deer"; it was on that day that he said the eleven men had plenty of provisions (pp. 35–36).

18. WI ended page [2] here; he numbered the next page "3" in the upper right corner and drew a half circle around it to the left.

19. Gist added that they were taken by "40 French Men, & twenty French Indians" (p. 37).

Jan 9[20] Further news of capture

Shawnees once protected by the Eng from the fury of the 6 Nations grateful therefore[21]

March 18 Lower salt lick 15 M from falls Boy & he alone[22]

This day we heard Several guns which made me imagine the French Ind were not moved but still hunting & firing thereabouts—Also saw traps newly set. Indian foot prints a day old

Great danger lest the French Inds should come upon our horses tracks or hear their bells. concludes[23] not to go to the falls ↑turned from salt Lick Creek↓—⟨travelled Southward till over little ⟨Cutawa⟩ Cuttawa river⟩ to a ridge of mounts that made toward the Cuttawa River & from the top of the mountain we saw a fine level country S. W. as far as our eyes could behold, and it[24] was a very clear day. Went down the mountain & set out S 20 &[?] W 5 m. through rich level land covered with small wallnut, sugar trees [? &c red ?][25] buds &c

19 Set out south crossed several creeks at about 12 Miles came to little Cut⟨a⟩tawa river—cross it and contd our course in all about 30 miles thro rich level land. This level is about 35 miles broad & as we came up the side of it along the branches of the little Cuttawa we found it 150 m long and how far to the S W we could not tell but imagd it held as far as the great Cuttawa which could be upwards of 100 m more and appeared much broader that way than here as I could descern from the tops of the mountains

20. WI wrote "Jan" in the left margin; he drew a line 1¾ inches long to separate ideas.

21. After skipping several pages, and almost a month's activities, WI copied this bit of information from Gist's January 29, 1751, entry, and his next note came from an entry more than 1½ months later.

22. Gist reported that on March 12 "after Breakfast my Boy and I got ferryed over [the Ohio]"; in the face of danger on the eighteenth, Gist wrote that he "was once resolved to leave the Boy and Horses" and go alone to the Falls, "but the Boy being a poor Hunter, was afraid he would starve if I was long from him . . ." (pp. 57–58).

23. WI here shifted from first to third person.

24. Page [4] concludes at this point; WI incorrectly numbered the next page "4."

25. Without the original journal from which WI was copying, transcription of the word or words would be impossible: it resembles "lurab." Gist wrote, "set out S 20 W about 5 M, thro rich level Land covered with small Walnut Sugar Trees, Red-Buds, &c." (p. 59).

20t—we did not travel Went up to the top of a mount. to view the country—very broken & mountainous but to East and by S W level

travelled along little Cattawa till ⟨29 April—having continually to go round the heads of the branches⟩
⟨blocks of coal⟩
⟨cut a passage thro towards for 2 miles⟩

↑April↓ 4th. Warrior camp
4th April plotted our course still 200 miles to home on a streight of line
⟨3⟩29—all the way along the Cattawa had continually to head the tributaries the banks being so precipitous[?][26]
Endless Mounts. beyond Konhawa ridge like Alleghany.[27]
30. Blue Stone river which falls into the big Konhawa

May 1 Killed Buffaloe ↑near Blue Stone↓ went up a very high mountain on top of which was a rock 60 or 70 feet high & a cavity in the middle into which I went & found there was a passage through it which gradu/ally ascended to the top with several holes in the rock which let in the light—when I got to the top of this rock I could see a prodigious distance & could plainly discover where the Big Kanhawa broke thro the next high mount. Came down & contind my course 75 N[?].
7 Get to the Big Konhawa ⟨? on island ?⟩ ‸↑8 miles above mouth of Blue stone↓[28] ⟨half way⟩ ‸↑crossed half way↓ campt on an island—made raft of logs & cross the other half[29]

Monday 13. Richd Halls farthest settler west of Konhawa
crossed dividing line betwn Carolina & Virg. Family frightened from Yadkin to Roanoke 35 miles further on as he was informed by an old man whom he[?][30] met near the place—[31]

26. Gist wrote that the branches "were so high" that they went "over the Heads of them" through "a continued Ledge of almost inaccessible Mountains, Rocks and Laurel Thickets" (p. 64).
27. Page [6] ends here, and WI incorrectly numbered the following page, "5."
28. The word "stone" is inserted between the raised line and the crossed-out words.
29. Page [7] ends here, and WI incorrectly numbered the next page "6" in the top left corner.
30. There is a loop touching the word which could produce the reading "having."
31. Gist ended this first journal with a May 9, 1751, entry saying that he found his family safe in Roanoke that night. WI went back to an earlier entry (twenty pages in this edition of *Gist's Journals*) in which Gist wrote, "From Thursday

From 31 Jan to Feb 11th.
at the Shawne town festival—In the Evg a proper[?] officer made proclamation that all the Ind marriages were desolved & a public feast was to be held for three succeedg days on which all the women were again (accordg to custom) to choose their husbands—

three days feasts—men & women running[?][32] by themselves round[?][33] the fires[?]—Women

Sing these lines alternately { I am not affined[?][34] of any[35] husband
I will choose what man I please }

Jan 31 to Monday Feby 11.—Stayed in the Shannoah Town, while I was here the Indians had a very extraordinary Kind of a Festival, at which I was present and which I have exactly described at the End of my Journal" (p. 46). In Darlington's edition of the journals, this portion of the journal apparently was not reproduced, but Darlington wrote in his notes that "Marriage and cohabitation with women amongst the savage tribes throughout the world present many similar features, curious, and often beastly, customs. A temporary interchange of wives is not uncommon among the Indians of the far North. A similar dance, etc., by a small party of Iroquois near Fort Cumberland, in 1755, is described in Sargent's 'History of Braddock Expedition,' p. 376" (pp. 122–23).

32. These letters could be "&c many."
33. This word could be "Covered."
34. This word could be "affiancd" or "affirmd."
35. This word could be "my."

Acknowledgment, (1859)[1]

This manuscript fragment is in the Beinecke Rare Book and Manuscript Library, Yale University, New Haven, Connecticut, where it is cataloged as Za Irving 21[1]. It is housed along with seven other fragments in a manila folder entitled "MSS. fragments (Gift of Miss Annie B. Jennings—11 June 1938)." It seems to have been torn away from its bottom half; it measures 3½ x 4 15/16 inches (the right edge measures 3¼ inches). The writing is in brown ink; the paper is white; and the verso is blank.

1. In his preface to the last volume of *Life of George Washington*, which he dated "*April*, 1859," WI wrote that his condition of "nervous indisposition" delayed the revision of the final volume; he continued that in this task "he has been kindly assisted by his nephew, Pierre Munro Irving, who had previously aided him in the course of his necessary researches, and who now carefully collated the manuscript with the works, letters, and inedited documents from which the facts had been derived. He has likewise had the kindness to superintend the printing of the volume, and the correction of the proof sheets. Thus aided, the author is enabled to lay the volume before the public" (V, 292). See STW, II, 238–39, for an account of WI's race with death to complete this volume of the work.

[*recto*]

The appearance of this volume has been retarded by illness on the part of the author; and it is only through the kind assistance of his nephew Mr Pierre M Irving in preparing it for the press that he is now enabled to lay it before the public

[*verso blank except for the accession number in pencil*]

MISCELLANEOUS MATERIALS

Fragments regarding Bracebridge Hall, Sketch Book, and A Tour of the Prairies

Manuscript Fragment, Relating to The Sketch Book *and* A Tour on the Prairies, *Undated*[1]

This manuscript leaf is in the Beinecke Rare Book and Manuscript Library, Yale University, New Haven, Connecticut, where it is cataloged as Za Irving 21[8]; it is housed with seven other fragments. Portions of the right edge of the page as well as most of the last three lines, are torn away; therefore, the measurement is only approximate: 5 x 6⅞ inches. The paper is off-white; the writing is in brown ink; and the verso is blank.

[*recto*]

"As I saw the last blue line of my native land fade away like a cloud in the horizon it seemed as if I had close[d] [*paper torn*] one volume of the world and its concer[ns] [*paper torn*] and had time for meditation, before I opened another. That land, too, now vanishing from my view, which contained all that was[2] most dear to me[3] in life what vicissitudes

1. WI quoted here from the third paragraph of his own essay, "The Voyage," in *The Sketch Book*; notice that he used quotation marks at the beginning of the passage (because the last word of the paragraph is torn off we cannot tell if he ended the quotation marks) and that he indicated "Vol 1." at the end. It appears that he added another sentence, perhaps a paraphrase of the beginning of the next paragraph, then crossed it out and gave the bibliographical reference. WI used this paragraph as the initial one in the introduction of the American edition of *A Tour on the Prairies* (1835), "By the Author of The Sketch Book." This page was probably penned by WI in January, 1835, when he was preparing the American edition of *Tour*.

2. Apparently, when copying, WI added the words "that was"; they are not in the Hudson Edition of *The Sketch Book*, but they are in the introduction of the first American edition of *A Tour on the Prairies* (p. vii).

3. The page is torn approximately 1½ inches from the right edge in line 8 through the word "me."

might occur in it or[4] what changes might take place in me before I should visit it again! Who can tell when he sets forth to wander, whither he may be driven by the uncertain currents of existence; or when he may return; or whether it may ever be his lot to revisit the scenes of his child[hood?] [*paper torn*][5]

[*verso blank, except for the accession number*]

4. In this copy, WI substituted the word "or" for the dash which appears in both *The Sketch Book* and *Tour*.

5. Of the final three lines of the page (approximately one inch), only a tab in the middle of the page, approximately 1¼ inches wide, remains. WI must have crossed out two lines: in the first only the word "reflection" is legible, and in the second, what may be "⟨? lics Set above ?⟩"; in the last line WI wrote, probably after the title, "Vol 1." In the introduction to the American edition of *A Tour on the Prairies*, this passage is footnoted "*Sketch Book, Vol. I."

Manuscript Fragment from "The Author's Farewell," Bracebridge Hall, *Relating to Irving's Feelings About England [1822]*[1]

This manuscript fragment is in the Beinecke Rare Book and Manuscript Library, Yale University, New Haven, Connecticut, where it is cataloged as Za Irving 21[2]; it is housed with seven other fragments. It measures 4½ x 7¼ inches; the paper is off-white; and the writing is in brown ink. The verso is blank.

[*recto*][2]

1. It is difficult to date exactly this fragment. It may have been a notebook entry, the manuscript used to set the American or the English editions of *Bracebridge Hall*, or one of the many revisions before and after the 1822 publication of that work. Herbert F. Smith, in the introduction and the textual commentary of his edition of *Bracebridge Hall*, discussed in detail the textual problems relating to this work. He pointed out that WI "was juggling revision of various states of the manuscript and the printed text simultaneously and probably worrying about getting a revised text to Ebenezer for the publication of [the second American edition]" (*Bracebridge Hall*, p. 351). Smith added that the "text seems to have been in a constant flux from March through May of 1822, with heavy revision being made by Irving in manuscript, and in proof . . ." (*ibid.*).

2. The paper may have been torn from a notebook along the left edge; if so, the writing is on the recto.

¶¶[3]

⟨⟨It will probably be said too by some that I view England with a partial eye. Perhaps I do; for I can never forget that it is my "father land." And yet the circumstances under which I have viewed it have by no means been such as are calculated to produce favourable impressions. For the greater part of the time that I have ⟨*L*⟩ resided in it, I have lived almost un-/-knowing and unknown; seeking no favours, and receiving none;[4] "a Stranger and Sojour/-ner in the land,"[5] and Subject[6] to all the chills and neglects that are the lot of the Stranger.

When I consider these circumstances, and recollect how often I have taken up my pen, with a mind crossed by care, and Spirits much dejected and cast down; I cannot but think I was not likely to err on the favourable side of the picture. The opinions I have given of English character have been the result of much quiet

[*verso blank except accession number in pencil*]

3. The paragraph indications and the double angle brackets are WI's own; they are in the left margin. This paragraph is the third in the essay "The Author's Farewell," in *Bracebridge Hall* (p. 308).

4. The theme of the stranger in an alien land is a recurrent one in WI's writings, especially during the unhappy years from 1815 to 1817 (see STW, I, 149–54, for a description of those years).

5. WI slightly misquoted Genesis 23:4, "I am a stranger and a sojourner with you. . . ."

6. There is an ink blot fingerprint which extends through this word and to the line above; there are several others on the page, the clearest of them in the first line of the next paragraph through the word "these."

Manuscript Fragment from "The Author's Farewell," Bracebridge Hall, *Relating to English-American Relationship [1822]*[1]

This manuscript leaf is in the Beinecke Rare Book and Manuscripts Library, Yale University, New Haven, Connecticut, where it is cataloged as Za Irving 21[3]. It is housed with seven other fragments. It measures 4½ x 7¼ inches; the paper is off-white, and the writing is in brown ink. The verso is blank except for the accession number.

[*recto*][2]

1. See p. 402, n. 1, for a discussion of the difficulty of dating exactly this fragment.

2. As in the previous fragment, this page could be recto or verso.

-cating[3] the cause of National Amity. To the intelligent and enlightened of my own country I address my parting voice, entreat-/-ing them to shew themselves superior to the petty attacks of the ignorant and the worthless; and still[4] to look with dis-/passionate and philosophic eye, to the moral character of England, as the intellec-/-tual source of our rising greatness; while I appeal to every generous minded Englishman, from the slanders which disgrace the press; insult the understanding, and belie the magnanimity of his country.[5] And I invite him to look to America, as to a kindred ⟨land⟩; ‸↑nation;↓ giving in the healthy vigour of its growth, the best of comments on its parent stock; and reflecting in the dawning brightness of its fame, the moral efful-/-gence of British Glory.

But however my feelings may be under-/stood or reciprocated, on either side of the Atlantic I utter them without reserve; for I have ever found that to speak frankly[6]

[*verso blank except for the accession number in pencil*]

3. In the Twayne edition of WI's essay "The Author's Farewell," in *Bracebridge Hall*, the sentence reads, "To pens more powerful than mine I leave the noble task of promoting the cause of national amity" (p. 311). This manuscript fragment begins with the final two syllables of a variant of the word "promoting," perhaps "predicating" or "advocating."

4. WI crossed out the word "still" and followed it with the same word; we have left the second attempt in the text, but it too may be crossed out.

5. WI was always sensitive to the negative attitude of the English press, particularly the *Quarterly*, to his native land. He wrote in 1824 to his friend Leslie that part of his isolation was due to his being in a country where "the very review of my publisher is hostile to everything American" (PMI, II, 224). In October, 1828, when Murray offered him an attractive financial package "to conduct a monthly magazine," and to write articles for that journal as well as for the *Quarterly*, WI wrote Peter that because the *Quarterly* "has always been so hostile to our country, I cannot draw a pen in its service" (*ibid.*, 346). Williams says that it was the brutality of writers like William Gifford of the *Quarterly* which prompted Irving to write "English Writers on America" (STW, I, 192).

6. This sentence ends with the words, "is to speak safely."

Manuscript Fragment from "Family Misfortunes" Bracebridge Hall, *Regarding a Storm's Aftermath [1822]*[1]

This manuscript fragment is in the Clifton Waller Barrett Library of the University of Virginia Library, Charlottesville, Virginia, where it is cataloged as #6256–m. It is fragment number 2 housed in a folder reading "Washington Irving: 4 fragments of unidentified AMs." The leaf has been torn from a notebook at the left; the top and right edges are straight and gilt, and the bottom edge seems to have been cut.[2] The yellowed paper measures 4⅜ x 2¼ inches. The writing is in brown ink; the verso is blank.

[*recto*]
my[3] window I beheld sad ravage among the shrubs and flowers; the garden walks had formed the channels for little torrents; trees were lopped of their branches; and a small silver stream that wound through the park, and ran at the bottom of the lawn, had swelled into a turbid yellow sheet of water.[4]

[*verso blank*]

1. See p. 402, n. 1, for a discussion of the difficulty of dating exactly this fragment.
2. This fragment and the one which follows it are probably portions of the same leaf: the width of the page is the same and there are similarities in ink, gilt edges, and the yellowing paper with darker splotches. Further evidence is the fact that the passages are from the first and third paragraphs of "Family Misfortunes" in *Bracebridge Hall* (p. 239). However, the cut edges do not match, perhaps because between these paragraphs in the essay is a short paragraph, the draft of which WI may have cut out.
3. The beginning of this sentence in the printed version of "Family Misfortunes" reads, "Nothing over-head gave traces of the recent storm; but on looking from my window . . ." (*Bracebridge Hall*, p. 239).
4. The page is cut horizontally after the line.

Manuscript Fragment from "Family Misfortunes," Bracebridge Hall, *Regarding a Squire at Breakfast [1822]*[1]

This manuscript fragment is in the Clifton Waller Barrett Library of the University of Virginia Library, Charlottesville, Virginia, where is is cata-

1. See p. 402, n. 1.

loged as #6256–m. It is fragment number 3[2] housed in a folder reading "Washington Irving: 4 fragments of unidentified AMs." The leaf has been torn from a notebook at the left; the bottom and right edges are straight and gilt, and the top edge appears to have been cut. The yellowed paper measures 4⅜ x 2¾ (outside edge; binding edge is 2½) inches. The writing is in brown ink; the verso is blank. In the top half is a watermark: "Turner."

[*recto*]

⟨[*page torn*] squire at his[?]⟩ ⟨Before the Squire had finished his breakfast in the great Hall he had received a⟩

While the Squire was taking his break-/-fast in the great Hall he was continually interrupted by some bearer of ill tidings from some part or other of his domains; he appeared to me like the commander of a besieged city, after some grand assault, receiving at his head quarters, reports[3]

[*verso blank*]

2. See p. 405, n. 2.

3. The end of this sentence in the printed version of "Family Misfortunes" reads, "of damages sustained in the various quarters of the place" (*Bracebridge Hall*, p. 239).

MISCELLANEOUS MATERIALS

Journal Fragments

Paris [1821]

This manuscript folio is in the Beinecke Rare Book and Manuscript Library, Yale University, New Haven, Connecticut, where it is cataloged as Za Irving 21[6]; it is housed with seven other fragments. Leaf 1 measures 4 x 6 inches, and leaf 2 is torn horizontally at approximately the center of the page, with only the bottom half remaining. The paper is off-white; the writing is in brown ink; and p. [3] is blank.

[*p. [1]*]
Moore[1] & Villamil[2] called on Kenney[3] at his appartments in the old chateau of Bellevue[4] & was told he was ill in bed—⟨for[?]⟩ They wanted him to dine with them but he ⟨could not⟩ complained of having Spasmodic headache—found out after-/-wards from Miss Holcroft that the Servant woman had taken away his inkbottle, whereat he was so afflicted as to take to his bed.

1. WI here referred to the Irish poet, Thomas Moore (see p. 208, n. 62).

2. Villamil was a Spaniard living in Paris, whom WI had met through Moore in 1820 (*Journals and Notebooks*, III, 210, n. 127). WI mentioned the Villamils often in his Paris notebooks, especially during 1824; in a January 8, 1824, entry, Irving said that when he called on Villamil, confined with gout, he heard the Spaniard deliver a dissertation on craniology (PMI, II, 182).

3. James Kenney (1780–1849), the dramatist, was another member of the Paris circle among whom were "the Forbeses, Lord John Russell, Luttrell, Sydney Smith, L'Herbette" (STW, I, 198). Reichart wrote that WI met Kenney through John Howard Payne, the American dramatist (*Journals and Notebooks*, III, 209, n. 122). In the journal entry recounting the visit which is the subject of this fragment, WI described Kenney as "a very worthy and a very pleasant fellow; a thin, pale man, with a gentleness of demeanor and manner, and very nervous. He gave some descriptions of scenes in London with admirable truth and character" (PMI, II, 46–47).

4. In a May 16, 1821, entry, WI wrote, "Accompanied Mr. and Mrs. Moore, and the Villamils to Mr. Kenney's, author of Raising the Wind, &c. He married the widow of Holcroft who had several children; her stock and his own make eight

Moore found him wandering in the Park of the chateau in great dejection—He evidently had something preying on his mind. Told Moore at length that he had been dreadfully annoyed—"you must know" said he "that Mrs Kenney has a cock"—Moore had some difficulty to keep his countenance—It turned out that this cock would get into the fossé[5] under his window, from whence he[6] could not get out again and would crow there, until Kenney would have to abandon the house—

[*p. [3] blank*][7]

[*p. [4], after the folio has been reversed*]
II[8] 159. double[?] chin—who being a slow man was considered a wise one, & never exactly &c—[9]

---

children. They have apartments in one of the wings, or rather the offices of the old chateau of Bellevue, built by Louis XV . . ." (PMI, II, 46).

5. WI used the masculine form of the word which means "ditch," "drain," "trench" or "moat."

6. Page [1] ends here.

7. Only the bottom half of this page remains.

8. WI began this line flush left, writing the "II" in the margin.

9. When the page is returned to its normal position, the accession number (in pencil) appears in the upper right corner of the portion of the page which remains.

Beychevelle [October 1825]

This manuscript folio is in the Beinecke Rare Book and Manuscript Library, Yale University, New Haven, Connecticut, where it is cataloged as Za Irving 21[7]; it is housed with seven other fragments. The pages measure 3⅝ x 4$^{13}/_{16}$ inches; the paper is off-white; and the writing is in heavy brown ink which has often faded through the paper. Page [3] is blank.

[*p. [1]*]

Becheville[1] M.[2]

The chateau is in the midst of the wine country, surrounded by the

1. The initial letter of this word resembles an *R*. WI's spelling is interesting in that it gives a clue as to his phonetic spelling, even in foreign languages. It was to Daniel Guestier's château near Bordeaux in southwest France—Beychevelle—that WI had come on October 3 and which he was describing in this fragment. In a letter to Thomas W. Storrow dated October 4, 1825, WI wrote, "Here we are safely housed in an old Chateau in the midst of the Vineyards of Medoc." He went on to describe in almost the same terms the château once belonging to Gaston

vineyards of Medoc. A long center building one Story high, containing a Great Hall paved with Tiles & a huge dining room, and[3] Flanked with two pavillions ⟨in⟩ ↑on[?][4]↓ which are ⟨Dining rooms & bed⟩ Drawing rooms & bed rooms. A great Stone terrace of vast width Stretches along the whole extent of the building, from whence ⟨S⟩ a flight of Steps lead down into the garden—⟨*illegible*⟩ a formal flat of ground, with clipped walks on each side & peopled with Statues—⟨*illegible*⟩ Armless[?] & ⟨*illegible*⟩ ↑legless[?][5]↓ of Marble, & baked clay—beyond is a Kitchen-garden and beyond that a great extent of lush green meadow Spreads out to the banks of the distant Garonne.[6]

[*p. [2]*]

The family have recently come in possession of the estate and have taken up their abode here within a month. The Servants ⟨being⟩ are for the most part English, but accustomed to the country. ⟨*illegible*⟩ ⟨They⟩ The family is as yet new in the old establishment and every day is big with some ⟨new[?]⟩[7] cir-/-cumstance or rumor. The ⟨old chambers⟩ Servants are full of Stories, not of Ghosts but serpents. according to the accounts they have picked up among the peasants the place must be ⟨dreadfully[?]⟩[8] fully infested with them. There is one Master Serpent which [*unrecovered*][9] over the meadow which several of the Servants profess to have seen. ⟨and⟩ They vary in their accounts of his size from the size of a bitch[?] to the size of a mans big[?] body. The gardiner has

---

de Foix, especially the physical description and the myth of the Master Serpent (*Letters*, II, 137–38). In WI's October, 1825, journal, there is a period between October 2 and 7 with no entries; Reichart explained that it was at this time that WI became a guest of Pierre F. Guestier (*Journals and Notebooks*, III, 527, n. 161); this fragment could be part of a missing journal.

2. The *M* might refer to Medoc; Pierre Irving mentioned the Irving brothers' "hospitable friend, Mr. Guestier of Chateau Margaux . . ." (PMI, II, 241).

3. Following the word "and," WI added another *d* or an ampersand.

4. This word could be "over."

5. In the letter, WI described them as "mutilated statues some of marble, some plaster of paris & some earthen ware . . ." (*Letters*, II, 137).

6. The Garonne River in southwest France rises just inside Spain in the central Pyrenees; it flows 402 miles northwest and is joined at the Bec D'Ambès by the Dordogne to form the Gironde estuary.

7. This word is marked through by an ink blot faded from the recto.

8. The first syllable is obscured by an ink blot from the recto.

9. The first letters of this ink-blotted word may be "dimis"; in his description to Storrow, WI changed the verb: "There is one master Serpent that haunts a meadow in front of the chateau, which . . . for size & length equals the Boa constrictor or the Sea serpent" (*Letters*, II, 137).

[p. [3] blank]

[p. [4] blank except for the accession number in pencil and one illegible word in the top left corner when the folio is reversed.]

Travel in Naples [March, 1805]

This manuscript leaf is in the Beinecke Rare Book and Manuscript Library, Yale University, New Haven, Connecticut, where it is cataloged as Za Irving 21[4]; it is housed with seven other fragments.[1] It measures 4⁷⁄₁₆ x 7¼ inches; the paper is faded off-white, and the writing on both sides is in brown ink which has faded through the paper.

[recto][2]
close by Nero's[?][3] ⟨tom⟩ baths are shewn the ruins of former palaces; the ⟨cold⟩ sea has rolled its cold[4] waves over them and they can be perceiv-/-ed in the bosom of its clear waters

The neighbourhood, ⟨like⟩ the very soil is rich with art & history—nameless tombs—urns filled with coins & medals; the ground is under

1. This fragment is written on the same paper and with the same ink as the following fragment entitled "Travel in Palermo, Naples, etc., [March, 1805]." It, too, is probably an early version of the entries in the 1805 Journal.

2. It is difficult to determine which side of the paper is the first; the underlined words "Harbor of Syracuse" at the top of the following page suggest that it is a title, but, it seems to have been added as an indication of the subject of discussion. WI arrived in Syracuse on February 2 and remained until February 11, 1805 (*Journals and Notebooks*, I, 179–95). Much of the material and, more important, the tone are duplicated in this fragment.

3. Because this first indication of place is difficult to decipher—it could begin with an *M*, *V*, or *N*—it is rather difficult to determine the date and place of this entry. In his March 17, 1805, journal entry, WI mentioned the "tomb of Caius Marius—The remains of antient Baia consisting of ruined temples &c"; Nathalia Wright pointed out that this ruin is not now called the tomb of Marius, but that the Roman ruins which do remain were evidently public baths (*Journals and Notebooks*, I, 247 and n. 249). More important for the dating of this entry as March 17 are the parallels in the description such as the fact that the boat "glid⟨ing⟩ed rapidly along the beautiful bay. Below us we could see thro the clear waters, the foundations of antient palaces—formerly the abodes of the highest luxury and ⟨voup⟩ voluptuousness—but long since passed away with the hands that erected them" (*ibid.*, p. 247). Later in this same entry, WI wrote, "Passing the foundations of several antient villas in the sides of the hills that bordered the sea we at length landed at the steam baths of Nero" (*ibid.*, p. 249).

4. WI added the word "cold" in the left margin.

tillage & the plow turns up fragments of vases, ⟨ar⟩ frezes, and now and then some ^↑nameless↓ dirty image to sunshine

⟨I pa⟩ our boat glided as if in air over the tops of ruined pallaces. I looked down to the ducts[?] ⟨once trod by horses and⟩ where roman luxury & beauty had once held their revels—the sea and [*unrecovered*][5] above these ruins—the fish plied ⟨through⟩ and lurked among the ruins—

Who shall tell me that I am extrava-/-gant in my conjectures—even in my slender experience what ⟨the⟩ monuments ^↑have I beheld↓ of human futility and the ⟨[*unrecovered*][6] transient⟩ passing dream of human greatness. ⟨have I not⟩ I have paced the Silent Shores of the bay where Syracuse once stretched her Spacious arms. The sad lay says—[7]

[*verso*]

Harbor of Syracuse

once[?][8] Surrounded by marble pallaces—Fleets would ride at anchor in the bosom of the city. Seven cities as it were locked their arms and made one mass of marble Splendid with all the riches of architecture; to look on this minute[?] Sea—I paced the shores of the ⟨fo[?]⟩ [*blank*] and they were Silent[—]the ⟨fo⟩ cities ⟨whic⟩ that locked their arms where were they?—the marble and the granite had disappeared—Stone was not [*unrecovered*][9] Stone to tell the Tale of these ancient glories—Yes it is true—There were the ruins of an amphithe-/-ater— with a few half defaced inscrip-/-tions—what [?god told?][10] thus the Solitude had once been cheerful—There were three Stupendous fragments of columns which had framd[?][11] part of a gigantic temple—⟨Inscribe[?]⟩ they only

5. These letters look like "flacinto" or "placentio," or combinations of both.

6. These letters could also be "passi," as WI searched for the right word.

7. In the lower right corner is the accession number in pencil.

8. This word could be "was."

9. Beginning with what may be the word "not," there may be three words written together, the last of which may be "paper." In his February 4 journal entry, WI described the type of stone from which the buildings of ancient Syracuse were built: "white freestone that is very easily cut but hardens on exposure to the air" (*Journals and Notebooks*, I, 181). In the same entry, he told of the "remains of an antient theatre . . . built on the side of a hill" and of a Greek inscription on one of the stone seats (*ibid.*, 184). On the following day, he wrote of the recently excavated "ruins of a temple supposed to have been dedicated to Venus. Several columns were laying near the hole" (*ibid.*).

10. The questioned words could be "sad tale."

11. This word could be "guarded."

remaind[?] the sublime indication of ⟨fo⟩ depart-/-ed glory–⟨Vesu[?]⟩ The ear of Dionysi-[12]

12. WI was fascinated by the Ear of Dionysius; there are several drawings in his journals of this tourist attraction near Syracuse which he had visited in February, 1805 (*Journals and Notebooks*, I, 180–84, 187–89, 518, 520–21, and figs. 12–13).

Travel in Palermo, Naples, etc. [March, 1805]

This manuscript leaf is in the Beinecke Rare Book and Manuscript Library, Yale University, New Haven, Connecticut, where it is cataloged as Za Irving 21[5]; it is housed with seven other fragments. It measures 4⁷⁄₁₆ x 7¼ inches; its paper is off-white; and the writing on both sides is in brown ink.

[*recto*]
left Palermo[?][1] in the evening–Orange boat– –passengers on board, return in the morning to [*blank*][2] get back to palermo[3]–red of eastern[?]

1. WI wrote in a March 1, 1805, notebook entry of embarking in the evening "aboard a small vessel loaded with fruit bound to Naples." In the night the violent motion of the vessel worked its worst on the passengers who "were crowded together higgledly piggledy," and in his March 2 entry WI said they "put about & stood back for Palermo." The wind did not allow them into port; they anchored in a bay ten miles east, went ashore, ate at a "miserable tavern," and he slept on a flea-filled mattress spread on chairs. On March 4, they returned to Palermo; WI was called back on board and set sail on March 5, and by the next day they caught sight of "Capre" and the erupting "Vessuvius" (*Journals and Notebooks*, I, 220–23). It seems clear that this fragment is an early version of this trip; there is also a mention of a hotel bill in Palermo which WI apparently paid on March 5, 1805 (*ibid.*, p. 551).

2. WI underlined the blank space; apparently he intended to name the bay where he spent two miserable days "on shore in a wretched hovel, where I had scarce any thing to eat, where I had to sleep in my clothes and great coat at night, for want of other covering" (PMI, I, 124).

3. One American "geography" and guide book published in 1832 described Palermo as follows: "the capital of Sicily, stands on a small bay in the northwestern part of the island. The streets are regular and wide; the houses elegant, and several of the public squares very beautiful. The city is built in a semicircular plain or valley surrounded by mountains. This little nook of land is called *Conca d'oro*, or the 'golden shell' and abounds with fragrant groves of orange trees and acacias. . . . Pop. 168,000" (S. G. Goodrich, *A System of Universal Geography*, p. 626).

—Sea—algerine—distant view of Vesu-/-vius ⟨*unrecovered*⟩ which ⟨fire-smok⟩ ^↑smoke↓ in the eveng—fire at night—morning pass by Prodica—promentories stretching out. Vessuvius—Naples—old convent—crowd of boats Forio[?].[4] Convent of [*blank*][5] Monks on the Shore—Corso. ⟨Marquis & his horses⟩ ride to Baia, by ⟨Pa⟩ [*blank*] visit to the convent on the summit of the hill.[6] As we approached the harbour the morning had advanced—the white walls of the convents among the trees and the houses which ⟨asc⟩ climb along the ascent of the ampitheater of hills ⟨*unrecovered*⟩[7] were brightening in the morning rays— —long Shadows from pinnacles and towers wavered in blue lines along the bosom of the Sea—between us & the shore were boats gliding with their picturesque latine sails and occasionally we heard[?][8] the song of the mariner. ⟨As we⟩ To our right we beheld Vessuvius sending up its thin column of smoke which spreads at top like a palm tree—down its sides

[*verso*]
were black Streaks of Lava, mingled with the green of vineyards, and along its base were the ⟨villa⟩ towns of Portici andc[9]

Stretching like a line of dotted white Specks. We passed under the island of Procida, which lays at the entrance to the bay; as we counted[?] it the Sweet fragrance of orange blossoms and [*blank*] were wafted from its bowers—⟨I beheld⟩ we beheld the crumbling ruins of palaces. [*blank*] which seemed buried in tufted shrubbery, for the soft climate of italy ⟨so⟩ over runs every thing with a ⟨[*unrecovered*] rich⟩ voluptuous foliage. The walls hang with myrtle; ⟨the [*two or three unrecovered words*]⟩ a thousand ⟨morsels[?]⟩ tender vines & ⟨weeds⟩ ^↑weeds↓ cling about the

4. Forio is a port on the north side of Ischia Island; to get to it, the boat would have to pass Procida, also a fertile island in the area. However, the word resembles "Fano."

5. WI underlined this blank space with a broken line; he mentioned in a March 13 journal entry that he visited "the Convent of St Martino, owned by a fraternity of Carthusians," and he described in detail the ascent and the convent itself (*Journals and Notebooks*, I, 231–33).

6. Also on March 13, WI wrote that the view from the window of the convent included Ciaja, Pausillipo, Ischia, "and a partial glimpse of the classic coast of Baia" (*Journals and Notebooks*, I, 232–33); on March 17, he discussed Baia in more detail (*ibid.*, pp. 245–48).

7. This word could be "has" or "had."

8. Apparently WI wrote "hear," then over the *r* wrote a *d*, and finally added another *d* after the original *r*.

9. WI wrote the word "and" and then after a looping ending to the right, he added what seems to be a *c* above the line; this configuration could be the longer version of his usual "&c." In the 1805 Notebook, WI mentioned "the beautiful villages of Portici, resina &c" (*Journals and Notebooks*, I, 238).

crevices of ruins and overwhelms the morsels of antiquity with their leaves. ⟨as we app⟩

To our left stretched the coast of Pausillippo;[10] ⟨? whi sa?⟩ we saw promontory stretching beyond promontory; Some crowned with towers; others with small forts at which we could discern the tall tapering latine mast. and the tower or fario[?][11] at the end of the mole which stretched into the sea[12]

10. See the March 12, 13, and 14 entries for detailed descriptions of WI's visits to Vesuvius and Posillipo (*Journals and Notebooks*, I, 228–43).

11. This word resembles "faces" or "faris."

12. In the lower right corner of this page is the accession number in pencil.

MISCELLANEOUS MATERIALS

Unidentified Fragments

Notebook Fragment, Variations on Goldsmith, Undated[1]

This manuscript sheet is in the Hellman Collection of the Manuscripts and Archives Division of the New York Public Library. It is cataloged as Washington Irving Autograph Letters, Mss & Etc., 43 M 122, Item #29; it is housed in a manila folder in a maroon manuscript box. The single sheet, which measures 14 13/16 x 12 1/16 inches, is folded in half; therefore, there are four pages of 7 13/32 x 12 1/16 inches. Only the first page of this folio has writing in brown ink; pages [2–3] are blank; and in the top left corner of page [4] is a pencil sketch of hills, church, and clouds. The paper is off-white, with tiny horizontal lines and seven vertical lines in the grain. In leaf 1 is a watermark with the numbers "1797," presumably the date, and in leaf 2 is a watermark seal consisting of a seated figure, holding torch and staff, in an oval enclosure.

[*p. [1]*]

When thus [*blank*][2] ↑creations↓ charms around combine
Amidst the store should thankless pride repine?
Say should the philosophic mind disdain

1. The New York Public Library dates this manuscript as ca. 1804, explaining that it was a part of the Salmagundi period and that it is the library's "earliest literary writings by Irving's hand . . . penned about 1804." In two letters (September 4 and 10, 1970) from Herbert L. Kleinfield to C. Hugh Holman, the date was discussed and Professor Kleinfield questioned the dating. In a May 9, 1805, journal entry, WI quoted six lines from Goldsmith's *The Traveller*, about the love which the Swiss have for their native land, but Nathalia Wright wrote that WI quoted from Coxe's *Travels in Switzerland*, I, 285, rather than from an edition of Goldsmith (*Journals and Notebooks*, I, 377–78, 378, n. 179).
2. Apparently WI intended to deviate from Goldsmith by adding a name; he left the space blank and then added Goldsmith's word above the line.

That *wig*[3] which makes each ↑batterd beau so↓[4] humbler
    bosom vain
Let school-taught pride dissemble all it can
These little *wigs*[5] are great to little man.
How wise then he[6]
And wiser he whose sympathetic mind
Exults ↑in all the good of all mankind↓[7] *to dress the heads*
    of half mankind!
                                        Goldsmith.[8]

⟨As some lone ↑barber↓ miser, visiting his store
Bends oer him a block head⟩[9]

My soul, turn from them—turn we to survey
Where Huggins[10] ⟨school⟩ ↑rooms↓ a nobler race display
Where ⟨stylish⟩ ↑dashing↓ bucks his stylish mansion tread,[11]
And to his hands commit the uncombd head

3. This underlined word was WI's first major deviation, excluding punctuation; he substituted "wig" for the word "good."

4. These three words are WI's above-the-line alternate reading; Goldsmith's line was quoted exactly.

5. Goldsmith's word here is "things."

6. WI apparently began the seventh line in the stanza with his own words, and then he dropped to the next line, quoting Goldsmith's seventh line exactly.

7. WI wrote Goldsmith's words above the line and his own words, which he underlined, on the line.

8. These eight lines are from Oliver Goldsmith, "The Traveller, or a Prospect of Society" (see *The Collected Works of Oliver Goldsmith*, ed. Arthur Friedman (Oxford: Clarendon Press, 1966), IV, 250, lines 37–44).

9. WI began to quote lines 51–52 in the same poem, inserting above the line his alternate reading, "barber"; after the word "Bends" in the second line, WI deviated from Goldsmith's words, "Bends at his treasure, counts, recounts it o'er," then struck the two lines and dropped to line 165 of the poem where he resumed copying.

10. The hairdresser's name, "Huggins," and the words "school" and "rooms" were substituted for the original "rougher climes." At the bottom of the manuscript page, in another hand, is the following:

	John Huggins	Listed as hairdresser
WASHINGTON IRVING	John R. D. Huggins	and haircutter
		N.Y. City Directories 1801–16

11. WI substituted between the first and last words of Goldsmith his own version; the original line reads, "Where the bleak Swiss their stormy mansions tread" (line 167); after the first word on the next line, WI left Goldsmith completely:

"And force a churlish soil for scanty bread;
No product here the barren hills afford,
But man and steel, the soldier and his sword" (*Traveller*, lines 168–70).

Thus to ⟨relieve⟩ ↑attend↓ the ladies is his pride
⟨And swift he ⟨w⟩ skips with iron by his side⟩
With comb & curling iron by his side
Firm in his duty—⟨proper[?]⟩ prompt at every call
He'll clip & snip, ⟨and⟩ he'll curl & twirl for all.

[*pp. [2–3] blank*]

[*p. [4] contains a drawing of an outdoor scene with church, hills, and clouds.*]

Manuscript Fragment, Regarding a Count's Wife, Undated

This manuscript fragment is in the Clifton Waller Barrett Library of the University of Virginia Library, Charlottesville, Virginia, where it is cataloged as #6256–m. It is fragment number 4 housed in a folder reading "Washington Irving: 4 fragments of unidentified AMs." The leaf has been torn from a notebook lengthwise; the yellowed paper measures 4⅜ x 7¾₆ inches. The writing is in brown ink; the verso is blank. In the top half of the leaf is an upside-down watermark: the letters "R T a s" are on one line and under the "as" is the number "18."

[*p. 8*][1]
to work to clear away the cloud of knavish parasites and faithless stewards that surrounded her husband, among which the most favourdable[?][2] was his own father confessor, a worldly and designing priest who had gained an ascendancy ⟨of⟩ over his mind & a control[3] over his very household.

A few years sufficed for this intelli-/-gent woman to reform the whole establishment, and under her[4] judicious management the old age of the count is ⟨easy and⟩ prosperous & void of care.

[*p. [9] blank*]

1. WI wrote "8" in the upper right corner of the recto; this manuscript page seems to be the end of a longer story.
2. These letters could be the words "favourd alli."
3. This word may be spelled "controul."
4. There is an ink mark over the *r* which may be a smeared dot of an *i*.

Notebook Fragment, No. 1, Regarding the Fall, Book, and Solomon, Undated[1]

This notebook fragment is in the Clifton Waller Barrett Library of the University of Virginia Library, Charlottesville, Virginia, where it is catalogued as #6256–a. It is fragment (b) housed in a folder reading "Washington Irving: Notes on Adam and the Fall." The leaf has apparently been torn from a notebook lengthwise; the holes from the stitching are evident at the left. It is also torn at the bottom; the yellowed paper measures $3\frac{15}{16}$ x $5\frac{7}{16}$ (outside edge; binding edge is $5\frac{1}{4}$) inches. The writing is in brown ink; the verso is blank. In the lower right corner is an upside-down watermark: a pointed shield with an orb topped by clasped hands with a design at the top of the shield.

[*recto*]

The old Jewish rabbins say that Adam after his fall recd from God as a consolation, by the hands of the Angel Raziel, a book which ⟨acquainted him⟩ contained all the secrets of the universe (the ⟨Sel⟩ Celestial Science or Cabala) the power of talking with the sun & moon; the knowledge of all maladies & of their cure; to overturn cities, excite earth-/-quakes, command good & bad angels, to interpret Dreams & prodegies & to prophesy.

—This Book passing from father to son fell into the hands of Solomon & gave him the power of building the temple, without using any instrument of Iron.

[*verso blank*]

1. At the conclusion of the sketch "St. Mark's Eve," in *Bracebridge Hall* (published in 1822), WI drew a line and then following three asterisks wrote, "In the foregoing paper I have alluded to the writings of some of the old Jewish rabbins. They abound with wild theories; but among them are many truly poetical flights; and their ideas are often very beautifully expressed. Their speculations on the nature of angels are curious and fanciful, though much resembling the doctrines of the ancient philosophers. . . ." (*Bracebridge Hall*, p. 86). He then related a part of the writings of Rabbi Eleazer (*ibid.*, pp. 86–87), the text of which Smith says WI likely translated directly from Balthasar Bekker's *Le Monde Enchante* (Amsterdam, 1694) (*ibid.*, pp. 325–26). This fragment may relate to that allusion by WI in "St. Mark's Eve," but it seems to be an earlier version of the more polished one which follows.

Manuscript Fragment, No. 2, Regarding the Fall, Book, and Solomon, Undated

This manuscript leaf is in the Clifton Waller Barrett Library of the University of Virginia Library, Charlottesville, Virginia, where it is cataloged as #6256–m. It is fragment number 1 housed in a folder reading "Washington Irving: 4 fragments of unidentified AMs." The leaf has been torn from a notebook lengthwise; the yellowed paper measures 4 x $5^{13}/_{16}$ inches. The paper is wrinkled as if it had been crushed and straightened. The relatively small, neat writing is in brown ink.

[*recto*]

The old Jewish rabbins affirmed that Adam, after his fall, received from God, as a consolation, by the hands of the Angel Raziel a book which contained all the secrets[1] of the universe, (the celestial science or cabala) the power of talking with the sun and moon; the knowledge of all maladies and of their cure; the power to overturn Cities; to excite earthquakes; to command good and bad angels, to interpret dreams and prodigies and to prophecy.[2]

This book passing from father to son fell into the hands of Solomon and gave him the power of building the temple without using any instrument of iron.

[*On the verso approximately two-thirds down the page is an unrecovered*[3] *word in brown ink.*]

1. There is an ink blot over the "re."
2. The word could be spelled "prophesy," but the questioned letter resembles more nearly WI's *c*.
3. This word resembles "sluicsing"; it could begin with "Sl," "sh," "Hu," or combinations of these or other letters. It ends with "ing."

MISCELLANEOUS MATERIALS

Notes Regarding Accounts, Publishing, etc.

Regarding Writing and Publishing Schedules [1850][1]

These four leaves are in the Beinecke Rare Book and Manuscripts Library, Yale University, New Haven, Connecticut, cataloged as Za Irving 110. Each leaf, measuring 4⅞ x 7⅞ inches, is kept in a separate manila folder, with superscripts "1" through "4" following the accession number; their order does not follow Irving's numbering of the pages. The transcription here follows the apparently intended order of Irving's numbering (pages 12–13, 20–25) rather than the library's designation of order. The white paper is faintly lined vertically, and the writing throughout is in brown ink, which has faded through the paper. On the verso of the leaf designated Za Irving 110[4] (Irving's page 22) is a tissue-thin piece of paper stuck to the paper in the center and bottom fourth of the page.

[*p. 12*][2]

Tales of a Traveller

1.[3] Commenced in Paris in the winter of 1823–4. Finished in England early in the summer of the same year[4]

2. Revised in the United States in 1850.

1. Ben Harris McClary wrote in his *Washington Irving and the House of Murray*, appendix 4, that in an August, 1850, letter, John Murray III asked WI twelve questions about each of the works Murray had published. WI's answers to these questions were based on these notes, and others obviously missing, and were sent in what McClary called Letter 64 (p. 217).

2. WI wrote "12" in the upper right corner of the recto of this leaf cataloged as Za Irving 110[3]; to the right of the number and on the page generally are markings from the ink's fading through from the verso. In the upper left corner are the small letters "cc," presumably in another hand.

3. WI underlined several of the numbers: "1," "2," "4," "5," and "7"; here the underlining seems to be under the period and we have regularized by underlining the number "1."

4. The paragraphing is generally block, with the number appearing in the margin, and the lines either under the first word of the first line, under the period following the number, or under the number itself; we have regularized the paragraphing.

3. Treated with Mr Murray for the work by Letter from Paris dated March 18, 1824[.] Bargain completed in London shortly afterwards
4. I agreed to sell it to him for 1500 Guineas[—]The agreement was verbal
5 I delivered the MSS. to him in ⟨England⟩ London in the course of the Spring and Summer of 1824 and in pursuance of the agreement.
6. I received in payt his notes for 1500 Gs. and gave him a receipt stating that it was for the copy regld[?] and that I would make a complete assignment of the same when required[.] Receipt dated ⟨E⟩London Aug 13th. 1824.

[*p. 13*][5]

7. I sent ⟨it⟩ ↑the MS.↓ to my Brother in US in portions[?] It was published[6] in New York in 4 parts[:] 1s part Aug 24th. 1824—2d Sept 9th. 1824[—]3d Sept. 25th[—]4th Oct 9th. 1824
8. Published in America by Carey Lea & Blanchard Philadelphia—dates as above.
9th. First published ‸↑in England↓ by Mr Murray[—]2 Vols Aug 24th. 1824
10. I intended the first part to be published in America Simultaneously with the whole in England
11. Published by Mr Murray on his own account
12. I resided in England at the time of its publication there.

[*p. 20*][7]

Companions of Columbus

1. Sketched out in Spain in 1827–8[.] Finished in England 1830
2. The revised edition corrected & completed in the United States in 1848, I residing there at the time
3. Treated with Mr Murray for the sale of ⟨original first⟩ work latter part of 1830.
4. ⟨A⟩Verbal agreement to sell it to him for 500 guineas—recd payt in notes.

5. WI wrote "13" in the upper left corner of the verso of the leaf; he underlined with a quarter circle. The ink from the recto has badly faded through to this page.

6. The word "published" has an unusual formation at the end; there is either an extra *d* and no *e*, or an unusually formed "&" and no *e*, or a line extending above the *e*.

7. WI wrote "20." in the upper right corner (and underlined with a quarter circle) of the recto of the leaf which is cataloged as Za Irving 110[2]. Ink from the verso has faded through to this page, particularly around the first four numbers in the left margin.

5. Delivered MS. to Murray in London 1830 in pursuance of agreet
6. I recd 500 Guineas, in notes—do not recollect about a receipt
7. Sent in sheets to E I in America. privilege to print an edition sold by him to ⟨C⟩Messs[8] Carey & Lea Philadelphia
8 First published in Am: by Carey & Lea Phila March 7, 1831.

[*p. 21*][9]
9. First publd. in England 31 Decr. 1830 By Mr Murray
10 Simultaneous publication intended in Engd and America
11. Publication by Murray was on his own account
12 I was residing in Engd. at the time of its first publication there

[*p. 22*][10]

Tour on the Praries

1 Composed in N York 1834.
2. Corrected for the last revised edition 1849, in the State of New York where I was then residing.
3. I first treated with Mr Murray for the work in the Spring of 1835.
4 I agreed to sell it to him for 400£ sterling[.] Col Aspinwall, my agent, gave a receipt for the same, dated March 3d. 1835, stipulating in my name to execute any formal instrument of sale that might be necessary.
5. The MS. was[11] delivered to Mr Murray by my agent in 183⟨4⟩5 ⟨in⟩ pursuant to agreement.
6 I received four ⟨thousand⟩ hundred pounds in promissory notes for which my agent gave a receipt

[*p. 23*][12]
7. I made an arrangt. for the publication in America with Messs.[13] Carey Lea & Blanchard of Phila.
8. It was first published by them April—11t or 14[?],[14] 1835

8. WI wrote the title with a superscript as "Mess^s^"; the final letter could be an *r*.
9. WI wrote "21" in the upper left corner of the verso of this leaf. Ink from the recto has badly faded through to this page, especially on the bottom half.
10. WI wrote "22" in the upper right corner (and underlined with a quarter circle) of the recto of this leaf cataloged as Za Irving 110[4]. There is a slight fading through of ink from the verso.
11. The word "was" is written over an illegible word or letters.
12. WI wrote "23" in the upper left corner of the verso and underlined with a diagonal line. The ink from the recto has rather badly faded through, especially at the bottom of the page.
13. WI wrote "Mess^s^."
14. This number could be "16."

9 First published in England by Mr Murray March 2d[15] 1835.
10. Publication in Engd & America intended to be Simultaneous
11 Published by Mr Murray on his own account.
12th I was residing in NYork at the time the work was first published in England.

[*p. 24*][16]

Abbotsford–

1 Composed in NYork 1834
2. Revised for the last complete edition of my works in 1848 or 9.
3. First treated with Mr Murray for the sale early in 1835.
4. An agreement was made with him through my agent Col Aspinwall. I do not recollect the price
5 The MS was delivered to him by my agent pursuant to agreement.
6. I do not recollect the sum—I presume a receipt was given by my agent—
[6½] I made an agreement with Mess Carey Lea & Blanchard Phila.[17]
⟨6⟩7. The work was published ⟨from same &⟩ under my ⟨eye in America⟩ ‸↑supervision.—↓
8.[18] It was first published by Carey Lea & Blanchard Philadelphia June 1, 1835.
9 First published by Murray ‸↑in London↓ May 1, 1835

[*p. 25*][19]

10. I intended the publication, in both countries to be Simultaneous
11. Published by Mr Murray on his own[20] Account
12. I resided in ⟨the US.⟩[21] ↑New York↓ at the time the work was first published in England

15. The line below the *d* seems to be an ink blot faded through the paper.
16. WI wrote "24" in the upper right corner of the recto of the leaf cataloged Za Irving 110[1]; in the upper left corner there is a faint Z or Q or "2." Below and to the left of the number 2 in the list is a tear; the ink has faded through from the verso.
17. This item, which we numbered 6½, was probably added later: the two lines are written in smaller letters in the space usually left blank between items.
18. The number "8" may be written over another number, perhaps a "6."
19. WI wrote "25" in the upper left corner of the verso and underlined with a quarter circle; ink has faded through from the recto.
20. To the right and below the word "own" is the small tear mentioned above.
21. Below the "US" is a mark which resembles WI's caret.

Disbursements while Building a Crib [1835]

This manuscript leaf is in the Beinecke Rare Book and Manuscripts Library, Yale University, New Haven, Connecticut, where it is cataloged as Za Irving 23a. It measures 7 13/16 x 9 13/16 inches, and the paper is off-white. On the recto, the first thirteen lines are in brown ink, and the final fourteen lines are in pencil. The verso is in ink except the initial number and the first column of figures.

[*recto*]

For every 100 feet in length it will require the following Materials for a Crib four feet high and four feet wide

6,000 ft of timber 10/. per hundred	$75 00
100 lb[1] Iron spikes—from 8 to 10 Cents per lb Say 9c.	9.00
Labour building Crib	15 –
If the stone can be obtained on the Beach of suitable sise it would Cost about $18 Dollars for 100[2] feet—	18 –
100 Braces or Chesnut Posts—	12.50
	$129 50
Expenses of getting timbers on the ground.	5.50
	135 "[3]

332
17
2424
332
5744[4]

332 Cubic feet a 10c pr cubic foot	33.20	Labor	30
50[5] lbs Iron Spikes a 8c	4.00		45
Labor building Crib	10 00		
			75

1. The *l* resembles a *t* in this abbreviation and in the one below it.
2. This number could be "150."
3. WI's indication of the numbers "00" was a mark which resembles a ditto mark or two short slashes.
4. This calculation is incorrect because of the error in multiplying.
5. WI wrote "⟨7⟩50."

Stone & do[6]	15.00	
		15
75 Chestnut Braces a 10c	7.50	
Expenses getting timber on the ground	5.00	90[7]
	74.70	
Contingent	5.30[8]	
	80 00	

[*verso*][9]

300

[*after the page has been turned one-quarter revolution counterclockwise*]

Washington Irving Esq
Greenburg

	84[10]	
42	16	
	504	
	84	
	1344	
	4.68 ¾	
	3.12 ½	
	7.81 ¼	
12.1.0		14.76
		8
		22.76

6. WI used his abbreviation here for the word "ditto."
7. WI wrote "⟨8⟩90."
8. The number "30" was written over an illegible number.
9. In the top right corner of the verso is the accession number in pencil, just above the number "300."
10. This one column of figures (as well as the number to the left of it) is upside down in smaller numbers in pencil.

Terms of Settlement with Publisher [1828][1]

This manuscript leaf is in the Beinecke Rare Book and Manuscripts Library, Yale University, New Haven, Connecticut, where it is cataloged as Za Irving 23b. It measures 4¾ x 7$\frac{1}{16}$ inches. The paper is off-white and has tiny lines in the grain; the writing is in brown ink. The verso is blank.

[*recto*]

Terms of Settlement for
the Conquest of Granada, as
by agreement.

Bills to be dated Jan 10th. 1829[2]

1st.	8 Months	400	due Sept 13
2d.	12 Mo.	400	Jan. 13/30
3d.	16. Mo.	400	May 13/30
4th.	20 Mo.	400	Sept. 13/30
5th.	24. Mo.	500	Jan 13/31
		£2100	

[*verso blank*]

1. On September 2, 1828, WI wrote to Peter from Seville that he had just sent by steamboat the manuscript of about half of the first volume of the *Conquest of Granada* and would send the remainder when he got it copied. He added that he had "authorized Col. Aspinwall to dispose of it to Murray, or to any other leading and respectable bookseller for 2,000 guineas, or as near that sum as he can get" (PMI, II, 341). On October 21, 1828, WI wrote to Alexander H. Everett that Aspinwall seemed "highly pleased with [the Conquest], and has put it in Murray's hands, from whom I await a reply" (*ibid.*, pp. 347–48). There was a slight delay in coming to terms with Murray; Aspinwall sent the letter to WI on December 20, 1828, and from December 22 to 24, WI rewrote from notes the missing two chapters which he had sent by mistake to Ebenezer in New York (*ibid.*, pp. 360–61). On December 27, WI received from Aspinwall a December 12 letter outlining the terms with Murray: "2,000 guineas, at long dates. . . . He gives you your own price, but the notes are to be at eight, twelve, sixteen, twenty and twenty-four months, from January 10, 1829; the last note for £500, and all the rest for £400 each (*ibid.*, p. 362).

2. WI actually wrote "Jan 10 ↑th↓. 1829." In the schedule, there is a vertical line separating the second and third columns, and irregular horizontal lines connecting items in the second and third and the third and fourth columns.

ACCOUNT BOOKS

1830-1831, 1841

United States Legation Disbursements and Personal Expenses

This manuscript notebook is in the Seligman Collection of the Manuscripts and Archives Division of the New York Public Library, where it is cataloged by halves as follows: the first part of the notebook is cataloged as Washington Irving Journals, Volume 24, and entitled "Journal: Disbursements for the Contingencies of the Legation of the United States at London, 1830, Jan. 6–1831, Jul. 2"; the second portion of the notebook (when it is reversed and read back-to-front) is cataloged as Washington Irving Journals, Volume 29, and entitled "Personal, House & Farm Expenses, 1841." The rust leather cover is not connected to the 34 leaves, and the off-white string between leaves 17 and 18 no longer holds the leaves together. The paper is a light green color, lined horizontally with blue lines and vertically with five red lines, the two in the center of the page closely approximate. The 68 pages measure 3⅞ x 6¹⁄₁₆ inches. In ink are the front cover, the inside front cover, pages [1], [3], [5] (these last two have several check marks in pencil), [6], [8–10], [12–14], [16–24], [26], [40–44], [46], [48], [50–54], [56], [62–68]; in combination of pencil and ink are the inside back cover, pages [7], [11], [15], [25], [27–30]; and blank are the back cover, pages [2], [4], [31–39], [45], [47], [49], [55], [57–61].

[*front cover*]

original
Disbursements
for the Contingencies of the
Legation of the United States
at London
From Jany 6 to
Washington Irving
Secy of Legation[1]

1. Irving learned on July 18, 1829, while he was at the Alhambra that he had

[*inside front cover*]
June[?] 19[2] Recd. from Mr M Lane his check for £64.7.9[3]

———

⟨Paid by⟩
Postage pd by Mr M'Lane

To Turner	2.
To Henry & Frank }	.19
	2.19

⟨Rcd. J⟩
Dec 29. Received[4] from Mr M Lane 5£

[*p. [1]*]
Mr M Lanes Dr[5] to W I.

[*p. [2] blank*]

[*p. [3]*]

Disbursements for Contingencies
of the Legation of the U.S. at London[6]

———

1830		
Jan. 6.	Turners a/c of Postage (See receipt No 1 }	2[7] 0 1
	^↑Customary↓ Christmas presents to the Keepers of St James Park }	1 1 –

been appointed secretary of the legation to London (PMI, II, 398). He took a leisurely journey to London, and in an October 6, 1829, addition to an August 10 letter to Brevoort, Irving said that he cut short his stay in Paris to meet Louis McLane, who was appointed minister to the Court of St. James in May, 1829, and began serving on September 21. WI said that he was "perfectly delighted with [McLane]," but the latter's illness had prevented their getting settled in a house (*Letters*, II, 462). McLane resigned in April, 1831, sailed for America in June, and became the secretary of the treasury in August; WI was "virtual head of the Legation from June 22, 1831, to April 1, 1832" (STW, II, 7).

2. The date could be "29."
3. WI drew a line 1¾ inches long; in the left margin is the number "20."
4. The first letters of this word were written over "Pd."
5. WI did not complete the debit list of McLane.
6. WI drew a double line 3½ inches long.
7. Check marks in pencil precede all the numbers in this list except the "2.2.9" and the total; there is also a check mark in the left margin below the date "14."

		£	s	d
9.	ditto to Lord Aberdeens[8] Servants	2	2	–
	Ditto to messenger of the Alien office	1	1	–
14	Turners a/c for Postage –See receipt no 2.	2	2	9
	Customary presents to the Ld Chancellors Servts	1	1	–
	ditto to Letter Carrier to the Foreign Ministers	2	2	–
	carried forwd.	£ 11	9	10.

L S.[9] Washington Irving

[*p. [4] blank*]

[*p. [5]*]

Disbursements for Contingencies &c[10]

		£	s	d
	Amt. brot forwd	£11	9	10
20.	Postage of letters pd by WI[11]		2	–
28	Turners a/c for Postage See receipt No 3.	3	6	1
"	Postage		8	–
Feb 7	Postage of a letter from Mr Wheaton[12] to ⟨se⟩ forwd. to Secy of State[13] &c		11	6

8. See p. 200, n. 19, regarding George Hamilton Gordon, Lord Aberdeen.

9. It is difficult to read these initials; the letters "L S" could be an abbreviation for legation secretary, or letter signed, or "locus sigilli," Latin for "place of the seal"; the letters could be "S S," standing for sworn statement; or the letters could be "S L," abbreviation for secretary of legation.

10. WI drew a double line 3⅜ inches long.

11. Written over the dash is "pd by WI." Preceding all the figures in the column of figures, except the first, last, and total, are check marks. The date "Feb 7" is in pencil.

12. Henry Wheaton (1785–1848) was chargé d'affaires to Denmark (beginning in 1827) and later to Berlin.

13. The U.S. secretary of state was Martin Van Buren (see Introduction, pp. xlvi–xlviii, and p. 182, n. 16).

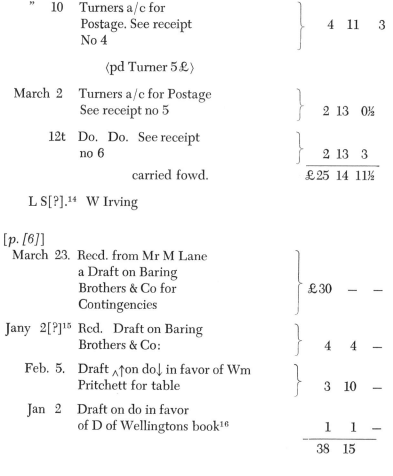

" 10	Turners a/c for Postage. See receipt No 4	4 11 3
	⟨pd Turner 5£⟩	
March 2	Turners a/c for Postage See receipt no 5	2 13 0½
12t	Do. Do. See receipt no 6	2 13 3
	carried fowd.	£25 14 11½

L S[?].[14] W Irving

[*p. [6]*]

March 23.	Recd. from Mr M Lane a Draft on Baring Brothers & Co for Contingencies	£30 – –
Jany 2[?][15]	Rcd. Draft on Baring Brothers & Co:	4 4 –
Feb. 5.	Draft ^↑on do↓ in favor of Wm Pritchett for table	3 10 –
Jan 2	Draft on do in favor of D of Wellingtons book[16]	1 1 –
		38 15

[*p. [7]*]

Disbursements for Contingencies &c[17]

———

Amount brot. forwd.	£25 14 11½

14. The second letter resembles an *E*.

15. WI could have written a "2" over a "4" or vice versa.

16. The political climate in England before the Reform Bill was passed in 1832 was full of turmoil, to say the least. Williams says that WI was intensely interested and "read widely in the writings of leaders on both sides" and talked with Wellington among many other principals (STW, II, 9).

17. WI drew a double line 3⅜ inches long.

March 25[18] ⟨23⟩	Turners a/c for Postage. See receipt no 7[19]	3	2	11½
28	Franking letters—		2	11
31	Turners a/c for Postage. Receipt 8[20]		19	2
	1 Quarters Salary of Office messenger	⟨30 20	0 —	0⟩
Jan. 4[21]	Fees to door keepers of the Foreign office	4 .	4	
Feb 5.[22]	writing table for the office	3	10	
Mar ↑⟨22⟩↓2	Fees to Duke of Welling/tons servants	1	1	
		58	15[23]	

[*p. [8]*]

June 4.	Recd. from Mr M Lane a draft on Mess Baring Brothers & Co. (for Contingencies—	£30	0	0
June 30.	Pd. by Mr M Lane 1 Qu Salary of messenger	20	—	—
		£50	—	—

18. This date could be "26"; beneath many of the words and numbers on this page are erasures, among them "March."

19. The "7" is written over a "2."

20. This and the following two lines were written and marked through in pencil, then written over in ink.

21. This date was corrected from "4" in ink to "2" in pencil; following the number is a check mark; to the left of the month is an ink mark resembling half of an "8" on its side.

22. WI wrote the "5" in pencil over a "7" or a "9" in ink; to the left and below the month is a check mark.

23. In the pounds column, WI wrote "5⟨9⟩8," correcting the sum.

[*p. [9]*]

1830					
April 10.	Turners a/c for Postage ^↑from 1. April↓ See receipt 1	2	1	8½
May ⟨6⟩4.	Turners a/c for Postage. See Receipt 2	6	19	5½
May 15.	Turners a/c for Postage. Receipt 3.	2	2	1.
May 19.	Turners a/c for Postage (Receipt 4	4	17	1
June 4.	Turners a/c for Postage (Receipt 5)	2	8	11
June 30	Turners a/c for Postage. (receipt 6)	5	7	0
	Sundry postages at various times pd in the office		10	6
		£24	6	9

[*p. [10]*]

Cr. Mr M Lane			
Amt brot forwd	£50		
	44	6	9
Balance due Mr M L	£ 5	13	3

[*p. [11]*]

Amt brot. forward.	24	6	9
1 Qus Salary of the office messenger[24]	20	–	–
	£44	6	9

24. WI wrote in ink over pencil the words "the office Messenger" over "office Messenger."

[*p. [12]*]

		£	s	d
	Due Mr M Lane			
—	Balance brot. from preceding page	5	13[25]	3
Oct 18	Recd. from Mr M Lane draft on Baring brothers & Co	30	0	0
Sept 30	Cr. Mr M Lane by 1 Qrs Salary of Messenger	20		
		55	13	3
		38	8	6
		£ 7	4	9[26]

[*p. [13]*]

		£	s	d
1830 July 13	Turners a/c for Postage (See rect. No 1)	3	8	10
15	Match box & tapers	–	2	0
24	Turners a/c for Postage (See rect. No 2)	4	15	6
Sept 2.	Turners a/c for Postage (See rect. no 3)	8	3	8
	Casual[?] postages paid in the office	1	2	6
⟨*illegible*⟩	Office pen Knife for Mr M Lane	–	10	0
	Pencils		6	0
Sept 30.	1 Qrs Salary of the office Messenger	20	0	0
		£38	8	6

L. S.[?]
Washington Irving
Secy of Legation

25. WI first wrote the number "15."

26. In the shillings column, WI wrote the "4" over another number.

[*p. [14]*]

Cr	Balance due Mr M Lane from last month the US.	7 4 9
	⟨By[27] overcharge in Turners postage a/c of Nov 25th. 1829. 10[28] or 2$ 22/100	⟨*number illegible*⟩
Dt	the US. to undercharge in transfering the balance from a/c ending 31. Month[?][29] last to the next. 30 Cents⟩	
Dec 2d.	By. Draft of Mr M Lane on Baring Brothers & Co 30£	30 0 0
		37 4 9

[*p. [15]*]

Oct 16	Turners a/c for Postage Since Sept 1. See receipt No. 1 £1[30]	7 16 11
22	Turners a/c for Do See rect. No 2	4 7 10
29	Note paper	1 –
30.	Cartridge paper for dispatches T.[31]	2 9
Nov. 3	Turners a/c for Postage see rect. 3	6 18 7

27. WI crossed out this section and the next one with one large *X*.
28. WI wrote "⟨2⟩10/."
29. This word may be "March."
30. This amount was added lightly in pencil.
31. This could be a "7."

Nov. 20.	Do. Do.[32] see rect. 4	5 0 4
Dec 2.	Do. Do. See acct. No 5	5 6 7
3		£29 14 0

carried forward
W Irving.

[*p. [16]*]

	Amt brot ford	37 . 4 9

carried forwd

[*p. [17]*]

Disbursements &c Contind[33]

———

	Amt brot forwd.	£29 14 0
Dec[34] 15.	postage of a letter	2 2
"	Turners a/c for Postage. Receipt 6	5 10 4
29	Christmas present to the letter carrier to the Foreign Minister	2 2 –
30	Do. to the General Postman	1 0 0
	Do. to the Court Reporter	1 1 –
	Do. to the Park Keepers	1 1
– 31.	Turners a/c for Postages. Receipt no 7	6 15 8½
	wrapping paper Porterages &c	6 6[35]
		£47 12 8½

carried forward
W Irving

32. Between "ditto" abbreviations, there are ink blots.
33. WI's line is 3¼ inches long.
34. There is a mark above the line after the *c*; it could be an *r*.
35. Above the numbers is an ink blot.

[*p. [18]*]

	Cr. M M Lane			
	By amt brot forwd	37	4	9.
	By 1 Qrs Salary of office messenger	⟨20⟩ 20	0	0
		£57	4	9

[*p. [19]*]

Disbursements &c[36]

——

1830.	Amt brot forwd.	£47	12	8½
Dec[?][37] 31.	1 Qrs Salary of the office Messenger	20	0	0
		£67	12	8½
	Amt from opposite Page	57	4	9
		£10	7	10½
	Balance due by Mr M Lane.[38]			

[*p. [20]*]

1831		
Jan. 1.	By Mr M Lanes draft in favor of W Irving on Baring brothers & Co	£30

[*p. [21]*]

Disbursements &c.[39]

——

1831.	Balance from last Qr.	10	7	11
Jan 1.	Christmas presents to the Ld Chamberlains Servants	1	1	–

36. WI's line is 3⅝ inches long.
37. WI's rendering of "Dec" is different from his usual; it could be an unusual "Jan" or "Decr."
38. Even though WI's items and figures do not correspond as usual, the "57.4.9" is the amount from the opposite page and the "10.7.10½" seems to be the balance due by Mr. McLane.
39. WI's line is 2¾ inches long.

3	Do. to Ld Palmerstons[40] Servants	3 0 0
”	Do. to Attendants to the Foreign office &c	5 0 0
4	Do. Attendants at the Colonial office	2 2 –
	Do. to Postman	10 –
	Do. to twopenny[?] postman	5 –
	Do. to Lord Greys Servts.	1 1 0
8	Do to Messengers of the Alien Departt.	2 0 0
		£25[41] 6 11
	carried forwd	

[*p. [22]*]

Amt brot forwd. ⟨recd. f⟩	£30

[*p. [23]*]

Disbursements &c[42]

1831	Amt Brot forwd.	25 6 11
Feb 23.	Postage from Jany 1. to Feb. 20. See Turners rect no 1	16 10 6
”	Freight & porterage of a parcel from France	– 3[43] –
March 14.	Postage from Feb 20th. to March 12 See Turners recd no 2	7 10 5.

40. Henry John Temple, third Viscount Palmerston (1784–1865), had been secretary of war in Wellington's Cabinet formed in 1828, and from 1830 was secretary of state for foreign affairs, a position he held with one interruption until 1841.

41. The bottom of the "5" is smudged.

42. WI's line is 3½ inches long.

43. In the pounds column, WI first wrote "3," then partially erased it and drew a dash through it; there is a smudge above the dash.

"	2 news papers		2	–
"	letter from Mr Van Ness (Spain)[44]		6	6
⟨2⟩19	Pd. post man		9	1
21	Letters from Spain		6	6
22	do.		6	6
"	Pd. Postman	1	3	1
		£52	4	6[45]

[*p. [24]*]

Recd. for[?][46] Mr M Lane

	amt Brot fowd.	30	0	0
March 23	Recd. Mr M Lanes cheque in Baring brothers & Co fav[?]	£30		
	Salary of office Mess.	20		
		80	0	0
		74	18	11
	Balance due Mr M L.	5	1	1

[*p. [25]*]

Dsbursements &c[47]

	Amt Brot forwd	£52	4	6
	Franking letters at various times and postages or [*unrecovered*][48] paid by WI. ⟨f[?]⟩	1	3	6
26.	4 letters fr 2d post			8

44. Cornelius Van Ness (1782–1852) was the American minister to Spain from 1828 until 1836.

45. The "4" and "6" are written over other numbers.

46. WI meant to write "fro[m]"; there is an ink blot in the margin to the left of the second line.

47. WI's line is 2¾ inches long.

48. This word looks like "indentalles"; the reference may be to the process of indenting which in England had to do with an official requisition or purchase order sent from a foreign country; rather than two words, Irving may have written "incidentalles" or "incidentally."

28	1 letter from Spain to Mr M Lane	10 10
	1 do Mr[49] Irving—	4 4
31	1 do from Mr Burton[50] Cadiz	4 4
April 1.	⟨Letter from⟩ ⟨Spain Mr Van Ness⟩	⟨3 6⟩
	↑Salary of↓ office messenger	20
		74 8 2[51]
	Postman	10 9
		74 18 11 ↑⟨13⟩↓

80.0 0
74.18.11
5. 1. 1

[*p. [26]*]

Due Mr M Lane

balance from former account.	5 1 1

[*p. [27]*]

Disbursments &c

April 1.	Letter from Spain from Mr Van Ness	3 6
2.	pd. Genl post man	3 4
4	Letter from Mr Van Ness—Madrid[52]	6 6
5	do d[?]	6 6
6	pencils.	11 6

49. It is difficult to distinguish between WI's "Mr," especially when he raised the *r*, and his *W*.

50. Alexander Burton (?–1860) was the U.S. consul at Cadiz from April, 1824, until June, 1859; WI had met him in the spring of 1828 and wrote, "Mr Burton . . . was unremitting in his kind attentions . . ." (*Letters*, II, 300). To the left of this line, in the margin, are three sets of numbers, apparently WI's calculations, the result being "4.5."

51. The "8" and "2" of this amount are written over other numbers, the "8" over "10" or "9," and the "2" over "4"; WI's sum is correct.

52. This item and the four following were written in ink over pencil.

11	Letter from Mr V Ness		6	6
12	do		6	6
13	Pd. Genl postman	2	13	0
	twopenny post 4 letts.			8
	Carriage of Coach parcel		3	8
20.	Postages— including 1 letter from Mr Van Ness 6/6		13	11
27.	Postages	1	15	1
	including 1 from Mr Van Ness 4/4	7	10	8[53]

[*p. [28]*]

	Ballance brot fr	5	1	1
June 10.	Draft of Mr M Lane for contingencies	20	0	0
		25	1	1[54]

[*p. [29]*]

	Amt brot fowd	7	10	.8
May 4	Postages	⟨4⟩3	19	11
19	do. to Harding[?]	2	11	8
21	do. (by WI.)		2	3
31	Do. to Harding	4	5	11
June 2	Pd Postage		6	4
June 9.	Postage	2	1	1
	⟨[? Replace cooler & ?] refurnishing office⟩			
16	Mr M Lanes present to coach horse Man on taking leave	5	0	0
	Postage of a letter			8
		£25	18	6[55]

53. The "6" in ink was corrected to "8" in pencil, also done at the top of p. [29].
54. The total is in pencil.
55. This subtotal, the subtrahend, and the result are in pencil.

⟨22	Porterage[?][56] of office⟩	⟨1 6⟩
		25 1 1
	⟨papers[?]–⟩	£ 0 17 5
	[*unrecovered*][57] &c &c &c	
21.	Carriage to attend the ⟨opening⟩ ↑Kings↓ opening of Parliament	
22.	Porterage of ⟨a letter[?]⟩ office papers[58]	1 6

[*p. [30]*]

June 31.	Postage pd Harding pd	2 10 8
July 2.	Fees to court news-/-man on being Presented to the King	2 2 0
	Porterage of [*unrecovered*][59] from [*unrecovered*] St to Argyle St[60]	2 6

[*lines 9–13 of p. [30] are in pencil and are very faded*][61]

[*pp. [31–39] are blank*]

[*At page [40] the notebook is reversed, and Irving wrote from back to front (pp. [68–40]), with only one exception, p. [67]. The two sections of the notebook were composed at different periods in Irving's life—the first half, when he was in London with the legation of the United States in 1830–1831, and the second part, when he was in the United States in*

56. This word could be "Contings."
57. This word could be "Balan."
58. See WI's letter of June 22, 1831, to Secretary of State Edward Livingston regarding his attending King William IV's "speech from the throne"; he appended a copy of the speech which is still attached to the letter (*Letters*, II, 608–09).
59. This word resembles "Oreheves"; it could also begin with a *G* and be "Grahams."
60. The unrecovered word resembles "Dearshu." In October, 1829, WI "took lodgings" at 3 Chandos Street, Cavendish Square, opposite McLane's house and less than a minute from the legation (*Letters*, II, 473); his letters included that address until February 3, 1830, when he wrote from his lodgings at 8 Argyll Street.
61. The items in the three lines seem to be "Wages to office / Messengs & dr / fr 20 to 30," and the numbers seem to be "1.5.7," "–.3.6.," and "2.4.5."

1841; p. [67] clearly belongs to this earlier time period, and for the convenience of the reader, it will be given at this point. Thereafter, the notebook will be transcribed from back to front.]

[*p. [67], which is in the normal position, or the same position as the first half of the notebook*]

⟨Drafts drawn by Mr M Lane

1830[62]			
Jany	4.	On Baring brothers & co in favor of Col Aspinwall[63] or Fund for relief of destitute Seamen	500 – –
	22.	do. do. in ↑favor↓ ⟨behalf⟩ of David Walker—Consul at Glasgow.[64] for Do	21 8 10
	22.	Do.[65] Do. in favor of Francis B. Ogden[66]	207 16 2 ⟩

[*p. [68]*]

1841

Personal.	
Servants	13.
Postage	50
"	44
Ink	25
Postage	1.10
"	18½
Steamboat	2.62½
Servants &c	5.–
"	1.–
Postage	12½
Omnibus	37½
Concert	50

62. To the left and below the year is an ink blot; this page is crossed out with a large *X*, beginning on the left just above the year.

63. Colonel Thomas Aspinwall was American consul in London; see p. 209, n. 66.

64. David Walker was U.S. consul in Glasgow from 1824 until 1831; see WI's letters of September 1, 1831, regarding his death in office (*Letters*, II, 649–51).

65. "Do." is written over another letter.

66. Francis Barber Ogden (1783–1857), a "childhood" friend of WI, was the U.S. consul to Liverpool from 1829 until 1840. Following nine blank lines is the word "Person." on the last line of the page and upside down and crossed out.

Servant.	1.–
Cab	50
Stage fare	1.50
Portuguese Dictionary	50
Steamboat	62½
News paper	6½
Postage	37½
	29.36½[67]

[*p. [66]*]

Personal Contind	29.36½
Charity	5 –
arranging Diamond[?] cont.[?][68]	6
Steamboat	31
Omnibus	50
Servts	2.–
Postage	22
Steamboat	25
lucifer Matches	6¼
Postage	7
Steamboat	1.39
Theatre	1.
writing paper	1.–
Shaving	12½
Omnibus & Coach	25–
Cab	37½
Postage	8
Steamboat	62½
Omnibus	75
Cakes[?]–	10
	$49.47¼

[*p. [65]*]

Personal Contind.	49.47½[69]
Steamboat	1.25
Lecture	50
Cab & omnibus	87¼
Exhibition	25

67. WI's total should be "29.66½."
68. This abbreviation could be "amt."
69. In carrying the balance forward, WI changed the fraction.

Lunch	5
Newspapers	8
Church	5
Oranges	12½
"	25
Subscript to church	5.–
Steamboat	25
Washing bill	1.
Servt.	1.
lemonade &c	75
Missionary[?] charts	50
Porterage	12½
National Gallery	87½
Panorama	1.12½
Omnibus	25
	$63.77¾

[*p. [64]*]

Personal Contind.	63.77½[70]
Servt	1
Paper	1.25
Pew Rent 1 year	15.–
Bear oil–	25
Gum arab	25
Tooth brush	25
Charity	2.–
Genl[?]	15
Charity	25
Steamboat	81
Postage	12½
"	79½
"	34[71]
Steamboat	1.56
Omnibus &c	69
Servt	25
Newspaper	6¼
Expenses to Hudson Canal	10.49
writing Paper	1
	$100.29¾

70. In carrying the balance forward, WI changed the fraction.
71. This number is written over another.

[*p. [63]*]

Personal Contind	100.29¾
Gave David Davidson	10.–
Postage	31
Steamboat fares	3.63
Omnibus &c–	1.–
Doctor Bill	29.19
newspapers–	10½
Stages omnibus &c	69
Steamboat fares	2.–
Servants–	2 –
writing Paper	2.–
Excursion Lake Mayopal[?][72]	7.12½
Steamboat	81¼
Sponge	1.75
Newspaper	5
Postage	21
Steamboat fares	3 50
Newspapers	– 9
Servants–	4.–
	$168.76

[*p. [62]*]

Personal Contd.	168.76
Book Poulling[?][73] yard	50
Omnibus fares	1.25
Gave Mary & Julia	5.–
St Nicholas Society	4.
– Dinner	5.
writing paper & pencil points	1.31¼
Cartman & Boatman	41
Gave Kate[?]	203.13
⟨Host[?]⟩ House Keep Fordhan[?]	75
Rail road tickets–	75
Porterage	50
Map Virginia	4.–

72. In *Appleton's Hand-Book*, there is a reference to a lake in the Highlands to which WI may have alluded: from Peekskill travelers can "take stages . . . in the hottest part of summer twice a day to Mahopack lake . . ." (p. 69). WI was in the Highlands during July and August, 1841.

73. This word could be "poulting."

Music	37½
⟨Servants⟩	⟨*illegible*⟩
Chestnut horse (and bit[?])[74]	3.50
Library Subscript	4.–
Postages (E I bill)	10 81
Church Tarry town	20.–
Protests[?]	6 –
	$440 4¾

[*pp. [57–61] blank*]

[*p. [56]*]

House	
Freight[75]	50
Half expenses Mrs Romeyns Ice House– }	7.50
Ackers bill for getting ice	6.25
Glass butter tub	4.50
Tennian[?][76]	4.19
Shad[?]	37½
Coffee	31¼
Drawg bowl[?][77]	1.87½
"	3.75
Bill for freight & 2 Hogs }	20.88
Wine bill	135.53
	$185.68¼[78]

[*p. [55] blank*]

[*p. [54]*]

	Farm	
Jan 9[?][79]	Work on lane	15 –
	Taxes	48.64
	Carpenter	75

74. This word could be "bill."
75. Below this word is a cluster of ink blots.
76. This word could be "tinman."
77. These letters could be "cont."
78. WI's sum should be "185.66¼."
79. This date could be "1," "2," or "7."

Putty	25
Clover[?] Seed	2.–
Nails	21
Timothy Seed	2.25
"	2.25
Protape[?] Potatoes 1 *Bushel*	50
Clover Seed	90
Nails	56
Putty &c	31
⟨Horse Harnes[?]⟩	
Work on lane	45.–
Ploughing drawg Hay &c	7.25
Plank for Bridge	2.–
Nails	70
Mending Plough	1.–
2 rifles for Scythe	12½
	$129.69½

[*p. [53]*]

Farm Contd.	129.69½
rope yarn	75
Nails	86
Barrack &c	11.–
Work in the Meadow (Acker)	16.65¾
Plank	2.25
Woodsaw	1.25
Nails	31¼
Road Tax	8 –
Nails	50
"	⟨50⟩
Mendg Spade & Crow bar	43
Nails	48
	$172.18½

[*p. [52]*]

Stable–	
Ginger	12½
Curry comb	44
oats ↑20↓ & Hay ↑10$↓	30
Mane Comb	18½
Ginger	25

Oats	5.80
Ginger	12½
Oats	20 –
Hay	10.37½
Shoeing Horses	3.44
do	7. 5
Oats	2.81
⟨Steamboat⟩	⟨75⟩
Oats	2.81
"	24.–
Horse doctor	50
Oats & Ship Stuff	28.75
Straw (Dearman)	5.–
	$111.96

[p. [51]]

Stable Contind.	111.96
{ Requas bill from Jan to Aug 21. Hay 11 000	68.75
Straw	5.85
Straw	80
50 Bush Oats (Sept 21)	28.50
⟨S⟩Horse shoing	1 25
"	5.64
Oats & Ship Stuff	65.50
Broo⟨t⟩m	18½
	$288.43½

[p. [50]]

Carriage & Harness	
Chamois leather	1.25
Mendg Carriage	6.13
Repairs of carriage	16.46
Saddlers bill	13.18
Repairs to waggons &c	12.29
	$49.31

[*p. [49] blank*][80]

80. There are ink blots which match those on the following page.

[*p. [48]*]

Garden	
Celery Seed	6¼
window glass & putty for frames	2.–
Seeds	37½
Rake	56¼
Seed	12½
Peas	12½
Beet [*unrecovered*][81]	6¼
Seeds	25
Grass Shears	2.–
Seeds	31½
"	75
"	1.50
	$8.12¾

[*p. [47] blank*]

[*p. [46]*]

Poultry	
⟨4 Buc[?] corn[?]⟩	⟨2 76⟩
⟨corn⟩	⟨5.16⟩
"	⟨68½⟩
Corn & Buck wheat	$65.59½
	⟨20⟩ –

[*p. [45] blank*]

[*p. [44]*]

Clothing	
Mending	68½
"	2 50
Gloves	1 –
Suspenders	1.25
India Rub ovrshoes	3 –
Watch hands	37½
2 pr Boots	13 –
Gloves	1

81. Ink blots obscure this word, which is probably "Seeds."

	Stock	3.25
	Pocket Comb	18½
Feb 22.	Pantaloons[?][82]	25.–
	repairs of watch	10 –
	Gloves	1
	HKfs	75
	Braces	37½
	Cloth cap[83]	3.–
	repairs of watch	1.–
	Spectacles	87½
	Eye Glass	2.50
	Gloves	31¼
		$71. 5¾

[p. [43]]

	Clothing Contind	71. 5¾
	Gloves	57
	Mendg Boots	75
	⟨comb⟩	⟨15[?]⟩
	Stuff for Pants	6.90
	Blk Silk Hkf	3.25
	Booties	2.75
July	Hat	4.–
	Gloves	⟨3⟩31
	Pantaloon[?]	20.–
	Taylors bill	5.25.
	Slippers	1.
	linen	1.50
	hemmings for Shirts	54
	Making Shirts	5.50
	Mending boots	1. 6
	[*unrecovered*][84] rasor	25
	Repairs to watch–	1.50
	Mendg Spectacles–	37½
Oct 29	Hat	5.–
	mendg	1.50
		$133 6¼

82. This word could be "pocketwatch" or "pocketvest."

83. There could be a final *e*.

84. This word resembles "Silking."

[*p. [42]*]

Clothing Contind	133. 6¼
Tooth brushes	50
Gloves	1.75
Pantaloons	13.30
Boots &c	10.25
Umbrella	1.25
Clothes–(E I. a/c)	96.15
Linen	9.11
Pants	4.50
Slippers	1.50
	$271.37¼

[*p. [41]*]

Personal	440. 4¾
House	185.68¼
Farm	172.18½
Stable	288.43½
Carriage & Harness	49.31
Garden	8 12¾
Poultry	65.59½
Clothing	271 36¼
Servants	378.
	1858.74½
House Exs	520
	$2378 74½

[*p. [40]*]

Servants.	
James	144
Patrick	138
Mary	96
	$378

[*Inside back cover, in its natural position, contains at the top, two lines of five unrecovered words which resemble "Rasn Wossenby" and "Marg. Tante Amors"; when the notebook is reversed, the following figures appear in pencil*]

337	50
50	6
287	300

50

33
40
———
13.20

110
20
———
130

156
13
———
143

[*back cover blank, except two blobs of red sealing wax, the bottom left one of which contains a partial seal*]

ACCOUNT BOOK

1840-1841

Personal Expenses

This manuscript account book is in the Manuscripts and Archives Division of the New York Public Library, where it is cataloged as Washington Irving Papers, Volume 29-A. It is housed in a maroon slipcase measuring 5$\frac{3}{16}$ x 8$\frac{1}{16}$ inches with a smaller maroon folder which folds twice into thirds (5 x 7$\frac{5}{8}$ inches) and slips into the larger case. The notebook, whose pages measure 4$\frac{7}{16}$ x 6$\frac{15}{16}$ inches, is bound front and one-half the back (the back cover is torn diagonally from top binding to approximately one-fourth of the distance from the bottom left margin) in a red morocco cover which is not attached to the pages of the notebook; the entire notebook is tied together with a red string. The off--white paper is lined horizontally with faded, almost imperceptible, blue lines and vertically with five red lines, two of them closely approximate. It seems that originally between each leaf there was a leaf of pinkish, soft blotter paper (more of the sheet remains between leaves 10 and 11 than between the others). The water mark appearing upside-down on most of the twenty leaves reads "G & R TURNER / 1828." Blank are the inside front cover, pages [12], [28–34], [36], [38–39], and what remains of the inside back cover. In pencil is the line preceding the total figure (which itself was written in pencil before apparently being traced over in ink) on page [6]; the last five lines on page [27] (a correction to the number "5" in the total is made in ink); a subtotal to the left of the column of numbers on pages [10], [14], [16], and [18]; the name "Brown" on line 5 of page [37]; and page [40]. In dark brown ink are the remaining pages, including the front and back covers; on many of the pages the heavy ink has badly faded through the paper.

[*front cover*]

	47
37½	
	154
	88
	289

[*inside front cover blank*]

[*p. [1]*]

18⟨3⟩40

Personal[1] expenses

Jany	1.	Servants. N Year Presents	
		Hugh McBride[2]	5.–
		Mary Gilhodly	4
		Susan Spear	4
		James Ryan	3
		David Davidson	3
		Sundries	.50
	16.[3]	Hostler	16[4]
		Rail road ticket	25
	17	Turkey	1.25
		Horse keeps[?]	37¼[5]
		Hostler	25
		Do[6]	10
	19	Soap	37½
Feb	1.	Omnibus tickets	75
		do	75
	12	tooth brush	18¾
		Oil	18¾
		Newspapers	12½
		Hostler	12½

1. This word is underlined twice.

2. Between the item and corresponding figure in the columns, WI used a series of periods or dashes in an inconsistent pattern; we have regularized by using no punctuation.

3. This number could be "1⟨5⟩6" or "1⟨6⟩5."

4. This number could also be "18," but the column totals correctly as "16."

5. Denominator of fraction is smudged, but ¼ produces the correct total.

6. WI here, as usual, raised the *o* of "Do" (ditto) as a superscript.

		Rail road	25
		Oyster Supper	56
	20	Hostler	37½
		[? Gabe Keets & Sarah ⟨P⟩ ?][7]	40.–
		omnibus	35
			65.91¾

[*not in Irving's hand, on the last line of p. [1]*]
Wormser June 3, 1940

[*p. [2]*]

		Personal Expenses Contind	
		Bro't over	65.91¾
Feb.	20	Concert	1.–
		Omnibus	25
March	5	[? Mr King ball ?]	3.25
		Mr Astors Servts	3.–
		omnibus	25
	10	Steamboat	44
		"	37½
		Omnibus	75
		Newspaper	2
	12	Steamboat	37½
	26	Do	75
		Newspaper	. 6
	30	Expenses to & from town	1.–
April	11	Subscription for family burnt out at Yonkers	10.–
		Do. for Gale[?] carriage maker burnt out	5.–
	13	2 Quires writing paper	.50
	14	Steamboat fares	75
		wild pigeons[?]	31
		Newspapers	8
	17	2 Steamboat fares	75
		Omnibus tickets	50
		Theatre tickets	2.–
		Steamboat fare	37½

7. These words could be "Gater Skeets & Sarah ⟨&⟩."

		Partition[?][8] & a/c	25.–
	21	Newspaper	6[9]
			$122.76¼

[*p. [3]*]

Personal Expenses

		Amt brot. forwd	122.76½[10]
April	24	Postage (7 Dram[?] bill)	1.89
	"	⟨I⟩ Paper	25
	"	Ink	12½
	27.	Steamboat fare	37½
	"	Omnibus tickets	1.–
	"	Theatre tickets	2.–
	28	Steamboat	37½
		fees for [*unrecovered*][11] pieces	75
	29	Charity	50
		Washing bill	.75
	30	Newspaper	6¼
May	4.	Steamboat	37½
		Porterage	25
		Stewart[12] of Steamboat	25
		Newspaper	6
		Steamboat to Albany	2.–
		lemonade &c	12½
	5–	Porterage	25
		Bill at Hotel	2.–
		Porterage	25
		do	18¾
		Newspaper[13]	. 9
			136.68

8. This word could be "postilion."

9. WI wrote "⟨7⟩6" with a mark over the corrected number.

10. The number "6" would not be legible without the total on the previous page; WI changed the fraction from "¼" to "½" when he carried forward.

11. The word resembles "Salesfaction" with the *f* crossed like a *t*.

12. WI probably meant to write "Steward" although the final letter is a *t*; there is an ink mark below the S.

13. In the margin below and to the left of this word, the ink has faded through.

[*p. [4]*]

		Personal Expenses ↓brot forwd↑–	136.68
May	6	Tea[14]	– 50
"[15]	7	Porterage	18¾
"		Steam boat	43½
"		Subscript towards ⟨worship[?]⟩[16] ↑new↓ Methodist ⟨*illegible*⟩ church	5.–
		Church Collect	5
	12	Steamboat fares	75
	13	Postage	1
	26	Writing paper	50
	"	Postage	2
	27	Steamboat	37½
	"	Ream of paper	4.50
	"	Priors Goldsmith[17]	1.–
	28	Rail road tickets	25
	"	Steamboat	37½
June	1.	Ink	12½
	4.	½ years Pew Rent	7.50
	10.	Postage	25
		Subscription to Church organ	25.–
June	15.	Steamboat tickets	1.50
		Newspaper	. 6
			185 6¾[18]

14. There is an ink mark above the line and following this word.

15. In the columns under the month and day, WI sometimes indicated ditto by a short dash or a period; in this edition we have regularized by using a quotation mark.

16. This word could be "washing."

17. Sir James Prior's biography of Goldsmith appeared in 1837. In 1840, WI prepared and published in *Harper's Family Library* an enlarged version of his own biographical introductions to editions of Goldsmith's works published in Paris in 1825, in Philadelphia in 1830, and in Paris in 1837. STW commented that WI left Prior's "factual records . . . intact, but he lifted, with a general acknowledgment, all personalia and anecdotes suitable for his superficial narrative" (II, 222).

18. The line above the figure is in pencil; the total was written in ink over pencil. The fraction is smudged.

19. The ink on the following page has faded through to this one rather badly, especially the numbers; this condition persists on pp. [6–10], [12–18], [20–26], and will not be noted further unless pertinent.

[p. [5]][19]

		Personal Expenses Contd	185. 6¾[20]
June	17.	Hostler	12½
		Barber[?] 3 days	37½
		Theatre (burning[?])	75
	"	Mace, oil	50
	"	Omnibus	12½
		Servs. chambs.	1.–
	18	Hostler	50
			10
		Theatre. Olympia–	50
	20.	Postage	6½
	21.	Church Collection	1.–
	22.	Steamboats	75
		Dinner	56
		Newspaper	6
	27	Mr Sheldons[21] Coachman[?]	50
	28	Steamboat	12½
		Rail road	18¾
		Newspaper	6
		Rail road	18¾
	29	Steamboat tickets	75
	30	Letter	6
			193.94[22]

[p. [6]]

		Personal Expenses ↓contd↑	193.94
July.	6.	church Collect	12½
	7	Steamboat	12½[23]
		Porterages	25
		Rail road tickets	56
		Stage fares	25
		Mr Astors Servts	3.–
		Washing	50

20. The fraction is badly smudged.

21. Probably Henry Sheldon, a merchant who lived in Tarrytown and whom WI mentioned several times in letters to his niece, Sarah Paris Storrow (see *Letters* III).

22. WI's total should be "193.34¾."

23. The fraction is illegibly smudged, but the total confirms the reading.

	16	Dinner	44
		Steamboat	12½
		lemonade	12½
Jan[?][24]	25	Insurance on Steryotype[?] plates for 1. year	12.25
		Rice food & Ind. meal[?]	4.63
		⟨*illegible*⟩ mendg pouch case	50
		do. Penknife	88
		do. Silver fountain pen	1.–
	19	church Collect	12½
	21	Gave Rent[?] as extra[?]	12½
	24	Steamboat fares	50
		Dinner	62½
		Newspaper	6½
	27	Steamboat fares	1.50
		Cab– do	37½
		Dinner	62½
		Newspaper	6
			$222.70

[*p. [7]*]

		Personal Expenses Contd.	$222.70
July	31.	Letters	18½
Aug	2.	Church Collection	25
	6	Steamboat fares	25[25]
		Dinner	62½
	"	Newspapers	6¼[26]
	7 –	Hostler	12½
		letter	6¼
	12	Bible Society	5.–
	15	Steamboat fares	.25
		Dinner	31¼
	20	Subscriptn to Presbtyn Church	3.–
	21	Steamboat fares	25
	"	Dinner	62½
		Lemonade	6¼

24. This word could be "Jun," but because a year's policy is mentioned, the "Jan" reading is probably correct.

25. The "5" includes an ink blot at the top.

26. WI first wrote "6" in the ten column, then erased and moved it to the right.

	2⟨3⟩2	Dinner at [*unrecovered*]	50
		Steamboat–	25
	23	Church Collection–	6½
	25.	Steamboat fare	37½
		Ice creams	37½
	30	Church Collection	10
			$235.42½

[*p. [8]*]

		Personal Exps. Contd.	235.42½
Sept	1.	Steamboat fares	43
		Books, map &c	2.–
		Dinner	31
		Postage	3
	2	Sheldons Groom[?]	25
	3	Ink.	12½
	6	Steamboat	31
	7	Rail Road	25
		Dinner	75
		Theatre	50
	8.	Steamboat	32
		newspaper	3
Sept to	9 23	Journey to Canandaigua & Niagara	120.–[27]
	26	postage	6¼
	29	Grapes	1.25
		Steamboat	25
	30	do	31½
		Theatre	1.–
		Omnibus	12½
		do tickets	1.–
		Mr Grinells[28] Servts.	1.–
		Steamboat	31½
		Salmon	1.75
			$367.79¾[29]

27. WI tried to erase and he actually wrote what seems to be "12020" with a line through the final "0."

28. WI probably referred to Moses Hicks Grinnell (1803–1872), who married Julia Irving, WI's niece, in 1836, and was a successful New York businessman.

29. The bottom right corner of the page with the fraction is torn off; the last digit could be a "0" or "9," but the addition and the balance carried forward to p. [9] support the reading.

[*p. [9]*]

Personal Expenses Cond

			367.79¾
Oct.	4.	Church Collection	1.–
	⟨9⟩8.	Steamboat	31¼
		Tarry town Lyceum[?]	5.–
		Rail Road car	6¼
		Theatre	50
	⟨10⟩9	Steamboat	31¼
		Newspaper	6¼
	15	Mr Boltons[?] Servt.	25
	19	letter	10
	20	Steamboat tickets	1.88
		Newspapers &c	12½
	28	Steamboat	1.25
		Dioramia[?]	1.50
		Cathn Irvg & Sarah Paris	75.–
		Opera tickets	6.–
		Servt.	1
	30	Steamboat &c	1.62½
	31.	Letter	6¼
Nov.	1	Church Collect	6¼
		Steamboat tickets	56
		gave away–	6¼
	10	Postage–	6¼
			$464.58¾

[*p. [10]*]

Personal Contd

				464.58¾
Nov.	12	Steamboat fares		56½[?][30]
		worstd[?] &c		36
	18.	Matches		4.
	20	Constants serv[?]		25
	24	Subscriptn. Dutch Church		10.–
	28	Steamboat fares–Breakfast &c		1. 6¼
		Theatre		1.–
Dec.	5.	Letter		6½[?][31]
	9.	Steamboat		94
		Porterage	477.92½	25

30. The fraction could be "¼."
31. The denominator is smudged; the total of p. [10] seems to be off by "1.20."

		Theatre & opera	10.–
		Omnibus ticket	75
		Steamboat ticket	1.50
		Breakfast	25
		Panorama tickets	87½
		Washing &c	1.–
		Mr Astors Servt	3.–
		Ink.	12½
		Society Library dues	4 –
		Expenses on Jaunt to Canandaigua	17
		Postages	3.75
			$522.56½

[p. [11]]

1840

House Expenses.

April	4.	Bbl[32] Lime	2.25
Jun	20.	Pd. D Mann for drawg Ice	2.50
			$ 4.75
June	11.	Plumbers bill for repairs	1.94
		Gilding weather cock	2 –
			8.69
July	17.	Freight Box wine	25
Aug.	10.	10 lb nails for Piazza	62½
	"	Planks & posts for do.	9.18
	"	Work on do.	4.50
	16[33]	6 Doz brass rings for awngs.	75
		4 " " awng hooks.	1.–
			$ 24.99½
		Carpeting	113.34
			$138.33½

[p. [12] blank]

32. Abbreviation for "barrels."
33. The number could be "15."

[*p. [13]*]

1840
Farm Expenses

		Taxes	$ 22.40
March	16.	Gate Hinges, Hasps &c [? Vide Lovetts ?] bill	1.15½
April	3.	James Ryan on a/c wages	20.–
	11[34]	Ernst Forster on a/c wages	5.–
	13.	Small nails	26
	15	Trees from Levys[?]	8.62
	20	Collar for Dog	2.50
	21	Grindstone	1.50
	24	Nails, ⟨a/⟩ (T. Deans bill)	2.50
	30.	Blk Paint	18¾
May[35]	1.	4 Mos. Interest on ‸↑Bond to↓ Isaac Lents[?] ⟨Bond⟩ for $3000 at 7 pr Ct	70.–
	8	9 lbs cut nails 7 cts.	63
	22	Small nails	29
		Tax for mending roads	9.50
Jun	20.	Acknowledge Deed & Sales factors price[?]	75
	"	David Manns bill for Ploughing	4.37½
		Do. drawg manure	1.87½
Jun	24	Paint for boat	2.46
		Paint brush	37½
			$154.37¾

[*p. [14]*]

	–	Farm Expenses Contind	
		Brot forw	$154.37¾
June	27.	Scythe 2.	1.–
–	–		$155.37[36]
July	1.	Pd. James Ryan a/c wages	10.–
	16	Small axe	75

34. There is a large blot to the left of the number, the ink having faded through from the next page.

35. There is a blot between the month and day.

36. WI dropped the fraction.

June	19.	Boat &C &c—33.25		33.25[37]
July	21.	Reuben for mowing 11½ days at 10/.		14.37½
	30	Conklin & Ashe for do. 1 Day		1.50
	31.	Shaft to Farm waggon		87½
Aug	7	Nails		18¾
	26.	Repairs of boat		3.50
			$219.80¾	219.80¾
Sept	1.	Mending boat		1.12½
Aug.	21.30	boards	12	3.60
Oct.	19	Nails		.50
Nov.	23	"		29
Dec.	30[?]	"		55
		Ploughing & harrowing[38]		5.52½
				$231.39¾
		Deduct wages		35
				$196.39¾

[*p. [15]*]

1840

Stable[39] Expenses

Feb	7	50 Bush. oats 40 Ct	20.—
March	6.	Grain 73 bush at [*blank*]	7.30
"	16	Shoeing horses &c Vide Lovetts bill	10 59
April	24.	50 Bushels Oats at .38—	19.—
		⟨&⟩ recd. ⟨about⟩ 13th. acct[?]	
	"	1956[40] H Hay—at 5/hand with expenses of weighing &c	11.12½
	"	Pane of Glass (T. Deans[?] Bill)	12½
	"	Broom "	25

37. WI rewrote the number to the left of the column because of an ink blot over the "33"; he followed the same pattern in the subtotal.
38. In pencil just above this word is the number "$25.32¼"; under the word are an illegible subtrahend, a line, and the result which has a "9" as the second number.
39. WI underlined twice.
40. The number could be "1756."
41. WI could have written the numbers "⟨2⟩13" or "⟨2⟩ 3."

May	13[41].	½ lb Ginger	6¼
	16.	Broom	25
	26	Bill for Shoeing horses	3.28
June	3	Shoeing horses	81¼
		2 Horses Keepg 3 days	3.75
	21.	D Manns Bill for drawing Hay	4.37
			80.91½
		Shoeing horses in town	4.50
July	14[42]	3 Bush oats. drawg. 28	.84
	16	50 " do. 45.	22.50
Aug	15	Stable lantern–	1.–
	19	2180 Hs[43] Hay. Paid last Spring.	13.62
			$123.37½

[*p. [16]*]

		Stable Contd.	$123.37½
Aug.	19.	50 Bush Ship Stuff –Paid[?] July 21[?].[44]	12.50
			$135.87½
Sept	1.	35 bundles oat Straw 4 Cts	1.40.
	25	65 do "	2.60
	16.	50 Bushels. oats 43	21.50
Oct	16.	Blacksmiths bill for Shoeing horses &c	7.38
	26.	50 Bushl oats. 45.	22.50
Nov.	10.	1 lb Ginger	12½
		Blacksmiths bill Shoeing &c	1.18¾
	18	Broom	25
		1 lb Ginger	12½
Dec	15	do.	12½[45]
	30	100 bush Ship Stuff	25 –
		Freight & Castg	3.–
		do of [*unrecovered*][46]	.50

42. The ink blot obscures the date, which may be "1⟨5⟩4."
43. These letters could be "lbs."
44. The date could be "2d"; the first word in the line could be "Recd."
45. To the left of the column at this point is the amount "92.93½" in pencil.
46. This seven-letter word seems to begin with "ri" and end with "fed."

	120 Bush Straw 6		7.20
	Horse Shoeing		1.86
			230.62¾[47]
	Drawing hay		62½
			$231.25¼

[*p. [17]*]

1840
Carriage & Harness Expenses

Feb	19.	Repairs to Sleigh & waggon See Gales bill	9. 6
		Carriage repairs, Curtain &c	21.–
March	16.	BlkSmiths work. Vide Lovetts bill–March 16	1.37½
	18	Part of Jones bill sadler ⟨for⟩	80
	22[?][48]	Newports[?] bill, repairing Wiffle trace of waggon	37½
May	20.	Mending whip	25
	22	do do	25
	26	Smiths work–repairg waggon	2.50
		Carriage maker for do.	1.10
		–Bates bills &c	81
		Mendg harness	62½
June	3.	do	1 31¼
		Mendg shaft of waggon	– 25
	24	Sadlers bill	1.34
	30	Mendg carriage pole	37½
			41.42¼
July.	3.	Mending reins & collars	2.25.
	16	Saddlers bill	2.25
	"	repairs to waggon.	17.25
			$63.17¼[49]

47. The "3" of this number is obscured by an ink blot, but the addition and the total confirm this reading.

48. Faded-through ink blots on this page make much of it difficult to read; WI may have written "2⟨5⟩4."

49. The lower right corner of the page is torn off; column totals and balance carried forward suggest this reading.

[*p.* [*18*]]

Carriage & Harness—Expenses

		Brot forwd	63.17¼
August	3.	Coach Makers bill for mendg waggon & for varnish	10.88
	"	Mending reins—	12½[50]
	10	Mending traces	25
	15	2 boxes Harness brackg	–75
			$75.17½
Oct.	12.	Repairs of Small waggon	10.94.
	"	" of Harness	95.
	19	Neats foot oil	25
		Repairing waggon	68¾
Nov.	14	Mendg Carriage	18¾
	18	" Harness	6¼
	23	Rope for halters	37½
Dec	30	Sadlers bill	45[51]
		Repairs of waggon	2.50
			$91.58[52]
		Gig bit & Curb	1.50
			$93. 8

[*p.* [*19*]]

1840

Garden Expenses

Feby.[53]	16.	Book of Gardening	.75
April[54]	13.	Garden Seed	25
	14	Do	56
	25	Bill for mending garden implements	1. 6[55]
	27.	Garden Seeds	–.50

50. The total is correct only if this fraction is read as "¼"; WI wrote the fraction "½."

51. To the left of the column is the number "88.62¾" in pencil, which is the subtotal.

52. WI rounded off the total from "91.57¾."

53. WI wrote "⟨Jan⟩Feby."

54. WI wrote "⟨M⟩April."

55. WI wrote "1"6," using a ditto mark rather than a decimal point.

May	16.	pint marrowful[?] peas	9
June	1.	Cucumber Seeds	12½
	21.	Drawg logs out of Garden	25
	22	Garden hoe	75
			4.33½
Aug–	6	Turnip Seed	12½
	21	lettuce Seed	6¼
			$4.52.[56]

[p. [20] blank]

[p. [21]]

1840.

Poultry.

Jany.	14	Corn & Buckwheat		3.75.
Feb.	17.	1 lb farm Sulphur		12½
March	12	6 Bush corn	.81.	4.86
		7 " Buckwheat	75.	5.25
	13.	8 " do.	"	6.–
		Rings for Pigs Vide Lovetts bill		12½
	18	6 Bush Corn at	7/	5.25
April	1	6 do.	7/.	5.25
	2	Potato a/c		1.–
	3	14 Bush Buck wheat	75	10.25
	11[57]	30 " do–auction	.44	13.20
	25	5 gooses eggs–		12½
May	12.	pd for 3 doz wooden Eggs		1.50
	30	6 earthen pans		37½
June	10.	Tin ware		50
	"	Rat trap		1.25
		Mouse do		25
	30	Steel trap		50
				59.56
June	25[58]	12 Bush corn.	58.	6.96[59]
				66.52[60]

56. WI added the fractions incorrectly.

57. To the left of the date column in ink WI wrote "55.5/." which is the correct subtotal through the number "13.20."

58. An ink blot obscures the "2."

59. WI wrote "⟨7⟩↑6↓."

60. WI wrote "6⟨7⟩6.52"; he also corrected the initial figure on the next page.

[*p. [22]*]

		Poultry. Contind.	66.52
Nov.	10.	Window Glass for Shed	93¼
	28.	2 Bushels corn at 75 Cts	1.50
		5 do. Buckwheat 62½ (Bot of Mr Hart).	3.12½
Dec.[61]	29.	8 Bush Buckwheat, do.	5.
	30	20 do. do. 4/6 (had of Requa some time since)	11.25
		14½ bush Corn—5/	9. 6
			$97.38¾[62]

[*p. [23]*]

1840.
Clothing

Jany	19.	1 pr Gloves	1.—
	22	Mending	18¾
Feb—	1.	Suspenders	87½
		Ind Rub over shoes	1.50
		Mending a pair of do	1.—
		Watch Glass	25
	20	Gloves—2 pr.	1.—
	27.	Pr. Pantaloons (blue)	14.25
		" Boots	7.—
March	26	Spectacle Glass	.25
April	14	Cloth Cap	2.—
	20	Gloves	75
		Cleaning watch (silver)	75
	24	Sundries as fr. T. Deans bill	2.29
May	4.	Silk Stock	1.25
	"	oil for hair	25
	10[63]	Mending clothes	50
	23[64]	1 pr Gloves	25

61. WI wrote "⟨Nov⟩Dec."

62. There is an ink blot between the dollar sign and the number; both "9" and "7" are written over other numbers, the "7" over an "8."

63. WI may have written "1⟨2⟩0."

64. The initial digit of this date is obscured by an ink blot.

June	13	Stuff for 2 pr pants	5.50
	15	2 pr Gloves	75
	22	Linen coat	1.75
		Boots	4
		Shoes	2 25
			$49.57¾[65]

[*p. [24]*]

		Clothing Contind	49.57¾
June	29.	Linen coat	1.75
		Straw hat	4.–
			55.32¾
			⟨65 ⟩
			⟨120.32 3⟩
July.	7.	2 pr Gloves	1.–
		Silk Stock	50
		Taylors bill for coat 2 vests & 2 pants	64.60
		1 Doz Half Stockg.	4.50
		1 Silk Hkf	87½
		Suspenders	75
		Linen &c purchd. by. Helen, Pierre	9.46[66]
	17.	Makg 2 pr pants.	3. 6½
	24	2 Silk Hkfs	2.50
Aug.	7.	Mending coat	43¾
	"	Pd for making Shirts	6.–
		NB.[67] The above will appear on my next a/c current with E.I	
	15	2 pr Gloves	50
	21	Silk Hkf	1.–
		Cotton Cover[?]	31¼
		Hooks of do	18½
		Gloves	37½
			151.38¾[68]

65. WI's total is incorrect; it should be "49.60¼."
66. There is an ink blot to left of the "9."
67. WI used the abbreviation for "nota bene," which calls attention to something important.
68. WI wrote this number at the bottom of the page, and the "38¾" is badly

[p. [25]]

		Clothing Contind	151.38¾
Aug.	21	pr Half Stockgs	25
	31	Watch Glass	25
			$151.88¾
Sept.	1.	2 pr Japan[?] Silk Gloves	62
	7.	Booties	3.–
	9.	Hat	4.–
		Hkfs. (Silk)	2.25
		Stock[69]	1.50
		Collars	1.–
Oct	2.	Sewing Silk &c	6¼
			$164.32
		Gloves	75
Nov.	6.	Cleaning & repairing watch	6.–
	12	Gloves	1.–
	28.	Bean[?] oil	.50
Dec.	12.	Hat	5.–
		Gloves	1.–
		Mendg boots	1.25
		do.	75
			$180.57
		Sleeve lining	1.50
		⟨Making Shirts⟩	⟨6⟩
			$182. 7

[p. [26]]

Servants wages.

Gardner.	10 Months & ⅔ at	15$	160
James Ryan	12	12.	144
Mary Gilhodly	12	8	96
			$400

---

smudged; the reading is suggested by the sum of the column and the balance carried forward to the next page.

69. This word could be "stick."

```
                    337½
                     32
                  ———————
                    674
                  1011
                     16
     365   |     10800       |   29.
           |      730        |
                  ———————
                   3500
                   3285[70]
                  ———————
                    215
```

[*p. [27]*]

Summary

Personal.	522 56½
House Expenses	138 33½
Farm	196 39¾
Stable Expenses	231 25¼
Carriage & Harness	93. 8
Garden	4 52
Poultry	97 38¾[71]
Clothing	182. 7–
Servants wages	400 –
Share House Exps.	520 –
	$2385.60¾
Wine (say)	60
	$2445 60¾
Moneys recd.	4244.54
	2448.60
	$1795.94

[*pp. [28–34] blank*]

[*p. [35]*]

Stocks.

12 Shares Mississippi Lan Cy. ⟨$50⟩ first cost $50 (raised to $100)	6000
Morris Canal Compy. first Cst	2500

70. The "2" and "8" are written over other numbers.
71. The "9" and "7" are written over other numbers.

10 Shares Mohawk rail road
purchased Oct 30, 1839 at 48 with Comms[?][72] 481.20
18 do. Aug 12 1841. 62¾ 1134
$1350 State 5 t.[?] (1858)[73] 81 with Coms[?] 1096.87

[p. [36] blank]

[p. [37]]

Property in 1841

House & land [? &c of ?] Sunnyside		15,000
Lots in Toledo. first cost–		12 000
Moneys falling due ⟨from⟩ these from[?][74] Mr Brown[?][75] }		3 000
Share in the Farm of Astor a twentieth of the whole. }	say	4 000
Balance due from Mr Godfrey for land at Ann Arbor^ ↑(Secured by mortgages)↓ }		2 000
Land at Milwaukie	say	300
Shares in Mississippi Land Compy.		11 000[76]
Shares in " bank Stock		700
28 Shares Mohawk Rail Road 65[?]		1 820
Morris Canal Stock		100
Due from Mrs. Romeyn		1 500
" Proprietors of Knickerhook[77]		1 000
" T. W. Storrow		5 000
		$57 420
Copy right property.		15 000
		$72 420

[pp. [38–39] blank]

72. This is WI's abbreviation for "Commissions."
73. The date could be "1838"; both "8" and "3" are written over other numbers.
74. The word is written over another, perhaps "Home" or "farm."
75. The name has been added in pencil, apparently later.
76. WI probably wrote "1⟨2⟩1000."
77. This word could be read as "Kinderhook."

[*p. [40]*]

1150	
50	Col
140	Gidfy[?]
⟨60⟩	gold
280	Stor
1620	
1600	
3220	

[*inside back cover blank*][78]

[*back cover blank except the number "87" written upside down*]

78. The inside and back cover is torn diagonally from the top of the binding edge to approximately a quarter up the outside edge.

ACCOUNT BOOK

1842

Personal Expenses

This manuscript account book is in the Manuscripts and Archives Division of the New York Public Library, where it is cataloged as Washington Irving Papers, Volume 30-A. It is housed in a maroon slipcase, measuring 5¾6 x 8¹⁄₁₆ inches with a smaller maroon folder which folds twice into thirds (5 x 7⅝ inches) and slips into the larger case. There is no cover and the pages measuring 4½ x 7¹⁄₁₆ inches are in a thin, worn, aqua cardboard folder tied with a new string; there have been single leaves attached with this string so there is no way to determine if the pages are in their original order. The paper is off-white and lined horizontally with very faint blue lines. There are sixteen leaves, the first of which is loose except for the string through the top hole. Blank are pages [16], [18], [21], [26], [28], and [30]; in dark brown ink are pages [5], [13–15], and [29]. In pencil are pages [20], [23–25], and [31]. Pages with some lines in ink, some in pencil, some numbers in ink and some in pencil or pages with numbers written first in pencil and then, over the figures, in ink are pages [1–4], [6–12], [17], [19], [22], [27], and [32].

[*p. [1]*]

April	1⟨2[?]⟩842
Wine on Voyage for Self:	£2.11.–
For Hector[1]	18
Stewards fees (Self)	1.10.–
(Hector)–	1.–
Passage on board Steamer Queen, for Hector & self	4.–
Dinners, wines &c	1.12.–
Porterage at Bristol	2.6

1. Hector Ames served as one of the attachés to the U.S. legation in Madrid from this time until June 13, 1843; see p. 198, n. 10.

Bill at Bristol Hotel.	17.–
Porter	1 ⟨*illegible*⟩
	£ 12.11.6
	53 4 7[2]
	3 8 6
	69 4 7
	12 10
	81.14.7

[*in the bottom quarter of page [1], at the left margin, written upside down*]

Day	24	71
Week	172	97

[*with the notebook again in its original position*]

77	8	
12	11	6
89	19	6

[*not in Irving's hand, on the last line of p. [1]*]
Wormser June 3, 1940 (40 M 36)

[*p. [2]*]

	May– *1842*	
	Omnibus fares to rail road	2.–
	two[3] Rail road tickets to London	3.⟨0⟩.–0
	–Cab to Leslies[?][4]	3.–
	Omnibus fares.	2.–
	Gloves–	3.–
	Fouchet[?][5]	5. 5
	Shaving box–	1. 7
	(Cab to Rail Road	3 –
	Fare to Birmingham	1.10 –
⟨9⟩.	Cab–	

2. This and the remaining figures on the page are in pencil.
3. The number, added later in the margin, could have been originally "One."
4. See the May 2, 1842, entry in the journal; WI called on Charles Robert Leslie, his old friend, the second night in London. The word could be "Lesters."
5. This word could be WI's spelling for the French "fourchet," a two-tined fork, or "fourchette," a table fork. This and the following nine items and corresponding figures are in pencil.

	9.	Stockings	8
		Buckles	9.
		[? Gum arab ?][6]	7
		Cab fares	3.–
		Exhibition	2.–
		Prestons bill for Clothes	12.5 –
		Moore for Hats–	9.13 –
		Shultz[?]	17.15[7]
		pr Silk Stockgs	10.6
		" Gloves	3.6
			£ 53.3.7[8]

[p. [3]]

		May	
		Amt Brot forwd	53. 3.7
May	13.	Shoes	18.–
		Servant at the Bandinels[9]	10.–
		Cabs to rail road	5.6
		Luggage (carriage in R Road)	5.
		Rail Road fare	1.10 –
			⟨3.8 ⟩[10]
		Bill at Thomas Hotel & servants For Self & H A.–	12.10 –
		Ticket at theatre	7.–
		⟨Ex⟩ Cabs at various times	1.10 –
May	17.	Pocket book	5.6
		Spectacle case	1.–
		Cab–Hire	3.6
		Lining Great coat	5.6
			71.14.7

6. In the space between this questioned word (which could begin "Earn") and the figures are ink blots from the following page.

7. WI has written "17.1⟨2⟩5" with the "5" written over the "2" in pencil.

8. The figure is in pencil, except for the "3" in ink; Irving "corrected" the number from "4" in pencil and carried the "3" to the next page; reading the seventeenth figure as "15," the total should be 53.4.7.

9. James Bandinel was a clerk in the Foreign Office whom WI had met during his earlier diplomatic stay in England; see p. 200, n. 20.

10. This total is both written and crossed out in pencil; the large bracket in the next set of items, the sum which follows, and the crossing-out of the final

		⟨ 5. 6
		1. 7
		8
		9
		12. 5
		9.13
		17.15
		[*two numbers illegible*] 6
		[*two numbers illegible*] 6
		18
		48.14⟩[11]

[*p. [4]*]

	Amt. brot. forwd.	71.14. 7
1⟨7⟩9	Postage	8 10[12]
	Pencil points	8
	Cab hire	3. 6
21	Cabs to Railway[13]	6
	Rail road for 2 to Weedon	1. 2. 6
	Newspaper	. 6
	Girl at Manor House ↑Sulgrave↓	2. 6
	Dinner	2. 6
	Servg Maid	2.–
	Turnpike gate	1.–
	Post Chaise 2/3 ds.[?]	1. 0. 6
	Postillion &c.	7.–
	Rail road to London (2)	1.17 –
	tea & sandwich	1.
22[14]	Beds & breakfast for 2. Victoria Hotel London	13.–
	⟨Rail⟩ Hackney coach to rail road & carriage of trunks	7.
	Toll Gates	1. 8
	Rail road to Southampton (2)	2. 2.–
	Hackney coach 2/6 Porter 1/6	4.–

column of figures on this page are in pencil. The next number, "12.10," is in ink over pencil.

11. In the blank space to the left of this column of figures are the number "240" and an illegible superscript in pencil.

12. There are two ink blots from the following page between the "8" and "1."

13. This and the following ten items and corresponding figures are in pencil.

14. To the left of this number WI wrote "77.8" in pencil.

	Steam Packet to Havre	2. 2.–
	Tea & Coffe 3/6. Stewards fees 4/	7. 6
		£ 83. 7. 3

£ 95.18. 9

[*p. [5]*]

	May Contind.	
⟨22⟩23	N Y Hotel fee [*three words unrecovered*][15] Francs	5.
24	Beasleys[16] Servt	5
	porterage	1.15
	2 Fares in Steamboat to Paris	49.10
	⟨Charity⟩ Subscription to Ship wrecked sailor–	5.–
	Music	1.10
	Sexton of Cathedral at Rouen	2.–
	Theatre–2 Stalls	10 –
25.	Bill for 2 at Hotel	18.–
	Servant–	2
	Porterage–	7. 1
	Resteraunt on board St boat	20. 4
	Servants	1.16
	Porter at Rail Road[17]	2.–
⟨26.⟩	Carriage & ⟨lug⟩ porterage ↑at Paris↓	7.30
26	Pd. Mr Storrow for Books bought last year	130.–
	Tickets at Theatre (Variete–	20.–
	Sundries	5.–
27.	Cab for 2½ hours &c	5.10
	francs	299.11

[*p. [6]*]

	May	299.11
2⟨9⟩8	Booties	15.–
	Theatre (Grand opera) 4 Seats	28.

15. The second and third words resemble "bueno maas."

16. Reuben Beasley, from New York, was American consul at Havre from 1818 until 1848; see pp. 218–19, n. 120.

17. An ink blot from the previous page makes these two words and the number "2" difficult to read.

	⟨3⟩29	Carriage to St Cloud		
		Dinner & Servts		25.
	30.	Opera 2 Seats		15
	31	Carriage [? & Boat ?][18]		
		Sattin Stock		9 –
		2 pr Gloves		6
		Silk Half Stockings		6
			5	403.11
			$[?]	80.71

£ 16.⟨6⟩0.6[19]

12.11.6
83 7.3
16. 0.6

£ 111.19.3

[*p. [7]*]

		June		
	1.	Robe de Chambre	Fr	100.–
		Garcon–		2.–
	3.	Guide at Invalids		5 –
		Picture Gallery		1.–
	5	Genl Cass' Sevt.		5.
	7	Collectn at St Roque[20]		5
		Domestic[?]		4
	8	2 pr half Stockgs		4.10
	13.	pr de Bettines		18.–
	14	cocher pour bain		5
		Pr Bettines[21]		20
		Dress Shoes		12
		Gaiters		9 –
	16	Coach at Versailles		6
		Cab		2 –
		Rail Road to Corbeil &c (2)		5.10
$40.40	20	Rail road to Paris 2		4[22]–

18. This word could be "Gent"; this and the following three items and corresponding figures are in pencil.
19. There is an ink blot above this figure from the following page.
20. The "7" of this line is in pencil and this and the next line and corresponding figures are written in ink over pencil.
21. This and the following nine items and corresponding numbers are in pencil.
22. The "4" is written over another number.

	Servant	2
	Fiacre[23] &c	4 –
	Theatre	6 –
		220

[*p. [8]*]

	June Contind.	220
21.	Cabriolet[24] hire	4.–
	hair cloth	70.–
	Carriage hire	224
	Excursion to Versailles	220 –
22	Cabriolet	40
	Theatre	5
	Hair Cloth	70
2⟨7⟩8[25]	1 doz half Stockgs	24
	Theatre (German)	5
2⟨8⟩9[26]	Cabriolet	4 –
30.	Ticket for [*unrecovered*][27] concert	20
		906
	⟨d⟩Robe de Chambre for Summer	32

[*p. [9]*]

	July.	
1	Note Paper Cards &c.	55.12[28]
3	Dinner & waiter	8.[29]
	Coffee &c	75
	Theatre	5 –

23. French word meaning a hackney-coach, cab, or small carriage.
24. Generally, a cab or one-horse chaise.
25. The "8" is in pencil; the "7," in ink.
26. This number is in pencil.
27. This word resembles "Thorns"; in his 1842 "Journal—Travels from the United States to Bayonne," WI omitted June 29 until July 11, so this occasion is not mentioned. He wrote Mrs. Paris that on June 13 he had attended a "magnificent fête given by our countryman, Colonel [Herman] Thorn. . . . His hotel was brilliantly lighted up, the extensive gardens fancifully illuminated, and singers and musicians stationed among the distant groves, who occasionally regaled the company with concerted pieces of instrumental music, or romantic choruses and glees" (PMI, III, 209).
28. WI wrote "55.⟨?⟩↑12↓."
29. This number, along with the corresponding item and those on the following two lines, was written first in pencil and then over in ink. The number "8" could also be a "5" or "3"; the number below it seems to have been "⟨15⟩⟨75⟩↓75↑."

		5 Neck kfs.	10
	4	Theatre 2 tickets	13.–
		Play book	12
		coach hire	1.13
	5	Chinon muslin	2.–
		Cab	2.15
		⟨5 muslin neck kfs⟩	
		1 Satin Neck kf	12 –
		" Stock	8
		Sponge & bag	6.10
	6.	⟨4⟩3 pr Shoes. 15 pr	45.
		1 " do 12	12.
		⟨Seams⟩ Mending Shirts	8.–
		Trunk	15.–
		Theatre	5.
		Play books	1.10
			212."7

[*p. [10]*]

		July Contind.	212 7
July	9.	Cabriolet hire	10 –
		Visiting cards[30]	6 –
		Cab	3 –
		Pd ⟨Louis⟩ ↑Lewis↓–consideration[?]–	75.
		Theatre 3 Tickets	2⟨?⟩
		Woodman & Co[mp]y Bill for Clothing	1399
		Forr[?]. Boot maker A/c for Boots &c	127[31]
		A/c for lamps–Glass China ^↑Linen↓ Candelabra &c	3953.11
		Bill for Silver plate	1040. 7
		" for Sword	43.10

30. In a letter to Henry Brevoort dated July 1, 1842, from Paris, WI said that their friend Colonel Thorn was concerned that WI was not paying enough attention to the social amenities "by neglecting to follow up the friendships proferred me in Saloons." Thorn strongly suggested that Irving leave a card the next day for the duchess of Grammont who had sought WI's acquaintance at a gathering and "at the same time read me a most affectionate lecture on my neglect of this piece of etiquette with respect to [var]ious other persons of rank" (*Letters*, II, 242).

31. The "2" and "7" are written over other numbers, the "7" over a "2."

Postages		63.18
		6919.13
Bill for Hector Ames lodgings[32]		115
washing bill		26 10
Charity		20
Carriage Hire		43
Porters a/c for connections[?] &c		29.13
Gave Lewis in addition		10. 7
Porterage		1.–
Expenses from Paris to Madrid		1602[33]
		8767. 3

[*p. [11]*]

Brot forward	8767. 3[34]
Carriage of trunk from Paris to Bordeaux & porters fee	23.10
Fees at Custom House[35]	10.–
Porterage	5.–
Crape[?]	

[*p. [12]*]

	August.		
1.	charity[36]	fr	5
	Bathing tub		5
	crape–5¼ reales		1. 6
	Carriage Hire		12.10[37]
5	Linen for Servants beds aprons, Towels &c $67.33/.		
	Iron bed stead $22 50/.		
	washing $2		
	Ices[?]		2.–
10	Pd. A Vail[38] on a/c of Furniture &c	$1000	

32. This line is ink over pencil.
33. This number, the line, and the total are in pencil.
34. This number is in pencil, and the following two lines are written in ink over pencil.
35. There is an ink blot between item and number.
36. To the left and above this word is an ink blot, the mirror image of "10" from the following page; WI subsequently crossed out the "10."
37. The "2" is written over what might be an "8."

11	Mattresses &c. $21.30/		
	Washing bill }	⟨5 fr⟩	5.
	Hector do. }		⟨3⟩7.0[39]
20	Washing		9.16
26	Christal mercht. ↑present to [blank]↓ ↓for glass escutcheon↑[40]	}	20.–
27.	Washing		8.16
2⟨7⟩9	Theatre		3.–

[*p. [13]*]

	Sept.		
3.	washing	⟨fr⟩	2[41]
10	"		1.84[42]
[*unrecovered*][43]			.80[44]
13.	Pd. Six months rent of apartments Calle de las Infantas, to Don Luis Ma. Rey, administrador of the Marquis de Mos		300.–
	Settee & 12 Chairs		22.–
	Voltaire chair		8
	office table		6
	Don Quixotte chair		1.
	Porterage		.40[?][45]
14.	2 Marble Slabs		10.
	Easy chair		6
	night table		1.50
	Old Table of nutwood		1.25
	Old Cabinet		1.30[?][46]
	Chinese table		1.20
	Kitchen Utensils		34.20

38. Aaron Vail (1796–1878) preceded WI as U.S. minister to Spain; he was the chargé d'affaires of the U.S. legation in London from 1832 until 1836.
39. WI may have marked out other numbers, intending a "0."
40. The words above and below the line are in pencil as is the bracket.
41. WI wrote "⟨10⟩↑2↓."
42. The "1" is written over either a "4" or "9."
43. WI wrote "⟨4?⟩.8⟨8⟩0."
44. This word resembles "Toros" or "Toror."
45. The first number could be "4," "9," "7," written over another number.
46. WI may have written "1.⟨2⟩30."

[*p. [14]*]

September Contind.

	14.	20 Chairs: common[?], 13½ reals	13.50
	"	12 " & Settee	9.
	"	12 " " " (maple)	22.
	"	Commode	10
	"	toilet table	9
	"	6 Kitchen Chairs	1.80
	"	Dinner at Geneiss[?]—for 3.	3.—
		⟨&⟩—garcon	.30
	16.	Opera	70
	17	washing bill	2.94
	20	Transportation of 4 boxes & trunks[47] from Cadiz }	20.90
		Freight, entry &c of do.	7.76
	23.	Iron Bracket for Marble Slab	8.—
		Netting[?]	95.35
	25.	Washing bill	13.60[48]

[*p. [15]*]

Oct.	17.	Pd. rent & porterage to 15 Sept of aparts. at house of I. S Lorenzo		
			840 Rs[49]—	$42.—
		present to porter	⟨$2⟩ 40 —	2.—
				Rs
Oct	14	Fairing[?]		20.
		Opera		14
	15	Washing bill		38.6
		Theatre del Venezia[?]		14.
		Cooks bill Commenceg Oct 9 to 15. Novbr[?]		503.21
		carbon		
	23.	Cooks bill to Oct[?] 22d.		387.24
		Charcoal—		80[50]

47. There are ink blots through these three words and in the blank space in the line above.

48. The five remaining lines on the page are blank.

49. Abbreviation for "reals"; there is a vertical ink blot from the "4" in this line to the crossed-out "2" in the line below.

50. The remaining ten lines of the page are blank.

[*p. [16] blank*]

[*p. [17]*]

Expenses—Commencing April 10, 1842

	Passage Money to Engd.		£ 30
	Expenses on the Voyage & in Engd.		22.8.0
			£ 52.8.0
			$261.60
	Expenses in France and on Journey to Madrid		435.86
Past.[?]	Expenses in Madrid to Oct 10		30.34[51]
	Clothing		658.30
	House Rent[52] ↑to Sep 15 St	131.30	172 97
	Lorenzo↓ Fr Mar to ↓Oct 10↑	41.67	
	House Expenses		500.
	Servants wages (porter 2$)[53]		115 30
	Stable		3.60
	Furniture		4278 28
	Carriage & Harness		925.
	Wine & Candles had of Mr Vail		271.70
			7657.65
	Deduct passage money pd in N York		150
			7507 68[54]
	Deduct amt unpaid of price of furniture		2066.30
			5447 38[55]

[*p. [18] blank*]

51. WI wrote "3⟨5⟩0.3⟨4⟩9" in pencil.
52. Following these two words, the added information and all the figures are in pencil; only the six items through the words "Mr Vail" and the bracket are in ink.
53. Parenthetical information is written in pencil.
54. WI wrote "750⟨4⟩7 68."
55. WI wrote "5⟨5⟩4⟨1⟩4⟨4⟩⟨7⟩1 ⟨6⟩38."

[*p. [19]*]

W. I.	Cr
By Expenditures in Engd.	111.60
By do. in France & Journey	329. 6[56]
By do in Madrid ⟨to Oct⟩	30.39
By Clothing	672.68
By Household Expenses	357.27
By pd for Furniture in Paris	1000.
By pd. Mr Vail on a/c Furniture	1017.40
By pd Mrs Storrow a/c Mr JTI.	7.10
By transportation of Effects from Paris	100.–
By do. from Cadiz	29.–
By furniture purchd in Madrid	608[57]
By Servts wages	113
By repairs of St Lorenzo House 89 30	21. 4
By rent of do. 42.	131 30[58]
By rent in adv of Marquis Mos	300.–
By Carpenters bill for Shelves	34.–
By China furnishd Mr Albuquerque	38.50
By pd Mr Storrow for Books bot last year	26.–
By Expenditures a/c Contingy Fund	93.52
By pd for 2 Exequaturs Bradley & Calhoun	36.50
	5056.36[59]

[*p. [20]*]

W I. Dr	
To cash on hand on leaving US.	40
To HA's Bill on Brown[60]	61.18.6
To Bill fr Freemans Exqr	4.–
To Cash Mr JTI	1.10.6
	£107. 9
	536.80

56. This number is in pencil over erased ink.
57. WI wrote in ink over erased ink.
58. The number, the next item, and corresponding figure are in pencil.
59. The sum is in pencil over other numbers.
60. On p. [2] of the later account book, [1842–1847], WI changed the name "Brown" to Freeman's bill.

		Cash on bills for Bradley & Calhouns Exqr	36.50
		To Do Recd from Mr Vail for McCreadys[61] Exq	17.40
		To Carson Brevoorts bill Exq	987.95
		To Recd of Qu[arter]s Salary	2250.
Aug	10.	To do	2250
Oct		To Salary to 1 Oct	1237.60
		To Dfts agst contg fund	149.20
		To cash from Albuquerque	38.50
			$7503 95

[*p. [21] blank*]

[*p. [22]*]

Candles, purchd of Mr Vail

200 lbs. 52 Cts.			104
Sugar.			66.30
Brown Sugar	389 lbs		
White do.	328		
37 loaves about 9 lbs each			
Brown Sugar	⟨15½⟩ ↑16↓ cts per lb.		
White	17.70	centimes	

	wine	417.90
⟨333[c]⟩	Candles	104
	Sugar	66.30
		598.20

wine	240
can	104
sugar	90
	434

[*p. [23]*]

		Rs dr[62]
Rent		12000
Fuel	at 81 pr week	5000

61. The more legible rendering of these expenses and this name in the later account book suggests "McCreadys" as the correct reading of this difficult word.
62. These initials are WI's abbreviation for "Reales Debit."

Cooks bills	60 pr day		21900
Milk			1980
Bread			1716
Fruit	at 52 pr week		2204
oil			744
washing–			3500
Stable			252
⟨Oats &c⟩			⟨192⟩
Oats			4326
BlkSmith			576
Servts			11520
Liveries			1800
		20	67518[63]
			3375.18
	Clothing		200
	Personal		250
		12	3825 18
	per Mo.		318.
	3 mos.	954	

[*column of two numbers at bottom of page unrecovered*][64]

[*p. [24]*]

	3456
Clothing	200
Personal	250
	3906
wine	300
Sugar	60
	4265

[*p. [25]*]

Rent		12,000
Fuel at 81. pr week		5 000
Cooks bills–	60 pr diem	21 900
Grocer	64 pr week	1 528[65]

63. This figure was written over the number "56574."
64. The initial two digits may be "25."
65. WI miscalculated: at 64 per week, the total would be 3,328.

Fruit	52 pr do.		2 204
Milk ↑& butter↓	165 pr m		1 980
Bread	143 " m		1 716
Oil			744
Washing	at 70 pr w		3 640
Horse feed	362 pr m		4 326
Blk Smith	48 " "		576
Servts. wages			11 520
Liveries			2 000
		Rs dr[?]	69 134[66]

$3456 pr an
864–qr
216–pr m

personal	⟨1⟩5 000
Clothing	1 000
pr ann $3756	75 134[67]
" qr 939	
" m 313	

[*p. [26] blank*]

[*p. [27]*]

2 doz	Lafitte[?][68]–	$5^{6.10}$ [69]	120
6 "	Beyeheville[?]	$3^{4.10}$	216
2 "	Marcobraun[?]	$5^{6.10}$	120
8 "	Champagne–	$5^{8.10}$	480
			936
216 Bot	Insurance 1 pr Ct		10
			946[70]

66. WI divided the year's reales debit subtotal by 20, apparently the rate of exchange, rounded off to the figure to the left, "$3,456," and then calculated his quarterly expenses; he miscalculated the monthly expenses (it should have been 288).

67. WI followed the same procedure as outlined in the note above.

68. This word could be "Lafille."

69. The superscripts are in pencil; the prices in the right column are unrelated to the superscripts.

70. The subtotal and three lines following are in pencil, except for the "250.20" in ink over pencil.

	Expenses	305
Expenses about 30[71] Sous[?] pr bot	fr	1251
$61 boxes as Exchg.		$ 250.20[72]
wine had of Mr Vail		167.70
		$ 417.90

[*illegible*]

216
30
6480

[*p. [28] blank*]

[*p. [29]*]
Stable—

English Coachman[?] getting Horses	160
Man who brought horses	120
Cloth for ⟨*illegible*⟩ Coachms coat	320
Horse Doctor	160
Hats for Coach & footman	100
Carpenters bill for Stables	68
Blacksmith for Feb	54
Break[?][73] wagon. 16 days	320
Straw & Barley 26 days	387.2
Boy who helped break horses	90
Tailor for makg. coat	240.—
Lorenzos Coat	440.—
English Coachman for breaking Horses—	320
Harness makers bill	575
Fodder for Horses (March)	444.2
Coachmans bill for do	74 —
Blacksmiths do	48 —
	3920.4
Coachmans bill for Jany	40.—

71. The number "30" was written over another number; expenses per bottle were 28.2 sous.

72. According to WI figures, the rate of exchange was five francs per dollar.

73. With one fewer loop, this word could be "Buck."

[*p. [30] blank*]

[*p. [31]*]

Butler	120	
Valet	120	
HouseKeeper	96	
Cook & aid	240	
		$576

Estimates of Mr Vail	
Marketing	2000
Groceries	450
Fruit	90
Bread	100
Butter	80
Milk	60
Oil	109
Candles	150
Wood	200
Charcoal	365
Water	24
Wine	365
washing	80
	$4073

[*p. [32]*]

4 Mos. Endg Nov. 25— House & personal	1131
	3
Year	⟨4⟩3393
Rent	600
Sevts.	579
Clothg—	250
	4822
Wine	280
	5102

⟨Storrow—Books 130 fr.⟩[74]

Expenses	416	month
	3	
	1248	qr.

74. WI wrote in ink and crossed out in pencil.

ACCOUNT BOOK

1842-1847

Personal Expenses

This account book is in the Clifton Waller Barrett Library of the University of Virginia Library, Charlottesville, Virginia, where it is cataloged by accession number 6256m. There is no cover; there were apparently originally 38 leaves—leaf 19 is loose and leaf 20 is missing. The notebook is tied between leaves 18 and 21. The pages measure $4\frac{15}{16}$ x $7\frac{1}{16}$ inches, and the paper is pale blue with 22 horizontal lines in the grain. On the loose leaf is a watermark of two lines, "Joynson/1842"; other watermarks are on leaves 13–14, 15 (partial), 16, and 18. Leaves 4–12 and 35–38 are cut out or torn out of the notebook. In ink are pages [56–58], [61], [66–68]; in pencil are pages [1] and [25]; in a combination of pencil and ink are pages [2–3], [5], [59–60], [65]. Blank are pages [4], [6], [26–38], [41–55], [62–64]. There are two pages inserted in the notebook, the first a notification of permission to draw money (the title and figures below the note are in Irving's hand). This piece of paper is blue, measures $5\frac{3}{16}$ x $8\frac{1}{16}$ inches, and is written in brown ink. It is folded horizontally, top to bottom edge, and then inserted (by the library) between pages [60] and [61]; however, because the mirror-image ink blot on the outside of the folded leaf matches the writing on page [56], and the information relates to that on page [57], it should be inserted between these pages. This blotting also helps to date the note and the notebook, as Irving had just written "1846/July 16th." when the note was inserted. The second inserted page is white and slightly larger than the notebook pages; its information parallels that of page [25] with some rearranging of the figures. It has been included at the end of the notebook.

[*p. [1]*]

3/5 Hous Expe 1 Y. 1778[?][1]

1. This writing in very light pencil begins at the top left margin; there is an ink smudge approximately one-fourth of the page below and to the right.

[*p. [2]*]

Dr.[2] W I.

		To Cash in purse on leaving US.	£ 40
		To. proceeds of H. Ames Bill Exchg.	61.18.6
		To. " of Bill on Brown for Mr Freemans Exequatur	4. --
		To–Cash from Mr J. T. Irving	1.10.6
			£ 107. 9
			$ 536.80
		To proceeds of bill for G. Bradley Exqr.	18.25
		To do. for Calhouns do	18.25
		To. Cash recd from Mr Vail for McCreadys Exeqr.	17.40
		To proceeds of Bill of Exchg of C Brevoort–	987.95
May	10:	To Cash on 1 Qrs Salary–	2250
Aug	10.	To do	2250
Oct.	1.	To proceeds of Dft of Rothschild for Salary to this date	1237.60
		To proceeds of dfts agst Con-/tingent fund to this date	149.20
		To Cash from Mr Albuquerque for part of Sett of china	38.50
			$7503.95[3]
		To. Carson Brevoorts Exchg on [*unrecovered*]	189.20
			7692.15

[*p. [3]*]

W I.	Cr
By Expenditures in Engd.	141 46[4]
Do. In France & on journey	329. 6
↑personal↓‸ in Madrid to Oct 10.	30 39
" pd for Furniture in Paris	1000
" pd. Mr Vail a/c Furniture	1017.40
" Mrs Storrow a/c Mr J. T. I	7 10

2. See p. [20] of the account book for 1842 for another listing of WI's debit column; in addition to that list, WI here added the last item.

3. The dollar sign is in pencil; the subtotal is in ink over pencil, and following the number is a dot of red sealing wax.

4. On p. [19] of the 1842 account book, WI recorded this amount as "111.60"; this and the following four numbers are written in pencil.

" transportation of effects from Paris	100
" " from Cadiz.	29
pd. Furniture purchd. in Madrid	608[5]
pd Repairs St Lorenzo house	21. 4
pd Rent of do	131.30
pd Rent pd. to Marques de Mos	300
pd. Carpenters bill for Shelves	34.
pd. China furnishd Mr Albuquer[.]	38.50
pd Mr Storrow for books bt last year	26.–
" Expenditures a/c contingy. fund	93.52
" Exequaturs. Bradley & Calhoun	36.50
Personal Expenses to Jany 1.	98.92[6]
House Expenses to do.	554. 5
Servants wages	249. 6
H. A.	1032.46[7]
	5877.75

[*p. [4] blank*]

[*p. [5]*]

	5877.75[8]
P C Brevoort	1266.50
McCreadys Exequatur	17.40
[*erasure*]	7161.65
Wine from Guestier	189.20[9]
Sugar	66.30
	7417.15
Clothing	658.–
	8075.15
Contingy Fund	185.88
	8261. 3

[*p. [6] blank*]

5. This number and "131.30" are in pencil.

6. WI wrote "98.⟨36⟩92"; this and the following two numbers were written first in pencil, and then after erasure, in ink.

7. This number, the line, and the total are in pencil.

8. There are erasures beneath this and the following four numbers, as well as the first four items.

9. This and the next line are the only two in ink on the page.

[*pp. [7–24] torn out*][10]

[*p. [25]*]

Supposed income	July 1847
Screw dock [11]	600
Storrow	500
New Jersey R Rd.	280
Aub & Roch R R.	320
Bank Commerce	126
Ohio 7th.[?][12]	140
Ohio Farm[13]	80
Kemble purchase[14]	125
Mississippi & Arkansas	250
Toledo[15]	150
Southern R Rd.	100
	2671
Funds on hand	100
Cabridgt[?] Columb.	30
Milwauke	
	2801

10. The pages are torn out in an irregular pattern, the remaining attached portions of the leaves varying from one-eighth to one-half inch in width.

11. By 1842, WI was discouraged about his investments, and in 1844 he wrote to PMI, who was handling his financial affairs in America, to retrieve what capital he could. In a March 24, 1844, letter, WI thanked PMI for getting $2,100 "out of the ashes and cinders of that once sanguine speculation," the town of Astor in Green Bay; in 1836 he had invested $4,000 in what he thought would equal Chicago in its rise (PMI, III, pp. 332–33, 89). On January 6, 1847, PMI wrote to his uncle that "the Screw Dock Company, in which he had an interest, had declared a *quarterly* dividend of five per cent," to which news WI replied that day, "I am glad to hear you are receiving such a snug little bag of money from the Screw Dock. In faith, the Dock deserves its name. I fancy there must be a set of Jews at the windlasses to screw the ships so handsomely. Tell them to screw on, and spare not!" (PMI, III, 397).

12. This superscript could be " ' ," *t*, or *h*.

13. WI apparently wrote "⟨7⟩Farm."

14. Of WI's investments, this land purchase of Western lands which he discussed in a January 10, 1838, letter to Gouverneur Kemble and which was handled by Mr. Godfrey (PMI, III, 119) was perhaps one of the most consistently profitable. In a February 5, 1852, letter to Kemble, WI said that he had just received "further remittance from the enchanted purse of Godfrey" (PMI, IV, 102).

15. WI wrote Pierre M. Irving on April 13, 1847, that he was "surprised and delighted at the windfall from Milwaukie, and shall now not despair of the sky's falling and our catching larks. Toledo, too, begins to crawl. There's life in a

[*pp. [26–38] blank*]

[*pp. [39–40] torn out and missing*]

[*pp. [41–55] blank*]

[*p. [56]*]
London Jany 15. [1846][16] Draw on Baring Brothers & Co favor John Miller for £5.18.6. on account of Contingencies—

1846
July 16th.
Draw on Baring Brothers & Co in favor of John Miller for £8.17.11½ on acct of Contingencies

W I.

[*p. [57]; written along the inside margin of the top quarter of this page after the notebook has been turned a quarter revolution clockwise is* "July 1. 1845."]

Miller qr[?] a/c Jan 11[17] 1845 £7.4.11 Draft on Baring Brothers & Co.
Draft on Barings for 464.17.6
a/c of Salary
" — — 20£—Contg fund
The above to remain in their[18] hands Subject to Dfts of myself & Pierre M Irving—Send Pierre notice—this Evg—

July 17. Write to Pierre Irving to draw on Messrs ⟨Baring Brothers & Co⟩ Palmer Mackillop Dent & Co London for 300£ on a/c of Henry O'Shea & Co of Madrid—out of which to pay Mr Grianole[?][19] ⟨for⟩ $963 57/ for Sperm candles shipped for the Count de Bresson[?], the residue to be passed to my credit

[*p. [58]*]
⟨Due W I Dec. 3d 1844

---

muscle! The screw, however, is the boy for my money. The dividends there are like the skimmings of the pots at Camacho's wedding" (PMI, III, 401).

16. In January, 1846, WI was in England at the request of Louis McLane.

17. WI could have written "Jany 1."

18. The *t* is written over another letter, perhaps a *P*.

19. This name could also be "Griancle" or "Grinach."

Postages in Am:	20
Metalic pans—	5
Paper	3.⟩
Expenses to Barcelona	486[?]$[20]
	514

Oct 1. 1845—Draw on Barings Brothers & C for £464.17.6 on a/c of Salary and £52 on a/c of Contingencies of the Legation.

The aggregate amt to remain in their hands subject to the drafts of myself and Pierre M Irving

Jany 1. 1846 Draw on Baring Brothers & Co for $2250 on a/c Salary and $250 a/c Contingencies.

The aggregate to remain as above.

[*p. [59]*]
1844
Octr. 1. Draw on Baring Brothers & Co. for $*2250* (Quarters Salary) to be placed by them to my credit—

Draw on same for $150 on account of Contingencies—to be placed to my credit. Authorize them to honor the drafts of Pierre M Irving, ⟨who⟩ to whom I have written to draw on them for $*1000.*

Octr 2d.—Write to the Consulate at Havre authorizing a draft on T. W Storrow Jr[?] of Paris for 403F ⟨4⟩35 centimes in discharge of postage account against the Legation

Octr 8. Draw on Baring Brothers & Co at Sight,[21] in favor of Henry V Wart Sons & Co. for sixty five Pounds sterling. (*65*£)

" Draw on ditto favor T W Storrow at 3 months date for 160£

Oct. 12. draw on Mr Storrow for 500 francs[?][22]

" Draw on OShea & Co Madrid, in favor of Jasper H. Livingston for 8000 reals.

20. In addition to a large ink blot over the third digit, WI has written over the second; the total suggests the reading.
21. The S seems to be written over an *H*.
22. The word is near the right edge of the page; it could possibly be "pounds."

" Draw on Mr Storrow for fr 208.50 for 5½ doz Gloves[23]

[*p. [60]*]
Octr 24. draft on Barings favor of John Miller for £7.11.10d[?].
29 draw[?] on Mr Storrow favor of Storrow for fr. 1030[24]

Nov. 9. Draw on Barings favor of T W Storrow 30 days sight for 40£ Sterlg–

Nov 20. Draft on OShea & Co. $100 for House rent.

April 1. 1844 Draw on Barings for $2250 Salary & 50$ Contg Exqr to be ⟨Sent[?]⟩[25] placed to my a/c subject to dfts of P M I.

[*p. [61]*]

1845.

March 1. Draw on Mr Petty Vaughan London[?] favor of Baring Brothers & Co for 10£5/. to be charged to a/c of Mr John K. Kane Philadelphia. Being amt. disbursed in procuring royal order for a commission in Manilla for Examination of his job[?] as Physician–

" Paid to Scrivner for copying manuscripts for Mr Obadiah Rich of London 10$.

[*pp. [62–64] blank*]

[*p. [65]*]

Paid

⟨Count de Bresson $190.10
For Sperm candles
Shipped by Grianole[?]
Nicolson[?] & Co–⟩[26]

Mem of Expenses from Madrid to Paris–[27]

23. This last line is in pencil.
24. This and the next day's entry are in pencil.
25. These crossed-out letters could be "Sub."
26. Only the crossed-out portion of the page and corresponding figure are in ink; everything else is in pencil. WI drew a line in pencil across the page to separate sections.
27. In a July 25, 1846, letter, WI wrote that in a few days he would leave Madrid: "Thus closes my public career." The August journey from Madrid to Paris was in a private carriage "in company with Mr. Weismuller" (PMI, III, 393).

3 Seats in Malle Porte to Bayonne	$81
Extra Baggage	1 40
Mayoral[?]	6 –
Hire of travelling carriage from Bayonne to Bordx	fr 80
Posting to Paris	84
From Paris to Bordx	195
Bridge & ferry	10
2 Passages in Steamer to Nantz	30
Fare onboard	10.15
Fare ⟨to⟩in Steamboat to Angers	10. 8
Fare to Tours	14
" " Orleans	15 14
2 places in Rail Road to Paris	25 –
⟨9⟩ (96 French Dollars)	

[*p. [66]*]

July 1. 1844

Draw on Baring Brothers. & Co for 2000$[28] ↑(a/c of this Qrs Salary)↓ favor of themselves—write to them telling them to hold this sum subject to the drafts of P M Irving of NY & to apprise him of the same

July 1. Draw on B. B & Co ⟨for⟩ favor of OShea & Co. for £25.5.4 balance of former a/c of Salary

" Draw on same for £51.13. the balance of this quarters salary after the above dft of $2000.

" Draw on Same for £18.6.8 for contingent expenses

After the 1st of July there will be in the ⟨*unrecovered*⟩[29] hands of OShea & Co about 23400 [*unrecovered*][30] I have their letter of credit on amts[?] from[?] Barcelona for 2000—

[*p. [67]*]

Mississippi Land Cy.

28. WI wrote "2⟨8⟩000."
29. WI crossed out what may be a date in the margin, "Jan 25"; the second part of the blot also may be a name and initials, "John T I" or "W I."
30. The letters are probably "Rs dr," WI's abbreviation for "reales debit."

1845 Lands unsold.
Mississippi—62,000 acres
Tennessee —18 000 "
In 1844 Mississippi land sold at $5 20/pr acre
Tennessee " " 1.65/.
It is supposed the prices will fall to
say Misspi. Land 3$ pr acre
Tenesse " 1.65
at that rate my interest in lands unsold[?] would amount to about $4,500
My share of outstanding debts drawing interest is $4500
I have recd in dividends—$2562

[*p. [68]*]

Mississippi Land Company

144,288 acres cost.	268 741.24
Expenses to Apl 10. 1840.	24 878. 9
	$293 619.33

Equal to $2 3½/100 pr acre.[31]

———

Land sold up to Apl 10. 1840	
30.129 76/100 acres	165,264.83
Equal to 5 45/pr acre	

Unsold Apl 10. 1840
114.159 acres

average sale pr acre as above	5.45
Deduct first cost & expenses	2. 3
	3.42
Do. 1/3 to Mr Orme (agent)	1.14
Net profit to Stock holders	2.28

My Share about 3206 acres cost abt.	6000$[32]
Whole profit at the above rate	$7309
profit on the 114,159 acres about	5782$

[*written along outside margin of p. [68] after notebook has been turned a quarter revolution clockwise*]
12 Shares on abt 45 part of the whole.

31. WI used a double line to separate items.
32. This and the following line are written in ink over pencil.

[pp. [69–76] have been torn out with the stubs approximately one-half inch wide. On p. [69] is written in pencil "Settled" along the inside margin after notebook has been turned one-quarter revolution clockwise; p. [72] has an ink mark; p. [74] has six numbers as if right column of figures.]

[*first inserted sheet, in another hand but with Irving's label at the top*]

Note *from John O'Shea*

M. Pierre M. Irving can draw on Messrs. Palmer Mackillop Dent & Co of London for £300— — on a/c of Messs. H. O'Shea & Co of Madrid—

[*in Irving's hand at the bottom center of the page*]

484[33]
300
———
784
5
———
3920
963
———
2947

[*second inserted sheet*]

Screw Dock	600
Storrow	560
New Jersey R Rd.	280
Aubn & Roch.	320
Bank Com.	126
Ohio 7'—	140
Ohio farm	80
Kemble	125
Mississippi & Ark.	250[34]
Toledo	150
	2631
	⟨1500⟩

33. The first, third, and fifth numbers in this column were written "48⟨6⟩4," "78⟨6⟩4," and "39⟨4⟩20"; WI wrote the "9" in the subtrahend beneath the "3," then marked it out. The result should be "2957."

34. WI wrote "⟨3⟩250."

	⟨4131⟩
	100[35]
	2731
Southn R Road	100
Milwauki	2831
Columb	30
	2861

35. WI wrote "1⟨3⟩00."

INDEX